The War Aims and Strategies of Adolf Hitler

OSCAR PINKUS

D1581859

McFarland & Company, Inc., Publishers
Jefferson, North Carolina, and London

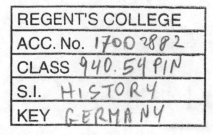
LIBRARY OF CONGRESS CATALOGUING-IN-PUBLICATION DATA

Pinkus, Oscar.
The war aims and strategies of Adolf Hitler / Oscar Pinkus.
p.   cm.
Includes bibliographical references and index.

ISBN 0-7864-2054-5 (softcover : 50# alkaline paper)

1. World War, 1939–1945 — Germany.
2. World War, 1939–1945 — Europe.
3. Strategy — History — 20th century.
4. Germany — Military policy — History — 20th century.
5. Hitler, Adolf, 1889–1945 — Military leadership.   I. Title.
D757.P53   2005   940.54 — dc22   2005011462

British Library cataloguing data are available

Cover image: Cover images © 2005 Clipart.com

Manufactured in the United States of America

*McFarland & Company, Inc., Publishers
Box 611, Jefferson, North Carolina 28640
www.mcfarlandpub.com*

Table of Contents

List of Terms, Codes and Abbreviations

Abwehr— Wehrmacht intelligence agency
ADC— aide-de-camp
AGC— Army Group Center (Mitte)
AGN— Army Group North (Nord)
AGS— Army Group South (Süd)
AK— Armia Krajowa, West-oriented Polish underground
AL— Armia Ludowa, Soviet-oriented Polish underground
Anschluss— annexation of Austria
BEF— British Expeditionary Force
Berghof— Hitler's home near Bertchesgaden
CiC—commander in chief
Dichtung— Hitler's smokescreen for his true intentions
EAM— Communist-oriented underground in Greece
EG— Einsatzgruppe — Execution Battalion
ELAS— Communist guerrillas in Greece
Feldherr— warlord
FTPF— Franc-Tireur et Partisans Francais (Communist)
FHO— Fremde Heer Ost: Army Intelligence: East
Flak— anti-aircraft artillery
GG— Generalgouvernement (German-occupied Poland)
Gestapo— German secret police
Gröfaz— Grösster Feldherr Aller Zeiten: nickname for Hitler meaning Greatest Warlord of All Times
Gulag— Soviet slave labor camp
Izba— Russian peasant room
Katyusha— Russian rocket battery
LSD (T)— Landing Ship Dock (Tank)
Lucy— Spy ring run by Rudolf Roessler
Luftwaffe— German air force
Maquis— generic term for French resistance
MUR— Mouvements Unis de Resistance

NLF— French National Liberation Movement (Communist)
NSDAP— National Socialist German Workers Party (Nazi)
OKH—(Oberkommando des Heeres) supreme German army command
OKL—(Oberkommando der Luftwaffe) supreme Luftwaffe command
OKM—(Oberkommando der Kriegsmarine) supreme German naval command
OKW—(Oberkommando der Wehrmacht) supreme command of German armed forces (Wehrmacht)
Ostheer— German army on Russian front
OUN— Ukrainian Nationalist Organization
Overlord—(D-Day) invasion of Normandy in June 1944
Panje wagon— Russian horse cart
Panzer— tank or armor
PM— Prime Minister Churchill
Politruk— political commissar in Red Army
PPR— Polish Workers' Party (Communist)
PQ— Allied convoys bound for Murmansk or Archangielsk
RAF— Royal Air Force
Rasputitsa— fall and spring mud period in Russia
RSHA—(Reichssicherheitshauptamt) SS security main office
Roundup— plan for a cross–Channel invasion in 1943
SA— Nazi storm detachment
SD— SS security service
Sitzkrieg— phony war in France, 1939-40
Sledgehammer— plan for a cross–Channel invasion in 1942
SS—(Schutzstaffel) Nazi guard detachment
Stavka— Red Army headquarters
Stuka— Ju-87 dive bomber

Torch— Allied invasion of North Africa in 1942

USAAF— US Army Air Force

USSR— Union of Socialist Soviet Republics (Soviet Union)

Wehrmacht— German armed forces

Weltanschauung— world view (philosophical)

Wolfschanze— Wolf's Lair, Hitler's headquarters in East Prussia

Preface

The main purpose of this work is to set down the nature and shape of Hitler's war, more than the war's course. It intends to show that the conflict's many seeming inconsistencies were but the logical consequence of a simple if unique master plan: the conquest of the vast landmass lying to the east of Germany up to, and perhaps beyond, the Urals. Hitler wanted no conflict with the West, in particular none with England. All this is not entirely new and has been proposed by Trevor-Roper, Hillgruber, and others. What is attempted here is to show that prior to and throughout the six years of war Hitler never wavered in his central aim and that all his shifts and convolutions were directly linked to it. Thus events that in most histories are presented as puzzling — Hitler's frustration after he was granted his wishes in Munich; the Germans' vacillation to invade the British Isles or their lack of interest in Malta, Gibraltar, and the Middle East; and the unfathomable "mistake" of hurling himself against Russia, without attempting to defeat the enemy still facing him in the West — all of these and other such mysteries were but manifestations of a specific kind of war Hitler planned and waged until his last days. Likewise such historiographical distortions as that the fight in Libya against two or three German divisions spawned more books in the West than the apocalyptic four-year struggle in Russia will be shown to be compensatory Western self-congratulation. Given the specific orientation of this book much will be omitted that otherwise would have required more attention. In essence this will be a history of the triangular confrontation between Germany, England and Russia, later to be joined by the United States, which buttressed, where it did not actually replace, the British side of the triangle.

Since Hitler's true objective was a crusade against the East with little interest in the Western powers, we shall next consider the means he employed in fighting the war. We shall see that even after he became embroiled in a war with both East and West, the tools and attitudes he employed in each case remained implacably welded to his original vision. Though it was France and England who declared war on him and it was British and American bomber fleets that turned his cities into rubble, Hitler treated their soldiers and civilians better than had the kaiser in the First World War, whereas in the Slavic countries — Poland, Yugoslavia and above all in Russia — both the POWs and the populations were butchered en masse. For to Hitler this was no ordinary war: It was to be a geoethnic cataclysm in which the Eastern peoples were to be half-exterminated and half-converted into serfs to toil in a vast Teutonic empire ruled by settled Nazi barons.

The book's second major theme is that from the winter of 1941-42 on, when the campaign against Russia had faltered and the United States had entered the conflict, Hitler knew that he had lost the war. In keeping with his stance of "all or nothing" — he would either have his way or he would drag the world into the abyss—Hitler's main exertions turned to implementing the second half of his agenda. This view was first advanced by Sebastian Haffner, and this volume documents that from 1942 onward, all of Hitler's demographic, political and even military decisions were geared to the goal of inflicting the maximum wreckage and bloodshed on friend and foe alike. This culminated in Hitler's known decision in the last months of the war — the Nero order — to turn Germany itself into a wasteland and doom the Germans to perdition. Having failed to win the war for him, they did not deserve to survive.

Finally, it will be seen how the hysteria of Hitler's schemes overwhelmed his own efforts at success, in that military victory was not kept as the main objective of his war. Hitler's ideological and personal obsessions took precedence over political, economic and military requirements, bringing defeats where there might have been victories. These were not errors in judgment or strategy, but deliberate acts undertaken with foreknowledge of their disastrous consequences— yet adhered to because of the pathological compulsions inherent in Hitler's personality. While the events will demonstrate Hitler's familiar role in imparting to World War II its genocidal dimension, the book will also show that the führer had a potent ally without whose dedication and zeal none of the horrors of the war could have been implemented. That ally, that necessary condition for the success of the criminal record of the Third Reich, was the character of the German people as it had developed over the first half of the 20th century, perhaps reaching back to the mid–18th century when Prussia wreaked its havoc on all its neighbors. It was a partnership of leader and nation sustained in times of triumph and defeat rarely encountered in recent history.

Since the goal of this work was to elucidate the overall shape of World War II, the main effort lay in understanding the dynamics of the conflict, the aims and motivations that fueled the events of the six-year conflict. The labors involved in this task took close to half a century, and yielded substantial benefits. As time went on the 30 or 50 years' moratoria on archival records lapsed, and the unexpected demise of the Soviet Union opened its wartime files. Thus, while at the end of the war the death toll in the USSR was given as 20 million and during Gorbachev's glasnost close to 30 million, Soviet archives revealed the awesome loss of life to be closer to 50 million — numbers rounded off in tens of millions. Another advantage this author enjoyed was that, willingly or unwillingly, he had become familiar with half a dozen languages. In the 50 years it took to complete the present work use was made of memoirs and documents written in Polish, German, Russian, Italian, Hebrew and Yiddish, the bulk of which had never been translated into English. Though often parochial, these sources revealed facts and facets of the war that had never appeared in the professional literature.

While the opening of archival material was a great boon to the documentation of the war's history one ought not to exaggerate its importance; to paraphrase Proust, who said that when a diplomat looks at you it is to stress that he has not seen you, one may likewise say that governments often produce documents *not* in order to tell but to hide the truth. Perhaps greater relevance to the present volume is that this author was an eyewitness to events that to this day remain subject to dispute and argument. For example, anyone exposed to Polish history knew that the "Corridor," so much peddled by diplomats and historians as the possible *causus belli*, was no corridor but ancient Polish land; it would have been more correct to call East Prussia an incursion into Slav territory than to call Polish Pomorze a corridor. After the war there was much hand-wringing about the bombing of Germany by the British and American air forces. But for those who lived through the

German-Polish war in 1939 there was no doubt as to who had initiated and practiced this sort of civilian slaughter. This writer lived in a small town in central Poland in which there was not a single industrial workshop, not a squad of soldiers, yet on September 9 German Heinkels bombed and strafed the town, setting it on fire and killing 50 civilians. The same thing happened in all surrounding towns, not to speak of Warsaw with its tens of thousands buried under the ruins. To this author, whose hometown was located next to the 1939 German-Soviet demarcation line, Hitler's attack on the Soviet Union could not have been considered a surprise by any twist of argument, as it is still being mooted in various quarters. In the days preceding the attack, every German soldier and every child in town knew that the attack on Russia would start at dawn on Sunday, June 22, 1941. In the four years spent under German occupation subject to the sadism of German civilians and soldiers, one learned firsthand of their total devotion to the Führer and of their readiness to do his bidding, whatever that bidding implied. The author's postwar participation in a Nazi trial in West Germany only confirmed the kind of outlook the Germans harbored when committing the most odious acts in the occupied East. When in 1944 the Soviet army swept the Germans from eastern Poland the sight of the oncoming Russian troops and the tales they told spoke a lot about the ordeal they had endured. These soldiers were not jubilant but rather subdued, sad that their victory had been bought with landscapes of desolation and butchery. They were terrified of what still lay ahead before reaching Berlin and the end of the killing. These personal experiences related in the author's two previously published war memoirs (*The House of Ashes* and *A Choice of Masks*) are not included here, but they did shed much light on the understanding of the history of the period.

Readers will benefit from knowledge of a few general conventions that are utilized throughout the text. Except for familiar place names, for example Warsaw and Munich, most localities are referred to by their native spellings. Upon first mention, the full name and position of individuals will be given; subsequently only their last names will be used. An appendix of names and ranks is included for further reference. The citation DGFP within the text is an abbreviation for *Documents of German Foreign Policy*, series D; DDR stands for *Das Dritte Reich*; and FNC is an abbreviation of *Führer's Naval Conferences*; all are included in the bibliography. The terms USSR, Soviet Union and Russia are used somewhat interchangeably.

Part One

THE WRONG WAR

· CHAPTER 1 ·

The Leader

Historians have long disputed whether it is circumstance or an individual that activates major historical events. The story of the Second World War should satisfy both camps: its outbreak is rooted both in the First World War and in an individual, Adolf Hitler. That is not to say that they had an equal input. Without Hitler there would have been no Second World War; but it is questionable whether without the legacy of World War I he would have been able to launch it.

The consequences of the Great War for Germany — the Versailles and St. Germain treaties, the installation of a republic, reparations, economic woes — all of these have been exhaustively argued in numerous works. However, they were not responsible for the outbreak of World War II, for, by the late '30s, most of these constraints had been abolished, including the Weimar Republic itself. There was, however, one aftereffect of the years 1914–18 that did help propel Europe toward a new war; it overwhelmed the statesmen, the generals, and the man in the street. That dynamic stemmed from the historical memory of the Great War.

The conventional understanding of the impact of the Great War is of the legacy it bequeathed to the Germans. But this is a severe delimitation of the role it played. While it undoubtedly left the seeds of another war in the hearts and minds of the German people, the Great War also had a profound impact on the Western Allies. In the Germans as well as in the French and the British, the Great War conditioned attitudes and reflexes that drove both sides on a converging course toward a new conflagration.

The Great War lasted four years, cost some 10 million lives, and ended with the defeat of Germany. A strange flip-flop mood settled over the opposing camps with the end of hostilities. The defeated Germans looked back on the war as a vigorous experience, a life-enhancing test of national will. Its veterans felt nostalgia for the days of combat when, as the German saying went, *Im Felde, da ist doch der Mann noch etwas wert*, whereas the postwar period was a letdown compared to the exhilaration and vigor of the fighting days. Moreover, they did not feel they had been defeated. Some nefarious conspiracy, a "stab in the back" perpetrated by traitors, had cheated them of victory. They tore at the leash for another round.

On the French and British the war left a sense of horror and revulsion at what had taken place in the pits and trenches of the battlefields. There was grief for the dead, and the memories of Flanders and Verdun were a nightmare for the living. Even though they were the victors, in the French and British consciousness the whole experience loomed as a depravity; victory achieved at such a price was not a victory. This postwar trauma was, of course, deeper in France than in England. The French, having lost 1.5 million men (plus

3 million wounded)—as compared with 680,000 for the English—feared that the biological core of their people had been undermined. Perversely, this contributed no less than the nostalgia of the Germans to the plunge into another world war.

In the thick of these disparate moods Adolf Hitler strode onto the German stage. Normally the historical relevance of a leader's personality in war or peace is overshadowed by a host of objective factors. In Nazi Germany this was not so. There the individuality of the führer stood out as the overriding determinant, the crux of its history. It is thus of the essence to be acquainted with Hitler's personal creeds and predilections, for in the affairs of state they ranked higher than the counsels of his experts or the weapons of his opponents.

Adolf Hitler was born in Braunau, Austria, in 1889. He was a slightly stooped man of medium height, with drooping shoulders and a pallid face. A square moustache and a forelock of black hair were his trademarks. He had extraordinary eyes; somewhat bulging, they were of an icy blue limpidity and it is a matter of record that they exerted a mesmerizing power on many of his admirers. His voice was shrill and raucous. His oversized raincoat, plebeian face and general resemblance to a clerk contrasted sharply with his speech, gestures and comportment meant to convey boldness and authority. Sulky, morbid and slightly unkempt, he looked to his admirers bohemian, and to others merely harmless.

If Hitler was vain about his physical image it was because it reflected on his role as a führer. In his Munich days he often wore leather breeches and carried a whip. After he became chancellor, he appeared a few times in mufti, but soon changed to military and party tunics. Because of his rather frail physical frame, he was rejected by the Austrians for military service and was furious when after the Anschluss the Gestapo failed to locate and destroy the incriminating record. When later in the war his eyesight deteriorated he avoided wearing spectacles and all papers submitted to him had to be printed in large-size type. He feared flying and distrusted the sea. He refused to indulge in any sport or competition, saying "A leader cannot afford to be beaten in games." Not unreasonably, he was apprehensive about assassination and from the earliest days surrounded himself with bodyguards, carried a revolver and moved about in a sly and conspiratorial manner. He was nocturnal in his habits, adhering to no special routine or order, for he loathed work and discipline.

Hitler led a simple life. He ate no meat, drank no alcohol, and did not smoke, nor would he permit others to smoke in his presence. Instead, he was fond of sweets. He was not interested in wealth and when he did build himself such grandiose places as the new Chancellery or the Berghof, it was done more in the spirit befitting a führer than for private pleasure. His relations with women were minimal. As to the reason, judgments vary from that he was impotent to the Nazi version of deliberate abstinence as a sacrifice for the nation. Of the six women with whom he was involved to some extent, five attempted or committed suicide, Eva Braun among them.

Hitler's education was rudimentary. The grades he received in school were poor and he failed to finish high school. For this he hated his teachers. Hitler thought of himself as an artist and tried to enroll in the Academy of Fine Arts in Vienna. He took the entrance exams twice and failed. For this he hated all Vienna. Except for newspapers and books on military tactics he had no interest in reading for, said he, "Only a confused jumble of chaotic notions will result from all this reading." He did not even read the works of his own cronies; when Rosenberg gave him *The Myth of the Twentieth Century*, the bible of Nazism, Hitler returned the book unread. He talked often about art and told his intimates that after the war he would become a full-time artist. Yet he never showed any interest in exhibitions or the works of contemporary artists. As an Austrian *petit-bourgeois,* he wallowed in a form of kitsch known as Vertico. Visiting his private quarters in Munich and at the Berghof, Speer commented, "It was full of richly carved oak library furniture, books behind glass, cushions embroidered with delicate party greetings, a bust of Richard Wagner in one corner, paintings of the Munich school in heavy gold frames, a canary in a gilt cage…" (Fest 1999, 44). As German chancellor he planned and built institutional behemoths, their overriding architectural features gigantic dimensions and miles of windowless cement. The statuary he scattered inside and outside these mastodons were, parallel perhaps to Stalin's aesthetics, a style of ideological realism — torsos of men meant to be gladiators, and females with bellies fit for procreation, two human ideals of Nazi theology. Whatever cultural diversions he indulged in were of the popular variety: operettas like *The Merry Widow* and *Die Fledermaus,* music hall shows, and most of all, the cinema. An exception to this fare was Wagner, whose *Die Meistersinger* he was reputed to have seen 100 times.

When he served on the French front in World War I Hitler loved the experience. Here are his feelings at the outbreak of the Great War: "To me these hours seemed like a release from the painful feelings of my youth. Even today I am not ashamed to say that overpowered by stormy enthusiasm I fell down on my knees and thanked Heaven from an overflowing heart for granting me the good fortune of being permitted to live at this time. For me, as for every German there now began the greatest and most unforgettable time of my earthly existence."* In a letter describing his first combat he rejoices at the sight of battle and the sense of killing. Hitler was twice wounded and was decorated with the Iron Cross, first and second class— the highest decoration to which a common soldier could aspire. Yet his fellow soldiers found him unpleasant. He shared in none of their camaraderie, indifferent to the ordeals and joys of the front-line soldier. Along with his bravery and dedication runs a streak of resentment for being at the front when he says, "In these times I felt for the first time the whole malice of Destiny which kept me at the front in a position where every nigger might accidentally shoot me to bits, while elsewhere I would have been able to perform quite different services for the Fatherland." In the army, as throughout his life, he had no close friends and no trusted advisers. His entourage consisted exclusively of people willing and capable of enduring his habitual monologues and perforce they were lackeys. A witness describes Hitler's presence in an aristocratic home before he became chancellor as "the stereotype of a headwaiter not quite daring to sit fully in his chair who talked endlessly…. He preached like a division chaplain, eventually beginning to bellow…. When he was gone (we) opened one of the big windows … to dispel the feeling of oppression … the unclean essence of a monstrosity" (Reck, 24).

Hitler saw himself as a man of destiny, willed to lead Germany on her greatest mission. A thorough pagan, he often invoked Providence as his backer; the two of them were, so to speak, in cahoots. He considered himself to be Germany's godsend. "I go the way Providence dictates with the assurance of a sleepwalker," he said in 1936. To Schuschnigg he remarked, "I have achieved everything I set out to do and have thus become, perhaps, the greatest German in history," which is a good sample of his logic. Much of his behavior was motivated by his sense of indispensability. His abstinence in food, fear of colds and infections, his avoidance of coffee and alcohol were due to a concern for his longevity. He worked hard to maintain his image of uniqueness. His speeches were prepared with the greatest care and he made sure that the crowd was not distracted or uncomfortable. His

In Chapters 1 and 2 all of Hitler's quotations are from Mein Kampf.

more important receptions and audiences were rehearsed. To enhance his prestige he arrived late at social functions and left early; his invitations, on the other hand, were commands which one was wise to obey. He officiated beneath a giant portrait of Frederick the Great; Michelangelo was his preferred sculptor; Wagner his composer. He built his Berghof with its vast rooms, oversized furniture, and the "largest window in Europe" high above the Bavarian Alps because that befitted his notion of greatness. Above the Berghof, on Mount Kehlstein, he built a holy of holies, the Adlernest, accessible via corridors hewn in rock and a lift rising 330 feet through the mountain to a gallery ringed with Roman pillars and bronze eagles floating over its roof. There, too, he wanted to be buried, like Barbarossa — a name we shall meet again. He scrupulously avoided situations in which he would be out-shone by others. When the German saboteur, Schlageter, was executed by the occupying French, he declined to speak in Munich because he was to be one among several speakers. Invited in 1926 by Mussolini, he refused to go because he would have been second fiddle to Il Duce. He likewise did not attend an evening with Churchill on the latter's visit to Munich lest he be outclassed by the formidable Bulldog. In fact, one of the reasons he joined the German Workers' Party, the forerunner of the National Socialist German Work-ers Party (NSDAP), was because it was very small and he could rise quickly to the top, just as, when he was in jail in 1924, he deliberately fostered schisms in his own party so that no one would replace him. Whatever substance the party was to have and whatever future awaited Germany, it would have to be indistinguishable from himself.

Hitler was a dazzling public speaker. Though his speeches were long and repetitious, he imparted to them a passion and a terror which made them overpowering. His greatness lay not only in his voice, but also in his acting stunts. In a rising pitch, lifting himself to the tips of his boots, his arms slashing the air, eyes flashing, hair flying, he whipped him-self and the crowd into a frenzy. While speechmaking was his one true gift, warfare was his one true passion. Yet there was in his love for the military the same dehumanized atti-tude he had exhibited as a corporal in the trenches of World War I. Hitler was not only supreme commander but, from December 1941 on, also commander in chief of the army and, at one time, even commander of an army group. Yet he rarely ventured to see his sol-diers, confining himself to the cloister-like isolation of his SS-guarded headquarters. On rare trips to his army group feldmarschalls he was impatient, insecure, anxious to return home. As with his love of the German people — which was an abstract vision of a nonex-istent Aryan entity — his love for the army was not a love of the camaraderie, campfires, marches which stir men fighting a war but, rather, for the remote game of divisions and conquests, the vision of a feldherr making history from the remoteness of a command post. He was indefatigable in his study of maps and campaigns, and he amazed and intimidated his subordinates with his memorization of dispositions of single battalions and the num-ber of weapons they had. After June 1941 he stayed buried in his eastern headquarters immersed in the tactical fortunes of individual divisions, ignoring allies, enemies, and all other affairs of state.

Hitler dismissed any outside expertise and counsel to a point that in the spring of 1942 he issued an order to the Oberkommando der Wermacht forbidding the dissemination of all intelligence unless the conclusions corresponded to his own opinions (Megargee, 176). From the beginning to the end of his rule he went about eradicating all vestiges of inde-pendent authority, demolishing in the process not only political, but also state institutions. He abolished the presidency, the war ministry and made a messenger boy out of his for-eign minister. He destroyed the general staff of the army, splintered its intelligence service and in the end began to replace the army itself with the Waffen SS. He maintained direct control over Germany's destiny via three independent channels: as chancellor through the traditional state machinery, as supreme commander via the armed forces, and as führer via the machinery of the Nazi Party and the police. Through all of them he intervened and acted at will at home and throughout the occupied territories. Everywhere the multiple channels of authority were kept in disarray so that he could be the ultimate arbiter.

Aside from being the supreme state authority, Hitler possessed personal attributes which made it possible for him to exercise absolute tyranny over his subordinates. His talent for intimidation was such that the next most powerful man in Germany, Hermann Göring, confided to Schacht, "I often make up my mind to say something to him, but when I come face to face with him my heart sinks into my boots." The same was true of Mussolini, who turned dumb in Hitler's presence. When Zeitzler took over as army chief of staff in September 1942, he was briefed by Keitel, "Never contradict the Führer. Never remind him that once he may have thought differently. Never tell him that subsequent events have proved you right..." (Cross 1993, 87). Hitler completely lacked what is a common human trait — a sense of shame. To quote Wheeler-Bennet, Hitler "always meant what he said except when he pledged his word." After each conquest he announced it to be the last and then went on to the next. On numerous occasions he said he would kill himself if he did not have his way; he sometimes did not prevail, and yet he survived. He repeatedly threatened that if this or that battle is not won the war would be lost; the battles were lost and he kept the war going for years thereafter. Consistent with these predilections he rarely committed himself in print. Vague, wary, secretive, he preferred endless talk. He had a remarkable memory and, taking advantage of this reputation, he employed false data and false facts and when discovered never flinched, arguing "The New Testament is full of contradictions but that did not prevent the spread of Christianity." He never convened a war council or cabinet meeting and was thus able to bamboozle his soldiers with arguments of diplomacy while silencing his ministers with military exigencies. When this approach failed he used what may be called the transcendental angle. When a commander pleaded for permission to withdraw from an imperiled sector of the front, Hitler, who on principle was against withdrawals, would suddenly ask the commander whether he had ever heard of a war being fought without peril, whether it was not the duty of the soldier to give his life for his country, life was brief, and so on. The commander had come to discuss a concrete point — instead Hitler talked about ethics, patriotism, and the fleeting nature of life. When none of these approaches worked and some astute officer — a rare specimen indeed — persisted in arguing his point not on the basis of metaphysics but in terms of the situation on the front, Hitler used his final weapon — hysterics. His eyes would turn wild, he would pound the table and fly toward his visitor with clenched fists, shrieking that he had been disobeyed, betrayed, whipping himself into an act of near collapse. The German officer, a stiff and unemotional breed, would be profoundly embarrassed and withdraw in confusion and distaste. Once, when the papal nuncio came to him pleading for the Jews, Hitler smashed a glass cup at the nuncio's feet (*New York Times*, April 24, 1966). Thus would many an interview between the head of state and his interlocutors be resolved.

It is easy to enumerate Hitler's many talents: his great skill as an organizer and leader of men, the sweep of his imagination, his iron will, his audacity. However, if statesmanship is measured by achievements, then all his undertakings are impressive only in the manner of their launching. He rearmed Germany at a dazzling pace, but also in a way which alarmed its neighbors and made it clear what was afoot. He was eulogized for winning the

Rhineland, Austria, the Sudetenland and Czechoslovakia — all bloodlessly — but he did it in such a predictable way that with each successive step he dragged England closer to war with Germany — an event he had screamed must be avoided at all costs. He brought about brilliant military campaigns, but in the process expanded the war into unprofitable regions with unintended enemies. His celebrated intuition was predicated on recklessness — on a number of occasions it had proved clairvoyant, but just as frequently it brought disaster. He was proven right in judging the strength of Poland and France but he was dead wrong on the strength of the Royal Air Force and the stability and power of the Soviet Union, not to speak of the might of America — and these were blunders that brought about his defeat. His spectacular tactics could never make up for a disastrous strategy, just as slyness is no substitute for wisdom.

In essence, Hitler can be described as a possessed psychopath — his compulsions accounting for both his strong and weak sides. Whatever he absorbed and formulated remained unaltered throughout his life and no counsels or facts ever altered it. He bent and slanted reality to suit his conceptions, for he held it a sign of weakness and diminution of authority to change one's mind. All major decisions were taken by Hitler, without any consultation with others. The process consisted of shutting himself off at the Berghof where, in the solitude of the Alps and a Wagnerian sunset, he planned the next move. After such a retreat the decision was announced and from then on it remained unalterable. Next was the fanatical ruthlessness of his methods that were pursued oblivious of the cost to his soldiers, his people, the world. His millions of victims were not war concomitants or excesses ordered for reasons of state. He exterminated by class, by nationality, by race; everyone with a university degree, all retarded people, all gypsies, all Jews, all Russian POWs — slaughtering entire populations according to his private demons. Hitler must be classed as a nihilist because he possessed not one positive idea or objective. All his creeds and actions were of a negative sort, including his professed love for the German people. He identified his low status and failures with a debilitated Germany of the '20s, but after seizing power he merely used it for his own megalomania. He had no love or loyalty to anyone or anything. In the Röhm Affair he sacrificed many of his staunchest Nazi comrades because they were a threat to his newly won chancellorship; his treachery in the affair was such that many of his friends died shouting "Heil Hitler." After all the splendid campaigns of the Afrika Korps he flung at Rommel the accusation that his soldiers had thrown away their weapons and ran. He called his own SS general, Sepp Dietrich, and his SS troops cowards, after most of them had died in battle. Nearly all his feldmarschalls were either sacked or executed. When at the war's end Baldur von Schirach begged him to declare Vienna an open city to spare the lives of the 90,000 wounded soldiers Hitler rejected the idea; instead he ordered that his collection of antique weapons be transferred to the Obersalzberg. He executed his own brother-in-law, SS General Fegelein, and in the end ordered Göring and Himmler to be tried for treason. Before he committed suicide he ordered the destruction of all services and facilities of the Reich, pronouncing the verdict that the German people had no right to exist, for they had proved inferior to the "Eastern Peoples."

In order to reconcile the disparate impressions he left on various people one has to view Adolf Hitler as a corpus of three distinct facets, each hermetically compartmentalized so that neither friend nor foe surmised the existence of the others. The first syndrome of his personality was that of the Austrian *petit-bourgeois*. This entailed kitsch *politesse* — flowers during visits, kissing ladies' hands, presents and felicitations on birthdays and holidays. Nearly all his aides-de-camp, secretaries, chauffeurs, valets, cooks and servants had nothing but praise for his attentiveness and generosity. This bonhomie and charm was often extended to visiting foreign dignitaries who left beguiled by his gallantry and seeming goodwill, carrying away the opinion that here was a statesman who craved nothing but a fair deal for his people. This posture of Austrian charmer was often reinforced by his stance as a bohemian. His impoverished, footloose existence as a youth, his interest in painting, his love for Wagnerian music, his passion for architecture — even if restricted to neoclassical and institutional behemoths— imparted to Hitler an "artistic" aura.

The second visage of Hitler, the one that the public had come to know, was that of führer. This consisted of the aura that in him Germany had found a statesman of genius, selflessly committed to the greatness and happiness of the nation. All his deeds and misdeeds— his dismantling of the state's constitutional and judicial institutions, his ideological travesties, his deceptions and aggressions— were all seen as a means of serving the German people. An entire nation — aristocrats, generals, bankers, academicians, philosophers, artists and clergymen — not to speak of the middle and working classes who not only supported but also loved him — all saw Adolf Hitler as a super–Bismarck who would obtain for Germany what neither the kaiser nor certainly the Weimar Republic had been capable of achieving. The führer's use of the concentration camp and the gallows for any deviation from Nazi ideas and practices; his claim to ultimate expertise in all spheres of knowledge whether armaments, economic theory, history, anthropology, or dietary medicine; the use of tantrums and screams to intimidate the high and mighty whether they were his own feldmarschalls or foreign heads of state and, above all, the total absence of dignity or self-respect which enabled him to repeatedly employ falsehoods and suffer defeats without embarrassment — all were practices for the alleged good of Germany and were so perceived by the German people.

For lack of a fitting neologism, the third facet of Hitler's persona will here be termed satanic. While the Viennese bourgeois was a veneer and the role of führer a studied pose for public consumption, the satanic facet constituted the true, inner core of the individual, permeating his entire conscious and subconscious psyche. It was the prime mover, the fountainhead of all his theories, schemes, and actions. The consequences of these satanic impulses have in scale and horror never been equaled in human history. What gave birth to this horrendous core of his person is unknown and, from a historical perspective, irrelevant. The results are only too well known. These gruesome deeds, all executed on his direct orders, include the euthanasia program which resulted in the deaths of some 100,000 "feeble" Germans; the order to kill off the Polish intelligentsia; the instruction that the invasion of Russia be not a war but a campaign of extermination in which Russia's "life force" must be extirpated; the murder of four million Russian POWs; the order not to occupy Leningrad and Moscow but lay siege to them so that they could be razed and the population starved to death; the slow strangulation of the men of the July 20 plot by means of piano wire looped over meat hooks so that he could later watch their agony on film; the program to exterminate the entire Jewish population of Europe which resulted in the assembly-line killing of six million men women and children; and finally, before his own suicide, his wish to have the entire German nation perish, declaring them unfit to live because they had not won the war for him.

• CHAPTER 2 •

The Program

In 1924, Hitler was spending time in jail for leading an abortive putsch against the Weimar Republic of Germany. Though his confinement in the fortress of Landsberg consisted of a flower-decked room with free visits from friends and admirers, the enforced inactivity was alien to his temperament. To relieve the tedium and to provide a program for his party, which was in the doldrums after the putsch, Hitler was led to do what he loathed doing—committing himself in writing. The result was *Mein Kampf.* Nothing that Hitler was later to pronounce, no known deed or scheme, substantially departed from what was spelled out in the pages of this book. It was an accurate portrait of its author and an oracle for the next 20 years of European history.

Throughout, the text hammers turgidly and repetitively at a few basic themes. Despite its verbosity the enunciated *Weltgeschichtlich* program for Germany's future can be subsumed under four headings:

1. Pseudo-Darwinism. Life is a perpetual contest in which only force can bring success and happiness and force is granted only to superior races of which the Germans are top specimens.

2. Brotherhood with England. Germany is never to war on or even compete with Great Britain because the Germans and the English are racial cousins, both fated to rule the inferior nations. Consequently Germany should not aspire to colonies or maritime supremacy because that would bring on a conflict with Great Britain. More generally, unlike the foolish kaiser, Germany should never wage a war in both East and West.

3. *Drang nach Osten.* In terms of world power, economic wealth and racial supremacy Germany's destiny lies in the East. This ranges over all Slavic lands east of the Oder, primarily the Russian landmass up to and beyond the Urals. A country can be a world power only when it rules an entire continent—vide North America, Great Britain, Russia. Germany's continent lies in the East, which must be conquered, depopulated, and settled with Aryan barons on vast *latifundias* worked on by hordes of local serfs.

4. Jews. Jews are the source of all misery and ugliness on earth and the only solution is the extermination of the entire race.

Now something has to be said about the affinity between the Hitlerian *Weltanschauung* and German history. On the surface it may seem that much of what Hitler advocated was but a resurrection of German proclivities prior to, during, and following the Great War. The Germans always detested the Poles, probably because if you harm someone you also begin to hate him—justifying thereby retroactively the inflicted injury. Even during the Weimar Republic with pacific, democratic Germans at the helm, there was a rabid desire

14

to dismember Poland, as Prussia had done on three previous occasions. There was a perpetual *Drang nach Osten* and the kaiser had flung himself against Russia in 1914 with all the glee of a would-be conqueror. In their paroxysm to become the leading European power there had been a similar disregard for the bloodshed and ruin inflicted on neighbors and a stunning devil-may-care attitude in engaging, at the same time, France, Belgium, Russia, England, Italy, and, eventually, America in a war Germany could not possibly win. So the parallels run deep simply because the kaiser, Weimar, and Nazism were all products of the same nation.

But despite the similarities there is no equating Hitler with what the Germans had produced in the past. In their aims and methods, the kaiser and Hitler are as different as a greedy banker is from a deranged gangster. The kaiser and his Germans wanted supremacy, glory, riches; Hitler craved ruins and blood. As an illustration of the basic differences one can cite Russia. After defeating it in World War I, Germany in the Treaty of Brest-Litovsk took the Baltic states, the Ukraine and Transcaucasia, their future to be determined "in agreement with their populations." But Russia was left as an independent state to rule its people. With Hitler Russia was to cease to exist, Moscow and Leningrad razed to the ground, its people either exterminated or reduced to slavery. Then the methods employed: the kaiser fought to win and whatever injury he caused to Russia, Belgium and France was part of an effort to achieve military victory. Hitler's methods were designed not for victory but for carnage and devastation as such. As will be shown later on, when ruin and extermination conflicted with the demands of military success he chose wanton slaughter over the demands of war. In Imperial Germany there was Germanization of the conquered Poles, anti–Semitism, chauvinism, greed — with Hitler it was gas chambers and genocide, a massacre of POWs, the extirpation of the "life force" of all Slavs. An affinity with the past perhaps lies only in the fact that the Germans who so devotedly followed Hitler saw in him initially a realization of their old national dreams; when later on they witnessed the slaughters and the purposeless destruction they proved to be too callous to bother about these "excesses."

To have had access to Hitler's printed and spoken views and yet to have the statesmen of the '30s misjudge Hitler so miserably is a bizarre tale. Naturally there were public figures who recognized Hitler for what he was— Churchill, Phipps, Dodds, Namier, Vansittard, to mention a few, — but they were in the minority and mostly men out of office. It is perhaps understandable that it was difficult for men of reason and conventional morality to accept as a possibility the ghoulish schemes Hitler proclaimed. However, statesmen are at their posts not to express beliefs or nurture hopes but to gauge the realities of the world and to safeguard the interests of their countries. In this they failed spectacularly. The failure was due not merely to weakness or ineptness in the execution of foreign policy but something more serious— dereliction of duty. Instead of application, scrutiny, and the utmost seriousness that the situation demanded they preferred the easy alternatives of optimism and procrastination. Whenever they did come face to face with Hitler and his deeds they proved to be men of piddling perspicacity for they drew mostly the wrong conclusions.

Ironically, the first grievous underestimation of Hitler occurs in the introduction to the American edition of *Mein Kampf* by Konrad Heiden, the Swiss eyewitness and early biographer of Hitler. Though aware of the nature of the book, which he calls a satanic bible, Mr. Heiden says, "*Mein Kampf* is packed with principles of foreign policy which have been taken more seriously by others than by the author himself.... Whether Hitler proclaims war against Russia or friendship with England … all these plans mean nothing. He has changed them again and again...." Others misjudged not only his intentions but also his murderous, fanatic willpower. Von Schleicher, Hitler's predecessor, opined in 1931 "Hitler knows how to distinguish between demagogy and national and international life. The policy to adopt is to use him." Von Papen similarly intended to make Hitler a tool of the Conservatives. For this misjudgment Schleicher paid with his life in the Röhm putsch; and von Papen, after twice escaping assassination on Hitler's orders, ended up in a concentration camp. Those were associates of Hitler who had unprecedented opportunity to observe him at close range. As for those who were not so close their verdicts often reached the comic, as when Baron de Ropp told the Anglo-German Fellowship in 1937, "Herr Hitler has given the church a free hand. He is a deeply religious man himself" (Gilbert & Gott, 65).

Nor was this myopia confined to Germans. From all corners of the globe flowed the considered judgments of important public figures. Vernon Bartlett, a veteran journalist, after seeing Hitler for the first time waxed lyrical over his brown eyes (which they were not) and wrote, in the summer of 1933, "Hitler, like Gandhi, wants a return to the spinning wheel, not only because he is an economic realist and a nationalist, but because he believes in simplicity." General Ironside, chief of the Imperial General Staff, after meeting Hitler on maneuvers in 1937 penned the following description: "The man struck me not at all. He made no more impression on me than would a somewhat mild professor whom I rather suspect of having a drop too much on occasions." He even flunked his physical diagram for he described Hitler's eyes as "watery, weak-looking" and his voice as "soft" (Ironside, 29). Poland's foreign minister Jozef Beck assured everyone that "Hitler had no wish to precipitate a general conflagration and that he certainly meant no harm to Poland." The renowned historian Arnold Toynbee after a chat with the führer said that he was convinced of Hitler's sincerity in desiring peace in Europe though he did not think, as Bartlett did, that he was another Gandhi. The pacifist Lansbury went to see Hitler to pray together for peace and after having put Hitler to sleep and being nearly shown the door announced "I return to England with the conviction that war will be avoided," a phrase Chamberlain was to repeat later on a more momentous occasion. Karl Burckhardt, the League of Nations high commissioner for Danzig, said that Hitler's boasting was due to fear and that as a person he struck him as "nervous, pathetic and almost shaken at times" (Gilbert & Gott, 262). As late as 1939, Göring's peacemaker, Birger Dahlerus, thought Hitler full of "good will," intent only on "saving face." Even after war broke out, Chaim Weizmann, scientist, Zionist leader and future president of Israel, judged Hitler as "confused who did not know what to do. He did not want war and was afraid of it in his soul." Lloyd George, the astute prime minister who led Britain through the ordeal of World War I, after being received by the führer in his study with a photograph of the old man flatteringly placed on the desk, later wrote "Germany no longer desires to invade any other land ... I only wish we had a man of his supreme quality at the head of affairs in our country today" and on another occasion he said, "He is the Washington of Germany.... The idea of Germany intimidating Europe ... forms no part of the new vision..." (*Daily Express*, November 17, 1936). The newspapers and entertainment media often did paint Hitler as the devil, but it was all caricature, like Chaplin's film *The Dictator*, which robbed the subject of its terror, its sole reality.

The most tragic consequences, of course, resulted from misjudgments made by the men in power. The people who set the moral and political tone of the '30s in Great Britain were men variously referred to as the Cliveden Set, the All Souls Fellows, or the Appeasers. They were a fraternity of high government officials and gray eminences whose uncanny uniformity of dress and mannerisms alone fills one with a suspicion of the obsolescence of their minds. They were not even aristocrats who, though conservative and supercilious, would, by adhering to their own code of honor, have recognized Hitler for what he was. They were men of the upper middle class, remnants of the Victorian era trying to approach aristocratic standards by imitating their superficial aspects. They were full of cant and high-mindedness and, while deploring the Nazi "excesses," remained unaffected by the tragedies they produced. They considered all continentals inferior and, if anything, thought of the Germans as the nation nearest to the English. And, of course, Soviet Russia was *the* menace. Though in the 15 years of her existence she had harmed no one but her own wretched people — yet to them the Soviet Union remained a menace worse than Nazi Germany. Nor did they want the Americans to have a say in their handling of the dictators, judging them naive; in the economic and cultural spheres they were even hostile to America. Throughout his years in office, and that includes the war period, Chamberlain was as much concerned with American financial rivalry as with Germany's political menace, perhaps to be expected of a manufacturer of bedsteads and a former chancellor of the exchequer. It was only when Hitler stepped on their patent leather shoes that they got haughty and shook their canes. The great turn in British foreign policy in March 1939 had probably as much to do with political realities as with the fact that Hitler had done the most dastardly thing he could possibly have done — breaking the word he had given to a British prime minister. When Hitler took Prague, Chamberlain pathetically exclaimed, "You don't do that to me" (Colvin 1965, 294).

What were these men's views of Hitler? For one thing, few of them had read *Mein Kampf,* nor did they really bother to learn anything about him. Still they had views. Lord Lothian, a veteran diplomat and author of the preface to the Versailles Treaty, said after seeing Hitler in 1935, "The central fact is that Germany doesn't want war and is prepared to renounce it absolutely as a matter of settling disputes" (Colvin 1965, 41). In 1939 when he finally saw through Nazism Lothian recalled that even with regard to concentration camps the attitude of his colleagues was that they were a "result of the denial to Germany of the rights which every other sovereign nation enjoys." Lord Halifax had this to say about the Nazi leaders: re Hitler: "I am sure Hitler was sincere when he said he didn't want war"; Göring looked "attractive, like a great schoolboy"; re Goebbels: "I had expected to dislike him intensely — but didn't" (Smith, 370). The German Captain Widemann quotes Halifax, the man destined to be foreign secretary in the crucial years of 1938–40, as having said in July 1938 that "Before his death he would like to see as the culmination of his work the führer entering London at the side of the English king amidst the exclamation of the English people" (Gilbert & Gott, 9, 128).

Of all these luminaries two deserve special mention. One is, of course, Neville Chamberlain. Not that he was duped more than the rest, but because he was prime minister. The kindest thing to say of him is that if he did not fathom Hitler it was because he was not interested in him. He thought him just another noisy continental martinet. The warnings of ambassadors that he may be dealing here not with what he, after first seeing Hitler, described as "the commonest-looking little dog," but a species of hyena that is neither common nor little, only evoked Chamberlain's disdain. Chamberlain felt superior to Hitler. That others should be frightened was natural, but he, Chamberlain, was British prime minister, older, wiser, reasonable and more persuasive and he would have no difficulty in handling the raw upstart. And so, when he came back from his visit to Godesberg he assured everyone "I had established a certain confidence ... and, on my side, in spite of the hardness and ruthlessness I thought I saw in his face, I got the impression that here was a man who could be relied upon when he had given his word." Put differently,

Hitler may be hard and ruthless to everyone else, but a word given to Chamberlain was holy.

The other worthy was Nevile Henderson, British ambassador to Berlin in the two and a half years preceding the war. Henderson succeeded Eric Phipps, whom Hitler loathed because, after an initial enchantment, Phipps quickly caught on and considered Hitler a menace. Henderson could not be called an appeaser for there was no need for appeasement. He was two-footed on the German side. Henderson's Germanophilia is too opulent to be quoted in full and some of his pronouncements will appear in the next two chapters. In the succession of crises over the years 1938–39 it was always the Austrians, the Czechs, or the Poles who were the reckless parties for, argued Henderson, by their reluctance to yield, they were endangering world peace. In his memoirs one finds repeatedly that it was never the Nazi chieftains, nor the ordinary German who craved war and conquest, but some hidden, mythical, all-powerful *extremists*. Unreachable, elusive phantoms, they were the ones pulling down the peaceful structure that Hitler and the German people so patiently strove to construct.

If in the preceding paragraphs the British official view of Hitler is emphasized it is done for good reason. They were the ones who, British reputation notwithstanding, talked most and loudest. And it was their opinion that mattered. The French had no policy effective enough to impact the course of events. As if in an intuitive acknowledgment of what was to happen later the French said very little. Whatever they thought of Hitler, and they thought less of him than their British friends, they kept silent, not wanting to upset the intricate construct of British diplomacy. Russia was kept at arm's length and whatever the Soviets said or wished to do was ignored and mistrusted, not without reason. America and the Benelux countries were "neutral." A few, like Poland and Hungary, aped the Germans. So the people whose judgment of Hitler mattered were the British statesmen, for they spoke for the Czechs, the French, and the Commonwealth. Their correct interpretation of Hitler and proper reaction would, certainly at the time of Rhineland, and very likely still during the Anschluss, have averted the Second World War. By March 1939, when they finally caught on, it was too late.

· CHAPTER 3 ·

The Bloodless Conquests

In the German elections of 1932, the NSDAP polled the largest popular vote of all political parties in Germany. As a consequence, on January 30, 1933, the president of the republic, von Hindenburg, appointed Adolf Hitler chancellor. In the Reichstag elections of December 11, 1933, with 95 percent of the eligible voters going to the polls, the Nazi Party received 92 percent of the votes, essentially taking over the Reichstag. In a series of swift, unconstitutional and uncontested measures, Hitler abolished the republic and all its democratic institutions. When Hindenburg died on August 2, 1934, Hitler abolished the presidency, too, and proclaimed himself supreme lord of a new Nazi state. In a subsequent referendum, 44 million Germans, or 90 percent of those voting, said yes to Hitler's Third Reich.

Fifteen years earlier, in 1918, Germany had been subdued in a world war, which she had ignited, by attacking Russia in the east and France and Belgium in the west. Subsequently a peace treaty was signed between the victorious Allies and Germany, the Treaty of Versailles. Its main provisions were as follows: Germany remained a free and sovereign state. In the east she was to return the territories she had acquired in the partitions of Poland during the late 18th century and in the west Alsace-Lorraine, Bismarck's conquest of 1870, was returned to France. Germany lost small slices of territory along her other borders: Schleswig-Holstein to Denmark, Malmedy and Eupen to Belgium, Memel to Lithuania. The Saar basin was to remain under the League of Nations until a plebiscite in 1935 decided its fate. Germany was deprived of all her overseas colonies. There were also domestic provisions. Germany was to pay reparations for the devastations she had caused in France and Belgium. The Rhineland was to remain demilitarized indefinitely. Conscription was to be abolished and the Reichswehr was allowed a maximum of 100,000 volunteers. Germany was allowed only a token navy and no air force. The allies had forbidden an Anschluss, a provision that was also written into the St. Germain peace treaty with Austria. The Allies reserved the right of intervention should Germany violate the treaty.

After planting the Nazi regime in the hearts and institutions of the German people, Hitler, as he had forewarned, started to unshackle Germany from the strictures of Versailles. He concentrated on the domestic provisions first, which was logical, but as we shall see, there was to this more than mere logic. The quick demise of the Versailles treaty at Hitler's hands can be understood better when it is set against the German view of it on the one hand and that of Britain and America on the other. According to the Germans, they had agreed to sue for peace in 1918 on the basis of Wilson's Fourteen Points, which the treaty allegedly violated. The clauses of the treaty were thus considered a breach of justice. The British and the Americans agreed with much of this. Furthermore, the German people

On the night of January 30, 1933, jubilant Berliners greet the new reichs chancellor, Adolf Hitler. (Used by permission of *Der Spiegel.*)

claimed that they had been beaten not by the allies but by traitors at home. In fact they had not been beaten at all. At Berlin University, a nest of World War I nostalgia, the war memorial erected there read, *Invictis Victi Victuri*— To the Unconquered the Conquered Who Will Conquer. On December 11, 1918, as the bands played *Deutschland Über Alles*, the troops returning from France passed in review under the Brandenburger Tor, with Friedrich Ebert, president of the Weimar Republic, proclaiming, "I salute you, who return unvanquished from the field of battle." Even in West-oriented Cologne crowds cheered the returning troops with Konrad Adenauer, the Allies' apostle of a reconstructed West Germany welcoming the soldiers in a speech to the city council saying "our brothers in field grey are coming home after four years of defending house and home … not defeated and not beaten" (Williams, 98). Now, if the Germans had not lost the war after all, and when even her former enemies felt Versailles to have been a miscarriage of justice, then the treaty was doomed *a priori*. Thus, by the time Hitler came to power most of its provisions had already been eroded. Reparations had been annulled, all occupation troops had long quit German soil and the Reichswehr under various disguises had armed itself beyond both the spirit and letter of the treaty. What is of interest in Hitler's handling of the treaty is not that he proceeded to undo it — the Weimar Republic with the connivance of England and America had been doing that for some time — but the selective attitude he adopted with regard to its provisions.

The years 1933 and 1934 were more or less devoted to consolidation of power. This meant not merely power of the regime but the personal power of Adolf Hitler. Thus, in addition to the purges of professional societies, labor unions, cultural institutions and the like, it extended also to any potential challenge from fellow Nazis which led to the decimation of the SA and the killing of its leader, Röhm. At the same time Schleicher was assassinated and von Papen banished, the two men who had handed Hitler the chancellorship confident that he would be a mere tool in the hands of the Conservatives. Then on March 9, 1935, Hitler, in conversation with the British journalist Ward Price, announced the rebirth of the German air force. On the 16th this was followed by the introduction of conscription in Germany and the raising of a standing army of 36 divisions, half a million men. On the 21st, Hitler decreed a secret defense law providing for the industrial and economic means of rearmament. In short, Germany served notice that she was building a new army, was building it fast, and intended to do so regardless of past agreements. To simplify things, she quit the League of Nations.

These moves struck alarm in the hearts of the French. The British, safe behind their moat, were not as alarmed but they, too, disliked this unilateral breach of international treaties and it led to an offer to come to Berlin for discussions. The first major conference between Hitler and the British statesmen is significant on account of both manner and substance; it is, in a way, typical of the future dealings between the two governments. The origins of the conference go back to the summer of 1934 when the French Foreign Minister Louis Barthou suggested to Eden an eastern Locarno, that is a joint guarantee of the status quo between Germany and her eastern neighbors. A joint Anglo-French note suggesting such talks was sent to Berlin on February 2, 1935. Instead Hitler proposed bilateral talks with England which the latter accepted. The trip — undertaken against the wishes of France — was set for March 25, 1935.

The British had two points on their mind. One was to grant Germany rights of rearmament provided she returned to the League of Nations, a spurious concession since Germany was well on her way toward full rearmament. The second, more important, objective

et Germany to join in a nonaggression pact with her eastern neighbors. On the
g of the 25th, Foreign Secretary Simon accompanied by Eden were shown into the
be. Chancellery where Hitler greeted them with the words, "I believe that National Socialism has saved Germany, and perhaps all Europe, from the most terrible catastrophe of all
time — Bolshevism." Simon, according to witnesses, looked at the führer with a paternal-
istic smile, though Eden, who a year ago had thought Hitler sincere, was beginning to have
qualms about him. In the talks Hitler rejected a return to the League because its covenant
was tied to Versailles. To Simon's suggestion that these two items could be divorced Hitler
bemoaned the lost German colonies. When the British hinted that this, too, was negotiable,
Hitler dropped the subject, saying that he could wait. An eastern Locarno he dismissed with
contempt, adding ominously that he preferred bilateral agreements with his eastern neighbors. If the visit did not fulfill British hopes it did fulfill one of Hitler's, for it was instrumental in producing the German-British Naval Agreement. At the meeting Hitler had told
Simon that while not prepared to put any limitations on the size of his army or air force —
in fact he bluntly told him that the Luftwaffe had already reached parity with Great Britain —
he was willing to settle for a navy only 35 percent as strong as England's. It was a gesture
certainly to be appreciated by his guests and this was what Hitler had hoped for. It was also
a gesture that put no hindrance on his future designs for Hitler needed no navy if he was
going to be true to himself, and he was nothing if not that.

Though the naval agreement was unpalatable to France, whose own navy was no larger
than Germany's proposed strength, England negotiated the treaty without consulting her,
and in June the naval agreement was signed. France sent London an angry note against what
amounted to England's connivance in a breach of Versailles, but a jubilant führer remarked
to Raeder, "Today is the happiest day of my life. First, the doctor has just told me that my
throat trouble is not of a malignant nature, and just now I have been informed of the completion of the naval agreement with England." Ribbentrop, who signed the document for
the Germans, later wrote in his memoirs: "After the naval agreement I concentrated on
building further on this foundation; I wanted to create even closer relations and possibly
bring about an alliance with Britain. For this was Hitler's ardent wish and also my own."
Characteristically Hitler never even took advantage of the provisions of the treaty. He who
had tirelessly exhorted his armed forces for bigger and better weapons restrained Raeder
in his naval ambitions. When war broke out he had fewer submarines than England even
though under the treaty he had been allowed parity. War with England, Raeder was told,
was unthinkable and he was given orders that such a contingency should never be made
part of any war games or exercises. The whole German naval blueprint, the so-called
Z-Plan consisting of a build-up of fast cruisers and battleships instead of submarines, was
based on the proposition of no war with England.

The reoccupation of the Rhineland by German troops on March 7, 1936, marks the
end of a phase. With this step Hitler completed the annulment of the domestic clauses of
Versailles. Now it is only natural that a defeated country should strive to rid itself of the
strictures of a punishing peace treaty; any leader in office is bound to work for it. However, it is one thing to rectify the economic and political consequences of a lost war and
another to prepare for a new one. For the primary purpose in all of Hitler's moves during
the years 1933–36 had been to create a potent military machine. This could not have been
achieved without overthrowing the multiple strictures of the treaty, which, of course, had
been set up with the purpose of preventing such a contingency. Actually, the reoccupation
of the Rhineland had deeper implications than merely the violation of Versailles or a fur-

ther increase in German military might. In Hitler's planned war with the east, the only other army capable of attacking Germany was that of France and as soon as he reoccupied the Rhineland Hitler began to build fortifications along the French border, the Siegfried Line, or Westwall. Now, Hitler was no exponent of trench warfare and the campaigns he planned and later conducted were blitzkriegs. The building of the Westwall was a waste of resources; Hitler never built an Eastwall on the borders with Poland or Czechoslovakia nor, after 1939, along the Soviet border. The Westwall was to protect his rear and as soon as he had taken the Rhineland he proceeded with its construction, a further violation of Versailles. All this was candidly conveyed in May 1936 by von Neurath to the American ambassador in Paris, William Bullit, who later quoted him as having said, "Until the German fortifications are constructed on the French and Belgian frontiers, the German government would do everything possible to prevent rather than encourage an outbreak by the Nazis in Austria and would pursue a quiet line with regard to Czechoslovakia. As soon as our fortifications are constructed and the countries of Central Europe realize that France cannot enter German territory at will, all those countries will begin to feel very differently about their foreign politics and a new constellation will develop" (Bullitt, 159). Thus the reoccupation of the Rhineland was more a step in Hitler's planned expansion to the east rather than the anti–Western move it seemed on the surface.

The reasons for the impunity with which Germany was able to break a treaty entered into with the world's most powerful states and guaranteed by the League of Nations were essentially two. First was France. Traumatized by the First World War, her fear and revulsion of a new war made her incapable of an active national policy. In addition, France had a half-paralyzed system of government in which the executive branch was at the whim of a legislature mired in partisan and budgetary squabbles; in the period 1932–40 France had 16 different governments. The only thing France did was to conclude in 1935 an alliance with the Soviet Union, a move that German diplomacy had been trying to prevent. This alliance had served Hitler as a pretext for the Rhineland but did not frighten him for he was convinced that France was no great power and would do nothing. The second reason for Hitler's impunity was the British. Their attitude to all German actions, including in the Rhineland, was predicated not only on expediency, but also on moral grounds. They felt that right was on the German side. "The Germans are merely going back into their own back yard," the British statesmen quoted a London cabdriver's reaction on the Rhineland crisis. This phrase was actually floated not by a cabdriver but by Lord Lothian (Colvin 1965, 96) and it reflected the attitude of the British government. The reoccupation of the Rhineland was not seen as a milestone on the road to war, but as the rightful clamor of a people becoming master in its own house. In this attitude the British were supported by the USA. For both England and America the coddling of Germany had strong financial underpinnings so that one may talk not only of political but also economic appeasement; when eventually war broke out there was to be also military appeasement.

Though certain gestures were made to protest the reoccupation of the Rhineland, including an official condemnation by the League, the British were essentially ready to acknowledge this latest German coup provided that was the end of it. They were encouraged in these delusions by Hitler himself who in typical fashion, after having gotten his bite, now talked of peace and friendship with all. The British government decided to take him up on it and on May 6, 1936, after consulting with a number of other governments, it instructed Ambassador Phipps to deliver a "questionnaire" to Hitler which in form and content must have been the most distasteful parcel ever dumped in the führer's lap. The

British wanted nothing less than written answers about Hitler's future intentions. They asked:

1. Is Germany ready for "genuine treaties"?
2. Does Hitler draw a distinction between the Third Reich and the German people, that is Germans living in Czechoslovakia, Austria, Danzig, etc.?
3. Does Germany ... now intend to respect the existing territorial and political status of Europe except insofar as they might subsequently be modified by free negotiation or agreement.
4. Is Hitler prepared for non-aggression pacts with Soviet Russia, Latvia, Estonia?

Forewarned of the missive, Hitler made von Neurath receive it and it was not until the 14th of May that he consented to see Phipps about the note. Earlier the Polish ambassador had already passed on the intelligence that Hitler was furious about the mention of a nonaggression pact with Russia. This was fully confirmed at the Phipps-Hitler interview. There was a violent outburst against the inroads Communism was making in Spain and France. He, Hitler, would conclude no pacts with the Soviet Union. The "questionnaire" was so distasteful to him that he would not answer it.

The questionnaire with its sacrilegious suggestion of respecting the status quo in Eastern Europe was not to be answered; the wooing of England, however, was to go on. In August 1936, Ribbentrop was appointed ambassador to London. Upon arrival there he confided that, though it was Hitler's intention to make him foreign minister, he felt that Ribbentrop's place was in London, for, being an expert on things British, he was to work on a rapprochement between the two countries. This reputation of Ribbentrop's stemmed from his successful conclusion of the naval agreement, as well as from his presumed social contacts. Actually, Hitler could not have picked a worse expert. A vain, humorless nonentity, Ribbentrop completely misunderstood the British. Worse, he indulged in private envies and phobias toward them over such things as the inability of his 11-year-old son to go to Eton and over other real or imagined social snubs. One of the things he did, sometime in 1937, was to request an audience with Churchill, who was then out of office and to whom he could talk in some privacy, yet be sure that it would reach official circles. Perhaps, too, he picked Churchill because the latter was known to be a staunch anti–Bolshevik. In a two-hour conversation at the embassy he told Churchill that Germany wanted friendship with England and, for that purpose, was ready to forego all claims to colonies. Furthermore she was prepared to stand guard over the British Empire. In return Germany wanted a free hand in the East; Danzig and the Corridor must be absorbed and so, too, White Russia and the Ukraine. All Hitler wanted from the British was that they not interfere. Churchill replied that even though the British may dislike Communism they would never let Germany annex Eastern Europe. Ribbentrop, who was standing with Churchill before a world map where he had been showing the territories Hitler wanted, then turned around and exclaimed, "In that case war is inevitable. There is no way out. The führer is resolved. Nothing will stop him and nothing will stop us." Churchill reported the conversation to the Foreign Office.

In *Mein Kampf* Hitler set down as the prerequisite for his drive to the east alliances with England and Italy. While there seemed to be no overt conflict of interests between Germany and England, vis-à-vis Italy there were questions of the Tyrol, Trieste, and above all, Austria, whose integrity was a cornerstone of Italian foreign policy. Yet it was the Italian alliance that Hitler found no difficulty in forging. On October 25, 1936, the Rome-Berlin Axis was born. Though there were a number of convergent elements to the

Rome-Berlin pact — the affinity of the two Fascist regimes and the strategic thrust of the two countries across the waist of Europe — yet on Hitler's side the main reason for its conclusion had something to do with his overall scheme of things. Hitler had no illusions about Italian military prowess, but he hoped that by posing a threat to England's extensive interests in Africa and the Middle East, Mussolini would distract and keep England in check. This was also partly responsible for his interest in the Japanese, whom he otherwise loathed, but with whom at the end of 1937 he set up the Anti-Comintern bloc. With England threatened in the Mediterranean by Italy and by Japan in the Far East, she would lack the focus and the resources to tamper with Hitler. Strangely enough, he did not count on Japan as an anti–Soviet ally, though this would have seemed a more natural alignment. The evidence suggests he did not want any competition in that future German subcontinent and was confident that he would need no help in conquering it. He didn't bother to consider what effect Japan's belligerence in the Far East might have on the USA.

The conclusion of an alliance with Italy was followed in the spring of 1937 by a visit of Feldmarschall Göring to Rome. After talks with his fellow airman, Ciano, Göring went to see Mussolini to whom he conveyed the central message of his mission: Austria must be annexed and the time for it was not far off. Il Duce was not delirious over the news but remained silent. It was a significant silence, for Italy had been the one country that had sent troops to the Brenner Pass during the unsuccessful Nazi putsch in Austria in 1936. It would have been most embarrassing to Hitler to lose his only ally on this first foreign venture.

The next step was to gauge the temperament of the British. In this, too, Hitler's luck held for, in the spring of 1937, two appointments were made in Great Britain which Hitler would have made himself had he been in a position to have done so. This was the ascendancy of the Neville & Nevile Company. On May 28, Neville Chamberlain succeeded Baldwin as prime minister; and a month later, Nevile Henderson replaced Phipps as ambassador to Berlin. Whereas Chamberlain was merely one among many, Henderson was unique even among the appeasers. A mustachioed, birdlike bachelor, he often sounded like the führer himself. On June 23 he told the U.S. Ambassador to Berlin, Dodds, "Germany must dominate the Balkan zone, which means she must dominate Europe. England with her empire is to dominate the seas along with the United States. England and Germany must come into close relations, economic and political, and control the world. France is a back number and unworthy of support" (Dodds, 421). Simply put, Henderson was in love with Germany. Love is an understandable emotion, even when the beloved is a vampire, but an ambassador in love is a useless ambassador. Whatever shortcomings he spotted in the Germans, such as brutality, he ascribed to the admixture of Slavic blood, for whereas Henderson merely disliked the French, he detested Slavs. Even after his mission collapsed and war had broken out he still wrote he believed in the decency of the German people because he had "felt at home among them more than among any other foreign people" (Henderson, x). Such and more succinct statements one can find the profusion in Henderson's memoir *Failure of a Mission* for which a more proper title would have been *Love's Labour's Lost*. Even the manner of his appointment is significant. Henderson was rewarded with the Berlin post as a compensation for a dull drag of duty in Argentina. Now, in 1937, to have given this appointment merely as a consolation to a disgruntled diplomat, instead of to the most astute man available, is in itself an indication of the frame of mind in which the British government approached the Hitlerian catastrophe. Henderson's only qualification for the job was that he spoke German and, given the circumstances, it was a fatal gift.

Broadly speaking, there were now two possible courses for the British government to follow. One was collective security. This posed problems of who and how, but at least the premise would have been sound, namely, that nothing but force was likely to halt Hitler's rush to war. Or, working on the assumption that Hitler's demands were reasonable and finite, one could negotiate and yield. Chamberlain was uncritically and stubbornly set on the latter. Furthermore, he was convinced that only he was capable of the job. Anglo-German relations had been cool since the Rhineland. All through 1937 the Germans had been trying to improve them and now, with Chamberlain in power, they succeeded. Göring was staging an international hunting fiesta and it was proposed that Lord President Halifax, a hunter like the rest of them, come to Berlin. Halifax's visit was approved by Chamberlain in the absence of Eden who had succeeded Simon as foreign secretary. Nor were the French consulted, and they were angry. Both the French and Eden were ignored and the trip took place as scheduled.

Halifax saw Hitler on the afternoon of November 19, 1937. There had been a nearly disastrous *faux pas* at the steps of the Berghof when Halifax continued sitting in his limousine waiting for Hitler, whom he mistook for a footman, to open the door for him, until von Papen with a hoarse prompting saved the situation (Read and Fisher, 38). In the vast salon, with the largest window in Europe, the Yorkshire clergyman and the madman sat down to fashion an understanding between their two countries. Another anxious moment arose when Halifax asked Hitler what he wanted. To Hitler this inquiry smacked of the past year's infamous questionnaire, but he controlled himself and went on to expound a very simple view of life and history. There are, said the chancellor, only two possibilities. One is the "free play of forces which may mean encroachment on the lives and destinies of other people and great convulsions," or, there can be a rule of reason, provided it led to the same results as the first course. Hitler cited Austria, Czechoslovakia and Danzig as areas where this doctrine applied. In addition, Germany must also extend economically into east and southeast Europe. Halifax, too, was candid. England, Halifax assured Hitler, would not stand in the way of changes in the status quo of Europe, provided this took place without the use of force. When Halifax proposed further talks, Hitler demurred. In a few months, he knew, would come the end of Austria and it would not be the most propitious time. What Hitler thought of Halifax can only be guessed. Halifax, upon his return to England, described Hitler as "sincere."

* * *

On the afternoon of November 5, 1937, Hitler called a meeting in the Chancellery which came to be known as the Hossbach Conference. Six men attended: Feldmarschall von Blomberg, minister of war and commander in chief of the Wehrmacht; General Fritsch, commander in chief of the army; Feldmarschall Göring, commander in chief of the air force; Admiral Raeder, commander in chief of the navy; Foreign Minister von Neurath; and Colonel Hossbach, Hitler's adjutant, who kept notes. It began at 4:15, lasted four hours, and to Hitler its substance was of such importance that in the event of his death he wanted it to be his testament. In the best tradition of *Mein Kampf* he opened with a turgid exposition on economics, geopolitics, and so on. Whereas the preamble was incoherent, the conclusions were ice clear. Germany needs *Lebensraum* and this is to be found not in colonies but in its immediate vicinity and can be gotten only by the use of force. He set a date for its implementation, the years 1943–45. By no means should the struggle be postponed beyond that period, for by then his armaments will have become obsolete, his secret weapons will have leaked out, and the enemy rearmed. To prepare for this it was the führer's unshakable determination to shortly annex, simultaneously, Austria and Czechoslovakia. This would meet several important objectives; it would provide a strategic base for subsequent operations; he would gain 10 million Germans, the equivalent of 12 divisions; and it would add resources and armaments to his arsenal. Incidentally, he added, 2 million Czechs and 1 million Austrians would have to be gotten rid of. There remained the question of what the Western powers would do. Britain, he said, embroiled with Ireland and India and harassed by the Italians in the Mediterranean and by Japan in the Far East, had already written off Czechoslovakia. And without Great Britain, France would do nothing. His commanders must be ready for action by 1938, a few months hence.

At the conference three men — Blomberg, Fritsch and von Neurath — expressed misgivings about the practical, if not the moral, aspects of the führer's blueprint. Within months all three lost their jobs. Not that their attitude at the Hossbach Conference was the sole reason. Getting ready for his foreign conquests, Hitler decided to purge the last of the old guard in government and the army. First he used the pretext of Blomberg's marriage to a floozie to dismiss him from his post. He then exploited the occasion to abolish the post of war minister altogether and to proclaim himself commander in chief of the Wehrmacht. In place of the war ministry he established an office called *Das Oberkommando der Wehrmacht*, OKW for short, and for its chief he appointed Wilhelm Keitel, a servile, robotlike general whom the military, themselves no giants of independent thinking, nicknamed *Lakaitel* (lackey). General Fritsch Hitler dismissed on trumped-up charges of homosexuality and replaced him by the colorless Walter Brauchitsch. As his new foreign minister he picked the expert on things British, Joachim von Ribbentrop. There were other changes. Hjalmar Schacht, financial wizard and minister of economics, who had been a persistent critic of the pace, though not the fact, of rearmament was, on December 8, 1937, replaced by Walther Funk. Sixteen senior generals were retired, 48 others transferred. All these latter shifts took place on or about February 4, 1938, after Hitler's return from a long, brooding sojourn at the Berghof.

Hitler lived up to the intention of the Hossbach Conference, namely the absorption of both Austria and Czechoslovakia. The case of Austria illustrates the interaction of Hitler's personal and political obsessions. As has been stated, unification of all ethnic Germans was not what drove Hitler on. Thus the persistent avowals that Austria must return to the fold was at most a partial reason for the Anschluss. This can be gleaned from the way Hitler made his demands for annexation. He said, "Vienna was and remained for me the hardest, toughest, most thorough school of my life…. Even then I had drawn the consequences from this realization: Ardent love for my German-Austrian homeland, deep hatred for the Austrian state…"(*Mein Kampf*, 16). It was the dark personal experiences in Vienna that made him want to reenter it as conqueror. He wanted to lay his hands on the heirs and relics of the Habsburg regime, which he detested; on the clerks who had thwarted his career as an artist; on the Slavs, Jews, Magyars and Gypsies who desecrated hallowed German soil. Then the political reason: it would be the first step of his eastern policy for after annexing Austria he had Czechoslovakia surrounded from nearly all sides.

Although Hitler was perfectly ready to wage war to get Austria and had issued orders that force be used in case negotiations failed, he preferred to annex the country without bloodshed. This was the exception to his future aggressions where not only was conquest the aim, but war the preferred means. In other circumstances one would credit sentimental reasons for these peaceful intentions; it was his homeland, the people were German. But this had no room in the führer's psyche. Baldur von Schirach, gauleiter of Vienna, was to recall a conversation when "the Führer began with what I might say, incredible and unlimited hatred to speak against the people of Vienna…. He said, 'Vienna should never have been admitted into the union of the Greater Germany.' Hitler never loved Vienna, he hated its people." His reasons were perfectly pragmatic. To be forced to fight the Austrians for what, presumably, they themselves longed for would have belied his arguments about the desire and right of all Germans for unity. While inside Austria the Nazis spread propaganda and subversion, von Papen, as one of his last ambassadorial duties, was ordered to hand Schuschnigg an invitation to visit the führer. Wary and deluded at the same time Schuschnigg journeyed to the Berghof where Hitler flanked by three generals took him to the room with the largest window in Europe. When the Austrian chancellor made the conventional remark about the beautiful view, Hitler snapped, "We did not gather here to speak of the fine view or the weather." Addressing him not by his official title but as Herr Schuschnigg, Hitler plunged into threats and vituperation, winding up the morning session with the cry "I give you once more and for the last time the opportunity to come to terms, Herr Schuschnigg. Either we find a solution now, or else events will take their course…. Think it over, Herr Schuschnigg, think it over well. I can only wait till this afternoon…."

In the afternoon Ribbentrop handed Schuschnigg a document to sign. This ordered him to turn over the Austrian government to a rostrum of Nazis, most of whom were in jail for treason. In addition, Austria was to integrate economically with the Reich. Flabbergasted and humiliated Schuschnigg said that even were he ready to sign the document he could not possibly do so without the constitutional authorization of the president. Schuschnigg was then summoned once again before the führer who told him that for the first time in his life he was going back on his word; he would allow three days to have the agreement accepted. In four days' time he wanted the agreement implemented. After declining Hitler's invitation to dinner, Schuschnigg returned to Vienna.

The steps leading to the Anschluss are worth retracing here only insofar as they demonstrate Hitler's rather obvious "diplomatic" acumen. For success this relied on a form of shock treatment: First a progressive escalation of unfillable demands which only a man contemptuous of a given word could resort to; then, due to both military and moral feebleness, the proclivity of his opponents to submit; and finally Hitler's very real readiness to go to war if not satisfied. Austria is a perfect example of this sort of escalation. Schuschnigg had seen Hitler on February 12, and on February 16 the Austrians agreed to meet the German demands. Even while the agreement was being implemented, the Nazis in Austria went on a rampage with the police under the newly installed Nazi interior minister, Seyss-Inquart, refusing to interfere. With the country in turmoil Schuschnigg decided to poll the Austrian people: "A free, independent, social, Christian, and united Austria — ja oder nein?" The plebiscite was set for Sunday, March 13. Such a referendum was holy water on Hitler's tail. On Friday, March 11, he ordered Schuschnigg to call off the plebiscite. At 2 P.M. Schuschnigg yielded. No sooner had he done so when he was told this was not enough; he must now resign. Schuschnigg resigned. Next, Hitler asked President Miklas to appoint Seyss-Inquart chancellor; by collusion with Berlin Seyss-Inquart was then to ask for German troops to help pacify the country. This Miklas refused to do. At that point, according to an eyewitness, "Suddenly the führer slapped his thigh, jerked his head back and exclaimed 'Jetzt geht's los.'" The order went out to implement Case Otto which read:

    1. If other measures prove unsuccessful, I intend to invade Austria with armed forces....

    2. The whole operation will be directed by myself.... The forces detailed must be ready on 12 March at the latest 1200 hours. I reserve the right to decide the actual moment of invasion....

This document had been issued early in the day and was signed by Hitler at 8:45 P.M. March 11. Just before midnight Miklas yielded and appointed Seyss-Inquart chancellor. By then the order to invade Austria on Saturday morning had already been set. Seyss-Inquart, an Austrian Nazi, was actually against the invasion and ordered the Austrian General Muff to request in his name that the Wehrmacht halt at the border. But he was ignored and at daybreak of Saturday, March 12, 1938, German troops rolled into Austria.

There were two neighbors of Austria to watch as Hitler deployed for his invasion. One was Italy. Mussolini, while silent during the Göring visit, had never given his official blessing. Hitler had dispatched Prince Hesse, son-in-law of the Italian king, with a letter to Mussolini informing him of the impending Anschluss. At 1:25 A.M. of March 12, a few hours before the invasion, he received the news that Mussolini approved. A jubilant and grateful führer bubbled over with emotion, crying again and again into the telephone that he would never, never, never forget it — remaining, indeed, to the bitter end Mussolini's steadfast friend, though at times against the latter's wish and certainly against his welfare. The other country to watch was Czechoslovakia. On the fateful evening of March 11 a diplomatic reception with wine and music was being held in the *Haus der Flieger*. There Göring sought out the Czech Minister Mastny and assured him that all this was nothing but a family affair between Austria and Germany. He hoped that Czechoslovakia was not mobilizing and wanted President Benes to know that should the Czechs lift a finger "one thousand bombers would reduce Hradcin to ashes." Mastny assured him there was no mobilization in Czechoslovakia.

As for Great Britain, her moral and political appreciation of the Anschluss was the same as during the Rhineland; the Germans were messing about in their own back yard. When Chamberlain had been informed of the Schuschnigg visit he summed it up as a dialogue whose main result would be an improvement of relations between the two countries. When on March 11 Schuschnigg cabled London for advice, Halifax answered that "His Majesty's Government cannot take the responsibility of advising the Chancellor to take any course of action which might expose his country to dangers against which His Majesty's Government are unable to guarantee protection." When six days after the Anschluss Russia proposed a conference to consider means of checking further German expansion Chamberlain's answer in the House of Commons on March 24 was that such an alliance would be "inimical to the peace of Europe." He also refused to extend any guarantees to Czechoslovakia.

In Austria delirious crowds greeted the arriving Germans. In Vienna, as mammoth torch parades filled the streets, 1,000 Jews committed suicide and 80,000 people, including Chancellor Schuschnigg, were shipped to jails and concentration camps. In Linz, in the presence of the führer, Article 88 of the Treaty of St. Germain which forbade an Anschluss was renounced and on March 13 Austria became a province of Greater Germany, to be called Ostmark. On April 2 England formally recognized the Anschluss.

* * *

Where Hitler would turn next is obvious from a look at Fig. 3.1 where it can be seen that after the Anschluss the Czechs were just prey in the jaws of the Greater Reich. Hitler

The Reichstag cheers Hitler's announcement of the annexation of Austria, March 12, 1938. (Courtesy the National Archives.)

had always been preoccupied with Czechoslovakia as a potential Russian air base and with her geographic location. As early as 1932 he told Hanfstängl, "Look at the way we have to travel round Czechoslovakia to get to eastern Germany. The whole thing is nonsense. Half the people on the other side are German anyway and it is all wrong to have this alien government placed across the lines of communication." This after he had first told his companion that "the most important thing in the next war will be to make sure that we control the grain and food supplies of western Russia." The above expresses Hitler's entire rationale with respect to Czechoslovakia. It even contains the tactics to be used, that "half the people there are German." But of course their plight was not what bothered him. Hitler lost little sleep over the suffering and spiritual craving of his numerous other compatriots in exile. On May 2 when Hitler traveled through the Tyrol to visit Mussolini, the local populace stared at him in resentment for having abandoned them to Italy. Hitler ignored them. In Rome he fixed their fate forever. "It is my unshakeable will and testament to the German people," he proclaimed, "that the frontiers of the Alps are erected by Nature, Providence and History between us and Italy and shall be regarded as eternally inviolate." There were also ethnic Germans in other parts of Europe — in Switzerland, Holland, Alsace-Lorraine, Schleswig-Holstein, and Belgium — but Hitler never called for their return. It was the Germans in Czechoslovakia, and later it would be the Germans in Poland, that wanted to and must return home. Hitler's patriotism was confined to Germans living in the east.

Hitler lost no time in getting at Czechoslovakia. It had been his habit to start brooding about his next move at the peak of some previous triumph and so even as the invasion of Austria was still going on he told Halder with his kind of humor, "This will be incon-

3.1. Europe at the beginning of 1938.

venient to the Czechs." Shortly after his return from Vienna, on March 28, already morbid and restless, he called Konrad Heinlein, the leader of the *Sudetendeutsche*, to a meeting at the Berghof. The directives Heinlein received were that, "We must always demand so much that we can never be satisfied." Furthermore, Heinlein was from now on to consider himself not a leader of an ethnic minority within the Czech state, but as a representative of the führer. Even while the talks were going on demonstrations, outrages and political sabotage were unleashed by the Germans in Czechoslovakia who now wanted nothing but union with Germany.

Having dispatched Henlein on his mission of internal disruption, Hitler on April 20 called in Keitel to give him a directive for the preparation of Case Grün, the plan for the invasion of Czechoslovakia. It was a problem which according to Keitel the führer said "would have to be solved sometime, not only because of the way in which the Czech government was oppressing the German population living there, but because of the strategically impossible situation that would develop should the time come for the big reckoning with the East and by that he meant not just the Poles, but particularly the Bolsheviks" (Keitel, 62).

What happened next is somewhat out of character with the past and future behavior of the various parties. On May 20 the Czechs, alarmed by the concentration of German troops on their borders and by rumors of an impending invasion, ordered a partial mobilization. Both England and France sent Germany warnings against war while France and the Soviet Union publicly reaffirmed their treaty obligation to go to the aid of Czechoslovakia. Hitler retreated. Rumors of troop concentrations were denied, the Czech ambassador was assured that Germany had no hostile intentions against his country and Heinlein, after another conference on May 22, was sent back with instructions to negotiate with Prague. In an almost grotesque aftermath, the defiance of the Western powers frightened them more than it did Hitler. They subsequently felt that they had gone too far in their show of strength, for had Hitler not retreated it would have threatened war. They considered their action to have been precipitous, blaming it all on Benes' "provocative" actions. So, if anyone learned a lesson from that refreshing weekend of May 20–22, it was not Hitler but Chamberlain — never again to be as audacious as on that spring occasion.

As soon as Hitler had reassured the world, he convened on May 28 another conference attended by Ribbentrop, von Neurath, Beck, Keitel, von Brauchitsch and Raeder. Bent over a large map Hitler indicated how he intended to wipe out Czechoslovakia. The draft of Case Grün had originally contained the phrase that it was not his intention "at this time" to attack Czechoslovakia. He now changed it to read "It is my unalterable decision to smash Czechoslovakia by military action in the near future" (Bullock 1962, 446). In a covering letter to the General Staff Keitel added, "The execution of this directive must be assured by October 1, 1938, at the latest." From then on German preparations for the attack continued apace. Within less than six months the strength of the German army doubled from 27 to 55 front-line divisions, the order of mobilization calling for a total of 96 divisions.

Hitler had spent most of the summer at the Berghof withdrawn and relatively quiet. He had made his decision and he was waiting. It was the Western powers who were now concerned with Sudetenland, it was they who were trying to find a "solution." As for resisting Hitler's impending invasion, this was even less likely in the summer of 1938. Britain was at the peak of its mood of appeasement; France at the bottom of dissension and fear. To quote the American secretary of the interior, Ickes, who had said it on another occasion, the French were so timid that "they walked without casting a shadow." The alliance with the Soviet Union, instead of an asset, had now become a steel ball around her neck. Poland would not dream of letting the Russians cross her territory to help the Czechs; nor would Rumania. Then on September 7 the *London Times* came out with an outright proposal of "ceding" the Sudetenland to Germany, something that went beyond what the Germans demanded. One would have expected Hitler to jump at the offer — but he did not and for good reason. In two of his last conferences, on September 3 and 9, Hitler had discussed with his top military men details of the impending invasion and had it fixed for September 30. This was to follow an uprising of the Sudeten Germans who had deliberately broken off all negotiations, though Benes had practically given in to all their demands. Nor did Hitler in his long, vituperative speech of September 12 make any mention of the cession of the Sudetenland; he made no demands of any sort. The thing he wanted was justice for the "traitor" Benes. The fact was that Hitler was not after the Sudetenland. He wanted Czechoslovakia.

However, the man who now did want to hand him the Sudetenland was Chamberlain. At 11 P.M. on September 13 a message for the führer arrived from London. When the führer read it he almost had a fit. "*Ich bin vom Himmel gefallen,*" he cried out. The message read that the British prime minister, 69 years old, who had never in his life been in an airplane, was willing to fly to the Bavarian Alps to settle the Czech problem. If Hitler's surprise was clear, his feelings were not. On the one hand it was a triumph to have the British prime minister rush to see him. More importantly it offered an opportunity to initiate those basic agreements with the British he had been seeking all along. On the other hand, he was leery of negotiations about the Sudetenland. Whatever his feelings Hitler could hardly have said no to Chamberlain's unconditional offer to visit him. As we shall see, Hitler somehow hoped to succeed in both directions, usurping Czechoslovakia while negotiating with Britain.

Chamberlain left London at 8:30 on the morning of September 15 in the company of Horace Wilson and William Strang of the Foreign Office and arrived four hours later at the Munich airport where he was met by Ribbentrop. As they rode by train to Berchtesgaden they passed trainloads of troops and guns heading for the Czech border. It had begun to rain as they reached the Berghof and, there, Hitler greeted his guest at the steps of the house. There were pleasantries and tea before they went up to the second-floor study. They talked alone except for the interpreter, Schmidt, whose record of the conference Hitler later refused to give to Chamberlain. The führer started off as usual with threats, saying that there was not much to negotiate, for he was determined to have his way come what may, deluge or war. Chamberlain asked, if that was so, why had Hitler agreed to his coming here? Hitler calmed down; he was speaking to the leader of a people he admired and feared, the only such people. Well, he said, if the Czechs were to commit themselves to relinquishing the Sudetenland, he was ready for discussions. Hitler later confided that when he had made the proposal he was convinced that Chamberlain would never ask this of the Czechs and, if he did, the Czechs would never comply. Hitler would then find himself aligned with Great Britain in demanding a cession of the Sudetenland which, when unfulfilled, would allow him to wage war on Czechoslovakia.

The problem of the Sudetenland would have posed a serious political and moral dilemma even if its surrender were to someone other than Hitler, to whom it was merely a stratagem in a more ominous scheme. In the first place, Czechoslovakia, like many another European state, was a union of minorities— Czechs, Germans, Slovaks, Ruthenians. Were one minority granted secession it would immediately call into question the existence of the state itself. Secondly, the entire Czech defense system was based on the existing borders with Germany and to abandon them would leave the country without walls. Also, some three-quarters of Czechoslovakia's industrial resources lay in the disputed territory and the entire country depended on the communication and transportation network passing through the Sudetenland. And lastly, should one accept the thesis that a state containing sizeable minorities is politically unacceptable, grave questions arose with regard to many other European states— Belgium, Switzerland, Poland, Yugoslavia, Rumania, and the Soviet Union. Even without Hitler's sinister motives the cession of the Sudetenland was far from the simple moral certainty Hitler's apologists claimed it was. Yet, as in the case of the Rhineland, this right of Germany to her 3 million people was at the core of England's attitude and it shaped its course more than did political or military considerations. Consequently, though Hitler's general strategy in the summer of 1938 with respect to Czechoslovakia failed, in one respect he attained his objective in that he managed gradually to shift the onus of a possible war onto the Czechs. When the British urged them to yield they resorted to the following language: "If it [Czechoslovakia] doesn't unconditionally, and at once, accept the Anglo-French plan it will stand before the world as solely responsible for the ensuing war." Henderson even argued that not only were the Germans not at fault, but they were being singled out for discrimination. Had the Germans been Hungarians, or Poles, or Rumanians, or the citizens of any small nation, he argued, all England would have been on their side. To the journalist Colvin Henderson cried out, "Benes is a traitor, a traitor to his people" (Colvin: 1965, 231, 239, 257), the very language Hitler used. In this mood the British found it possible to first suggest, then press, and finally threaten the Czech government into accepting the German demands.

On September 22 Chamberlain once again went to see the führer, this time at Godesberg. From his hotel, on the eastern bank of the Rhine, he was ferried at dusk across the river to the Hotel Dreesen, a hangout of Hitler's, to meet him. For the past few days Hitler had been in a rage. On that morning the savage mood persisted; there were dark patches under his eyes and he had a tic. He was having premonitions. Two days before, when he had urged a Hungarian delegation to put forward territorial demands on Czechoslovakia, something he was also urging on the Slovaks, they heard him say that, "in his opinion action by the army would provide the only satisfactory solution. There was, however, the danger that the Czechs would submit to every demand." Hitler was confirmed in his premonitions at 11:30 on September 21 when he learned that the Czechs had given in, though how far he was not certain (Shirer 1959, 392). Chamberlain, on the other hand, as he sat down with Hitler in the board meeting room of the hotel, was in excellent spirits. He had been given a historic mission and had carried it out with aplomb. The British and French governments and the Czechs, he told the führer, had agreed to meet his conditions. In some ways the concessions went beyond Hitler's demands, as, for example, the offer to dispense with plebiscites in the predominantly German areas. The Czech-Soviet alliance, presumably so much resented by Hitler, would be dissolved and replaced by a joint guarantee for the new Czechoslovakia, which would thereafter remain a neutral state. For almost an hour a proud Chamberlain went on talking of his achievement. When he had finished the führer asked whether he had heard correctly that the Czechs had agreed to cede the Sudetenland to Germany. Yes, replied Chamberlain, yes. The führer looked at him and announced, "I am exceedingly sorry, but after the events of the last few days this solution is no longer of any use." To extricate himself from the trap he himself had helped set, Hitler now made the proposed cession humiliating and impossible. The original arrangement had been for an orderly transfer of the Sudeten areas under appropriate safeguards. These included plebiscites in the mixed regions, an exchange of populations, compensation for property left behind — all under international supervision. Now Hitler demanded immediate occupation. An indignant Chamberlain jumped to his feet, asking what had brought about this sudden change. To this he received no answer. Chamberlain retired to his hotel across the river, but not before hearing Hitler confess that he "never believed himself that a peaceful solution could be reached and that he never thought that the Prime Minister could have achieved what he had" (Gilbert & Gott, 153).

The following day Chamberlain, instead of attending a scheduled meeting at 11 o'clock, sent the führer a letter rejecting an immediate occupation. Hitler repeated his demands: the Czechs were to begin evacuation by 8 A.M. on September 26, two days hence, and complete it by September 28. Though in the morning Chamberlain had stood pat, later on as the day waned so did his determination. He now agreed to convey Hitler's demands to the Czechs. His efforts were now aimed mainly at softening the wording of the demands and to gain a few more days for the Czechs. Half an hour before midnight Chamberlain saw the führer again to receive from him a proposal which required the Czechs to clear most of the Sudetenland by October 1. In the mixed Czech-German regions plebiscites were to decide their future; what were, and what were not, mixed areas, had been decided by Hitler on a map, which he now handed to Chamberlain. The two statesmen, quite amicable now, parted at 2 A.M. and in the early morning of September 24 Chamberlain flew home.

This time the Czechs rejected the German demands. The news was brought to Hitler in the form of a letter from Chamberlain. As the letter was read to him Hitler threw one of his hysterical fits, shrieking unprintable threats, and rushing for the door. A few hours later he delivered in the *Sport Palast* one of the most virulent speeches of his career. Yet, while threatening obliteration of everything Czech, he did not fail in the same breath to praise Chamberlain. With regard to the Sudetenland he announced, "It is the last territorial claim which I have to make in Europe.... I assured him [Chamberlain], moreover, and I repeat it here, that when this problem is solved there will be no more territorial problems for Germany in Europe" (French Yellow Book, 8). That night a second letter arrived from London in which Chamberlain guaranteed to obtain Czech concurrence if Hitler abstained from using force. The letter was delivered to the führer early on September 27, but he refused to discuss it. Instead, he delivered an ultimatum: either the Czechs accepted his demands by 2 P.M. the following day, or he would invade by October 1, which had been his invasion date all along. Horace Wilson, who had brought Chamberlain's letter, then said that the prime minister had instructed him to deliver a second message which he proceeded to read to the führer: "If France, in fulfillment of her treaty obligations, should become actively involved in hostilities against Germany, the United Kingdom would deem itself obliged to support France" (Schmidt, 164). Hitler responded that he did not care. That evening, however, he wrote a conciliatory answer to Chamberlain's letter. This was the second time, the first having taken place at the Berghof, that Hitler had shrunk from slamming the door on further negotiations in face of a clear stand by the British prime minister.

Wednesday, September 28, was the critical day of the Sudeten crisis. Direct negotiations were suspended, the German ultimatum was to expire at 2 P.M., the Czechs had mobilized and Hitler stood torn between his twitch for war and his dread of British belligerence. That morning two interventions took place which swayed Hitler toward accepting a peaceful cession of the Sudetenland. At 11:15 Hitler saw François-Poncet, the French ambassador, who brought new proposals for immediate occupation of substantial parts of the Sudetenland, though these did not yet have the official concurrence of the Czechs. Hitler wouldn't hear of it. Poncet then told him in a measured voice to which the führer seemed to have listened very carefully, "You deceive yourself, Chancellor, if you believe that you can confine the conflict to Czechoslovakia" (Schmidt, 106). The words were, of course, a repetition of those he had heard the day before from Chamberlain, a day when Great Britain had mobilized her fleet. A number of authorities attribute Hitler's acceptance of a peaceful solution also to the lack of enthusiasm for war on the part of the Berliners and to the opposition of his generals. There is no evidence and not a single hint from Hitler himself that this had in any way influenced him. And, knowing Hitler, this is most unlikely. A similar lack of enthusiasm for war was presumably observed before the invasion of Poland; nor were his generals more enthusiastic about the Rhineland, or the invasion of France or Russia and that had not made him change his plans. But whether this had an effect or not, everyone agrees that the crucial intervention was that of Mussolini. At 11 o'clock that morning he called Hitler and, after expressing his own wish for peace, suggested a Four Power conference to settle the issue. By now the pressure of his only ally and his anxieties over a rift with Great Britain combined to make Hitler accept Mussolini's proposal, which he did at 11:40, some two hours before the expiration of the ultimatum. The result was the Munich Conference which made the Czechs transfer 11,000 square miles with some 3 million Germans and 800,000 Czechs to the Third Reich.

The conference was a defeat for all concerned and that included Hitler. It was clearly a disaster for the Czechs. They lost a sizeable portion of their country with its industry, resources and system of fortifications, and it brought into question the existence of the state itself. Far from bringing homogeneity, it sent other wolves snapping at their territory—the Poles, the Hungarians—and it set in motion separatist movements of its Slovak and Ruthenian minorities. For France it was a loss of a loyal and well-armed ally. The Czechs fielded 34 divisions, 14 of them motorized, backed by an excellent armament industry, and for all practical purposes it wrecked the Franco-Soviet alliance. It was a defeat for England, for it had once again taken a political decision based on the wrong appreciation of the issues involved, bringing Europe and herself closer to war, not to speak of the ignominy of having delivered a democratic state to a loathsome regime. It prostrated her and the other democracies with disrepute, produced a hostile reaction in the USA, and made Russia more than ever wary of an alliance with England. And, finally, Hitler's defeat was that he didn't want a settlement. He wanted Czechoslovakia as a strategic southern pincer against Poland, and beyond. His methods here had been similar to those used with Austria. By making unfulfillable demands he had hoped to find a pretext to invade Czechoslovakia. What Hitler discovered to his dismay was that what he considered exorbitant turned out to be acceptable to the British and enforceable on the Czechs. He was not to make a similar mistake again.

In retrospect, the most fateful consequence of Munich lay in its psychological effect on Hitler. As we have seen he had unflinchingly insisted on never going to war with Britain. Munich seemed to have shaken his awe of the British and for the first time he felt contempt for them. When on October 28 Ribbentrop visited Rome he told Il Duce, "The Czechoslovak crisis has shown our power.... As from the month of September we could face a war with the great democracies" (Bullock 1962, 475). Whereas previously England's reaction had been Hitler's predominant concern, after Munich the German diplomatic papers contain little about what possibly Chamberlain might do. When in connection with Poland later on he was cautioned against possible British intervention Hitler replied with contempt, "I have seen my opponents in Munich. They are little worms." He had let fall similar statements on other occasions. For a while, at least, he had ceased to respect them, and his fear of them waned. It was a most crucial mental shift, for if there had been one way of averting war it was Britain's unequivocal stand coupled with Hitler's commandment of no war with her. Were these brakes to fail, as they seemed to have done after Munich, there was nothing to stop him. This flush of disrespect for Chamberlain and the likes of him did not last and Hitler was eventually to regain his healthy and not mistaken respect for the venerable lion — but it had been enough.

The diplomacy leading up to the cession of the Sudetenland, with Munich as its apogee, is referred to by everyone as the Period of Appeasement. Here, too, the term has been used to denote this particular policy and its practitioners. The word has subsequently come to evoke censure and opprobrium. In summing up this period it should, however, be made clear that the failure of the leaders of those days lay not in appeasement as such. If by conciliating Hitler another world war would have been avoided, that policy would have gone down as a statesmanlike act. The dereliction of the men of that period lies in that they failed to realize that Hitler was not after the Rhineland or the Sudeten Germans but after a whole continent and entire nations; and that the earlier he was taken on the better the chances of preventing the subsequent catastrophe. By providing him with the confidence that he would get away with his consecutive aggressions, they eased the way to the Second World War. And this they did because they were men of limited imagination, insular in their morality and intellectual horizons so that they applied themselves with great vigor to fictitious crises, missing the deeper reality around them. There remains the argument that these leaders resorted to their form of conciliation to gain time for rearmament. But this was not what motivated them. In the available records of meetings and interoffice memoranda there is nothing about compromising with Germany and prolonging negotiations in order to boost Western defenses. Even if this were so, it would not have been a sufficient rationale for appeasement because the crucial question was not whether England rearmed — and she did rearm — but who gained more from the delay. Certainly not the Western powers, if we go back to 1936; and even if the reference years are 1938–39 it is still questionable, given the loot Hitler scooped from the Czechs. There is no available document, no staff paper, in which the crucial question of who would gain more from a postponement of the conflict was studied in depth or even broached. At the time of the Anschluss France, England and Czechoslovakia had a total of 99 divisions and 2,748 planes to Germany's 57 divisions (plus another 24 untrained and under-equipped Landswehr divisions) and 1,820 planes; at the outbreak of the war France and England had 90 divisions plus 40 questionable Polish divisions and some 3,000 aircraft (the 500 Polish planes were mostly obsolete), while Germany had 120–130 divisions and 4,210 planes. In addition, with Austria and Czechoslovakia annexed, Nazi Germany had a block of 90 million industrious, obedient subjects. Given the Western armies' antiquated generalship and tactics, Germany may still have beaten them even in 1938 but it was not rearmament that was the main motivation for appeasing Hitler.

It has been said previously that had the Western powers chosen war early enough they would have prevented a world war. The retort, often heard, is that at that stage public opinion would not have endorsed such a step. That is true. This only raises more fundamental issues, moral and pragmatic. Is it the role of leaders to follow misguided popular sentiment, or rather to inform and enlighten the public about what is at stake? A similar view was voiced by an unlikely individual, the anti-war US ambassador in London, Joseph Kennedy, who, commenting on his son's book, *Why England Slept* (ascribing it to the public mood), had this to say: "The basis of your case — that the blame must be placed on the people as a whole — is sound. Nevertheless ... a politician is supposed to keep his ear to the ground; he is also supposed to look after the national welfare and to attempt to educate the people when ... they are off-base. It may not be good politics but is something vastly more important ..."(Kennedy Letters, 434). This from an archappeaser and an arch-politician. Moreover, is it the prerogative of leaders to spare their people a small cost in life and lead them instead into a national catastrophe, because the earlier option would have entailed an unpopular move? One can construct a set of parallel equations to express what this issue implies for a nation and its leaders: for the rulers this amounts to a conflict between personal interests (politics) and national interests (statesmanship); for the nation the consequences of these two choices are a cataclysmic war versus a police action. If regard for public opinion was behind their appeasement policy, then the paradox arises that it was for the sake of the public that the British leaders opted for a world war. Moreover, as will be seen, when England did go to war she was not capable of waging — never mind winning — a war against Nazi Germany.

* * *

After Munich Hitler was plunged into one of his blackest moods. He felt outmaneuvered and cheated — toadies had knocked the torch of war and conquest from his hand. Already on taking leave of Chamberlain on the 31st of September when the two signed a document "never to go to war with each other" Schmidt found him "pale and moody." Next day, on his way back to Berlin, Schacht overheard him muttering, "that fellow [Chamberlain] has spoiled my entry into Prague" (Shirer 1959, 427). He spent the last two months of the year at the Berghof, where he sulked in frustration, talking to his entourage about the paltriness of his adversaries and his frustrated mission. On October 17, when François-Poncet saw Hitler on his aerie he heard him say that the crisis was not over.

Hitler then set about recouping what his own mistakes and the spinelessness of his opponents had deprived him of during the fall. As usual, he did not fail to inform the world about his intentions. In a speech of November 8, he said, "If the rest of the world obstinately bars the way to recognition of our rights by way of negotiations, then there should be no surprise that we secure for ourselves our rights by another way." Hitler's failure in Munich consisted in that by striving to retain the confidence of the British he had forfeited Czechoslovakia. He was now to flounder in the opposite direction; he was to win Czechoslovakia all right, but at the cost of forfeiting, irrevocably, the trust of the British. His anger at the British now made him scornful of his own principles, a rare thing for him. There was little bother and very little maneuvering in his next steps aimed at the occupation of Prague. It was almost an anticlimax to the Sudeten crisis, though it was this move that clinched Hitler's fate.

On September 29 when Hitler dipped his pen to sign the Munich agreement, the inkwell proved to be empty (Colvin 1971, 169). It was a portent of things to come. The morning following the conference Chamberlain met Hitler in his private apartment in Munich, a unique honor on part of the führer. The purpose was to get Hitler to sign a joint declaration of good intentions. After Hitler was read the translation Chamberlain inquired if and when this could be signed. "Why not now?" asked the führer. This document, which Chamberlain was later to wave before the crowds at the London Airport and at Downing Street, read in part, "We regard the agreement signed last night ... as symbolic of the desire of the two peoples never to go to war with one another again. We are resolved that the method of consultation shall be adopted to deal with any other questions that may concern our two countries...."

Characteristically, Chamberlain did not tell Daladier of his tête-à-tête with Hitler. The French, naturally, were eager for a similar statement. There was no difficulty in obtaining it. Ribbentrop made a special trip to Paris where, on December 6, he and Bonnet signed the French-German declaration which in paragraph 2 said that "Germany solemnly recognizes as permanent the frontiers between their two countries"; and in paragraph 3, "Both governments are resolved, without prejudice to their special relationships with Third Powers ... to have recourse to mutual consultation in case of any complications arising." Thus the utmost sense of security and cooperation had been granted by Germany to the Western powers. Later on, when France reaffirmed its guarantees to Poland and Ribbentrop objected, France pointed out to him the phrase about third powers in paragraph 3. Ribbentrop's answer was that the clause did not apply to the states of Eastern Europe (French Yellow Book, 213).

At the time of Munich, one other document had been signed by all four participants. This concerned guarantees for the boundaries of the truncated Czech state. Both England and France gave their guarantees as of the moment of signing; Germany and Italy were to join them after the claims of Poland and Hungary were settled. The Poles got their bite — Teschen — on October 2. The Hungarians got theirs on November 2 in the so-called Vienna Award. This was a conference chaired by Ribbentrop and Ciano when they allotted Hungary a wide swath of Czech territory along its southern borders amounting to some 4,600 square miles and a mixed population of Magyars, Slovaks and Ukrainians, 1 million strong. Thus within a month of Munich the claims of Poland and Hungary were met, largely by German manipulation.

Still, the guarantees for Czechoslovakia failed to materialize. The reason for this was given to the Czech foreign minister, Chvalkovsky, during his visit to Berlin at the beginning of February. Both Hitler and Ribbentrop told him that it was impossible for Germany to give guarantees to a country which doesn't do away with its Jews (French Yellow Book, 56). When France complained about it in a official demarché in Berlin, its embassy reported back to Paris on February 18 as follows: "The conditions which the Reich lays down to the Czechoslovak Government for an effective guarantee of the Czechoslovak frontiers by Germany may be summed up in the following ten points:

1. It [Czechoslovakia] must adopt complete neutrality.
2. Its foreign policy must be brought in line with that of the Reich.
3. It must leave the League of Nations.
4. It must drastically reduce its military effectives.
5. A part of its gold reserves must be ceded to Germany.
6. Czech currency in the Sudetenland must be exchanged for Czech raw materials.
7. Czech markets must be opened to German industries in the Sudetenland and no new industries may be created in Czechoslovakia if they compete with those in the Sudetenland.
8. It must promulgate anti–Semitic laws analogous to those of Nüremberg.
9. It must dismiss all Czech Government employees who may have given Germany grounds for complaint.
10. The German population in Czechoslovakia must have the right to carry Nazi badges and fly the Nazi flag [French Yellow Book, 60–61].

Instead of guarantees Hitler issued, on October 21, three weeks after Munich, the following top secret directive: "The future tasks for the armed forces and the preparation for the conduct of the war resulting from these tasks will be laid down by me in a later directive. Until this directive comes into force the armed forces must be prepared at all time for the following eventualities: 1. The securing of the frontiers of Germany. 2. The liquidation of the remainder of Czechoslovakia. 3. The occupation of the Memel district" (Shirer 1959,

428). The text is of particular interest as it hints of "future tasks." This time the pretext for invasion was to be the clamor for independence of the Slovak and Ruthenian minorities, irredentist movements the Germans had been inciting throughout the summer. After Benes had resigned as president of Czechoslovakia on October 5, the Slovakian and Ruthenian minorities were given autonomy, including local governments. On orders from Berlin, these now launched a campaign of subversion demanding full independence. Simultaneously the Hungarians were pressing further demands on Czech territory. In this they were vociferously supported by the Poles, desirous of having a common frontier with Hungary. Whenever the Slovaks slackened in their drive for secession Hitler threatened to hand them over to the Hungarians and whenever the Czechs tried to put the Slovaks in place they were threatened with war.

The whole issue came to a head on the Ides of March. Dismissed from his job as premier of Slovakia, Monsignor Tiso, who would eat half a pound of ham each time he was tense, came to see the führer on March 13. He was ordered to go home and proclaim an independent Slovakia, which he did the following day. Hitler then set 6 A.M. on March 15 as zero hour for the occupation of Prague. Concurrently, Dr. Hacha, a professor of history who had replaced Benes as president, had asked to be invited to Berlin to discuss with the führer his country's troubles; he was told to come, by all means. His visit was the ultimate spectacle of diplomacy transformed into opera buffa; Hacha had been scheduled to attend the Russian opera *Rusalka* in Prague that day, but he had to cancel in order to attend the German performance. Accompanied by his daughter, Hacha arrived at the Anhalter Bahnhof at 10:40 P.M. on March 14, where he was greeted by Ribbentrop with a bouquet of flowers. At the Adlon Hotel there were sweets for Miss Hacha, a personal gift from the führer, who was at that time watching a film appropriately titled *Ein Hoffnungsloser Fall* (A Hopeless Case). When informed of Hacha's arrival the führer ordered that the gentleman be made to wait and went on watching the movie. Hacha wasn't summoned until 1:15 in the morning when he was made to inspect an SS honor guard in front of the Chancellery. Inside, Hitler informed Hacha that in view of the disturbance to peace the Czechs were causing in Europe he, the führer, had ordered his troops into Czechoslovakia; this they would do within a few hours, at 6:00 A.M.; Hacha would be well advised to telephone Prague not to put up any resistance, otherwise there might be bloodshed, which no one wanted. With this Hacha was dismissed. In the antechamber Göring and Ribbentrop pressed Hacha to sign a document legalizing the invasion. When Hacha hesitated Göring said he was about to bomb and pulverize Prague. Whereupon Hacha fainted. Revived by the führer's personal physician, Hacha telephoned his government and asked that there be no resistance. At 3:55 A.M. in the presence of the führer he signed a declaration whose pivotal lines read, "the aim of all efforts must be the safeguarding of calm, order and peace in this part of Central Europe. The Czechoslovak President declared that, in order to serve this objective and achieve ultimate pacification, he confidently placed the fate of the Czech people and country in the hands of the führer…. The führer accepted…" (Shirer 1959, 447).

At six in the morning the German army crossed into Czechoslovakia; in some parts they had been there since the previous night. Fifteen hundred airplanes, 500 tanks, 43,000 machine guns, a million rifles, and Skoda, after Krupp the finest armament works in Europe, passed into German hands. In addition, they scooped 10 million pounds sterling in gold; subsequently the Bank of England shipped in another 6 million pounds sterling deposited with it by the Czech government. It was a substantial military and economic boost for Germany, sorely strapped for foreign exchange needed to stock up on raw materials from abroad. As evening fell, Hitler followed his troops into Prague, after first announcing to the German people "Czechoslovakia has ceased to exist." He slept that night in the Hradcin Palace.

The next day Bohemia and Moravia were declared German protectorates. The same day Slovakia, after enjoying its two days of independence, was likewise ordered to request protection, which was granted immediately, and German troops entered Slovakia, too. Ruthenia's independence, proclaimed on March 12, was snuffed out shortly thereafter when its territory was handed over to Hungary.

The occupation of Prague is taken to be the turning point in Great Britain's attitude to Hitler. Actually, there was no change in policy, for, as before, the British were willing to negotiate and fulfill Hitler's various demands in order to prevent the calamity of a new war. What had changed, though, was their comprehension of him. What they finally realized was that fulfilling Hitler's demands had no bearing on war and peace. They had finally gleaned that it was not the Rhineland, the Sudetenland, or Danzig or Memel, that Hitler was after, though this was what he said, but some vast new conquest that would reshape the continent. They would go on as before negotiating and urging concessions but no longer under the illusion that this would satisfy Hitler and were prepared, should he use force to get what he wanted, that they would have no other recourse but to go to war with him. The basic tragedy of the Europe of the '30s, aside from Hitler himself, was that at the helm of Great Britain were men who needed 15 years to decipher what Hitler had clearly enunciated and acted out ever since *Mein Kampf*. It is perhaps only fair to add that Chamberlain's break with Hitler may have occurred at the first Godesberg meeting when Hitler uttered those fateful words, "I am exceedingly sorry." Already then Chamberlain's smugness had been punctured. When he returned from that trip he told the House of Commons that Hitler's retraction of his word "was a great shock to me." When he came back from Munich, even as he peddled his "Peace in Our Time" and waved his scrap of paper, he told Halifax as he rode with him through the cheering crowds, "All this will be over in three months," though there are conflicting views about what he had meant by it. For a few days before Prague he was still issuing statements that the situation was hopeful and disarmament discussions might begin before the end of the year. In his diary he noted that "all information seems to point in the direction of peace." When the British cabinet met on March 15 to ponder the events of that day and the issue of guarantees to Czechoslovakia came up for discussion, Halifax stated that the guarantees "had come to an end," because Czechoslovakia had ceased to exist, as if it had not been killed but had died a natural death. However, the indignation of the country was now beyond Chamberlain's power to keep in check. Public opinion, and nearly the entire press, were in revolt against the government's procrastinations. And so was the House of Commons, including many of the Conservatives. They not only denounced but taunted the prime minister for his failure to buy off the dictator. The furor in the Parliament was such that there was a chance the Chamberlain cabinet would be ousted. These events, together with the sense of personal affront suffered by this haughty, narrow-minded man, brought about *a volte face* rarely seen in British statesmanship. On the afternoon train to Birmingham, where he was to deliver a speech on March 17, Chamberlain discarded a prepared, cautious text and, referring to Prague, penned the following words: "Is this the end of an old adventure, or is it the beginning of a new one? Is this the last attack upon a small state or is it to be followed by others? Is this, in effect, a step in the direction of an attempt to dominate the world by force? ... No greater mistake could be made than to suppose that because it believes war to be a senseless and cruel thing, this nation has so lost its fiber that it will not take part to the utmost of its power in resisting such a challenge if it is ever again made." That very day Chamberlain spoke these words to the entire world; it was all very circumspect, but clear nevertheless.

· CHAPTER 4 ·

Gate to the East

As with the Austria-Czechoslovakia sequence, a look at the redrawn map of Europe revealed in which direction Hitler would move after he entered Prague; it was Poland's turn. But unlike his previous conquests, Poland presented a more complex challenge for reasons that were partly objective, partly of Hitler's making.

Geographically Poland was the platform from which to debouch upon the landmass of European Russia, the ultimate goal. It was the necessary prelude to reaching a contiguous border with Russia. In that sense Poland was only a means to an end. Yet Poland was herself part of Hitler's contemplated *Lebensraum*. It was a large agricultural country inhabited by Slavs, it ranked highest in the ethnic antipathies of the ordinary German, and, prior to Versailles, much of Poland had been under Teutonic rule for nearly 150 years. She was, therefore, not merely a stepping stone, but a solid part of the Nazis' projected geopolitical map. Nor did Poland make it simple for Hitler to implement his scheme. For, unlike Austria and Czechoslovakia, she was not content to be a warden of the great powers, east or west. Poland preened herself as a major political factor in Eastern Europe, so much so that she pursued a vision of a "Third Europe" with her in the lead, independent of Germany, the Soviet Union, and the Western powers. She inserted herself with a will of her own into the political maneuvers of the 1930s. These ramifications were reflected in the several shifts Hitler followed in his attempts to pry open the gate to the East.

On January 26, 1934, Marshal Jozef Pilsudski, the father figure of a resurrected Poland, concluded a nonaggression pact with Hitler. Although at the time of signing the then German foreign minister, von Neurath, had stipulated that the pact "in no way implies the recognition of Germany's existing eastern boundaries," the Poles considered the pact a diplomatic success. This bilateral treaty was a blow to the Western powers' policy of collective security and Poland's reprisal for Rapallo where France had reached a *rapprochement* with the Soviet Union. When in 1935 Eden, and subsequently others, broached the subject of an eastern Locarno aimed at a general acceptance of the postwar status quo in Eastern Europe, Poland, like Nazi Germany, opposed it, perhaps not to alienate Germany. Poles feared the Soviets more than all other countries combined. This attitude only worsened with the death of Pilsudski in 1935, when power passed into the hands of a clique of colonels with Jozef Beck, the foreign minister, himself an erstwhile colonel in Pilsudski's Legion, at the helm. Not only were they all congenitally chauvinistic but, catering to the fashion of the times, they propelled the country into some sort of native Fascism. A typical example of their thinking was their Paris ambassador's cable that the Sudeten crisis "is being inflamed by Jewish and Communist circles who want war against Hitler" (Lukasiewicz, 99). It was thus natural that while planning the destruction of the Polish state Hitler should at times have been tempted by the possibility of the gate to the East being opened by the Poles themselves and, moreover, having them as allies in his drive into Russia. The trouble with this tempting alternative was that it would have impeded the annexation of those parts of Poland the Germans considered their due; that Hitler would have had to grant some semblance of statehood to the Poles; and that, unlike the Germans, the Poles may not have been willing or capable of going along with the ghoulish plans Hitler had in store for the conquered territories. Thus even as vassals to the Germans, the Poles may have presented more trouble than they were worth.

There were numerous occasions when the subject of a common crusade against the East was broached, Poland being offered Ukraine while Germany was to retain the rest of Russia. The first approach occurred soon after the Nazis came to power, in December 1933. In a talk with Lipski, Goebbels stressed that Communism compelled Germany to seek an understanding with Poland. Soon thereafter, on January 24, 1934, Lipski had a long conversation with Hitler. In it Hitler underscored Communist Russia's danger, not only to Poland, but also to Western civilization, and for its defense he considered Poland's role "momentous" (Lipski, 113, 125). While there were certainly other reasons, this potential alliance may have been a stimulus for concluding the nonaggression pact with Poland.

In the Sudeten crisis Poland sided with Germany. It enabled her to claim and annex Teschen, a slice of land 40 × 40 miles in size. For this she blackened her name in Western eyes and at one point was even threatened with a cancellation of her defense treaty with France. The larger reason for her siding with Germany had to do with her pretensions to a Third Europe. This was to be an alliance of neutral states from the Balkans to the Baltic, possibly including Scandinavia, all of them forming a buffer primarily against the Soviets. Since the Czechs had a defense treaty with the USSR, it was Poland's goal to dismember Czechoslovakia, with Ruthenia going to Hungary, and Slovakia seceding and joining the Third Europe. Poland was not to see any of these goals realized during the Sudeten crisis, but later on she did assist Germany in dismembering Czechoslovakia. Following Munich, Hitler saw a renewed opportunity of hitching the Polish horse to the German tank. On October 24, 1938, Ribbentrop asked Lipski to visit him and for the first time the Pole heard the demand for Danzig and an extraterritorial link with East Prussia, along with the old proposal for a joint venture against the Soviets. This seemed to be an opportune time to raise both issues because, on the one hand Poland, due to her anti–Czech stand, seemed alienated from the West, and on the other hand the demand for Polish territory was the whip which would drive the Poles to acquiesce in an anti–Russian crusade. This was followed on December 17 by a conversation between Ribbentrop and Burckhardt, the League's high commissioner for Danzig, to whom the reich's foreign minister proposed that Germany obtain Danzig, and for good measure also the Polish provinces of Torun and Poznan, in exchange for giving Poland large territories in Russia. (Cienciala, 201).

Barely had this piece of intelligence reached the Poles when Beck, on a health cure in Monte Carlo, received a summons from the führer to see him at the Berghof. Also present at the meeting were Ribbentrop and Ambassador von Moltke, who journeyed from Warsaw especially for the occasion. While the führer did mention Danzig and the link with East Prussia, the main topic was the mooted joint venture against Russia. Said the führer: "A strong Poland is absolutely necessary for Germany.... Every Polish division engaged against Russia is a corresponding saving of a German division" (Watt, 391). On the following day Beck had further talks with Ribbentrop, who hammered away on the same topic. Hoping perhaps to improve the atmosphere, Beck reminded Ribbentrop of his promise to pay an official visit to Warsaw. This the reich foreign minister did on January 25,1939 — significantly on the fifth anniversary of signing the nonaggression pact. The reich minister was extravagantly dined, wined, and fêted, but it did not make him relent on his mission of urging Beck and Pilsudski's successor Rydz-Smigly to join the anti–Comintern pact and of together marching east. Besides the Ukraine Ribbentrop promised Slovakia (a hint of things to come) and access to the Black Sea. In pressing his proposal the dour Ribbentrop even managed a witticism. When Beck wouldn't budge on the corridor and proved equally recalcitrant with regard to a war against Russia, Ribbentrop exclaimed: "You are so stubborn about maritime issues — the Black Sea is also a sea" (Zeszyty, Vol. 20, 71).

Ribbentrop's visit to Poland in January 1939 was the high-water mark of Germany's efforts to enlist Poland in an anti–Russian crusade. Only once more, on March 26, did Ribbentrop mention the subject to Lipski. The reason for this is probably that after the occupation of Prague and the inclusion of Slovakia in the German orbit, Poland was strategically cornered and the Germans thought she would yield. She did not. Henceforth Hitler returned to his plans for an invasion which, most certainly, was his preference all along.

With the advent of 1939 the task facing Hitler was twofold. He had to proceed so as not to repeat his Munich mistake when he had ended up with only part of the loot. He needed not part but all of Poland, because what he was reaching for was a border with Russia. Then, too, he wanted to accomplish this not by diplomacy, compromises, or even surrender, but by war. The waging of war was an end in itself and for excruciatingly simple reasons. He had rebuilt the Wehrmacht from scratch, he had honed new weapons, and, as would be seen in September, he had developed a new concept of warfare, later to be known as the blitzkrieg — and before he took on the USSR, or possibly France, he had to test it in the field. He clearly stated this at an August lecture to his generals when he said, "it is necessary to test the military machine" (Shirer 1959, 530). This was the rational element; there was also an atavistic one. To wage war, to kill, destroy, and terrorize, were the private, innermost cravings of the chancellor of the Third Reich.

That he was bent on nothing less than war Hitler had, as usual, revealed on a number of occasions. During both the Czech and Polish crises he instructed the Foreign Ministry that no negotiations should end in agreement. Hitler provided periodic briefings, or lectures, to his top commanders — Göring, Raeder, Brauchitsch, Halder, and others. On May 23,1939, in the Chancellery, with his adjutant, Schmundt, keeping notes, the führer expounded: "Danzig is not the subject of the dispute at all. It is a question of expanding our living space to the east…. The answer, therefore, is Poland…. We cannot expect a repetition of the Czech affair. This time there will be war" (Mendelssohn, 88, 90). On August 28, Il Duce, concerned about his partner's relentless drive for war, sent Ciano to put some restraints on the Germans. Over a good dinner Ciano asked his host, "Well, Ribbentrop, what do you want, the Corridor or Danzig?" "Not anymore," Ribbentrop replied, "we want war." This, of course, was not Ribbentrop but his master's voice speaking. At another meeting held on August 22, 1939, Hitler specified the kind of warfare he demanded of his soldiers and mulled over his fears that something could yet derail his planned attack, scheduled to start "perhaps next Saturday," three days away. Said the führer: "I shall give a propagandist's cause for starting the war. Never mind whether it is plausible or not. Have no pity. Adopt a brutal attitude. Right is on the side of the strongest. Act with great severity. Our first aim is to advance to the Vistula and the Narew. There will be a new German frontier according to healthy principles" (Mendelssohn, 101–105). "I am only afraid that at the last

minute some *schweinhund* (a swine; literally, pig dog) will produce a plan of mediation"
(Mendelssohn, 101–105; Shirer 1959, 531).

As previously noted, along with the objective difficulties in dealing with Poland, there
were also problems due to the führer himself. This had to do with the way he went about
achieving his successes from 1933 onward. His political astuteness had always consisted of
a mixture of threats and escalation. In the case of Austria and Czechoslovakia it had started
with a demand that the German minority not be mistreated, then for autonomy, then for
incorporation into the *Vaterland*, up to a point where there was no way of satisfying him
but by handing over to him, not only the German minority but the host country itself, otherwise there would be war. By now these tactics had become transparent not only to the
man on the street but even to diplomats trained not to see them. And yet, as we shall see,
he now resorted to the same stratagems, for he had no other intellectual resources to draw
on. Nazism was brutality and conquest, and Hitler could unearth no fresh thought, idea,
or vision that he could claim, however deceptively, as a reason for starting a world war.

The first German demands on Poland date back to the immediate post–Munich days.
On October 24, 1938, the Polish ambassador met Ribbentrop for lunch. The subject on
Lipski's mind was Ruthenia, which the Polish government wished to have transferred to
Hungary so as to stomp out any potential independent Ukrainian state for which there was
a strong irredentist movement in Poland. Instead, Ribbentrop turned the conversation to
something else; it was time, said he, to settle any outstanding issues between the two countries. For the moment these were Danzig and a link with East Prussia across the Corridor.

The term "corridor" will henceforth appear innumerable times in the negotiations, documents, and moralizations of the Germans and nearly everyone else. It is therefore important to take a look at this issue because formally it loomed as the crux of the German
grievances. However, it represents, more properly, a glaring example of a distortion due to
historical illiteracy and relentless sloganeering. Fig. 4.1 shows the boundaries of Poland during the 18th century. It will be seen that Poland had a substantial maritime province with
a shore extending over 100 miles. This province was called Pomorze—Land by the Sea;
Danzig, the Polish Gdansk and the later East Prussian town of Olstin were part of it. In the
short span of 1772–1795 Poland's three neighbors—Prussia, Austria, and Russia—in what
is known as the Three Partitions, usurped the entire country and extinguished Poland as
a state. While subsequently the boundaries between the three invaders underwent some
changes, the land taken by Prussia in 1772, which included all of Pomorze, remained annexed
to Germany. In the 145 years that Germany had ruled the usurped parts an intensive Germanization strove to stomp out their Polish identity. This lasted until the collapse of Imperial Germany in 1918 when the Allies reconstituted Poland as an independent state. A look
at the above map will show that in 1918 Poland got back only a part of Pomorze territory
with the enclave of Danzig made into a free city under the League of Nations. Poland's access
to the sea now shrank to less than half. This reduced Polish Pomorze, the Germans now
branded "corridor," implying an incursion into German territory. Given that East Prussia
had come into existence as a result of repeated armed onslaughts by the Teutonic Knights
into the East, it would have been more correct to say that East Prussia was an implant into
centuries-old Polish and Lithuanian territory.

But no, the Germans and everyone else—journalists, historians, diplomats, most
official notes and demarches—referred to it as the corridor. The Poles kept protesting that
it is not some corridor but Polish Pomorze, but it did them no good. So fixed was this historical mendacity that when on May 2, 1933, Hitler talked to the then Polish ambassador

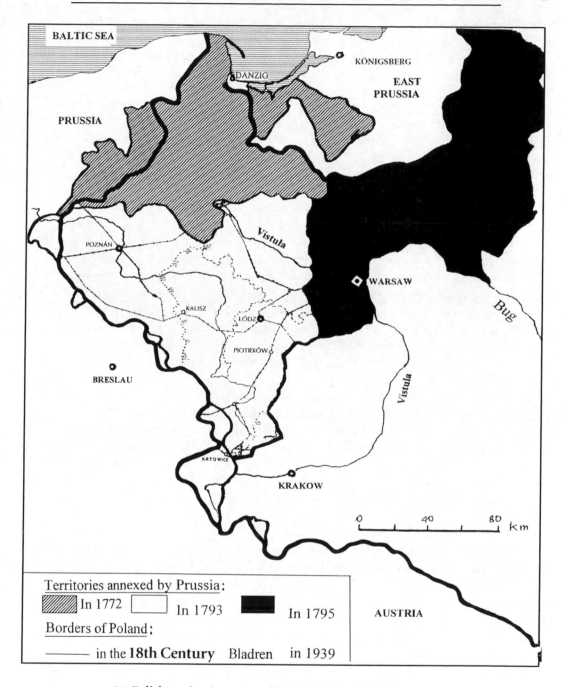

4.1. Polish territories annexed by Prussia in the 18th century

in Berlin, Wysocki — a man who certainly knew the history of the area — he had no qualms
in saying to the ambassador that relations between Poland and Germany would have been
much easier had Versailles allotted Poland a corridor to the east instead of to the west of
East Prussia (Lipski, 78). Hitler often used this argument in his speeches and interviews
to show his magnanimity on the issue and to the uninformed it seemed a reasonable proposition. Henderson, of course, considered the corridor "a real German grievance" and he

ludicrously argued before the British cabinet that, "Were Scotland separated from England by an Irish Corridor we would be demanding the same that Hitler is demanding" (Strauch, 214). The reality of this manufactured crisis was best expressed by the Poles themselves. At a high strategy meeting attended by the President, the Prime Minister, Rydz-Smigly and Beck, the situation was understood to be as follows: "If the Germans maintain such pressure in matters that are so secondary for them as Danzig and the highway, one can have no illusions that we are threatened with a large scale conflict. These objectives (Danzig) are only a pretext, and in view of that, a vacillating position on our side would lead us inevitably toward a slide, ending with loss of independence and the role of Germany's vassal" (Martel, 196).

The first stage of German demands on Poland can be said to have ended in January 1939. This was the period when Ribbentrop still hoped to exchange the Baltic for the Black Sea — that is, to swap the Corridor for the Ukraine and beyond. The manner in which this project was approached on the German side, tentative and subdued, raises doubts as to whether Hitler had ever meant it seriously. At any rate, it stopped after Ribbentrop's visit to Warsaw. There was now a seven-week hiatus in contacts, the period when Hitler was getting ready to occupy the rest of Czechoslovakia. Soon after, on March 21, Ribbentrop complained to Lipski that he had had no response regarding the German approaches on Danzig and the Corridor link. His tone was sharp. The issue, he announced, brooked no delay. There was a danger that the chancellor could conclude there was no hope for good relations with Poland. He asked that Lipski persuade Beck to come to Berlin for talks with Hitler (Gafencu, 42).

A day later, on March 22, Hitler swallowed another piece of territory, the Lithuanian port city of Memel. He then visited the new conquest and delivered a speech in which he promised "protection to all Germans living abroad." This was more ominous than the demand of Danzig. Indeed, when Ribbentrop saw Lipski a day after the latter returned from Warsaw with the message that at the moment it was inconvenient for Beck to travel to Berlin, Ribbentrop, linking up with Hitler's speech, for the first time put forward the complaint that the German minority was being mistreated in Poland.

* * *

Hitler's breach of the Munich agreement and occupation of Czechoslovakia on March 15 had triggered a momentous change in Britain's perception of him. Now the steadily increasing pressure on Poland by Hitler's use of familiar tactics prompted the British government to replace appeasement with something that it hoped would prove more effective in halting his rush to war. On the day that Ribbentrop told Lipski that the demands on Poland could not brook further delay, the British ambassador in Warsaw delivered to Beck a memorandum which said that "the absorption of Czechoslovakia shows clearly that the German Government is resolved to go beyond its hitherto avowed aim to consolidate the German race" and that consequently, "there is no state in Europe which is not directly or ultimately threatened." It was proposed that a declaration be issued on behalf of Poland, France, Great Britain, and the USSR which, *inter alia,* would state that "in case of any action that constitutes a threat to the political independence of any European State, our respective governments hereby undertake to consult together immediately as to what steps should be taken to offer joint resistance to any such action" (Docs.Pol. Min., 69–70). The proposed declaration, conceived by Chamberlain, was endorsed by France and the USSR, provided Poland accepted it.

The Poles rejected this declaration, arguing that it would have little effect on Hitler; an unstated reason was that the Poles would not join an alliance that included the Soviet Union. Instead, in his instructions to London, Beck broached the idea of a bilateral pact between Poland and Great Britain. With unheard-of alacrity the British agreed. The rationale behind the guarantee was that an unequivocal commitment by Britain might deter Hitler from his aggressive course. It was also triggered by strong public opinion and the stand of the House of Commons, where a faction of the Conservative Party itself had had enough of the government's vacillation, which was as distasteful as it was ineffective. As a result, on March 31, Chamberlain delivered a statement in the House of Commons, in which the key sentence read: "in the event of any action which clearly threatened Polish independence, and which the Polish Government accordingly considered it vital to resist with their national forces, His Majesty's Government would feel themselves bound at once to lend the Polish Government all support in their power. They have given the Polish Government an assurance to that effect."

Following Chamberlain's announcement Beck went to London where, in a typical Polish gesture, he insisted that the commitment be made reciprocal, that is, Poland be obligated to help Britain if the latter is threatened. The British accepted this and on April 6 a joint communiqué was issued about a mutual commitment to go to each other's help in case of aggression on either country. The details, said the communiqué, were to be worked out before the agreement was ratified. A secret protocol attached to the treaty limited the guarantees specifically to aggression by Germany (Doc Brit.For.Rels., 37–8). In April, British guarantees, identical to those given Poland, were extended to Rumania and Greece.

The French had several defense treaties with Poland, going back as far as 1921. During Locarno in 1925, the French again signed a defense pact with Poland, which was to hold even if the League of Nations did not support their joint stand against aggression (French Yellow Book, 407–8). In announcing Britain's guarantees Chamberlain added that he was authorized to state that the French were party to these commitments; this Daladier publicly confirmed on April 13. Given the actuality of the German threat, it was high time to work out the specifics of French military assistance in case Poland was attacked. For this purpose a delegation of Polish officers, headed by War Minister Kasprzycki, left for Paris to confer with their French counterparts. The military protocol signed on May 19 by Kasprzycki and the head of the French armed forces, Gamelin, specified that in case of an attack on Poland France was committed to the following:

1. The French Air Force would act against Germany immediately with the declaration of war by France.
2. The Army would start operations on the third day of the war.
3. A full-fledged offensive would start on the 15th day of the war.

An interesting contingency in the agreement, insisted on by the French, stipulated that the military protocol was to come into effect only with the signing of a corresponding political agreement. As it transpired, a political agreement was not signed till September 4, four days after the invasion of Poland. The military agreement with the British took place in Warsaw and was signed on June 1. Its military commitment was a massive use of the air force immediately on the declaration of war (Jurga, 112–14).

The British guarantee to Poland flew in the face of Hitler's entire strategy. It is worth speculating about an alternate approach that may have offered Hitler his chance of invading Russia without bringing about a war with Great Britain. The manner in which he first reoccupied the Rhineland, then took Austria, then the Sudetenland, then Czechoslovakia, then Memel, and eventually threatened Poland — practically dragged England against her will into war. By occupying Prague he humiliated the appeasers, tore up a state agreement to which the British prime minister had put his signature, and, by later invading Poland, with whom Britain had a treaty of mutual assistance, he left the British no choice but declare war. If, instead, he had foregone the nasty intermediate steps but after remilitarization had taken the direct route across Poland into Russia, his chances could have been much better. All the propaganda Hitler had used for the Sudetenland applied with greater force to the Corridor and Danzig, as the argument for being reunited with East Prussia, false as it may have been, was very persuasive. Without the stigma of Czechoslovakia, had Hitler invaded Poland there was a good chance that Britain would not have gotten involved. She would have been indignant, she would have protested as she had done in the case of Austria and Czechoslovakia, but would have done nothing. Once Germany had Poland she could, at will, have started her march into Russia and it is most unlikely that Great Britain would have intervened to save the Soviet Union. It was one thing to later accept the USSR as an ally when England was desperately alone at war with Germany and another to go to war to save Stalin. While it is an open question whether the Poland-Russia strategy would have worked, the fact is that Hitler's chosen strategy ended in failure. But even had he considered the latter option, it is likely that he could not have resisted grabbing Czechoslovakia as he later fell to invading Denmark, Norway, Holland, Yugoslavia — areas he did not need for the prosecution of his war. We are dealing here with an example of the führer's compulsions overriding the exigencies of his private master plan.

The British guarantee threw Hitler into a state of paroxysm. Canaris, who was with Hitler when the Chamberlain statement was brought to him, relates that, "with features distorted by fury he had stormed up and down his room, pounded his fists on the marble tabletop and spewed forth a series of imprecations. Then, his eyes flashing with an uncanny light, he had ground out the venomous threat, 'I'll cook them a stew they will choke on'" (Read & Fisher, 70). The next day, off to Wilhelmshaven for the launching of the *Tirpitz*, he announced that despite the guarantee he would not be swayed from the path he had chosen. Gafencu, who saw him on April 19, found him calm until the subject of the guarantee came up which "made him furious, propelling him out of his chair and making him shout.... If the British really want war he is prepared for it" (Gafencu, 78). It was in that state of rage that all his admonitions to himself and his cohorts that Poland must be isolated and that there must not be a conflict with the West seemed to have begun to crumble. Perhaps it had been so all along. For if he had to choose between giving up his scheme of an eastern empire and of risking war with England — being Hitler, the choice was obvious. If he couldn't launch a war against the East he might as well emigrate to Argentina. Of course, thus far it was only a risk of Western intervention; following his vaunted instinct he gambled that England was bluffing.

It is at this stage that Hitler, on April 15, received Roosevelt's peace appeal addressed to him as well as to Mussolini who, a week earlier, had invaded Albania. Among the usual exhortations for peace and harmony, Roosevelt inquired whether Hitler would give assurances of not invading the independent countries of Europe, 30 of which Roosevelt listed by name, among them —*horribile dictu*— Poland and Russia. The guarantees, said Roosevelt, could be given for 10, perhaps even 25 years.

The response was not long in coming. Reeling under these twin Anglo-Saxon blows— England's guarantee against aggression and America's plea for peace — Hitler convened a special session of the Reichstag on April 28. He then delivered his longest peacetime harangue — two and a half hours. It was also the most vituperative, sprinkled with hefty doses of ridicule and sarcasm on Roosevelt's account, for which he received roars of applause. The speech also contained progress on the Polish question. He recalled that he had been offering reasonable terms with respect to Danzig and the Corridor, which the Poles had rejected; he would no longer repeat that generous offer. Then he announced that he thereby renounced Germany's nonaggression treaty with Poland.

Hitler next ordered the General Staff to prepare a plan for the invasion of Poland under the code name Weiss. The first such directive bears the date of April 11 and its preamble addresses both political and military matters. In the diplomatic area it points out the imperative of isolating Poland to avoid a war with the West. The military is directed to use surprise in launching the attack and aim at the complete destruction of the Polish armed forces. The plans were to be worked out so that the invasion could start any time after September 1. Within five weeks, on May 23, Brauchitsch and Halder presented the Weiss plan to Hitler. This was the meeting quoted earlier in which Hitler said that war was what must ensue and war was what he wanted. On June 22 the OKW had a detailed timetable for the attack, including the calling up of reserves under the guise of fall maneuvers.

To strengthen his hand while preparing for war and try to keep England out, Hitler pressed Mussolini to reinforce their alliance with a military pact. Mussolini had been evading this but now the Germans insisted. Following trips by Ribbentrop to Rome and Ciano's to Berlin, the military protocol, named Pact of Steel, was signed in Berlin amid great pomp on May 21. The key provision of the pact, contained in Article III, reads that if "it should happen that one of them is involved in hostilities with another Power or Powers the other contracting party will immediately come to its side as an ally and support it with all its military forces." This alliance was accompanied by an agreement to transfer the ethnic Germans from South Tyrol to the reich. As a consequence 70 percent of the 267,000 Tyrolian Germans had to leave their homes; those who chose to stay had to adopt Italian citizenship (DDR, XIV, 84). So much for the führer as champion of the German race.

Having committed themselves to the defense of Poland, the Western powers, too, looked for allies. Given the trauma of World War I and their unspoken but very real determination not to get into a bloodbath with the German army, England and France were looking for a continental power to do the actual fighting should Poland be attacked. They turned to the Soviet Union. Although on the surface such an alliance seemed perfectly natural, there were serious impediments to its realization. The British, after 20 years of anti–Bolshevik policies, were loath to change their stance; Poland refused to join any alliance that involved the Soviets, fearing Communist subversion if not outright annexation; and the Russians perfectly understood why the West suddenly turned to them after ignoring them throughout Hitler's ascent, particularly at Munich. Yet there were compelling reasons for all parties to erect a common front. Even the Soviets, much as they distrusted and resented the West, knew the West would never attack them; Hitler was the peril that threatened not only their regime, but the very existence of their country.

While in office, Litvinov had once broached the possibility of a triple alliance. But on May 3 Litvinov was dismissed and Molotov became foreign minister. It was the first bad omen for the West's chances of engaging Russia. Litvinov was a Jew and an advocate of collective security; Molotov could be anything. Typically, the British had vacillated in responding to Litvinov's earlier proposal and when they did consent — the talking partner was Molotov. On May 27 the British ambassador and French charge d'affaires presented Molotov with the draft of a proposed pact. It aimed at negotiating a political agreement, a military convention, and the issuing of guarantees to several Central and East European countries. Molotov asked that Halifax, his counterpart, come to conduct the negotiations. The latter declined and instead sent William Strang, a member of the Foreign Office, who arrived in Moscow on June 4. Almost immediately difficulties sprang up all along the line. The Russians wanted a full-fledged alliance, all partners to engage in fighting the moment Germany attacked East or West. In the east this was to include not only Poland and Rumania but also Greece and Turkey in the south, and the Baltic states plus Finland in the north. The British wanted only a commitment to "consult" on ways and means when aggression occurred. When he eventually agreed to an alliance Chamberlain did not want the Soviets to automatically come to the aid of the victim but only when "invited." He also did not agree to include in the agreement cases of indirect aggression, such as a Nazi coup or other forms of internal subversion. Finally, the British wanted the pact to be under the auspices of the League of Nations, subject to its legalities and voting procedures. In view of these complex conditions the Russians proposed that they commence military talks while the deadlocked political issues were thrashed out. But the British insisted that the political agreement come first. The French, who had a greater stake in involving the Russians—otherwise they would have to do all the fighting—managed to get the British to relent. It wasn't until July 31 that Chamberlain agreed to the Soviet position. Despite rumors of German approaches to the Soviets, the British military mission was sent off by slow boat, so that it did not arrive in Moscow until August 11. The head of the British mission was a retirement-due admiral; his full name was Sir Reginald Aylmer Ranfurly Plunkett-Ernle-Erle-Drax. Chamberlain's instructions to him were to drag out the military talks till progress was made on the political front. The Soviet delegation to the military talks was of the highest caliber: Voroshilov, minister of defense; Shaposhnikov, chief of the General Staff; and the commanders in chief of the air force and navy. Vis-à-vis them the Western delegates were of substantially lower rank and the Russians felt slighted. The talks started on August 12 and on the 14th reached an impasse. If the Germans invaded Poland, asked Voroshilov, would the Red Army be allowed to cross Polish territory to engage them? The Western delegates had no answer and cabled home for instructions. After three days a directive came to procrastinate—for at home, too, they had no answer. When at the next meeting on 17th the Western delegates again dawdled, Voroshilov suspended the meeting, stating that a clear answer to his inquiry constituted the key to possible Soviet participation in the alliance. In the meantime inquiries were made in Poland. The Poles replied that they did not want Soviet guarantees, nor would they permit the passage of Soviet troops even along proscribed corridors; besides, they did not believe that the Red Army would be of any help, they did not think highly of it (Rumania likewise opposed the passage of Soviet troops). Pleas and pressures, particularly from the French, failed to change their mind. The attitude of the Poles is best reflected in Rydz-Smigly's aphorism: "With the Germans we risk losing our freedom, with the Russians our soul" (Jurga,136). When the French continued to press, Beck delivered an official reply: "I do not admit that there can be any kind of discussion whatsoever concerning the use of part of our country by foreign troops. We have not got a military agreement with the USSR. We do not want one" (Shirer 1959, 537). When on August 21 the parties met again, Voroshilov asked the talks be adjourned *sine die*. August 21 was, of course, the eve of Ribbentrop's arrival in Moscow to sign the Nazi-Soviet pact.

* * *

The history leading up to the signing of the Nazi-Soviet pact extends over a considerable period and is buried in a multitude of hints, soundings, and obfuscations. We shall go over those phases which shed light on the motivations of the two sides in striving for it, and on their effect on the British-German confrontation. Again we mention only the British because the French had no independent policy.

According to Hilger, a member of the German embassy in Moscow for many years, the USSR tried throughout Hitler's reign to bind Nazi Germany in a pact with the East European states. Hitler rejected them all (Hilger, 278). Von Neurath quotes a conversation with Hitler when the latter told him of an approach by Stalin in 1937, made via David Kandelaki, chief of the Russian trade mission, which was rebuffed. These approaches intensified in the summer of 1938 when Hitler annexed Austria and the Sudetenland. As part of this campaign the Soviet press toned down its anti–Nazi propaganda. The main spur to an accommodation with Hitler came with Munich from which the Soviets were excluded even though they had a defense treaty with Czechoslovakia. This left them with a conviction that the West had no intention of resisting Hitler, and might in fact support him in his drive east. This is corroborated by Litvinov who in his memoirs says that Stalin's switch to a rapprochement with Germany occurred as a result of Munich and that already in January 1939 Litvinov received indications that being an advocate of collective security he would soon be removed from office (Shirer 1959, 480).

The most authoritative hint to the Germans, however, came from Stalin in his March 10, 1939, speech before the XVIII Party Congress. In it he made clear his suspicion that the Western powers were trying to involve him in a war with Germany and his determination not to fall for it. He said that in the realm of foreign policy the task of the USSR was "to observe caution and not to permit our country to be drawn into a conflict by the *provocateurs* of war, who are accustomed to having others pull the chestnuts out of the fire for them." It is as succinct a statement of the basic motive behind the pact as any other source. This speech was followed by the dismissal of Litvinov, who as a Jew was not suitable for negotiations with Nazi officialdom.

To make sure that the speech and the switch in foreign ministers were not lost on the Germans, the Soviet charge d'affaires, Georgi Astakhov, in a meeting of May 5 with Julius Schnurre, the German expert on East European economic affairs, was reported to have asked whether the removal of Litvinov was likely to cause a change in the German attitude to the Soviet Union. He also invited the Germans to resume the trade negotiations which had been suspended since February. This was expanded at a higher level when on May 20 in a meeting with Molotov the German ambassador Schulenburg was told that the USSR would resume trade negotiations when the necessary "political bases" had been created.

Two months of hesitation followed in which both sides mulled over their conflicting interests and emotions. On the Soviet side this included Russia's awareness of Hitler's designs on her; the negotiations going on with the Western powers; and the possible damage to Communism at home and abroad by a pact with Hitler. On Germany's side first and foremost was Hitler's personal aversion to such a partnership; the screeching halt, even if temporary, the pact would impose on his plans for the East; the existence of the anti–Comintern pact; the effect on its allies, particularly Italy and Japan; and the ideological shock to the Nazi regime. But the central calculation, that the removal of Russia from a possible alliance with the West would leave England stranded and stop it from going to war over Poland, overwhelmed everything else. So at the end of July, on instructions from Ribbentrop, Schnurre informed Astakhov that "German policy in the East has now taken an entirely different course," and that Germany is ready for "a far-reaching arrangement of mutual interests with consideration of vital Russian problems," a message which Astakhov post haste conveyed to Moscow (Shirer 1959, 501).

There were, perhaps, two reasons for this particular timing. One, tentative, was the impending dispatch of the allies' military missions to Moscow; the other, obvious one, was that if the treaty was to work its effect on the English it would have to happen before the attack on Poland on September 1. Hitler thus had only one month to accomplish it.

That the Germans were not only ready but eager to conclude a treaty with the Russians became abundantly clear on August 3. Schulenburg was scheduled to see Molotov late that day and at 1 P.M. Ribbentrop rushed off a cable to his ambassador instructing him to inform Molotov that on the German side "there is a wish of remodeling German-Russian relations and that from the Baltic to the Black Sea there was no problem which could not be solved to our mutual satisfaction" (Shirer 1959, 505). Molotov's answer conveyed via Astakhov on the 12th was that the USSR was ready to discuss the German proposals, and suggested Moscow as the seat of negotiations. Two days later came the high point of Germany's race to conclude the pact. On the evening of the 14th, Schulenburg was instructed to inform Molotov that Ribbentrop was prepared to come to Moscow to deal with the treaty; in addition, the ambassador was to request an audience with Stalin in order to communicate to him this important message. Schulenburg saw Molotov at 8 P.M. on August 15 and on the following day cabled Berlin that Molotov was amenable. Before agreeing to the trip, however, Molotov wanted to know whether in the contemplated agreements the Germans would agree to:

- conclude a nonaggression pact.
- a joint guarantee to the Baltic States.
- influence Japan to stop her attacks on the USSR in the Far East.

Within a day, Ribbentrop accepted all demands and proposed that he come to Moscow by plane any time after August 18. In a personal memo to Schulenburg he stressed it was important the visit take place at the end of that week or, at the latest, the beginning of next. The reason for this rush was that Hitler was now planning his attack on Poland for August 26, leaving only a week for the pact to exert its impact on the British.

Before Molotov heard of the Germans' agreement to his stipulations, he informed Schulenburg that while the USSR was prepared to negotiate the treaty it preferred less publicity and a more methodical pace. Then he learned of Ribbentrop's offer to come to Moscow. This was supplemented on August 18 by another cable of his in which, hinting of impending war, the emphasis was on haste. Schulenburg, seeing Molotov at 2 P.M. on August 19, tried to impress him with the need for haste but Molotov preferred orderly work. When Schulenburg persisted, Molotov said that he had nothing to add and terminated the interview. Half an hour later Schulenburg was called back to the Kremlin where Molotov agreed to Ribbentrop's hasty visit. The ambassador surmised that Molotov had talked to Stalin, who grasped the reasons for Hitler's insistence, and made Molotov agree to the visit. Still, Ribbentrop's date for the visit was too tight and the Russians proposed either August 26 or 27. Efforts by Schulenburg to advance the date were unsuccessful.

Within a day came another bombshell—a personal letter from Adolf Hitler to Josef Stalin. It was sent on August 20 and received in Moscow on the 21st; the instructions were to deliver the letter to Molotov on a sheet of paper without a letterhead. Its text read:

Berlin, August 20, 1939

Herr Stalin, Moscow

    1. I sincerely welcome the signing of the new German-Soviet Commercial Agreement as the first step in the reordering of German-Soviet relations.

    2. The conclusion of a nonaggression pact with the Soviet Union means to me the establishment of a long-range German policy. Germany thereby resumes a political course that was beneficial to both states during bygone centuries. The Government of the Reich is therefore resolved in such a case to act entirely consistent with such a far-reaching change.

    3. I accept the draft of the nonaggression pact that your Foreign Minister, Herr Molotov, delivered, but consider it urgently necessary to clarify the questions connected with it as soon as possible.

    4. The supplementary protocol desired by the Government of the Soviet Union can, I am convinced, be substantially clarified in the shortest possible time if a responsible German statesman can come to Moscow himself to negotiate. Otherwise the Government of the Reich is not clear as to how the supplementary protocol could be cleared up and settled in a short time.

    5. The tension between Germany and Poland has become intolerable. Polish demeanor toward a great power is such that a crisis may arise any day. Germany is determined, at any rate, in the face of this presumption, from now on to look after the interests of the Reich with all the means at its disposal.

    6. In my opinion it is desirable, in view of the intentions of the two states to enter into a new relation to each other, not to lose any time. I therefore again propose that you receive my Foreign Minister on Tuesday, August 22, but at the latest on Wednesday, August 23. The Reich Foreign Minister has full powers to draw up and sign the nonaggression pact as well as the protocol. A longer stay by the Reich Foreign Minister in Moscow than one or two days at most is impossible in view of the international situation. I should be glad to receive your early answer.

Adolf Hitler

    Timing was so important that Hitler decided to intervene personally, distasteful as it undoubtedly was for him to write that letter. It shows in its tone. He addresses Stalin as *Herr*. In any bilateral reference he puts Germany first. He also cannot refrain from being two-faced when he says "the conclusion of a nonaggression pact with the Soviet Union means to me the establishment of a long-range German policy." In contrast Stalin addressed Hitler as chancellor and wrote a reply which was both polite and factual. This letter, forwarded from Moscow at 7:30 P.M. on August 21, reads:

Moscow Aug. 21, 1939

To the Chancellor of the German Reich, A. Hitler

    I thank you for your letter. I hope that the German-Soviet nonaggression pact will mark a decided turn for the better in the political relations between our countries.

    The people of our countries need peaceful relations with each other. The assent of the German Government to the conclusion of a nonaggression pact provides the foundation for eliminating the political tension and for the establishment of peace and collaboration between our countries.

    The Soviet Government has authorized me to inform you that it agrees to Herr von Ribbentrop's arriving in Moscow on August 23.

J. Stalin

At 11 P.M. on the day Hitler received Stalin's letter the German radio announced the news of the treaty and that Ribbentrop was on his way to Moscow. Hitler was in a hurry to announce it even though the pact hadn't been signed yet in order to let the blow sink in and do its work. Ribbentrop arrived in Moscow at noon on August 23 and after a brief stopover at his embassy went to the Kremlin. There, he was received by both Molotov and Stalin. The meeting lasted three hours and, after a break, continued long into the night. At 2 A.M. on the 24th the treaty was signed. There followed some jovial banter that lasted till dawn. Ribbentrop again managed a joke that now Russia could join the anti–Comintern Pact; Stalin laughed heartily.

The agreement signed that night consisted of a nonaggression treaty, which stipulated that neither party would attack the other, nor join in any hostile alignment. At Hitler's insistence a clause was included that, without waiting for ratification, the treaty would come into force immediately. This part was made public. There was also a supplementary deal bound in a secret protocol which did not surface till after the war. This secret protocol provided for the partition of Eastern Europe among the two signatories, as follows:

1. In the event of a territorial and political rearrangement in the areas belonging to the Baltic states (Finland, Estonia, Latvia, Lithuania), the northern boundary of Lithuania would represent the boundary of spheres of influence of Germany and the USSR.

2. In the event of a territorial and political rearrangement of the areas belonging to the Polish state, spheres of influence of Germany and the USSR would be bound by the line of the rivers Narew, Vistula, and San.

3. With regard to southeastern Europe, attention was called, by the Soviet side, to its interest in Bessarabia. The German side declared its complete disinterestedness in these areas.

A proviso in the above treaties was Hitler's stipulation that Stalin hand over all those émigré Austrians and Germans who had sought refuge in the Soviet Union after the Nazi seizure of power (Volkogonov, 387). Their impending fate can be surmised. A similar requirement was later entered into the armistice clauses with France. That this loomed of such importance to him as to include it in international treaties tells much about Hitler's inner makeup described in Chapter 1.

The reason for the USSR's signing the pact was what Stalin had said in his March 10 speech. Had Russia joined the Western powers, its fate would have been similar to that of Poland when in September it was left alone to fight and lose, with the English and French standing by as if there were no war. The Russian historian L. Bezymierski provides a convincing scenario. "The Germans invade Poland. England sits behind its water moat. France sits behind the Maginot line. They have thus achieved their aim; the USSR is at war with Germany. The Wehrmacht overcomes Poland into which the Russians are not allowed to enter. The Germans are on the borders of the USSR already in 1939. It could even be that the West would not even have declared war" (Jurga, 133). In the words of Cripps, had Russia "come in on the side of the allies she would have been doing all the fighting in the east and France and Britain would no more be able to assist her than they had been able or willing to assist Poland" (Gorodetzky, 3) Another calculation for signing the pact, an inversion of the first, was that instead of Russia bleeding in a war with Hitler why not let the Western powers do it, they who for so long had abetted and strengthened him. The capitalist world, which to Stalin included both Germany and the West, may exhaust itself in the process, yielding territorial and other gains for the Soviets.

The closest enunciations of Hitler's motive behind the pact is contained in what h said to Burchkhardt as early as April 11 when he received him at his aerie — an indication of the importance he attached to the exchange. Burckhardt was to be his messenger to England and he lectured him for two and a half hours, in the course of which he said, "I want to live in peace with Britain. If they give me freedom in the east I will happily conclude a pact with the British and guarantee their possessions all around the world.... Everything I am doing is directed against Russia. If the West is too obtuse to grasp this, then I shall be forced to come to terms with Russia and turn against the West first. After that I will direct my entire strength against the USSR" (Read & Fisher, 184).

As soon as he knew Stalin had agreed to a nonaggression pact Hitler embarked on the final steps for the invasion of Poland and set a date for the attack — all under the conviction that the pact with Russia had knocked England out of the game; moreover, he expected the British cabinet to fall as a result of his scoop. On August 22 he gathered his top military chiefs at the Berghof. He was in a euphoric mood. It was a beautiful summer day outside; inside Hitler stood behind a large desk, his generals in front of him. Hitler harangued and prophesied. He thought the West would probably not fight, but the risk had to be taken; had he not taken risks there would have been no Rhineland, Austria, Czechoslovakia. In announcing the Moscow Blitz, he said: "The enemy had hoped that Russia would become our enemy.... The enemy did not count on my great power of resolution.... The day after tomorrow Ribbentrop will conclude the (nonaggression) treaty. Now Poland is in the position I wanted her" (Shirer 1959, 530–1). Hitler then plunged into a general exhortation, reminiscent of the most bloodcurdling pages of *Mein Kampf.* He even falsified the regime's economic record in order to justify the war to his robotlike generals. Said Hitler on that day:

"The decision to attack Poland was arrived at in spring. Originally there was fear that because of the political constellation we would have to strike at the same time against England, France, Russia and Poland. This risk, too, we would have had to take. Göring had demonstrated to us that his Four-Year-Plan is a failure and that we are at the end of our strength, if we do not achieve victory in a coming war.

"Since the autumn of 1938 and since I have realized that Japan will not go with us unconditionally and that Mussolini is endangered by that nitwit of a King and that treacherous scoundrel of a Crown Prince, I decided to go with Stalin. After all there are only three great statesmen in the world, Stalin, I, and Mussolini. Mussolini is the weakest for he has been able to break the power of neither the Crown nor the Church. Stalin and I are the only ones who visualize the future....

"Our strength lies in our quickness and in our brutality. Genghis Khan has sent millions of women and children into death knowingly and with a light heart. History sees in him only the great founder of States. As to what the weak Western European civilization asserts about me, that is of no account. I have given the command and I shall shoot everyone who utters one word of criticism, for the goal to be obtained in war is not that of reaching certain lines but of physically demolishing the opponent. And so for the present only in the east I have my death-head formation in place with the command to relentlessly and without compassion to send into death many women and children of Polish origin and language....

"Poland will be depopulated and settled with Germans. My pact with the Poles was merely conceived of as gaining time. As for the rest, gentlemen, the fate of Russia will be exactly the same as I am now going through with in the case of Poland. After Stalin's death —

he is a very sick man—we will break the Soviet Union. Then there will begin the dawn of the German rule of the earth....

"I have but one worry namely that Chamberlain or some other swine (some recorded that he used the word *Schweinhund*, others *Saukerl*) will come at the last moment with proposals or some switch (*Umfall*). He will fly down the stairs even if I shall personally have to trample on his belly in the eyes of the photographers.

"No, it is too late for this. The attack upon and the destruction of Poland begins Saturday (the 26th) early.... For you gentlemen, fame and honor are beginning, as they have not for centuries. Be hard, be without mercy.... And now on to the enemy, in Warsaw we will celebrate our reunion..." (Adamthwaite: 119–20).

The speech so inspired Göring that he jumped on a table and "danced like a wild man" promising obedience to the führer; Göring, of course, denied this at his trial at Nüremberg. All the other participants kept quiet.

For the rest of August 22 and throughout the next day Hitler stayed at the Berghof waiting for the signing of the treaty with Russia. Bad news arrived as Ribbentrop was still winging his way to Moscow. This was a letter delivered by Henderson at the Berghof at 1 P.M. on August 23. In it Chamberlain informed Hitler, "The announcement of a German-Soviet Agreement is taken in some quarters in Berlin to indicate that intervention by Great Britain on behalf of Poland is no longer a contingency that need be reckoned with. No greater mistake could be made.... If the case should arise, they are resolved, and prepared, to employ without delay all the forces at their command." This was followed by a memorable sentence, both eloquent and pathetic, which encompassed much of the nature of the war that followed. Said Chamberlain in the above letter, "It has been alleged that, if His Majesty's Government had made their position more clear in 1914, the great catastrophe would have been avoided. Whether or not there is any force in that allegation, His Majesty's Government are resolved that on this occasion there shall be no such tragic misunderstanding."

With the signing of the pact confirmed, Hitler returned to Berlin on the 24th. All that day he expected that, as a result of the pact, the Chamberlain and Daladier cabinets would be replaced, as he put it, by "friends of peace." He told this to Weizsäcker on August 23 and he was so certain of it that he had instructed his press chief, Dietrich, to bring him directly the news of the fall of the allied governments the moment it was announced (Bregman, 47–8). The press and Goebbelses propaganda machine, too, led the German public to expect that England would now abandon her commitment to Poland. Instead next day, Friday the 25th, a profound crisis materialized. Hitler had on that day given the final word for the attack on Poland to begin at 4:45 the next morning. That Friday morning Chamberlain delivered a speech publicly affirming England's guarantee to Poland. Hitler instructed Schmundt to find out from the General Staff what was the latest possible hour to cancel the ordered attack. He was informed 3 P.M. He asked that Henderson be summoned immediately. The ambassador arrived and, interrupting his lunch, Hitler received him at 1:30. The important message he had for him was that he, Hitler, was an artist, he preferred art and architecture to war and with the end of the Polish crisis he would settle down to live the life of a bohemian. He was offering England an alliance and a guarantee of her empire. More than that, he was prepared to assist England "in any part of the world where such help might be needed" (Schmidt, 149). When Henderson demurred that this was not much to go by, Hitler told him that there was not much time to lose and that he was providing Henderson with an airplane to fly to London and submit his offer to the

British government. Henderson flew to London. At 5:30 that afternoon, Dietrich, brought Hitler the devastating information that in London the Polish-British defense treaty had been ratified just 15 minutes earlier. Soon after, Attolico brought Hitler a letter from Mussolini saying that if the Polish crisis led to war with the West Italy would not participate in it. Hitler sent for Keitel and ordered, "Stop everything. At once. Get Brauchitsch immediately. I need time for negotiations." Göring later testified that on that afternoon Hitler called him and said that "he had stopped the planned invasion of Poland. I asked him whether this was temporary or for good. He said 'No. I shall have to see whether we can eliminate British intervention'" (Mendelssohn, 106).

It took some doing to stop the impending invasion, for by then the armies were heading for their jump-off positions. By light plane and dispatch riders they had to be reached and turned around. Some border skirmishes had already taken place, particularly by the special detachments. One, at the Jablonka Pass, had failed to receive the order to halt, and had crossed the border at midnight and seized the Mosty Station at the entrance to the railway tunnel. No other troops followed them and the German Command disowned them, claiming they were a Slovak unit (Read & Fisher, 279).

The goal of "negotiations" with England now assumed frantic forms and it was pursued along two venues: the diplomatic via Henderson; and informally via Birger Dahlerus. The latter was a Swedish businessman and a friend of Göring's whose mission was not revealed to the public, not even to Ribbentrop, in the hope, perhaps, of making it easier for the British to yield. Another reason for the employment of Dahlerus was that he acted on behalf of Göring. At home and abroad Göring was known as the Nazi with a human face; in fact he was a ruthless, totally immoral thug. He was one of the main figures in engineering the annexations of Austria and Czechoslovakia and he was party to most of the atrocities committed by the Nazi regime. His personal debaucheries— gluttony, drugs, greed, flashy uniforms and his frequent clowning in front of the public — made him, unlike Hitler, familiar to the masses. It was therefore thought that this "moderate" might help sway the British.

Dahlerus was summoned from Stockholm on the 24th and instructed to tell Britain that, despite the Nazi-Soviet pact, Germany was ready for an understanding with the British and, like Henderson, was packed off to London. At first Halifax would not see him but after some urgent calls to and from Berlin, he received him on the 25th and told him that the issue was not the British Empire but Poland. This message Dahlerus delivered to Göring on Saturday, the 26th. Despite the lack of specifics in the message, Göring took him to see the führer that night. The führer was already asleep. Göring asked that he be woken up. After a long night's harangue Hitler sent Dahlerus back to London with the same message — friendship with England. On Sunday, Dahlerus saw Chamberlain and Halifax. The answer they gave him was that England was ready for friendship with Germany but before this could take place, the cooked-up Polish crisis must be settled not by war but by negotiations, and decent negotiations at that. Being unofficial, no record of the Dahlerus talks were kept, but at some point in these discussions, perhaps at the suggestion of Dahlerus, it was decided to keep Henderson in London till Monday, while Dahlerus gave Hitler an oral report on the British insistence on negotiations. Should Hitler's attitude be favorable the British proposals would be given to Henderson in writing to deliver in Berlin. Sunday evening, Dahlerus returned from Berlin and reported that Hitler accepted the British stand. Since the proposals were to contain a commitment on behalf of the Polish government, Halifax cabled Kennard to check with Beck; the phrase for which Halifax sought Polish concurrence was that the Polish government was ready "to enter at once into direct discussions with Germany." Beck's answer was "Yes." The note, which Henderson, upon his return to Berlin, handed to Hitler at 10:30 P.M. on August 28 emphasized the following points:

- Agreement to conduct negotiations is conditioned on the "nature of the settlement and the methods by which it is to be reached." The British government would not acquiesce in any settlement that puts in jeopardy the independence of Poland.
- Hitler had not specified his demands on Poland. What were they?
- Any use of force would result in what Chamberlain had stated on August 22 (Cadogan, 203–4).

Following the delivery of this note Hitler, in his talk with Henderson, reverted to his old ploy of escalation. He stated that his previous magnanimous proposals were no longer valid. He now demanded Danzig; the whole of the Corridor; and rectifications in Silesia. No longer a link with East Prussia but the whole Corridor; and now Silesia which had never before been mentioned. When Henderson left at midnight he was accompanied out by Meissner, head of the Chancellery. Henderson remarked to him that it was a great pity that Hitler still did not believe that the British would fight. Meissner reported this back to Hitler who shrugged his shoulders and muttered, "They will think it over" (Strauch, 290).

The official German reply was given to Henderson at 7:15 P.M. on Tuesday. In paraphrased form it contained the following demands:

1. Danzig to be returned to Germany.
2. The Corridor to be returned to Germany.
3. Germany could not tolerate "the disorganized state of affairs in Poland" and it must provide "protection" for the German minority which was being treated "in a barbaric fashion."
4. Germany could not renounce its "vital interests."
5. In order to guarantee the boundaries of Poland the concurrence of the USSR would have to be secured.
6. Germany agreed to direct negotiations provided that a Polish representative with full powers to sign an agreement — a plenipotentiary — arrived in Berlin no later than the next day, Wednesday, August 30.

In the above document there is again a replay of Hitler's worn-out tactics. As practiced with Schuschnigg and Hacha when, by a combination of threats and humiliation, they were made to submit, this was now being tried on the Poles. Then, in addition to phrases such as that Hitler could no longer tolerate the "disorganized state of affairs in Poland," that he had to "protect" the German minority, and could not renounce "vital interests" — all open doors to subsequent aggression — there were in the above document two conditions impossible to fulfill. It was impossible for any Polish representative, without having seen the German demands, within a day to come, negotiate and sign an agreement. And secondly, not even Hitler could secure a Soviet guarantee for Poland's boundaries, particularly in view of what was contained in the secret protocol of the Nazi-Soviet pact.

All of these moves by Hitler were meant, of course, not to open negotiations, even on his terms, but to avoid them. Following the annexation of Czechoslovakia, there had never been direct approaches to Poland. The maneuverings and the magnanimous offers were all addressed to London. As the critical month of August approached, Hitler had made sure that there would be no accidental encounter with the Poles. At the beginning of the month he had ordered Ambassador Moltke home and he was to have no contact either with his embassy in Warsaw or with the Polish Embassy in Berlin. In Warsaw the embassy staff was permitted only to receive communications from the Poles. Likewise, the Foreign Ministry was told to avoid all contact with the Polish Embassy in Berlin (Read & Fischer, 173).

The most intensive efforts to resolve the German demands peacefully came from Mussolini. The spur to it lay in his dilemma of being tied to Germany by a military pact, yet having neither the desire nor the means to wage war with the West, which he thought inevitable. During July, Il Duce planned to see Hitler in order to dissuade him from attacking Poland. However, before meeting him he decided first to test the waters. In a letter of July 24, Mussolini gave his view that an attack on Poland would lead to a European war and he proposed convening an international conference of the Big Powers to settle the German demands. Ciano on his own tried the idea of a conference on Ribbentrop, who talked to Hitler. Hitler rejected it. Moreover, in view of these Italian designs, Hitler on July 31 cancelled the projected meeting with Mussolini. Caught between his alliance with Germany and his unwillingness to be dragged into war, Mussolini sent Ciano over the Alps. At his first meeting with Ribbentrop at Salzburg on August 11, Ribbentrop, in Ciano's words, "rejected any solution which might give satisfaction to Germany and avoid the struggle" (Ciano, 115,119); it was in line with his outburst that it's not Danzing but war that Germany wants. Ciano subsequently saw Hitler twice on the Berghof. When he arrived on August 12, Hitler was stooped over a table covered with military maps. Ciano wanted to talk about negotiations and conferences; the führer lectured him on grand strategy. "I personally," said Hitler, "am absolutely convinced that the Western democracies will, in the last resort, recoil from unleashing a general war." Ciano gently broached Mussolini's wish for an international conference; if not a conference perhaps direct diplomacy to arrive at a peaceful solution. Hitler ignored the suggestions. On the last day of August, when he knew war was imminent, Mussolini again offered to mediate the dispute. Hitler declined.

Several other interventions for peace were launched in the last days of August. On the 24th Roosevelt wrote to Hitler. Noting that he had not received an answer to his April appeal, he proposed that Germany and Poland resolve their differences either by direct negotiations, arbitration, or conciliation with the help of a neutral party; an identical note was addressed to President Moscicki. Poland answered accepting either direct negotiations or conciliation procedures. Roosevelt wrote again on the 25th informing Hitler of the favorable reply from the Poles. It was not till August 31, when war had already been set for next morning, that the German charge d'affaires in Washington handed Roosevelt a reply which said, "Owing to the attitude of the Polish Government ... all these (peace) endeavors have remained without result" (Peace and War, 477–80). Also, on August 28, the queen of Holland and the Belgian king jointly offered their good offices for mediation. The Poles accepted; the Germans rebuffed them (Docs.Pol Min., 109).

* * *

The missive of August 29 in which the Poles were given one day to come to Berlin and deal with the German demands can be considered Hitler's last shot in his campaign to appear in British eyes as willing to negotiate. The British answer to that one-day ultimatum was that these were unreasonable conditions and England could not presume to demand this of the Polish government; urgent and direct talks between the parties, yes, but arranged via customary diplomatic venues, to which Britain would lend a hand.

From then on all subsequent notes and meetings were merely codas in a play that had run its course. On the afternoon of the 28th, at the time he was drafting his one-day ultimatum, Hitler talked to Brauchitsch and fixed the new invasion date for Friday, September 1, the exact hour still to be determined. At 3:22 P.M., Brauchitsch passed this on to the General Staff. Hitler's expectations or delusions of England staying out now extended beyond the outbreak of war. After Henderson had left the Chancellery carrying the one-day ultimatum Hitler told his entourage, "In two months Poland will be finished. And then we shall have a great peace conference with the Western Powers" (Lipski, 309–14). Speer recalled that "Hitler did not consider war as inevitable. He, and Göring, too, said at the time that England would declare war only nominally. Afterward, the English would soon settle things by political methods, and would yield again" (Overy, 2001, 330).

At noon on Thursday, Hitler issued his first war directive:

1. Now that the political possibilities of disposing by peaceful means of a situation on the Eastern Frontier which is intolerable for Germany are exhausted I have determined on a solution by force.

2. The attack on Poland is to be carried out in accordance with the preparations made for Case Weiss....

The time for the attack in this directive is given as 4:45 A.M. September 1. At 4 P.M. the order was passed down to all units in the field and they started for their jump-off positions.

During the 30th of August a list of extremely "reasonable" demands was assembled by Ribbentrop, undoubtedly with the führer's help. These were to provide proof that Germany's offer to Poland was magnanimous and that the Poles had been recalcitrant, leaving Hitler no choice but the use of force. In this the Germans had the help of Henderson, who to the very end attempted to resurrect within the British cabinet the phantoms of appeasement, castigating the Poles for the way they responded to the German demand for a plenipotentiary.

At 2 A.M. on August 30, Halifax instructed Henderson to inform the Germans that "it was unreasonable to expect that we can produce a Polish representative in Berlin today and the German Government must not expect this." At that very hour Henderson got Lipski out of bed and urged him to have Beck or Rydz-Smigly come to Berlin. Lipski said he would call Warsaw. The attitude of the British government had been conveyed to the German Foreign Ministry already by 4:30 that morning; and when the formal British reply arrived that urgent negotiations yes, but one-day compliance no, Henderson asked to see Ribbentrop. They met at midnight of August 30-31. Henderson handed him the British note; he also complained that, though promised, he had not been given the text of the demands the Germans were to place before the expected Polish delegate. The notorious exchange between the two then took place. First Ribbentrop exclaimed, "The time is up. Where is the Pole your government was to provide?" (Schmidt, 151). He then read out the German demands, of which there were 16. He read them fast and in German. Henderson did not grasp or understand most of them. When at the end he asked for a written copy Ribbentrop refused. Henderson then asked that Lipski be called and given the German demands. It is too late, Henderson was told; it was now midnight and a Polish plenipotentiary had not shown up. When two days later Henderson inquired why he had been refused a copy of the German demands, Ribbentrop answered that "he was not authorized" to do that (DGFP, 505). At some point following Ribbentrop's presentation of the no-longer-valid offer Hitler commented to Schmidt, "I needed an alibi…. That explains my generous offer" (Gilbert and Gott, 294).

Then came the last day of peace, Thursday, August 31. The Germans were silent. By morning Henderson had received informally via Göring — the good cop — the text of the 16 points and he judged them "reasonable." Throughout that day, even though he had been told by the Germans that it was too late, Henderson kept pressing Lipski and London for the Poles to produce a negotiator. In the end Halifax did ask Beck to inform the Germans once again that the Polish government was available for negotiations. After some hesitation Beck agreed and at 1 P.M. instructed Lipski to deliver a message to the German government. As soon as he received these instructions Lipski asked to see Ribbentrop. He was kept at bay for most of the day. After more than five hours, at 6:15 P.M., Ribbentrop agreed to receive him. Lipski cut a lonely figure as he headed for the German Foreign Ministry. There he read to Ribbentrop Beck's communication:

"Last night the Polish Government were informed by the British Government of an exchange of views with the Reich Government as to the possibility of direct negotiations…. The Polish Government are favorably considering the British Government suggestion and will make them a formal reply on the subject during the next few hours."

Lipski added that he had been trying to deliver that communication since 1 o'clock. Ribbentrop's only question was whether Lipski came as a plenipotentiary. Lipski replied "for the time being no." Promising to inform the führer of the visit, Ribbentrop terminated the interview.

A few hours later, at 9:15 in the evening, the 16 points were broadcast over the German radio and beamed abroad by all German and foreign media. On the logic that when one loses a leg it is a stroke of good luck not to have lost both, the German offer was considered by all and sundry as a mild set of conditions. One of these mild points was that in the Corridor a plebiscite was to determine whether it was to belong to Poland or Germany. According to Article (3) of the German memorandum the people entitled to vote were only those inhabitants and their offspring who had lived there in January 1918; those Germans who had left the area before 1918 were entitled to come back and take part in the plebiscite. In other words, no Poles and their offspring who were expelled from Polish Pomorze following its annexation by Prussia; nor those Poles and their offspring who had settled there following the reestablishment of an independent Polish state could vote. It was not far from saying that only English colonials could decide whether India was to belong to the Indians or to Great Britain. But, as Ribbentrop had said, even those conditions no longer held.

When Lipski returned to the embassy after his meeting with Ribbentrop and tried to contact Beck he found that all communications with Warsaw had been cut. In the ambassador's files lay an invitation dated August 11 to attend a hunting party with Göring in which the ambassador was asked whether October or November would suit him better. This was the night of August 31 and to the east, tight against its borders, 57 German divisions waited for dawn to start the invasion of Poland.

· CHAPTER 5 ·

The September Weekend

AT 4:45 on Friday, September 1, 1.5 million German troops, 2,700 tanks, and 1,300 airplanes were hurled across the Polish frontiers. It was the start of the war Hitler had sought since midsummer of 1938 and had been robbed of by Munich. This time he had not let it happen.

The dawn attack was preceded by several staged incidents which were to prove to the world that it was Poland that started the war. On Thursday night SS men dressed in Polish Army uniforms faked an attack on the German radio station Gleiwitz in Silesia. After the "seizure" of the station an anti–German tirade was broadcast in Polish. Later the Germans "counterattacked" and repulsed the Poles who left behind a dead soldier. This dead Polish soldier was a concentration camp inmate whom the SS men had killed during the faked attack. This incident was reported by all of the media abroad, according to the German version. Sixty more SS men disguised as Polish soldiers attacked the German customs post at Hochlinden, destroying the building and the stores inside. Here six dead "Poles" were left behind — all Sachsenhausen camp prisoners. Similar incidents were staged at other locations.

On Friday morning at 10 o'clock Hitler delivered a speech to the Nazi-appointed Reichstag, especially convened for that historic day. Since the burned-out Reichstag building had never been restored, this took place in an appropriate substitute, the Kroll Opera House. Dressed in a new hybrid military and party tunic which he swore not to take off until victory or death, Hitler plunged into an *Apologia per Bellum Suum*. He cited the generous offer of the 16 points; his patience in waiting in vain a whole day for a Polish delegate; and, besides, it wasn't the German Army that attacked first but the Poles, viz. Gleiwitz. The first German military communiqué of World War II issued that day by the OKW plied the same line: "to check Polish aggression, troops of the German Army have counterattacked early this morning across all the German-Polish frontiers."

While Hitler was talking, a new brainstorm struck Henderson. After passing on to London Göring's intelligence that the Poles had attacked first, he cabled that now the only hope for peace would be for "Marshal Smigly-Rydz to announce his readiness to come immediately to Germany to discuss as soldier and plenipotentiary the whole question with Field Marshal Göring." This, when the Germans were pushing deep into Poland and scores of towns far behind the lines had been bombed, causing many civilian dead and wounded. Along with Henderson, Dahlerus continued throughout that day and the next to bombard London with telephone calls that Göring was prepared to come to London, and so on. On September 2 Ribbentrop himself, on instructions from the führer, phoned the press attaché at the German Embassy in London, Dr. Fritz Hesse, to see Horace Wilson with an offer of "withdrawal" if Poland would yield this and that (DDR XIII, 623). Then Mussolini went into high gear again and his efforts are worth retracing because they reveal the terrible state into which France was plunged in those days.

This goes back to August 23 when Stalin, France's erstwhile treaty partner, signed up with Germany. On hearing this, the French government panicked. While Foreign Minister Bonnet was known as an archappeaser, less is known about Daladier. A stubborn, taciturn politician, given to long silences and murky speeches, he was a typical casualty of the First World War. The son of a provincial baker, he spent four years in the trenches, took part in the battles of Verdun and at one point suffered a poison gas attack. It was said of him that "the country keeps a mediocrity in power for fear of something worse." Soon after the announcement of the Nazi-Soviet pact Daladier convoked a meeting of the Council of National Defense. Its members were Daladier, Bonnet, Gamelin, the chiefs of the air force and navy, and four others. The question before the council was: Given the defection of the Soviets, can or should France keep its Polish commitment? When Gamelin was asked about the state and plans of the army, he answered that the army was all right. As for plans, in case of hostilities the French would immediately mobilize, forcing Germany to withdraw troops from the Polish front; arrangements were being made with a view for a long war during which France would expect considerable British forces and American arms; after two years of preparations the French would start an offensive. All this was nothing new. Ever since 1918 French military strategy was based on a defensive phase lasting some two years; it was with this in mind that France had invested a treasure erecting the Maginot Line. In sum the council's decision was to honor the French commitment to Poland but not get involved in any fighting (Shirer 1959, 609–10). One can only wonder what had made the Poles trust the promises given to them in May.

At noon on August 31, Ciano had called the French and British ambassadors and informed them that Il Duce proposed to convene an international conference on September 5 in order to "examine the clauses of the Versailles Treaty which are the cause of the present troubles." While this was being read in the two capitals, Hitler at dawn the next day launched his war. Still at 11:45 that Friday, Bonnet called Rome to say that he was in favor of the proposed conference. He then inquired of the Poles whether they agreed to Mussolini's proposal. The Poles answered "We are in the midst of war.... It is no longer a question of a conference but of common action which the Allies should take to resist" (Shirer 1959, 605–6).

The British stepped in and made the French drop all talk of a conference and go along with their next move. This was a common note to Germany. At 9 o'clock Friday evening Henderson handed Ribbentrop the following note from the British government:

"Unless the German Government are prepared to give His Majesty's Government satisfactory assurances that the German Government have suspended all aggressive actions against Poland and are prepared promptly to withdraw their forces from Polish territory, His Majesty's Government will without hesitation fulfill their obligation to Poland."

Ribbentrop's comment on the note was that Germany had not committed any aggression but that "the previous day regular and irregular Polish units had invaded German territory" (DGFP, 505). An hour later Coulondre delivered an identical note from the French government. The British and French ambassadors requested an immediate reply. Ribbentrop said he would report this to the führer.

The delivery of these notes did not end France's attempts to avoid war with Germany. The trouble was that while she was unhappy about following Britain's determined stand —

she could not think of any alternative. France was so demoralized that she was incapable of formulating a policy of her own, even one of surrender (this would come later). She therefore grasped at anything that gave the illusion of an escape from the terror imposed by Hitler. This showed up the very next day after Coulondre delivered his stern note to Ribbentrop. On Saturday, Mussolini had Attolico deliver a message to the Germans saying that Italy could get Britain and France to the conference table on the basis of an armistice, which left the German armies in Poland where they were. It is not known whether this was presumption or a result of a nudge from the French. When Ribbentrop met Attolico at 12:30 P.M. he asked whether the notes the Western powers delivered yesterday were ultimatums. Attolico ran off to see the Western ambassadors and returned with the happy news that no, they were only warnings. Ribbentrop then promised Attolico an answer by noon Sunday. At 2 P.M. Ciano telephoned both Paris and London and, while Bonnet as usual equivocated, Halifax told him that for the British to consider Il Duce's proposal, a prior condition was that the Germans pull out of Poland and Danzig be restored to the status quo ante. This, Mussolini knew, Hitler would not do. Attolico then had to inform Ribbentrop that the British would not enter any deal that was not conditioned on a pullout from Poland, and therefore Il Duce's mediation efforts were at an end. To this Ribbentrop made no reply. Still at midnight Bonnet woke Ciano and said that he was prepared to wait for Hitler's response promised for noon Sunday and proposed that perhaps everything could still be salvaged if the Germans staged a "symbolic" withdrawal. In his memoirs Ciano says he threw this proposal into the wastebasket.

The next difficulty between Britain and France arose over the timing of an ultimatum to Germany. The British proposed issuing an ultimatum at midnight Saturday to expire at 6 A.M. Sunday the 3rd. The French resisted. They had mobilized 360,000 reserves on August 24 but refrained from ordering general mobilization so as not to annoy Hitler. They now argued they needed at least 24 hours to get this mobilization under way; to the demurring British they pointed out that they would have to do the fighting and that at the moment there was not a single English soldier on French soil. However, that evening Chamberlain ran into his own difficulties when he faced an angry House of Commons who castigated him that the invasion was now two days old and England was doing nothing. Consequently at 9:50 P.M. Chamberlain called Daladier, and later on Halifax called Bonnet, proposing a joint ultimatum to be given at 8 the next morning to expire at noon. Both Daladier and Bonnet said no.

Chamberlain was to appear before the House of Commons again the next day at noon. Both he and Halifax now feared that they would be unseated. So Halifax called Bonnet again to inform him that, regardless of the French position, Britain was going to deliver its ultimatum next morning. Next, Halifax instructed Henderson to arrange for a meeting with Ribbentrop for 9 o'clock Sunday morning; the text of the ultimatum had been delivered to the Berlin embassy already at 5 A.M. When Henderson tried to set up the appointment, Ribbentrop refused to see him; he could not even get to see Weizsäcker. So it transpired that the declaration of war was delivered to Hitler's interpreter, Paul Schmidt. Henderson arrived at the Foreign Ministry punctually at 9, declined to take a seat, and standing in the middle of the room read out the British ultimatum. He then gave Schmidt a copy, which read:

> Although this communication (the warning of September 1) was made more than 24 hours ago, no reply has been received, but German attacks upon Poland have been continued and intensified. I have, accordingly, the honour to inform you that unless not later

than 11 A.M. British Summer Time, today September 3rd, satisfactory assurances to the above effect have been given by the German Government and have reached His Majesty's Government in London, a state of war will exist between the two countries as from that hour.

At noon in the House of Commons Chamberlain announced that there had been no response from Berlin and that consequently Great Britain was at war with Germany.

The French presented their ultimatum at 12:30 P.M. to expire at 5 o'clock Sunday evening, characteristically lagging England by 6 hours.

Upon receiving the British ultimatum Schmidt immediately carried it over to the Chancellery. There he found Hitler sitting at his desk and Ribbentrop near the window. Standing in front of them, Schmidt translated the text of the ultimatum into German. For a while there was total silence in the room. After a long interval, which to Schmidt "seemed an age," Hitler turned to the standing Ribbentrop and with a "savage look" asked, "What now?"

It was a cogent question. Hitler had screamed his head off to be an ally of Britain and make war on Russia; he ended up in an alliance with Bolshevik Russia and at war with Britain and France.

• CHAPTER 6 •

Blitzkrieg in Poland

The war the Germans unleashed against Poland was a preordained contest. In all respects— weaponry, generalship, tactics, morale, numbers— the Germans were by far superior. Still, it is relevant to retrace, however briefly, the circumstances and course of the Polish campaign because it anticipates the performance of most future opponents of the Wehrmacht. The defeats that they suffered on the battlefield were, of course, due to the power of the German war machine but to various degrees they were also self-inflicted. It tells of a malaise in the military domain consistent with the failures of Europe's interwar statesmanship.

The problematics of the Polish army again hark back to World War I. For the Poles the traumatic years were not 1914–18 but 1920 when they fought and won a war against the Bolsheviks. As a result two notions became fixed in their minds. One was that their main enemy was the Soviet Union. In the 20 years between the two world wars all their efforts were directed toward a possible conflict in the east; Pilsudski even forbade his General Staff to work out plans for a war with Germany. It was not until late in 1938 that a frantic race began to map out a defensive strategy in the west. Not only was this somewhat late in the day but even had the Poles had such plans they would have been partly obsolete given that by occupying Czechoslovakia the Germans were now deployed also along their southern border, a situation the Poles themselves had helped to create.

The second legacy of 1920 was horses. In the Russo-Polish war cavalry had played a prominent role, both on the Russian side when Budyenny's Red Cavalry broke into southern Poland, and then in Pilsudski's counterstroke which drove the Russians out. There was also an indigenous element in this devotion to cavalry. Poland was a land of peasants and gentry and they knew and loved horses. Emotion and tradition mingled with martial experience and caused them to build an army out of kilter with military realities. The Poles had some 12 cavalry brigades of three regiments each, perhaps 100,000 horsemen armed with sabers and lances. They were a splendid sight on parades and maneuvers but how they were to operate against the German armored divisions posed a question the Poles preferred not to examine.

Nor were the 45 other wartime divisions fit for modern combat. They were foot soldiers equipped with bayonets, rifles and machine guns. Barring a few demonstrative units sporting light and obsolete models, the Polish army had no tanks, no modern airplanes, and no motorized transport; nor did it have enough artillery to support the million strong soldiery Poland put into the field. It had no independent means of communication and had to rely on civilian telephone and telegraph services. Ostensibly the reason for all this was that the country could not afford it. But this does not explain why the army had so few antitank or flak guns; during the war the entire Polish army fielded 126 antiaircraft guns. Not only that, but the generals had failed to train their troops how to deal with the enemy's armor; the war was a week old and nearly over when instructions went out to the infantry about how to fight the German tanks. Likewise the absence of modern aircraft was due less to Poland's economy than to military myopia. In April 1929, Pilsudski issued an ukase that "aviation is to serve only for reconnaissance and only in this direction should it be used"; officers who pressed for combat airplanes were dismissed. Poland's military budget in the years preceding the war allotted twice as much to its cavalry as it did to the air force (Cynk, 101). Poland, in fact, had some skilled and imaginative aeronautical engineers and much of the equipment could have been built at home. It was primarily the incompetence and lassitude of its leadership which, on top of Poland's economic straits, had produced an army unfit for even a limited war with the Wehrmacht.

In case of war Poland's mobilization schedule was to be conducted in two stages, a secret stage followed by a publicly announced call-up. The secret part was put through on April 23. When full mobilization was announced on August 29 the Western allies demanded that Poland rescind it so as not to "provoke" the Germans. The Poles complied but, as the threat intensified, mobilization was reinstated next day at 10 A.M. It was then too late for an effective integration of all reserves. Even those who reported for duty were stomped by the Luftwaffe, which wrecked the trains, depots, and assembly areas of the called-up men. Particularly affected were the strategic reserves of the Supreme Command, which never came up to their projected strength. In effect, when hostilities opened only 39 Polish divisions were in line, amounting to some 800,000 to 1 million men. In numbers of troops alone the Germans had a superiority of 2:1 and, as will be seen later, in the combat zones the ratio was considerably higher.

The Poles had a total of some 320 warplanes, half fighters and half bomb-carrying machines. The Polish air force was under the command of the army but just before the war it was split in two, one part placed under the Supreme Command as a strategic force, and the other assigned to the land armies—a dispersion of means contrary to military principle. The mainstay of the Polish fighters was the P11C, a machine of the early '30s with a nonretractable undercarriage, capable of a maximum speed of 220 mph and armed with two machine guns. Their opponent was the modern Me-109, at least one and a half times as fast and armed with two cannons in addition to two machine guns.

The most wrenching decision for the Polish leadership was the disposition of its troops. As with the army's combat effectiveness the strategic position of the country vis-à-vis Germany was precarious in the extreme, but, as we started off by saying, the Poles made it considerably worse. Fig. 6.1 shows the deployment of the forces on the eve of fighting. As can be seen, the troops were pressed tight against all borders, forming a box enveloped on three sides by the invader. Moreover, the greatest concentration was in the west, the side farthest from the center of the country and most exposed to the enemy, whereas the southern and northern borders were lightly manned. It almost begged for an envelopment from the wings. This particular line-up was chosen by the Polish leadership for domestic and political reasons because the western parts of the country were the most settled and developed. A deployment offering some chance of holding out against the German armada would have been along the Vistula or even the Bug river, a shortened linear front not easily susceptible to outflanking maneuvers. This, however, would have implied a loss of prestige and a readiness to abandon half the country. That the alternative of defending everything meant losing everything did not sway the leadership. With this all-around defense, the plan was

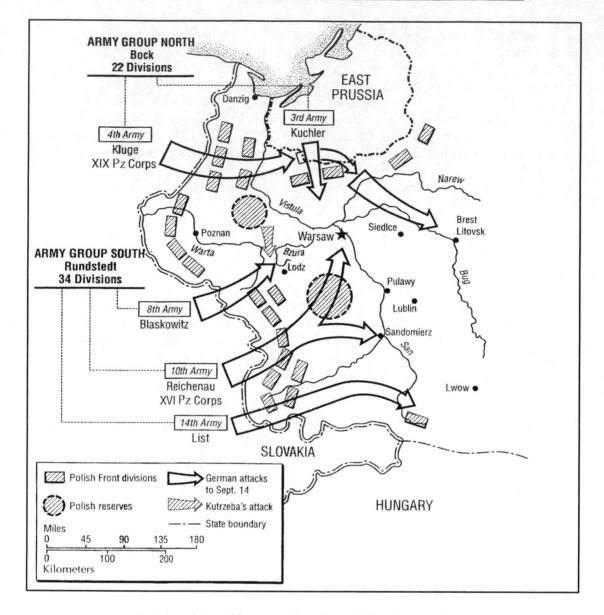

6.1. Disposition of forces and invasion of Poland, September 1939

to fight along the borders and, when necessary, retreat gradually to new defense lines. This was to last until the French opened their promised grand offensive forcing the Germans to withdraw the bulk of their divisions from Poland.

That these tenets of Polish strategy — orderly withdrawal and a French offensive — were wishful thinking should have been clear to the General Staff. Any competent military professional knew that the Germans' tanks and airplanes would not allow a foot and horse-drawn army to stage organized withdrawals; it was also known to the intelligence community that the basic strategy of the French was to do no fighting for at least two years. These German and French doctrines must or should also have been clear to the Poles. The Allies' war strategy was reiterated as recently as May 4, 1939, during a British-French conference, at which it was agreed that in case of war no offensive would be undertaken against the Germans but most available forces would be directed to the Mediterranean. Why the Poles chose to believe otherwise is explainable only by the psychology of those who, deprived of hope, resort to self-deception.

As shown in Fig. 6.1, the Germans concentrated their forces at two sectors, the corners of the box. In the southwest von Rundstedt's army group had 34 divisions organized in three armies, the 10th Army with its XVI Panzer Corps in the center being the strongest. The two other armies were screens for this central prong. Von Rundstedt's mission was straightforward; thrusting in a northeasterly direction he was to head for Warsaw. In the northwest the army group under von Bock had a more complex task. Von Bock's two armies were initially separated by the Corridor. The 4th Army in West Prussia was much the stronger and it had under its command most of the armor, the XIX Panzer Corps. Its mission was to sever the Corridor from the rest of Poland. Upon reaching East Prussia it was to hand over the XIX Panzer Corps to the 3rd Army which would then drive south to the rear of Warsaw, link up with von Rundstedt coming up from the southwest and so trap the entire Polish army in the western half of the country.

Outside the two concentrations the Germans left only border guards. Thus on the opening of battle von Rundstedt's 34 divisions faced anywhere from seven to 10 Polish divisions; and von Bock's 22 divisions faced six to eight divisions. The Poznan Army plus large parts of the Pomorze Army were to be bypassed. Metaphorically, the German attack can be visualized as that of two pitchforks thrusting into Poland, one from the southwest the other from the north and both aiming at the heart of the country. For the campaign the Germans concentrated 78 percent of their armed strength, leaving barely a fifth of it to face the West (Moczulski, 150).

Integral to their overpowering equipment and deployment were the projected German tactics, a method of warfare soon to be known as the blitzkrieg. This was not an entirely new concept. It had been bandied about in France and England but it was the Germans who adopted and perfected it to a degree that it had become a uniquely German tool. Its tactics actually originated during the last German offensive in 1918. These used special storm units whose mission was to bypass nests of resistance and penetrate deep into enemy territory without worrying about the flanks. Instead of pummeling at the opponent's muscles the blitzkrieg aimed at his nerves and blood vessels so that the demise was quick and total. To achieve this the enemy is attacked not frontally but is instead penetrated at his weakest point. The assault is then carried forward at a furious pace — at the greatest speed and most concentrated firepower — heading for the enemy's infrastructure with the aim of encircling him. Such deep thrusts into enemy territory violated all orthodox precepts of military science which forbade exposing one's flanks to the enemy. All this was made possible by the employment of tanks and aircraft. The tanks were not to be used as support for the infantry but as independent armored wedges; likewise the air force was to be used not so much in support of the troops as in demolishing the enemy's rear — his transportation, communication, headquarters, signal centers, supplies, and assembly areas. In addition to disrupting the enemy's logistics and disorienting its leadership the Luftwaffe was to attack civilian centers with the aim of spreading terror and chaos. For the principle of the blitzkrieg was to exert not only military but also psychological pressure and cause a general breakdown of the enemy's will and ability to resist. An example of this sort of fighting was the German dive bomber Ju-87, the familiar Stuka, which under its wings carried a siren to be turned on during the dive (some were in the fins of the bombs) so that in combination with its plunge from the sky and the burst of bombs, the terrifying shriek would paralyze the enemy. The confidence of the Germans was such that before hostilities began they had sent into the rear 1,200 volunteers to prevent industrial destruction by the retreating Polish troops.

The Germans crossed the Polish borders at 4:45 A.M. on Friday. Even before this hour the Luftwaffe was already over Polish territory. Its primary mission was elimination of the Polish air force. In this it failed. The Poles had moved their planes to makeshift airfields and did a good job of camouflaging the parked machines. This, combined with fog and low clouds that Friday morning, frustrated the Luftwaffe's effort. They did, however, bomb and destroy depots and stores on the permanent air bases. And already on that first day they bombed scores of open towns ranging as far as Brzesc in the eastern part of the country. The Polish pilots flung themselves with great audacity against the German aircraft and despite severe handicaps shot down a number of them. But already on that first day the strategic fighter group lost a quarter of its strength.

The German army spent some time probing the Polish lines. With fair weather in the southern parts of the country, von Rundstedt made better progress than the 3rd Army attacking from East Prussia. But during the second day Guderian's XIX Panzer Corps fought its way across the base of the corridor trapping three Polish divisions north of it. Guderian ignored them and went on to link up with the 3rd Army, which he did on September 3 and together they launched an assault to the south. During the following days the drive into Poland from both north and south progressed on schedule as if the Germans were on maneuvers. Their method of attack proved irresistible. First came a wedge of massed armor; then a phalanx of motorized troops equipped with both light and heavy weapons; and then infantry divisions whose task it was to widen the breach made by the tanks. The spearheading armor, assisted by squadrons of bombers and ground-attack planes, pulverized everything ahead and to the sides of it so that the Poles rarely got a chance to give battle. The masses of scattered and demoralized Polish troops were subsequently mopped up by the infantry divisions following the tanks.

The advance was such a success that the Germans did not even bother to encircle the enemy. The Poles were repeatedly forced to abandon their positions to avoid being trapped. Once in the open they were pounced on by the Luftwaffe and subjected to a relentless bombing and strafing until they ceased to be a fighting force. Throughout the entire campaign the Polish army was incapable of a single offensive action or of any tactical defensive move that would have interfered with the Germans' timetable. In a little over a week the German northern and southern pincers were approaching Warsaw.

The only major encounter between Polish and German forces, unplanned by either side, occurred toward the end of the campaign. As noted, the Germans deployed in such a way that the Poznan and most of the Pomorze armies were bypassed. By the end of the first week the two Polish groupings, still

Friday, September 1, 1939. With the break of dawn German bombers head for Poland, starting World War II. (Courtesy the Polish archives.)

unbloodied and stranded in western Poland, were ordered to retreat behind the Vistula, the new defense line. As these divisions, led by General Kutrzeba, retreated eastward they moved parallel to Blaskowitz's 8th Army. All along Kutrzeba was aware that the German 8th Army, its attention focused on Warsaw, had its left flank exposed to his troops. On the second day of the campaign Kutrzeba had asked the Supreme Command for permission to attack Blaskowitz but was refused. It is not clear to what extent he was permitted

The first victims of World War II — fallen Polish soldiers in a common grave. (Courtesy the Polish archives.)

to do so now. But attack he did. From an operational standpoint the attack made no sense. At that stage a defensive front was being formed along the Vistula; the capital was being invested; and, most important, Kutrzeba's retreat was being cut off and would soon be blocked completely. The called-for direction of attack was eastward to break through to the Vistula. Instead, tempted by the Germans' open flank, Kutrzeba struck out to the south.

The battle opened on the evening of September 9 along the lower Bzura River. The assault came as a complete surprise to the Germans who had come not to expect anything of the sort. The Poles had a local superiority of 3:1 in manpower and 2:1 in artillery. The Poles crossed the Bzura and for the first day or so gained ground to a depth of perhaps 10 to 15 miles. The main blow fell on the German 30th ID which lost 2,300 men while its commander, General Briesen, lost an arm in the fighting. Under attack Blaskowitz tried to contact Rundstedt's HQ but was unable to reach it. On his own he stopped the march on Warsaw and turned north to face the enemy. Elsewhere, too, the Germans recovered quickly and by the 11th managed to stabilize the front. Then the forces investing Warsaw, including the XVI Panzer Corps, were turned westward to face the Poles; even the 4th Army to the north was diverted to join the battle, with Rundstedt himself taking command of the converging forces. Kutrzeba, realizing that he was about to be trapped, shifted his attack eastward but it was too late. He was stopped by the powerful 10th Army which closed the ring for good. On the 17th the Germans passed over to the offensive in which tanks, airplanes and artillery converged from all directions on the encircled troops. Under an avalanche of fire descending on the ever-contracting cauldron the Polish armies were ground to pieces. By September 19 the fighting, known either as the Battle of Kutno or Bzura River, was over. Of the original 200,000 troops 15,000 Polish soldiers were killed; 40,000, including General Kutrzeba, escaped into beleaguered Warsaw; and the rest were either taken prisoner or scattered.

Already on the night of September 4 the Polish government started to evacuate Warsaw. The Supreme Command transferred to Brzesc where it arrived on the night of the 6th. Rydz-Smigly was quartered in a damp cellar screened from other personnel by a blanket. The Supreme Commander was not given much time in Brzesc for the Germans were circling Warsaw from the east and the notion of a Vistula-San defense line had to be abandoned. The new plan was to set up a defense perimeter embracing the two southeastern provinces of Volhynia and Podole. Accordingly, on September 12 Rydz-Smigly moved to

Wlodzimierz Wolynski. This lasted barely a day when news came that the Germans were approaching Lwow. Significantly on that very day the Western Allies held a top-level meeting in Abbeville in the presence of Chamberlain, Daladier, Gamelin and Ismay at which it was decided to halt all skirmishing at the Westwall. The last Polish scheme was to form a Rumanian beachhead — a small enclave in the southeast corner of the country abutting the Rumanian border. Through it, it was mooted, war supplies sent by the Allies would come in while the French opened their grand offensive. On September 15 Rydz-Smigly, President Moscicki, and the entire government transferred to the vicinity of Kolomyja, just this side of the Rumanian frontier.

The clinching day for the Poles was September 17. By the secret Nazi-Soviet agreement the Russians were to take possession of all territory east of the Narev-Vistula-San rivers. This was one of the reasons the German pincer movement was originally directed along the Vistula. As the campaign progressed Ribbentrop kept pressing Moscow to do its bit of invading. But the Russians demurred. They wanted to be sure that the Poles were indeed defeated; they also probably didn't care to appear as Germany's war partner. As will be seen later, they had their own ideas about how to portray their part in the latest partition of Poland. Hitler, however, was worried lest the Soviet delay enabled the Poles to organize some sort of permanent resistance in eastern Poland. Orders went out to initiate a new enveloping sweep down the right bank of the Bug River and liquidate any troops escaping to the eastern parts of the country. This the German army accomplished in no time at all. Guderian lunged south and on September 13 took Brzesc. Four days later he linked up with von Rundstedt near Wlodawa, some 30 miles south of Brzesc. With German troops deep into what was to be Soviet territory, Stalin finally made his move.

On the early morning of September 17 the Red Army crossed into Poland. The intervention of the Soviets was a puzzle to nearly everyone. This was magnified by the behavior of the Russians, who in general did not fire on the Poles but fraternized with them. The Soviet air force was also forbidden from bombing any settlements. By order of Rydz-Smigly the Polish troops, too, were instructed, unless attacked, not to engage in fighting with the Red Army. The Russians were expected to reach Kolomyja within a day, so an urgent meeting took place with the participation of President Moscicki, Rydz-Smigly, Prime Minister Slawoj-Skladkowski and Beck. After some painful discussions the decision taken was to leave. That very night they all crossed the border into Rumania.

When the government and supreme commander left Polish soil fighting was still going on near Lwow, in the Kutno cauldron, and a few other localities. But the main drama was being played out in Warsaw. Still on the 16th the Germans demanded the city surrender. Following a meeting of the city's president, Starzynski, with the local commanders the demand was rejected. There were some 100,000 troops in the city and the Germans' initial venture into the built-up metropolis ended in failure costing them some 60 tanks. But what the city lacked was air defenses. The strategic fighter force had originally been stationed near the capital. Throughout the first week the Polish pilots, with great dedication, continued to take a toll on the German airplanes bombing the city. But as German troops approached, the squadrons were moved to safer locations. This spelled the end of the Polish air force. The fuel, ordnance, and ground services that were to follow were bombed and scattered by the Luftwaffe, which had a free run of the country.

The taking of Warsaw was assigned to Blaskowitz; he in turn gave the job to the Luftwaffe. Brimming with experience from mauling towns, villages, refugee columns, food queues, and even farmers in the field, it fell upon its prey with glee. For days Warsaw was swept by indiscriminate bombing, assisted by artillery, eventually leaving it without food, water or electricity. The assault on the city started on September 19 with a continuous air and artillery bombardment. The culmination came on September 24 when 1,150 airplanes plastered the city with explosives and incendiaries. The fires were such that a plume of smoke 10,000 feet high stood over the city. On September 25 Hitler together with Brauchitsch and Halder visited Blaskowitz at his headquarters, some 10 miles southeast of the capital. Hitler was then taken for a ride over the city. Flying at an altitude of 6,000 feet he watched for half an hour as swarms of Ju-52 transport planes hung over Warsaw with men shoveling incendiaries onto the burning city (Giziowski, 142). Nearly half of the residential buildings were either destroyed or heavily damaged. An indication of the kind of warfare the Germans unleashed on the city is that while 2,000 soldiers fell defending it, civilian dead numbered at least 10,000 and by some accounts 40,000; the exact number could never be established because later on the Germans murdered more than half of its 1.5 million inhabitants. Three days later Warsaw surrendered.

On September 23 the OKW issued a communiqué that "the campaign against Poland is over." In a subsequent report it gave the German casualties as 10,000 dead and 30,000 wounded. Throughout the war German military communiqués proved to be pretty accurate both as to the course of fighting and the casualties suffered by both sides. Thus, while some sources cite the German losses as high as 16,000 killed, the figures given by the OKW are correct. The Polish military casualties were 70,000 dead and 133,000 wounded. The Germans took 420,000 prisoners while another quarter million fell into Russian hands. About 75,000 Polish soldiers made it to the neighboring countries from where most of them eventually reached France.

* * *

As darkness fell on blacked-out Berlin on September 3, five heavy cars, their headlights dimmed, drove into the courtyard of the Chancellery. Hitler, dressed in a field uniform and heavy army boots with a revolver strapped to his belt, a steel helmet and gas mask slung over his shoulder (Ball, 237), strode out and mounted one of the cars. The cars drove off to Hitler's special train, perversely named *Amerika*. It consisted of a dozen coaches fronted by two locomotives and guarded front and rear by armored wagons mounting 20 mm antiaircraft guns. Next to Hitler's private coach was a command car with a map section and a communication center linked to the OKW and field headquarters. Accompanying the train was a personal guard company, the SS-Leibwache, commanded by General Rommel, a fervent admirer of the führer. The train headed northeast, in the direction of the Polish border. Hitler was going to the front.

After a short trip the train halted amid a pinewood, just inside Polish Pomorze. For the next several weeks Hitler toured the battlefields. It was what he had dreamed of all his life — a Feldherr commanding a mighty army at war. Although at this stage he was not yet teaching his generals how to fight, the fact that there was a war at all was his doing and the strategy of driving pincers down the middle of the country so as to encircle the entire Polish army was also his — the very personification of Hitler's popular image as a super–Bismarck. There was, however, also something else: wreckage left by the shattered Polish divisions, blown bridges, overturned civilian wagons, burned-down villages, dead men and dead horses; Hitler's innermost soul exulted. The very next day he watched troops crossing the Vistula near Topolno and, overwhelmed, he called out to his generals, "What this

Hitler reviews a victory parade in the fallen Polish capital on October 6, 1939. (Courtesy of the United States Army.)

means to me!" (Bock, 45). On September 6, seated with von Bock in a six-wheeled heavy Mercedes, he toured the 4th Army plowing its way into the detested Corridor. The next day he visited Guderian, with whom he traveled as far as Grudziadz where he gazed over the Vistula into the misty east — a replica of Napoleon staring across the Niemen. Two days later his *Amerika* rolled south to see how von Rundstedt was doing. There he spent some time with the 10th Army's commander, General Reichenau, the most Nazi of his generals. When the battle near the Bzura flared up he rushed north again. Worried about the sudden life that had come into the Poles he appeared on September 13 at Blaskowitz's 8th Army to make sure that everything was done to achieve that ultimate of blitzkrieg warfare — a cauldron.

Hitler, of course, made a point of visiting the place that was the "cause" of the war, Danzig, incorporated into the reich on the first day of the war. On September 19 he delivered to the city's jubilant and flower-tossing crowds a speech in which, referring to the land he had in the nick of time liberated from the Poles, he expostulated, "Thirty years would have been sufficient to reduce again to barbarism those territories which the Germans had saved from barbarism…. What was for us and also for me most depressing was the fact that we had to suffer all this from a State which was inferior to us" (Bullock 1962, 551–2) but already then, with the campaign still on, he offered England peace. September 25 found him at the perimeter of besieged Warsaw where Blaskowitz's artillery batteries were pounding the city. Perched high atop a sports stadium, his eyes glued to field glasses, Hitler watched the bombardment.

On September 26, after three weeks "at the front," Hitler returned to Berlin. There was some business to settle with his Soviet partner. As noted, the Russian troops had encountered only sporadic resistance (DDR, XIV 50). So already on September 18, one day after their invasion, the Russians were near Brzesc where they met the Germans. There Guderian and Russian general Chuikov reviewed a parade of German-Soviet troops. In fulfillment of the Nazi-Soviet pact the Germans began to pull back behind the Vistula-San line. The Soviet troops were already approaching Warsaw when a change of minds occurred in Moscow. It is unclear why the reasons that now motivated the Russians to revise the original agreement had not occurred to them when signing the Nazi-Soviet pact in August. But as soon as Hitler's lightning victory became evident, the Russians started to insist on changes in the division of Poland. The main element of the new proposals was that the Soviets cede to Germany the territory west of the Narew-Bug line in exchange for having Lithuania assigned to the Soviet sphere of influence. After first broaching these new ideas with Schulenburg, Ribbentrop was eventually asked to come to Moscow to arrange the new deal. The probable reason for the switch was that the Russians wanted to occupy only areas heavily populated by Byelorussians and Ukrainians, nationalities represented by USSR republics. In addition to the ethnic angle the Russians also had historical claims to the invaded territories. When after the Great War Poland was reconstituted as an independent state, the designated eastern borders were what is called the Curzon Line, corresponding closely to the Narew-Bug line now proposed by the Soviets. The liberation and safeguarding of the Byelorussian and Ukrainian populations would later be used by the Soviets as the official justification for annexing eastern Poland, a state the Soviets claimed had "ceased to exist" (reminiscent of Halifax's statement in March that Czechoslovakia had ceased to exist). Less clear is the nonchalance with which Hitler agreed to the exchange. When Ribbentrop cabled from Moscow on September 29 for a decision, Hitler immediately granted the Soviet wishes. This readiness to accept Stalin's latest demand was in keeping with the ease and speed with which he had accepted Stalin's demands in August when the pact was signed. The best explanation that comes to mind is that, then as now, Hitler told himself, "let them take whatever they want; in due course they will disgorge it — this and much more besides." Another exchange revealing the thoughts running through the minds of the two dictators was what to do with the indigenous Polish territories. On September 25 the erstwhile ambassador to Poland, von Moltke, suggested the formation of a rump state between the new German borders in the east (after the annexations) and the Bug river, arguing that when given such a statelet the Poles would strive to regain the eastern lands seized by the Soviets and thus become a German satellite. Evidently Stalin anticipated such a possible evolution. When Ribbentrop broached the subject, Stalin's view was it would generate "friction" between the two new friends, and said, "We consider it wrong to have an independently run Polish state" (Moczulski, 491).

The Narew-Bug demarcation line as agreed on September 29 gave each side almost exactly half of Poland. Germany took over a population of some 22 million, nearly all Poles, except for 2 million Jews. The Soviets got 13 million people, a mixture of Poles (40 percent), Ukrainians (34 percent), Byelorussians and Jews (8.5 percent each). This the Soviets got at the cost of 737 dead and 1,860 wounded men lost in the invasion. From Hitler's standpoint the main accomplishment was that in addition to gaining extensive agricultural land with its subhuman labor pool the occupation of Poland provided a common boundary with Russia, a stretch of flat, open country 350 miles long.

Of the territory taken by Germany close to a half — 32,000 square miles out 71,000 —

Elite German troops parade before the führer in occupied Warsaw. (Courtesy the National Archives.)

was annexed to the reich. These areas included the provinces of Pomorze, Poznan, Silesia and places that not even in 1914 belonged to Germany, such as Lodz. A rump was left amounting to a quarter of original Poland with a population of over 10 million. In the territories annexed to Germany there immediately began mass expulsions of Poles and Jews so that by the end of the year the population of rump Poland rose to 14 million. The status assigned to leftover Poland was that of a Generalgouvernement (GG), a political nonbody which at most meant that a governor would rule it. In Nazi parlance it was referred to as the Nebenland. Literally it means nearby-country, but its implications come closer to that of a byproduct, if such a thing is conceivable when applied to political entities.

The official decree establishing the Nebenland came out on Oct 12. For its ruler, the generalgouvernor, Hitler chose Hans Frank, a jurist. Frank had been Hitler's private attorney in the days when the führer needed such services and he subsequently held numerous posts as editor, academy president and minister in Germany's judicial system. Hitler's instruction to him with regard to rump Poland was "to ruthlessly exploit this region as a war zone and booty country, to reduce it, as it were, to a heap of rubble in its economic, social, cultural and political structure" (Fest 1999, 216). In a conversation prior to taking office Hitler told him that he didn't want Warsaw as the capital, in fact he didn't want Warsaw rebuilt, and that the seat of governorship was to be Krakow. Frank took up his post on November 7. He settled on the Wawel, Poland's revered castle housing the tombs of past Polish kings and of Marshal Pilsudski, over which Frank now hoisted the Nazi flag.

Whatever it was called, GG, *Nebenland* or, after June 22, 1941, *Zwischenland* (Inter-mediate-land), this rump territory constituted in reality Nazi Germany's laboratory for geopolitical and demographic apocalypse. As on September 1 the five German armies drove into Poland from north and south, they were followed by five *Einsatzgruppen*, whose literal translation would be task forces but were, in fact, execution battalions. The importance of these units in Hitler's scheme of things is indicated by the fact that Eicke, commander of the *Totenkopfverbände* (part of the Einsatzgruppen) directed his units from Hitler's special train (Sydnor, 38). Originally they comprised 2,700 men; with auxiliaries from the police and the army they grew to some 4,000 strong. With them they brought a *Fahndungsbuch*, a prepared list of some 60,000 Poles to be done away with. These SS troops were later on to emerge as the ultimate in Nazi horror and here was their baptism of slaughter. Under the code name *Unternehmung Tannenberg* they had several tasks to fulfill. One was to exterminate the Polish intelligentsia or, as Hitler expressed himself, anyone capable of a "leadership role." This embraced teachers, clergy, doctors, dentists, veterinarians, administrators, writers, journalists, prominent merchants and landowners— or, to simplify matters, anyone with a university or gymnasium degree. In September and October alone 20,000 Poles were murdered. As they went about their work they were assisted by the army, particularly the rear area troops; of the 764 executions that took place, 311 were staged by the Wehrmacht (Gross, 68). In those instances where the Einsatzkommandos couldn't identify "leadership" types they shot Jews so as to meet their assigned quotas (Pinkus 1990, 29).

Already on September 21, with the war in Poland still on, Heydrich sent head of RSHA to the chiefs of the Einsatzgruppen an order which constituted the first step in the implementation of what history came to call the Holocaust. Along with a plethora of sadistic and denigrating ordinances to be applied to Jews the more significant parts read:

The Jewish Question in Occupied Territory

I refer to the conference that took place today in Berlin and remind you once more that all measures taken (also the final goal) must be kept absolutely secret.
We must differentiate between

1. The final goal (long-term) and
2. The stages leading to the implementation of the final goal (short-term).

As a first step toward the final goal all Jews are to be concentrated in large towns.... It must be assured that the selected towns are near railroad hubs, or at least along railroad lines [DDR, xiv, 159].

The GG being in the nature of a proving ground for Nazi plans and practices, many of their essential features emerged already in the first months of the occupation. With the campaign over, the German occupation troops were organized into a command named Oberost with General Blaskowitz its commandant. He moved into Spaha Palace, a tsarist hunting lodge halfway between Lodz and Warsaw. Blaskowitz, of course, was subject to orders from the OKH. In October Frank became governor and by the führer's edict was to take orders only from him. The Einsatzgruppen were subordinated neither to Blaskowitz nor Frank but to Himmler, specifically so arranged by Hitler. These three agencies, the Wehrmacht, the Civil Administration, and the SS Security Services overlapped in their functions in the course of running the conquered territories. From the very beginning conflicts arose over jurisdiction and authority causing fights over power, loot and turf which later on many Germans, particularly the military, converted into presumed acts of opposition on moral rectitude. Thus when the *Einsatzgruppen* started their executions behind the army's back, Blaskowitz protested to Brauchitsch against this incursion into army territory, arguing that it affected the discipline of the troops. But to no effect. Soon after Frank's appointment, SS Obergruppenführer Friedrich Wilhem Krüger arrived in Krakow to set up his Police and SS network, taking orders directly from Himmler. When Frank protested that Krüger did things without his approval he was told that if he cared to remain governor he better cooperate. These triple or quadruple layers of authority were Hitler's deliberate ploys to keep decisions in his own hands.

While the population of the GG was handed over to Messrs. Blaskowitz, Frank and Krüger, Hitler in a talk with Keitel on October 20 expounded on the future role of the occupied territory. He explained that the GG hadn't been incorporated into the reich so that actions taken there would not be hampered by whatever legal constraints still existed in Germany. He was not going to establish there any Polish entity; it was, instead, to be a dumping ground for unwanted populations. The most important task, however, one that concerned directly Keitel and the OKW, was to see to it that railroads, highways, and communications in the GG were bolstered and improved because it was to be a base for future military deployment (Aufmarsch) (DDR, xiv, 105).

· CHAPTER 7 ·

Sitzkrieg in the West

It is ironic that neither England nor Germany had achieved its primary objective by the pacts they had concluded just prior to the war. England had given Poland guarantees hoping that, after all the past compromises and evasions, this determined stand would deter Germany from attacking Poland. It didn't. On his side Hitler concluded the Nazi-Soviet pact certain that without Russia's support England would not go to war with Germany. He was so certain of it that he had made no preparations in the West. Jodl, chief of operations in the OKW, was about to go off on a cruise in September and he later said that "none of the soldiers I had spoken to expected a war with the Western powers." Schacht, too, recalled, "Hitler had invariably assured them [the generals] on the possible intervention by the western powers in the event of a war with Poland" (Ball, 85,163). The surprise was such that on Sunday half a million Germans had to evacuate their homes within two hours, leaving behind their belongings, to make room for the troops arriving by train to man the pillboxes in the Westwall.

When Hitler returned to Berlin he still could not believe that the Allies had actually declared war. The situation in the West seemed to confirm it. The guns were silent, there was no activity whatsoever from the Allied side. So he fell back into his old stance, peace after one more killing. On the very day he returned to Berlin Hitler talked to Dahlerus about the latter's contacts with the British. Dahlerus had seen Ogilvie Forbes, counsellor of the British Embassy in Oslo, who told him Britain wants peace. "They can have it in two weeks—without losing face," replied the führer. He was ready to guarantee everything but there was to be no Poland. He suggested that Dahlerus fly the next day to continue his efforts (Shirer 1959, 639). On the 29th Dahlerus saw Roberts, the Foreign Office expert on Germany, and subsequently conferred with Cadogam, Halifax and Chamberlain himself. Two days later Hitler persuaded the Soviets to issue a joint statement that now, with the Polish problem solved, it was in everyone's interest to call off the war. He followed it up on October 6 with a much-trumpeted speech before the Reichstag, saying, "Germany has no further claims against France…. I have devoted no less effort to the achievement of an Anglo-German understanding, nay, more than that, of an Anglo-German friendship…. Why should this war in the West be fought?" While offering peace right and left to the West, guarantees to France, England, Belgium and Holland, he stressed in the same breath that Poland would never be resurrected. On October 10, when launching the *Winterhilfe* in the *Sportpalast*, Hitler repeated his "readiness for peace" and said he had "no cause for war against the Western Powers." The German press and radio went into high gear to sell this latest peace offensive. On October 12 Chamberlain officially rejected Hitler's bid for calling off the war.

81

While pushing his peace offensive — and this would continue through the winter in more indirect ways — Hitler worked on his war option in case the Allies did not yield. Hitler had always preached not to get Germany into a war with both East and West. With Russia bound by a treaty of friendship, it seemed to everyone that he had succeeded. But he knew better. He knew that as soon as possible he would strike eastward where his life's mission beckoned. And here, dumped on his back, was a war with the West. He would have preferred not to be sidetracked, but now the French army had to be dealt with before the East could be taken on. Looking ahead, over the period between the conquest of Poland and the invasion of Russia during which he faced various crises and new fronts, Hitler's way of dealing with his quandary adds up to a sort of a pattern. His acts of commission and omission prior to June 22, 1941, suggest a strategy based on the following rule: If he couldn't restrict his war to one enemy — the one in the East — he would see to it that he fought on only one front. From now on all his maneuvers and conquests would be guided by the principle that before he took on Russia there would on the European continent be no armed force likely to interfere or strike him in the back; he would create what he later designated Fortress Europe. In the fall of 1939 that continental enemy was France and she would have to be beaten. A defeat of France might in fact mean much more than eliminating the one army menacing Germany. It could collapse the whole basis of England's grand strategy, of having the French fight and bleed while England indulged in her customary stratagems of blockade, bombardment, and economic strangulation. A defeat of France might mean the end of the war with the West.

With his customary haste and zeal Hitler proceeded to plan his western campaign. As early as September 27 Hitler had a conference with his three Wehrmacht chiefs in which he announced his intention to open an offensive in the West this very fall. Although he had only a month before guaranteed the neutrality of the Benelux countries, the offensive would ecompass Belgium, Holland and Luxemburg. Already then he sketched out his strategy of not following the old Schlieffen Plan but to strike across the northern flank of the Allies for the Channel coast. He ordered his chiefs to let him know how soon the troops could be assembled. On October 9 he drafted the directive for the attack in the West codenamed *Fall Gelb* — the third color in his chain of aggressions.

After two weeks Brauchitsch and Halder informed him that no offensive was possible before November 26. Without inquiring into the reasons for his experts' judgment, Hitler told them no, he wants the attack to be launched on November 12 with the corresponding orders to go out to the units on November 5, a week before the invasion. This peremptory schedule of what seemed then the major battle of the war disconcerted the generals. Mindful of what had happened in 1914, they were not as eager for this venture as they had been about Poland. On November 5, an hour before the orders were to go out, Brauchitsch, at the prompting of his colleagues, appeared at the Chancellery and asked to see the führer, in private. After half an hour of conversation, Hitler summoned Keitel. Brauchitsch read them a hand-written memorandum stating the generals' apprehensions that the army was not ready and that the French have a mighty this and that. As Brauchitsch went on, the führer cut him short and told him, "I place a low value on the French Army's will to fight. Every Army is a mirror of its people. The French people think only of peace and good living and they are torn apart in parliamentary strife. After the first setbacks it will swiftly crack up" (Perrett, 81). Brauchitsch returned from this meeting with his commander in chief close to a nervous breakdown.

The same day Hitler issued orders for the attack to begin on November 12, as scheduled. Two days after he had issued the order, Hitler postponed the attack. Originally the delay was for two days, then for another 10 days. Eventually the number of such postponements during the fall and winter mounted to 14. To straighten out his generals as to their place vis-à-vis the führer, Hitler convened a meeting on November 23, in which he told them, "History teaches that when a nation does not employ force against the outside, it uses it against itself, to the point of killing its own children.... We will be able to move against Russia only when we are free in the West.... I must mention my own person; it is irreplaceable, neither a military nor a civilian person can replace me. I am convinced of the power of my brain and my own power of decision.... The fate of the Reich depends only on me" (DDR, XIV, 312). There were no further memoranda on what the generals thought about war and peace.

Numerous reasons are cited for Hitler's vacillation in preparing the western campaign. The most common is the weather. Others, that the army needed more training; that after the Polish campaign the tanks had to be refurbished; that the rail transports were slower than anticipated; and that on January 10 a Luftwaffe major landed by mistake in Belgium with the plans for the attack which the Belgians handed over to the French and British (who suspected it was a plant). It would be atypical for the führer to have been swayed by any of the above reasons. The most likely motivation is that Hitler remained tuned in to any possible chances for an accord with the West. The period after the Polish campaign was rife with such attempts from various quarters. Since mid–September Franklin Delano Roosevelt had been in contact with Göring through an American businessman, W.R. Davis, regarding the possibility of a settlement which continued well past Hitler's peace offer of October 6 (Kennedy, 394). On November 7 the Belgian king and the queen of the Netherlands offered to mediate. On January 13 Mussolini sent a long missive suggesting that chances for peace would improve if the führer reconstituted some sort of a rump Poland. To punish Il Duce for this sacrilege the führer did not respond till March 8, informing him that he had no intention of resurrecting Poland in any form.

The most important peace initiative came at the end of February when Roosevelt's envoy, Undersecretary of State Sumner Welles, arrived in Europe to look into the possibilities of ending or rather preempting the war. The details of his mission remain murky. In his 1944 book, Welles simply says that he cannot reveal the substance of his talks. But that it was a most serious initiative is attested by his itinerary. Welles spent more than three weeks conferring with the top leaders of Italy, Germany, France and England. When on February 26 he met with Mussolini and inquired whether, from the Axis' side, a conference such as had been proposed on August 31 was still possible, the answer was a clear yes. Il Duce suggested that, after visiting the other capitals, Welles come back to see him at which time he would have had time to consult with the Germans. Welles spent three days in Berlin conferring with Ribbentrop, Weizsäcker, Hess, Göring and the führer himself. The guidelines that Hitler handed down to his associates for these talks were to stress that it was not Hitler who had started the war; that he demanded nothing from the West; that, if forced, Germany would fight; and that there was nothing to be said or done about Poland. When Welles saw Hitler on March 2, he was told straightforwardly, "I did not want this war. It was forced upon me against my will" (Welles, 108). Welles was also told what the führer did want — there was to be no state in the east that could "menace" Germany and that Germany must be given economic supremacy in eastern and southeastern Europe. With his unique brand of logic he announced that Germany's triumph in the coming battle was "inevitable," but if not, "we will all go down together." If the world did not yield to him, complete destruction would descend on Germany and everyone else. With this Sermon on the Mount Welles flew off to Paris and London.

In the West the American envoy talked to anyone of importance — Daladier, Gamelin, Blum, King George VI, Halifax, Chamberlain. Simultaneously tremendous activity bubbled over in the Axis camp. Ribbentrop came to Rome and saw Ciano, Mussolini, and the pope. Hitler then phoned Il Duce and asked to meet him; this was set for March 18 at the Brenner Pass. When Welles returned to Rome on March 16, Il Duce received him the same day and informed him of the pending summit meeting and asked that Welles delay his return home till he had conferred with the führer. In the meantime Il Duce inquired whether Welles would authorize him to say that in case of negotiations Hitler would be assured of lebensraum in the east. The American responded he could do no such thing. The next day Welles conferred with the pope, whom Ribbentrop had seen a few days before. On March 19, with Ciano's impressions of the Brenner meeting in his pocket, Welles flew home to brief Roosevelt on the results of his mission.

* * *

The peaceful war that the Western Allies waged against Germany during 1939–1940 is named differently by the three belligerents, but the German appellation Sitzkrieg (sitting war) is the most appropriate because it corresponds to a physical reality; one could, indeed, observe French and German soldiers sit on chairs with rifles across their laps looking at each other as if involved in a stare-down contest. This form of warfare was enacted not out of some whim, or to amuse future historians; it rested on deep national dilemmas. Hitler did not want this war; he would rather be facing east and not in a stare-down contest either. For the French the Sitzkrieg was an expression of their grand strategy, logically formulated over 20 years of Gallic analysis. They would keep honing themselves for two or three years, accumulating allies and resources, while a blockaded Germany would see its depots depleted, its army starved. When this process had ripened, say in May 1942, they would start fighting the war they had declared on September 3, 1939. Like the Poles, who had mapped out a strategic retreat of their armies bunched up along the borders, the French, too, seemed not to have asked themselves the simple question: Would the Germans allow all that?

The Allies' Sitzkrieg performance commenced when the Polish war was still on. Historians would have been kinder to them had the Allies admitted that they had not prepared themselves for fighting and hoped not to have to do any. This would have come as no news to their enemy and would have sounded credible to their friends. Instead they indulged in prevarication and self-delusion. Contrary to their agreement with the Poles there was no grand offensive on the 15th day of the war. All of Germany's Panzer divisions and all its motorized and front-line infantry divisions were in Poland; 44 reserve divisions under von Leeb were left in the West facing an Allied army at least twice its size with all its armor and air force on hand. The French had also promised to shuttle across Germany a number of air squadrons to help Poland fight the Luftwaffe; these never took off. When, on September 10, the Polish military attache' inquired about the inactivity of the French, Daladier told him "More than half of our divisions are engaged…. The Germans are opposing us with vigorous resistance…. It has been impossible to do more" (Shirer 1971, 2,512). There are two untruths in the above reply; only nine out of the 85 French divisions stepped over the border; and there was no resistance at all, not to speak of vigorous resistance from the Germans. Worse news came next day when Polish Ambassador Lukasiewicz talked to

Gamelin and the latter elaborated on the reasons for not starting an offensive. Italy's stand — said Gamelin — is unclear, tying down French forces; the neutrality of Belgium prevents a vigorous attack; and, he confided, England is gearing up for a long war (Jurga, 522). This was no longer a tactical but a strategic-political rationale for the inactivity of the Allies. Gamelin summed up the situation the way Daladier did — nothing more can be done.

The "fighting" Daladier referred to in his talk with the Pole was what the French staged during the second week of September. On the 9th, French troops in battalion strength crossed the border near Saarbrücken on a front of 15 miles. There was some skirmishing. By the 12th, when the French had advanced some five miles, Gamelin ordered a halt and the French entrenched in front of the Westwall. That afternoon, at a meeting of the Allied Supreme War Council in Abbeville, Gamelin informed the British that he had stopped the advance. "My report brought a sense of relief to everyone," he recorded. As the Polish war ended and German divisions started to move west, the five-mile conquest began to worry the French commander in chief and he told Daladier he wanted to pull back his troops. Daladier agreed but advised to do so surreptitiously because it would be bad for morale. The retreat, which took place under the cover of darkness, leaving behind only screening patrols, was completed on October 4. The story ends on October 16 when the Germans moved to regain their strip of land. The French patrols withdrew so that by late October the situation reverted to what it had been in peacetime.

This "fighting," which some saw as a gesture to Poland and which Gamelin described to Ironside as "a little test," was duplicated by the British in their fashion. On September 4, 29 RAF bombers attacked several naval bases in northern Germany; this was repeated on the following day. The raids were ineffective and the British lost some 10 machines in each raid. That was the sum-total of British warmaking for some time. From the description of these initial raids it is clear that they were more in the nature of a test of the crews' ability to deal with meteorological and navigational problems than an act of war. As far as real warmaking was concerned the exact opposite was enforced. For fear of retaliation the French and British pilots were forbidden to bomb German territory. The Poles, too, had been told not to overfly Germany and not to cross the German border. Even during the subsequent Norwegian campaign British planes, while searching for elusive German supply ships, were forbidden to bomb the depots and loading facilities in German ports, lest there be civilian casualties. Reciprocating, Hitler kept his surface raiders away from British waters because, in his view, hurting British pride might have prejudiced the chances of restoring peace. When sinkings did take place, such as by the pocket battleship *Graf Spee* in the south Atlantic, the crews were first permitted to take to lifeboats before the ships were sunk. When the British proposed to drop fluvial mines on German rivers and canals, they were stopped from doing it because, argued the French, they, too, have rivers. Instead, an intensive program to reeducate the German people was set in motion. This was done by nightly leaflet dropping — the *Paper Bullet* campaign. On the very first night of the war the RAF dropped 6 million leaflets over Germany. Prior to Christmas the British staged 22 more leaflet raids, an activity which was vigorously pursued throughout the winter (Kaufmann, 102).

The most memorable visage of the Sitzkrieg followed the initial French fighting gesture. As soon as the old lines were reestablished, both sides refrained from initiating hostilities and artillery bombardments were expressly forbidden. Trains transporting coal from the Ruhr trundled peacefully along the front in sight of French troops; when a local commander once tried to interfere he was severely reprimanded (Fonvieille, 194). German working parties performed their jobs next to the French without being disturbed. Using loud-speakers the German troops blasted slogans and played songs—perhaps lullabies—to their opposites. Signs and billboards appeared proclaiming the Germans' love for France and desire for peace. The French were invited to come out and do their laundry and, after ini-tial hesitation, French soldiers did wash their laundry in the open with the Germans benignly looking on. There was regular traffic on the Rhine, the bridges across it were not blown, French and German sentries posted at either end as at peacetime. Some German parties would actually cross the river to fraternize with the French soldiers and give them the führer's peace proclamations. The Kembs power station on the Rhine continued to oper-ate, supplying electricity to both Germany and France (Chapman, 58). When in February 1940 the European Danube Commission met in Galatz, Rumania, the German, British and French delegates sat together at the conference table (Dallin 1942, 210). This French lassi-tude eventually led to a most bizarre proposal. Since there was no fighting, and none was contemplated till 1941 or later, it was proposed that France start demobilizing, so that the armament factories could be supplied with enough manpower. The proposal was seriously considered by the government but the military were opposed as it could damage morale (Beaufre, 162). It took three months of warfare before the British suffered their first casu-alty—a corporal was shot on December 9 while on patrol.

There was also a serious aspect to the Sitzkrieg, pursued with great perseverance by the French. It amounted to no less a strategy than to transfer the war somewhere else. While on its border with Germany the French stuck their heads in the sand not to see or smell danger, when it came to fighting elsewhere they became ferocious firebrands. They exhumed and pressed on the British the wildest schemes as long as they promised to divert the Germans from the French border. On September 11, at the first meeting of the SAWC, Dal-adier proposed to establish an "eastern front" at the other end of Europe, at Salonika. The French claimed that the Greeks and perhaps also the Turks were eager for it. The British demurred, arguing that it might "alienate" Italy, which was still neutral. Next, when the Soviets attacked Finland, an obsession took hold of both France and England to shift the war to the Arctic Circle. The trigger for this idea lay in the blockade syndrome, designed to undo Germany. Two vital raw materials that Germany had to import to stoke her war industries were iron and oil. More about this will be told in connection with the invasion of Norway, but suffice it to say here that a substantial portion of the iron ore Germany imported came from Sweden via the Norwegian port of Narvik. The idea was that under the pretext of aiding Finland the allies would occupy northern Scandinavia and cut off the Swedish ore supply. Not only couldn't they possibly persuade or force the Scandinavians to let them occupy their northern provinces but sending troops to Finland would have involved them in hostilities with the USSR. Yet, they persisted in that scheme with mulish obdu-racy.

Even more bizarre was the scheme of bombing the Caucasian oil fields in order to deprive Germany of the oil delivered by the USSR. While the godmother of the Scandina-vian obsession was Britain, the idea to bomb the Caucasus was a French brainstorm. This lacked the pretext of helping Finland but otherwise it was identical to the Scandinavian aberration; the Allies had no means of destroying the Caucasian wells and a bombing would have caused a war with the USSR. For the French, this scheme was even sweeter than Scan-dinavia because the Caucasus was twice as far from France as Norway. The idea was first broached by Daladier on March 19 and within a month Gamelin presented a detailed plan. In its various options it involved air raids, naval bombardment in the Black Sea and, according to some sources, even land troops converging on Moscow from both the Caucasus and Finland (Shirer 1971, 537). It had gone sufficiently far to have Wygand and Wavel, the Allied commanders in the Middle East, plan a campaign from bases in Turkey, Iran and Iraq. The Caucasian aberration was kept alive well into April and was abandoned only after the Norway debacle.

What all this in reality amounted to was that their prewar experimentation with pusillanimity vis-à-vis Germany had brought France and England to a state that while afraid to fire across their own frontiers, they were willing to take on the Russian colossus thousands of miles away, as long as it did not mean tackling the Wehrmacht. It represents an instance — and there would be others— where procrastination and loss of will combined to produce a state of physical and mental enfeeblement. Although the Allies' Scandinavian expedition was never realized, it turned out to be more than a comic episode in the history of the Sitzkrieg, for the mere talk of it triggered the first military defeat Germany inflicted on the Allies.

CHAPTER 8

The Occupation of
Denmark and Norway

Of Germany's three Wehrmacht services the navy was destined to be the most frustrated during World War II. This was partly so because the sea was one of the führer's many phobias. He used to say that while he had a Nazi Luftwaffe he inherited an Imperial Navy — stodgy and old fashioned. The navy's rearmament program was not to be completed until 1944 and here Hitler had launched his war in 1939 and, immediately after Poland, had started planning another land campaign in the West. To Raeder, the navy's commander in chief, who assumed England to be the main enemy, all this was maddening. That he hadn't bothered to fathom the mind and intentions of his führer is no more a discredit to the grossadmiral than it was to the other statesmen and generals of that period.

As soon as war broke out, Raeder, the memory of World War I etched in his mind, broached to the führer the idea of seizing Norway. The potential benefits for Germany were prodigious. It would break the British stranglehold in the North Sea, and open the gates into the Atlantic for German raiders and submarines. It would supply bunkering and supply facilities for German ships as well as safe harbors. It would be a boon to the Luftwaffe, too, for it would bring most of Britain and its northern sea lanes within range of its bombers. It would constitute a complete reversal from World War I when the German fleet remained bottled up in the Baltic, enabling the British to impose the blockade that became a potent factor in Germany's collapse.

The führer listened and dismissed it all. He told Raeder a neutral Norway suited him fine. German ships were using Norwegian territorial waters, which was preferable to having to defend them against the Home Fleet, and certainly better than to provoke England into occupying Norway. Raeder wouldn't give in and ordered his staff to conduct a study which was completed on October 9. The next day, during a routine naval conference, Raeder brought the subject up again. However, on the same day in a memorandum setting forth his ideas on the prosecution of the war, Hitler specifically stated that the neutrality of the Nordic states was to be assumed even in a war of long duration (Greenfield, 40). The subject surfaced again on the occasion of Vidkun Quisling's visit to Berlin in December. Quisling, a Norwegian politician and former minister of defense, was also a Nazi whose name was to become a synonym for traitors and collaborators in general. During his visit in Berlin he talked to Hitler three times. First he relayed what he knew about British attempts to use Finland as an excuse to occupy northern Norway and Sweden. He then proposed to stage a coup d'etat in Oslo, request the help of German troops and bring Norway into the Fascist orbit. This was very much Hitler's kind of statesmanship and the führer listened.

Still, even though he ordered a small staff to prepare plans for a possible Norwegian campaign he refused to commit himself to its execution.

But while Hitler was content with Norway's neutrality the Allies were not. The problem was iron ore. Germany's consumption of the ore was 15 million tons per annum (mt/a), three quarters of which came from Sweden. During summer the main outlet was the Swedish port Lulea on the Baltic but from December to mid–April the Baltic froze. The export to Germany then went via the ice-free Norwegian port of Narvik, which had a capacity of 3 mt/a. The merchantmen that hauled the ore to German ports used Norway's territorial waters, called the Leads, where they were immune from British warships leery of violating Norway's neutrality. All the Allies' sound and fury about Norway was aimed at cutting off these 3 million tons of iron ore. If successful, this would have deprived Germany of 20 percent of the ore it needed. Even this was optimistic. At the outbreak of war Germany had a reserve of 2 million tons. Thus after one year it would have been short of 1 million tons, or 7 percent of its needs assuming that Germany wouldn't have found alternate sources or other means of transport.

The Allied attempts to deal with this problem are too tedious to relate in any detail. It is a sordid tale of endless chatter, of plans born and buried, of retreats ordered ahead of advances, and decisions taken that verged on the frivolous. The Norway project was under British tutelage and their decision-making apparatus encompassed five august bodies: the Ministry of Economic Warfare; a Chiefs of Staff Committee; a Military Coordination Committee that included the three service ministers and the Chiefs of Staff; and the War Cabinet, which had the final word. In addition it had to have the approval of the SAWC, which consisted of top-ranking members from both Britain and France. All this was fully realized by some of the men who were themselves party to these shenanigans. Winston Churchill who as first lord of the Admiralty was a member of the war cabinet, said in a memo of Jan 13, "First the objections of the other Economic departments, Supply, Board of Trade, etc. Secondly, the Joint Planning Committee. Thirdly, the Chiefs of Staff Committee. Fourthly, 'don't spoil the big plan for the sake of the small'. Fifthly, the juridicial and moral objections…. Sixthly, the attitude of the neutrals…. Seventhly, the Cabinet itself…. Eighthly, when all this has been smoothed out, the French have to be consulted. Finally the Dominions and their consciences…. All this makes me feel that … we shall be reduced to waiting upon the terrible attacks of the enemy" (Harvey, 19). Here is a bit of self-analysis that was also prophetic.

The major phases of the schemes that were mooted and never implemented as well the two minor acts that were actually committed can be briefly told. The Allies toyed with four scenarios. The most ambitious was the Finnish scheme. After demanding and being refused some territorial concessions, the Soviet Union on November 30 went to war with Finland. This event provided the Allies with the idea of offering aid to the Finns. Since there was no direct access to Finland, the solution was to ask Norway and Sweden to grant the Allies passage. Once in, some troops would indeed go to help the Finns but the bulk would stay in the north of Norway and Sweden, home to the ore mines and railway to Narvik. The problem was that the Scandinavian countries had no intention of complying. The French then had the idea of landing in Finland's northernmost port Petsamo, from where they would filter into the ore fields and Narvik. When Gamelin proposed it on January 4, the Russians had already captured Petsamo but this did not faze the French commander in chief, because he was prepared to take on any army as long as it did not speak German. By the time this project went through the mill, the Finnish war was winding down.

On March 12, the very day that Finnish delegates were on their way to Moscow to negotiate a peace agreement, Ironside sent the Finns a note offering them 57,000 troops and a swarm of bombers. The Finns declined.

The end of the Finnish war may have killed the pretext but not the wish for a Scandinavian incursion. The Allies continued to scheme and connive to get a foothold in northern Scandinavia. They sent countless demarchés, notes and hints to the two Nordic states. The answer was always a blank refusal. In frustration Churchill came up with a moral justification for the proposed occupation of the two neutral states. In a memo to the cabinet of December 16 Churchill noted, "We are fighting to … protect the liberties of small countries. Our defeat … would be fatal not only to ourselves but to the independent life of every small country in Europe…. Small nations must not tie our hands when we are fighting for their rights and freedom" (Harvey, 16). In return the British government received its own lesson in morality. Said the Swedes in one of their many rebuffs, "The British Government had the fate of a sufficient number of small states on its conscience as it is" (Petrov, 14) — as if it was England and not Germany that had invaded Austria, Czechoslovakia and Poland. Norway, although it was not pro–German as were the Swedes, also had a moral lesson for Mr. Churchill saying that violation by Germany of Norwegian neutrality does not justify similar behavior on the part of England. Needless to say, no Allied expedition ever sailed for Norway prior to the German assault.

The third scenario was to have British warships enter the Leads and sink the German merchantmen cruising up and down the Norwegian coast. It would seem to have been a much simpler and more elegant option; it would constitute less of an infringement on Norwegian sovereignty; it would have deprived Germany not only of the iron ore but of a good part of its merchant fleet; and it would have been a job the British knew how to do. Perversely, this approach never acquired the fervor of a land operation. Like the two land options this, too, never materialized.

The fourth scenario was that of mining the Leads; Churchill even wanted to mine the Baltic off the Swedish coast. This was the minimal option involving the least violation of Norway's neutrality and the least likelihood of serious fighting — a surreptitious act after which one could vanish from the scene of crime. As we shall see later on, this was implemented when it was too late and no longer of any use to the Allies.

Information of these goings-on was, of course, bound to reach Germany. In particular the exchanges with Norway, Sweden and Finland, countries with strong pro–German sympathies, provided the Germans with a rich if muddled picture of Allied intentions. As was seen, on December 12 Quisling briefed Hitler about Allied plans to seize Norway. Also, the reports of the Swedish naval attaché in London were regularly leaked to the Germans by Swedish Intelligence. At about the same time the German naval attache in Oslo informed Raeder, who told Hitler, of an imminent British landing (Harvey, 42). Imminent was an undeserved compliment but the report, following the outbreak of the Finnish war, did correctly reflect the Allies' rumblings about an expedition.

The event that finally decided Hitler to forestall the British was the *Altmark* incident. The *Altmark* was an 11,000-ton German auxiliary tanker. In September the ship was loading oil at a Texas port. In the event of war the captain had instructions to head for the southern Atlantic and serve as a tender for the German raider *Graf Spee*. Overnight the *Altmark* changed colors from battle grey to yellow, renamed itself *Sorge* and hoisted the Norwegian flag, hoping thereby to elude the British. At one of its rendezvous with the *Graf Spee*, in exchange for fuel the *Altmark* received 299 British prisoners the *Graf Spee* had collected from merchant ships it had sunk. In mid–December, off Montevideo, the British caught up with the German raider and, after a much-written-about battle, the wounded *Graf Spee* was scuttled by its crew. Before doing that, she released all remaining British prisoners aboard. From these men the Admiralty learned of the "Norwegian" oil-cow and its cargo of POWs. Expecting a hunt, the *Altmark* loitered in the Atlantic for over a month, until she headed for home at the end of January. Soon after entering the Leads near Trondheim she was spotted by a British plane. Three times Norwegian personnel boarded to inspect the ship and although the prisoners below deck shouted and banged, the Norwegians pretended not to hear a thing, exchanged salutes with the captain and allowed the *Altmark* to proceed. At Bergen there was a hitch because its enclave was a naval security zone and off limits to foreign warships. The German captain was ordered to circumnavigate the enclave. He refused because this would have brought him into international waters and under the British guns. When the Norwegian rear admiral on the scene telephoned the Foreign Ministry about the affair he was rebuked for provoking an incident. The naval chief then recalled that once before a German warship had been allowed to sail through the Bergen enclave, a most handy precedent. The diplomat in the Foreign Ministry congratulated the rear admiral on his splendid memory and the German ship was let go.

The *Altmark* was now close to the southern tip of Norway and would be home soon. But on February 17 a squadron of British warships appeared off Jossingfjord. A destroyer entered Norway's territorial waters and despite interference from Norwegian torpedo boats drove the *Altmark* into the frozen fiord. With the *Altmark* stuck in ice the British sent a boarding party onto its deck. In the brief scuffle six Germans were killed while the captain and the rest of the crew scampered across the ice to safety. The British ship took off the 299 prisoners and sailed for home.

This was for Hitler clinching proof that Britain would not let Norway alone; it was in fact the only instance — and there would soon be one more in Norwegian waters — when Britain indeed violated the neutrality of a European state. There was also a touch of humiliation in it and Hitler was furious, exclaiming, "No resistance. No British casualties." He called Jodl, shouted to get ready for an attack on Norway and asked for someone to lead the invasion. The OKW dug up General von Falkenhorst, a corps commander who in World War I had fought in Finland. Hitler received him on February 21, four days after the *Altmark* incident. Following a brief chat about the general's experiences in the north, he appointed him on the spot commander in chief for the impending invasion — a mighty title for a corps commander. He then led him to a spread-out map of Norway, told him what it was all about and ordered him to prepare an appropriate plan. The general was not given any staff, yet by nightfall he had his strategic blueprint ready. The next day Hitler approved what he had been shown. On March 1 Hitler issued the official order and but for a date, the invasion of Denmark and Norway was on.

While for the Allies, given their geography and resources, a Norwegian expedition would have been an ideal operation, for the Germans it was a most hazardous undertaking. The plan they prepared was, as usual, audacious and all-encompassing. It aimed to occupy Denmark and Norway at one stroke. All this despite the fact that Germany had no navy to confront the combined might of the French and British fleets; that for an invader Norway has perhaps the most forbidding topography on earth; and that the distance from the nearest German port to Narvik was 1,200 miles, well beyond the reach of the Luftwaffe. In addition, like the blitzkrieg in Poland, the Norwegian campaign was an untried form of warfare. It was the first time that a combined operation involving land, naval and air forces was resorted to in a single campaign. It is a cliché of strategy students to say in connection with some military scoop that the "element of surprise" was behind it — there was no surprise in this case. But there was nonconventional thinking executed with speed and resolve, the very attributes the Allies lacked. The reward was a fast and total victory.

The German scheme called for landings at five major cities, extending over the entire length of Norway. Since Narvik was a thousand miles north from the southernmost point, the convoys had to be so echeloned that, despite the varying distances, different ship speeds, and the vagaries of the weather, they would all reach their targets simultaneously. As shown in Fig. 8-1, five flotillas were readied to sail for Narvik, Trondheim, Bergen, Kristiansand and Oslo, each group ferrying from 1,000 to 2,000 troops. For reasons of speed and safety the troops were to be carried on warships. One of Raeder's concerns was to get his naval ships back once the troops had disembarked because, following the landings, the Home Fleet would head for the Norwegian coast and the Germans were no match for it. One problem was that the ships bound for Trondheim and Narvik would by then be out of fuel. Another problem was that the troops crammed below the decks of the warships needed supplies. It was decided to load transports with food, fuel and ammunition, and send them up the Leads to arrive at the debarkation points ahead of the troops. The warships were to sail close to the coast of Norway but in international waters. When near the landing sites they would dash into the fjords. Should the Norwegians challenge them they were to pose as British ships and signal "Coming for a short visit. No hostile intentions." Simultaneous with the landings, paratroopers were to capture two airfields; Ju-52s would then land and disembark 3,000 troops at Oslo and 2,500 at Stavanger. The invasion was to be carried out by a total of 14,200 men, 8,700 coming by sea and the rest by air. With the air and sea landings accomplished, reinforcements would follow to occupy the country in a leisurely land campaign.

When told on April 2 that the preparations were complete, Hitler set the invasion date for April 9. At about the same time the British cabinet, after deliberating for seven months, finally authorized the mining of Norwegian waters at two places; the Vestfjord, opposite Narvik, and at Standland, north of Bergen. Consequently, the battleship *Renown*, accompanied by eight destroyers, sailed for Norway. Should the Germans respond with a landing in Norway two brigades of British troops were loaded aboard warships to stand by for a counterinvasion. It was under the impact of these daring moves that a beaming Chamberlain boasted before his cabinet that "Hitler missed the bus," a phrase that along with "peace in our time" sums up the man's leadership in war and peace. As Chamberlain was speaking the German transports were already at sea. Flotillas I and II, designated for Trondheim and Narvik, slipped out of Wilhelmshaven at dawn on April 7. Their route being the longest and most hazardous they were given an escort of Germany's two battleships, *Gneisenau* and *Scharnhorst*. Thus on April 7 both the British and German fleets were at sea headed for Norway, one to scatter mines and the other to take over the country.

Four hours after Flotillas I and II left Wilhelmshaven they were spotted by a British reconnaissance plane. The Admiralty was uncertain what they were up to. Since they saw warships, but no transports, the first guess was that it was a sortie and the ships would soon return to port. When the Germans kept heading north the British dispatched the Home Fleet to sea. By then seven hours had elapsed since the Germans had been spotted and 12 since they had left port. Scapa Flow being on the same parallel as southern Norway, the German ships after 12 hours were well to the north of their pursuers. The next day came definitive confirmation of German intentions when a Polish submarine sank a transport

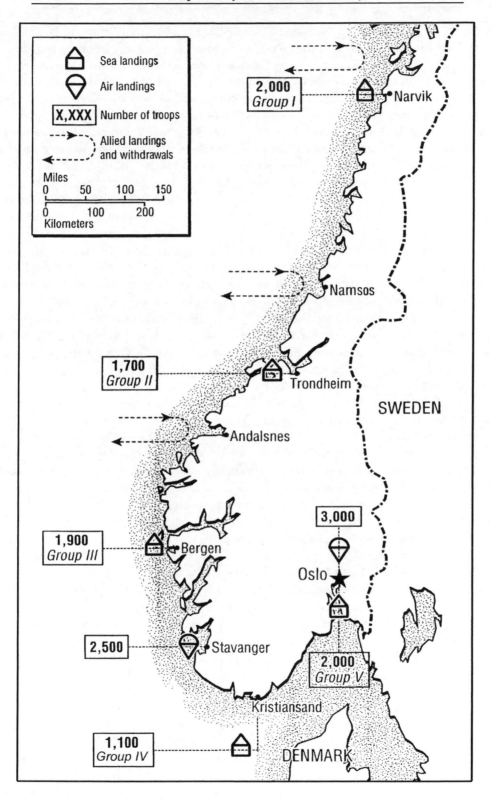

8.1. German invasion of Norway, April 1940

carrying troops for southern Norway. The survivors, soldiers in full combat gear, were taken to Norway where they said they were going to protect Norway from the British. Even prior to that, agents and German sources, such as Colonel Oster from the Abwehr, had conveyed information that an invasion was imminent. As usual, the reaction was both lethargic and wrong. The Home Fleet, under the command of Admiral Forbes, first headed northeast to intercept the German ships, but soon two inexplicable things happened. As noted, the British had loaded troops aboard several warships to be ready for a counterinvasion in case the Germans attacked Norway. Now these ships were ordered to unload and join Forbes. Thus the troops that had been embarked for the contingency of a German attack on Norway were speedily disembarked when that contingency in fact occurred. Next, Forbes, at first sailing north for the Norwegian waters, at some point reversed direction and headed south. All this was provoked by the phantom of World War I. Forbes feared the German fleet was bent on breaking out into the Atlantic, as it had tried in 1915. The Admiralty, though not as sure of it as Forbes, also thought it likely. All available ships were then rushed off for the expected great sea battle à la Jutland. When on April 8 the *Renown* squadron finally did lay the mines off Narvik—though the mission at Standland was aborted—this squadron, too, was ordered away from the Norwegian coast. While all these mighty British ships searched for the enemy presumably headed for the Atlantic, the Germans plowed their way steadily for their targets along the Norwegian coast. To help the British in their misconception, the *Gneisenau* and *Scharnhorst*, the moment they had brought their charges close to Narvik, separated from them and headed northwest, hoping to lure the British fleet away from the troop-laden destroyers.

On the morning of April 9, with the British fleet strung out all over the waters, the German ships unloaded their troops at all five designated Norwegian ports, on schedule. The Norwegians had six active and four reserve divisions. The reserves had never been mobilized and the active troops either scattered on sight of the disembarking Germans or surrendered, often jovially so and frequently against specific orders to fight. One such case happened at Narvik. The invaders there were General Dietl's mountain troops, 2,000 strong. Upon landing Dietl and the local Norwegian commander, Colonel Sundlo, exchanged salutes and conducted a cordial conversation during which the German suggested the Norwegians surrender. The colonel thought he ought perhaps to consult headquarters. When he telephoned he was told Norway was being invaded and the orders were to resist. Colonel Sundlo returned to General Dietl and told him, "I hand over the town." Whereupon the Norwegians departed and Dietl's mountain troops occupied Narvik without a shot.

The only place where things went wrong for the Germans was at Oslo. What happened there illustrates another attribute of the German army the Allies lacked—perseverance in fulfilling an assigned mission. Two powerful ships led the invasion fleet in Oslofjord, the heavy cruiser *Blücher*, the flagship, and the pocket battleship *Lützow*. They passed the entrance to the fjord unscathed but when they got close to Oslo the coastal guns and a torpedo battery opened fire. The *Blücher*, torn by internal explosions, capsized and sank with the loss of a thousand soldiers and sailors. The *Lützow*, now in command, ordered the invasion fleet to retreat and to discharge its troops some 50 miles south of Oslo. The scheduled air landings at Fornebu, Oslo's airport, also miscarried, because of heavy fog. The planes with the paratroopers had to turn back and consequently the follow-up air transports, too, could not land. When the bombers and fighters assigned to support the parachutists appeared over the airfield, they too, ran into trouble. Of the bombers three crashed in flames and the fighters ran out of fuel. What happened next is probably unique in the history of warfare. Eight fighters landed at Fornebu airport, the pilots trained the planes' machine guns on the Norwegian defenders and drove them off, securing the airfield for the troop transports.

Even though the coastal batteries prevented the invaders from reaching Oslo, King Haakon and the government fled the capital at 7:30 that morning. By 8 A.M. Oslo was an abandoned city, free of any authority. At noon the Ju-52s arrived at Fornebu and disgorged eight battalions of infantry. A commercial airliner followed, bringing a military band and its instruments. The German infantry in parade formation, music blaring, entered and took over the Norwegian capital. That afternoon General Falkenhorst arrived. In half a day the job was completed with a German commander in chief established in Oslo in place of the king.

The story of the Allied reaction to the German invasion is best begun with an exchange between Gamelin and Prime Minister Reynaud, who in March had replaced Daladier in consequence of the "Finnish" fiasco. Gamelin arrived at Reynaud's office on the morning of the invasion and found him and his aides poring over a map of Norway. When Reynaud asked what Gamelin thought of the news, the latter replied, "You are wrong to get excited. We must wait for more complete information. This is a simple incident of war. Wars are full of unexpected news." Reynaud looked at him and asked, "You consider the invasion of Denmark and Norway entirely unexpected news?" When pressed what he intended to do, the French commander in chief settled the issue by saying, "The British have been put in charge of this operation. It is up to the British Admiralty to make the decisions. I have no business intervening" (Shirer 1971, 555).

From now on it was a purely British show, and a poor show it was. The decision was to land at Trondheim and Narvik and thus recapture central and northern Norway. A convoy carrying a British brigade left on April 12 but instead of Narvik the troops landed at Harstad, an island off the Vesfjord devoid of Germans. As for landing at Trondheim, this too was avoided. On April 17 and 18 a brigade each was disembarked at Namsos and Andalsnes, north and south of Trondheim with the intent of encircling the city. The landings took place without opposition. The northern pincer at Namsos never got far from its landing site due to lack of artillery and strong attacks by the Luftwaffe. At Andalsnes another inexplicable thing happened. Its mission was to swing north to join up with the Namsos arm. Instead the troops attacked southward where they were thoroughly beaten by the Germans coming up from Oslo. One week after the landings it was decided to evacuate. By the beginning of May British troops had withdrawn from central Norway.

Following the landing at Harstad considerable reinforcements poured into the Narvik area. At the end of April the French shipped in three battalions of Alpine Chasseurs, two of the Foreign Legion and four of Polish troops. Soon the total Allied strength there exceeded 26,000 men. Compared with this Dietl had his 2,000 mountain troops plus 2,600 sailors rescued from the 10 destroyers the British had sunk in the Vestfjord. These sailors were more of a burden than a help because they were untrained and without weapons. Moreover, Dietl's transports had failed to arrive and he was without supplies, cut off by sea and by land. Dietl got some help from the Swedes, who had agreed to ship him via the Narvik railroad supplies from Germany and to evacuate some of the stranded sailors. Thus Sweden ended up preventing help from reaching Finland, its Scandinavian neighbor to the east, and actually assisting in the invasion of Norway, its Scandinavian neighbor to the west.

It is symptomatic that while General Falkenhorst arrived in Norway the same day as his troops, the commander of the Allied forces in Norway, General Massy, sat in London throughout the Norwegian venture. His CO in the Narvik area, General Mackesy, refused, despite repeated urgings from London, to launch a direct assault on the town though his forces outnumbered the enemy 10 to 1. He planned, instead, a methodical campaign of encirclement from all four directions. In the meantime the Germans, having chased the British from central Norway, were moving north to relieve Dietl. To block them a combined British-Norwegian force placed itself at Mosjoen, some 200 miles south of Narvik. The story of that fight adds another song of praise for the German soldier. The terrain around Mosjoen and up the Norwegian panhandle is for an attacker the most difficult piece of terrain to conquer. There was a single road heading north, cut by fjords negotiable only by ferry. The road itself is hemmed in by mountains, at that time of the year under deep snow and ice. The country here is at its narrowest, at some points no more than 15–20 miles wide. The landscape is harsh and desolate. There is no chance of outflanking the enemy by either maneuver or deception. Up this road the Germans advanced. The tactic of the British and Norwegian units was to stage ambushes from the sides of the road. As soon as a German column appeared they fired on it, causing casualties only to the point squads. When struck by these ambushes, the response of the Germans was to climb the hills on either side of the road and to continue forward. Soon they were on the flanks and in the rear of the defenders who scampered to avoid being encircled. The Norwegians, native to these mountains, claimed they could not move or fight in these snowy wastes and, if they couldn't, certainly the British couldn't. But the Germans could. On skis, snowshoes, or their standard jackboots they marched and fought across mountains and fjords defeating the allied contingents over and over again. In the end they forced the Allies to fall back beyond Bodo and to their remaining beachhead at Narvik.

That beachhead, too, did not endure long. Since General Mackesy refused to follow orders from London, he was replaced by General Auchinleck who was going to be more energetic. But once on the scene, he, too, opted for caution and followed Mackesy's plan. By the time Allied troops approached Narvik, the Germans on May 10 launched their assault on the western front. With disasters piling up faster than the Allies could count them, the British made two decisions. One was to pull out of Narvik; the other was to proceed and capture it. The decision to evacuate Narvik was taken on May 22 and why it was thought proper to still press for its capture remains inexplicable. The final two-pronged attack on Narvik was carried out by French and Polish troops. Auchinleck, watching what he considered the great dash of these foreigners, was heard to remark, "I wish the British were here, too." Narvik was taken on May 28. However, Dietl and his troops escaped. They retreated along the railroad toward the Swedish border and stayed in the mountains, waiting for a better day.

Five days after the troops captured Narvik, the retreat began. The Norwegians who fought with the Allies were kept in the dark about the planned evacuation and were left behind; they promptly surrendered to the Germans. However King Haakon and his government were taken aboard a cruiser to England. On June 8 the last Allied troops departed. The Norwegian saga was over.

The cost of the Norwegian intervention in troops was slight. The numbers of men killed on land was 1,317 for Germany and 1,869 for Britain. In a war that lasted two months, this indicates that no serious fighting took place. The casualties at sea were for both sides nearly double those on land. The naval losses were about equal, but the impact of these sinkings was more severe for Germany. Ten German destroyers were sunk by the British and two had been sunk by their own bombers so that out of a total strength of 22 Germany was left with 10 destroyers. Nearly all major German ships were damaged during the campaign and had to retire for repairs. While victory was achieved on land, Germany emerged from the Norwegian adventure with its naval strength cut in half.

The Norwegian fiasco led to a change in the top leadership of the two Allies. Blamed for his muddle in the Finnish episode, Daladier was replaced on March 21 by Reynaud, though Daladier retained his post as minister of defense. And on May 10 Chamberlain was finally ousted with the words, "For God's sake, let's be done with you" and replaced by Winston Churchill. While the switch in French premiers had no effect on the course of events, Churchill's stewardship proved to be momentous.

• CHAPTER 9 •

The Collapse of France

With the fall of Poland the Allies had lost their eastern front, yet the Polish campaign could and should have been of enormous assistance to them. To any sane government and General Staff there revealed itself in the course of that war a treasure of information on the German war machine which usually takes years of exploration and intelligence to acquire, if it is acquired at all. For here ahead of the main confrontation in the West, the Germans had demonstrated the kind of war they intended to wage, the organization and tactics they had assigned to their armored formations, the role that the Luftwaffe and particularly the dive bombers would play on the battlefield, and the panic and death its bombers would inflict on the civilian population in order to clog the roads with refugees and prevent the troops from either reaching the front or escaping to the rear. Yet no such lesson was learned and no measures taken to counteract the German strategy. Gamelin, the French commander in chief, was a man with the manner and temperament of a bishop. In earlier days when François-Poncet had warned him that Germany was capable of raising 300 divisions, he scoffed that they could never train enough NCOs for such an army. When François-Poncet said there would be no need to train NCOs since "the Germans are born such," the truth and humor of it missed the generalissimo. When the word blitzkrieg was mentioned, Gamelin, with his studious equanimity, dismissed it with, yes, on the flatlands of Poland and against Polish troops the Germans could show off their blitzkrieg, but it would not work in France. The German concentrations opposite the Ardennes he dismissed too; in that region no offensive was possible. The terrain there, he claimed, would "defend itself." In January 1940 Gamelin appointed Gen. Alphonse Georges commander of the Northeast Front — that is, of all the armies likely to be engaged in combat. Thus while content to hold in peacetime the august title of commander in chief, when it came to fighting Gamelin shed all responsibility for it; during the Norwegian campaign he had assigned it to the British, and now to a subordinate general. Consequently, there were now two headquarters, that of General Georges and Gamelin's at Vincennes, near Paris. Here in his subterranean compound Gamelin did not even have any radio communication with the outside world, which led some staff members to dub the place as "a submarine without a periscope" (Goutard, 99).

While the French hunkered down behind their Maginot Line, Holland and Belgium hunkered down behind their neutrality. The legacy of the Great War played tricks with their psyches, as it did with everyone else's. In the 1914 invasion of France, Holland had been spared. Although it was clear that its reason was the Germans did not need Dutch territory to carry out their Schlieffen Plan, the Dutch preferred to attribute it to their policy of neutrality. They, therefore, remained religiously neutral throughout the interwar years.

When in 1937 Hitler offered the Netherlands guarantees, the Dutch government declined, saying that by accepting they would appear to condone the notion that someone indeed contemplated to violate their territory. Dutch territorial inviolability, declared the Dutch foreign minister, is "an axiom" (DGFP, 358). To show how seriously she took her neutrality, Holland guarded not only her border with Germany but also that with Belgium, and had even stationed troops along the coast against a seaborne invasion — by England? America?

Belgium, despite its neutrality, had been invaded by the Germans in the very first days of the 1914 war. The lesson, therefore, was that neutrality guarantees nothing, and in the postwar years the Belgians joined in signing the Locarno Pact and other mutual defense treaties. This fortitude lasted as long as there was no potential aggressor in sight. When in 1935 Hitler started rearming and then occupied the Rhineland, the Belgians quit all their international commitments, scrapped their defense treaty with France and pronounced the country's strict neutrality. From then on they refused all French approaches for staff talks or any common preparations against a German attack. When in response the French considered extending the Maginot Line along the western Belgian border — which would have left the Belgians to fend for themselves — they vociferously objected. Moreover, should the Germans attack, the Belgians reserved the right to request Allied aid. This attitude was maintained throughout the winter of 1939-40 even though reliable intelligence flowed into all Western capitals that in their invasion of France the Germans intended to attack all three Benelux countries. When alarmed by the German invasion of Norway, the French on April 9 proposed stationing troops along the contemplated Allied defense line in Belgium, not only was the request denied but the Belgians rushed reinforcements and mined the roads along the French border. Much of this attitude was due to King Leopold III, commander in chief of his army. The king was an aloof, morose man of uncertain political views. Some of this was due to an unhappy private life — his father, King Albert, had died in a mountaineering accident and his young wife was killed in a car crash with the king at the wheel. Much of it was domestic politics; by his neutral stand he appeased both ends of his society — the Left which fought against rearmament and the Flemings with their pro–German sentiments. But most of it was a result of the memories of World War I when Belgium had been invaded, despoiled, and Flanders stayed a battlefield for over four years. When the king in his speech of October 14, 1936, announced his switch to neutrality, he said that "an invasion would penetrate deeply into Belgium at the very beginning and she would be devastated. Afterwards friendly intervention might, of course, ensure final victory but in the process the country would suffer ravages such as would be infinitely worse than those of the war of 1914–18" (Doc. Belgian For. Min., Appendix p. 5). These sentiments, undoubtedly, contributed later to the king's precipitate decision to order the capitulation of the Belgian army.

The result was that, as we shall see later, Holland and Belgium each fought and lost its own separate war. Due to Holland's preferred neutrality there had been no cooperation between Holland and Belgium. When the Germans struck at Belgium there was an interlude of reluctant Belgian-Allied cooperation which soon collapsed, the Belgians, like the Dutch, going down to defeat and occupation. This was paralleled by the behavior of France and England themselves. At the beginning the two allies cooperated and fought in unison. But as soon as the French started to wobble, the British, with good reason, began looking over their shoulder toward the evacuation ports. Consequently, after a brief brotherhood of arms, each went its own way — France to defeat, and England to its disengagement from the continent.

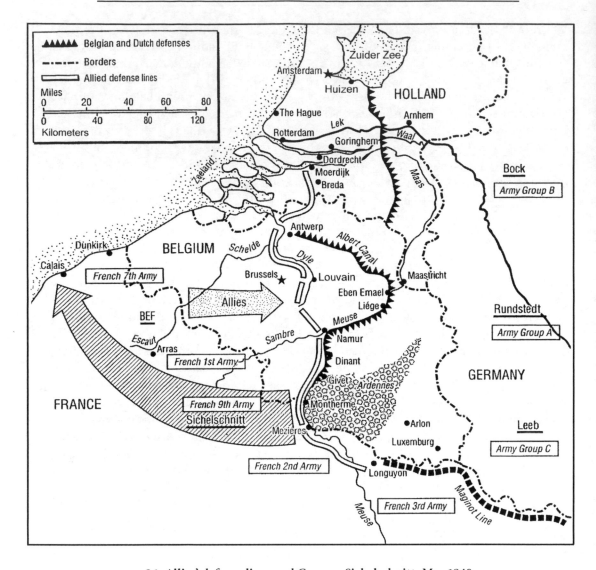

9.1. Allies' defense lines and German Sichelschnitt, May 1940

Fig. 9.1 shows the defensive schemes worked out by the Low Countries and France against a German invasion. The Dutch, with a population of 9 million, fielded an army of 10 divisions, about 300,000 men. This weakness dictated their contingency plans. They had resigned themselves to abandoning the northern and eastern parts of the country, some 60 percent of their territory. They drew a first line of defense from the Zuider Zee to the Belgian border — the serrated line on the map. However, at its southern terminus, where it abutted the Belgian border, the line hung like a tail in midair. This was a result of lack of common planning with the Belgians, whose own forward defense line arched westward at some distance from the Dutch frontier leaving an open corridor between the two defense systems. The ultimate resistance was planned for what the Dutch called Fortress Holland. This was a rectangular bastion surrounded on three sides by water with its front from Huizen to Gorinchem 40 miles long. This defensive box contained Holland's three most important cities: The Hague, the seat of government; Rotterdam, Europe's largest port;

and Amsterdam. Here, shielded on three sides by various estuaries, the North Sea and fronted by rivers, canals, dykes, and deliberate inundations, the Dutch hoped to be able to hold out.

Although its population of 7 million was smaller than Holland's, the Belgians had an army of 22 divisions, 650,000 strong; they were also better trained and equipped. Their strategic plans were more complex. When Belgium had an alliance with France, the plan had been that as soon as war threatened, French troops would come in and man the line Arlon-Liege with the Belgians positioned along the Albert Canal (Shirer 1971, 577). This lapsed with the abrogation of the treaty in 1936. The Belgians went ahead and constructed a formidable defense line stretching from Antwerp along the Albert Canal to the gigantic fortresses of Eben Emael and Liege, thence along the Meuse to the French border. This enclosed most of Belgian territory except for its southeastern corner protected, as was believed, by the impassable Ardennes forest. This was later claimed by the Belgians to be merely a "covering line" so as to give the Allies time to take up defensive positions in the rear. But it is hard to accept this Belgian version of their intentions. The Eben Emael fort, erected at the confluence of the Albert Canal and the Meuse, was considered by military experts as the most formidable fortification on earth. Liege too was an awesome fort. It is difficult to believe that so much expense and effort had been invested in what was to serve merely as a delaying line. Furthermore, at the outbreak of hostilities the Belgians had 10 divisions along the Albert Canal. It is more likely that this fortified line following pretty much Belgium's border with Holland was meant to defend all of Belgium. This in spite of its serious shortcomings stemming mainly from its configuration. The line resembled a triangular salient projecting eastward from whence the attack would come. It was twice as long as a linear north-south frontage; it was prey to envelopment from either wing; and it was far from the French border and the Allied troops meant to come to Belgium's rescue. When war broke out in September, though remaining neutral, the Belgians opened secret contacts with the French General Staff. They wanted, as soon as the Germans attacked, the Allies to rush in and man the covering line. The French said it was too far from the border and they could not possibly reach these lines in the teeth of a German advance. On their part the British were willing to advance no farther than the Schelde.* The French compromised by agreeing to advance and man the line Antwerp-Namur, or what is often called the Dyle line, which encompassed only 30 percent of the country. With this the Belgians had to be satisfied.

A France safe behind its Maginot Line seems a spurious notion when one realizes that its border with Belgium — along which there was no Maginot Line — is almost as long as that with Germany. In the south its border with Switzerland and Italy is even longer — but there, at least, were the Alps. Not so in Belgium which is a perfect platform for invasion. France's defense strategy, worked out soon after the end of the First World War, was as follows. Along the border with Germany a Maginot Line was built consisting of two parts; where the Rhine separated the two countries the fortifications built were of moderate bulk, relying on the river to bolster the defenses; where the border departed from the Rhine the Maginot Line was at its most formidable. The latter ran northwest to the point where the Belgian-French-Luxemburg frontiers meet. Further north France had no fortified line.

There is likely to be some confusion with river names. What the Germans call the Lower Rhine, the Dutch call the Lek; what in France and Belgium is called the Meuse is called the Maas in Holland; and what is the Schelde in Belgium is the Escaut in France. For consistency the names Lower Rhine, Meuse and Schelde will be used here.

When the French-Belgian alliance was in force and when it was not, a tenet of French strategy remained that should the Germans enter Belgium, Allied troops would rush in to man the Dyle line. This line stretching from Antwerp via Namur to Givet the Belgians considered their main defense. From Givet to Longuyon where the Maginot Line terminated, there were no fortified positions for, as was claimed, the Ardennes would "defend itself." As soon as Belgium was attacked the Allied forces, pivoting on Mezieres, were to execute a rotation of some 50 degrees and join up with the Belgian armies pulling back from the covering line. This implied a march of 50 miles at the center, and more than 100 at the extreme north. Should Holland, too, be invaded the northernmost French forces were to go beyond Belgium to assist the Dutch in holding Fortress Holland.

Including the BEF, the Wehrmacht faced four opponents, and it dealt with them as if they were one. The original plan had the German army launch an offensive via Holland and Belgium with its main effort on the right. The bulk of the forces had been given to Army Group B under von Bock, with its neighbor to the south, von Rundstedt's Army Group A, providing support. While working on this plan, Rundstedt's chief of staff, General Manstein, conceived of an alternative approach. Attacking on the right, he surmised, would merely push the Allied armies inland, offering little prospect of a decisive blow. His idea was to switch the main effort south, to Army Group A. By assigning to the latter large forces and the bulk of the armor, he proposed to drive across southern Belgium for the Channel coast so as to trap all Dutch, Belgian, British and most French forces in a northern cauldron. An additional advantage of the Manstein idea was that the attack by Army Group A would be across the Ardennes where there was a gap between the Maginot Line and the Meuse fortifications and where no attack was expected. Knowing his soldiers, Manstein was not too concerned that the difficult terrain — woods, hills, rivers, poor roads— would stop the German army. This plan was later dubbed Sichelschnitt — a sickle cut. When Manstein presented his plan to the OKH it was rejected. Furthermore, for disagreeing with and denigrating the existing OKH plan Gelb, Manstein was reassigned to an army corps in Stettin. It was common procedure for corps commanders to be received by Hitler prior to taking up their new assignments. This took place on February 17 when Manstein broached the Sichelschnitt idea to Hitler. Hitler was instantly enthused by it. There are some indications that he himself had toyed with this concept but there is no doubt that it was only on February 24, after his talk with Manstein, that he issued the order to revamp Gelb in line with the Sichelschnitt idea; this was accomplished by March 7. Though Manstein's plan seems radically new, we have here, once again, the shadow of World War I. In March 1918 during their last great offensive in the West, the Germans, following the old Schlieffen plan, broke the Allied lines and headed for Paris. When Allied resistance stiffened the closer the Germans got to the French capital, Ludendorff switched his objective. With the French armies on his left and the British and Belgians to the north he swung his main effort toward the Channel coast aiming to sever the French from their allies to the north. As it happened Ludendorff ran out of steam and stalled, but we have here the very idea of the Sichelschnitt. It would have been strange had Manstein and Hitler not been aware of all this.

There should be no surprise that Sichelschnitt was instantly embraced by the führer, for aside from its military virtues the new plan carried great political potential. By cutting into French territory along Army Group A axis, the Germans would isolate in the north the Dutch, the Belgians and the British, leaving south of the Sichelschnitt only French forces. It carried the vision not only of a military triumph but of shattering the Western alliance.

North of the Maginot Line where the main fighting was to occur, the distribution of the opposing forces was in inverse ratio to each other. While Army Group A had a powerful concentration of 45 divisions, including seven of Germany's 10 Panzer divisions—the French forces facing them were at their thinnest; moreover, these divisions consisted of poorly trained reservists. The main French forces, including its mobile units and the BEF, were concentrated in the north, ready to plunge into Belgium. There von Bock, after giving up 11 divisions to AG A, was left with only 21 divisions which faced 11 Dutch, 22 Belgian, 25 French and some 15 British divisions, a total of 66 divisions giving the Allies a local superiority of 3:1 (Bock, 116). The Maginot Line, facing practically no German forces to speak of, was garrisoned by nearly 50 divisions, a huge army destined to be mere spectators in the coming contest. Whereas the Germans with a total of 136 divisions kept 42 of them, or a full third, as reserves, the French had a reserve of only 17 divisions, less than a fifth of the Allies' total strength. Most French commanders had been opposed to the plan of sending Giraud's 7th Army into Holland, preferring to keep its seven divisions in reserve, but Gamelin would not yield. Probably the motivation to send the 7th Army into Holland, as well as the willingness to get into Belgium deeper than did the British, reflected Gamelin's old compulsion to displace the fighting as far away from French soil as possible.

Except for airplanes, the two armies were of equal strength. There were 136 German against a total of 142 Allied divisions. The Germans deployed some 2,700 tanks, while the French had 2,400, many of them heavier and better armored than the German vehicles. The ratio of aircraft was 2:1 in favor of the Germans, and in bombers more like 3:1. Of course, these numbers do not reflect the actual potential of the two combatants. After the Polish campaign the German armored divisions improved their proficiency. Instead of three, each Panzer division now had only two tank regiments, augmented by a brigade of motorized infantry with its own self-propelled artillery. The French tanks were broken up into 54 battalions, half of them in support of the infantry; even their independent armored divisions were merely amalgams of three existing battalions. The same with the air force. While the German air armada was grouped into two Luftflotten under independent command which assigned their aircraft in concentrated mass wherever the need arose—the French planes, like the tanks, were distributed among the land armies. Worst were the antiquated tactics of the tanks which bore no resemblance to the concentration, speed, firepower, flexibility and generalship of the Panzer divisions.

* * *

On the evening of May 9 Hitler left the Chancellery and boarded his special train. The train first headed north so as to give no hint where the führer was headed. With nightfall the train changed direction and proceeded west toward Hitler's new field headquarters, Felsennest, 25 miles southwest of Bonn. Hitler arrived there at dawn and in the brilliant early morning stood in a state of euphoria and watched German columns heading down all roads to the Belgian border, the sky black with airplanes. It was Friday, May 10, the date of Hitler's onslaught on the West.

There had been no need for the deceptive maneuver of Hitler's special train. The night before all three Western capitals had received information, most specifically from Colonel Oster again, of next morning's scheduled attack . In Holland the alarm was passed on to the border troops, though not to those of Fortress Holland; there would be time for that (Maas, 28–30). Holland was also the first to notice the tentacles of the hydra that was about to strangulate the West. During the night its inhabitants were awakened by the roar of passing airplanes. The planes flew on and disappeared — the Dutch surmising that they were bound for France or England. Once over the North Sea the German squadrons turned around and about 4 A.M. came in over Holland from the west. While in common with all Western strategies the Dutch had prepared defense lines and fortresses facing east, the Germans skipped these preliminaries and reached for the heart of the country. Some 4,000 paratroopers dropped into Fortress Holland, followed by an airborne division. The task of those dropped near The Hague was to seize the capital and cajole the queen and her government to cooperate with the invaders; otherwise they were to ship them to Germany. The coup failed when Dutch troops prevented the Germans from reaching the city. However in their operational tasks the Germans scored full success. One objective of the air landings was to pry open the southern gates of Fortress Holland so that the troops coming from the east could enter the Fortress and debouch into northern Belgium. For this the various bridges over the Lower Rhine, Waal and the Meuse had to be captured. Assisted by troops that had debarked from hydroplanes at the Rotterdam estuary, all these bridges were in German hands that very morning. The troops were also to disrupt any attempt at organized resistance. The paratroopers that landed in scattered parts of western Holland holed up on farms, dykes and ditches, repulsing all attempts to dislodge them, for, as their foreign minister explained, Dutch troops had been trained only for defense. In their work the Germans resorted to all kinds of deception and treachery such as dressing in Dutch army uniforms, driving captured prisoners in front of them, and making use of local Germans and collaborators. Stunned by the airborne landings and frustrated by vain attempts to clear out the German pockets, there was practically no resistance to the main body of German troops invading the country from the east. When Giraud's 7th Army reached Breda he found no Dutch troops there and, pounced upon by the Germans who had arrived there ahead of him, he quickly withdrew into Belgium.

The forces of Army Group B that entered southern Holland consisted of four infantry divisions and one Panzer division. They reached the area south of Rotterdam after two days and there they linked up with the paratroopers. Although all the bridges at Moerdjik, Dordrecht and south of Rotterdam were in German hands, the access to Rotterdam itself was still held by the Dutch. Instead of fighting, the Germans resorted to a familiar weapon — terror bombing. They had threatened Hacha with bombing Prague, they had subdued Warsaw with their bombers, and they had intimidated Copenhagen into surrender with their planes. On the morning of May 14 the Germans delivered an ultimatum to Rotterdam: surrender or it will be obliterated by the Luftwaffe. The Dutch agreed to hand over the city but there was a bureaucratic hitch. The ultimatum bore no name and before they surrendered the Dutch asked for an authorized signature. This cost the Dutch dearly. While they fussed about securing a signature, the Germans launched their air attack which killed 900 people and burned down the center of Rotterdam. At 4 P.M. the city surrendered.

On the morning of May 13, Queen Wilhelmina, carrying only the clothes she had on and a steel helmet, left the capital for England, followed soon by her government. The commander in chief of the Dutch army, General Winkelman, was left with the option to continue fighting or quit. Soon after Rotterdam surrendered General Winkelman ordered his troops to cease fire. Von Bock, driving through Holland, reported that the population was friendly and the POWs happy it was over. Following the capitulation Dutch sentries presented arms wherever he appeared. At Doorn he was forbidden by Hitler to pay a visit to the Kaiser who had been living there in exile since 1918 (Bock, 140). The official capitulation of the Dutch army took place on the morning of May 15. As a reward, Hitler ordered that Dutch soldiers not be made prisoners but sent home. The Dutch casualties were 2,100 killed and 2,700 wounded (Maas, 42). The war in Holland lasted four days.

Some 100 miles south of the air armada that had rumbled over Holland in the early hours of May 10, another air fleet, towing 40 gliders, was at the same time heading toward Belgium. Like the Dutch, who had thought of various bulwarks against a land invasion but not about their skies, the Belgians too had erected stupendous walls against a frontal attack but left the roof of their house open. And this was where the airborne Germans, some 500 men, were heading. Their mission was to seize the three bridges over the Albert Canal north of Eben Emael — Veldenwelt, Vroenhoven and Canne — and to capture Eben Emael itself. They were to hold out there until the main invasion force coming from the German border 30 miles away reached them, tentatively in four hours. In essence, these few airborne commandos were to smash in Belgium's most formidable bastion and open the way for the regular troops.

At dawn 30 gliders landed at the bridges and their troops overpowered the Belgian defenders. The two northernmost bridges were taken intact but the one nearest to Eben Emael, Canne, the Belgians managed to blow up before retreating. A great German feat of arms was then enacted. Eben Emael was the strongest fortress, or rather system of fortifications, on the globe. In sheer bulk, complexity and sophistication it has never been equaled. It consisted of 12 concrete casemates topped with revolving, 12-inch thick steel cupolas mounting 120 mm and 75 mm guns in armored embrasures . These dome-shaped cupolas could be raised for firing the guns and retracted to avoid enemy fire. The forts had multilevel underground galleries and tunnels housing generators, ammunition depots, supplies and hospitals. In addition to the canal the fort was defended by concrete-lined moats, machine gun nests and infantry trenches. Eben Emael's role was to block the approaches into Belgium as well as to the bridges further north. It had a garrison of 1,200 men under the command of Major Jottrand. However, on the fatal day there were only 800 of them in the battlements, the rest being on leave or in training (Mrazek, 25–8).

The team assigned to capture Eben Emael consisted of 85 men under the leadership of a Lieutenant Witzig. When still over Germany the towrope of Witzig's glider snapped and he was left behind. The remaining gliders continued on their way and in a steep dive descended and landed on the roofs of Eben Emael. Although the Belgians had flak and heavy machine guns, not a single one of the 41 gliders assaulting Eben Emael and the bridges was shot down. After the commandos had disgorged from the gliders and silenced the machine guns they discovered that their leader was missing. No matter! A sergeant named Wenzel took command of the group, now reduced to 77 men, and they set about demolishing the fortress. The weapon they used was hollow, or shaped charges. These were heavy 110-pounds packs of explosives containing at the bottom a hemispherical void lined with a steel cap; when placed against a surface and detonated most of the explosive energy was directed toward the steel cap which melted and was impelled against the contact surface. The temperatures and pressures of the resulting implosion were so high as to drill a hole in the thickest concrete or steel wall. Divided into groups of three to four men the commandos now went about attaching these explosives against the casemates. After the men set the fuses and ran for cover, the explosions shattered and cracked the cupolas, driving concrete and steel shrapnel and poisonous fumes into the interior of the forts. These unexpected blasts drove the gun crews from their stations and terrorized the men in the galleries below. Within a short time most of the Belgians in Eben Emael abandoned their positions and escaped into the underground chambers, sealing themselves in with the automatic steel gates that isolated the various levels of the fort. Subsequently the Germans placed charges into the muzzles of the guns and blew them up, while most of the 800 defenders cowered in the catacombs of the fortress. A full Belgian division stationed in the vicinity did not attempt or failed to drive off the 80 or so German dinamiteros.

By midday the job was done. Deep inside Belgium, with only hand weapons to defend themselves against a sea of Belgian soldiery, the Germans sat on the roofs of the forts or astride the captured bridges, waiting to be relieved. The German army reached the Albert Canal in the afternoon, well beyond the planned four hours. But while for the Germans at the bridges the ordeal was over, for those at Eben Emael rescue was further delayed because of the blown bridge at Canne. It took all night to secure a crossing and it was not until dawn of May 11 that the commandos of Eben Emael were relieved. They had been alone for 24 hours and had suffered six dead and 20 wounded. Before the regular German troops entered Eben Emael, Major Jottrand gathered his men and proposed to break out of the fortress. The men refused to obey and insisted on surrendering. The major lined up his men and under a white flag marched them into captivity (Mrazek, 164, 157).

After the Germans breached the Eben Emael complex, King Leopold recalled most of his troops from the Ardennes, leaving it practically undefended. The impulse to pull his troops northward persisted throughout the campaign. It was motivated probably by a desire to keep the Belgian army together and shield the major cities—Antwerp, Brussels and Ghent. Thus the four Belgian divisions stationed south of the Meuse retreated toward Namur to join the troops falling back from the Albert Canal. Already at 6:30 on the morning of May 10 the Belgian government had appealed to the Allies for help. According to plan three French armies and the BEF moved into Belgium. When Hitler was told of this mass movement of Allied troops toward the Dyle line, he exclaimed, "I could have cried with joy. They have fallen into the trap. The attack through Liege had been a good move" (Goutard, 106). The last sentence reveals a basic ingredient of the German master plan. Given that the intent was to trap the Western armies between the sea and the Sichelschnitt, it was superfluous to attack southern Holland and the Albert Canal, easy as it proved to subdue them. With a successful Sichelschnitt Holland and northern Belgium would have automatically fallen into German hands. From Hitler's remark about Liege, it transpires that the Germans did everything possible to assure an Allied plunge into Belgium. They launched what seemed a serious offensive on the Low Countries to confirm the Allies in their long-held presumption that this would be the Germans' main effort. The Allies were also nudged into the trap by a tactical ruse. Originally, the Allies intended to march only at night. In view of the fiasco at the Albert Canal they decided to speed up their deployment by moving also in daytime. To their relief they were not molested by the Luftwaffe, which everywhere else was causing the greatest havoc. It should have given the generals pause, but preoccupied as they were by a collapsing Belgian front, they paid no attention and hurried on. And indeed by the 14th, two days sooner than anticipated, they were on the Dyle where they joined up with the Belgians falling back from their covering line. The Belgian army now deployed from Antwerp to Louvain; next to it was the BEF; and further south the 1st, 9th and 2nd French armies. Here they waited for the main German assault. It never came.

The subsequent fortunes of the Belgians are linked to the actions or inactions of the French army. As early as March intelligence had informed the French General Staff of an increase from 23 to nearly 50 German divisions facing the Ardennes, including seven Panzer divisions. This was confirmed on the night of May 8/9 by French aircraft out on a leaflet-dropping mission over Germany; at this late date the Allies were still trying to transform the Germans into Quakers. The pilots reported seeing German armored columns, 60 miles long , their headlights on, bound for the Ardennes. When on May 10 Rundstedt's phalanxes crossed the border, they found some toppled trees and scattered mines but no opposition, neither Belgian nor French . And yet it was ideal country for delaying tactics , harassing fire, and ambushes. The German tanks and vehicles were hemmed in on primitive, narrow roads abutted on both sides by forested hills. They were even vulnerable to hand weapons, not to speak of artillery and air attack. None materialized. General Blummentritt later commented, "This advance through the Ardennes was not an operation in the tactical sense but an approach march" (Goutard, 118). The Ardennes presented the Germans with no more than a traffic problem.

On the afternoon of May 12 the Panzers emerged from the Ardennes, 24 hours ahead of schedule, approaching the Meuse on a front of 80 miles. The German battering ram consisted of three Panzer corps: Hoth at the northern end and Reinhardt in the center, each with two Panzer divisions, and in the south, opposite Sedan, Guderian with three Panzer divisions. The bridges on the Meuse had been blown and the river with its wooded steep banks was lined with pillboxes, flak batteries and artillery positions. Assisted by Stukas, Guderian struck the initial blow at the junction of the 2nd and 9th armies. The French broke without giving battle, the flak crews abandoning their guns, some troops fleeing the moment they saw German tanks, others at the mere rumor of their approach. The officers followed their men in flight, infecting with panic the troops in the rear. After storming the Meuse on rubber boats, four bridgeheads were established across the river on the 13th and engineers immediately began to build pontoon bridges. Some French artillery tried to interfere but it did not stop the Germans; 24 French bombers attacked and were all shot down. That same evening, when General Beaufre, a member of the General Staff, saw Georges—the effective commander of the fighting front—he saw a broken man mumbling, "There has been a collapse." He then fell into sobbing.

Tuesday, May 14, was the fatal day in the campaign. Debouching from the bridgehead at Sedan an avalanche of tanks broke into French open country. Near Sedan the Meuse runs east-west so the breakthrough was first directed south. But as soon as the Panzers were across the river they turned west, their left flank leaning on the Aisne and Somme rivers. Guderian's tanks were soon joined by those of Hoth who broke through at Dinant creating a 60-mile breach in the French lines. The total might of the three armored phalanxes, nearly 2,000 tanks strong, struck the 9th Army of General Corap. The army disintegrated and northern France was open to the invaders. As the seven Panzer divisions, three columns abreast, raced ahead, the French armies on either side of the armored wedge merely retracted in parallel with the Panzer corridor neither interfering with their movement nor counterattacking the enemy's flanks. On the 15th, the diary of the 9th French Army reads, "No information—communications cut—liaison unworkable—back areas blocked with convoys and wrecked columns—petrol trains in flames—wholesale chaos" (Chapman, 152)—blitzkrieg incarnate which Gamelin opined could never happen in France. On the same day General Corap was replaced by Giraud. This was a typical scapegoat gesture, for neither General Huntziger to the south nor General Blanchard to the north attempted to deal with the collapse of Corap's 9th Army. The day was capped with a telephone call from Reynaud to an incredulous Churchill informing him that they were beaten. "Last evening," said the French premier, "we lost the battle" (Kaufmann, 230).

As in Poland, the four Allies neither singly nor together managed to stage a single attack that would have achieved some operational objective, nor any maneuver that would have interfered with the Germans' advance or timetable. In fact the Poles did better, when Kutrzeba's flank attack at the Bzura did deflect the Germans from their attack on Warsaw and delayed its capture by a week or so. Soon the Germans' Panzer wedge was extended to a length of 175 miles. In addition, the tanks were so far ahead of the infantry that it would have taken the latter days to catch up. It was thus not beyond the strategic thoughts of a small boy playing at soldiers to conceive of what was required; cut the head of the snake attached to the body by a mere thread. The very daring of the Sichelschnitt made such an operation almost self-demanding. Here was this narrow German wedge, head and body not quite connected, while to the north and south, lurked massive concentrations of enemy troops— 50 divisions in the north and 40 to the south. And indeed Gamelin did plan such a pinching stroke in the area of Arras where the Panzer corridor was no more than 25 miles wide. But before he got going he was replaced on May 19 by Weygand, a more assertive though older man. On the same day Marshal Pétain was called into the cabinet so that the two might put some life into the crumbling republic.

Later on there were fierce debates about the strategic mistakes committed by the French Command in the campaign; if only they had done this or that they might have prevailed, or won a stalemate. From the performance of both the troops and the generals this seems to be an empty post-mortem. When one reads the reports of the top- and lower-echelon commanders why they failed either to resist or attack the reasons consist of one of the following: the troops were not ready, there was a shortage of fuel or ammunition, their neighbor did not cooperate, the orders arrived late or not at all. Thus it was never an essential operational factor—defeat in battle, enemy superiority, poor tactics, or bad luck—that defeated the French but trivia that are a systemic part of any military organization; they might as well have claimed that their soldiers lacked shoes. Judging by the performance of the French military, the German army would have probably defeated the Allies even if it had fought according to its original Gelb plan, with the main effort on the northern wing. One can even argue that its victory would have been even greater because by pushing the Allied armies into the interior it would have prevented the evacuation of the BEF. From the performance of the 80 German commandos at Eben Emael one may speculate that the Wehrmacht would have won even had they struck the Maginot Line head-on. Breaches similar to those at Eben Emael could have been made on a wide scale in the forts of the Maginot Line through which the Panzers would have thrust into the interior of France. As subsequently agreed by nearly everyone, including the French themselves, the defeat was not due to strategic mistakes. It was a result of 20 years of civilian and military retreat from reality with a resultant sclerosis of will and competence. The defeatism of the French extended from the government and top military leadership down to the ordinary soldier and civilian. When at the beginning of the war it was suggested that the Allies float riparian mines in Germany, Daladier said he would resign if the project was adopted. The Germans simply could not keep up with the escaping French troops and when they did catch up they would disappear into civilian houses and barns. Brest, a powerful fortress which the Germans in their defeat in 1944 defended for two months, was taken from the French by a platoon of German motorcyclists. All localities with a population over 20,000 were declared open cities (Bloch, 131.) In many places when the troops did try to put up resistance the local residents objected that it would only end up in the destruction of their towns and villages; on the airfields peasants drove carts and lorries onto the runways to prevent French aircraft from taking off, fearing retaliation by the Stukas. A French officer was murdered by civilians for refusing to abandon the defense of a bridge over the Cher at Vierzon. On June 20 a French colonel who ordered his unit to break through encircling German forces was shot by his own men (Rings, 59). Even when it came to fighting the Italians the local authorities near Marseilles prevented 48 bombers from taking off, fearing a response by the Italian air force; General Vuillemin, commander in chief of the French air force, himself stopped the bombers from taking off for the same reason (Churchill Vol. 2, 299, 304). When the armistice was announced French officers clapped and tossed their caps into the air, jubilant it was all over. It was a most "democratic" collapse, extending as it did from the top leaders to the entire armed forces and the populace in general. The exact opposite was true with the Germans; when the troopers who took Eben Emael were interviewed how they felt about assaulting such a fortress, their leader said, "We were so enthused and charged that we felt we didn't need all the explosives. We could have taken the fort with grenades and rifles." (Mrazek, 65), which tells half the story; the other half was that they were given the best tools available. All this in contrast to the overall record of the West, for the British, in the various campaigns they subsequently fought and lost, performed little better than the Norwegians, the Dutch, the Belgians and the French.

On the evening of May 20, Guderian's tanks took Abbeville and a few hours later Noyelles on the coast. While the tankists, covered with oil and grime from 10 days of continuous battle splashed in the sea, Guderian pored over a serious problem; he was so much ahead of schedule that he knew not which way to turn, up or down. On the 21st orders arrived to go north and his tanks struck out along the coast toward Boulogne and Calais.

Weygand could think of nothing better than Gamelin's pinching attack at Arras and he fixed it for May 23. The forces assigned to it were the BEF and French troops that abutted the Belgian divisions. That night Billotte was injured in a car crash and died two days later. While a successor was being appointed the attack was postponed by another day. On that very day Gort reported that his part in the attack could amount to no more than a "sortie" as he didn't have enough ammunition; the truth was that by then he was already thinking about evacuating the BEF. When General Blanchard took Billotte's place the new date for the attack was rescheduled for May 27. While all this was going on, the Germans on May 24 captured Arras. As if relieved, Weygand cabled Blanchard, "If this [capture of Arras] makes operation as ordered impossible, try to form as big a bridgehead as possible covering Dunkirk" (Goutard, 24). Thus the single contemplated counterattack died before it was born.

With the German breakthrough at Sedan the floor had been pulled from under the Allied forces at the Dyle. Henceforth they kept retreating, first to the Scheldt and then to the Lys River. After the failure to launch the Arras counterattack, the Belgians quickly pulled back to the north, opening a big gap between themselves and the Allies. By then the idea of capitulation had already crystallized in King Leopold's mind. On May 27 he requested an armistice. The führer demanded unconditional surrender. The king accepted and the Belgian army laid down its arms at 4 A.M. of May 28. The king's decision was taken without consulting his allies (DDR, XV,152) and against the wishes of his government which, as a constitutional monarch, he was bound to obey. His apologia was that as commander in chief he wanted to share the fate of his troops. This was somewhat of a sham for while half a million Belgian soldiers were marched off to POW stockades, the king moved to the Chateau de Lacken where he was allotted a retinue of 20 courtiers and 100 or so servants and he later found the times appropriate to marry his second wife. The Belgian populace acclaimed him a hero while its government in London, which urged continued resistance, was vilified. However, when the Allies won the war the Belgians drove King Leopold from the throne.

Though the BEF under General Gort was subject to French command the two governments had originally agreed that should Gort feel the French placed his troops in any sort of peril, he had the right to appeal to London. It was a wise stipulation for soon enough Gort felt that his BEF was in for disaster. When the Germans took Abbeville, the British troops started planning for a withdrawal to the coast and the Admiralty in London began mobilizing ships for their evacuation. By May 24 the northern armies had been compressed into a triangular enclave with its base at the coast astride Dunkirk, some 60 miles wide, and its apex at Valenncienes, 70 miles inland. This salient was being attacked by Army Group B from the east and by Army Group A's Panzer divisions from both west and south. It was at this point—with the British readying for reembarkation—that an order arrived from Hitler—for Army Group A to cease its offensive, the famous "halt order," the motives for which have been and are a matter of controversy. The various reasons given for having issued it are: It was not Hitler but Rundstedt who originated it, a version the latter denied; Hitler wanted to save his Panzers for operations at the Somme; the canal-crossed and water-logged terrain was not suitable for armor; Göring had persuaded Hitler to let him finish the job, thus garnering glory for the Luftwaffe; Hitler wanted to spare the Flemish population the havoc of battle; and variations thereof. There is no evidence whatever of Hitler citing any of the above as reason for the halt order; they are also out of character with Hitler or his generals. There is, however, much recorded verbiage from the führer, spoken at the time and on later occasions, that it was his wish and will to spare England the humiliation of defeat and thus promote peace. These sentiments are contained in the following utterances:

• Halder's diary quotes Hitler saying on May 21, "We are seeking contact with England on the basis of a division of the world."
• According to General Blumentritt's recollections, at Charlesville on May 24 where Hitler met Rundstedt and confirmed the halt order, "Hitler was in a very good humor ... and gave his opinion that the war would be over in six weeks. After that he wished to conclude a reasonable peace with France and the way would be free for an agreement with Britain.... He concluded by saying that his aim was to make peace with Britain on a basis that she would regard as compatible with her honor to accept" (Shirer 1959, 734).
• Ribbentrop's representative at the führer's headquarters left on record the following remarks: "Hitler personally intervened to allow the British to escape. He was convinced that to destroy this army would be to force them to fight to the bitter end."
• Toward the end of his career, reminiscing to his intimate circle about things that went wrong, Hitler said in February 1945, "Churchill was quite unable to appreciate the sporting spirit of which I had given proof by refraining from creating an irreparable breach between Britain and ourselves. We did indeed refrain from annihilating them at Dunkirk" (Lukaczs 1991, 80,86).

Perhaps what is most relevant is not what a given general or some quotation may imply, but how the unquestionable fact of having stopped the Panzer offensive against the BEF

British prisoners taken at Dunkirk, June 1940. (Courtesy the National Archives.)

when it was ripe for plucking fits in with the overall strategy of the führer who had single-handedly dictated the course of German history for the past eight years, including the ongoing war. As will be related in Chapter 11, already in May an impatient Hitler had rebounded to his basic Weltanschaung and taken up again his plans for a crusade against the East. Assured of victory in France, he had already started musing about preparations for war against Russia. Tied to this with an almost atavistic chord was the issue of peace with England, as it had been all along. Set against a 20-year-old history of the führer's innermost obsessions and intentions, there seems no escape from concluding that the halt order was one more step in his campaign to induce England to make peace with him.

The British, unaware of the führer's good intentions (actually there is one claim that Hitler deliberately sent the halt order in the clear and that the British did intercept it) frantically utilized the days of reprieve to escape. They erected strong defenses around their coastal perimeter and from bases in England Spitfires appeared in force to protect the troops on the beaches and the ships in the Channel. The evacuation started on May 27 reaching a peak of 68,000 men embarked on May 31. On that day the size of the enclave had shrunk to five miles in depth and 20 miles along the coast. The Germans bombed Dunkirk, killing some 3,000 civilians, even though the actual embarkations were taking place not in the port but from the outlying beaches. By midnight of June 1 the entire BEF was back in England; on the following two days it was mostly French troops that were taken off. The Germans entered Dunkirk on June 4, taking prisoner 40,000 men that had covered the withdrawal. This marked the end of Operation Sichelschnitt.

On June 3 the führer transferred his headquarters to Bruly de Peche, a Belgian village that had been cleared of its inhabitants. Hitler wanted to be close to the scene of action when the coup-de-grace was administered to the enemy. The new headquarters was named Wolfschlucht (Wolf's Gorge); on Hitler's orders Felsennest was to be made into a national monument (Warlimont, 101). The attack on the Aisne-Somme line, defended by 50 second-rate French divisions, had been scheduled for June 5. The Panzer divisions as they raced for the sea had the presence of mind to establish bridgeheads south of the rivers and these now served as staging areas for 163 German divisions, including all their Panzer formations. There is little to say about the course of that battle. Within a few days the Germans were across the Somme and inundated France in every possible direction. The French army dissolved as the Germans took city after city, entering Paris on June 14.

What is of interest are some of the political reactions attending the death throes of the Third Republic. The first notable event was Italy's joining the war. Il Duce, as usual, was torn between his Latin temperament and envy of Teutonic prowess. Eyeing the drama in northern France he saw a loophole to resolve this dichotomy; he would start a war that would be over by the time he joined it. At the end of May he informed Hitler that he was ready to march on June 5; he was advised to hold off for a while. Mussolini had ambitions to inherit French and British possessions in the Mediterranean, whereas Hitler's mind was on peace and Il Duce's demands would cause complications. Trying to forestall Italy's entry into the war, Halifax on May 25 informed Il Duce that England would meet any of his "reasonable demands" and that Italy would be treated as one of the victors (Cadogan, 289). Roosevelt, too, tried his hand. On May 26 he inquired of Il Duce what were his demands in the Mediterranean, or elsewhere; he, Roosevelt, was prepared to pass these on to the Allies. Forewarned, Mussolini refused to receive Ambassador Phillips carrying the president's message and it had to be given to Ciano. When no reply was received, Phillips was instructed on May 30 to see Ciano and inform him that Italy's entry into the war would constitute "a hostile act against the USA," intimating that eventually America would find itself ranged against the Axis. On June 1 Ciano had to inform Phillips that Mussolini rejected the thesis that Italy's going to war would affect American interests; that if the USA wanted to fight the Axis it was her business; and that Il Duce requested not to receive "any further pressure" from Roosevelt (Peace and War, 536–8). On June 10 Italy declared war on France and England.

As the situation catapulted toward catastrophe, the French government did things that merely reflected the despondency of its leaders. Several times they appealed to America for aid — thousands of guns, tanks and airplanes to be shipped immediately to stave off defeat. On June 14 Reynaud sent Roosevelt a last and desperate cable stating, "if you cannot give France in the coming days a positive assurance that the US will come into the struggle within a short space of time … you will then see France go under" (Shirer 1971, 805). The French were told this was an impossible request and, aside from speeding up orders already placed with American factories, there was little the USA can do. But though disengaging itself from its woes, still America had something to ask of France. On June 17, with French surrender in the wings, Roosevelt demanded that under no circumstance should the French hand over their fleet to the Germans. If they did, the message read, this would mean the end of American friendship, the end of the French Empire, and France would not be admitted to the circle of victors at the end of the war (Peace and War, 538). The French government assured Roosevelt that the fleet would not be surrendered.

The strangest step the French took occurred on May 28. Minister of Public Works De Mezieres approached the French Communist Party — outlawed since the Nazi-Soviet Pact — to join in the war effort (in Communist jargon an imperialist war). Its response was that if France was serious it should fire all appeasers in the government and the General Staff, arm a civil militia, erect barricades in Paris, and so on — a hint of how in the future the various Communist undergrounds would fight the Germans. Moreover, De Mezieres and Air Minister Laurent Eynach sent an official note to Moscow saying that since a defeat of France would have the direst consequences for the Soviet Union, they were appealing for help, particularly aircraft; Pierre Cot, a former minister of the Popular Front, was ready to go to Moscow. The startling thing was that Moscow agreed to such talks (Fonvieille-Alquier, 181–7).

There had also been a series of appeals to England to increase her share in the fighting, primarily by sending over more squadrons of airplanes held on the island. With good reason the English would not comply as, in case of France's defection, only the fighter command and the navy stood between them and the Germans. But it created resentment and acrimony. Thus when after the evacuation of the BEF Churchill kept pressing France to remain in the war and fight from North Africa, such appeals seemed facetious in French eyes. Churchill even went to the point of proposing a Franco-British union. Whatever else it meant, it certainly meant continuation of the war and was ignored by the French cabinet, which was thinking along entirely different lines.

On June 10 the French government left Paris and transferred to Bordeaux. On the 16th Reynaud resigned and the premiership was taken over by Marshal Pétain, a man who remembered better fighting days and who despised France's prewar political system. With Bordeaux about to fall into German hands Pétain on

French civilians watching German troops enter Paris on June 14, 1940. (Courtesy the National Archives.)

June 17 asked the Spanish Embassy to pass on to the Germans French readiness for an armistice. For two days there was no reply; Hitler was conferring in Munich with Mussolini about conditions to be submitted even though Hitler already had in his pocket a draft of the proposed terms. At 6.25 A.M. on June 19 the French were notified of the Germans' readiness to conclude an armistice.

* * *

About a hundred miles northeast of Paris the Forest of Compiegne contained a French national shrine. In a clearing ringed with cypresses rose a statue of Marshal Foch, savior of France in 1914; a museum housed a Pullman car in which the German delegation signed the armistice of 1918; and inscribed slabs commemorated the Allies' blood-drenched struggle to stop the Germans in World War I. In June 1940 Hitler chose this spot to have the French sign their submission to Germany.

On June 19 Army engineers arrived and demolished one wall of the museum in which Foch's wagon-lit was kept. They pushed the car out onto the now rusty tracks to the same spot where it had stood on November 11, 1918. At 3:15 P.M. on June 21 a convoy of cars came down the shaded lanes of the forest and out of his Mercedes stepped Adolf Hitler. He was followed by Göring, Raeder, Brauchitsch, Keitel, Ribbentrop and Hess, all in uniform. Hitler's car had stopped near a plaque commemorating the liberation of Alsace-Lorraine but it was covered with swastika flags so he didn't see it. But when entering the clearing he stumbled upon a 3-foot high granite memorial which in chiseled large letters proclaimed:

> Here on the 11 of November, 1918 succumbed the criminal pride of the German Empire vanquished by the free peoples which it tried to enslave.

Hitler read the inscription then silently walked toward Foch's railroad car. Eyeing it he fell into a familiar pose, hands on hips, legs firmly spread apart. Then he climbed into the car, seating himself in the chair Foch had sat in. On either side of him ranged his companions. Across the table four empty chairs awaited the French delegation.

The French emissaries were General Huntziger of the 2nd Army; air force General Bergeret; Vice Admiral Le Luc; and Leon Noel, erstwhile ambassador to Poland, the only man in civilian dress. They had left Bordeaux the previous day, had stayed overnight in Paris and were then taken north without being told where. The sight of the Compiegne clearing was a shock that they were barely able to conceal as they passed a company of German soldiery who stood to attention but did not present arms. At exactly 3:30 they entered Foch's car. The Germans rose, Hitler, imitated by Ribbentrop and Hess, giving the Nazi salute. When all were seated Keitel read the preamble to the armistice. Neither before nor afterward did Hitler speak and as soon as the reading was over, he left. As Hitler strode toward his car a military band struck up "Deutschland Über Alles," followed by the "Horst Wessel Lied."

That evening and on the following day Keitel, assisted by Jodl, discussed with the Frenchmen the 24 clauses of the armistice. The Germans had stipulated that these could not be argued or modified; the French could only ask for clarifications. The French delegates were actually not authorized to sign; they had been told to convey the terms to the government, which alone could approve it. The text was passed on across the still belligerent armies by telephone. The cabinet's debate of the armistice terms dragged on through the day; an added twist was that General Huntziger, head of the delegation, did not want to be "authorized" but "ordered" to sign. At 6:30 an impatient Keitel issued an ultimatum giving the French one hour to decide, whereupon Huntziger was told to sign. This took place at 6:50 P.M. on June 22.

The agony of the Frenchmen was not over yet; the agreement was to take effect only after an armistice with the Italians had been signed. The French delegates were therefore taken by plane to Rome. There, with Ciano presiding, a French-Italian armistice was concluded. The Italians retained several hundred yards of French territory they had conquered in their 10-day war; and a 50-mile demilitarized zone was imposed on the French side of the border. This was signed at 6:35 P.M. of June 24. Six hours later, a little after midnight of June 24-25, the guns fell silent throughout France.

The major clauses of the armistice stipulated:

- A demarcation line was drawn from the Swiss border through Tours parallel to the Atlantic coast to the Spanish border. The territory south of that line, enclosing about 40 percent of France, was to remain unoccupied with Pétain's government in charge.
- The fleet was left in French hands with those in home ports to be immobilized under German supervision. The Germans made a "solemn promise" not to seize them.
- The nearly 2 million French POWs were to remain in camps; Frenchmen were forbidden to take up arms against Germany.
- The French armed forces were to be demobilized except for the requirements of internal security.

Although the stipulation was not to try to modify the text, one item the French objected to was a requirement to hand over all refugees from Germany residing in France or anywhere in its possessions; this embraced a motley group of socialists, pacifists, labor leaders, intellectuals and Jews. Another clause the French wanted to modify was that instead of handing over all their aircraft, they ground them. It is a striking example of the führer's mindset that while he agreed to changing the airplane clause — which meant a loss of 1,000 or 2,000 military machines— Hitler refused to eliminate the clause about the refugees. Later on the Vichy regime with great zeal rounded up hundreds of these people and shipped them back to Germany and the executioner's ax.

At his meeting with Hitler about the armistice Mussolini had put forward a plethora of demands; he intended to occupy the south of France; he wanted to have its fleet; occupation of Corsica, Tunisia, Dijbouti and Malta; and an outlet to the Atlantic across Morocco. Hitler brushed all this aside and told Il Duce that they must at all costs prevent France from continuing the war from North Africa. Real as it was, this was not the main reason for Hitler's treating the French kindly. The bigger theme was spelled out by Ribbentrop who told Ciano in great confidence that the führer's conditions for peace had already been conveyed to England via Sweden. Struck by this news— only 10 days after Italy went to war to capture the French and British empires— Ciano asked, "Does Germany at the present moment prefer peace or the prosecution of war?" Ribbentrop's point-blank answer was "Peace" (Bullock 1962, 590).

For a change Ribbentrop had told Ciano the truth. The restrained terms of the French-German armistice were certainly motivated by a desire to see France leave the war. But the bigger objective in Hitler's overall strategy, as we shall see later, was the conflict with Great Britain. With France out of the war there seemed now to be no choice for England but to quit. Hitler was determined to do everything to facilitate it and his restraint with France

Table 9-1
Casualties in the Western Campaign during May-June 1940

Country	Killed	Wounded	POWs (millions)	Duration of fighting (days)
Germany	27,500	110,00	0.018	43
France	90,000	200,000	1.9	43
England	3,500–6,500	20,000	0.015	21
Belgium	7,500	15,800	0.5	18
Holland	2,900	6,900	0	4
Total Allies	105,00	353,000	2.4	86

Based on Perrett, 54; Shirer 1971, 909; Kaufman, 308

was one such step, a hint that he would be quite magnanimous in terminating the war with England.

Mussolini, no more than others, never caught on to the führer's grand design. Consequently, after only 10 days of comradeship-in-arms, he was reduced to the role of the paltry retainer he was to remain for the duration. After he was forced to relinquish all his demands, he sent the following message, "Führer: In order to facilitate the acceptance of the armistice by the French I have not included ... the occupation of the left side of the Rhone, or of Corsica, Tunis and Dijbouti , as we had intended at Munich. I have limited myself to a minimum — a demilitarized zone of 50 km. For the rest, I have used the clauses of the German armistice" (Shirer 1971, 909).

Some time after signing the armistice the three-foot slab commemorating the Allies' victory in 1918 was, on Hitler's orders, dynamited and Foch's historic wagon-lit dragged to Berlin where it perished in a bombing raid. In France Marshal Pétain proclaimed June 25 a day of national mourning.

The casualties suffered by the belligerents in the Western campaign of 1940 are shown in Table 9-1. The defeat of the four allies cost Germany 27,000 killed and 110,000 wounded. It inflicted about three to four times that number on the Allies. The Germans took over 2 million prisoners, later to be converted into forced labor to toil for the success of the Third Reich.

CHAPTER 10

The Aftershocks

The elimination of France from the war constituted Hitler's one true strategic victory in World War II. Aside from its being his greatest military achievement, he came close to ending the war. It generated an earthquake which shifted the ground under countries large and small, all the way from America to the Far East. It was Hitler's greatest triumph, and he reached during June the peak of power and glory, a warlord possessed of a seemingly infallible historical prescience. The German people were ecstatic and the adulation of the führer reached godlike proportions. Flags were ordered flown for 10 days and church bells tolled for a week throughout Germany. Hitler returned home to frenzied ovations from the crowds such as the Nazi leader, who had seen plenty of them, had never encountered.

Hitler had opened the Western campaign with two objectives in mind. One was to eliminate the French army as a military threat in the west, just as he had gone to war in Norway to forestall the allies from establishing a foothold in the north. This was in line with his master plan to avoid fighting on two fronts when the time came to start his crusade in the East. The second objective was to induce England to quit by depriving her of a continental army to fight the war for her. While he was quite certain of defeating the French, the peace angle had been only a hope. Given the scale and speed of France's collapse hope became an expectation, at times a certainty. France was eliminated not only on the continent — she was out of the war. England had been deprived of French Mediterranean bases in North Africa and the Middle East while Italy joined in the war; the occupation of the Channel and Atlantic coasts grievously jeopardized British home security, the first by bringing the Luftwaffe to her doorstep, the latter by opening the Atlantic to U-boats and surface raiders— Germany's most cherished naval dream come true; and new dangers loomed in the Far East. There seemed to be no prospect for the British to continue the fight.

There followed now the dizziest peace offensive the war had seen. Pacifist doves took wing as soon as Sichelschnitt tasted the cool ocean breeze at Abbeville on May 20. Jodl noted in his diary on that day that Hitler "is working on a peace treaty" (Shirer 1959, 727). On May 30 Dr. Carl Clodius of the Foreign Ministry was instructed to prepare drafts of peace treaties not only with France but with England, too (DDR, XV 231). Hitler raced ahead of himself. Brushing aside Italy's territorial demands on France, Hitler made plans to offer England whatever she wanted of the French Empire, once she sat down to talk peace (Hillgruber 1965, 144).

German moves aimed at terminating the war ranged far and wide. On May 28, the British ambassador to Japan, Robert Craigie, reported that he had met Japan's foreign minister, who broached the subject of peace with Germany. On June 14 Hitler received the chief correspondent of the Hearst press, Karl von Wiegand, and talked to him at length about

Adolf Hitler in Paris, June 28, 1940; on the left is Albert Speer. (Courtesy the National Archives.)

his readiness to end the war. "I want—he said—peace with England. You know I have always wanted it." In his diary of July 13, Halder notes, "The Führer is obsessed with the question why England does not yet want to take the road to peace…. If we smash England militarily the British Empire will disintegrate…. With German blood we would achieve something from which only Japan, America and others will derive profit" (Shirer 1959,

748–52). This is quite revealing in connection with the controversy whether Hitler ever meant to invade England, aside from the fact that he never attempted it. It shows that even if he could, he wouldn't have wanted it because in his view the existence of the British Empire was a must and no one, not even Germany, could replace it. The ambassador to Sweden, Victor Mallet, had been approached by a Dr. Weissauer, reportedly a secret emissary of Hitler's, which Halifax reported to the war cabinet on September 11; and as late as January 20,1941, the British minister to Berne reported talks between Göring and a Swedish courier, Carl Barde, about peace moves (Churchill Papers Vol. 1:99, Vol. 3:100). To assist in all this the Germans indulged in a bit of appeasement of their own. On Hitler's orders a planned victory parade in Paris was called off; Göring's proposal to retaliate for British bombing attacks on Germany was vetoed; and when on July 2 Mussolini offered Hitler troops and planes for an invasion of England the führer ignored it (Ciano, 272).

Hitler planned to deliver a victory speech before the Reichstag but kept postponing it, hoping to hear good news from the British. But except for rumors and wishful mongering nothing concrete materialized. So Hitler set July 19 for the event, a day when as victorious warlord he would officially proffer peace, similar to that of October 6, 1939, after he had wiped Poland off the map. The speech lasted two hours and 20 minutes and mixed pride of achievement with generosity of spirit. During the ceremony he had 12 of his generals mount the podium and promoted them to the rank of feldmarschall. This was accompanied by his statesmanlike call for an end to bloodshed. Said Hitler, "It almost causes me pain to think that I should have been selected by Fate to deal the final blow to the structure which these men [Churchill, et al.] have already set tottering…. In this hour I feel it to be my duty before my own conscience to appeal once more to reason and common sense in Great Britain as much as elsewhere. I consider myself in a position to make this appeal since I am not the vanquished begging favors, but the victor speaking in the name of reason. I can see no reason why this war must go on" (Bullock 1962, 592). The official British reply came on July 22. In a broadcast to the nation Halifax announced that Britain would not make peace with a Hitler ruling over a subjugated Europe.

Still the peace doves kept fluttering to and fro. One of the British complaints was that Hitler's peace offer gave no hint of terms or conditions. So on July 24 Göring approached Albert Plesman, head of the KLM, offering specifics; it was the usual partnership with Britain in exchange for a free hand in the East. Utilizing Swedish Embassy channels this message reached London at the end of August in the middle of the Battle of Britain. Then came the Windsor game, the Germans having gotten it into their heads that the Duke's unorthodox views and personal resentment would make him turn against his homeland. Finally there was the Hess-Haushofer interlude which was to end eight months later with the deputy führer's sensational flight to Scotland. On September 8 Hess inquired of Haushofer, a German expert on geopolitics, whom he would suggest as contacts in Great Britain for an approach about ending the war. Among various names the Duke of Hamilton was mentioned. On the 23rd Haushofer was prevailed upon to write a letter to the duke but received no answer. That very autumn Hess started taking flying lessons eventually to become the most famous peace buzzard attempting to strike a deal with the British.

There was considerable activity by outsiders; by the apostolic delegate to Britain, Godfrey, which elicited only silence; by Inönu from Turkey; and several from Switzerland. The Swedish king, too, had written to King George VI with an urgent appeal to restore peace to which Churchill replied that the efforts of "the ignominious King of Sweden as a peace maker after his desertion of Finland (to the Russians) and of Norway (to the Germans) …

is singularly distasteful" (Churchill Papers Vol. 2, 603). Strangely, it was the presumed impartiality of these "neutrals" which alienated Hitler. He suspected that in their professed fairness they might dig up taboo issues, such as the restoration of Czechoslovakia or Poland. Hitler, therefore, ignored third-party offers. He wanted direct talks with the British who, he thought, would be more susceptible to his unholy mixture of love for their empire and hatred of Slavs.

There is one note to add to this picture of Hitler begging for peace. One can find here and there contrary statements, asserting Germany's dismissal of peace talks and threats to crush England. This was a tactic reminiscent of the German vocabulary when talking to Sumner Welles. If the Allies wanted war Germany was ready and the Allies would be sorry. In Hitler's talk with Alfieri; with Ciano on July 7; and in Weizsäcker lecture to Foreign Office personnel; in all these instances the message was that Germany would demolish England the way it had demolished France. This was to show that the alternative to peace was tackling an infallible führer and an invincible Third Reich. The crux of the matter was whether the British believed that the führer was infallible and the reich invincible. Evidently not.

* * *

The period of May–June 1940 was the most fateful in the history of World War II. It was during these two months that the question whether the war was to continue or to be wound up was decided. This choice was made by the British, due primarily to the stewardship of Winston Churchill.

On October 28, 1937, just before Hitler started his series of conquests, Britain's Imperial Defense Committee had reviewed the country's strategic situation. The cogent part of its report reads, "Without overlooking the assistance which we should hope to obtain from France and possibly other allies, we cannot foresee the time when our defense forces will be strong enough to safeguard our territory, trade and vital interests against Germany, Italy and Japan simultaneously" (Colvin 1971, 64). This was somber enough. Now with the collapse of France a still graver situation developed. While the General Staff concluded that a sufficiently strong air arm in combination with the Home Fleet should be able to repulse a German invasion, England's ability to defeat Germany was another matter altogether. The consensus of the British leaders seems to have been that England alone could not do it. Moreover, the defeat of France and Holland left their possessions in Indochina and the Dutch East Indies up for grabs. These areas brimmed with oil and other natural resources the Japanese both needed and coveted as part of their Asian coprosperity empire. It was thus only a matter of time before the Japanese would move into these territories and on the way step on British toes in Malaya, the Indian subcontinent, and elsewhere. There was, therefore, a good chance that England would shortly face Japan, too, a hopeless case for Britain.

Even the assessment that Britain could fend off an invasion was hedged by reservations. Britain depended on overseas imports not only for raw materials but also for food. With a war on, England would have to defend its sea lanes practically throughout the globe and foremost in the Atlantic and the Mediterranean. Even with Britain's powerful navy the call on warships and merchant vessels was likely to be beyond her means, particularly with the French west coast available to German U-boats. In addition, England after only one year of warmaking was financially bankrupt; the Treasury had already informed the Cabinet that after December England would be unable to pay for the armaments she had ordered in the USA (Reynolds, 147). Thus even if England could defend itself against an invasion, it did not answer the crushing question how she would defeat Hitler and, even if she did no fighting, how she would withstand a drawn-out conflict. Even with France at her side Britain had not felt strong enough to conduct a fighting war the way the Allies had done in World War I. A week after war broke out, Chamberlain wrote to his sister, "What I hope is not a military victory—I very much doubt the feasibility of that—but a collapse of the German home front." This he repeated in a letter to Roosevelt on October 4, 1939 (Reynolds, 74). In December 1939 Halifax echoed Chamberlain by stating that without the French "we should not be able to carry on the war by ourselves" (Lukacs 1991, 92). Ejected from the continent, without an army to speak of, there was seemingly no way for England to continue the war.

The straits in which Britain found itself in May 1940 produced a serious crisis in the cabinet. A peace faction emerged advocating the war be terminated. These were the same men who had produced the late '30s appeasement policy, had led England into war and instituted the Sitzkrieg. Chief among them were Halifax, supported by Butler, his undersecretary; Chamberlain, now lord president; Lothian, ambassador to the USA; Sir Samuel Hoare, ambassador to Spain; and the gray eminences John Simon and Horace Wison. Already in mid–May Churchill had been told by Reynaud that France had lost the war. Following Holland, Belgium had capitulated, the BEF was evacuating, and the French were talking surrender. On May 15, the day Reynaud had called, Chamberlain offered his view that without France he could not see how England could go on, for she would be "fighting only for better terms, not victory." On May 25 Halifax drafted a letter to Roosevelt aimed at obtaining peace terms from Hitler. The letter asked that the president warn Hitler that if his terms jeopardized England's independence, the USA would throw all its might against him (Reynolds, 103,109). Churchill held up the letter. Through the next two days, May 27 and 28, the cabinet met numerous times to debate the issue of war and peace. The occasion was the arrival of Reynaud with a proposal that Mussolini be approached about asking Germany for peace terms. Halifax tabled his view, that, provided Britain's independence was guaranteed, England should terminate the war. He agreed with Reynaud that Mussolini be asked to find out what Hitler's terms were. Halifax urged that the appeal be made before France fell, for later the conditions would most likely be harsher. It was a disingenuous formulation because Halifax knew very well that, far from wanting to deprive England of her independence, Hitler was compulsive about becoming her ally and defender; the clause about independence was sugarcoating for the motion to pass. In this sort of doubletalk Halifax found in Churchill more than his equal. Churchill's answer was that he would not take the initiative in asking for terms, because it would show weakness; however, if the terms were known he would consider them, hence producing a paradox: England would be willing to settle if the terms were favorable; however, asking for terms would elicit harsh terms; therefore no satisfactory offer could be obtained by asking. Churchill reinforced his argument by adding that if England fought and achieved some successes it would be in a position to insist on a better deal. The war cabinet, consisting as it did of five men — Churchill, Halifax, Chamberlain and the two Labour ministers Attlee and Greenwood — was split. Churchill then interrupted the May 28 meeting and convened the full British cabinet where he succeeded in persuading them to continue the fight. With this decision Churchill had no difficulty in having Chamberlain half switch to his view. The Labour Party members in the cabinet, too, came down on Churchill's side. Reynaud then had to be informed that

Britain would not participate in asking for terms. Still this was not the end of the struggle for on June 17, with Halifax's knowledge, Butler conferred with Bjoern Prytz, the Swedish minister to London, telling him, "No opportunity would be neglected for conducting a compromise peace" (Lukacs 2001, 182; 1991, 132). Prytz passed this on to Stockholm adding his own view that Halifax might soon replace Churchill. It was probably this exchange that Ribbentrop referred to when he told Ciano about the Swedish contact. Also in late July when Lothian got wind that Halifax was about to deliver a major speech he telephoned "wildly" from Washington begging Halifax not to say anything that might foreclose the door to peace (Nicolson, 104). As stated, on July 22 Halifax officially rejected Hitler's bid for peace.

What then was the basis for Churchill's determination to go on with the war? Alone, without allies, without an army, financially broke, facing the Wehrmacht just across the Channel, what made him ready to face down the Germans? The answer is—the USA. Churchill realized that England by herself had no chance of continuing, not to say, winning the war and concluded that the only way to go on was to assume that sooner or later America would be drawn into the conflict. He set this down as an axiom of British policy and strategy. England, he postulated, must do everything possible to engage the USA; until then she must endure alone and carry whatever burden was imposed on her, for when the USA came in there would be no doubt about the outcome of the conflict. Even if this prognosis were a certainty it was a long-range view that required fortitude and steel nerves to simultaneously face the menace of a Hitler on England's doorstep and the fickleness of American politics involving as it did its president, Congress, the media and US public opinion. But, as Churchill saw it, this was England's strategic reality in the summer of 1940. From now on whatever helped draw America in would, on Churchill's orders, be done; as required, England would pose as either weak or strong; it would submit to any US demands and ignore the complaints of its generals, diplomats and Commonwealth members if these tended to jeopardize American support; it would take whatever the US offered and cede anything she demanded if this brought the hoped-for moment of US involvement a bit closer; and Churchill personally, as assertive and proud an Englishman he was, would subordinate himself to the dictates of the American president in order to promote an Anglo-American alliance.

In addition to sharing military and political plans with the Americans, this accommodation descended to the most personal level. When in early 1941 Roosevelt sent to London his confidant Harry Hopkins to review England's needs, Churchill on hearing his name asked "Who?" When enlightened, he ordered a Pullman railroad car to pick him up, with conductors wearing white gloves and refreshments and dinner served aboard the train — unheard of luxuries in wartime Britain. The very next day he was invited to 10 Downing Street to meet the prime minister where, by chance or design, the two hit it off splendidly. In his usual manner Churchill described the frail Hopkins as "a crumbling lighthouse from which there shone the beams that led great fleets to harbor" (Berthon, 97–8). Hopkins was able to report to FDR, "I have spent twelve evenings at Cherwell with Mr. Churchill dining, drinking and conversing on the most weighty issues, this in a addition of meeting Cabinet ministers and Commanders of the Armed Forces." Moved by the prime minister's lonely struggle Hopkins, entirely on his own, quoted to him from the Book of Ruth: "Whither thou goest I will go; and where thou lodgest I will lodge; thy people shall be my people" and very quietly added his own words, "Even to the end," whereupon Churchill burst into tears (Churchill Papers Vol. 3, 77, 91). Similar treatment was extended to other visiting Americans such as the US ambassador John Winant who, at the beginning of 1941, replaced the Anglophobe Joe Kennedy; and to Colonel Donovan, in England on a purely military mission, leading the natives to complain that evenings at Cherwell had turned into American parties.

The most conspicuous such hospitality was extended to Averell Harriman who had come to London on March 15 as chief expediter of Lend-Lease. Churchill literally took the man into his household. They dined and played cards together and weekends Harriman was repeatedly asked to come to Chequers. Harriman went to London accompanied by his daughter, who was lodged with young Pamela, recently married to Churchill's son, Randolph, sharing homes both in London and in a country house. These intimacies eventually led to Harriman becoming the lover of Churchill's daughter-in-law, Pamela. She would often relate to her father-in-law Harriman's views and opinions and he would compliment her on her efforts to improve Anglo-American relations. In later years there was acrimony between father and son, Randolph Churchill bemoaning that his parents "tolerated adultery under their own roof" (Abramson, 316).

One wonders, though, whether this total reliance on future American intervention was solely the product of Churchill's foresight or whether during the crucial months of May and June 1940 there had been an intimation or even commitment from Washington to that effect. Churchill and Roosevelt had started a correspondence soon after the outbreak of the war. It was an unusual exchange, private and secret, particularly so from the president's side. Was there behind Churchill's rocklike determination to stand fast a secret assurance that the USA would come into the war provided Britain held out? There is no such available evidence, although there is a report of Lothian cabling on May 27 that Roosevelt had told him that if Britain was *in extremis* the USA would come in (Brown, 256). This is a very unlikely piece of confidence from the kind of man Roosevelt was. Even if this or another such promise had been given, realistically it would have meant little for without public support and congressional approval Roosevelt could have done nothing to fulfill the role Churchill had unilaterally bestowed on the USA — declaring war.

There is a poignant scene described in Churchill's Papers (Vol. 2, p. 700) dated May 18, 1940. Churchill is shaving and his son Randolph comes to say goodbye before leaving for his assignment. Churchill turns to his son and says:

"I think I see my way through."

"Do you mean that we can avoid defeat? Or beat the bastards?"

"Of course I mean we can beat them."

"Well," said Randolph, "I'm all for it, but I don't see how you can do it."

With great intensity Churchill replied, "I shall drag the United States in."

With rising and resounding emphasis Churchill now launched a rhetorical campaign aimed both at his own people and the USA. Discarding the playful argument about asking or not asking for terms, reliance on the USA became the principal weapon against the peace advocates. Churchill kept forecasting that within weeks, months, after the November elections, or next year the USA would come into the war. This was to keep the British people in the fight although he must have known that at best its realization was a matter of years, if it was to happen at all. In nearly every speech and message he never failed to reach for the hearts and minds of America to convince them how much they would lose should England go under. To speed up the date of possible American participation, Churchill was prepared for nearly any sacrifice. Visiting the prime minister in August de Gaulle recalled the following exchange:

CHURCHILL (raising his fist): "So they [the Germans] won't come...."
DE GAULLE: "Are you in such a hurry to see your towns smashed to bits?"
CHURCHILL: "You see, the bombing of Oxford, Coventry, Canterbury, will cause
such a wave of indignation in the US that they will come into the war" (Reynolds,
107).

Confronting Churchill's strategy was America's stance as dictated by its own moods
and interests. The starting point here, too, was the shock produced by the fall of France. A
safe and smug USA had been watching the conflict in Europe convinced that whatever
might befall England and France nothing serious was likely to strike America. Effectively,
the Americans had been spectators to a boxing match with no more commitment than an
occasional cheer for the preferred pugilist. Overnight — and perhaps to an exaggerated
degree — the Americans found themselves in perceived danger. The strategic gloom they
visualized was the following scenario. Germany would get hold of the French and British
fleets, which together with the Italian (and Japanese) navy, would surpass what the USA
could put to sea. German troops would secure the west coast of Africa abutting the shortest distance to South America, where Germany enjoyed support in a number of dictatorships, and among the sizeable German communities there. Its warships and long-range
bombers from France could reach the USA across the Atlantic. Thus German naval and air
power in combination with a subversion of South and Central America would pose a direct
threat to the USA, not to speak of the political, economic and cultural isolation were Europe
to become a Nazi dominion.

There were several conflicting currents in the American willingness and ability to provide help for England. One was the uncertain prognosis of England's survival. While everyone recognized that England had become for the USA what the Rhine had once been for
England — a forward bastion to be defended in its own interests — the question was whether
that position would hold. If the prospects looked good, then, of course, it should be supplied and strengthened. If the chances were slim then all the weaponry and munitions
plowed into it would be lost. The USA itself was at that period practically unarmed, having no more than a quarter of a million troops. Thus some people in the administration
advocated that all the weaponry America had and whatever came off the assembly lines be
kept for hemispheric defense. The view of others was that everything possible should be
done, even at risk, to bolster England, for she represented an irreplaceable forward base,
an unsinkable aircraft carrier, for the defense of the USA.

The other conflict resided in the president himself. Here a word must be said about
the personality of Franklin Delano Roosevelt. Perhaps a clue to his character can be inferred
from the fact that the man was either intensely disliked, even hated, or rapturously admired.
He was an opaque, devious politician par excellence, with no loyalty or sympathy for any
cause or individual, including his wife. In Harry Truman's words, "He was the coldest man
I ever met. He didn't give a damn personally for me or you or anyone else in the world"
(Meacham, xvii). In the familiar pattern of power hoarding he chose colorless associates,
a prime example being his wartime secretary of state, Cordell Hull. In June 1943, his eye
already on the 1944 elections, the president dismissed the undersecretary, Sumner Welles,
who effectively ran the State Department, and retained Hull who due to illness and temperament was a nonfunctioning secretary, but who was a heavyweight in the Democratic
machine and in Congress — this at a time when weighty issues of war and peace preoccupied the Allies vis-à-vis the Axis powers and the Soviet Union. When Churchill became
first lord of the Admiralty FDR initiated a correspondence with him writing inter alia, "I

want you to know that I shall at all times welcome it if you will keep me in touch personally with anything you want me to know." This launched an intimate correspondence that lasted throughout the war years. Yet his impression of Churchill was that of "a coarse, aggressive bibulous cad" (Brown, 260). At the time FDR started this correspondence, Churchill was on his way to become an illustrious warlord and statesman, a time when as in World War I England was expected to win and become the arbiter of the ensuing peace. After 1943 when the US was in the war as the major partner and Stalin emerged as the leading personality both as warrior and statesman, FDR sidled up to Stalin to the point of trying to arrange, behind Churchill's back, twosome meetings with the dictator to the chagrin and personal hurt of the prime minister. The same with de Gaulle. Churchill was considerably piqued by the pretensions and personality of Charles de Gaulle — a thorn in his side since June 1940. Yet he had admiration and sympathy if not for the man then for his cause. No such sentiments on the part of the president. He had no consideration for the loneliness and tragedy of the man or France in defeat. He made sneering remarks about him, called him Joan of Arc, or the "bride," and the reason for this neglect was that, as Stalin had said about the pope, "how many divisions does the Pope have?"; de Gaulle had no army and no political clout. The same went for the Poles. When elections were pending he told his Polish constituency he would be the prime defender of Polish interests. After winning the elections he dismissed it from his agenda. Churchill wept with Mikolajczyk when it became apparent that the Soviets were going to keep Poland's eastern territories— there was no such sentiment from the president. When in 1943 Jan Karski, a delegate from the Polish Underground, came to America to report on the tragedies in occupied Poland — the decimations of the Polish population and the ongoing Holocaust — it took some efforts to prevail on FDR to receive him and when he relented he did not want to hear about the above "problems." Instead he pressed Karski for "adventure" stories about the feats and heroics of the partisans. His response to the massacre of 20,000 Polish officers at Katyn and elsewhere was that "The graves...question wasn't worth such a fuss" (Olson and Cloud, 270). And of course FDR did nothing about the ongoing extermination of European Jewry nor about admitting to America the few wretched survivors that escaped the Nazi death mills.

Roosevelt's overriding concern was to remain president, which he did for four terms. To secure reelection he was prepared to forget all principle, jettison allies, mislead friends and enemies, and make commitments he knew he couldn't, and wouldn't, keep. Often this amounted to plain prevarication. When Churchill asked for the 50 destroyers late in 1940, the answer was an outright no because it was an election year. In late 1942 he insisted that Torch be launched in October because 1942 was a year of congressional elections. He kept Joe Kennedy as an ambassador in Britain till the end of 1940 even though he was a misfit as an envoy because FDR wanted to be assured of the Irish vote. Just before elections that year he asked Kennedy to come to the States and prevailed on him to make an important political speech endorsing FDR's candidacy; only after that was Kennedy informed that he was being removed from his job. Yet this was the man who seemed to be doing all the "right' things. He pulled the country out of the Great Depression, instituted lasting social and economic reforms, and led the country to victory against the three dictatorial powers. Like Churchill he had a visceral loathing for Nazi Germany and Hitler in particular. This duality of the man played a considerable part in the evolving role of America in World War II. When the question of helping England arose, Roosevelt was campaigning for a third term. Given the strong isolationist, even anti–British, attitudes in the country and the often vehe-

ment opposition to Roosevelt's liberal views and actions, he was concerned lest any overseas commitment rebound on his chances of being reelected. The country's attitude was
that Wilson had unnecessarily dragged the USA into World War I, and up to the fall of
France the majority was against letting it happen again. It was an old stance to let the Europeans stew in their own mess, or even, in Jefferson's phrase, have "the new world fatten on
the follies of the old."

Reflecting these American crosscurrents and presidential ego, the winds from the new
world blew hot and cold on the embattled British island. However, the USA acted promptly
whenever threats, however remote, loomed close to its shores. There were small Dutch and
French possessions in the Western Hemisphere, primarily in the West Indies, and fear arose
that these might be transferred to Germany as part of the capitulation agreements. So, even
before the French armistice was signed, the US on June 18 notified Germany that it "would
not recognize any transfer of a geographical region in the Western Hemisphere from one
non–American power to another non–American power and that it would not acquiesce in
any attempt to undertake such a transfer" (*Peace and War*, 560). An equally determined
step would be taken later on to occupy Iceland — a Danish possession — and place American troops there to guard against any threat from that island.

Just as England had worried about the French fleet, so now Roosevelt tried to make
sure that the Home Fleet wouldn't end up in German hands. On May 23 Roosevelt asked
Mackenzie King, the Canadian prime minister, to suggest that Britain send her fleet to
Canada. The Canadian said the president should address Churchill directly. Roosevelt was
not shy and did so. There followed now a poignant exchange on the subject. In addressing
Churchill Roosevelt talked as one talks to a cancer patient about preparing a will. Repeatedly the president urged that steps be taken for a safe transfer of the Home Fleet to the
Western Hemisphere. Churchill played all available chords not to rebuff the president and
yet bolster England's cause. One argument he repeatedly used was that such a commitment
was not solely in his hands because if England went down he would not be at the helm and
others may want to use the fleet as a bargaining item in extracting favorable peace terms .
The only way to avoid this was to see that England didn't come to such a pass.

A silence lasting from mid–June to early August followed. No correspondence flowed
between the two leaders, and no help arrived. Roosevelt was not confident that Britain
would survive and he was biding his time. Yet, he was scheming of ways to help if this would
be called for. Responding to Churchill's appeal of May 19 he ordered the army to take from
its stocks 250,000 rifles, 130 million rounds of ammunition, 80,000 machine guns, 900
75mm cannons and 140 bombers to be held for shipment to England. This Roosevelt did
against the wishes of his military which wanted this materiel for its own arsenal. Moreover,
since the Neutrality Act forbade such transfers, a scheme was set up whereby these weapons
would be resold to the manufacturers who were then free to sell them to the British (Reynolds, 109). He also went to work on the request for 50 destroyers, consummated on September 2. To circumvent the Neutrality Act this was arranged in the form of a barter deal;
in exchange for the destroyers, England ceded a number of bases in the West Indies. In
addition, the agreement contained a clause that no matter what happened the British Fleet
would neither be sunk nor surrendered. By this time the Battle of Britain was over and
England was here to stay. From then on the USA would be reinforcing England on a steadily
rising scale — a partial fulfillment of Churchill's prediction of the course the war would take.

However, the road ahead was far from smooth. Ironically, the greatest snag occurred
in the weeks following the German attack on Russia. Euphoric as he was about the Ger-

man plunge to the east, Churchill had serious concerns about its effect on the attitude of America. And he was not mistaken. On two occasions, August 19 and two weeks later, the American public's response to the query, "How would you vote on the question of the USA entering the war against Germany?" the results were nearly identical — 20 percent for 74 percent against. In writing to his son Churchill articulated the reason, saying "Germany's involvement with Russia renewed sentiments in America that 'they need not worry'.... The President is thought by many.... to move with public opinion rather than lead it" (Wilson, 228, 232).

Concerned with this development Churchill proposed a summit meeting. Codenamed Argentia, the summit took place in Placentia Bay off Newfoundland August 9–12, 1941. It was the first face-to-face meeting of the two leaders. Churchill's purpose was nothing less than to induce the USA to enter the war and he looked forward to it with great expectations. In contrast, FDR seems to have treated it as a respite from the bustle of Washington, an occasion to bask in the company of his illustrious guest; the president was known at that period to be in a low mood and in a state of some indecision. The trip was arranged in great secrecy and not one of FDR's associates had any clue what it was all about; Secretary of State Cordell Hull did not even know it was taking place. During the cruise to Canada FDR talked about all kinds of things except the impending conference. But to Harry Hopkins he gave specific instructions: "Economic and territorial deals — NO.... No talk about war" (Wilson, 22). During the four-day meeting the leaders shuttled from ship to ship, dined and wined, their assistants trailing them in utter bafflement as to what was happening. The highlight of the conference was a religious ceremony on Sunday with the two leaders — both of them agnostics, at the least — attending, Bibles in hand. On his way back FDR exulted about "the remarkable religious service" where everybody sang "Onward, Christian Soldiers."

The fact was that in mid–1941 the USA was farther from entering the war than it had been in late 1940, relying now on Russia to do the job it had in the past expected of France. If anything, its attention was focused more and more on Japan's inroads in the Far East. However, if neither Churchill nor Roosevelt managed to bring America into the war, there was always Adolf Hitler to accomplish it — as he was to do a few months later.

⁂

Following the German occupation of large parts of Europe, London became the seat of a number of governments in exile. These included Czechoslovakia, Poland, Norway, Holland, and Belgium, as well as what came to be known as the Free French under Charles de Gaulle. Formally, the latter was a rebel group splintered from the legitimate Pétain government in Vichy — but in the later stages of the war it assumed the authority of a quasi-government. Until the Free French became a force to speak of, which happened only after the Allied invasion of North Africa at the end of 1942, the most prominent among the various exile governments was that of Poland. This was partly because they had the largest fighting contingent, but more so because, after the German invasion of Russia, it played a conspicuous role in the relations between Britain, the USA and the Soviet Union.

The September '39 defeat sent a stream of Polish exiles into Rumania and, to a lesser extent, Hungary. By prior agreement Rumania was to treat Polish soldiers and officials crossing into its territory as allies, free to stay or move on as they chose. But as soon as a German victory became apparent Rumania on September 6 switched from nonbelligerence to neutrality and reneged on her word with regard to Polish escapees. This she did principally because of German demands that the Poles be interned. Submission was made easier for the Rumanians by a similar intervention of France, done for entirely different reasons, but with the same result. The French considered the prewar Polish leadership an embarrassment. They had been portrayed in the Western press as a semi–Fascist clique, they had assisted Germany in the dismemberment of Czechoslovakia, and — in French judgment at the time — they had botched the war in the most incompetent way. The French were assisted in this by Polish emigrés who, before the war, had either been opposed to the regime or had been professionally shunned by the colonels, chief among them Gen. Wladyslaw Sikorski. The net result was that the prewar Polish leadership was interned and prevented from leaving for the West.

The internment of two of the top men had a sad ending. Marshal Rydz-Smigly was an appealing man who in his youth had studied art and philosophy, was a fair painter, read poetry, and had served as a competent regimental commander in Pilsudski's First Brigade. Interned like the others in Rumania he escaped a few months later to Hungary where he stayed in a Budapest outskirt, tolerated as long as he didn't try to leave the country. But he had never made peace with himself for abandoning his army. In the fall of 1941 he eluded the Hungarians and with the help of a guide crossed on foot the Carpathian Mountains into Poland. There is a poignant description of the erstwhile marshal dressed in peasant garb making his way on a horse-drawn cart across German-occupied Poland. He reached Warsaw on October 30, 1941, where he offered his services to the Polish Underground. The latter, being part of the London government, refused his services. He then tried to organize his own underground group to fight the Germans. The marshal suffered from angina pectoris and the conditions he lived under and lack of medical attention aggravated the illness. He died in December of that year, aged 55. He was buried secretly in a Warsaw cemetery under a false name and his grave stayed that way for the next half century.

Foreign Minister Beck was confined to a small schoolhouse in Stavesti, Rumania, where he lived with his wife and daughter. Beck suffered from tuberculosis and all his pleas for better accommodations and medical care were ignored, particularly after Rumania became a German ally. He died on June 5, 1944, not quite 50 years of age. President Moscicki did succeed in reaching Switzerland but died one year after the war ended.

Some 50,000 Polish soldiers made their way to France. They formed two divisions and two more were being trained, utilizing manpower from the local Polish community. Some of these troops fought in Narvik. When Narvik was evacuated the Poles were disembarked in France where together with those attached to the French army they were either captured or dispersed. Of a total of 85,000 men, only 20,000 reached British shores. Thus within less than a year they endured two defeats. However, there was for the Poles one consolation in the second debacle. Up to that time the rapid demise of the Polish army was considered a uniquely Polish achievement, ascribed to its nonliberal regime and the ignorance of its generals — in short to the peculiar incompetence of the Polish state machinery. The Poles had to agree with all this. The ease with which President Moscicki, the government and the leaders of the army relinquished their posts to a new generation of men under General Sikorski attested to this feeling of guilt. Now the Poles could raise their heads again and wipe away the imposed September stigma. The vaunted French army fell apart just as totally and just as quickly. Given the potent arms it possessed and an incomparably better strategic position, they in fact did worse than the Poles. Nor did the British do much better in Norway. The new Polish government, now established in London, could proceed without a feeling of inferiority to gather again its forces for the upcoming struggle.

* * *

The greatest panic engendered by the French surrender occurred in the Soviet Union. One can judge its intensity by the steps taken in consequence of that event. That it was bound to produce extreme disappointment and anxiety is clear. The disappearance of the French front shattered the foundation of Soviet policy promoted by the Nazi-Soviet Pact — the expectation of a drawn-out conflict between the capitalist states which would spare Russia from war and bring political benefits. Suddenly, after barely 10 months, the contest on the continent was over and the Soviet Union was left to face, all alone, an unemployed Wehrmacht.

To deal with the German threat, the USSR took a number of steps in the diplomatic, military and economic spheres. As usual Stalin pushed these through with ruthless thoroughness. But while proceeding with what was necessary, he was at the same time concerned lest these very steps even trigger a German attack. He therefore pursued simultaneously a precautionary and conciliatory course, which explains some of the contradictory moves taken at that time by the USSR. As the German danger grew this to and fro maneuvering would follow a progressively more errant pattern, until just before the German attack on Russia it assumed on Stalin's part pathological forms with tragic consequences for the Russian people.

The immediate initiative taken by the USSR was to occupy along its border with Germany a buffer of additional territory to keep the Germans as far away as possible from its vital centers. Back in 1939 Stalin had forced the Baltic states to grant the USSR military bases, stationing 25,000 troops each, in Estonia and Latvia, and 75,000 in Lithuania. With this Stalin had secured the southern approaches to Leningrad. He then tried to achieve similar results in the north, demanding from Finland both territory and bases. Finland refused, which led to the Winter War. When after three months Finnish resistance crumbled, Stalin took Karelia adding a 100-mile zone to the north of Leningrad; a strip of territory near Kuolayarvi to cushion a possible enemy drive to the White Sea which would have cut off Murmansk, Russia's only ice-free port in the north; and a 30-year lease of the Finnish naval base in Hanko, at the entrance to the Gulf of Finland. With this Stalin had rested his case.

All this changed in June. Within a few days of the entry of German troops into Paris, the USSR occupied all three Baltic countries and, after the usual Communist elections, incorporated them into the Soviet Union. At the end of June an ultimatum went out to Rumania demanding Bessarabia and Bucovina. The first territory had been assigned to Russia by the Nazi-Soviet pact but not Bucovina. The Germans objected and a deal was struck whereby only North Bucovina was taken by the Soviets. The Russians were in such a hurry that they used paratroopers to occupy the newly won Rumanian territory. By this act the Russians also became a riparian partner of the Danube River and by occupying a few small islands in its estuary could block the outlet to the Black Sea, which she considered of strategic importance to her security.

In August 1940 Stalin also turned once again to Finland and made two new demands on her: to demilitarize the Aaland Islands near Hanko, and to grant Russia transit rights on Finnish railroads. Both of these requests were granted. Ironically, when the Russians began using the Finnish railway on September 25, it was one day after the Finns had granted Germany similar transit rights although by the Nazi-Soviet pact all of Finland had been assigned to the Russian sphere.

In extending its defense perimeter Stalin cast eyes also on the Balkan peninsula and attempted to buttress his position there. He advised Bulgaria — traditionally a friend of Russia — to demand Dobrudja from the Rumanians — a step that would have cut Rumania off from the Black Sea and given Russia a common border with Bulgaria. This move was blocked by Germany, which by that time was herself on the march into the Balkans. Also, after a long break, Stalin established diplomatic relations with Yugoslavia, another potential Slav ally. The Soviets' move into the Balkans was very tentative and, as with Bucovina, they did not press their demands when there were objections from Germany. While Stalin was careful in his moves in this uncharted area, the Germans, as we shall see in the next chapter, were not so reticent.

The internal measures taken by the Russians concerned the armed forces and the heavy industries. In the early '30s the Red Army, influenced by the new trends in Europe, subscribed to the concept of massed armored formations. This changed in 1939 when the Russian tank expert Pavlov returned from Spain and stated that by the experience of the Civil War tanks were good only for infantry support. The Soviet armored formations were then broken up and assigned as auxiliary arms to the infantry. The German blitz in France shattered this Pavlovian doctrine and the Red Army embarked on a crash program to create massive armored corps each composed of two divisions of tanks and one of motorized infantry (a Russian corps was equivalent to a German division and a division to a regiment). This conversion barely got going when the Russian war started.

Other important changes, initiated in the wake of the Finnish war, were considerably accelerated after June 1940. On May 7 Timoshenko replaced Voroshilov as defense commissar and one of the first changes he introduced was to limit the role of Politruks to propaganda, leaving operational matters in the hands of the soldiers. Some 4,000 high-ranking officers were released from the gulags, among them Rokossovsky, to emerge in the coming war as one of the top Soviet marshals. The arms industry was put on a war footing and the first steps were taken to transfer some of the plants beyond the Urals. But interestingly enough the big military dumps stored in the Western territories Stalin refused to move lest it provoke the Germans (Read and Fisher, 480).

So Stalin used his boots but treaded softly. Throughout the summer *Pravda* made no mention about the possible consequences of the French defeat, as if it did not concern the USSR. When the Germans started penetrating into the Balkans and Finland it evoked no reaction from the Soviets. When as a result of deliberate policy shipments from Germany lagged behind those of Russia which punctiliously delivered what they had promised, Stalin was willing to postpone outstanding German payments. The most striking event reflecting the changed constellation in Europe occurred on May 16 when Maiski approached Butler to suggest negotiations but "by word of mouth and not by notes" (Gorodetsky, 30). Following the Soviet attack on Finland England had had no ambassador in Moscow. Now England proposed to return the envoy. The Soviets insisted that it be Cripps, a leftist considered sympathetic to the Soviets and the British agreed. Cripps brought with him a letter for Stalin in which Churchill said that Hitler was obviously on the point of gaining hegemony over all of Europe and constituted, therefore, a danger to all still independent countries. Churchill suggested that perhaps the time had come for improving relations and "that we [England and the USSR] are better enabled than others … to resist Germany's hegemony" — a replay of what had been mooted a year earlier. But a wary Stalin answered that he was unaware of any German drive for European hegemony and saw no reason for a change in relations. Significantly, Stalin handed Churchill's message and his own response to Schulenburg, who passed this interesting information to Berlin.

• CHAPTER 11 •

The Turnabout

The battle in France was still on but with the smell of victory already in the air when a new and puzzling motif began to appear in the führer's pronunciamentos. At first these allusions had the ring of incautious slips, then as accompaniments to other themes, but soon enough they took center place. The subject was Russia.

Several elements, all complementing each other, made it easier for Hitler to turn his back on the war with England. One was doubt that Germany had the means of staging a successful invasion; even if a landing succeeded, there were deep reservations about being able to reinforce and sustain it. Another factor was that in his infatuation with England as the only suitable companion to rule the globe he didn't want to destroy her. And there was the unextinguished hope that once he took on the Bolsheviks, England would see the merit of the case and if not officially then surreptitiously let the war in the west fade away.

The first time Hitler mentioned Russia during the French campaign was on June 2 when he told Rundstedt, "Now that England will presumably be willing to come to a sensible peace agreement I shall at last have my hands free for the real major task — the conflict with Bolshevism." An identical statement was recorded on June 5 by Rundstedt's chief of staff, General Sodenstern (Lukacs, 108). These sentiments were echoed by Weizsäcker in a conversation with Halder on June 30 when he told him, "It needs only a little more force before England yields and so free our rear for an attack in the East" (Hillgruber 1965, 208). The diplomat must have picked this up from his boss, Ribbentrop, who picked it up at one of the führer 's seminars. On June 26 Speer overheard the führer say to Keitel, "Now that we have shown what we are capable of, believe me, Keitel, a campaign against Russia would be a child's game" (Read and Fisher, 485–8). These projections must have leaked out, for on June 27 Churchill wrote to Smuts, "If Hitler fails to beat us he will probably recoil eastward. Indeed he may do this without trying invasion." To have foreseen in June 1940 what in fact happened a year later has to be attributed either to a gift of prophecy — withdrawn by the Maker from the human race after the destruction of Jerusalem in AD 70 — or to a piece of accurate intelligence. In either case it did not do the British harm to know it.

Hitler went to Berlin on July 6 and there waited for signs that England was responding to the multiple peace feelers floated throughout Europe. But nothing concrete materialized. He departed two days later for the Berghof where he locked himself into one of his solitary meditations. In his *Table Talks*, Hitler told his entourage that it was at that time that he had made his final decision to proceed with the invasion of Russia (Hillgruber 1965, 216). These Berghof meditations are reminiscent of Cromwell's periodic withdrawals where he claimed to have communicated with God, after which there was, of course, no further argument about the merits of his decisions. Hitler returned to Berlin to deliver the twin of

131

his Russian plan—the July 19 peace offer to Britain. Soon after, on the 21st, he called in Jodl for a closed meeting and instructed him to look into the feasibility of launching a campaign against Russia still this autumn. Jodl passed the request on to Halder. The experts at the General Staff concluded that the task of transporting several million men from west to east combined with the poor state of the transportation network in the GG precluded launching a campaign in the fall. Hitler then rescheduled the attack for May 1941.

July 31 was one of those grandstand performances by the führer when as a super–Bismarck he lectured his generals on the politico-strategic parameters of Germany's situation. The meeting took place at the Berghof in the presence of Keitel, Jodl, Brauchitsch, Raeder, Halder and the navy's representative, von Puttkamer. "Britain's hope — said Hitler — is Russia.... Russia's destruction must therefore be made part of the struggle." Later he explained the kind of struggle he had in mind, which was to be nothing like the military campaign just conducted in the West. This, he told the generals, is not a matter of military victory but a war for "the extinction of Russia's life force" (Leach, 68; Hillgruber 1965, 226). All of the Ukraine, White Russia and the three Baltic states would be annexed. He outlined his operational plan—a two-pronged attack, one through the Baltics, the other along the Dniepr, the two to meet east of Moscow. He needed for it 120 divisions. The campaign would start in May 1941 and be over by winter.

While we have traced the reemergence in June 1940 of the führer's designs on Russia, this, as we know, was no new twist. Wintherbotham of British Intelligence recalls that on a 1938 visit to Rastenburg in East Prussia he saw "a massive concrete base for Hitler's headquarters rising from the sandy woodland soil" (Wintherbotham, 146). As early as 1938! We also recall that in October 1939 Hitler had told Keitel that the GG was to serve as a deployment area for future operations against the East. In his famous harangue to the generals on November 23, 1939, he had told them that the campaign in the West was only an intermediate step to the real thing. "We can oppose Russia only when we are free in the West," the führer had said (Shirer 1959, 796). When informed about the plans for invading Russia, Raeder on August 11 requested an interview with Hitler and asked for the reasons for this puzzling change in the direction of the war. Hitler's reply was that, "he never lost sight of the inevitability of a clash ... that he didn't believe it could be avoided ... and that it was better for him to shoulder this grave burden now ... than for him to bequeath it to his successor."

Three separate study groups were given the task of preparing an eastern campaign. On July 29 Jodl told Warlimont about the projected war in the East and asked him to work out an appropriate OKW plan. On July 22 Halder asked his chief of operations, General Greiffenberg, to work out the OKH approach to the campaign. Independently General Marcks, chief of staff of the 18th Army, was asked to do a similar job. When on September 3 General Paulus became quartermaster general he took over the staff work assigned to Greiffenberg. This was typical of the German army's approach to operational problems; let separate groups or individuals come up with alternative schemes and then choose one or combine the best features of all.

Hints surfaced of what was coming. The Russians had granted Germany the use of their ice-free port of Murmansk as a base for naval forces; it also aided German raiders to sail via the Polar Sea to the Pacific Ocean; it even supplied icebreakers to help them negotiate the ice-locked stretches on their passage. On September 6 the Germans terminated its use, claiming that Norway — which they had had for close to half a year —could replace Murmansk. The economic offices were instructed to withhold trade deliveries to Russia after the spring of next year. When in January 1941 Rumania asked Berlin for permission to ship the USSR 100,000 tons of gasoline the answer was that yes, of course, but that the deliveries not start until July (DGFP XII, 3). And an order went out on August 2 to stop the building of fortifications along the Russian border. Instead, on November 15, the Todt organization was instructed to complete the führer's headquarters in East Prussia. Temporary headquarters were to be built also in the northern, central and southern sectors of the eastern border (Hillgruber 1965, 358).

Along with the operational studies the movement of troops began. The 18th Army under von Küchler was ordered east as soon as the French campaign was over. An official directive went out on August 9 coded Aufbau Ost — Buildup East. This concerned the building of roads, bridges, railroad lines, barracks and dumps for the reception of mass armies in the GG. By August 19 there were 15 divisions in the east with six Panzer and three motorized divisions en route. On September 6 orders went out to shift von Bock's entire Army Group B to Poland. Bock's headquarters moved to Poznan on October 6; List, commanding the 12th Army, settled in Cracow; and Kluge commanding the 4th Army moved his headquarters to Warsaw. Up till then General Blaskowitz had been military commandant in the GG. On October 30 he was replaced by von Bock; the GG had become a deployment area for the upcoming invasion.

There was a brief interval following the defeat of France when some 40 infantry divisions had been scheduled to be disbanded (from 110 to 120). This was soon countermanded when Hitler, at the end of his July 31 tour d'horizon, ordered instead the establishment of 60 new divisions and an increase from 10 to 20 in the number of Panzer divisions. Hitler apportioned 120 divisions for the invasion of Russia, and 50 divisions for occupation and guard duty in France and 10 divisions each to the Low Countries and Norway (DGFP X, 375). It thus seems that the original plan to disband a large portion of the army soon after the fall of France was that in June and July he still counted on peace with England and did not need the 60 divisions for occupation duty; when peace did not materialize Hitler reinstated and, in fact, increased the number of active divisions. In doubling the number of armored units each Panzer division was reduced from two to one regiment of tanks, although these were now equipped with the heavier Mark III and IV models instead of the lighter tanks which proved vulnerable during the French campaign.

Elaborate measures were taken to camouflage the scale and intent of the buildup. This effort was one of great irony, for it employed a double inversion. The Germans' disinformation attempted to give the impression that the concentration of forces in the east was aimed at deceiving the British by pretending that an attack on Russia was being planned — whereas in actuality the Germans were preparing a landing in England. Thus the truth was being peddled as a deception to mask the truth. Other elements of disinformation were that the troops were being transferred to Poland for rest or that they were there to escape British air raids, or that the GG was about to be incorporated into Germany, with the troops sent in for security reasons. Within the Wehrmacht the number of people initiated into these plans was kept to a minimum so that at the end of July only 16 people were aware of it. On the other hand steps were taken to learn more about Soviet dispositions. After much hesitation Hitler on September 1 gave approval for reconnaissance and photographic flights over Russian territory to a depth of 300 miles.

Along with the military preparations allies were canvassed for his eastern campaign. Hitler had a low opinion of all foreign armies — with the exception of the British — but still he wanted them. The nature of the upcoming war — a crusade against Bolshevism — provided an ideological banner for all of Europe to join in stomping out that ungodly nest. Then there were geographic factors. The southeastern countries had long borders with the Soviet Union and they offered good access into Russia, particularly when the Pripet marshes and the Carpathians precluded using large stretches in Poland as staging areas. Finally there were economic considerations, of which the most critical were the Ploesti oil fields which, if left to the Rumanians, would likely be lost as soon as the first shots were fired.

In order to draw the Balkans into his orbit Hitler began to support revisionist claims of those countries which had lost territory after the Great War. A major grievance was Transylvania, an area populated by ethnic Hungarians but a part of Rumania since 1919. In the so-called Vienna arbitration award of August 30 Rumania was forced to cede most of this territory to Hungary. Rumania also had to return to Bulgaria the southern part of Dobrudja. As an inducement to accept these decisions Hitler offered Rumania guarantees of her new borders. With this Germany had bound to herself Hungary, Bulgaria, and Rumania which, after the loss of Bessarabia and Northern Bucovina had automatically become an enemy of Russia. King Carol, a friend of the West, bent to the demands of the times, dismissed his quasi-democratic cabinet and appointed Gen. Ian Antonescu to the premiership. On September 6 the new prime minister forced the king to abdicate in favor of his teenage son, Michal, and assumed dictatorial powers in Rumania with himself bearing the title of conducatorul — leader. On September 23 Rumania adhered to the Axis Pact and "requested" German troops for the defense of the country. The arriving troops had instructions "to prepare for deployment from Rumanian bases all the German and Rumanian forces in case of a war with Soviet Russia." By October there were 50,000 German troops along the Rumanian-Soviet border with depots and airfields being built at a rapid pace in the hinterland.

Contacts between Germany and Finland dated back to the Winter War but these did not surface until after the French campaign. In September the two governments signed an agreement for the transit of German troops, ostensibly for Kirkenes in Norway. In reality they were concentrating near Petsamo — a vulnerable area for several reasons, most conspicuously because of the nickel deposits there, an important item in the arms industry. This metal was coveted by the British, the Soviets and the Germans. At the end of the Winter War the Russians left Petsamo in Finnish hands not to tread on British interests. Now Finland agreed to ship Germany substantial amounts of their nickel output. Both the transit of German troops and the nickel deal trespassed the provisions of the 1939 pact, which had assigned all of Finland to the Soviet sphere.

Thus by the fall of 1940 Germany had aligned Bulgaria, Hungary, Rumania and Finland on its side. Although none of these countries were officially told about German intentions, this was not necessary. Their readiness to cooperate was based not solely on fear of a vengeful Third Reich but also on the political and territorial prospects resulting from a defeat of the Soviet Union.

Of the various blueprints for a Russian campaign, the one adopted was that of Paulus, completed at the beginning of November. Maneuvers were held to resolve outstanding problems in the proposed plan. The results were then discussed at several meeting during the next few weeks. On December 18 Hitler issued Directive No. 21, code-named Barbarossa, which remained the master plan for the invasion of Russia.

• CHAPTER 12 •

The Wrong Enemy

The events or rather lack of events in the next half a year or so have to be seen against the background of German *Dichtung und Wahrheit*, literally poetry and truth, or in our context, appearance and reality. The reality was that Hitler found himself in a quandary wherein with each passing week England was less likely to end his unwanted war in the West. He had to look for a solution to the strategic bind into which he had stumbled at the moment of his greatest triumph. What he fell back on while waiting for Barbarossa, scheduled for May 1941, was a vast subterfuge campaign to give the impression that he was doing what everyone expected him to do. Hitler once described himself to an intimate thus: "I have three ways of being secretive. One is when the two of us are alone; the second is when I keep it all to myself; the third are problems of the future which I do not think through to the end" (Detwiler, 167). Here then was Hitler in his mode number three. Regardless of what his chieftains advocated; regardless of what it meant to his beloved German people; regardless of what he himself was able to project, he was off into the East, while still at war with England and with a clash with America looming. The obvious problem in the late summer of 1940 was how to defeat England, the sole obstacle to ending the war. Hitler was aware that this was what everyone expected and he spelled out his concern about it when at his first mention of Russia he had told Rundstedt, "The problem is how am I going to explain this to my people." Much of the activity that now followed, and many of the mooted but never executed plans, were thus aimed at bamboozling his audiences, including his own generals and diplomats, that he was indeed bent on resolving the problem of English belligerence. We will in the next pages a multiplicity of plans and moves— Seelöwe Felix, Isabella, Attila and others—conceived, abandoned and resurrected, which served the purpose of giving the appearance that the führer was as sane as the rest of them and fully at work on terminating this malicious British war. He even used the real thing — his planned Russian campaign — in the service of this pretense when he argued that England's remaining hope and sole reason she wouldn't make peace was Russia. The truth, of course, was that England was betting not on Russia but on the USA. The British had mixed feelings about a possible Russian-German war. While welcome for many reasons the event carried considerable risks. The British had a poor opinion of the Soviets— in 1939 they had rated the Polish army higher that the Red Army — and a Russian defeat would have provided Germany with a cornucopia of resources and manpower. A Soviet defeat would have prolonged the war but would not have changed England's reliance on the USA in eventually winning it. Hitler's argument about subduing Russia in order to defeat England was a fraud. But to his generals and diplomats, whose intellect was such that after eight years of dealing with Hitler they had never fathomed him, his reasoning smacked of high statesmanship.

Conceptually, England could be fought via three strategic venues. The most direct blow would have been to invade the British Isles. Being in possession of the entire French coastline, with the English shore 10 to 100 miles away , the Germans possessed good launching sites for an invasion. In midsummer of 1940 England had no army to defend itself with. The forbidding aspect of such an undertaking was crossing the Channel in the teeth of the British Navy. Still, by a combination of the Germans' customary daring, skill and willingness to pay the price they may, if done early enough, have been able to carry it off the way they had done it in Norway and were to do it later in Crete and Tunisia.

A variant of the above would have been an invasion of Ireland. Officially neutral, Ireland's sympathies were with the Germans. During World War I there took place in 1915 an uprising in the Free State of Ireland against the British then, too, busy fighting the Germans. One of its operatives was Sir Roger Casement, an Irish civil service official, who left for Germany there to organize a Liberation Legion from Irish POWs. Along with the nationalistic impulse, an additional element in this anti–British stance was religious; nearly all other Catholic countries— Austria, Hungary, Croatia, Italy, Spain and Vichy France — were in the German orbit. Irish complicity with Germany worked on two levels: via government policy and via the IRA, the illegal opposition to de Valera's government. De Valera's fondness for Germany, laced with a touch of malice, had a long record. He had endorsed Hitler's takeover of the Sudetenland comparing the case to that of Northern Ireland; he castigated Roosevelt's appeal for peace in 1939 as "inept"; on September 12, 1939, he informed Eden that Irish territorial waters were out of bounds to British ships (Duggan, 72). These sentiments survived the demise of the Nazi state. With all its horrors now public knowledge, de Valera on May 3 paid a visit to German Ambassador Hempel to express his condolences on the death of the führer, the only case of a European statesman to have done so.

As for the IRA, they were direct participants if not instigators of the various German plans to invade the British Isles. As soon as war threatened the IRA launched an extensive terror campaign against British targets, including public utilities and military installations; it was directed by Jim O'Donovan, the chief Irish agent employed by the Abwehr (Duggan, 147). A plan called Kathleen visualized a German landing in Northern Ireland to be timed with an insurrection throughout the island. Had the Germans succeeded by air or sea in setting foot on Irish soil, their chances of success were good. For Britain the consequences of an occupation of Ireland would have been grave.

The next option available to Germany was to sever England's sea-lanes across the Atlantic and past the Cape of Good Hope. A vigorous offensive against British shipping could have left the island starved and shorn of the resources needed for prosecuting the war. While such a campaign could not have been carried out by German surface ships, there was nothing to stop a horde of U-boats— given their professionalism and dedication — to accomplish this task. That the U-boats were capable of such a performance would be shown in 1942 when they took on, not only Great Britain, but the USA as well. In 1940 this was potentially the most decisive form of warfare Germany could have waged in an effort to win.

A wide-open field for German warmaking was the Mediterranean basin. Here the strategic areas were Gibraltar, Malta and the Suez Canal. Gibraltar and Suez were accessible by land; and Malta was practically in Sicily's backwaters. Given the base in Libya the German army could have taken the Suez Canal with a minimum of effort. Between Libya and the French Levant lay the key British possessions in the Middle East, the base of British operations in the Mediterranean. In this region also lay the Iraqi and Iranian oil fields, fueling the vast naval, air and motor fleets of the British armed forces. Gibraltar, in turn, could have been taken from Spanish territory either with or without the acquiescence of Franco.

These were the options available to Germany in prosecuting the war against England at a time when America was still not a factor in the conflict. The Germans, in fact, had sufficient means to undertake several of these steps simultaneously and to carry on a concentric assault on British power. We will now take a look at what Hitler did with all these options available to him in the summer and fall of 1940.

* * *

Until the end of June there had been no talk and no interest in an invasion of England. Nothing had been prepared to deal with the problem in the event England did not capitulate, as France had. When on June 21 Raeder inquired of the OKH what it thought of a possible invasion the answer was it "considers its execution impossible ... General Staff rejects the operation" (Shirer 1959, 758). At the beginning of July Hitler ordered a study of invasion prospects. This was buttressed by a Jodl memorandum of July 13 setting down the prerequisites for an invasion. These were the elimination of the British navy from the Channel, chasing the RAF from the skies, and a massive employment of ground troops. Otherwise, Jodl's brief stated, an invasion would be "a desperate" gamble for which there is really no need. Three days later Hitler issued Directive No. 16 ordering that military preparations for an invasion be completed by mid–August. The resulting OKH plan specified an assault by 41 divisions, nearly a million men, over a 200-mile stretch from Ramsgate to Lyme Bay (the Normandy landings were only 50 miles wide). On the 21st and also on the 29th Raeder informed Hitler the navy could provide neither shipping nor escorts for such an invasion front. Raeder proposed it be postponed till May 1941—a horrible suggestion as the date coinciding with the planned attack on Russia, of which the grossadmiral knew nothing. In a meeting with his military chiefs on the 31st Hitler set the landing for September 15 but added that a decision whether or not to go ahead would depend on the performance of the Luftwaffe whose offensive was to start on August 6. On August 7 and 10 there were acrimonious debates between the OKH and the OKM about the coastal extent to be invaded, each claiming the other's version meant catastrophe. On the 27th Hitler reduced the invasion front to a stretch from Folkestone to east of Portsmouth, half of what the OKH demanded.

The logistics of Seelöwe involved the most intimate cooperation of all three branches of the Wehrmacht. The crux of the expedition was shipping, which posed three problems. Ships were needed to transport the hundreds of thousands of men, their supplies and heavy weapons like tanks and guns. Of these Germany had pitifully few. Next came the craft required for disembarkation over the beaches and variable tides, the kind of LCs the Allies later built in the thousands and never had enough. Of such landing craft the Germans had none. Finally the problem of naval escorts to protect the invasion fleet. Germany had never had enough warships to take on the British navy and after Norway had even fewer.

Lacking all of the above the Germans resorted to river shipping for crossing the sea — and a rough sea at that. Within a short time they assembled 170 transports totaling 700,000 BRT; 2,000 barges with 400 tugs and over 1,000 motorboats (Hillgruber 1965, 169; DDR, XV 537–38). These were all river and canal flotillas, half of them of Dutch and Belgian origin. The 500 800-ton barges were for the most part not self-propelled and had to be towed or pushed by tugs or motorboats. The bows on the barges were removed and ramps installed to provide gangways for men and vehicles. Many were given concrete flooring to support tanks and heavy equipment, which worsened their seaworthiness, poor to start with. Their maximum speed was four knots. The problem was so critical that the Germans had to use aircraft engines to propel the barges (Winterbotham, 72). By all accounts not only was it questionable whether they could withstand maneuvering and explosions during battle, but it was doubtful they could even make it across the Channel. In addition, once at their destination, tides would imperil disembarkation while the receding tide would ground them for the next 12 hours. No solution was found for transporting artillery so that the disembarking troops would have no covering fire either from their own guns or warships. Also, there were to be no motor vehicles. Instead 4,500 horses and some mules were assigned to the infantry. Lacking motorized transport, provisions were packed in large containers equipped with wheels and straps to be manhandled by the troops. The invaders were given 240 amphibian tanks. The light models could swim short distances from ship to shore; the heavier tanks were made submersible by equipping them with periscopes and air intakes and were expected to crawl on the sea floor to reach the beaches. Characteristically, while neither the ferries nor the amphibian tanks were ever employed against England, they were used against Russia; the tanks in crossing the river Bug and the ferries on Lake Ladoga to tighten the blockade of Leningrad.

To fend off the British navy, minefields were to be laid on either side of the invasion stream, one at the Dover straits and another, 60 miles long, at the western side. These mine belts would have to be kept in place for weeks while the troop echelons and supplies were ferried across the Channel. What the tides and British minesweepers were likely to do to the mine belts was left to the winds of war.

In mid–July the plan had been for 41 divisions to invade 200 miles of England's southern coastline; these included six Panzer and three motorized divisions. At that time there were only some 13 trained but poorly equipped British divisions that had escaped from France plus another 13 in training—a pitiful force against the projected million-man German army. At that time, too, for some reason the British had concentrated whatever forces they had on the east coast where they thought the invasion would strike. In September the German order of battle was reduced to nine seaborne plus two air divisions aimed at a stretch of coast of less than a hundred miles, which the OKH claimed invited defeat. The first wave was to consist of only 6,700 men from each division, or a total of 60,000. It would take the nine divisions 11 days to disembark. Subsequently they could be reinforced at the rate of one division every two days (Fleming, 253). But in mid–September the British already had a well-equipped army of 20 divisions of which four were armored. Also by the latest intelligence and the concentration of German barges in French ports the British knew the attack would be across the Channel. Thus a countershift was generated by the führer's leadership. When in July the British had only the rescued BEF—demoralized, without heavy weapons, half of them without rifles—the invasion plan foresaw a mighty armada of 41 divisions. When in September the British could field 20 combat divisions deployed along the endangered coast, the Germans reduced their forces to 11 divisions to be landed piecemeal over a span of 11 days.

Next the führer's Directive No. 17 instructed the Luftwaffe to "destroy the RAF." The air offensive, which started in mid–August, had in the course of its prosecution degenerated into a bombing and terror campaign lasting well into the spring of 1941. Here we shall look only at that phase of it which bears on the invasion, a span of three to four weeks.

When on August 8 Göring issued an order of the day for the opening of the offensive this was immediately picked up by the British, who by then had been reading the Luftwaffe's Enigma ciphers. The main assault was by Luftflotte 2 under Kesselring and Luftflotte 3 under Sperrle; at some stages they were assisted by the much smaller Luftflotte 5 stationed in Norway. They had a total of 2,500 planes: 1,500 bombers and 1,000 fighters. Against them the British could field 700 to 800 Spitfires and Hurricanes. The initial phase of what is known as the Battle of Britain was fought for air superiority seemingly linked to the projected invasion. This stage lasted from August 13 until September 6 when there was a switch in the Luftwaffe's strategic targeting. Up till the Battle of Britain the Luftwaffe had been employed primarily in a tactical role on the battlefield; now their planes had to fly to England to do a semi-strategic job and they were unsuited for this mission. The bombers carried too small a bomb load and the fighters had too small a range. The Me-109's time in the air was one hour which left them only 20 minutes over England; when dogfighting or zigzagging to stay with the bombers, this was reduced even further. In addition planes that crash-landed and any pilots that bailed out over England or the Channel were lost to the Luftwaffe, whereas this was not so for the British. Added to this was Britain's technologically advanced air defense system, including radar, sector stations to report progress of the raiders, and a central control system for the entire Fighter Command. In England the Luftwaffe encountered a heretofore unaccustomed challenge and suffered accordingly.

The target during the early phase of the offensive was the infrastructure of Fighter Command — radar, airfields, sector stations, command posts and the fighters themselves. The first massive raid occurred on the afternoon of August 13 with the result of 39 German planes shot down for 15 British losses. During the next two weeks the ratio of downed planes settled down to a fairly constant 2:1 in favor of the British. Even though the purely numerical score was strongly in favor of the RAF, yet by the end of August the effect of attrition on the Fighter Command was beginning to tell. One reason was that the RAF had fewer fighters to start with; also many of the shot-down German planes were bombers whereas on the British side they were predominantly fighters, and the British pilots were beginning to show the strain of flying too many sorties. By the end of August five forward airfields and six out of the seven sector stations were severely damaged. In only two weeks between August 23 and September 6, 466 British fighters were lost or damaged. Even with replacements the net loss was close to 200 fighters (Wheatley, 82). The air superiority battle was slowly tilting in favor of the Germans.

Then at the beginning of September the Germans suddenly switched their main effort to a bombing campaign. The commonly given explanation is that it was retaliation for a raid by 83 British bombers on Berlin on the night of August 25. If the German air offensive was meant to be preliminary to an invasion it is difficult to accept this as a reason. The damage to Berlin was trivial. Certainly if strategic goals were involved all this would have been ignored and the Luftwaffe kept to its mission of clearing the skies for the invasion. Instead on September 7 Göring arrived on the French coast to watch 300 bombers accompanied by 600 fighters — nearly the entire fighter force of the two Luftflotten — sally forth against London; at night another 247 bombers went out to stoke the fires. Hundreds of civilians died and considerable damage was done. Significantly, the main area bombed was East London, a concentration of the city's Jewish population. According to Raeder, this switch to terror bombing had been previously approved by Hitler (Raeder, 330). From now on, the Luftwaffe was busy bombing mainly civilian and economic targets. Thus as far as the struggle for air superiority the Luftwaffe withdrew from the field at the beginning of

September — at a time when the invasion was scheduled for September 15. There was thus no coordination between what the Luftwaffe was doing and what the invasion fleet waited for, events lamented at the time by the other branches of the Wehrmacht. On September 5 at a conference of the Operations Branch of the OKW it was reported that "Göring is not interested with preparations for operation Seelöwe as he does not believe the operation will take place." And on September 12 the Naval Staff complained that the air offensive "cannot assist preparations for Seelöwe. No effort can be discerned to engaging units of the British Fleet which are now able to operate almost unmolested in the Channel" (Wheatley, 60, 79).

As in all other political and military affairs of Nazi Germany, the deciding voice in the invasion was that of Adolf Hitler. Unlike in Norway where he had picked Falkenhorst to lead the invasion, here Hitler himself was to be in command. He established an invasion headquarters in Schloss Ziegenberg north of Frankfurt a/M and ordered his three service chiefs to move to nearby Giessen, where they would report directly to him (Fleming, 48). As commander of the land forces he had appointed Rundstedt. Yet while taking over direct command of the multiservice operation, Hitler took no part in any of the deliberation by the navy, army or air force on the modalities of their plans (Leach, 230). And, significantly, neither he nor his Wehrmacht chiefs ever moved to the prepared invasion headquarters.

While on July 16 the führer issued the directive for Seelöwe and on August 1 ordered the Luftwaffe against England, any intent to implement these directives is belied by everything that Hitler subsequently said or did. This shying away happened not because he failed to defeat the RAF. He failed because, atypically for him, he did not persevere as he usually did in the past and would do so again in the Balkans, Crete and Italy. Many of his deeds and words preceding the September 7 date when the Luftwaffe switched to bombing London, indicated that the invasion was a subterfuge. Thus in a letter to Mussolini of July 13 he declined Il Duce's offer of planes and troops for the impending invasion; certainly the planes Hitler could have used if in no other role than to distract the RAF pilots. Even when he issued Directive No. 16 it didn't read like the führer's prose. It opens with the following sentence: "Since England, despite its military hopeless situation, still shows no signs of willingness to come to terms, I have decided to prepare a landing operation against England, and if necessary to carry it out." Three days after issuing Directive No. 16 Hitler told Runsdtedt that Seelöwe was only a "Scheinmaneuver" — a ploy in an effort to induce England to make peace (Hillgruber 1965, 170). Rundstedt's chief of staff, Blumentritt, expressed a similar view as did Kesselring who was "convinced that the operation would never start" (Fleming, 238). Kesselring, in addition, pointed out that there had been no coordination between the air offensive and the invasion troops. And Dr. Schramm, the meticulous keeper of the OKW diary, stated after the war "Seelöwe was a deception" (Detwiler, 149).

During the air offensive the invasion date stood at September 15. On September 3 a Hitler order went out delaying the invasion for the 21st. Next more than a delay was involved. On September 6 Raeder saw Hitler and recorded in the Naval Staff diary, "The Führer's decision to land in England is still by no means settled, as he is firmly convinced that Britain's defeat will be achieved without a landing." For the invasion to take place on the new date, the go-ahead had to be issued on the 11th, to give the expedition forces 10 days' warning. On September 10 the go-ahead date was postponed for September 14. On that day Hitler met with his Wehrmacht chiefs and launched into a monologue piling inconsistencies on top of non-sequiturs. According to Halder's diary the führer explained, "A successful landing followed by occupation would end the war.... A landing need not necessarily be carried out within a specified time.... We have already achieved everything that we need.... The operations of the Luftwaffe are above all praise.... We have a good chance of bringing England to her knees.... (But) the enemy recovers again and again.... In spite of all our successes the prerequisite conditions for Operation Seelöwe have not yet been realized.... Decision: The Operation will not be renounced yet" (Shirer 1959, 768–70).

On September 17 Seelöwe was indefinitely postponed. The mobilization of shipping was to be stopped, those in the Channel ports dispersed. On October 12 a directive went out to maintain an appearance of invasion threat "for political and military pressure" on England. This remained on the books till February 1942 when the operation was officially cancelled. The story of Seelöwe is well summed up by Rundstedt who after the war testified, "The proposed invasion of England was nonsense.... Our navy was not in a position to cross the Channel ... nor was the Luftwaffe capable of taking on these functions.... I had a feeling that the Führer never really wanted to invade England ... he hoped the English would make peace" (Cookridge, 42).

It is not difficult to claim, as is done in most histories on the subject, that Hitler was serious about the invasion and that it was defeat in the Battle of Britain that stopped him. First the Battle of Britain. It has been shown previously that the struggle for air superiority — the only part pertinent to the invasion — was not lost but abandoned, or even spiked by Hitler himself. Its launching, conduct and termination was not linked to any timetable the army and navy may have had. Next, the seriousness of Seelöwe is argued on the basis of the extensive effort invested, particularly the requisition of shipping craft, which presumably played havoc with the German economy. There is no disputing the fact that the various branches of the Wehrmacht went about their tasks with customary German industriousness. Even Himmler's agencies were engaged. They had prepared lists of people to be apprehended in England and had even appointed a Dr. Dix to be the top SS chieftain in occupied Britain. This simply says that what Hitler had ordered the Germans executed with zeal and alacrity. The point under discussion, however, is whether Hitler intended to invade England or whether all this was only meant to give the impression of an impending invasion and thus intimidate England to make peace with him. The major moves by Hitler described in the previous paragraphs are far from conveying the plethora of orders, qualifications, changes, and delays Seelöwe had undergone in the two months between July 16 when it was first ordered and September 26 when it was cancelled. A mountain of activity was what Hitler instigated to convince everyone that an invasion was afoot. The alleged economic dislocation due to the requisition of barges and other river craft was an argument that Raeder used in trying to dissuade his chief from going ahead with a venture the navy had no means of implementing; no other agency complained about the alleged economic hardships. In fact it was nothing of the sort. Germany's economy worked at great slack in those days; two years later, even under heavy bombing, its economy would double or triple the output of planes, tanks and U-boats. It surely could have made up for the thousand or so barges requisitioned for the invasion. That it was not an economic burden is easily shown. In the first place, most of these small craft were taken from Dutch, Belgian, and French owners so that only 40 percent of the requisitions affected Germany. This domestic inroad amounted to no more than 30 percent of Germany's inland shipping (Wheatley, 44). But the best proof of it is that after the invasion was cancelled most of the barges were not returned to their owners but retained by the Wehrmacht.

Two other points should be mentioned. Hitler persistently referred to bad weather as an impediment in crossing the Channel. Bad weather is inherent to the English Channel and this was known when the invasion was conceived. As it happened, in 1940 the weather during September and October was exceptionally favorable —cloudy, with occasional rain, moderate visibility and light wind (Fleming, 253). These were suitable conditions for the German invasion fleet, as the sea was not too rough and visibility murky enough to partially hide it from the RAF and British warships. The other point relates to the dating of Directive No. 16, Hitler's one clear order for an invasion. This was issued on July 16. At that stage Hitler was planning the attack on Russia to take place in the autumn (only at the end of July was he told it was impossible). Thus if the invasion of England was meant seriously, he was preparing a simultaneous war on British soil and in Russia — not just a two-war but a two-front struggle, patently something he did not seek.

After Hitler was told that the attack on Russia could not be launched till May 1941 he faced a whole unemployed year ahead of him. It was a dismal prospect, particularly since he could not tell his people, not even his generals (at that time only 16 people knew about Barbarossa) of the glories awaiting them in the summer of 1941. He thus went on with Seelöwe, as in the eyes of ordinary humans this was the thing to do next. There were perhaps two side effects to the invasion subterfuge that had a real purpose to them. One was the hope that the threat of invasion, combined with the terror bombing started on September 7, would sway England to give up the fight. But as it happened even that missed its mark, for Churchill never believed there would or could be an invasion. He kept the specter of invasion alive to sustain the English people in the war effort and perhaps, too, to scare the USA. He told this frankly to his cabinet and to his intimates but admonished them not to say so in public. Thus, ironically, neither Hitler nor Churchill took the threat of invasion seriously, but floated its imminence for their own purposes (Wintherbotham, 72). The other reality lay in using the invasion phantom to obscure his preparations against Russia, a deception made official in a subsequent directive.

* * *

Two other alternatives for a war against the English homeland were the occupation of Ireland and a U-boat offensive. Aside from Kathleen, an invasion of Ireland was laid out in an independent plan, appropriately codenamed Grün. Two corps under Gen. Leonard Kaupisch were to embark from northern France and land on the southeastern corner of Ireland. From there they were to head for Dublin and the high ground west of it. The operational orders for this attack were issued on August 12 (Duggan, 121) but it is unclear whether this was to be a bona fide landing or a feint for Seelöwe. It never took place. The subject did not blow away even after Seelöwe was cancelled. For on December 3 Hitler told Raeder that "the occupation of Ireland might lead to the end of the war" (Coogan, 570). As with Seelöwe the Naval Staff's view was that such an operation was beyond Germany's capacity. The führer then turned to others. On Jan 23, 1941, he summoned Göring and Student — the future conqueror of Crete — to the Berghof and discussed the possibility of an air invasion of Ireland. In May 1940 the Abwehr had parachuted into Ireland its star agent, Dr. Hermann Goertz, who with Irish help established wireless contact with Germany. At the time of Hitler's meeting with Student, Goertz was asked by orders "of the highest authority" to provide information about Irish defenses. After leaving the meeting Göring told Student not to bother, as the führer was not serious about Ireland. No more was heard of the subject.

It was only natural that before the war Raeder and Dönitz should have argued the construction of a large U-boat fleet. Theirs was not the pleading of interested bureaucrats— it was indeed Germany's most promising weapon against England. Employed on a massive scale from the start it could conceivably have proven decisive in bringing England to its knees. After the fall of France Raeder on several occasions urged Hitler to forget an invasion but embark instead on a rush program of U-boat construction. But such a program was launched neither before nor after the outbreak of the war. In December 1940, when Raeder again argued the U-boat case, Hitler told him that once Russia was defeated he could have all he wished; at the moment German industry must cater to the needs of the army and air force in preparation for Barbarossa. Dönitz had estimated that to be effective he needed at least 100 operational U-boats (Hillgruber 1965, 160). The actual number at the time was closer to 10. What is particularly relevant is that after France fell and the time had come to knock England out of the war for a whole year the number of operational boats had not noticeably changed; there was, in other words, no effort to launch an effective U-boat offensive. While the number of U-boats did not increase, the toll on British shipping took a considerable jump. This was not due to increased submarine activity. The Germans' failure to achieve whatever success they could have had at the beginning of the war was caused by defective torpedoes and poor tactics. In mid–1940 the torpedo problem had been solved and new tactics in the form of wolf packs were introduced. Also, a good part of the increased sinkings was due to surface ships and the Luftwaffe, released from their Seelöwe duties (Terraine, 237). When Raeder did learn about Barbarossa he begged Hitler to postpone it till after victory over England— a voice in the wilderness if there ever was one. Eventually he moaned that as commander in chief of the navy he came to feel that Germany had abandoned sea war altogether (FNC, 222).

* * *

The southern periphery along which Germany could have taken on England embraced the two gateways to the Mediterranean, Gibraltar and the Suez Canal; the bone in the Axis' throat, Malta; and the Middle East— Egypt, Palestine, Iraq and Iran. There was also an outer arc of strategic posts: the Portuguese Azores and Madeira Islands at the approaches to Western Europe, and the Spanish Canary and Cape Verde islands guarding West Africa. Although in the vast canvass of anti–British strategy these islands do crop up in the deliberations of German planners, their capture required a strong navy and long-range aircraft which the Germans did not possess. They can therefore be left out of the available options. The taking of the Suez Canal seems to have been the easiest to accomplish since Libya was an Italian base from which a land campaign could have been launched— yet the Germans' most extensive activity centered on Gibraltar. It is also a strategic puzzle because closing the Suez Canal along with Gibraltar would have bottled up the British Fleet in the Mediterranean, whereas closing Gibraltar alone would not; ships could sail around the Cape of Good Hope, which they had been doing most of the time anyway. But nothing was lost because Hitler, though extremely active, was not serious about Gibraltar either, as events will show.

A southern periphery campaign was urged on the führer by his own OKW, the Army General Staff and, of course, Raeder. As early as June 30, one week after the fall of France, Jodl presented a comprehensive plan for further conduct of the war. To the north a siege by air and sea was to be imposed on England and its cities bombed, to be followed by an invasion. To the south he advocated the inclusion of Italy, Spain, Japan, the Arab countries and Russia in a concerted drive against the Mediterranean and the Middle East (Hillgruber 1965, 157). On July 30 a nearly identical blueprint for winning the war was presented by Brauchitsch and Halder. Since these men knew about Hitler's Russian designs they added, "the question whether, if a decision cannot be forced against Britain, we should in the face of a threatening British-Russian alliance and the resulting two-front war, turn first against Russia must be answered thus: we had better keep on friendly terms with Russia.... We could deliver the British a decisive blow in the Mediterranean ... and with the aid of Russia ... confidently face war with Britain for years" (Ansel, 17). Somewhat later, on September 26, Raeder pushed for a similar approach; Gibraltar, Suez and the Canary Islands should be taken and an attack through Syria and Palestine launched. The attacks should exploit French North Africa and Syria; were the French to decline, force should be used (Hillgruber 1965, 52–3). In his presentation Raeder even presciently warned that failure to intervene in the Mediterranean would lead to the collapse of Italy. Hitler listened to his naval chief and said that he would approach Il Duce and the leaders of Spain and France about this program. In his report on the conversation Raeder noted, "The Führer agrees" (Ansel, 5).

Talks and plans now followed in hectic succession. In the course of the second half of September Hitler and Ribbentrop saw Spain's foreign minister, Serrano Suner, four times and discussed at great length the capture of Gibraltar where the British presence presented not only a strategic stranglehold but a blot on Spanish national honor. In the meantime military preparations went ahead. On July 22 a Wehrmacht mission disguised in civilian clothes went to Spain to investigate its road and rail infrastructure as well as the approaches to the Rock. With this information Warlimont had his staff prepare a plan for a Spanish expedition, which he presented to Jodl on August 20. On November 12 the führer issued Directive No. 18, encompassing a Mediterranean strategy that was to involve Spain and France. The directive ordered the following preparations:

- French territory in Africa was to be secured for German warmaking and the French required to support these measures with their own forces.
- Spain would be made to join the war against England. German troops would enter the country under the code name Felix in order "to drive the English from the Western Mediterranean." Gibraltar would be captured with the help of Luftwaffe planes stationed in French North Africa and German troops in Spain. After Gibraltar, occupation of the Madeira Islands and the Azores would be considered. If necessary, Portugal, too, would be occupied.
- Italy would be supported by one armored division sent to Libya and by Luftwaffe units whose task would be to "close the Suez Canal to English warships."
- The Balkans. Greece would be occupied from Bulgarian territory after which the Luftwaffe would launch an offensive against the eastern Mediterranean.

The 12th of November when Directive No. 18 was issued was the date of Molotov's arrival in Berlin. Therefore, one other significant paragraph was added. Since Jodl and others were urging the inclusion of Russia in the new *Drang nach Süden*, Hitler in his directive stated the following: "Political discussions for the purpose of clarifying Russia's attitude in the immediate future have already begun. Regardless of the outcome of these conversations all preparations for the East for which verbal orders have already been given will be continued" (Trevor-Roper 1964, 41–43).

This impressive directive dealing with the Mediterranean from Portugal to Greece was followed by one concerned specifically with Felix—the takeover of the Iberian Peninsula.

At the outbreak of the war Spain had declared its neutrality but, mesmerized by the German victories, it switched on June 12 to nonbelligerence. It declared itself ready to join the war, the price being annexation of a number of French possessions in Africa. These conditions were conveyed to the Germans on June 19, the armistice date with France. Hitler ignored the Spanish demands and ordered that Germany proceed without Spanish cooperation. The Spaniards had an army of 500,000 but were under-equipped and exhausted. By August 9 Warlimont had a plan for a cross–Spain attack on Gibraltar, which Hitler approved on August 24. The Felix directive specified the army would enter Spain on January 10; special troops, including those that had captured Eben Emael, would assault Gibraltar on February 4; after the Rock had been taken one Panzer and one motorized division would cross the straits and occupy Spanish Morocco (Detwiler, 83). On December 6 Hitler discussed the technical ramifications of the operation in the presence of Reichenau, in overall charge of Felix; Richtoffen, who was to command the Luftwaffe; and General Küchler, who has trained the troops for assaulting the Rock. While these briefings went on, Canaris in Madrid pressed Franco for an agreement to the January 10 date set for entry of German troops into Spain. Franco wouldn't commit himself. When Canaris pressed for an alternative date, the Caudillo said that Spain would enter the war when England was about to collapse (DGFP, XI 817). Having previously announced that in case of refusal he would use force against Spain the führer now would not hear of it. Instead, on December 10, Keitel issued an order that since "the necessary political situation no longer exists," Felix is cancelled.

This by no means ended Hitler's being busy with Gibraltar. Some time in January Hitler called in Student and discussed with him the possibility of an airborne capture of Gibraltar. Next, Hitler asked Mussolini to try his hand with the Spaniards. Mussolini met with Franco on February 12 in an attempt to induce him to go along with the German plan. Without waiting for the results of Mussolini's intercession, Hitler ordered that the units held for Felix be reassigned to Barbarossa. With this the Spanish saga, stretched over seven months, fell silent.

The story of Gibraltar bears a striking resemblance to the Norwegian episode — not to Hitler's role in it, but, ironically, to that of his opponents. As with the British, there was fumbling, prevarication, endless discussions and hectic preparations, but no action. There were arguments by Hitler that the Spaniards were too tough for the Germans. There were even moral scruples (Hitler and scruples!) about invading a sovereign country. The British had been fortunate in that the Germans by their swift action in April 1940 had terminated England's agonizing bluff; Hitler was not so fortunate and he himself had to call it off.

On July 15, 1940, the Pétain government received a startling note. It demanded that France provide Germany with bases in Morocco, including eight airfields near Casablanca, unrestricted access to French ports and the use of Tunisian railroads. All these facilities were to pass under the command of the German military. The führer asked that France communicate its assent "immediately." Vichy refused and the startling thing is that Hitler accepted it without demur. Yet the military was quite busy with plans and preparations to take over not only Morocco and Tunisia but much of French Northeast Africa. The German navy had made preparations to have U-boat facilities in Dakar and to transfer troops and supplies via Gibraltar to Spanish Morocco and hence to the French colonies (Goda, 16, 67,197).

A discussion at the naval conference on September 26 laid down the following imperatives for German warmaking during the fall and winter:

a)   The Canary Islands had to be secured
b)   The Suez Canal had to be taken because the Italians would never manage to do that.
c)   An advance from Suez via Palestine and Syria as far as Turkey was necessary.

Accordingly, Hitler was exceedingly busy in the late fall and winter of 1940-41. He set in motion grandiose plans involving Portugal, Spain, North Africa, Greece, Bulgaria, the Middle East, and even the Soviet Union. One thesis, propounded by Goda, argues that all the activities and plans involving the Atlantic islands, the Mediterranean and Africa were all a post–Barbarossa contingency lest England and America, even after a defeat of Russia, still refuse to end the war. It was for a future era when a war with the Anglo-Saxons would have to be fought that all these sought-after land, air, and sea bases were meant to serve. And indeed in July–August 1941 when victory in the East seemed imminent that discussions were held by the führer about far-reaching changes in arms production and troop deployment which emphasized the need for sea and air weaponry. If so, it was a reenactment of the familiar children's story about the girl hopping around with a basketful of eggs dreaming about purchasing of a castle with the proceeds from selling the eggs till she tripped and broke the eggs along with her castle.

* * *

After the fall of France, as German strategists searched for ways to carry on the war against England, there emerged from their various proposals, in an unintended way, an entirely novel strategy. Although it sprang from the familiar elements of a peripheral campaign — Gibraltar, Suez, etc, — it grew into a radically fresh conception, which transcended and eclipsed any piddling Mediterranean operation. It amounted to nothing less than the creation of a new supercoalition to fight World War II. It was in a way an odd procedure. Normally one gathers allies and then goes to war; here Hitler was at war and looking for partners. For reasons that will become clear later, we shall refer to the new constellation as the Eurasian bloc.

The idea for this supercoalition emerged from several branches of the Wehrmacht, the OKW, the Army, and the Navy. We had seen how Jodl, already on June 30, advised that Germany ally itself with the potential inheritors of a broken-up British Empire — Spain, France, Italy, Russia and Japan. Brauchitsch and Halder advised likewise. In stating their opposition to war on Russia they had implored that a "visit to Stalin would be desirable. Russian aspirations in the Straits and Persian Gulf need not bother us…. In the Balkans … we could keep out of each other's way" (Ansel, 17). Raeder added his view that heading toward the Middle East would not trigger Russian hostility but would, on the contrary, induce it to come closer to Germany. Said Raeder in his September 29 brief, "Fundamentally Russia is afraid of Germany…. It is doubtful whether an advance on Russia from the north [i.e., a German invasion] will be necessary" (Salisbury, 58). Thus within three months after the French armistice a consensus emerged as to what the next political and military moves ought to be. This fell in nicely with the views of Hitler's consultant, the philosopher-geopolitician Karl Haushoffer who, as a counterbalance to the maritime Anglo-Saxon powers, advocated a continental block stretching from the Atlantic to the Pacific.

Japan's place in the emerging concept of a Eurasian bloc had been in the making for some time. Germany had long been trying to wean Japan away from its war with China and redirect its thrust southward, against England. Ribbentrop even discussed with the Chinese ambassador the possibility of a compromise peace with Japan (DGFP, XI 515). What eventually swayed the Japanese were the aftershocks of the French defeat. With a collapse of Dutch and French power the Japanese suddenly faced defenseless, lucrative regions in Indochina and Indonesia. They immediately took advantage of it. By agreements of August 9 and September 22 they forced Vichy to acknowledge the "preponderance of Japanese interests in Indochina" and to grant them air and land bases in the Tonkin (Salisbury, 13–15). With this change in direction of its martial ambitions Japan aligned itself with the war aims of the Axis powers. Since the steps the Japanese took risked a conflict with the USA, Japan concluded on September 27 the Tripartite Pact — a political and military alliance with Italy and Germany. This aimed primarily at deterring the USA from getting involved in the expanding conflict. Its key paragraph 3 read that "they undertake to assist one another with all political, economic and military means if one of the Contracting Powers is attacked by a Power at present not involved in the European or in the Chinese-Japanese conflict." Paragraph 5 then specifically excluded Russia. As England was already at war and Russia had been excluded, its only target was the USA. Thus in the fall of 1940 an alliance bound together Germany, Italy and Japan. The buildup of a Eurasian bloc could then proceed on the basis of this coalition.

After the signing of the Tripartite Pact Hitler met Mussolini on October 4 at the Brenner Pass and told him of his plans to include Spain and France in a European alliance. As usual, Mussolini had nothing to add or subtract. At the end of October the führer embarked on an untypical for him diplomatic junket in which he conferred with Laval, Franco, Pétain and Il Duce again. It is difficult to extract any substance from the record of these conversations. On October 22 Hitler met Laval at Montoire-sur-le-Loire. Laval offered France's participation in the war against England at the price of a peace agreement with Germany. Hitler told him this was not possible before the end of the war. Laval's offer had some precedent to it. Sometime in July Pétain had written to Hitler in response to the demand that France cede Germany bases in Casablanca. Although, said Pétain, this was not in the armistice agreement, he was willing to consider it provided Germany offered some concessions (DGFP, X 274). It is an indication of the führer's commitment to the Mediterranean war that neither this offer nor Laval's at Montoire was taken up. After one hour of talking to Laval, Hitler's special train trundled off to Hendaye on the French-Spanish border. Nine hours of conversation and dining followed during which Hitler told Franco that his purpose in coming was to effect a wide-ranging front against England which ought to include Spain. He also informed him that he had seen Laval and was to meet Pétain the next day in order to get France, too, to join the new Europe. The Caudillo was to raise no objections even though it might limit Spain's eventual inheritance in Africa (DGFP, XI, 371).

On the following day Hitler's train thudded back to Montoire to meet Pétain, whom the führer likewise tried to persuade to join an anti–British coalition. Aside from a generalized endorsement of the need to fight British imperialism, Hitler did not extract much from the silent marshal, who left most of the talking to Laval — a man Hitler disliked. Hitler then left Montoire to meet Il Duce, from whom he had received an alarming letter about an impending attack on Greece.

While not reaching any immediate results in the West, Hitler easily obtained adherence to the pact at the opposite end of Europe. Following the Vienna Awards, Hungary joined the Tripartite Pact on November 20 and Rumania one day later. The Bulgarians, in deference to an old ally, Russia, hesitated for some time but on the 1st of March the following year gave in and joined up. After being summoned to Hitler, Regent Paul was given a few days to fall in. On March 25, 1941, Yugoslavia, too, signed the Tripartite Pact.

The missing big link in the Eurasian constellation was the Soviet Union. And here lies a tale to be told. Hitler's feelings on the subject have been adequately covered to need any repetition. It will thus come as no surprise that the main architect of this tale was Joachim von Ribbentrop. An arid man himself, he most likely stole the idea from the Japanese. In July 1940 a new Japanese cabinet was formed under Konoye, which included Matsuoka as foreign minister — the man who later concluded the nonaggression treaty with Stalin. The cabinet laid down its foreign policy as follows: Japan was to have hegemony in Asia, Germany was to dominate Europe, and the USSR should set its ambitions toward India and the Middle East (Friedlander, 130). Ribbentrop's enthusiasm for this idea harks back to the Nazi-Soviet deal of August 1939. Not fully conversant with Hitler's mind, Ribbentrop took the 1939 pact seriously and was even fond of it. Vanity was a large part of it. The feasting and entertaining at the Kremlin left its mark to a point that upon his return he had told Hitler that in Stalin and Molotov's company he felt like being among old Nazi "comrades." As the Eurasian bloc construct began to emerge from the late 1940 political fog, with the USSR the missing link, Ribbentrop leaped at the opportunity to close the gap with a zeal his führer certainly did not share.

Ribbentrop went to work the moment the ink dried on the Tripartite Pact. Informing the Soviets of this event, he added that he intended soon to write an important letter, not to his counterpart but to Stalin himself. This he did on October 13. Equating importance with verbosity the missive was 3,000 words long. Starting with a "My Dear Mr. Stalin" and aping his master's didactic style he at tedious length enlightened Stalin on the ongoing war which, he claimed, Germany had already won and went on to say, "I should like to state that in the opinion of the Führer, also, it appears to be the historic mission of the four powers — the Soviet Union, Italy, Japan and Germany — to adopt a long range policy and to direct the future development of their people into the right channels by delimitation of their interests for all ages.... We would welcome it if Mr. Molotov would pay us a visit in Berlin soon." Leapfrogging the possible results of such a visit, he added, "I should be happy to come to Moscow again personally in order to resume the exchanges of ideas with you my dear Mr. Stalin, and to discuss — possibly together with representatives of Japan and Italy — the bases of a policy which would only be of practical advantage to all of us."

Stalin's reply on October 22 was brief, one-tenth of Ribbentrop's. He agreed to the visit and added that while not opposed to discussions with Italy and Japan, he felt that a settlement of issues with Germany should precede any four-power talks (DGFP, 291–7, 353–4). Ribbentrop was elated by the renewal of contacts with the Soviets and in a communication of November 8 to his embassy in Moscow he reminded Schulenburg that he had been promised a signed photograph of Stalin which he hoped the Molotov delegation might bring with them (Brüghel, 254).

Molotov journeyed to Berlin on Tuesday, November 12. It was Molotov's first visit to Berlin and he brought with him a party of 65. Schulenburg and Hilger of the German Embassy in Moscow came with him. The train arrived at the Anhalter Bahnhof at 11 o'clock to be met by a large delegation including Ribbentrop, Himmler and Keitel. They were all in uniform and they raised Nazi salutes as Molotov in a rumpled blue suit walked past the reception line tipping his homburg. The station was decked in red flags and, instead of the "Internationale," a tune forbidden in Germany since 1933, the band played military marches and the "Horst Wessel Lied."

The opening exchange with Ribbentrop lasted only one hour. Referring to the Tripartite Pact Ribbentrop informed his visitor that now Japan, too, was oriented southward.

Thus all three powers had their sights set in the same direction: Japan toward the South Pacific; Italy on the Mediterranean and North Africa; and — a bombshell — Germany's interest lay in Central Africa. Germany was proposing that the Soviet Union align itself with this new political constellation and direct its ambitions southward, toward the open sea.

"Which sea?" asked the Russian.

"The Persian Gulf, the Arabian Sea, the waters south of the Asian continent," said Ribbentrop. The Soviet visitor replied that he had not expected anything so far-reaching; he had come unprepared for talks of that caliber. The purpose of his visit was to settle issues that concerned Russia in Eastern Europe and not in South Asia where there were no problems between Russia and Germany.

It was with this as an opening that they went to see the führer in the Chancellery. Hitler repeated to Molotov the set piece: the war against England was already won and the time had come to take over the real estate of its empire. Germany and Italy, together with France and Spain, were to take Europe and Africa, over which a kind of Monroe Doctrine would be imposed so no one would dare touch it. At the moment when this inheritance was being parceled out he would like to see the Soviet Union direct its activities toward her own sphere of interests— the south Asian continent. The USSR is invited to join the Tripartite Pact and take an active part in a subdivision of the British inheritance.

Molotov answered that in principle he was not averse to joining the pact. However Stalin had given him "exact instructions" and these were to clarify certain events that had taken place on Russia's western borders in the months following the collapse of France. These fell into two categories. One concerned German incursions into what had in 1939 been designated as the Soviet sphere of influence, such as the presence of German troops in Finland and the Petsamo nickel concessions. The other related to German activities in the Balkans. That area had not been assigned to either side but some of the German moves there were inimical to Russia's vital interests. These were troop concentrations and guarantees given to Rumania and the transfer of Rumanian territory to Hungary and Bulgaria — acts which by the 1939 pact required prior consultation with the USSR. It was issues like these that he had come to discuss. Hitler answered that these acts were due to the war Germany was waging. In Finland the troops were only in transit to Norway. There was always the danger of the British getting a foothold in Finland or Sweden and Germany had to take precautions. When unable to get a more satisfactory explanation, Molotov retorted that since he had heard the war against England was already won, these reasons were not fully convincing. Hitler tried repeatedly to steer the conversation to the Eurasian bloc — but with an impassive face the man in the rumpled blue suit persisted in discussing only issues affecting Russia's security. After three hours of wrangling, Hitler looked at his watch and said that in view of the late hour and the likelihood of a British air raid, the discussions should be adjourned till the next day. The interpreter, Schmidt, later wrote that "no one had ever spoken to him [Hitler] in that way in my presence" (Shirer 1959, 805).

That night Ribbentrop gave a reception for Molotov with the participation of Göring, Hess, Himmler and Frick. Hitler refused to attend. Following dinner the Russians were taken to their opulent residence, Schloss Bellevue in the Tiergarten, one of the Hohenzollerns' royal palaces. That night the Russians cabled home the trend of the discussions. The reply from Moscow was to stick to the instructions Molotov had been given.

On Wednesday morning Molotov paid a courtesy call on Göring, with whom he discussed trade issues; and on Hess, with whom the common interest was the problem of coordinating party and state affairs. Molotov then went to the Reich Chancellery for more discussions with the führer. These continued to orbit the divergent aims of the two sides—but on a rather exacerbated level. When Hitler repeated his war-dictated reasons for the military incursion in Finland, Molotov simply said that there must be no German troops there. To forestall any possible Russian countermove in the north Hitler resorted to a threat: "There must be no war with Finland because such a conflict might have far reaching repercussions." Molotov replied that with this "a new factor had been introduced." Ribbentrop tried to defuse the situation by commenting, "there is no reason at all for making an issue of the Finnish question. Perhaps it was a misunderstanding only." After Hitler once again took up the prospects of a Eurasian bloc Molotov repeated that before they moved on to Asia there were other problems to settle besides Finland. If Germany claimed that her presence in Rumania was directed against a possible English incursion in Greece, the USSR had always been attacked by England via the Bosphorus. The USSR would, therefore, like to bolster its security there. Similar to the Germans' action in Rumania, one way to achieve it would be for Russia to give Bulgaria guarantees and keep a Russian presence near the straits. Hitler's answer was that whereas Rumania requested German guarantees, he was not aware that Bulgaria asked the USSR for them. On that note the discussions with the führer ended.

Following the two-day talks the Soviet Embassy arranged a Russian-style banquet. For this festivity, too, the führer did not show up. When following Molotov's toast Ribbentrop rose to reply, an air-raid alarm sounded. The Russian Embassy had no shelter, so Ribbentrop took his guest to the Foreign Ministry bunker. There Ribbentrop pulled out of his pocket a draft of the proposed treaty. It consisted of one public and two secret protocols. Paraphrased, the public part stipulated that:

1. The USSR concurred in the principles of the Tripartite Pact.
2. The signatories would respect each other's sphere of influence.
3. They would not join in any alliance against the four powers.

The secret part pertaining to all four participants specified,

1. Aside from revisions in Europe, Germany' sphere of influence would be Central Africa.
2. Italy's sphere would be the Mediterranean and North and East Africa.
3. Japan's sphere would be south of the Imperial Islands.
4. The USSR's sphere would be south of its territory in the direction of the Indian Ocean.

The second secret protocol concerned a revision of the Montreux Convention to give Russia the right to have warships pass the Dardanelles at any time, a right not granted to other countries.

Following the reading of the document Molotov returned to a host of European problems to be settled before Russia could commit itself to the Quadro-Pact. This included a real and not a paper arrangement for security in the Dardanelles, which meant a foothold in Bulgaria. The issues in Finland and Rumania would have to be settled, perhaps also those of Yugoslavia and Greece, as well as the question of the Skagerrak and Skattegat straits, which kept the Russian fleet bottled up in the Baltic Sea. To this Ribbentrop could only murmur that he was "überfragt" (swamped). So once more he asked: Is the USSR interested in a Quadro-Pact or not? Molotov replied that in principle yes, but with regard to the assigned spheres of interest he would have to discuss it with his colleagues in Moscow. Even if the answer were yes—the issues in Europe would have to be resolved first. He would be in contact through diplomatic channels. And on a light note Molotov added that he did not mind the air raid as during the long stay in the cellar he got such a clear exposition of German intentions (DGFP, XI 533–69).

The time was midnight, November 13. The next day at 11 A.M., 48 hours after his arrival, Molotov left for home seen off by a solitary Ribbentrop.

Was the project of a Eurasian bloc meant seriously by Hitler? What justifies having gone into Molotov's visit in some detail was that this formidable continental bloc stretching across Europe and Asia and including the world's three greatest military powers offered Hitler the only chance of winning the war. The 800 or more divisions available to Germany, the Soviet Union and Japan when let loose against the southern hemisphere would have swamped it. Left unconquered would be the two American continents. Whether the USA would have undertaken to liberate Europe, Asia and Africa in an immensely difficult and protracted conflict remains moot.

But it is very doubtful whether Hitler believed Russia would join him in a such a venture or that he wanted it in the first place. It would have been contrary to all the hatred he felt and later practiced with respect to Russia, and contrary, too, to the exalted role he assigned to the British Empire in his future world order. Nor do the specifics of the plan's history speak for its seriousness. There was nothing for Germany in the suggested division of the spoils; it is ludicrous to believe that Central Africa was what Hitler wanted. This he could have had without war; it was offered to him on many occasions. Nor does the manner of negotiations with Molotov suggest an eagerness to reach agreement—it was perfunctory and dismissive. Compared to the grand potential of a Eurasian bloc, issues such as Finnish nickel or guarantees to Bulgaria were trivial.

Proof of Hitler's disingenuousness is evident from what followed. After two weeks the Soviet Union in effect said yes to the proposed scheme. The November 25 reply from Moscow stated that "The Soviet Government is prepared to accept the draft of the four power pact ... subject to conditions." With regard to German-Soviet issues these were:

1. German troops were to be withdrawn from Finland.
2. Russia be given long-term leases for bases in the vicinity of the Dardanelles. As part of this Bulgaria was to be assigned to the security zone of the USSR (DGFP, XI 714–15).

To this offer there was no response from the German government. Hitler forbade Ribbentrop to send any reply. On January 17 Molotov inquired why he had not received an answer to his memorandum. To this, too, there was no reply. Instead Molotov's demands on Finland, Turkey and Bulgaria at the time of his visit had been tape-recorded and passed on to these governments to facilitate their enlistment in an eastern crusade, the preparations for which proceeded at full gear while the Eurasian bloc was being bandied about.

What then was the purpose behind this elaborate diplomatic campaign? One possible motivation was that by raising the specter of an alliance with the USSR Britain would be thrown into a panic and perhaps agree to make peace with Germany. That Britain indeed kept an eye on events is attested by the air raid on Berlin staged on the night of Molotov's visit—this at a time when the RAF did not yet venture that deeply into Germany. Although later Churchill jocularly wrote in his memoirs that "though not invited, he won't want to be left out of the proceedings entirely" (Churchill Vol. 2, 584) perhaps indeed the bombing raid was a reminder to Molotov that Britain was still in the war and kicking. But most likely the Eurasian bloc scheme was an attempt to get the Soviet Union on a collision course with England. In his talk with Mussolini on October 28, Hitler had informed him that Molotov would be coming to Berlin and that its purpose was "to divert the Russians to India" (DGFP, XI 417). Had Russia joined the Quadro-Pact and pushed into the Persian Gulf, not to speak of India, she would have ended up at war with the Anglo-Saxon powers. A happier situation Hitler could not have dreamed of. It would have been back to *Mein Kampf*— he and England against the Bolsheviks.

Hitler's deception about the Eurasian bloc may, however, have exacted a perhaps fatal price on his megalomanic schemes. Since Hitler never told the Japanese about the impending attack on Russia, but had instead peddled his *Dichtung*— the pretense of fighting the British Empire — this helped push Japan toward a thrust into South Asia instead of against Russia. One result was the Neutrality Pact with the Soviet Union. In concluding the pact Matsuoka as late as April 12 still advocated the merits of the Quadro-Pact, saying to Stalin, "Should you want access to the Indian Ocean via India this shall be permitted.... If the Soviet Union shall prefer the port of Karachi Japan will close its eyes (Bix, 393) Had Japan been told about Barbarossa it may have decided to join Germany and drive north instead of south with incalculable consequences to the course of the German-Russian war and as to whether or not America would have entered the war — the two pivotal events that decided the outcome of World War II.

CHAPTER 13

Fortress Europe

Having covered Hitler's pseudocampaigns against the British Isles, Ireland and Gibraltar, we will next examine how he exercised his options in the Mediterranean and the Middle East. Here the war on England was tied to Italy's martial fortunes. When during the French armistice Il Duce arrived with a shopping list for French spoils he received nothing. The Italians then went off to grab what they could on their own. It was to be Italy's parallel war. While the Germans would gobble up the continent, the Italians would rearrange things in their mare nostrum. Mussolini's legions were soon on the march in three widely separated areas— East Africa, Libya and Greece.

After the conquest of Ethiopia in 1936 the bulk of Mussolini's Roman Empire was in East Africa, a subcontinent nearly 1,500 miles in width and breadth. Here Il Duce disposed of 90,000 Italian and 182,000 native troops, commanded by the a cousin of the Italian king, Duke d'Aosta, viceroy of Ethiopia (DDR, XVI,1). Wedged against Ethiopia was British Somalia, upon which, on August 3, 1940, the Italians launched an attack. Strapped as the British were during that lonely summer for men and equipment they did not put up much of a resistance. After two weeks the British withdrew and on August 19 Italian troops entered Somalia's capital, Berbera. What that conquest meant was dubious. Even with Somalia Italian, East Africa remained surrounded on all sides by English territory. Furthermore the Italians were cut off by land, sea and air from their homeland and could count on no supplies or replacements beyond what they had at the outbreak of the war.

One month later the Italian army took the offensive in Libya. Here the stakes were higher. Five hundred miles to the east beat the heart of the British Empire — the Nile delta, Alexandria with its naval base and stores, and the Suez Canal. An advance there could form the southern pincer aimed at Britain's Middle East bastion. Here, unlike in East Africa, the Italian army was close to home, supplied across a waterway dominated by their planes and ships which could operate with equal facility from Sicily, Albania, or the Dodecanese islands. The Italians in Libya were led by Marshal Graziani, conqueror of Ethiopia and a dedicated Fascist. Within a few days they advanced 40 miles into Egypt and came to a place called Sidi Barani. There they halted.

Six weeks later Mussolini embarked on his third campaign. Deploying from his Albanian base, he launched himself on October 28 into a conquest of Greece, once more Rome versus Athens. In attacking a neutral country he aped Hitler's methods. The Greek prime minister, Metaxas, was woken up before dawn and presented with an ultimatum: unless Italy was given strategic bases in Greece, war would follow in three hours, at 6 A.M. When Metaxas inquired how he could possibly get the cabinet together in three hours, the Italian ambassador had no answer; when Metaxas inquired what Greek bases Italy demanded, the ambassador did not know. At 5:30, half an hour before the ultimatum was to expire, Italian troops attacked (Zotos, 6–7). Hitler was on his train back from a frustrating talk with Pétain, when Mussolini cabled him, "Führer, we are marching. This morning a victorious Italian Army has crossed the Greek frontier." When Hitler read this news, a witness recalled that he "raged and cursed ... saying that this ruined his *Rezept* (recipe or formula)" (Hillgruber 1965, 286).

The attack on Greece, with its opportunities to exploit either the land route across Turkey or the islands of Crete and Cyprus, formed the northern pincer for the conquest of the Middle East. Together with the offensive in Libya these were the two parallel thrusts urged on Hitler by his strategists—which Mussolini now launched on his own. But in November the weather in the Epirus region was vile, either torrential rain or snow gales; the mountains were steep and roadless; and the Greeks fought well. In the first surge of the invasion the Italians penetrated a few miles into Greek territory but 10 days later the offensive bogged down. On November 14 the Greeks took the initiative. In sustained close fighting they drove the Italians from Greek soil and went on to capture Koritza and Leskovik in Albania. By the time winter stopped operations, the Greeks had advanced along the frontier with Albania to a depth of some 30 miles.

The next blow came in Libya. On December 6, employing only two divisions, the British went on the offensive. As usual, they were slow. It was also a feature of desert fighting, whether it was with the Italians, the English or later the Germans, that the farther their armies progressed the more cumbersome were the logistics and more difficult to maintain the advance. It took the British 10 weeks to defeat the Italian army but when it ended, it was— starved as the British were of any success— a spectacular victory. On January 22 they took Tobruk, and on February 6 Benghazi. In two days of fighting, the cut off Italian 10th Army was destroyed at the western end of Cyrenaica. For a loss of 500 killed and 1,373 wounded, the British captured 130,000 prisoners, 380 tanks, and 91 undamaged airplanes (Playfair, 362). The Italian army in Libya was no more.

The battle in Libya was still on when at the end of January 1941 the British also took on the Italians in East Africa. Given the distances, the topography and the other hazards of tropical Africa, this would prove an even more prolonged affair. The campaign, launched in stages and from all possible directions by land and sea, lasted four months. On February 25 Mogadishu was taken, and on April 25 Addis Ababa. The Duke d'Aosta together with 185,000 men surrendered at Amba Alagi on May 16, and Haile Selassie, the Lion of Judah, was restored to his imperial throne. It was indicative of the nature of the campaign that while the British suffered 1,154 battle casualties, the toll due to sickness and accidents was 74,550, with 20,000 lost to malaria and dysentery alone. With the campaign over not only was East Africa cleared of the enemy but ships could now safely use the Red Sea on their way to the Suez Canal and the eastern Mediterranean.

The defeats on land were accompanied by similar flops at sea. For a long time the Supermarina avoided the British fleet sortieing out of Gibraltar or Alexandria. Failing to bring the Italians into the open, Cunningham, the commander in chief of the Mediterranean Fleet, went looking for them in home waters. The place was Taranto, Italy's main naval base, which harbored six battleships and a swarm of cruisers and destroyers. On the night of November 11 the carrier *Illustrious* approached Taranto and while bombers dropped flares to silhouette the Italian ships against the east, 21 torpedo-carrying Swordfish attacked from the west in two waves. Three of the Italian battleships were struck by torpedoes and put out of action for nearly half a year. At the same time escorts sank four merchant ships just outside Brindisi. The British lost two planes in the operation (Playfair, 37).

Following this debacle the Italians were more wary than ever in venturing onto the open seas. However, when the British started to ferry troops to Greece in anticipation of a German attack in the Balkans, the OKW began to press the Italians to attack the convoys sailing from Alexandria to Crete and Piraeus. Reluctantly the Italians complied and sent out a force consisting of the modern battleship *Veneto*, six cruisers and a number of destroyers to the waters between Crete and Greece. On learning of the Italian sortie Cunningham left Alexandria with three battleships, an aircraft carrier, four cruisers plus destroyers. The sea battle that took place March 29 south of Cape Matapan resulted in damage to the *Veneto*, which escaped, and the sinking of three Italian cruisers and two destroyers. The British suffered no casualties. After this Mussolini confined his fleet to home waters (Ansel, 133). It was symptomatic of the course of World War II at sea that both at Taranto and at Cape Matapan, the damage was inflicted primarily by aircraft launched from carriers.

To round off the picture of Italy's parallel war one should mention the performance of its air force. Soon after they joined Germany the Italians intensively bombed Malta — in June alone 63 times. From then on their activity progressively decreased until at year's end it had dwindled to zero. Their attacks on British shipping likewise amounted to little. Mostly their planes shrank from coming close enough to their targets to launch an effective attack. British warships and convoys sailed relatively unobstructed between Gibraltar and Alexandria. On the other hand, the Italian transports heading for Tripoli were being sunk at an ever-increasing rate by planes and ships stationed in Malta.

As Hitler watched Mussolini's misfortunes on land and sea he must have felt that not only was England the wrong enemy but that in Italy he had the wrong ally. But then the führer never counted on Italy's help, nor did he now feel that her defeats mattered much. As Italy floundered, Hitler did nothing to help her. He would not get involved in campaigns over islands and colonies; it was not in the south that Germany's destiny was to be fulfilled. This aloofness was buttressed by the sentimental streak in Hitler. Ever since the Anschluss, when a complacent Duce had let the führer gobble up Austria, Hitler had remained devoted to him not least because Il Duce became a Dictaphone into which the führer could, without ever being challenged, pour all his views and prophecies. He knew how desperately Mussolini craved war laurels for his new Roman Imperium and would have resented any German aid. So Hitler let things slide without interfering.

All this fit in with Hitler's own reluctance to make war on England. Instead of new campaigns, he tried to prevent or extinguish those that simmered. Prior to his invasion of Greece, Mussolini had contemplated attacking Yugoslavia. Since the Italian border with Yugoslavia was too narrow for a grand offensive he considered attacking also from the German side. When the Italians inquired at the OKW about Yugoslav fortifications along the German border, the request was passed on to Hitler. The reply of November 15 stated, "The Führer is completely uninterested in the Italian wishes regarding an attack on Yugoslavia. He wishes peace at the southern frontier of Germany and warns against giving the English an opportunity to establish their Air Forces in Yugoslavia … information … on the Yugoslav fortifications are not to be passed on to the Italians." Likewise, in December it was suggested to the Greek minister in Berlin that Athens ask for German mediation, promising Greece an "advantageous" peace (DGFP, X, 483; XI, 929). On December 12 Canaris told the Greek ambassador in Spain that Germany was prepared to put a buffer force between the Italian and Greek armies, the Greeks keeping the territory they had captured in Albania.

Germany's only stipulation was that Greece get rid of the British forces on her soil (Hill-gruber 1965, 289–90). Contacts aimed at stopping the war in Greece continued well into February.

But as the Italian defeats on land and sea piled up, a new concern arose—fear of a col-lapse of Germany's ally. On December 8 the führer conferred with the Italian ambassador, Alfieri. When the latter tried to explain away the Italian failures, the führer interrupted to say that one way to stop the rot was "by using barbaric means such as by shooting gener-als and colonels" (DGFP, X, 820). Alfieri ignored the suggestion, but hinted that by now Italy was ready for help. Hitler now began to fear a collapse of the Fascist regime. Even so he was against sending ground troops. When on December 28 the Italians asked for a mountain regiment to stabilize the front in Greece, Hitler refused it (Hillgruber 1965, 341). In his view the main problem at the moment was to safeguard the sea lanes between Italy and Libya and he agreed to support the Italians only with airplanes. Even this was hemmed with restrictions; Milch was told that he wanted the planes back by February. The unit selected was Fliegerkorps X in Norway, initially some 180 machines, trained for attacks on shipping. At the end of the year they were transferred part to Sicily and part to the Dode-canese. They remained subordinate not to the Italians but to Göring. Their mission was to guard the sea lanes to Tripoli, interrupt British convoys, bomb Malta and sow mines in the Suez Canal, multiple tasks that ultimately proved too much for Fliegerkorps X.

In the meantime a military envoy that had been sent to Libya reported back that the four remaining Italian divisions were incapable of defending Tripolitania. This brought up the danger that, when in control of Libya, the British might try to land on the continent (a profound misjudgment). On January 11 Hitler ordered ground troops to Libya, one Panzer and one motorized division. For their commander he appointed Erwin Rommel. Hitler's instructions to Rommel were to defend Tripolitania; if it was too late for that the troops, plus reinforcements, would have the task of guarding the southern coasts of Italy and France against a possible British landing (Hillgruber 1965, 347). Thus with iron consistency Hitler refused to be drawn into any offensive operations in the Mediterranean. His main objec-tive was to see that no opponent set foot on what was being built up as Fortress Europe.

Although the aid package to Italy was limited both in size and mission, the results were immediate. During the first major Luftwaffe attack on British shipping on January 10, the aircraft carrier *Illustrious* was gravely damaged and the cruiser *Southampton* sunk. More serious was that for months thereafter British east-west traffic was interrupted. On the other hand shipping between Italy and Tripoli, nearly severed by attacks from Malta, was resumed. In the two months that German land forces were being transferred to Libya, 15 convoys carrying 25,000 men, 8,500 vehicles and 26,000 tons of supplies reached Tripoli safely. Of the total of 220,000 BRT of Axis shipping only 20,000 were lost (Playfair: Vol. I, 319; Vol. II, 53).

Rommel alighted in Tripoli on February 12. Three days later the first German contin-gents started to disembark. They immediately moved out of Tripolitania and pushed on to Sirte to establish a blocking position against any further British advance. By mid–March the two German divisions, together with their equipment and stores were in place. Despite the führer's orders that he was there on a defensive mission only, Rommel on March 30 struck out against the British. Within two weeks, in a quarter the time it had taken the British to do it, Rommel recaptured all of Cyrenaica. Rommel then wanted to push on to the Suez Canal but Hitler ordered him to stop on the Egyptian border (Hillgruber 1965, 472).

This was also the time to tackle the main strategic objective in the area—Malta. But just as he had not let Rommel take Suez, Hitler made no attempt to capture Britain's vital pivot in the Mediterranean. The island fulfilled for the British many offensive and defensive functions. Located midway between Alexandria and Gibraltar, the island contained naval and air bases, a submarine pen, dry docks, repair and refueling facilities and stores of all kinds. Only half an hour's flying time from Sicily, it had, in June 1940, no fighters and few antiaircraft guns. Its ground troops consisted of six British battalions plus one regiment recruited from the local populace. All armaments and stores as well as three-quarters of the food had to be imported. The assaults by the Luftwaffe in March 1941 were effective enough to interrupt British convoys across the Straits of Sicily. After the heavy attacks of March 5 and 7 the British were compelled to ship back to Egypt the one squadron of bombers they had on the island lest they be destroyed on the ground. By the end of March Fliegerkorps X had been increased to some 440 machines and a study Hitler had ordered on February 15 for the capture of the island was ready. But no attempt to take Malta was ever undertaken.

From the end of March onward the story begins to reverse itself. The squadrons assigned to Fliegerkorps X were drawn off to the fighting fronts in Libya, the Balkans and Barbarossa. While the German forces were being depleted those of the British increased. By April the British already had 110 fighters on Malta and 2,000 additional ground troops had been shipped in. By June 1941 no German planes were left in Sicily. The task of defending the convoys to Libya and keeping Malta under siege was handed back to the Italians—with predictable results.

* * *

With the recapture of Cyrenaica Hitler had mended one of Il Duce's broken wings. There was the other one of Greece, but Greece was not a matter of bucking up a faltering ally but something that affected Hitler's own designs. Following the Italian attack British troops had landed on Crete and RAF squadrons were stationed on the mainland. This ran against the führer's determination of not having enemy troops on the continent when he turned east. The first mention of a possible German intervention in Greece came in Hitler's directive of November 12; a month later he gave it the code name Marita, scheduled for March 1941. Since such an invasion could be launched only from Bulgarian territory, Hitler had talked with King Boris and Prime Minister Filoff, to whom he promised Thrace and access to the Aegean Sea. In exchange Bulgaria had tacitly agreed to let its territory be used against Greece, provided it be kept secret until shortly before the invasion. To secure its flanks Bulgaria needed the acquiescence of Yugoslavia in the west and Turkey in the east. This was accomplished when, on February 17, Turkey signed a nonaggression treaty with Bulgaria. Yugoslavia by then had joined the Tripartite Pact. On February 28 pontoon bridges were thrown over the Danube and German troops started crossing into Bulgaria, and deployed against Greece.

Back in April 1939 the British had given Greece a guarantee similar to the one offered Poland. When it became clear the Germans were going to intervene, England launched a most intensive diplomatic offensive to build up a Balkan coalition against the expected attack. Churchill, Eden, the chiefs of staff and Wavell kept pressing Yugoslavia and Turkey to join in a common front. They even tried to enlist the Soviets. They sent Cripps a number of notes addressed to Stalin with the intent of entangling the Russians in the Balkans. Some of them were so transparent that Cripps refused to deliver them. In early April

Churchill directly asked Stalin whether he was going to let the Germans take over the Balkans. When Cripps objected to such a note Churchill forced him to deliver it and in his exchange with Stalin Cripps was to tell him that he should "give material help to Turkey, Greece and … Yugoslavia" and that by doing so "they [the Russians] would be acting in no one's interest but their own [and] that Hitler intends to attack them sooner or later" (Churchill Papers Vol. 3, 447). Nothing came of all the trips, insinuations and conferences. In the end the British had to do it alone. They had agreed that the moment the Germans crossed into Bulgaria they would send an expeditionary force to Greece. The first British units arrived in Greece on April 1 and in the course of the next six weeks 58,000 troops had been disembarked. These troops, under the command of General Wilson, were designated Force W.

On March 27 an internal coup led by General Simovic overthrew the Yugoslav government that had signed the Tripartite Pact. The regent left the country and the young son of King Alexander, assassinated by a Croat nationalist in 1934, became King Peter II. It is difficult to understand the white fury this event ignited in the führer. The new government pledged to honor the Tripartite Pact; it did not rush to help the Greeks— in fact, it did nothing to help itself. The German army in its plans for invading Greece had not counted on Yugoslav territory or facilities. Everything was based on an attack from Bulgaria and the troops there were already in place. But a rage was consuming the führer to "punish" the Yugoslavs. The invasion of Greece was postponed. Orders went out to erase Yugoslavia "militarily and as a national unit" and "the city of Belgrade to be destroyed from the air" (Trevor-Roper 1964, 60–61).

Yugoslavia with a population of 16 million was a large, mountainous, rugged country. Its army fielded 800,000 men. Yet within 24 hours the German military machine produced a plan for its conquest. It assigned to it 10 divisions drawn mostly from the troops assembled in Rumania for Barbarossa. The Germans did not even bother to wait for the assembly of all its divisions. They were still on the march through Austria and Hungary when on April 6 they struck out. The first thing they did was to launch a terror attack on Belgrade, which the Yugoslavs had declared an open city. The Luftwaffe staged five raids that day using a total of 500 bombers. They plastered the city at random, killing at least 15,000 civilians; 50,000 others were wounded. There is practically nothing to be said about the Yugoslav war because no war took place. The unanswered questions are not when and how the Yugoslav army lost the battle but where it was hiding. Some of the explanations given are that the units containing large numbers of Croats (3 million in the total population) deserted and welcomed the Germans. But the bulk of the army and most of the officers were not Croats and they had completely absented themselves from the battlefield so that the Germans occupied the country without resistance. The best indicator of what did or did not happen is that in the period up to April 17, when the Yugoslav army capitulated, 150 Germans were killed, taking in the process 360,000 prisoners of whom a quarter million were Serbs. Given the topography of the country and the massive traffic one would have expected more fatalities due to road accidents alone.

The battle for Greece that commenced on the same day as the attack on Yugoslavia is a revealing example of the kind of war England and its successive European allies waged starting with Poland in 1939. From the moment of the Italian attack, the possibility of Germany joining in was clear to all. The direction from where the invasion would come was also clear— the Bulgarian frontier. The country along this frontier consisted of a narrow strip some 20 miles wide and 200 miles in length. It was imperative not to try to defend it, because a single thrust on its western end would cut off all the troops manning the Bulgaian border. But to abandon it meant evacuating part of Greek territory (the Polish argument); and since Bulgarians were always the potential enemy this is where the main fortifications were — the Metaxas Line (the French argument). Consequently, the Greeks insisted the strip be defended. It was manned by the Greek Second Army, 70,000 strong.

When following the German entry into Bulgaria the British sent in Force W it was placed left of the Metaxas Line; this back-up position was named the Aliakmon Line. The rationale here was that, should the Metaxas Line break, the Greek divisions would withdraw and join Force W — a maneuver the Germans had never allowed any of its foes. When it became clear the Germans would also invade Yugoslavia, its border with Greece became open to an enveloping thrust, perhaps even the main one. Although the Allies had two weeks to adjust to the new situation, nothing was done. Instead of evacuating Albania, the main Greek forces, 14 divisions strong, stayed in place facing the Italians. Thus, on the eve of battle the Greek-British forces were hunkered down in three separate pockets. Some Greek divisions were in the Metaxas Line. Separated from them was Force W on the Aliakmon Line. Then the Greek division on the Albanian front, completely apart from Force W. Between them were unmanned stretches of country. When the British requested that the Greek army in Albania pull back and link up with Force W the Greeks refused. It was, they argued, against their honor to abandon positions they had won with so much blood. So, as in Poland and France, the Germans had their job cut out for them. The isolated Allied troops sat in their positions waiting for the Panzer divisions to drive between and roll them up. And that is what they did.

The assault on Greece was carried out by List's 12th Army. Its 11 divisions assembled in Bulgaria had five Panzer and three motorized divisions. As was to be expected, one prong moved west of the Metaxas Line, reaching Saloniki on the coast three days after crossing the border. This isolated the Greek armies in the Metaxas Line still bravely fighting off frontal attacks by German mountain troops. The main German forces moved first into southern Yugoslavia and turned sharply south. One prong passed through the Monastir gap and got on the flank of Force W. The other prong, after taking Skoplje on April 8, debouched into the back of the Greek army fighting the Italians in Albania. The German tanks performed prodigious feats of conquering both the enemy and the terrain. They plunged through swift running rivers and negotiated precipitous trails, keeping up the pace and momentum, steadily heading south.

The 13th of April was the crucial day in the campaign. The Germans made contact with the British forces and Wilson, after one day's battle, started a withdrawal that never stopped. On the same day the Greek army in Albania started to pull back but found itself cut off. And it was on the 13th that the British command decided to evacuate Greece. On the 21st the Greek army capitulated; two days later the king and his government left for Crete; and on the 27th the Germans entered Athens. The British evacuations lasted to the end of the month, succeeding in saving 40,000 of their own troops as well as 10,000 Greeks. While the toll in the Italian-Greek war had been heavy for both sides, that during the German blitz was very light, indicating there was little fighting involved.

Most of the British forces evacuated from the mainland landed on Crete. There were 32,000 British troops there as well as 10,000 Greeks. For Hitler they represented a potential threat to the just-conquered Greek peninsula. Furthermore, there were RAF squadrons there and their bombers had sufficient range to reach the Ploesti oil fields — a tender spot in Germany's war economy. The British had to be gotten rid of and Fortress Europe sealed and locked against any possible incursion.

In the fight for Crete all advantages but one were with the British. They had combat-experienced troops; they were well entrenched for a defensive battle against a numerically inferior enemy who, being on the offensive, should by conventional military wisdom, have had a 3:1 superiority; the British also got help from the local populace, who took an effective part in rounding up the German parachutists, killing some in the process; and their navy, of course, dominated the seas. Their only handicap was that while, unlike in Norway, they did have airfields, their air force was substantially inferior to the Germans' which, operating from interior lines, could employ as many of their airplanes as they wished. But the Allies' biggest advantage was that the Germans had to come by sea or air — in either case a most hazardous venture. Finally, there was Enigma. It provided General Freyberg, commander of the Crete forces, with the utmost detail of the impending attack — zero hour, the number of incoming planes, the direction of the assault and much else.

The German plan was to drop one parachute division of 9,500 men, commanded by General Süssman, whose primary task was to seize one or more airfields; a mountain division of 8,000 men, commanded by General Riegel, would then be landed by air; and finally 6,000 men would come in by sea. The 23,500 troops would be supported by 720 planes. The 35-mile-wide island is fairly mountainous so its airfields were on the coast and this was where the parachutists would have to drop. The waters separating the island from Greece were, of course, patrolled by the British Fleet.

Early on May 20, in fine weather, swarms of transport planes, some towing gliders, descended on Crete. There were three airfields on the north shore: Malame west of Suda Bay, Retino and Heraklion to the east. The main target was Malame where most of the 5,500 men of the first wave were dropped. Three thousand five hundred more paratroopers came in the second wave. It was not a successful operation. General Süssman and his staff were killed before they reached ground. The paratroopers were scattered over a wide area and had difficulty collecting their weapons and supplies. By the end of the day nearly a third of the division were casualties. Most important, none of the airfields were captured, so no reinforcements could follow.

The pivotal position in the fight for Malame was Hill 107, a dominant height located to the southwest of the airfield. It overlooked the runways, the beach and the sea beyond. It was manned by a battalion of troops under the command of a Colonel Andrew. Even though the Germans had been unable to reach any of their objectives, scattered units held out around Malame and Hill 107, probing and harassing the British positions. However, all their attacks had been repulsed. As evening descended on Crete, Colonel Andrew decided that next morning more German parachutists "would" be dropped and that he "would" be defeated; the time had come to withdraw under cover of darkness. Without either getting permission to do so or being stopped by his superiors, whom he had informed of his decision, Colonel Andrew during the night withdrew his men from Hill 107. With this the battle of Crete was decided. Early the next day as the scattered German units probed Hill 107 they found it abandoned. The news was immediately flashed to General Student. Although no longer under direct fire from Hill 107, Malame was still being pounded by artillery but this did not faze the Germans. Amid bursting shells and disintegrating airplanes, hundreds of Ju-52s kept landing on and across the runways, at the edges of the airfield and even on the beach, disgorging thousands of troops of Ringel's mountain division.

The last scheduled operation involved the seaborne troops. The first contingent of 2,300 sailed on the night of May 21 in 25 caiques. Spotted by British warships they were scattered by gunfire; 300 men drowned and the rest escaped or were fished out of the water. A second German flotilla, ferrying 4,000 men, too, had to return to Greece when it ran into British ships. But these delays no longer mattered for by then the British were in full retreat — some to the east, some over the mountains to the south coast. Without mules or any other transport the German troops climbed along paths that were not even trails and over heights considered unscalable, to fight and supply themselves, in temperatures up to 130 degrees F and altitudes ranging up to 7,000 feet — a hot duplication of the Germans' performance in the snows and glaciers of Norway. It was all over by the end of May by which time 18,000 Allied troops had been evacuated from the island. Although Crete was a sideshow, the losses suffered by both sides were much heavier than in the Greek campaign. The British suffered 1,820 killed and left behind 12,000 prisoners. Particularly heavy were the naval losses, all inflicted by the Luftwaffe; three cruisers and six destroyers were sunk and 17 other vessels, many large ones, were damaged, with a loss of 1,830 lives (Playfair, 104). The Germans suffered 2,000 dead with another 2,000 missing and presumed dead; 2,100 were wounded. In addition half of the Ju-52 transport fleet of 500 machines was either destroyed or damaged. The highest price was paid by Crete's civilian population. By the time the occupation ended out of a population of 400,000 islanders, 25,000 were executed by the Germans (Kiriakopolous, 368).

If the führer were to follow in the footsteps of Il Duce, who thought he had entered the war against England to expand his imperium in Africa and Asia, then after the capture of Crete and Rommel's successes in Libya the time had come to do it. Simultaneous with the conquest of Crete there opened up a breach in the Middle East, beckoning the Axis powers to come and grab it. With the outbreak of World War II nearly the entire Muslim world turned to Nazi Germany for rescue from British imperialism, oblivious to the racial policies and kind of "independence" they would enjoy under the Axis boot. The sympathies for Hitler extended all the way from the Islamic Bosnians and Albanians in Europe to the Arab countries in Africa and Asia, including the Shiites in Iran. Thus as Rommel approached the Egyptian border King Farouk sent Hitler a message welcoming the event and expressing the hope of being liberated from the British yoke (Hillgruber 1965, 472). The erstwhile mufti of Jerusalem, now mufti of Iraq, had been badgering von Papen and the Italians for some time about enlisting the Arabs as allies, and an Arab committee composed of Iraqis, Syrians, and Palestinians had been formed to cooperate with the Axis powers. On January 20, 1940, a letter addressed to Hitler from the mufti promised "loyal cooperation in all spheres." The führer's answer expressed sympathy for the Arab cause and promised to supply them with arms once a proper contact had arrived in Berlin (Schechtman, 106–7). When subsequently the mufti was received by Hitler, the mufti intimated, among other fervent hopes, that his countrymen would be forever thankful if the führer applied the same methods to the Palestinian Jews as were being implemented in Europe. The mufti then traveled to Bosnia where he reviewed the Muslim battalions mobilized for the struggle on the Balkans.

As part of this budding Arab-Nazi alliance an anti–British revolt broke out in Iraq. This started with the eviction of the ruling regent by a military junta under General Rashid Ali. The British reaction was prompt. Ground troops were rushed overland from Palestine while forces from India landed in Basra. While the mufti declared a jihad against the British, Rashid Ali appealed for German help. This could come only via Syria, which was under

Vichy rule. On May 6 the French gave permission to use Syrian airfields and ports for transshipment of German arms; they also agreed to give Iraq munitions from their own stores (Playfair, 195). But the führer dismissed the revolt with a directive of May 23, which said that aside from token assistance there should be no direct military involvement in Iraq. More generally the order explained, "Whether and how the English position between the Mediterranean and the Persian Gulf ... shall be definitely defeated, is to be decided only after Barbarossa" (GFPD, XI, 862). Within a week the revolt in Iraq collapsed.

The final episode in Hitler's refusal to take on the British in the Mediterranean was played out in Syria itself. Perturbed by the Iraqi revolt the British, fearing a takeover by the Germans, invaded Syria and Lebanon. Three British divisions plus a contingent of Free French troops launched the attack on June 8. The Vichy French not only resisted stubbornly, but pulled in reinforcements from North Africa. Here the Germans had an ideal opportunity to establish themselves in the Middle East where they would have had allies in the Vichy French and in the surrounding Arab countries. With this in mind Hitler's generals urged him, after capturing Crete, to take Cyprus from where it would have been simple to reinforce Syria; this could also have been done from Rhodes, in Italian hands all along. Hitler would not hear of it (Hillgruber 1965, 468). Not only would he not reinforce Syria but while the fighting was still on he ordered that the planes and arms the Germans had stored there be withdrawn. After resisting for five weeks, Doentz, the resident French commander, asked for an armistice. This was signed on July 10 and the Middle East passed completely into British hands.

Thus, with regard to all the possible targets— the Suez Canal, Iraq, Syria — none were taken nor was an attempt made to capture them. The extensive discussions and planning that went into targeting them and the elaborate preparations invested for assaulting some of them — when viewed against the known politico-strategic objectives of the führer — leave no other conclusion but that they were all meant for internal and external consumption to create the impression that this was what was intended, whereas what was in fact being prepared was a war against the East.

* * *

The end of fighting in Greece concluded one phase in the history of the Second World War. By the end of May Hitler had completed a series of campaigns forced on him by the declaration of war by Britain and France. He had not wanted it and, more gravely, had not envisaged it. Unable to prevail on Britain to make peace and never considering giving up on his mission of conquering Russia he thus faced enemies east and west, something he had sworn never to let happen. The only thing he could now do was to ensure that nothing on the continent was likely to stab him in the back while he marched East. When the British threatened to land in Norway Hitler swiftly eliminated that danger. Next he dealt with the French army, his greatest accomplishment in the war. When Il Duce opened the door to a British bridgehead in Greece, he had turned south and cleaned out that nest.

With the conclusion of the Greek blitzkrieg, Hitler also ran out of the kind of opponents he had faced thus far. Up to May 1941 Hitler defeated or occupied some 10 countries, diverse in size, topography and national temper. Yet they all exhibited a strikingly similar behavior prior to and during the assaults on their statehood. What characterized them before their own demise was indifference and often glee at the misfortune of their neighbor, a morbid self-congratulation that this was not happening to me! States do not act on moral principles and the above is not to imply that any should have taken on Hitler in order to rescue a neighbor. The point is that they were deluding themselves— it wasn't happening to them *yet*. And it was indeed self-interest that called for a different reaction, if not action. But in no case was such a response exhibited until one by one, as if ducks in a shooting gallery, these states fell under the guns of the Germans.

When Austria was occupied in 1938, Czechoslovakia and Yugoslavia looked on in silence although it affected profoundly their security; Italy too did not wish it but tolerated it. When Czechoslovakia's turn came there was not merely indifference on the part of its neighbors, there was celebration and both Hungary and Poland feasted on the carcass of Hitler's kill. When Poland's turn came, France, facing a border relatively empty of troops, did nothing to help her and the USSR, of course, swallowed half the country. When France was fighting for its life, there were only seven German divisions on the Russian border and it would have been a walkover for the Red Army to take Berlin. Even if the Germans had switched half their army from west to east, quite a difficult thing even for them, a two-front war would have ensued, saving Russia untold grief. Had Yugoslavia joined in when Mussolini invaded Greece, the Italians would most certainly have been driven into the sea, and the possibility cannot be excluded that Hitler would have silently approved of it, sparing Greece and Yugoslavia the ravages of war. Instead, when the British started sending aid to Greece the regent of Yugoslavia objected lest it "provoke" the Germans. Prince Paul had even threatened the Greeks that if they let British forces into Greece he would allow the Germans to attack Greece from Yugoslavia. The Greeks had informed the Yugoslavs that they would request British help only when the Germans crossed the Danube into Bulgaria. The Yugoslav government promptly passed this information to the Germans. Even after the putsch the Greeks and Yugoslavs never established a joint command or consulted each other about the imminent fighting. In his first broadcast to the USA Churchill spoke of it all when he said, "There was no unity. There was no vision. The nations were pulled down one by one while the others gaped and chattered" (Churchill Papers Vol. 3; 99). And finally, as we shall shortly see, when Russia was invaded Britain and America looked on for three full years before, with the Normandy invasion of 1944, they deigned to open a second front. Diplomacy and warmaking are often compared to chess but a basic rule of the game is to consider as many moves ahead as possible. The astonishing thing about the above events is that no one was capable of visualizing even one move ahead. This was not the best the countries' leaders had to offer their peoples and it was not — as they would claim — done in their interest; it was done because it was the easy thing to do, requiring the least courage and imagination. In the end, out of 24 independent countries in Europe 20 were attacked or occupied by Hitler, including his own allies, Italy, Rumania and Hungary. Ironically, the only country Hitler didn't occupy, even though he had cogent reasons to do so, was Finland, perhaps because, though an ally, it never became an abject vassal.

There is also a depressing consistency to the incompetence, if not actual negligence, with which Hitler's foes fought their wars. We have seen how the Poles, for reasons of public sentiment, had placed their army in a sack, preferring to lose the entire country than evacuate part of it. The French had their well-thought-out plan to block a German invasion that could come "only" via central and northern Belgium. When they learned the Germans were concentrating opposite the Ardennes, they would not budge from their mould-encrusted blueprint. They stayed along the Dyle while the Germans conducted their blitz elsewhere. And in Greece General Papagos, like Rydz-Smigly, would not evacuate the hopeless position in Thrace, actually a small part of the country, while on the Albanian front the Greeks would not pull back because it was contrary to honor. Together with General Wilson they did the job for the Germans by grouping their forces in three pockets ripe to be gobbled up. Greece, like Norway, is ideal country for waging a defensive war and had the British and Greek forces combined to form a line either below Macedonia or on the Pelopenesos, virtually an island, there would have been some chance of staging an effective resistance. This was even more likely when it became clear that the Yugoslavs, too, were to be in the fight. When the Greeks asked the Yugoslavs to concentrate their forces in the southern part of the country, which is where the German breakthrough eventually occurred, the Yugoslavs refused (Cervi, 271).

A pattern also seems to have emerged in British maneuvering whenever they fought the Germans. It can be called a strategy of dispersion. As has been stated, the British were determined not to get into a bloodbath similar to that of World War I. They knew they could not match German military power on land and, although they would never say so, they did not have the generalship for the kind of war the Germans waged. The British generals were of a Kitchener mentality, one foot still in the colonial wars, the other in the trenches of Flanders. Like the pre–Churchillian diplomats they were a supercilious and mediocre lot and they stayed that way to the end. Yet the British seem to have provoked the Norwegian expedition and when they intervened they did so with insufficient forces, almost frivolously, knowing beforehand their effort would fail. Two blatant examples of "dispersion" being a deliberate policy is provided by the Greek episode and when Italy's capitulation was being thrashed out by the Allies. De Guignand, later Montgomery's chief of staff, relates in his memoirs that had Britain told the Greeks they were incapable of stopping the Germans, the Greeks would have released Britain from its guarantees. But the British not only did not ask for it but pressed Yugoslavia and Turkey to join the fight, promising help. Nearly all those involved in preparing the Greek expedition knew it was a doomed venture. Moreover while troops were still being landed and before the Germans even attacked the Joint Planning Services were already preparing plans for evacuating the British troops (DeGuignand, 71). It was sometime later, at the Casablanca conference in January 1943, that the rationale behind this sort of warmaking was elucidated by Eden. The Casablanca meeting, where the whole strategy against the "soft underbelly" of Europe was being laid out in the presence of Roosevelt and Churchill, took place after the invasion of North Africa by the Allies. What was being visualized was an invasion of Italy with the aim of knocking her out of the war. Although the "soft underbelly" strategy was the favorite brainchild of Churchill's it turned out that even this was not meant seriously if it involved fighting the Germans. A memorandum submitted to the conference by Eden said that it was the view of His Majesty's Government that "our aim must be to knock Italy out of the war as quickly as possible and this could be achieved with almost equal effect whether Italy makes a separate peace or ... the Germans are forced to establish a full scale occupation. In the latter event it is to be expected that the Germans not only would have to provide troops for the occupation of Italy, but would also be forced to replace Italian troops on the Russian front, in France and in the Balkans.... The view of His Majesty's Government is ... that we should not count on the possibility of a separate peace but should aim at provoking such disorder in Italy as would necessitate a German occupation" (Higgins 1968, 40). In fact when Italy did surrender in September 1943, vast areas in Italy, Yugoslavia, Greece and the Dodecanese that had been under Italian rule could — with some effort — have been taken by the Allies. Instead, they were all left to the Germans. The British had even been against landing on the heel of Italy, the only slice of territory the Allies did take.

There was, perhaps, an additional rationale behind this British strategy of dispersion. It was mooted that the more countries were subjugated by the Nazi regime, the more intense would be the Americans' reaction, feeling as they would of being deprived of their customary world of travel and commerce with Europe. This effect on public opinion was expected to be of considerable help to the USA administration in deciding to arrest Nazi rule over Europe. And indeed in deliberating whether or not to send British troops to Greece, in addition to trying to embroil Turkey and Yugoslavia, was the motivation that it would produce a "favorable" reaction in the USA (Churchill Papers Vol. 3, 256). The main strategic idea was to let the Germans occupy as many countries as possible and thus disperse their forces. Dispersion was thus one plank of British strategy in World War II, along with those of blockade, bombing and revolts by the subjugated continentals. Certainly in their goal of dispersion the British scored full success. By June 1941 Hitler had dispersed his forces over the entire European continent.

Part Two

THE HOLY WAR

• CHAPTER 14 •

Barbarossa

With his sense of histrionics Hitler should have refrained from giving his eastern crusade the code name Barbarossa. There was some reason for picking that name. In 1162 this German emperor, after capturing Milano, had the city destroyed and the land it stood on plowed under; and in 1190 he led an army of 200,000 bent on liberating the Holy Land from the infidels. But on the way Emperor Barbarossa tumbled from his horse and drowned in the turbulent waters of a Syrian river. It was a portent of things to come.

The area of the Soviet Union, 8.5 million square miles, occupied one-sixth of the earth's land surface; from end to end it measured 4,000 to 6,000 miles. In 1941 including the annexed territories its population was 195 million. Historically, once it had been formed into a unified state, the country had never been conquered by a foreign invader. When this was attempted — by the Swedes in 1709 or the *Grand Armée* in 1812 — it had ended in disaster for the invading armies. Russia fought and lost wars, but they always ended in a compromise that hardly dented the bulk of the country.

Aside from its size, which tended to swallow an invader, there was the weather. Russia has an extreme continental climate, with scorching summers punctured by cloudbursts and dust-laden storms, and icy, snow-laden winters with long nights of polar darkness. Roads were mostly wagon ruts, or worse; in 1941 only 3 percent of them were paved (Fugate, 101). What roads did exist vanished in spring and autumn when the rasputitsa converted them into rivers of mud; in winter they disappeared under ice and snow. The movement of people and goods was mainly by a rail system that functioned relatively well. But this was no comfort to an invader. Mindful of the lure that their plains had for all sorts of foreigners — Swedes, Frenchmen, Germans, Poles, Japanese, Turks, and even Americans (in 1919) — the tsars introduced a wide-gauge rail track, unusable for European rolling stock. By 1941 the Russians had extended this wide-gauge rail into the absorbed Polish territories all the way to the Bug. To use the Russian system an invader, who could expect to capture little of local stock, would have to rebuild the entire network of railroad tracks.

This was the country Hitler was going not just to defeat militarily — not to get a chunk of it, but to conquer and possess as a province of his projected super-reich. Leaving out Finland, where contact with the enemy would occur only at a few isolated spots, from the Baltic to the Black Sea the Germans faced a frontage of 750 miles. While in general the land was flat and open there were several impediments the Germans had to reckon with. One, as shown on Map 14-1, were the Pripet Marshes, 300 miles long and 100 miles wide, impenetrable to a modern army. This forced them to split the army into northern and southern groupings, unable to support each other. The other problem was the Carpathian Mountains which in turn split the southern grouping in two, one to operate from Poland, the

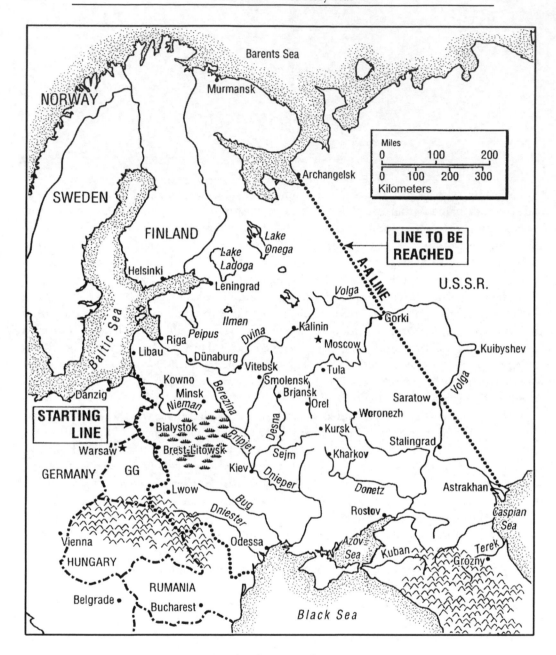

14.1. Geographic features of Western Russia

other from the Rumanian lowlands. Then there was the "funnel" effect; as the Germans advanced eastward Russia's land mass opened up, sucking the invader into an ever-widening frontage. For the objective of the campaign Hitler set the Archangielsk–Astrakhan (A–A) axis, the dotted line on map 14.1. Should the war not be won in the interim, the Germans would face a frontage nearly twice as long as the 750 miles they had started from. These were some of the terrain and climatic features of Russian geography and it was up to the craftsmen of the German General Staff to devise a plan to carry off the invasion.

The first plan worth mentioning is that proposed by Hitler himself back in July 1940.

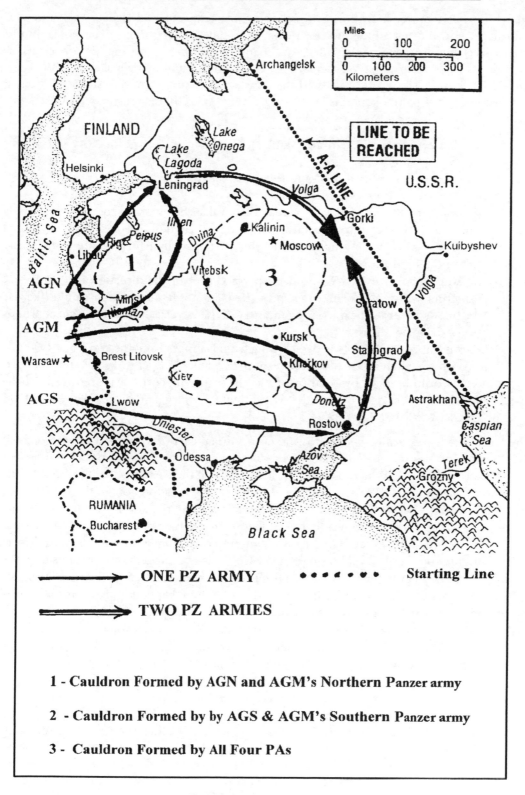

ONE PZ ARMY   • • • • • •   **Starting Line**

TWO PZ ARMIES

1 - Cauldron Formed by AGN and AGM's Northern Panzer army

2 - Cauldron Formed by by AGS & AGM's Southern Panzer army

3 - Cauldron Formed by All Four PAs

14.2. Hitler's plan for the conquest of Russia

Like his architecture, his homicidal schemes, his range of knowledge, this, too, was grandiose, Hitler often alluded to this plan and so did Goebbels in his diary notes. But its most direct explication was provided by Göring in Nuremberg during his conversations with the German journalist Werner Bross, who recorded and made a sketch of the campaign's basic aspects. Göring was livid that this scheme, sure to have resulted in victory, had been vitiated by the generals. Referring to Fig. 14.2 Hitler's master-plan was as follows:

- Four Panzer groups were to be established, one for AGN, two for AGC and one for AGS.
- AGN was to reach Leningrad and then turn south.
- AGS was to reach Rostov and swing north.
- The northern PG of AGC was to reach the Valdai heights and together with AGN form a Kessel (cauldron) south of Leningrad. Its liquidation would be handed over to the follow-up infantry while the two joined-up Panzer groups would head inland behind Moscow.
- The southern PG of AGC would push via Gomel in the direction of Rostov and together with AGS form a Kessel in the Ukraine. Its liquidation would likewise be handed over to the oncoming infantry division, releasing the two Panzer groups for a drive northeast.
- All four Panzer groups—the two coming from Leningrad and the two from Rostov—would then drive east of Moscow to form a super–Kessel whose western periphery would be held by infantry divisions while the entire armored force of the Ostheer would destroy the Red Army caught in the gigantic encirclement around Moscow (Bross, 82–83).

The Germans were to slice deep into Russia to join up east of Moscow and with one fell swoop trap and destroy the entire Red Army. What is revealing in this master plan is that had it been tried it would have aggravated many-fold all the elements that eventually contributed to the failure of Barbarossa. The thinness of the invading forces, the shortness of the campaigning season, the distances, the lack of adequate rail and motor transport, the breakdown of logistics due to weather—all factors that helped doom Barbarossa—would have been considerably exacerbated had one attempted to implement this fantasmagoric scheme. Evidently the generals thought likewise for it was never seriously considered—though the führer never forgot it. Later Hitler would claim that had the Prussian generals followed this plan Germany would have won the war. The other major plan considered was that of General Marcks, chief of staff of the 18th Army. In this scheme the main force was to debouch from near Brest-Litovsk and head for Moscow via Vitebsk and Smolensk. Its aim would be the annihilation of all Soviet forces north of the upper Volga. Two weaker wings would aim one at capturing Leningrad, the other Kiev. After taking Moscow a force would turn south so as together with the southern wing form a pincer around Ukraine. In the final phase all three army groupings would head for the Volga. In his commentary to the plan, General Marcks noted that it would be impossible to defeat the Red Army in one blow; that if by the time the Germans headed for the Volga the Red Army had not collapsed, it would be necessary to continue to the Urals. Even then, given that there would still be 40 million inhabitants plus millions of evacuees beyond the Urals, there was no assurance that the Soviets would collapse in which case the war would go on for an "indefinite period."

Hitler rejected Marcks's approach partly because of its pessimism and partly because

Marcks had been press officer to General Schleicher whom Hitler had ordered killed in 1938. The plan adopted was that prepared by the OKH. The entire front was parceled out among three Army Groups (AG), that in the North would start from East Prussia and head for Leningrad; AG Center concentrated in northern Poland would move along the Minsk–Smolensk axis; and the southern group near Lvov assisted by a prong from Rumania would head for Kiev. The largest concentration of forces and the line of main effort was assigned to AG Center with Moscow as its objective. It had none of the enveloping features of the Marcks plan; it also did not agonize over what to do if the Red Army did not collapse. A prodigious task faced the Germans in the matter of logistics. Normally their army needed two supply routes per corps, which for the forces envisaged required 15 such lanes. Given the unsuitability of the railroad gauge in Russia and that roads there were mere sand tracks, the Army would have to look after itself. And indeed that was what the troops were ordered to do—live off the land. The objective of the campaign was to reach the A-A Line. In the OKH estimate the campaign could start around mid–May and would last three to four months.

Following the presentation of the plan, exercises were held on the practicalities of the campaign. It was learned that if after reaching the line Kiev-Smolensk-Lake Peipus the war was still on, the German army would not have sufficient forces to fill the funnel opening up toward the A-A Line. This lesson was ignored, both by Hitler and his Prussians. Nor did any of the strategists consider the possibility of the war against Russia requiring perhaps two campaigns stretched over two fighting seasons.

When presented with the OKH plan Hitler added to it a few ideas of his own and instructed Halder to make the appropriate changes. The final draft was prepared by Warlimont of the OKW and presented by Jodl to Hitler on Dec 17. Hitler signed it and it was issued next day as Directive No. 21 under the code name Barbarossa. Its highlights can be summarized as follows:

- The war against Russia was to consist of a "lightning campaign," the Red Army to be trapped and destroyed close to the borders.
- The main effort was to be with AG Center. Following the destruction of the Russian forces facing it, strong formations would pivot left and together with AG North encircle the Baltic states and take Leningrad. Only after this task was completed would AG Center resume its march on Moscow.
- The Luftwaffe was given the exclusively tactical role of supporting the ground troops. It was specifically forbidden to bomb industrial targets because the advance was to be swift enough to foil any Russian attempts to either move or destroy them. Once at the A-A Line the Luftwaffe would start strategic bombing and destroy the enemy's leftover industries in the Urals.

On February 2 Hitler received von Bock, commander of AG Center, the largest of the three groupings. Bock said that it was clear to him how to force the Red Army to give battle and defeat it but how, asked the feldmarschall, can the Russians be forced to make peace? To this the führer answered, "We have such an abundance of materiel that we had to reconvert some of our war plants…. The armed forces have now more trained manpower than at the beginning of the war." And before Bock managed to ask more questions, Hitler exclaimed, "I shall fight!" (US Army 20-261, 30).

The major change introduced by Hitler into Barbarossa from that drafted by the OKH was that after the initial assault AGC was to swing its direction of attack toward the Baltics.

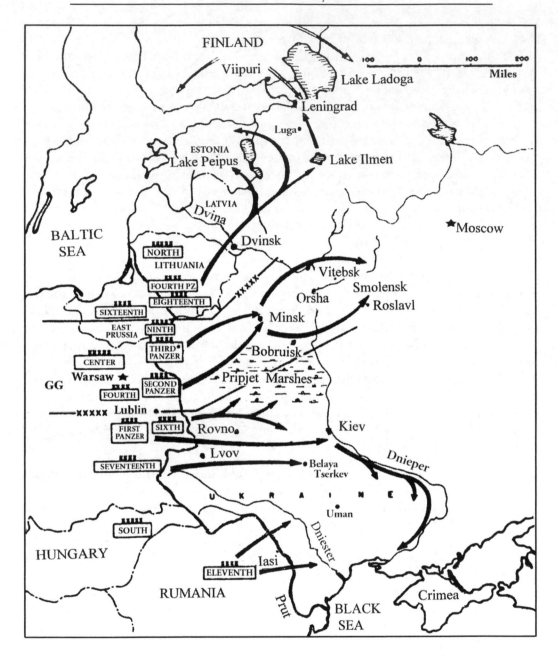

14.3. Final Oberkommando der Wermacht plan for Operation Barbarossa
(Source: US Army pamphlet 20-261a, p. 36.)

At the end of March Hitler also changed the role of AG South. While the first change was due to the führer's strategic insight, the second was dictated partly by the Balkan diversion. Instead of two prongs only the left one coming from near Lvov was to conduct an enveloping movement along the Dniepr. The panzer divisions of the 12th Army that originally were to make up the right-hand drive from Rumania had gone to Greece and could not be recalled for the start of operations.

The Balkan affair also forced a change of the starting date, originally set for May 15.

For in addition to the armor of the 12th Army, the entire 2nd Army of von Weichs was in the Balkans. This Army had been designated as the main reserve of AG Center and it could not be shipped back to the Bug on time. After both Yugoslavia and Greece capitulated, Hitler on April 30 fixed the new starting date for June 22. This delay was due to Hitler's whim of attacking Yugoslavia, a gratuitous act, for after the occupation of Greece, Yugoslavia would have been hemmed in on all sides by the Axis powers and would have remained in their lap anyway. Thus, aside from the subsequent troubles with Tito's partisans, this private campaign of his resulted in a postponement of Barbarossa of close to six weeks. Given that the entire campaigning season in Russia was only four to five months, the delay amounted to a 25 percent reduction of available time, something that was bound to affect the chances of success in the critical summer of 1941.

The conduct of military operations against Russia was not the only task Hitler imposed on his generals. Entwined with and parallel to it was the genocidal program he had mapped out for the coming war. Back in July 1940 and subsequently on December 5 he told his generals that the objective of this war was not merely the defeat of the Red Army, nor the overthrow of the Soviet regime, nor the occupation of territory. This was to be a crusade to "extirpate the life force" of the Russian people. He now proceeded to invest this vague principle with concrete and specific instructions. On March 3 Keitel issued a set of directives in which he spelled out the führer's orders to be followed by the military during the eastern campaign. This, it said, was not to be a military action as the generals understood war and it would not be sufficient to defeat the enemy forces. Instead "the Jewish-Bolshevist intelligentsia must be ... eliminated." Nor was a nationalist Russia to be allowed to emerge from the ashes, nor any independent Baltic states. The army was not to establish the customary military administration in the rear areas. Instead reichskommissariats would be set up taking orders direct from Berlin. Throughout the rear areas as well as in the front line zones special SD troops commanded by Himmler were to have complete freedom of action. The army was not to interfere with their activities; nor should the army punish its own troops for crimes committed on the civilian population. All "communist functionaries" captured at the front were to be handed over to the Einsatzgruppen for "special treatment"; if combat conditions made such a transfer inconvenient the captured men were to be killed by the troops. These orders were repeated to the generals on March 30 in a meeting with the führer himself. The generals also met with Himmler and Wagner, the quartermaster general, and with Heydrich, who further elaborated on the extermination program to be conducted in the east in parallel with the military operations (*The Holocaust*, Vol. 7, pp. 99–101).

Although the subject will be taken up more fully later on, it is relevant to clarify already here one aspect of the German army's complicity in the genocidal campaign in Russia. Much has been made of the Commissar Order, which instructed the army to hand over to the SS or shoot on the spot captured politruks of the Red Army. Were the killings confined to the execution of politruks, even if adhered to 100 percent, the record of the German army's criminality in the East would have been a paltry affair. There were not that many politruks to start with, most of them were never captured, and when on the point of capture, many killed themselves rather than fall into German hands. The elaborate arguments about the army's implementation or nonimplementation of the Commissar Order is a smokescreen hiding a much vaster landscape of odious crimes. Probably the single greatest atrocity committed in Russia was the extermination of close to 4 million Russian POWs—conscripts without office, rank, ideology, or social standing. The POW camps were under army jurisdiction, formally and factually. But in accordance with the wishes of the führer the army saw to it that out of the close to 6 million Russian POWs two-thirds perished in captivity.

* * *

Now, that one pillar of his life's mission — the launching of his eastern crusade — had been put in place, Hitler resurrected its twin — peace with England. If he could achieve that, his historical role would, to the strains of a Wagnerian crescendo, have soared as the greatest triumph in history. In a way it was back to the summer of 1939 when with his armies poised eastward he had inveigled, cajoled and begged England for friendship and acquiescence in his plans. He now tried again.

As soon as Barbarossa was signed into order contacts with various intermediaries were intensified. On December 23 the RSHA agent Jost reported to Ribbentrop that he had had talks with the British minister in Stockholm, Victor Mallet; Jost was instructed to continue his efforts (DGFP, XII, 931). Then in his Sportpalast speech of January 30, 1941, Hitler returned to the theme when, with a touch of chagrin, he said, "I have offered Britain my hand again and again. It was the very essence of my program to come to an agreement with her…. We have been drawn into war against our will. No man can offer his hand more often that I have." In May, von Papen approached Turkish foreign minister Saracoglu with a request to act as intermediary between London and Berlin. To sweeten this peace offensive the Germans on May 13 halted their air raids on London, which had been quite heavy in the preceding two months, and the press was ordered to tone down their anti–British tirades (Dallin 1942, 370–1).

The most spectacular event of that period was Hess's flight to Scotland. This took place on the evening of May 10, leading to talks with representatives of British Intelligence and the British cabinet. Like the halt before Dunkirk this event is a favorite topic of controversy as to whether Hitler was party to it. One can construct a generous list of particulars arguing for or against it. Some of the most telling facts are as follows: for the purpose of shuttling Hitler, his personal pilot, Baur, was given a most confidential map showing closed zones of flying over Germany and other restrictions applicable to aircraft. He was, of course, forbidden to share this information with anyone. Yet Baur, in cooperation with Milch, had given Hess such a map (Sweeting, 150). Hess also had no difficulty in procuring a Messerschmidt 109 for the trip. He had taken off for Scotland three times before without being stopped but returned because of bad weather. On May 10 he had flown from Augsburg the entire width of Germany and far into the North Sea without being intercepted by Germany's air defense system. What matters most, however, is that the message he delivered to the British and the vocabulary he used are straight out of his master's mouth. The gist of Hess's mission was that Germany was about to launch a war against the USSR and that this was the time for England to make peace. Speer testified that upon hearing of Hess's deed the führer let out an "almost animal-like scream." However, in a meeting with party chieftains on May 13 Hitler told them that a few days before his flight Hess asked him if he still stood for cooperation with the British the way he expounded it in *Mein Kampf* and he had answered yes (Kershaw 2000, 375–6). After the war Gauleiter Bohle of the Auslandsorganisation testified that Hess acted with the führer's knowledge and encouragement; so did Bodenschatz, Göring's adjutant. Perhaps the most authoritative testimony on the subject came from Britain's intelligence chief, Menzies, who reached the unpublicized conclusion that "Hess was sent to England with Hitler's permission to arrange a truce" (Brown, 348).

A circumstantial piece of evidence in this direction is that since the British did not announce Hess's presence for several days the Germans likewise withheld the news from the public, hoping perhaps for a success of the mission. It was not until 8 P.M. on May 12, two days after Hess's disappearance that, following Britain's announcement, an official German communiqué revealed that the deputy führer went crazy and flew to the enemy.

The most likely scenario is the familiar one of such schemes; had Hess succeeded in his mission Hitler would have taken credit for a bold move; in case of failure, Hitler would disown the man and his deed. To cap this story a document was delivered to Hitler on May 12 — two days after Hess's flight — from Professor Karl Haushofer, Hess's geopolitical mentor, in which the professor informed the führer of his peace contacts with various British individuals. In the memorandum he asked Hitler to receive him in order to pass on orally further details of those contacts (DGFP, XII, 783).

The hope for England's acquiescence in an eastern crusade persisted into the start of the campaign. On the first day of Barbarossa, Halder quotes a Weizsäcker scenario with regard to the German-English-Soviet triangle. First, said the Foreign Office staatssekretär, England will feel relieved at having found a fighting partner; then, with German victories piling up, England will sober up; it will then make peace with Germany and give it a free hand in the East (Halder, Vol. II, 3). On the same day the Foreign Ministry instructed von Papen to approach the British ambassador in Turkey with an offer of peace (Goerlitz 1954, 394). One fall-out from Hess's escapade, as well as of the other peace contacts, was to increase Stalin's suspicions that a plot was being hatched between Berlin and London. It made him more wary than ever of British warnings about an impending German attack.

* * *

The stream of intelligence reaching Moscow — first about preparations for a German attack, and eventually of its exact date, June 22 — is too extensive to record. Its very proliferation almost made it suspect, except that it was all true, and easily verified. It arrived from all possible directions, friend and foe alike. It came from the Red Orchestra, the Soviets' most elaborate spy network with excellent connections to the German military, to whom the Luftwaffe lieutenant Schulze-Boysen had delivered in January the full text of Barbarossa (Read and Fisher, 603–4). The Soviets' second best network, Lucy in Switzerland, informed them in April that the date had been set for the last week in June. Sorge, in Japan, who on May 2 had cabled the Soviet Military Intelligence (GRU) about the decision to invade, followed it up on June 15 with the exact date of attack. It came from the Soviet Embassy in Berlin where a German Luftwaffe major informed the ambassador that the Luftwaffe had been moving from Africa to Poland in preparation for an invasion of Russia. When General Proskurin, head of Red Army Intelligence, persisted in trying to persuade the Politburo about Barbarossa, Stalin had him shot; nor was he the only agent to suffer that fate — so were some German deserters that brought such "provocative" news (Miner, 126). Schulenburg and Hilger, both opposed to the war, openly revealed the secret to Molotov imploring him to do something to mend fences — a heartfelt message wrapped in a hopeless plea.

Both America and England kept sending a stream of warnings. After carefully confirming received intelligence about Barbarossa, Sumner Welles called in the Soviet ambassador on March 20 to inform him about the existence of the plan. At the beginning of June, the US ambassador in Moscow, Steinhardt, was given the exact date and he too passed it on to the Soviet government. Even more specific information came from the British. Their warnings dated back to 1940, but on April 13, based on Enigma decrypts, Churchill provided Stalin with the most concrete information yet. Between that date and mid–June Eden met Maiski five times with further warnings. Finally, on June 10 Cadogan called in Maiski, told him to sit down and take notes; based on Enigma intercepts he proceeded to give him the entire deployment of German forces along the Soviet borders (Read and Fisher, 604–10).

There were facts on the ground that corroborated everything intelligence said. There was the steady and massive build-up of German troops along the border. There were the Luftwaffe reconnaissance flights over Russian territory, hundreds of them. Due to a malfunction, one of these planes landed on April 15 near Rovno; in it the Russians found maps, cameras and photos taken 100 miles inside their territory. On the night of June 17 Soviet troops intercepted several German saboteur parties whose mission it was to destroy rail lines and bridges west of Minsk to isolate Russian frontier troops from the hinterland; during interrogation the Germans revealed the date of the scheduled attack. And on the last evening before the attack, June 21, when the troops had moved to their jump-off positions, several German deserters swam the Bug telling the troops to expect an attack within hours. According to Soviet archives opened after the fall of the USSR, in early June Schulenburg at a private luncheon at the German Embassy in Moscow revealed to Dekanozov that Hitler has definitely decided on war with Russia, and added, "You will ask me why I am doing this.... I was raised in the spirit of Bismarck who was always an opponent of war with Russia." When this was reported to Stalin he sneered, "Disinformation has now reached Ambassadorial level" (Andrew, 83).

In fact there was no need for any elaborate intelligence or Enigma code-breaking to know for certain what was coming on the morning of June 22. The entire civil population along the Russian border was party to the "secret"; it was a literal case of the saying that every child knew it. On the Saturday afternoon of June 21, in all the communities along the Bug, one could see swarms of German soldiers selling their accumulated loot — watches, blankets, trinkets—which they could not take with them into the field, and then vanish toward the river. They had all informed the populace that tomorrow, Sunday morning at 3:15, they would invade Russia. Thus while the Soviet colossus was doing nothing, the ordinary people along the Bug prepared themselves for war. With a few belongings and parcels of food they abandoned towns and road junctions and headed for the countryside, to avoid the air and artillery bombardments expected from the Russian side when the Germans attacked (Pinkus 1990, 43). That all this did not stir the Red colossus is a study not in history but in pathological psychology.

Stalin's reactions to the German preparations for war against him represent the case of a leader's rational behavior collapsing in step with the escalating threat. We have seen previously how, following the collapse of France, Stalin had embarked on a crash program of occupying territories on his western borders— Estonia, Latvia, Lithuania and large slices of Rumania. This was a safe and useful precaution because it created a buffer zone to absorb the shock of a possible attack, and being within the terms of his 1939 pact with Germany, it was also prudent. The next stage in Stalin's moves commenced around the time of Molotov's visit to Berlin when Stalin endeavored to rein in the German incursions into Finland, Rumania, and Bulgaria. At that time he even tried to restrain Hitler's war preparations in the GG. In his discussions with Ribbentrop, Molotov reminded him that the August 1939 pact left open the question whether "the interests of both countries make it desirable the retention of an independent Polish state" (Bregman, 123). In 1939 Stalin had dumped the entire Polish question in Hitler's lap. But in November 1940, when echelons of German troops kept arriving in the GG as part of Aufbau Ost, Molotov raised the issue hoping to restrict the use of Polish territory for the German build-up. The Soviet attempts were an idle exercise; Stalin wielded no handle and was not prepared to take any action to force Hitler to abandon his buildup in the countries adjoining the Soviet Union. Failing in this and then witnessing the demise of Yugoslavia and Greece, as well as the inclusion of Bulgaria in the German orbit, Stalin's responses rapidly went askew. Unable to stop Hitler's military preparations and frantic to avoid war, Stalin resorted first to his own brand of appeasement, followed by the spectacle of curtsying and scraping practiced on all levels of Soviet-German relations, economic, diplomatic, military and even personal.

One of the great boons for Germany of its pact with the Soviet Union was the trade agreement, which pumped prodigious quantities of foodstuffs and raw materials into the German war economy. For Stalin it constituted the most reliable fetter by which he hoped to make Hitler honor the nonaggression pact. Russian shipments provided all the grain needs of the Wehrmacht and a quarter of its fuel needs (Rich, 207). During 1940 the USSR shipped Germany half a million tons of phosphates, nearly a million ton of various grades of iron, and 100,000 tons each of chromium and cotton. Moreover, it transshipped rare materials from the Far East including critical rubber. On January 10, 1941, a new trade agreement that provided for even heftier deliveries was signed. The supply of grain was boosted to 2.5 million metric tons. Metals crucial to the German armament industry were added to the list, including 6,000 tons of copper, 1,500 tons of nickel, and 500 tons each of tungsten and molybdenum. The Russians, after having long bickered over Finnish nickel, agreed on January 31 to supply Germany with 60 percent of the Petsamo mines' output (DGFP, XII, 960,1060,1235). The Finns were informed not to worry any longer about Soviet demands on the Petsamo mines and, full of smiles, Stalin promised the visiting Paasikivi to supply Finland with 20,000 tons of grain (Krosby, 164). While the German payments, mostly machinery, were scheduled for delivery at a later date, the Russian shipments began immediately. They in fact exceeded commitments. In March, Schnurre reported that Russian deliveries increased "by leaps and bounds" (DGFP, XII, 475). He also reported that Kostikov, the commissar for foreign trade, complained that the Germans were not providing enough trains to pick up the available goods (Brügel, 302). This hectic pace of deliveries was kept up to the very hour of the German attack.

The last instance of Stalin trying to restrain the Germans from expanding into the Balkans occurred on January 17, 1941. Russian ambassador Dekanozov handed Weizsäcker a demarché which, taking note of German preparations for entering Bulgaria, stated "the Soviet Government regards it as its duty to give warning that it will consider the appearance of any foreign armed forces on the territory of Bulgaria ... as a violation of the security interests of the USSR" (DGFP, XII, 1122). This occurred at the same time that Molotov kept inquiring why there had been no response to the Soviet offer to adhere to the Four-Power pact (Eurasian bloc). No response came to the Bulgarian demarché any more than to the previous note. In March the Germans did enter Bulgaria and the Soviets sat and watched it happen, the delivered "warning" a scrap of paper in the wind. Then came the German blitz against Yugoslavia and Greece and Soviet diplomacy went down on its knees. One year after their occupation by Germany the USSR withdrew its recognition from Norway and Belgium and expelled their ambassadors—a quirky diplomatic move as the Germans had not abolished these two states. This was followed by the withdrawal of USSR recognition from Yugoslavia and eventually also from the Greek government-in-exile. Instead, the USSR recognized the rebel regime of Rashid Ali of Iraq — a government destined to expire within a month — and exchanged ambassadors with the Vichy regime of France. None of this was ever requested by the Germans. Hitler's response was to instruct the press not to report these Soviet moves and to withhold the news of the new trade agreement with the USSR. When Göring heard of all these Soviet recognitions and nonrecognitions he remarked, "Der Russe kommt zu Kreuze gekrochen" — the Russian comes crawling to the Cross (Williams and von Narvig, 252).

As part of his sycophantic offensive, Stalin for the new year of 1941 replaced his Berlin ambassador with one Vladimir Dekanozov. Hitler would not receive him. News was also passed on to Schulenburg that, except for Maiski in London, Stalin had now purged all Jews from high positions and, in a grand gesture of breaking the ice, Stalin himself took over from Molotov the premiership of the Soviet government (till then he was merely secretary of the party). In a long dissertation to Ribbentrop, Schulenburg expounded on the meaning of this move: Stalin was ready for a radical upturn in relations with Germany, which Molotov ostensibly had bungled.

During May and June, as Hitler made his last preparations, Stalin addressed to Germany a number of appeals mixing professions of love with imprecations for pity. As the news of the impending attack became an open secret in the Moscow embassies, Molotov called in Schulenburg on June 14 and handed him a statement which, he said, TASS and Pravda were to publish next day. In it, blaming the English press and Ambassador Cripps for rumors about an "impending war between the USSR and Germany," the Soviet government branded them as "a clumsy propaganda maneuver of the forces arranged against the Soviet Union and Germany.... In the opinion of Soviet circles rumors of the intention of Germany ... to launch an attack on the Soviet Union are completely without foundation" (Shirer 1959, 844). Stalin, of course, hoped to elicit a similar denial from the Germans. None came. This, like the freight trains rumbling over the Bug, was kept up to the last hour, and beyond. At 9:30 of the evening of June 21 Molotov called in Schulenburg again and declared, "There were a number of indications that the German Government was dissatisfied with the Soviet Government. Rumors were even current that a war was impending.... He would appreciate it if he [Schulenburg] could tell him what had brought about the present situation in German-Soviet relations" (Shirer 1959, 847). Schulenburg could offer no explanation.

As part of this diplomatic kowtowing Stalin personally indulged in a number of embarrassing gestures. He called Dekanozov home for the May 1 parade and put him on the podium next to his own exalted person, the photograph of the event splashed next day on the front page of Pravda — a hint that if one loves the envoy to the emperor, the emperor himself must at the least be adored. Stalin even invited the führer's artistic companion Speer to help out with his building projects in Moscow, an invitation Hitler immediately scotched (Fest 1999, 79). And there was the frequently described April 13 scene at the railway station when Matsuoka was leaving Moscow after signing the neutrality pact. Suddenly Stalin appeared — the rarest of occasions in Soviet history. Joining Matsuoka he uttered the strangest pronouncement: "Now that Russia and Japan have fixed their problems, Japan can straighten out the Far East; Russia and Germany will handle Europe. Later together all of them will handle America." Stalin then asked for Schulenburg and when he came over, threw his arm around him, saying, "We must remain friends and you must now do everything to that end."

The Soviet military reaction to the German war preparations was in keeping with its diplomatic and economic sycophancy. No troop movements and no defensive measures were permitted that would have constituted a response to the mounting threat. When the Russians protested the hundreds of overflights by their reconnaissance planes, the Germans promised to "investigate" and no more was heard from them; the flights continued unabated. The Russian border troops were ordered never to fire on the encroaching aircraft and the plane that had landed at Rovno was released. When in mid–June General Kirponos, commander of the Kiev Military District, in response to the heavy German deployment opposite his sector, had moved some units closer to the border, he received a blistering rebuke from Moscow: "Report on what grounds you ordered the units ... to occupy the forward zone. Such actions can immediately provoke the Germans to armed conflict.... Cancel the order immediately and report who, specifically, issued that arbitrary order" (Read and Fisher, 615). The punishment that awaited the officer in charge was in keeping with similar events in the past, when intelligence agents were executed for bringing bad news. Bock reported that in his sector one could see Russian soldiers waving across the Bug and shouting that there would be no war because Stalin and Hitler have agreed on everything. "Unbelievable!" remarked the feldmarschall (Bock, 217).

All these pathetic acts pale when compared to the negligence exhibited on the day of the outbreak of the war, for on the morning of the attack, as the greatest land armada rolled across the Soviet frontiers, Russian troops were asleep in their barracks; Soviet aircraft stood parked in rows; all depots, rail and road junctions were unprotected; sentries on the frontier had been neither reinforced nor alerted; the strong points along the border were not manned; and none of the bridges were blown and fell undamaged into German hands. It was so peaceful that Guderian, commanding the most powerful Panzer Group opposite Brest-Litovsk considered foregoing the planned preparatory artillery bombardment in order not to wake up the Russians (Guderian, 127). On Sunday, June 22, with the Germans already on Russian soil Berlin intercepted a message from Moscow asking Tokyo to mediate the "economic and political differences" with Germany and requesting the Japanese to make contact with the German Foreign Office (Halder Vol. II, 4). The Germans surged into a country asleep, inflicting the most horrendous devastation on the Russian troops that had been neither prepared nor warned of what was coming. And when the blow fell they were abandoned to their fate.

As we have seen there was no surprise in the German attack on that Sunday morning — neither on the strategic, tactical, or any other level. What happened to the Man of Steel to have things come to such a pass? Stalin's name is used advisedly because in that period he and he alone dictated policy. The easiest thing to say is that there is no rational explanation, no more than for the mass executions Stalin had ordered for his own people and army during the preceding 15 years of his rule. But if one must enter the labyrinth of motivation one can, on the basis of previous events and utterances, paint the following mental landscape.

Several elements, both objective and abnormal, combined to weld iron shackles around Stalin's ankles and prevent him from responding rationally to the coming onslaught. In the spring of 1941 Russia was catapulted back into the situation, perhaps even more critical than she had faced two years earlier. Stalin was frantic in trying to avoid a war with Germany; he had nothing to gain from it and everything to lose. He was terrified of the German army, particularly after witnessing what it was capable of in its campaigns against the Polish, French, English and assorted other armies. Whereas the Wehrmacht, a honed killing machine, was at its peak in terms of experience, armaments and esprit-de-corps, the Red Army was in the midst of reorganization and refurbishment, in need of at least another year to complete it. The German army faced no opponent on the continent and could employ its entire might in the East. And Stalin knew that should he find himself at war with Germany Russia would be left alone to fight and bleed. England, he knew, would and could help no more than she did during the Polish campaign. There is an illuminating confirmation of this from the record of a meeting in early June with Soviet ambassador Maiski, when Churchill and Eden had tried to pull Russia into cooperation. Churchill promised Maiski that should the Germans invade the Soviet Union Britain would assist her by bombing Germany and forming an economic blockade — things she had been doing with little effect for some time — and by way of additional help Britain would immediately send to Moscow a military mission (Langer, 529). This is what Stalin feared and this is what subsequently happened. For three years Russia had been fighting a devastating and blood-soaked war alone against the German army and it wasn't until the latter was a spent force that, in summer of 1944, the Western Allies entered the European continent in force. Stalin had anticipated all this and, to avoid it, was prepared for any humiliation, any collaboration, if that could save him from the catastrophe of a clash with the Germans.

The above was the rational and objective component of Stalin's behavior. The next element, not in the realm of statesmanship but metaphysics, was that Stalin could find no explanation why Hitler would want to go to war with him. Hegelian dialectician and hard-nosed horse dealer that he was, he could find no *rational* motive for Hitler taking on the Soviet Union when the war with England was still on — as indeed there was none. Stalin would not countenance the possibility of a country going to war due to the mental kink of its ruler. True, the Bolshevik state with him in the lead also subscribed to an ideology, perhaps even more fervent than Nazism, but Stalin knew perfectly well that all his moves were based on realpolitik and profit, with emotion and dogma jettisoned whenever they conflicted with state interests. Cast in this pragmatic mold Stalin would not accept the notion that Hitler might go to war because of a weltanschauung, and even more perversely because of his private compulsions. He could not understand it and therefore disbelieved it. Another element in Stalin's escape from reality was his suspicion that England may attack him. In late 1939 the Allies indeed mooted action against the USSR, first via Finland and then from the Black Sea on Baku. Now, in 1941, the British were landing in Greece and the Greek islands, and tempting Turkey to join in a common Balkan front. So he was almost as suspicious of British intentions as of the threat from Hitler. That after the fall of France Stalin could still harbor fears of a British expedition against the USSR only shows the dislocation of Stalin's psyche. This was further fueled by a possible German-British collusion — a separate peace and a joint attack on the USSR — particularly in view of Hess's sudden flight to England (Gorodetsky 1999, 110, 232). This also made Stalin inclined to mistrust all the hints and warnings from the West, suspecting a conspiracy aimed at provoking him to do things that would give Hitler a pretext for attacking Russia.

From this second element — a reliance not on reality but on rationality — followed Stalin's descent into a state of mental catalepsy. It stems for a process when one's needs and wishes are of such intensity that one is incapable of perceiving the moment when they become a delusion. Stalin was so committed to avoiding war that when it became a certainty he would not acknowledge it. Psychologically traumatized by the turn of events so contrary to all his efforts and to the vital interests of the USSR, he fell into a panic lest the slightest move on his part trigger the very thing he so obsessively feared. In his memoirs

Zhukov writes that Stalin's fear of provoking the Germans became "maniacal" (Volkogonov, 400). There is a medical description of what happens to the attacker and its victim minutes before the kill. Whereas the killer brims with adrenaline, the victim becomes catatonic and goes into shock, induced when the body is flooded with a paralyzing neurotransmitter called acetylcholine. By June 1941 Stalin was a dazed rabbit sitting with folded ears under the shadow of the coiled viper, waiting to be struck.

* * *

One-thirty P.M. of Saturday, June 21, had been set as the last hour for a possible cancellation of Barbarossa. The hour passed with no recall from Berlin — the invasion of Russia was on. Of the total German army strength of 3.8 million men, 3.2 million, or 85 percent, were arraigned against Russia and so was 60 percent of its air force. The hour of the attack was set for first light, 3:15 in the morning.

In Berlin on that Saturday afternoon Hitler sat in the Chancellery composing a number of proclamations: to the German people to be broadcast at 5:30 in the morning, to Mussolini and Horthy inviting them to join the crusade, and statements to be handed out to Dekanozov in Berlin and to Molotov in Moscow. The troops were told that the fight they were embarking on was not only to "provide the means for ending this Great War for all time ... but for the salvation of the entire European civilization and culture." It ended with "May the Lord God help us in this struggle." Eight hundred thousand leaflets were delivered to the front lines to be read to the troops before opening fire.

Late that Saturday night the telephone rang in the Soviet Embassy, the caller requesting the ambassador to appear at the Wilhelmstrasse at 3:30 in the morning. The Russians thought that Ribbentrop had finally agreed to receive the communication they had been trying to deliver all that day. This concerned three issues: a protest against reconnaissance flights, a warning about the repercussions of an armed attack, and a readiness to embark on negotiations with Germany. Thus, when Dekanozov, accompanied by Berezhkov, arrived at the Foreign Ministry, he started reading his memorandum. Ribbentrop waved him to a stop, saying that he had something more important. He then let Schmidt read out a long litany of Soviet sins committed against Germany, in consequence of which, the statement concluded, "The Soviet Government has broken its treaties with Germany and is about to attack Germany from the rear in its struggle for life. The Führer has therefore ordered the Wehrmacht to oppose this threat with all the means at their disposal." As the significance of this delivery sank in, Dekanozov, according to his memoirs, replied, "You will regret this insulting, provocative, and thoroughly predatory, attack on the Soviet Union. You will pay dearly for it." Reportedly, as the Russians were leaving, Ribbentrop called out, "Tell them in Moscow that I was against this attack." According to other reports, after delivering the declaration of war Ribbentrop simply strode out of the room.

At nearly the same time Schulenburg in Moscow asked to see Molotov. The latter received him as soon as the request came in. It was daybreak in Moscow when Schulenburg read out his statement. It was a condensed version of the one given Dekanozov but it ended with the identical announcement that "by the order of the Führer the Wehrmacht is to oppose the Russian threat with all the means at their disposal." Molotov listened in silence and when Schulenburg finished he asked, "This is war. Do you believe we deserved it?" Schulenburg answered that he had been ordered not to enter into any discussions.

At 5:30 A.M., two hours after the Ostheer opened fire, the German people heard on the radio trumpets of a Liszt fanfare, followed by Goebbels reading the führer's proclamation about the start of his crusade against Russia.

In 1940 when he set out to entice his generals into attacking Russia he had told Rundstedt that he would "kick in the door and the whole rotten structure [the Soviet Union] will come crashing down" (Clark, 43). In a conversation with Hewel on the evening of June 20, one day before the start of the campaign, the führer returned to the same metaphor, although with a different prognosis: "I feel as if I am pushing open the door to a dark room, never seen before, without knowing what lies behind that door" (Read and Fisher, 629).

On the eve of the Polish campaign Hitler had thrown overboard one of his holy caveats—that of never going to war with England. With the start of the Russian campaign he was jettisoning his second holy maxim — never to wage war against both East and West. All his "do-nots" shriveled when confronted with implementation of his central mission. And so the amok-like spasm to destroy Russia overwhelmed everything else.

• CHAPTER 15 •

The Black and the Red

On Saturday night nearly the entire German army lay pressed against the Russian frontier. Complete radio silence had been imposed on all units. The troops were told not to jangle their equipment and to shield their cigarettes—so they lay and listened to the croaking frogs and the sounds drifting in from the other side. Each camouflaged tank had 10 jerricans of fuel strapped to its sides and towed a trailer with three additional drums—ready for a long, nonstop haul. Motor vehicles carried rolled up fascine mats for crossing swamps. By a previous order the troops were forbidden to read the history of Napoleon's march on Russia. But the date fixed for Barbarossa was the same as when the *Grand Armée* crossed the Niemen 129 years earlier. At 9 o'clock that evening the soldiers were gathered round their commanders, who read to them the führer's message. They were given chocolates and cigarettes and every four men received a bottle of schnapps. Then they waited for dawn.

The largest concentration of troops was opposite the Bug river. Across it the Germans could see the lights blinking in Russian towns, the largest glow coming from Brest-Litovsk, a formidable fortress meant to guard the road and rail bridges spanning the Bug. When earlier Guderian came to inspect the front line troops, he recorded that "the behavior of the Russian troops convinced me that they know nothing of our intentions ... the strong points along their bank of the Bug were unoccupied" (Kershaw R., 26). At about 2 A.M. those crouching opposite the city heard the sound of an oncoming train. It was a freight train ferrying goods from Russia to Germany. It clattered over the iron bridge and disappeared in the interior of German territory (Carell 1963, 22). Likewise a Soviet airliner on the Moscow-Berlin route was on its way across the Bug and the order was to shoot it down. However, the Germans failed to intercept it (Knoke, 42).

Although the onslaught had been set for 3:15 in the morning, the Russians had been struck the first blows before that hour. Commando squads had slipped across the Bug, knifed or strangled the sentries manning the bridges and removed the demolition charges. Special bomber formations had taken off during the night and crossed the border so that the first bombs fell just before the invasion started. At 3:15 the entire frontier lit up with a snake of fire from 72,000 guns as the Germans opened up the one-hour preparatory bombardment. Simultaneously, over 1,000 bombers and fighters flew across the border, headed primarily for Soviet air bases. Already some planes were returning from Russia, having dropped sabotage troops in the interior during the night.

The artillery bombardment was still on when 3,000 tanks followed by millions of German troops rushed the border. All bridges over the Memel, Niemen and Bug were taken intact and over them the Panzers rolled to the other side. The tanks that had been built

German troopers at their peak during the invasion of Russia, June 1941. (Courtesy the National Archives.)

ostensibly for the invasion of England were finally put to use; 80 of them were at the Bug and within minutes after plopping into the water they emerged on the other shore, joining those clattering off the bridges (Carell 1963, 25). Three hours later Guderian, commanding PzG 2, joined his soldiers on Russian soil, flagging his divisions to an ever-faster pace. Both here and elsewhere the advance of the Germans proceeded with little or no opposition from the disoriented and leaderless Russian troops.

In Berlin that morning the German people were awakened at 5:30 by the booming voice of their propaganda minister, Goebbels, who read over the radio the führer's proclamation. The proclamation was later published with an addendum of OKW and SD documents revealing that the Bolsheviks had indulged in "political agitation" and Germany had to act. The same morning 12 German missions abroad were instructed to notify their host governments about the latest deed; in addition to the Tripartite members and sympathizers notes were sent to Turkey, Afghanistan and Iran — all neighbors of the USSR (DGFP, XII, 1072–3). The führer himself did not speak nor did he convene the Reichstag, as he had done at the start of the Polish campaign. At 12:30 the following day he quit the Chancellery and boarded his train for his headquarters in the woods of East Prussia, where he was to stay holed up for the next three and a half years until he was flushed out by approaching Russian troops.

In Moscow a deadly quiet reigned on the morning of June 22. When after his meeting with Ribbentrop Berezhkov returned to the embassy and tuned in to Moscow radio, all he heard was music; he tried several hours later — still the same music. It was not until 7:15 — four hours into the war — that the Defense Ministry was heard from. While it issued an order to fight back, it forbade the army to cross into German territory (Petrov, 221). The Soviet air force was ordered to launch bombing raids on the invader. Since the bombers' bases were further inland than those of the fighter planes, a number of them had escaped the initial attack. As the bombers headed for the German lines, 500 of them were shot down on that Sunday alone. The next day General Kopets, chief of the Soviet bomber fleet, committed suicide.

The fog that hovered over Stalin's behavior prior to June 22 persisted during the initial days of the war. Reports on his reactions vary but the most common view is that he slid into a depression and was incapable of action. Just before the attack he had left for his dacha at Kuntsevo. When the first air raids were reported Stalin was asleep but Zhukov insisted he be woken up. When Stalin answered the phone Zhukov told him the news but elicited no reaction. "Did you understand?" Zhukov repeated, but there was only Stalin's heavy breathing on the line. Finally Stalin asked to convene the Politburo and returned to the Kremlin. To his generals who had arrived to tell the Politburo about the German encroachments, Stalin replied that he had received no demands from the Germans, no ultimatum, no declaration of war. Facing the Politburo, Timoshenko and Zhukov told them that war was imminent and urged the issuance of an alert to the troops, to which Stalin replied, "It would be premature to issue that order now. It might still be possible to settle the situation by peaceful mean." Then he added, "Isn't this a provocation by German generals …? If a provocation needs to be staged then the German generals would bomb even their own cities. Hitler knows nothing about it for sure. What is needed is to urgently contact Berlin" (Volkogonov, 401; Axell 1997, 162). The German Embassy was called. The German ambassador said that in fact he had just requested a meeting with Molotov, for whom he had a communication. Upon Molotov's return from the meeting with Schulenberg with the news that yes, it was war, Stalin retreated again to his dacha and was not seen or heard from for the next three days.

The desperate attempts to "cancel" the war persisted for some time. In July, Stamenov, a Soviet agent employed in the Bulgarian Embassy, was approached by Sudoplatov of the Secret Service with an offer to the Germans of a Brest-Litovsk kind of truce (Trotsky's *Neither War nor Peace*). In a follow-up with the Bulgarian envoy the Soviets offered the Germans the Baltic states, Moldavia and large parts of Ukraine and Belorussia (Volkogonov, 412–3). This report emerged only after the fall of the Soviet Union and if it sounds far-fetched, one must keep in mind that this happened at the height of Russian defeats on all fronts, and that the territories offered had already been captured by the Germans anyway.

It was not Stalin who stepped forth to tell the Russian people about the calamity that befell the country. It was Molotov who at 12:15 that June 22 announced over the radio the news of the war. The speech and its delivery were in keeping with the personality of the man but he did end the address with a touch of poignancy. "Our cause" — said Molotov — "is just. Our enemy shall be defeated. Victory will be ours."

* * *

As implied in Directive No. 21 the general concept of the campaign was to trap the bulk of the Red Army in the western borderlands and annihilate it in a series of vast encirclements so that only minor pacification operations would be left to complete. This was to be accomplished during the four months of July to October — the season suitable for blitzkrieg operations. No thought was given to a possible strategy should this scenario go awry. It expressed the ideological approach of this war because to suggest that a Slav army directed by a Judeo-Bolshevik state could not be smashed in four months by a German army at the peak of its strength would have been blasphemy vis-à-vis the führer and German history.

The deployment of opposing forces on June 22 is shown in Fig. 15.1. Here a general comment is necessary about citing relative strengths of the two sides. While the Russian forces, too, are given and many historians are prone to cite precise numbers of Soviet divisions, armored corps and air fleets—this is often a profitless exercise. Due to organizational differences and subsequent catastrophic losses Russian regiments, divisions, corps, etc., in 1941 were nowhere near their German counterparts; thus a Russian division in terms of manpower and weaponry was closer to a German regiment and a Russian tank army was equivalent to a Panzer corps. In 1941 the corps was, in fact, eliminated from the Russian table of organization so that an army had no more than three to four divisions (Seaton: *Moscow*, 63). Likewise it is no use citing numbers of Russian tanks or airplanes—at least at the beginning—when their models, armament and equipment were woefully outmoded. It would be totally misleading to say that 10 German faced 30 Soviet divisions and from it conclude that a 3:1 ratio prevailed on the battlefield when in fact the forces would be about equal. Thus wherever possible, comparisons will be made by gross numbers. At the start of hostilities the Germans fielded over 3 million men, within a month or so boosted to 3.4. They disposed of some 600,000 motor vehicles as well as about 650,000 horses for their artillery and supplies. The Red Army had in western Russia a total of 4.5 million troops, of which 2.9 million were close enough to the frontier to face the initial onslaught.

The commanders of the three army groups (AG) were the same men who led the German army in the Polish and French campaigns. Unlike in the West, here the major role was assigned to von Bock in the center. Of the entire Ostheer he had 40 percent of the infantry divisions, 53 percent of the armor and 910 of the available 2,000 airplanes, roughly half of the invading forces. The objective for his AG, as laid down by the OKH operational directive of January 31, was to head in the direction of Smolensk from where he was to detach "strong fast forces" for cooperation with AGN aiming at Leningrad. Following "complete destruction of the Russians" in the north these detached forces would be freed for "further operations." The overall operational plan is sketched in Fig. 14.3.

Bock positioned his PzG 3 under Hoth in the Suwalki triangle, just south of East Prussia while Guderian's PzG 2 took off from north and south of Brest-Litovsk. The city itself was bypassed as the tanks, flanked by infantry, rushed ahead along the Bialystok-Minsk axis. Bock himself was across the bridge at Brest the very first day of the war. Since already in the first few days the infantry lagged behind the Panzers, Bock decided on a double envelopment of the Russian armies trying to escape the battlefield. The infantry would close one ring east of nearby Bialystok while the Panzer divisions far ahead would form an outer ring east of Minsk.

During the first three days the Luftwaffe concentrated on stationary targets, primarily airfields, but starting on June 25 it switched to ground support of the troops. Then, in perfect summer weather, along the plains and roads of Poland and Byelorussia an immense carnage was inflicted on the retreating Red Army by the 1,000 or so planes crisscrossing the vast battlefield. The German bombers and pursuit planes flew from five to eight missions a day without any opposition from either Soviet fighters or organized ground defenses (USAF, 153–9). One week after the start of the campaign the two cauldrons around Bialystok and Minsk, containing at least half a million men, were sealed.

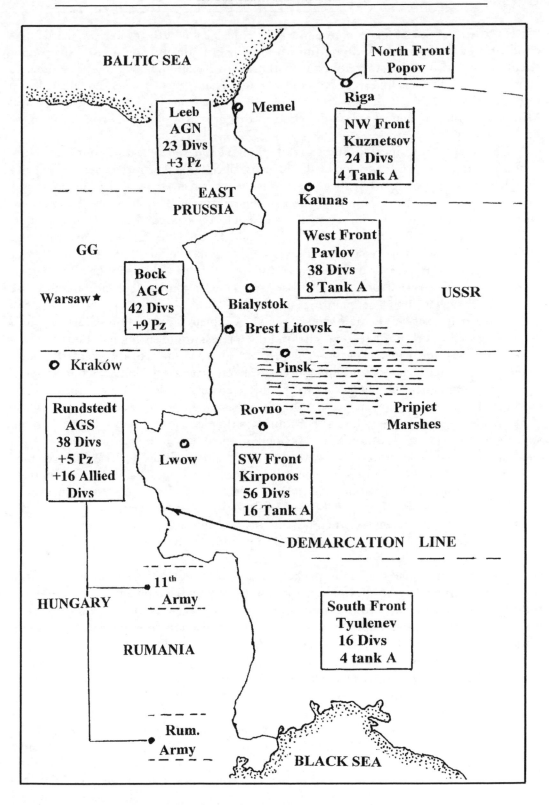

15.1. Disposition of opposing forces on the Eve of Barbarossa

Of the total Soviet forces commanded by Timoshenko in the center two-thirds were concentrated at Bialystok, and one-third near Minsk. It was only on June 25 that Timoshenko ordered his Bialystok troops to withdraw to the Slonim-Lida line. The order to retreat and the fallback line were both out of date because the Germans had taken Slonim a day earlier and closed the ring. On June 28 Guderian and Hoth joined hands east of Minsk and trapped Timoshenko's divisions in that area as well as those that escaped the Bialystok cauldron.

But already, at the peak of these breathtaking victories, new features of the war were becoming apparent. In France or in the Balkans, once the Germans had achieved operational success, and quite often ahead of it, the enemy retreated, or, if surrounded, simply surrendered. Not so here. Though encircled, the fighting at Bialystok and Minsk swayed and swirled for 10 days without letup. The Russian forces kept counterattacking, attempting to break out either by various ruses or by suicidal frontal charges, and in the end some did escape. Even when overwhelmed, individual groups melted into the swamps and forests to continue the war as partisans. It wasn't until July 8 that the fighting in the Minsk pocket died down. The Germans took 100,000 prisoners in the Bialystok and 288,000 in the Minsk cauldron, as well as immense quantities of booty.

Another instance of the new kind of war the Germans faced was Brest-Litovsk. Guderian bypassed it, certain that left far behind the fortress would surrender. It was a typical case of this war in many respects. When the attack came most of the garrison troops, together with their artillery and tanks, were away on maneuvers. Only 3,500 men out of the usual complement of 8,000 were in the fortress (Kershaw R., 48). Even their officers who usually slept in town were away. Still, when the 45th Infantry Division moved to take it, it was repulsed with heavy losses. For four days the Germans tried to subdue it without success. Only after an incessant two-day bombardment by artillery and bombers, as well as a Karl howitzer, which fired 60 cm two-ton shells, did the leveled fortress fall; even then isolated groups fought on in the ruins till the end of July. It took eight days to eliminate that stranglehold on the road and rail junction on the Bug and it cost the Germans 482 killed and 1,000 wounded. It was the second time Guderian had captured Brest-Litovsk, the first time in September '39 when he took it without losing a man. Symptomatic, too, of this war was that of the 7,500 Russians taken prisoner in the fortress, 400 survived German captivity (Carell 1963, 43).

The fighting around the Minsk pocket was still on when the two PzGs were faced with their first dilemma. Should they plunge forward to keep up the momentum or wait for the infantry to secure the ring around the cauldron? The infantry was still a long way back and it would take time to catch up. On June 30 the OKH decided to order the Panzers forward. This is certainly what Guderian preferred. Within days his divisions were at the upper Dniepr and had secured a crossing. He was now so far ahead that he estimated it would take the infantry two weeks to reach him. But he kept going and on July 16 attacked Smolensk from the south. By the end of the day this important city was in German hands. All along resistance was light and casualties were low but as the Germans advanced it kept stiffening. With the taking of Smolensk he was 500 miles into enemy territory and Moscow was just 200 miles away. Ahead of him was Yelnaja, an important road junction and a high-ground platform pointing at the Russian capital. Guderian ordered his Panzers to storm it. It took four days of bitter fighting to accomplish it but on July 19 Yelnaja, 180 miles from Moscow, was in German hands. Unbeknownst to him that thrust opened up a 12-week struggle that was to have serious consequences for the course of Barbarossa.

The tactical situation of AGC was now as follows: Guderian had driven a deep wedge into Russian territory with his right wing stretched westward all the way to the Pripet marshes, an open flank 600 miles long, and to the north separating him from Hoth's PzG 3 were concentrations of several Russian armies. These Russians were enveloped from the north, west and south and it was expected that Guderian would pivot left, link up with Hoth and close the ring from the east. However, he could not do it. The fighting on his flanks and particularly in front of him was growing fiercer by the day. The battle at Yelnaya had turned into a prolonged positional struggle with all the frightfulness of trench combat. The artillery barrages loosed by the Russians were so intense that officers who remembered World War I likened it to Verdun. Guderian could proceed neither forward nor sideways to effect the encirclement at Smolensk; in fact, he could barely maintain his position at Yelnaja. There was talk of abandoning it but Guderian wouldn't hear of it.

Hoth's original axis of advance was in the direction of the upper Dvina, at a slightly divergent angle from Guderian, with the aim of later joining AGN in its fight for Leningrad. But with the right wing of AGC bogged down, it was Hoth who had to turn south to close the Smolensk cauldron. This he did on July 27. In the meantime sizeable portions of the encircled 16th and 20th Russian armies escaped to the east; even after the ring was closed furious attacks from within and without the cauldron made breaches in the ring and enabled more troops to escape. It is estimated that about 100,000 Russians got out of the Smolensk cauldron. The fighting there lasted nine days at the end of which the Germans reported the capture of 309,000 prisoners, 3,200 tanks and 3,000 guns (Fugate, 147, 167).

In the end Guderian's struggles at Yelnaja proved to be in vain. On August 30 the Russians launched a counterattack against Yelnaja and forced the Germans to evacuate it on September 5. The battle at Yelnaja was the Russians' first success in the war; it was, symbolically, the first German retreat; and operationally, by staging their scattered but persistent attacks, the Russians prevented the AGC from mounting any strategic offensive, whether alone or in conjunction with AGN. At the end of these battles AGC had to withdraw its Panzer divisions for refitting; Guderian's combat strength was down to a quarter of his initial 747 tanks and Hoth's to 40 percent of his initial complement of 783.

By the middle of August, that is, after seven weeks, the AGC had reached more or less the line assigned to it by the OKH. However, whether it fulfilled its strategic role within the overall framework of Barbarossa can be gleaned only after a look at its neighbor to the north. AGN's task was to cut off and annihilate the enemy forces in the Baltics and capture Leningrad. The main effort was to be on the right wing, which was to proceed in the direction of Dvina-Opochka. In this task AGN's commander von Leeb was to be assisted by elements of AGC. In keeping with his past assignments—he had sat out the Polish and French campaigns on the Maginot Line—von Leeb was given the smallest force, 22 percent of the infantry and 18 percent of the armor. Von Leeb also had an uncomfortable deployment base. The direction of his attack was northeast so to shorten his distance to the Gulf of Finland his troops were crowded into the small enclave of Memel. The leader of his PzG 4, Hoepner, had two armored corps, one under Reinhardt on the left and one under Manstein on the right. The Panzer Group was shielded north and south by infantry armies. Manstein's was to be the main effort and as was typical of him he started off with great skill and daring. His main target and key to farther operations was the broad river Dvina. Straddling it was the city of Dvinsk with its rail and highway bridges. The city was more than 200 miles from his starting line and no conventional attack could have secured the bridges for him. If not legal warfare then let it be illegal and Manstein resorted to a deception. On June 26 selected troopers, some of whom spoke Russian, dressed in Red Army uniforms, boarded captured Russian trucks and sped off in the direction of the city. At the bridges they bantered with the Russian guards and then mowed them down. They quickly removed the demolition charges and within an hour Manstein's Panzers clattered over the intact bridge to the right bank of the Dvina. The coup was a severe blow to the Russian defenses. In a series of suicidal waves the Red air force tried in vain to destroy the bridges; on one day alone the Germans shot down 64 bombers (Manstein, 182–4).

Manstein covered 220 miles in four days, but at Dvinsk he ran into the same problem as had Guderian at Minsk. His infantry lagged 60 to 100 miles behind and his right flank was unprotected. OKH ordered him to halt at Dvinsk until the 16th Army, his infantry screen, caught up with him. He spent six idle days there after which he was given the green light to proceed. Both armored corps now moved northeast, parallel to the Dvinsk-Leningrad railway. Reinhardt was allocated the one good road leading to Luga. Manstein was to branch off eastward toward the old Soviet frontier and its Stalin Line stretching from Lake Peipus to the Dvina. The objective of this side thrust was to eventually invest Leningrad from the east. Once off the Dvinsk-Luga road Manstein bogged down. The terrain east of the Baltics is the edge of thickly forested and marshy country stretching from the White Sea to the approaches of Moscow. In the second week of July both Reinhardt and Manstein lived through their first crises. First Reinhardt was stopped at Luga and repeated attacks on the Russian positions there brought only casualties and failure. Any time his tanks got off the road to execute an enveloping maneuver they were stuck in the mud, not to speak of the untracked vehicles. Then when Manstein reached Lake Ilmen his entire corps was cut off and surrounded. It wasn't till July 19 after three days of fighting that he managed to extricate himself. Hoepner now resorted to a version of musical chairs. Reconnaissance had reported that south of Narwa the Russian defenses were weakly manned. Hoepner thus took Reinhardt off the high road and switched him to the left and Manstein was put in his place on the Luga highway with the task of resuming the advance on Leningrad. After a difficult march across roadless swamp that required building corduroy tracks and causeways, Reinhardt reached the lower Luga river south of Narwa and managed to capture intact the bridges across it whence he immediately established several bridgeheads on the eastern side. He was then in a good position to continue his advance. But he was ordered to remain in place and was kept there for nearly three weeks. The familiar reason given was that Reinhardt's left flank was exposed. The 18th Army, which was supposed to be shielding Reinhardt, was still battling the Russians withdrawing from Estonia. It wasn't until August 7 that German spearheads reached the sea at Kunda, east of Tallin, isolating the Russian forces in the Baltics.

On the Luga road Manstein did no better than his predecessor. On August 10 he stormed the Luga defenses but was repulsed. Effectively then in mid–August the AGN was blunted in its offensive thrust. Faced with this situation von Leeb arrived on August 15 at Hoepner's headquarters for a discussion. The decision was taken to combine the two armored corps by having Manstein join Reinhardt at the Luga river bridgeheads and from there resume the attack on Leningrad.

While these shifts were being considered Voroshilov attacked on August 10 south of Lake Ilmen. Manstein's place there had been taken by the screening 16th Army. After a short time the infantry divisions there were threatened with being overrun, the peak danger occurring the very evening Manstein had arrived at Hoepner's headquarters. Thus instead of discussing the new concentrated offensive Hoepner ordered, Manstein had to rush back to help the 16th Army restore the situation. Manstein did his job with aplomb. As the Russian forces facing north were about to push the German divisions into the lake, Manstein's Panzers struck at their flank and smashed them. It was the only place where a sizeable number of Russian troops were taken prisoner, some 20,000 of them. The Germans then marched north and on August 20 took Chudovo, Voroshilov's erstwhile headquarters. By September 11 the Germans were at Duderhof Heights, with a view of the sea and metropolis of Leningrad, with its 3 million inhabitants.

One day later an order originating with Hitler arrived at von Leeb's headquarters instructing him not to capture Leningrad but to lay siege to it and starve it. The soldiers were not to be told of this ukase so as not to affect morale while being driven to attack the city. But as will be discussed later, it is doubtful that this late in the campaign and given the formidable defenses erected there, the Germans could have taken Leningrad by storm.

Of all three army groupings the prospects for AGS were the dimmest. Though it had roughly a third of all infantry and armor (as compared to one-fifth for AGN), plus two Rumanian armies, in all other respects it faced a more difficult task than the other commands. Its right Panzer wing in Rumania had been shunted to the Balkans, and in its place AGS had been given the 11th Army. Also, contrary to what German intelligence estimated, the bulk of Russian forces was not in the center but in Ukraine. There too Kirponos seemed to have been more alert for what was coming than the other fronts. Operationally, AGS was in a relatively difficult position from the start. It was squeezed between the Pripet marshes and the Carpathain Mountains and had no contact with the 11th Army in Rumania. In the drive into Ukraine the AGS was thus dangling between Russian forces to the north and the open spaces of southern Ukraine. Its position was not made easier by the task assigned to it. According to the operational plan it was to breach the border fortifications, head in the direction of Kiev, and execute a wide sweep to the south along the bend of the Dniepr to trap all the Russian forces west of the river (Halder Vol. II, 465). It was a loop of some 500–600 miles in circumference and it was to be executed by a single prong of Kleist's PzG 1 flanked by the 6th and 17th Armies.

Predictably von Rundstedt, commander of AGS, ran into difficulties from the start. Strong enemy armor engaged him the moment he crossed the border and heavy fighting developed along the Russian positions on the Rovno-Tarnopol line. Heavy battles continued for eight days and it wasn't until Kirponos had expended all his tanks that he gave way. Then the Germans ran into the Stalin Line on the old Polish-Soviet border, which held them up for another week. In two weeks the AGS advanced some 200 miles without achieving any envelopments and fighting heavily all the way. On July 7 Kleist broke through the Stalin Line at Zhitomir and headed east. But the severity of the fighting did not let up. Out of the Pripet marshes the Russian 5th Army attacked the German flanks and heavy rains turned roads into quagmire, impeding the flow of supplies. At this point, three weeks into the campaign, Hitler got worried and suggested giving up the idea of a large cauldron and aim instead at smaller encirclements. For this purpose he wanted to break up Kleist's PzG into task forces and form several kettles in the area the AGS had reached. Rundstedt opposed it and he resumed his drive to implement the original plan.

Ukraine is excellent tank country and once through the Stalin Line Kleist's Panzers pushed on towards the Dniepr. On July 16 he took Byelaya Tserkiev, 40 miles from the river. This was barely halfway round the river's semicircle and a long way from the 11th Army which only on July 1 had crossed from Rumania in order to link up with Kleist along the Dniepr. Rundstedt then decided to meet Hitler's suggestion halfway and execute a smaller loop in the area of Byelaya Tserkev. Without waiting for the 11th Army he ordered Kleist to wheel south, and once past Uman turn west again to link up with the 17th Army to the south. For Kleist this was waging battle with a reversed front but the Germans managed it, though at a cost of incomplete success. On July 25 Kleist met his southern prong, enclosing in the ring three Russian armies. The fight around the Uman cauldron lasted till August 7, by which time the Germans tallied 103,000 POWs, including two Army commanders— their first major success. On August 3 the 11th Army from Rumania finally made contact with the main forces and AGS was poised for a coordinated advance eastward.

During August the Germans reached the Dniepr bend from below Kiev to the seashore. The 11th Army moving along the coast crossed the Dniepr Delta on August 21 and cut off the Crimea. Isolated from the mainland, the Crimea was almost an island and could not have played much of a role in the war. To take it required the use of the 11th Army's entire stock of artillery and antitank guns and all its aircraft. The reasons Hitler gave for storming Crimea were statesmanlike. One, he explained, was to intimidate Turkey, an argument that lacks any relevance to Turkey's military or political designs. The other reason was to safeguard the Rumanian oilfields from the Red air force. The Russians had no strategic bombers and had not bombed Ploesti when they were on the Rumanian border, never mind from Crimea, at a range of 600–700 miles. The third argument was that by capturing Crimea it would be possible to cross over from Kerch into the Kuban to join up with the forces coming from Rostov for the conquest of the Caucasus. To this there was some sense but the cost bore no relation to its potential, and it was woefully premature, as events would show. But Crimea was one of Hitler's pet projects; as in his colonization schemes for Russia the Crimea was to become a German Riviera. So Crimea had to be taken.

On September 12 the commander of the 11th Army, Ritter von Schobert, landed his plane in a Russian minefield and was killed. As a replacement Manstein was brought down from the north. In addition to German troops he was given command of the Rumanian 3rd Army, of which he held no high opinion. The task assigned to Manstein was twofold: to storm the Crimea and advance on Rostov. This, he felt, was too much for the forces he had been given. Whether on his own initiative or that of the OKH, Manstein opted for the Crimea, leaving the task of taking Rostov to Kleist, positioned north of him.

* * *

Five countries joined Germany in its crusade against the Soviet Union. These in order of their contribution to the cause were Finland, Rumania, Italy, Hungary and Slovakia. At a later date Spain contributed a fighting contingent, the Blue Division. On the first day of the war Germany had asked Sweden for permission to transport troops from Norway to Finland on Swedish railways, which was granted three days later; also a Swedish volunteer battalion joined the Finns opposite the island of Hanko. None of the countries were told the exact date of attack, nor did most of them want to emulate Germany in simply being the aggressor but looked for some pretext. Consequently some of them went to war several or more days after the start of the campaign.

Unlike the others Finland was of substantial importance. One key objective was Murmansk handling Lend-Lease, and if not the port itself, its railroad—cutting it would have served the same purpose. Next, by linking up with the Germans east of Lake Ladoga it would have provided great operational freedom for the two armies and by advancing west of Ladoga the Finns could help take Leningrad with all that it implied.

And indeed, the original dispositions of forces seemed to reflect the pull of these strategic opportunities. One concentration was near Petsamo opposite Murmansk; the other, farther south, was opposite Salla, the closest approach to the White Sea. The divisions in these two locations, 27,000 men near Petsamo under General Dietl, and 41,000 near Salla under General Feige, were primarily German troops under the overall command of Falkenhorst, brought over from Norway. The bulk of the Finnish army, some 12 divisions, was deployed on the flanks of Lake Ladoga and were led by the Finnish feldmarshal Mannerheim. In total the Germans had 80,000 troops in Finland while keeping 150,000 in Norway for fear of a British landing. Here was one penalty for Hitler's invading countries he didn't really need and a payoff for the British strategy of dispersion.

At the outbreak of hostilities Finland declared its neutrality. But the next day Luftwaffe planes took off from Finnish bases and bombed Murmansk while German patrols crossed into Soviet territory. In response the Russians bombed Petsamo and Rovanienni. With this Finland had its pretext and on June 26 declared war. Mobilization had been going on since June 17 and by the time Finland was at war it had mobilized half a million soldiers, 80,000 women auxiliaries and 30,000 men for road work, a respectable effort for a country of 4 million.

Military operations commenced on June 29 with an attack by Dietl in the direction of Murmansk, 56 miles away. The forces in the center under Feige went over to an attack on July 1 with the aim of taking Kandalaksha. Both attacks bogged down after advancing some 15–20 miles. The terrain was forbidding, the Germans had great difficulty with their supply lines and, unlike on the main front, here the Russian soldier proved to be a more skillful and enterprising fighter. With the Germans unable to make any headway the right wing of Feige's troops, the III Finnish Corps, was asked to try. Its objective, too, was the railroad abutting the White Sea. The Finns made better progress but on August 25 their commander, General Siilasvuo, had to report that his troops had reached the end of their strength. Nowhere did the Germans come close to endangering the Murmansk railroad which in addition to its future role in transshipping aid from the West was also a vital lateral artery bringing supplies and reinforcements to the Russian troops. On October 8 the OKW ordered all German operations on the Finnish front stopped.

After two and half months of fighting the Germans in Finland had suffered a total of 21,500 casualties, nearly a third of the engaged forces, with little to show for it. The troops were spent. The two divisions in the Petsamo area were withdrawn and replaced by a single mountain division. Hitler was so dissatisfied with Falkenhorst that he disbanded his headquarters and sent him back to Norway. His place was taken by Dietl at a new headquarters designated Army of Lapland. Dietl was a good field officer but no operational brain and he hesitated to take on the job. But ever since Narvik Dietl had become a protégé of Hitler and therefore fit for the highest office (Ziemke 1950, 188–208).

For the Finns the main theater of operations was in Karelia. This was where the bulk of their forces was concentrated and this was the land they had lost to the Soviets in the Winter War of 1939-40. Mannerheim, in fact, referred to the present conflict as the Continuation War — a slogan meant to assuage Finnish qualms about joining Hitler. In conformity with German plans of assigning the main weight to AGN's right wing, the OKH asked the Finns to concentrate their main effort east of Lake Ladoga. This conformed to Finnish thinking. From the beginning the Finns were reluctant to be overly active on the isthmus, the land bridge between the Gulf and Lake Ladoga. This, too, was a function of their moral stance. One of the Soviet justifications for the Winter War was the Finns' proximity and threat to Leningrad, a city which had nearly as many people as all of Finland. The Finns, therefore, didn't want to validate this Soviet claim, though on a number of occasions they confided to the Germans that they would not mind it if the city was depopulated and razed — but they themselves wouldn't be party to it. As it turned out they had the right address.

The Finnish army opened its offensive in eastern Karelia on July 10 and were soon on the march. They had been supplied with modern weapons by the Germans and had plenty of experience in fighting their opponent. More importantly, the Russians, being in great straits elsewhere, had denuded that front of all its reserves so that the Finns in Karelia had a numerical superiority of 3:1 (Ziemke 1950, 190). After two weeks of fighting they were on the Tuloksa River, 10 miles east of the old border. This offensive was still on when Keitel urged Mannerheim to also start an attack on the isthmus, which he did on August 22. After one week the Finns entered Viborg, Karelia's main city lost to the Russians in the last war, and were close to the old border. Keitel kept pressing them to join up with von Leeb. To Keitel's importuning Mannerheim cited economic dislocation at home, high losses of his troops and other reasons for his hesitation. On September 4 Jodl arrived at Mannerheim's headquarters to bring him an Iron Cross and persuade him to resume the advance on both sides of the lake. Mannerheim gave in and resumed the offensive. On the east side of Ladoga the Finns advanced all the way to the Swir River, an incursion into Russia of over 50 miles but on the isthmus they merely crossed the border until they came up against the old Russian fortifications, where they halted.

To terminate the wrangling Mannerheim notified Keitel on September 25 that the Finns had suffered losses larger than in the previous war; that his army would have to be reorganized to release men to the crippled economy; and that the Finns would go no further than the old border on the isthmus and the Swir east of the lake. In the time remaining before winter the Finns extended their left flank to Lake Onega so as to position themselves in a more defensible line. But as of December the Finns stopped all offensive operations.

There were also some significant diplomatic moves as far as Finland was concerned. In mid–August the Soviet government offered Finland peace terms, including territorial concessions, which were passed on to Helsinki by Sumner Welles. The Finns did not respond. In her effort to sustain Russia in the war, England pressed Finland not to invade Russian territory once it had recovered its lost lands. When the Finns continued their advance this was watered down to a request that they quietly cease hostilities. This too passed without a positive answer. When on November 8 Finland joined the anti–Comintern Pact, Britain delivered an ultimatum that she cease hostilities. When she did not, England on December 6 declared war on Finland, just a few days before the USA, too, found itself at war with Germany.

Rumania's situation was in some respects similar to Finland's. She, too, had lost territory to the Soviets in 1940, giving her a motive for going to war. Antonescu handed over governmental business to Mihai Antonescu and named himself, figuratively, commander in chief of the German-Rumanian 11th Army. Imitating the führer he, too, departed for the front in a special train, *Patria*. The commander over the 11th Army's German troops was von Schobert who had a German liaison staff attached to the Rumanians. Initially the Rumanian front stayed quiet, which was dictated by military considerations. The main German forces were some 300 miles to the north and it wasn't until they reached the Dniepr bend that the forces from Rumania were to march forth to meet them. The other reason was that the Rumanians were not ready. But they did declare war on June 22, terming it a "holy war" for the liberation of Bessarabia and Bukovina.

The German 11th Army, flanked on the north by the 3rd and in the south by the 4th Rumanian Armies, crossed the Prut on July 2. The Russians gave ground, some of them withdrawing to Odessa, others retreating along the Black Sea coast. By July 26 all of Bessarabia was reconquered and on August 14 Odessa was surrounded. Up till then both the Germans and the Rumanians were under the formal command of Antonescu who, in effect, took orders from Rundstedt. Now the forces were split. The 4th Army came under Rumanian command with the task of investing Odessa and the 3rd Army was subordinated to the Germans.

At one of his meetings with Antonescu, Hitler took out a piece of red chalk and asked the Rumanian to indicate how much of Ukraine he would like to own (Gheorghe, 188). Antonescu hesitated for reasons that were not entirely noble. Rumania's visceral grievance was Transylvania, taken from her in 1940 and given to Hungary. Antonescu feared that the offer was a compensation for accepting the status quo, whereas one of his reasons for joining Hitler was to accumulate enough credits with him to later reclaim Transylvania. Eventually, at a meeting with Hitler on August 6, he consented to take a slice of Ukraine from the Dniestr to the southern Bug, known as Transnistria. In return, Antonescu promised his continuing participation in the Russian campaign.

The Rumanians now moved to capture besieged Odessa. On August 18 the 4th Army attacked but failed to take the city. Subsequent attacks likewise ended in failure and brought the Rumanians severe losses. They increased their strength to 21 divisions and replaced the commander but still could not defeat the Russians. It wasn't until the Luftwaffe came to help and German troops converged on the beleaguered port that the Russians decided to evacuate Odessa. This they did on October 16 removing by sea some 75,000 troops and all their heavy arms. Following this fiasco the 4th Rumanian Army settled down to occupational duty in Transnistria, which they converted into a vast killing ground, exterminating either on their own or in cooperation with the Germans a quarter million Rumanian and Russian Jews, as well as countless POWs. The 3rd Army stayed with the Germans and helped storm the Crimea. By the end of October the two Rumanian Armies had suffered 70,000 dead; this compares with 117,000 German dead for the entire Russian front. After this the 3rd Army was reduced to just one mountain and one cavalry corps with the rest sent home for rehabilitation (Hillgruber 1954, 138).

Mussolini, as usual, had been neither consulted nor informed about the upcoming conflict. The führer's letter written on the afternoon of June 21 was delivered to Il Duce in the middle of the night. "I do not disturb even my servants at night," fumed Il Duce as he read the letter which, *inter alia*, said, "Whatever may come, Duce, our situation cannot become worse as a result of this step," a remarkable sentence indeed (Bullock 1962, 649). And, as usual, though hurt to the core by this nonchalance, Il Duce jumped to the call of his partner and immediately declared war on the USSR. Italy's initial contribution was three divisions, which were later augmented to a full army. Like the other satellites, the Italians, too, were employed on the southern front and like them suffered catastrophic losses in their encounter with Russian troops.

The regent of Hungary also received a personal letter from Hitler. The reply, as conveyed by the German envoy Erdmannsdorff, was that the regent thought the news "wonderful. For 27 years he had longed for this day" (DGFP, XII, 1072). Hungary's eagerness to join, aside from the customary East European distaste for Russia, particularly since the Magyars were not Slavs, had also much to do with Transylvania. Hungary didn't declare war on the first day. Instead it watched with consternation as the Rumanians marched shoulder to shoulder with Germany, fearing the very thing Antonescu hoped to achieve. Consequently, the Hungarians decided to compete for Hitler's favors, but first looked for a pretext. This came on June 26 when an air raid was staged on Kosice. There is uncertainty as to who the raiders were — Soviet, German or Hungarian planes — since the markings on them were "misleading." But the next day, on June 27, Hungary declared war. Three motorized brigades and one cavalry brigade as well as 10 battalions of alpine troops were dispatched to the front (Fenyo, 29). They were attached to the 17th Army, the right wing of AGS. Since the Rumanians were to the left of the 11th Army they were neighbors of the Hungarians. The enmity over Transylvania was such that in case of contact there was danger of fighting breaking out between the two cobelligerents. The Germans therefore had to shuffle these contingents around so as not to bring them within rifle shot. The danger did not last long for soon the regent had second thoughts and requested the withdrawal of his troops. The Germans held back but after a meeting between Hitler and Horthy on September 7 the three mobile brigades were sent home. The remaining Hungarian units were subsequently used mainly for occupation and antipartisan duties.

Although Japan was not an ally of Germany in its war on Russia — if she was an ally at all — she does appear, albeit fleetingly, on the canvas of this conflict in a most revealing way. It would have seemed natural for Germany to have tried to induce Japan to attack Russia in the east while the Germans attacked in the west. But this was not so at all. Long before Barbarossa was launched Germany kept urging Japan to go to war against England by attacking Singapore and for that purpose had even encouraged Japan in signing the neutrality pact with the USSR. The rationale behind it is contained in a Hitler memorandum of March 5, 1941, which says "The aim ... [is] to bring Japan into active operations in the Far East. This will tie down England's forces and the focal point of the USA will be diverted to the Pacific." In the same directive he ordered that Japan be given no hint about Barbarossa (Rich, 228). On April 20 the führer said he was for a Soviet-Japanese nonaggression pact as this would redirect Japan toward British possessions in the Far East (FNC, 193). According to some the neutrality pact signed that month was aimed on Stalin's part not only to secure his rear but as late as it was still aimed at convincing the Germans that he was ready to join the mooted Four-Power bloc. The potential consequences of a Japanese attack on England, including the likely reaction of the USA, will emerge in the course of the actual events that took place later that year. But to have preferred the uncertain prospects of a war on England over the tangible impact of a Japanese attack on Russia simultaneously with one in the West can attest to one thing only — Hitler's conviction that he didn't need any help in defeating Russia. He may, in fact, have resented such possible help. This being an Aryan crusade against the subhumans of the East, he may not have wanted the participation of the Japanese who, whatever else they were, certainly weren't Aryans. As it turned out the Japanese for their own reasons obliged. Even though the Germans later changed their mind and pressed her to attack Russia, Japan ignored them and stayed neutral throughout the war. Some of the consequences of this pilpulic scheming were discussed at the end of Chapter 12.

* * *

While Stalin went offstage his chieftains tried to cope as best as they could. Molotov had given his speech on Sunday and the top military leaders began to issue orders, however tentative. On the second day a general defense headquarters was established as well as a committee in charge of evacuating endangered industrial plants. Whatever else had struck Stalin, he presumably expected to be removed or even executed — a fate he was shortly to mete out to lesser sinners. But such thoughts were far from the minds of his cohorts. On June 30 a Politburo delegation led by Molotov went to his dacha asking Stalin to form a state defense committee and serve as its chairman (Bullock 1992, 729–30). From that moment Stalin slowly returned to life. His resurrection became official when on July 6 he delivered a nationwide radio address. The speech contains two noteworthy themes. Already, barely two weeks into the war, he imparted to the conflict two features that were to become hallmarks of Russian resistance to the Germans. He christened it a "patriotic" war, a fight not for Communism, empire or any other abstract cause but a war in defense of the Russian homeland. The second point he stressed was that this would have to be a struggle fought not just by the Red Army but by every man and woman throughout the Soviet Union.

The effects of this policy would show in the future but at the moment the fate of the Russian soldiers was one of unmitigated defeat and tragedy. In the first weeks the Red Army soldier was simply abandoned to the steel and fire of the German behemoth. At the start of the fighting the commanders were either absent, asleep or at Saturday night parties. When awake they found their signals and telephone lines had been severed by bombing or sabotage and they could not communicate either with their superiors or the units in the field. Pavlov, the commander of the central front bearing the brunt of the invasion, was on

Wounded, a Russian infantryman fights on. (From *The Russian War 1941–1945* by Daniela Mrazkova and Vladimir Remes copyright ©1975 by Daniela Mrazkova and Vladimir Remes. Used by permission of Dutton, a division of Penguin Group [USA] Inc.)

June 22 at his headquarters in Minsk, 200 miles to the rear. Communications were so poor that Stalin learned of the Bialystok-Minsk disaster from the German radio; he asked Pavlov whether it was true, and the answer was that indeed yes, it was. On June 30 he was recalled to Moscow. During his interrogation on July 7 by the NKVD he was asked how things happened the way they did and Pavlov answered: "At 0100 of June 22 I was summoned by front HQ ... I spoke to Timoshenko on the phone. He said, 'Be calm. Don't panic.... Something could happen this morning. But beware. Don't give in to provocations'" (Fugate and Dvoretsky, 355). But the interrogation was meant to show that Pavlov had been a "traitor." Together with his chief of staff and several other officers Pavlov was shot — an execution in effigy of Stalin himself. Those commanders who were at their posts did not dare take any initiative — a legacy of Soviet centralization made worse by Stalin's prewar admonitions not to fall for the provocations of capitalist agents.

In the meantime the troops were bombed out of their billets and camps, cornered by packs of Panzers and cut to pieces. Those who managed to reach the roads were plastered by a neverending stream of fighters and bombers piloted by men who knew their job to perfection and against whom the Russians had only their rifles. The roads in eastern Poland and Byelorussia that first week of the war were a spectacle of infernal devastation and slaughter with whole divisions — men, horses, wagons, tractors and guns — mangled into smoking debris, their only contribution to the war the precious time the Germans lost in bulldozing away the mountains of wreckage. The Russians had no way to fight back — they could only run. And run they did, only to find that the Germans were already ahead of them. Ambushed and encircled they went down by the tens of thousands in a carnage that was more like a mass execution of entire armies. There were for the Russian fighting man in those days only two choices — suicidal stand with rifle and hand grenade against a phalanx of tanks and Stukas, which many chose to take; or giving up, which they did by the hundreds of thousands.

The consequences of this initial collapse persisted well into that first summer of the Russo-German war and beyond. Due to the huge losses the Russian command had to use up its strategic reserves in piecemeal engagements. They also found that the troops in the field desperately needed tanks and were forced to break up their large armored formations, which they had started reforming after the fall of France, and assign them to the infantry. An additional reason for doing so was that the Russians could not handle large armored formations. This was only partly the commanders' fault. Russian tanks carried no radios and had to communicate by flag signals — not to speak of the fact that most of their tanks were mere iron boxes and no match for the Panzers. It is estimated that in 1941 about 80 percent of the Russian heavy equipment was obsolete.

Draconian measures replaced planning and strategy. Order No. 274 declared that in the Red Army there was no such thing as surrender — all POWs would be considered traitors (Seaton 1971, 97). Masses of men without training, without uniforms and often without weapons were thrown in the path of the Germans. When a commander complained to Molotov that in his units only one man in five had a rifle the reply he received was, "Let them fight with bottles" (Berezhkov 1994, 202). Tanks were rushed to the front straight from the factory with their civilian drivers used in combat. Men were sent over minefields with the purpose of exploding them so that the next wave could forge ahead. Dogs carrying satchels of explosives were trained to charge tanks and hopefully destroy them and naturally they often attacked their hosts' tanks. Attacks were repeated over and over again in routine fashion and with catastrophic results. The German machine guns became untouchable from the amount of firing and killing they did. Up to the summer of 1943 the Russian infantryman was given an initial ammunition ration for 10 days only as he was not expected to live longer (Cross, 65). For lack of better means it seemed that by such attacks the Russians hoped to make the Germans use up their ammunition and wear out the barrels of their guns.

However backward their ground equipment was it pales in comparison to the performance of the Soviet Air Force; and unlike the other branches of the armed forces this deficiency persisted to the end of the war. The main problem was the training and tactics of the Russian pilots. According to almost unanimous reports the performance of the Russian bombers and fighters in the summer of 1941 verged either on the suicidal or the farcical. German infantry would stop to watch air combat as one watched a circus. The Red air force was not a separate service. Its regiments and divisions served under the army the way the artillery and tank units did. The standard Soviet fighter was the I 15 or I 153, both biplanes, and the monoplane Rata. The first had a top speed of 200 mph and the Rata up to 285 mph. Because of a lack of aluminum the planes were made of canvass and wood so that even an incendiary bullet would set them on fire. Fighters flew three abreast making them easy prey to the Germans who flew in a loose vertical stack-up. These fighters as well as the bombers carried no radios, not even for internal use. To communicate they fired flares or executed flight maneuvers. For navigation they relied on terrain features and were unfamiliar with map and compass flying. Quite often the crews flew without parachutes. When off on a bombing mission only the leader was told of the objective so all the Germans had to do was shoot down the lead plane and the mission had to be aborted. When in formation they rarely resorted to evasive tactics but flew a straight line until shot out of the skies. On the other hand German bombers were rarely attacked. For one thing they were often faster than the Russian fighters and had greater firepower. Even when damaged the Russians left them alone. As for the German fighter planes the Russians avoided them at all cost. Should they run into them the Russians resorted to one of two techniques. When they were few they tried to escape by diving to treetop level and heading for home. When there were many they closed up into what the Germans called a *Schlange*—a snake. As soon as they spotted the Me-109s the Russians formed a circle whereby each plane had another guarding its tail while covering the plane in front. Keeping this formation they translated as a group toward their own lines constantly lowering their altitude in order to bring the Germans over their own front lines where flak and possibly shortage of fuel would make the Germans turn back. When their own airfields were attacked the fighters would take to the air and assemble some distance away and watch the bombing until it was over. When ordered to intercept German bombers they often cheated. Approaching the raiders they simulated combat by firing their guns and appropriate aerial acrobatics but never coming close to the attackers. Whatever losses the Germans incurred were due to flak. (USAF, 61; 175–184).

Like their desperate methods on the ground the sense of failure and anger led some Russian pilots to resort to ramming. During the battle of Moscow a combat directive was issued, stating, "If machine guns jam in the air, if cartridges are spent prematurely, if the enemy is out to destroy an important state object, go and destroy the enemy by ramming." It was emphasized that this was not meant to be a suicide mission but the supreme act of aerial heroism (Axell 2000, 122). One technique was to approach the enemy from the rear and with the propeller shear off his tail assembly. The other was to come alongside and tip the enemy's plane with one's wing. Ramming usually resulted in the destruction of both planes and the only hope lay in bailing out. By the end of September the Red air force lost 96 percent of the aircraft it had at the outbreak of the war (Volkogonov, 425–6).

The record of the Soviet Navy in 1941 is similar to that of the air force. The ships were obsolete, the advances in gunnery, sonar and radar nonexistent. They even lacked an effective defensive capacity such as minesweepers or the ability to lay mines themselves. In the Baltic the Germans had no warships at all but by the use of mine belts and the Luftwaffe they inflicted crushing blows on the Soviet Navy and practically paralyzed it. When the Germans encircled Tallinn they trapped there a whole Soviet army. Four large convoys carrying troops escaped port, headed for Kronstadt. They were accompanied by a cruiser, 18 destroyers, six submarines, and 34 other naval craft. On August 27, they were attacked by Stukas while simultaneously running into minefields, some of which had been laid by the Germans prior to June 22. During the day the Russians lost 17 transports, five destroyers and three submarines; the next day seven more transports were lost to mines. Altogether, the Russians lost 35 transports (Haupt 1997, 72–3). The extent of the disaster can be judged by the fact that 12,000 men were fished out of the water or taken from the surrounding little islands—the remainder of the three divisions that had embarked at Tallinn (Ruge, 19). In the Black Sea they had one battleship, five cruisers and 30 destroyers versus no German warships—yet they never staged any operational sortie and after losing Sevastopol retired for the duration to their Caucasian ports.

The Soviets had the largest submarine fleet in the world then but their performance was pitiful when compared to that of the Germans or the Americans, the latter mainly against Japanese shipping. The Germans transported overland to the Black Sea three 250-ton U-Boats which sank two-thirds of the Russian transport fleet. The Russians had 50 submarines and sank 300 GRT of enemy shipping.

On September 17 Stukas attacked the prize of the Soviet Fleet, its two battleships anchored off Leningrad. One, the *Marat*, was sunk in shallow waters and the other, *Red October*, was badly damaged. But typically for the Russians the battleships did not give up; if not as dreadnoughts they would fight as artillery. Within a short time the turrets on the *Marat* were fixed and its twelve 30-inch and sixteen 12-inch guns kept firing throughout the siege of Leningrad helping to keep the Germans away from the city. Also, the sailors that survived the sinkings turned into land commandos and when the Gulf of Finland froze, launched attacks on the icebound Finnish and German ships—probably the only case of ships being attacked by infantry. While a failure against the Germans, Soviet ships did well in their confrontation with the Rumanians in the Black Sea. Throughout the siege of Odessa they remained offshore, bombarding the Rumanian positions and keeping them away from the city. And when the time came to abandon Odessa, Soviet ships evacuated 86,000 soldiers and 150,000 civilians, leaving the Rumanians a bare 6,000 prisoners (Ruge, 66).

By the end of July some semblance of control of the front armies made itself felt. Perhaps in imitation of the Germans the Soviets consolidated their original five fronts into three groupings. In the north Voroshilov became commander of the Northwestern Theater, subsuming under him the north and northwest armies. In the center Timoshenko took over Pavlov's front as well as the strategic reserves. In the south Budyenny integrated the southwest and south armies under a Southwestern Theater. A separate command was established for the air force with its own commander though still subject to the army. Shaposhnikov, an old Tsarist general, replaced Zhukov as chief of staff, the latter becoming Stalin's roving representative to coordinate operations on the most vital sectors of the front. In the fall rifle brigades were formed counting some 4,000–5,000 men which gave the Red Army officers more flexibility in controlling the units during battle. To their luck three weapons that proved outstanding on the battlefield, and that were superior to their German equivalents, began to roll off the assembly lines and reach the troops. One was the T-34 tank, with superior armor and tracking, firing the excellent 76 mm gun and comprising almost 70 percent of Soviet tank production. They were so effective that in 1942 Hitler authorized the use of hollow-charge projectiles against them even though these were still a secret weapon. The other weapon was the Katyusha, a truck-mounted battery of electrically triggered rockets, which could fire in salvos of 16 projectiles. And finally the ground support airplane Sturmovik appeared; although not a match for the German fighter planes, it was to prove an excellent tactical plane on the battlefield. Attacking from their march routes the Russians began concentrating on the Germans' flanks and rear, learning to find their weak spots and to cope with breakthroughs by picking on the infantry following the tanks. Though still uncoordinated these attacks harassed and frustrated the Germans, preventing them from undertaking initiatives of their own. Given the condition they were in, these crude and piecemeal methods may have saved the day for the Russians.

* * *

At the beginning there was euphoria. By mid–July the Germans thought they had carried off the greatest blitzkrieg yet, had won the war in Russia. On July 3 Halder noted in his diary, "one can already say that we have carried out our job of smashing the bulk of the Russian Army…. I am therefore not exaggerating when I say that the campaign in Russia was won in 14 days." On the same day Hitler told Schulenburg, just repatriated to Germany, "By August 15 we shall be in Moscow. By October 1 the Russian war will be over" and on the following day he reiterated that, "to all intents and purposes the Russians have lost the war" (Read and Fisher, 647). Goebbels on his visit to the Wolfschanze on July 8 was told by the führer that "the war in the East was in the main already won." He ordered that planning commence for the reduction of the army except for the tank forces which would have to be kept strong to roam the occupied spaces (Warlimont, 179–80). On July 14 the OKH began studying the disposition of the army for occupation duties and future tasks in Europe.

As resistance, instead of petering out, grew in intensity, there ensued a period of puzzlement and indecision as to what to do with a situation that did not conform to what only yesterday had seemed a certainty. For by the end of August the Barbarossa scenario had played itself out. Its main objective had been to pin down and annihilate the Russian armies within the western borderlands. Of the four sectors, when one includes the Finnish front, only the AGC can be said to have accomplished its mission. By the end of August it had penetrated deep into Russia, getting to within 200 miles of the Kremlin walls and taking in the process 800,000 prisoners. But not so the two other groupings, not to speak of Finland. AGN was supposed to have destroyed the Soviet forces in the Baltics, but it let them escape; it was to have taken Leningrad and failed to do so; it was to link up with the Finns but never succeeded in doing so. After the initial dash to the Dvina it bogged down in the forests, lakes and marshes of northern Russia. And in Finland the Germans failed to take either Murmansk or sever its vital rail line. In the south AGS got off to a late start and likewise failed to trap the Russians in Ukraine. Their proposed large sweep down the Dniepr bend had to be given up for the lesser sweep of the Uman pocket; the 100,000 prisoners taken there was small compared to AGC's tally particularly when nearly half of all Russian armies were in the south.

Although the AGC did carry out the intent of Barbarossa, yet it, too, failed in one important respect. As stressed in Directive No. 21 AGC was to have sent its armored forces north to help von Leeb. It did no such thing. But the führer had not forgotten it. On July 23 there was a conference in the Wolfschanze in the presence of a worried Halder. Early in July he had estimated that of the original 164 divisions available to the Russians only 46 were left; now at the end of July, following all their defeats, this estimate rose to 94 divisions. Halder asked the führer what the *Endziele* of the campaign were — a strange question to ask one month after it had been launched. Hitler answered that "regardless of the enemy and other events" he would stick to his program; Bock would give up PzG 2 to help von Leeb because his main interest was and remained Leningrad (Halder Vol. III, 97). Within the next few weeks Hitler issued three directives: 33a (July 23), 34 (July 30) and 34a (August 4), each canceling the previous one. In the one of July 23 he deprived AGC of its main role and assigned Hoth to AGN and Guderian to AGS, a switch from the center to the wings. Bock, left with infantry divisions only, was to defeat the Russians east of Smolensk and capture Moscow (Bock, 260–1). Von Leeb, reinforced by Hoth's armor, was to destroy the Soviet forces in Estonia and surround Leningrad. With Guderian's help Rundstedt in the south would occupy the Donetz Basin then swing south to invade the Caucasus. The July 23 directive seems to have originated under the midsummer euphoria for it also stipulated that planning be started on returning the bulk of AGN and parts of AGS to Germany — in preparation for post–Barbarossa needs! The directive also reminds the military of the ideological context of the war: "The security troops in the rear areas are to operate not by legal punishment of the guilty but by striking such terror into the population that it loses all will to resist" (Trevor-Roper 1964, 89–90).

Directive No. 34 of July 30 makes a complete about-face from the one of a week before. The führer suddenly discovered that Russian resistance was strong; the flanks of AGC were dangerously exposed; supply problems were mounting; AGC's two Panzer groups were in need of rehabilitation; all of which, says the directive, makes it impossible to implement 33a. All army groups were now to cease offensive operations and AGC's two Panzer groups were ordered withdrawn for refitting. A screeching halt was thus imposed upon the Ostheer six weeks into the campaign. The order also amounted to a postponement of any decision of how to proceed with the campaign. In his diary Halder commented, "This decision frees every thinking soldier of the horrible vision obsessing us these last few days, when the Führer's obstinacy made the final bogging down of the eastern campaign appear imminent" (Boog, 81).

The above was followed by Directive No. 34a on August 12. It cancelled the halt order and directed von Leeb to lay siege to Leningrad and with the help of Hoth's armor join up with the Finnish Army in Karelia. The orders to AGS were to avoid capturing Kiev but, as soon as supply conditions permitted, destroy it with incendiary bombs and artillery fire (Trevor-Roper 1964, 94). In his entry of August 18 Halder quoted Hitler that Kiev must be leveled into "rubble and ashes" and he estimated that "to do the job" 17 trainloads of explosives would be required. When the threat from the flanks was eliminated and AGC's Panzer Groups were refurbished Directive No. 34a foresaw an attack on Moscow. Its aim would be "the removal from the enemy before winter of the entire state, armaments and communication center around Moscow."

While these directives flowed from the führer's pen, the mood at the OKH continued to darken. On July 26 Halder heard from Hitler an evaluation of the war that shook him. Contrary to all that the German army knew and practiced, Halder now heard from the commander in chief of the Wehrmacht a new principle of warfare. "The Russian — said Hitler — cannot be beaten with operational successes; he simply does not acknowledge them. (That England was already beaten but didn't know it Hitler had likewise told his previous visitors.) The solution? He must be broken in a series of small tactical defeats." Halder noted that after hearing this he began to doubt the success of the campaign. As the north-south tug of the führer's directives continued, Halder asked Jodl on August 7 whether the führer wanted to defeat the enemy or go after industrial targets. Jodl answered that in the führer's view both could be gotten at the same time (Halder Vol. III, 143,167). But Halder's concerns deepened to a point that in his entry for August 11 he summarized the situation by saying that all efforts were now being aimed at avoiding a slide into positional warfare.

The situation came to a boil during the third week of August. Frustrated by the deadlock, Halder made Brauchitsch recommend to Hitler that the next stage be a concentrated push on the central front with Moscow as the objective. Hitler angrily dismissed it, saying "the OKH plan is not in accordance with my intentions" (Trevor 1964, 95). This was followed by a furious memorandum from the führer which said that operations at the front were not being conducted according to his wishes and that the OKH did not follow a plan but let the army group commanders run the show according to their self interest.

Stung by this rebuke the General Staff made a feeble attempt to salvage its honor. Since a situation developed whereby neither the OKH nor Hitler were assuming leadership Halder recommended that both he and Brauchitsch submit their resignations. Brauchitsch refused to have any part in it. Halder then persuaded Guderian to present the army's case to Hitler. Guderian met the führer on August 23 and came out of the meeting saying that he agreed with the führer. When Halder remonstrated with him for failing in his mission, Guderian replied that since Hitler was determined to have his way, it was his duty to acquiesce and "make the impossible possible" (Halder Vol. III, 194–5).

The problems afflicting the Russian campaign as a whole were reflected in the war in Finland which contained all the sins martial wisdom teaches leaders to avoid. The forces there were too small for a 620-mile-long front. They were dispersed so that nowhere did they have a preponderance of strength and were unable to assist each other. There was no unified command for the Germans and the Finns were led by different commanders in chief. And the Germans themselves were subordinated to two different headquarters, von Leeb to OKH, Dietl and Feige to the OKW. This, on top of the German contempt for the northern terrain and the capacities of the enemy.

Problems such as these, but on a grander scale, afflicted the Ostheer on the entire Russian front. The invasion forces were too small to start with. They were not mobile enough for the spaces involved and what motorized transport the Germans had was unsuitable for the Russian terrain and climate. It is symptomatic that the only army group to have fulfilled its assignment was von Bock's which had two Panzer groups; the other two AGs had only one each. As the three groups moved into Russia they advanced along diverging axes, northeast, east and southeast, with von Leeb sometimes heading straight north and Rundstedt straight south. Consequently huge gaps developed between them, which the Russians exploited for attacks on their flanks. Von Bock could reasonably argue that in addition to the heavy fighting that had developed near Smolensk and Yelnaya he also had to fight off the Russians on his flanks. After Smolensk, Guderian had to be sent off to Roslavl and Gomel to secure von Bock's southern flank, and Hoth had to be dispatched to Velikye Luki on the boundary between AGC and AGN to eliminate a threat to Bock's northern flank. Hoth also correctly argued that it would have been no good to send him to AGN from

Smolensk because he would just have sunk into the morass there; the axis to have followed north was from Minsk into the Baltics where the terrain was good and the place swarmed with Russians. But no one had ordered that, neither Hitler, nor the OKH, nor von Bock. The Barbarossa Directive was vague on when and where the turn north was to take place. This was in keeping with the general vagueness that afflicted the grand design itself. For Barbarossa never bothered to provide a contingency plan in case the Russians did not collapse where the Germans wanted them to collapse.

Then, the question of leadership. First there was the General Staff under Halder, who, even though he himself had prepared the operational plan with its swing north, thought Moscow when he wrote Leningrad. Then came the commander in chief of the German army, Feldmarschall von Brauchitsch. He thought Halderlike when in the presence of Halder and Hitlerlike in the presence of Hitler. The stature of the man is indicated by his statement at Nüremberg that "Hitler was the fate of Germany, and this fate could not be halted" (DDR, XVII, 436). There was also a private matter here, as so often is to such loyalty. Involved in 1938 with a mistress and unable to divorce his wife, Brauchitsch had been helped by the führer with both money and the divorce and Brauchitsch never forgot the debt he incurred. Next came Generaloberst Jodl who was Hitler's chief advisor on operational matters. But Jodl, part of the OKW with no responsibility for the Ostheer, was considered an interloper by the OKH. Since Hitler would not tolerate any sort of supreme council where things could be thrashed out collectively, a thing contrary to the führerprinzip, everyone cogitated in isolation. Hitler considered all his generals to have "fossilized minds" and had ordered that periodically front line officers (*Sendlinge*) be sent to him to give him a true picture of the situation. In its ultimate reality, it boiled down to two polar opposites; the generals functioning in terms of operations, armaments, and logistics; and the führer, who operated in terms of a jihad. Consequently field commanders were given either puzzling ideological orders or were left to their own devices. Thus PzG 2's dash to Yelnaya in July had not been planned or ordered but was due to the ambitions of Generaloberst Heinz Guderian. It was his entanglement with the Russians in front of him and on his flanks that forced Hoth to help close the Smolensk pocket and remain part of Bock's central axis. In France, Guderian's breakneck dash to the Channel proved a military masterpiece but this was due to the French, who refused to fight. At Smolensk, where the Russians did fight, a private war such as Guderian's rush to Yelneya was more akin to recklessness.

All through August the war in Russia remained in limbo, an orphan. The planned total annihilation of the Russian army obviously had not occurred; on the contrary, the Russians seemed to fight more tenaciously by the day. Clearly, too, the projected combined operation of the central and northern army groups had not been implemented. At the end of July the German casualties were 180,000 with replacements amounting to only 50,000 (Halder Vol. III, 143). By the end of August the casualties rose to 440,000 with 110,000 men dead or missing (Halder Vol. III, 213). Guderian's armor was down to 25 percent of its original strength while for the entire eastern front it fell to 47 percent (Müller-Hillebrand Vol. III, 205). The problem of supplies was acute. Partisans became a sufficient menace to require whole divisions to combat them. And more than half of the fighting season was gone.

• CHAPTER 16 •

Untermensch and Übermensch

On the day following the start of the campaign Hitler left Berlin, arriving at his field headquarters late in the evening of June 23. It was a portentous move. By settling down in this place, he essentially abandoned the war in the West. England was not doing much to him and he had no intention of doing anything to England, so he removed himself from this sideshow. At his eastern headquarters he was finally and completely in the place and role he aimed at. He was commander in chief of the most powerful army ever assembled waging a war of annihilation against the East. Amid feldmarschalls and maps, he kept all his fingers and every fiber of his brain on the crusade he had launched against the infidel. He was not to abandon that mission until the last breath was squeezed out of the German army and his own life.

The location of his HQ was in the Mazurian woods of East Prussia, some eight miles east of Rastenburg. It was not a headquarters in the sense of a field command close to the front from which armies are maneuvered and led in battle. It was a monastery — 400 miles from Berlin — away from its distractions of Italian ineptitude, a looming war with America and the devastations to be caused by Allied bombing; and 600 miles from the front with no hint of the bloodshed and ordeals suffered by the soldiers. Located in pinewoods infested with mosquitoes, it consisted of barracks and concrete bunkers ringed with multiple fences of barbed wire, mine belts, machine gun nests and flak. The dwellings were camouflaged with shrubbery so that from above the forest seemed pristine. The name Hitler chose for it was the *Wolfschanze* (Wolf's Lair).

Not only had Hitler abandoned the capital but the entire top military, state and party apparatus of Grossdeutschland also followed him into seclusion. The epicenter of the Wolfschanze was *Sperrkreis* A, housing Hitler, installed in a hut with all its windows facing north for he did not like the sun. The hut was sparsely furnished except for a large portrait of Frederick the Great which Hitler lugged with him to any of the multiple headquarters he happened to be occupying, east or west. He also brought with him to Rastenburg his dog, Blondi, as well as a trainer to prepare Blondi for "service at the front" (Sweeting, 163). With Hitler in *Sperrkreis* A were the chiefs of OKW, Keitel and Jodl; the party boss, Bormann; Germany's press chief, Dietrich; as well as his two private physicians, Brand and Morell, the latter a dispenser of assorted drugs and palliatives to the führer. Göring, in his capacity as commander in chief of the Luftwaffe, had his own headquarters nearby, but as Hitler's top nabob he also had a *pied-à-terre* in *Sperrkreis* A. The OKH with Brauchitsch and the General Staff was located in Mauerwald, 10 miles to the north. A railroad connected OKL and OKH with the Wolfschanze and while the army officers commuted on ancient railroad cars, Göring had his own deluxe train, white-gloved waiters serving meals in a lux-

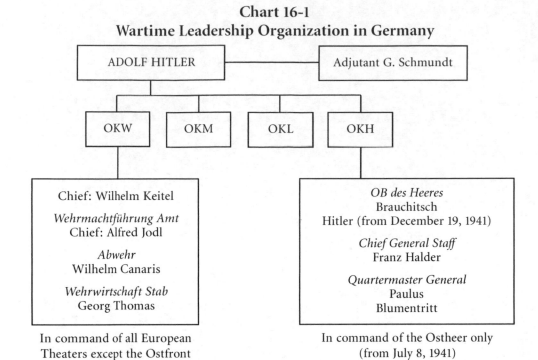

Chart 16-1
Wartime Leadership Organization in Germany

| ADOLF HITLER | Adjutant G. Schmundt |

OKW   OKM   OKL   OKH

Chief: Wilhelm Keitel	OB des Heeres
Wehrmachtführung Amt Chief: Alfred Jodl	Brauchitsch Hitler (from December 19, 1941)
Abwehr Wilhelm Canaris	*Chief General Staff* Franz Halder
Wehrwirtschaft Stab Georg Thomas	*Quartermaster General* Paulus Blumentritt

In command of all European   In command of the Ostheer only
Theaters except the Ostfront   (from July 8, 1941)

(Source: DeGolyer and McNaughton.)

urious dining salon. OKL headquarters were in Rominten Heide, the kaiser's erstwhile palace and hunting grounds, on which Göring promptly built himself a new palace. Ribbentrop and Himmler, too, established residences in the neighborhood; for trips to the führer they shared Himmler's private train, the *Heinrich*. It is symptomatic that while all military branches had relocated to the vicinity of Wolfschanze, the OKM stayed behind in Berlin. With England expelled from the war, Hitler did not need a navy.

In conformity with the significance of his move to the woods of East Prussia, Hitler now revamped the top military command. The OKW and OKH were officially divorced, as sketched in Chart 16-1. From now on the OKW commanded all military theaters throughout Europe and North Africa, while the OKH and the army General Staff were to confine themselves to one and one thing only — Russia. The army's high command was thus deprived of any voice in the operations of its troops outside the eastern front, and sometimes even of them. Thus the troops in Finland, coming as they did from Norway, were under the OKW even though they were fighting Russia.

Hitler commanded the wide-ranging horizon of military matters through two daily conferences. At midday Jodl presented to him an overall situation report. OKH sent in its report in the morning, which was combined with those from the other theaters by Jodl. Thus the eastern front was part of Jodl's presentation, which he did over a map of 1:1,000,000. Occasionally Halder or Warlimont was called in to report on the Ostfront, over a map of 1:300,000. The midday conference lasted two to three hours. This was followed by lunch and at 5 P.M. by coffee with his two secretaries, Christa Schröder and Gerda Daranowski. In the late evening a second situation report brought Hitler up to date. During these presentations Hitler expostulated at great length on his views and predictions, concluding with instructions to be drafted into orders. Between these two daily conferences

Hitler conferred sometimes with Bormann but most often with Himmler, who reported on items he had been charged with by Hitler Persona Number Three. At 7:30 supper was served to the führer in the company of a dozen or more associates. Sitting in the middle of the table he routinely had Jodl on his right, Dietrich on his left and facing him Keitel and Bormann; the others were representatives from various service branches, the SS and personal cronies. At these suppers there was no conversation. Without looking anyone in the eye Hitler lectured on scientific, historical and artistic matters flung out in the form of oracles or verbal formulas. He used a similar approach when on rare occasions army commanders were allowed to present a situation report or argue a point. He would make them appear during the daily briefings so that the large number of people present would cramp the visitor. Since he usually did not care to listen to complaints or suggestions he himself would soon start talking at great length and when this did not intimidate his interlocutor he would resort to one of his familiar rages. That would usually conclude the interview. This routine was practically invariable as was the attending company. Commented Christa Schröder, "We are permanently cut off from the world.... It's always the same limited group of people ... (we are) losing contact with the real world" (Kershaw 2000, 397).

Hitler rarely made a trip to the front and never spent time with his fighting troops. He occasionally visited Army Group headquarters—four such visits in the first four months. These were undertaken not to inform himself on the situation or on the views of his commanders but to express dissatisfaction with the course of events or to press for the implementation of a particular brainstorm of his. The visits were usually brief during which he was apprehensive and eager to get back to his lair. Though the OKH was only 10 miles away, he went there only once throughout that year. Cooped up with Jodl, the maps before him pinned with a steady 200 divisions, even if they had been reduced to tatters, he pressed on, oblivious of allies, enemies and in a way of his own fighting troops.

The wretchedness that awaited the Germans in Russia was total, encompassing the entire gamut of a soldier's experience in war, and beyond. The troops came from an unbroken series of easy and exhilarating victories fought in splendid countries like Norway, Holland, France and Greece where the circumstances of combat were civilized and life thereafter in the boulevards, cafes, country estates and beaches were for the victors not merely good but posh. Even in Eastern Europe, Czechoslovakia, Poland and Rumania, the occupiers had a fat and flattering time. It is probably correct to say that for most Germans the brief wars and the following occupations offered them more "fun" than at home. Suddenly they were in Soviet Russia, and what they faced was a new universe of life and death.

Initially it seemed that it would be a close second to past experiences. The first large cities they entered — Lvov, Vilnuis, Riga, Kaunas, Tallin — bore the tastes and architecture of their previous owners. The populations in the borderlands were nations forcibly incorporated in 1939–40 into the Soviet Union and had been for decades hostile to their eastern neighbor. This certainly applied to the Poles, Lithuanians, Latvians and Estonians. The Ukrainians, those of former Poland and those that had been part of Russia, harbored irredentist ambitions and as recently as the Russian Civil War had fought against the Bolsheviks and with the help of the Germans in World War I briefly witnessed an independent Ukraine. Inevitably the Germans were treated as "liberators" by these ethnic groups. In some places the usual ceremonial of proffered bread and salt and flower-decked maidens greeted the Germans. The misconception was two-sided. Little did the Balts and Ukrainians realize that Hitler had not come to liberate them, or anyone else, and that soon enough all attempts to establish any sort of national entity, be it a Lithuania, Latvia or Estonia, not to speak of a Ukraine, would be rubbed out with the same finality as Poland. One can forgive that naive faith for it was a reasonable thing to expect; in the fight against the Soviet Union this would have been in Germany's interest. But reason and self-interest were not what propelled the führer, and, soon enough, the Balts and Ukrainians would be fully enlightened on that score. The German troops on the other hand, seeing the attractive cities and the blond and beflowered girls recruited by the Ukrainian separatists, thought this was the country they were invading. The war at that time was easy and casualties light; the weather was splendid, fields of sunflowers swayed under white clouds, and the air was filled with scent of herbs and fruits. The Germans, their sleeves rolled up, their hair blowing in the breeze, marched deeper and deeper singing to the trill of harmonicas their Erika, La Paloma and Heimat songs—tunes most popular with the troops that first summer of the Russian war.

But soon the Baltics and the western Ukraine were behind them and ahead was Russia, a continent that had trodden its own ways for a thousand or more years. First of all, the maps the Germans had of Russia were misleading, or as Rundstedt complained "they were false." Marked highways turned out to be mere tracks and major industrial areas proved to be agricultural hamlets. To Germans such blasphemy against printed official maps were enough to drive them to distraction. The infantryman carried a pack weighing 55 pounds and the marches were so grueling that men fell asleep on the march. When the roads were dry and the sun shone the landlocked heat of Russia was intense. The tens of thousands of men and vehicles churned up the tracks raising a permanent wall of dust. The convoys of tanks and trucks spewed exhaust gases, fumes of burned oil and burned rubber. The smoke of villages, forests and grain fields set on fire by the fighting obscured the horizons, mixing with the fumes emitted by engines driven perpetually in low gear. This was what the infantry and the grenadiers in the open trucks and armored carriers inhaled and lived in for weeks and months on end. The dust turned their faces into gray masks; it entered their ears, nostrils, mouths, made their eyelids bleed; and the men swallowed it with the food they ate. Along the roads in the scorching heat lay heaps of dead Russians and, what was more upsetting to the Germans, mangled and disemboweled horses, emitting the stench of a cosmic slaughterhouse. In many instances the fields of cadavers had to be sprayed with quicklime before the Germans could settle down to rest and eat. The effects of dust on the vehicles had an immediate impact on their combat-worthiness. It clogged the filters, penetrated the bearings, seals and piston rings damaging the engines. Supply columns lost a third of their transport on the way to the dumps. Since the Germans had no tank transporters the Panzers moved on their own power, wearing out the tracks. The road conditions and the traffic usually forced the tanks to drive in low gear and as a result the consumption of fuel and lubricants was from two to three times higher than under normal conditions.

These were the good times. When rain came it was not of the European sort but downpours that dumped cascades of water and produced floods. Immediately the roads became impassable. In the summer the sun would come out and after several hours movement resumed. Not so in the fall when the Rasputitsa set in. Then rain and mud were as permanent as the dark skies. It was a struggle for the men to pull their legs out of the morass and later the dried-out clay doubled or tripled the weight of their boots. The soldiers called it buna, after the synthetic rubber produced in Germany. It was so deep that artillery shells that plopped into it often failed to explode. Vehicles, tracked or untracked, could not negotiate these quagmires and soldiers harnessed to ropes were employed like Volga boatmen to extricate them. Tanks often sank so deep that when pulled out they had to be returned for overhaul. Everything that could be gotten hold of, trees, telephone poles, straw were dumped into the mud; oftentimes houses were disassembled and the boards placed under the wheels to provide traction. Corpses of fallen Russian soldiers were stacked in the morass over which supplies had to travel. The horses the Germans brought with them were no match for the Russian roads either. One thousand horses died every day from shelling and other causes, 200 of heart failure in their exertions to pull their loads or extricating stuck motor vehicles (Lucas 1979, 113–4). The German wagons sporting rubber tires and ball-bearing mounted axles proved unsuitable for the muck and rivers of water. The Germans started replacing them with the high-slung panje carts and skinny horses taken from the locals. Unlike the oat-eating horses from Germany and Belgium these Russian horses when needs be survived on bark from the trees and straw from the thatched roofs. It was a landscape filled from horizon to horizon with waterholes and mud such as no German had ever seen or dreamed of.

In the central and northern sectors, these vicissitudes were increased by swamps and forests. Corduroy log roads, causeways and countless new bridges had to be laid to enable the troops to move or maneuver in battle. In the marshes swarms of mosquitoes, gnats and other insects plagued the men during the day and robbed them of sleep at night. In the southern parts the flies were so thick that they had to be brushed off in layers and even then men swallowed them with their food. A third of Byelorussia was covered with forests of oak, beech, and lime. These were nothing like the woods Germans with rucksacks and Lederhosen loved to visit in their homeland. This was a primordial wilderness preserved in its virgin state for millions of years, decomposed trees and giant undergrowth forming impenetrable thickets for hundreds of miles. They were so dense that when forced to enter them the Germans usually followed the spoors and trails of the larger animals. All movement was on foot, the men had to carry drinking water and, in the absence of a sky overhead, navigation was by compass. Coping with the semidarkness, strange sounds and lurking ambushes were features of a war that the German soldier had to learn for himself.

Either because there were so many corpses around or because of the starvation that gripped occupied Russia the Germans were inundated with rats. They were in all their quarters and dugouts. They infested the hospitals where they fleeted across the operating table during surgery and the doctors and medics had to cover their heads at night with blankets to protect themselves from the ceaselessly scurrying rodents (Bamm, 65). They even found their way into the tanks where they chewed up the electrical wiring and other equipment.

The infantry divisions and the horse-drawn columns of artillery and supplies showed great stamina in their rush to reach the encirclement areas staked out by the Panzers. The Germans marched for weeks and months 20–30 miles a day. Even when the roads were dry these were reserved for motor vehicles and off limits to the infantry, so the men marched in the roadside ditches or cross country — a winding endless stream of dust-caked soldiery snaking its way from horizon to horizon. It wasn't much better when the rapid advances ended and the divisions settled down in their permanent front or rear areas. The cities they occupied were rubble and ashes — either due to the scorched earth policy of the Russians or to the indiscriminate work of German artillery and bombers. The streets were desolate, the remaining inhabitants sullen and silent. There was no nightlife of any sort since there were curfews for all civilians. It was not safe for Germans to move about at night for there were urban guerillas and soldiers were occasionally killed or kidnapped when they ventured out in small groups. Most villages were burned to the ground and those that escaped destruction consisted of shacks and huts that were a revelation to the German soldier. Made of roughhewn logs and thatched roofs, they consisted of a single room, in Russian izba, with an earthen floor and bare walls, occasionally pasted over with newspapers. A big clay stove was the centerpiece of the abode on top of which the whole family slept. A wooden bench, wooden utensils, an icon or portrait of Stalin in a dim corner complemented the furnishings. Quite often a pig or goat shared the hovel with its owners, kept either in a small vestibule or in the corner of the izba itself. The air was foul but more vexing was the vermin that infested the izba and its inhabitants. Lice, bedbugs and fleas were an inseparable feature of these dwellings, all feeding on human blood. This they did primarily at night when they would descend in columns on the sleeping denizens. In addition to the bites and itches lice were also carriers of typhus, a common epidemic of the war years. While in the summer many Germans preferred to billet outside — when winter came they considered themselves lucky when they could squeeze in amidst the dozens of soldiers huddling in these infested dens that sheltered them from the icy winds and blizzards howling outside.

Beyond the exertions against heat, dust and mud, what oppressed the German soldier most was the seeming endlessness of it all. After long, backbreaking marches what they usually reached was a landscape identical to the one they had just left. Ahead there was no end in sight, no familiar destination like the Seine or Athens. They may have heard of Smolensk or Kiev but the hundreds of localities with unpronounceable names they were asked to fight for they never heard of, nor wanted to know. While some officers— usually of aristocratic caste — had traveled and appreciated the unique beauty of the Russian landscape, to the young and middle-aged German soldier — accustomed as he was to the manicured villages and cuckoo-clock interiors of his homeland — this land seemed of another planet, without charm, sense or limits. It was denuded and stark; they felt lost in these monotonous horizons ringed with black forbidding forests. And beyond these forests, as they marched on, the scene was of another flat landscape ringed with forests. Officers reported moods of depression plaguing troops exposed for too long to the Russian experience.

And there was the problem of women. Most young Russian women had left with the Red Army or the evacuated industries. But even had they stayed the problem would have existed. To the Germans the women of Russia were as uninviting as their homes and climate. Barefoot in the summer and wearing volanki in the winter, wrapped in padded jackets and heavy woolen scarves, in the misery of wartime conditions lacking food and doing heavy labor, it was difficult to tell their shape, age and sometimes even their sex. Then the ideological angle. Although not specifically forbidden the soldiers were told that Russian women were unworthy of a German lover; in addition such a liaison posed a security risk because most of those consenting were Communist agents. Should a German soldier succumb to his sexual needs, the woman involved would usually be hauled before the SD and shipped off to forced labor if not to a worse lot; sometimes the German, too, would be punished.

Because of the mud and subsequently the ferocious winter the German soldier began to lose his proud look — tight jacket and hobnailed boots. They began to wear anklet boots, baggy pants and the famous *feldgrau* gave way to a more practical green uniform, in which they looked more like mechanics than the vaunted *Soldat* of past and recent glory.

As the blitzkrieg turned into positional warfare most of the troops ended up in dugouts and bunkers familiar from World War I. But they were not as solid or comfortable or safe. Russia at war was a country denuded not just of shelter, but of nearly everything, no paper, matches, shoelaces. Lacking either bricks or wood the German dugouts were flimsy affairs. Water and wind penetrated the foxholes, lamps had to be improvised from shell casings using foul-smelling kerosene. Since the troops were thinly spread, these dugouts were wide apart. The Russians were experts in infiltration and to guard against it and protect their flanks prolonged guard and patrol duty were imposed on the men, leaving little time for rest or sleep. Nor could they hope for speedy relief because most of the time the Germans had no reserves for it.

All this was mere background to the ordeal of fighting the war. The Germans, as usual, were superb soldiers combining competence, ruthlessness and physical bravery. They were no novices to cunning, treachery and cruelty in combat — much of which they had invented. But they were not prepared for the kind of apocalyptic struggle that came to characterize the fighting in the east. The new physiognomy of this war stemmed from two congruent elements: Hitler's decision to extirpate the life force of Russia, and the Russians' traditional tenacity in defending their homeland, augmented by the norms of Bolshevik leadership.

The Russians did not subscribe to the textbook notion of battles won and lost or of military sense and nonsense. They attacked ceaselessly regardless of casualties and achievement. They overwhelmed the Germans by the mere stubbornness of their infantry charges. They laid down unaimed artillery barrages that deafened one by the mere noise of it. Once they succeeded in coming to grips with the Germans, once past their tanks and flamethrowers, they proved formidable fighters. They endured conditions the Germans thought an insect could not survive. They lived through the heaviest bombardments, they went without food and water, endured floods, ice and frost, stoically took their wounds — and fought on. They were masters of camouflage; whole regiments would in the blinking of an eye vanish from the surface of the earth. The Germans would enter seemingly empty villages, they would search and probe and no sooner settle down than the whole place would erupt with machine gun and mortar fire. Ahead of them would be a dead and silent marsh and all at once its dead clumps of weed and piles of peat would turn into floating ramps firing machine guns. They would cautiously enter a forest and cross it only to discover that the Russians were dug in not at the front but at the end of the thickets, starting to fire as soon as the Germans emerged into the open. Carrying tsarist rifles with their triangular bayonets, without steel helmets, gas masks, or even canteens, the Russian soldier faced the German wall of steel and fire without flinching, dying en masse but extracting a price. To win a skirmish or a battle was not the end of the story but rather the beginning — following which there began a debilitating war of harassment, attrition, ambush and sabotage. Following the evacuation of Kiev and Sevastopol the Russians mined extensive parts of the cities and exploded the mines by remote control the moment the Germans occupied them. When Odessa was abandoned, Russians in its sewers and tunnels fought on for another two years. After Kerch was taken they holed up in the disused mines and fought until liberation. Men stayed in their dugouts and when the tanks passed they lobbed Molotov cocktails into their exhaust pipes. Beaten, some Russians remained as nuclei for future infiltrations, as partisans in the woods, as sabotage units in the cities. A typical feature of this relentless defiance was the U-2, also designated PO-2. Unable to match the Germans in the air, thousands of tiny planes, flying at no more than 100 mph, swarmed like mosquitoes over the German lines every night in a ceaseless harassing offensive. Penetrating a few miles into the rear these flimsy biplanes, dating back to 1927, would cut their engines, glide down to a few thousand feet and shower bombs on barracks, billets and parked vehicles. They did little damage but they deprived the Germans of sleep and forced them to run night after night to the air-raid trenches. This they kept up in 10- to 15-minute intervals over the entire length of the front.

Unlike in other wars there was no alleviating thought that in case of a mishap or defeat one would end up a prisoner and somehow survive. The Germans made sure to forsake this option. Stalin had issued his no-surrender order, not for any humane reasons, but the Red Army man would have been well advised to heed it. In 1941 the chances of a Russian prisoner surviving captivity were close to nil. Immediately at the front German soldiers shot them at will. In many cases, for reasons of discipline or in order to encourage desertion from the other side, officers inveigled the men not to do it, but it had little effect (Bartov, 114). When Russians were captured en masse in the giant encirclements they were exterminated in stages. They were first left in the broiling sun for days or weeks without food or water; then they were marched long distances and whoever could not keep up was shot; then they were herded into freight trains without food; then they were put behind barbed wire enclosures where, in addition to starvation and epidemics, mass executions took place by shooting or gassing. German witnesses describe huge *Lager* of prisoners sitting in the open over whom occasionally "a wind of sighs" would pass; or when they marched all that could be seen was a moving mountain of dust followed by myriad flies. A doctor in the Crimea, when confronted with a mass of wounded Russians, approached his commander, a Viennese, for help; the Viennese asked him, "Would a machine gun do?" (Bamm, 70).

Although Hitler had not issued an order similar to Stalin's he, in fact, expected the same from the German soldier. When letters from POWs in Russian hands arrived via the Red Cross he ordered them confiscated and they were never delivered to the families of the prisoners (Stahlberg, 192). He did not want his soldiers to believe that they could survive by surrendering. As the Germans advanced, they would now and then come across prisoners killed by the retreating Russians. In a most peculiar mindset they considered these to be barbaric acts, in no way connecting them with their own thousandfold murders of Russians. When they encountered corpses of their comrades they vowed "revenge." All together the mentality of the Germans was such that not only were they indifferent but oblivious of the hatred they evoked by their deeds in a country they had gratuitously invaded. They also never blamed their leaders for the snafus and disasters that overtook them. If there was some failure they felt that perhaps the generals had goofed — never the führer (Bamm, 62).

Caught in a morbid land amid the hatred of sullen and inscrutable peasants, ceaselessly attacking or being attacked with no quarter asked or given, the Germans ceased to be an army conducting a military campaign, becoming a pack of cornered animals. The grim physical conditions and the almost unnatural endurance of the Russian soldiers dovetailed with the Nazi views they had swallowed and made them agree that, indeed, they were fighting a subhuman race. Not being particularly empathetic people to start with, this atavistic level of warfare converted the German soldiers into ghouls.

* * *

It is tempting to compare Stalin to Hitler because superficially there were many similarities. Supreme rulers of their countries, they were both responsible for the murder of millions of people. Both were feared and obeyed without the slightest contradiction or opposition from their underlings. Both had established a god-like idolatry of their persons while despising the masses. Even some of their personal backgrounds and habits were alike.

Chart 16-2
Wartime Leadership Organization of the USSR

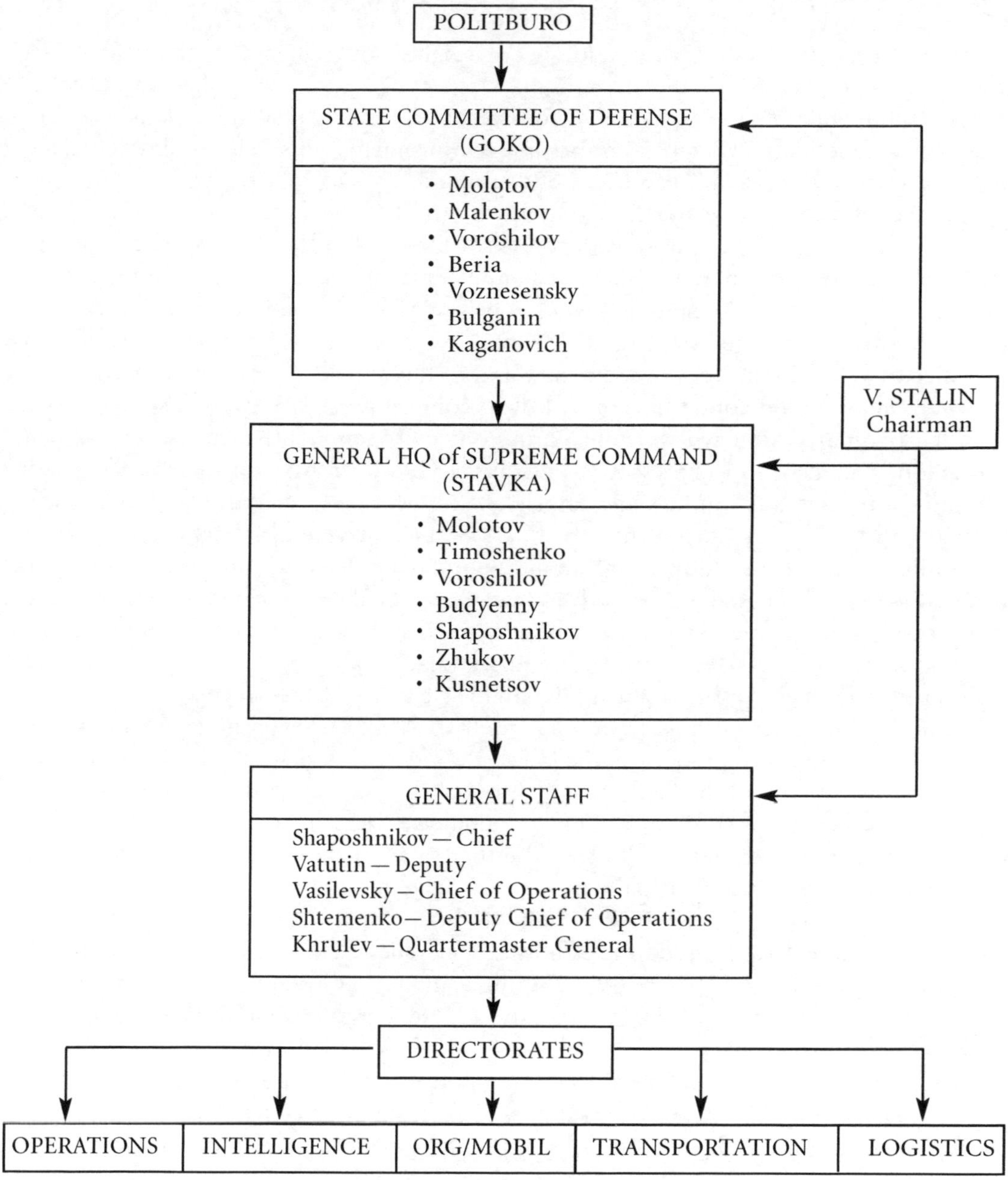

```
                        ┌─────────────┐
                        │  POLITBURO  │
                        └──────┬──────┘
                               ▼
        ┌──────────────────────────────────────┐
        │   STATE COMMITTEE OF DEFENSE          │◄──────────┐
        │             (GOKO)                    │           │
        ├──────────────────────────────────────┤           │
        │        • Molotov                      │           │
        │        • Malenkov                     │           │
        │        • Voroshilov                   │           │
        │        • Beria                        │           │
        │        • Voznesensky                  │           │
        │        • Bulganin                     │           │
        │        • Kaganovich                   │           │
        └───────────────┬──────────────────────┘    ┌───────────────┐
                        ▼                            │  V. STALIN    │
        ┌──────────────────────────────────────┐    │   Chairman    │
        │  GENERAL HQ of SUPREME COMMAND        │◄───└───────────────┘
        │             (STAVKA)                  │
        ├──────────────────────────────────────┤
        │        • Molotov                      │
        │        • Timoshenko                   │
        │        • Voroshilov                   │
        │        • Budyenny                     │
        │        • Shaposhnikov                 │
        │        • Zhukov                       │
        │        • Kusnetsov                    │
        └───────────────┬──────────────────────┘
                        ▼
        ┌──────────────────────────────────────┐
        │          GENERAL STAFF                │◄──────────┘
        ├──────────────────────────────────────┤
        │ Shaposhnikov — Chief                  │
        │ Vatutin — Deputy                      │
        │ Vasilevsky — Chief of Operations      │
        │ Shtemenko — Deputy Chief of Operations│
        │ Khrulev — Quartermaster General       │
        └───────────────┬──────────────────────┘
                        ▼
                 ┌──────────────┐
                 │ DIRECTORATES │
                 └──────────────┘
```

OPERATIONS	INTELLIGENCE	ORG/MOBIL	TRANSPORTATION	LOGISTICS

Both came from humble origins, had no formal education and functioned late into the night. Yet they were as different as was Caesar from Caligula. In capsule form it can be said that while Hitler exercised his tyranny over the Germans in order to fulfill his private hysterical compulsions, Stalin with caution and calculation used his tyrannical powers to win the war.

Russia's leadership ladder during the war is shown in Chart 16-2. The highest decision-making organ was the State Committee of Defense — GOKO. It had eight members representing the diplomatic, economic, and military purviews of the state; its edicts took precedence over all state and party statutes. The strategic-military decisions of GOKO were passed on to a General Headquarters of State Defense, Stavka, made up of seven of the country's top military men. Though both GOKO and Stavka were chaired by Stalin, they were genuine consultative bodies where issues were weighed and argued, though the final decision rested with the chairman. The military decisions of Stavka were then passed to the army General Staff under Shaposhnikov for execution. On July 19 Stalin took over as commissar of defense and on August 8 he became commander in chief but this did not change the procedures of the established chain of command.

These offices as well as the more important ministries were located within the Kremlin walls. The General Staff was outside, on Kirov Street; after the Germans started bombing Moscow and its building was damaged and people killed the General Staff moved into the Kirov subway station. There they worked behind partitions and slept in a parked train. Stalin's premises, the same as before the war, consisted of a secretariat next to which was the office of Poskrebyshev, Stalin's secretary and factotum who also operated a signals center where Stalin could communicate with field commanders. This led to a security room attended by guards after which came Stalin's office. Its conference area was an oak-paneled oblong hall. Next to Stalin's seat was a globe and Lenin's death mask under a glass cover. In addition to portraits of Marx and Engels, Stalin, when the war started, added those of Kutuzov and Suvorov. Across the street was Stalin's private apartment, described by Churchill as modest — a study, bedroom and living room. Even within the Kremlin Stalin moved about accompanied by two bodyguards; otherwise there were no searches or inspections of people that came to see him. Stalin remained in these quarters throughout the war.

Stalin's workday started a little before noon. First he called the Operations Directorate to find out what had happened during the night. He followed their reports on maps hung in his office, duplicates of those at the General Staff. At 4 P.M. Shaposhnikov either sent or personally brought over a report on the latest military events, delivered in the presence of the GOKO members and the Politburo. A third briefing took place about midnight, delivered in person by Shaposhnikov and the commanders whose reports were relevant to the day's events. During delivery Stalin would either sit and listen in silence or walk up and down the room smoking; he usually broke two cigarettes and used the tobacco to fill his pipe. After listening to the reports he would on the spot issue directives and orders. These nocturnal sessions lasted three to four hours after which Stalin still went to his office so that work was not finished before 6 A.M. While Stalin was at his desk none of his immediate subordinates and none of the latter's subordinates dared leave; only when he quit did they, too, go home.

In their encounters with Stalin friends and enemies alike left with similar opinions of the man. Despite his short height, pockmarked face and crippled left arm the impression he gave was of dignity and poise. He was polite and hospitable, never raised his voice either with guests or subordinates. When he was dissatisfied with a delivered text he so told its author and taking a pencil would himself redraft it. When angered he would calmly and in few words give his reasons. When bad news was brought to him — like Churchill's message that there would be no second front in 1942 — there was no outburst and no rebuke to Churchill, though no hiding that it may have grave implications. Everyone was particularly impressed by his quick grasp of subtle points and his gift of formulating policies in succinct, precise phrasing. He knew how to deflect grave questions or lighten tense moments by a morbid humor. Along with other generals, Rokossovsky had been released in 1941 from a gulag to take command of Russian troops. When Stalin saw him he asked where he had been and when Rokossovsky explained, Stalin said, "It was a good time to be away." In a similar vein when Molotov let him know that his wife had been arrested, Stalin's rejoinder was "I don't understand, they arrested my relatives too." Sometime these acerbic repartees became reality. Dissatisfied with his English interpreter, Stalin asked that Berezhkov, erstwhile first counselor in Berlin, be assigned in his stead. When Molotov pointed out that Berezhkov's specialty was German, Stalin dismissed that by saying, "I will tell him to interpret into English and he will." Berezhkov soon interpreted for him during the conferences with Churchill and Roosevelt (Berezhkov 1994, 201).

Through his chairmanship of the Politburo, GOKO, and Stavka and by being commander in chief, prime minister, and commissar of defense, Stalin had his hand on all the levers and buttons that activated the Soviet colossus. Despite the very defects in his makeup Stalin turned out to be one of the greatest war leaders in history. He had a supreme sense of long-range strategy and the keenest eye for future possibilities. With ruthless consistency and willpower he orchestrated the utilization of industry and manpower, extracting the last ounce of devotion, effort and blood from every man, woman and child in the USSR — harnessing it all to the single task of overpowering the German army. Stalin was adamant about the buildup of strategic reserves. He hoarded not only troops, but artillery and air force parks, keeping them directly under his own control. These were recorded on tally boards by his desk and were not disclosed to the front commanders lest they start clamoring for them. He then doled them out as he saw fit. At the lowest point of the Red Army's fortunes, in the deepest crises, he kept his attention on political issues, skillfully maneuvering the progress of the war and relations with the West so that when Russia had paid its terrible price for victory she would be rewarded with territory, power and prestige in the postwar world.

At the beginning Stalin liked to meddle in the business of his generals, perhaps with reason since the generals weren't much good at it. This, too, was partly Stalin's fault for his best military men were killed off in the purges and when the war started those at the top were all Stalin's cronies. The three front commanders, Budyenny, Voroshilov and Timoshenko were descendants of the Red Cavalry Army of the Civil War, enshrined as a myth in Soviet history. Budyenny was a relic, belonging more to Genghis Khan's hordes than to the tank armies he commanded on the southwestern front. Voroshilov was a politician rather than a soldier. But again to give Stalin his due he learned his lessons quickly and learned them correctly. The cavalry marshals were soon cashiered. Young, professional men like Zhukov, Konev and Rokossovsky and half a dozen others took over and were to prove themselves great commanders throughout the wrenching, four-year conflict. While on the German side the generalship, under Hitler's whip, went downhill, with the Russians it steadily improved until at war's end they were as confident and skillful as were the Germans at the beginning.

The Russian soldier, too, kept improving though slowly and at an excruciating price. As in the past he was tenacious, facing privation and danger with a stoic stubborn bravery. But due to the negligence of his leaders and the inadequacy of his weapons he had to endure conditions that taxed his innate fortitude. At the beginning there were cases when whole villages were flung as a unit into the front, many without weapons, which they were told to procure from their fallen comrades or the enemy. A Russian infantryman was given a supply of ammunition for only 10 days as he was not expected to last longer. A saying in the Red Army went that a platoon leader or lieutenant survived, on the average, one attack and a half; a tankman one battle and a half; a pilot one and a half combat missions (Axell 2001, 245). Most regular troops had no steel helmets, carried no gas masks and lacked even trenching tools. With a canvas pouch over his shoulder that carried all his military and personal utensils he was sent to face a wall of steel and fire and it is no metaphor to say that hundreds of thousands of Red Army men resisted the Germans with their naked flesh. The soldier was aware that he had to defend his home and he knew that with a Politruk in the rear he could not bow out and he also knew surrender meant death, so his only alternative was to fight to the limit. When defeats multiplied troops in the rear were ordered to shoot at frontline soldiers forced to abandon their position or running away; the orders were to shoot at the feet or over the heads but in many cases retreating soldiers were killed in these fusillades (Loza, 19). With his innate cunning and gift of improvisation he resorted to tactics and stratagems that in their primitiveness and ferocity tended to make up for the glaring technical disparity between the two armies. Wherever they halted the Russians immediately disappeared from sight; they could camouflage their dugouts and bunkers to look no different from meadows and thickets. They utilized retreat for staging future attacks by leaving behind pockets of men which were then reinforced to serve as jumping-off points for combined assaults. Russian infiltrations were a never-ending headache to the Germans. In a steady trickle, silently and invisibly, men would filter across the German lines, lie low for days and weeks, accumulating reinforcements to suddenly attack the German rear. Whether retreating or advancing across rivers they formed little bridgeheads, which from company size quickly swelled to regimental proportions. The Russians would cross marshes crawling on their bellies and could nest for weeks on clumps of weeds and peat piles. One of their great skills was their ability to negotiate the widest rivers. The simplest technique was when thousands of men grabbed boards, tree trunks, empty drums or tires and paddled across pulling with them raft-mounted horses, machine guns and mortars. The other technique was to build underwater bridges using inflatable bellows on which they laid tracks one foot below the water surface, invisible even from the air. Some of these bridges could be lowered to the river bottom by day and lifted up at night. Altogether the Russians' ability to handle haulage of troops and supplies—given that initially they had little motorized transport—was one of their great achievements. Trains moved in convoy within sight of each other, unmindful of safety, all this in the face of great shortages of locomotives and fuel. In case of need both tracks were used for one-way traffic and during offensives when reserves were being piled up in great haste the emptied cars were thrown off the tracks to enable the oncoming trains to unload their cargos. Every possibility was utilized to bolster resistance. Fake maps were planted with the Germans. Men about to become prisoners were given false information to have it passed on during their interrogation. Unlike the Germans who sought shelter during air raids, the Red Army was ordered to lie on their backs and fire on enemy planes, partly as a morale booster and partly due to the weakness of their air force. Lacking armored carriers for the accompanying infantry, handrails were welded to the tanks to which the infantry clung during combined attacks. Against magnetic mines that the Germans used, the Russians smeared cement on the hulls of their tanks. On the other hand, the Germans often found Russian crews locked in their tanks to prevent desertion.

To make up for their inadequacy in aimed firepower the Russians resorted extensively to the use of mines. Men marching to the front were each given an artillery shell or mine to carry to the forward positions. When civilians were sent to build fortifications every man, woman and youngster carried a shell or mine for delivery to the troops. They were equally proficient in clearing enemy mines. Quite often they not only eliminated German minefields, but brought back with them the retrieved mines for their own use; this forced the Germans to lay minefields behind their forward positions and pull back during Russian attacks (US Army, 20–230). The Russians also somehow found a way of employing tanks in their own fashion. They would rush behind the German lines and, like their infantry, hide in hollows, haystacks and houses to attack the German flanks. They were the first to use "hull-down" positions by burying the tanks into the ground and using their cannon as artillery or an antitank weapon. Otherwise the tanks were forbidden to engage the German armor if they could avoid it.

In their inability to handle combined-arms formations the Soviet Command resorted to the simple solution of instituting separate infantry, or what they called rifle divisions, and separate regiments of artillery, rocketry and tanks. During combat these specialized units were attached to the riflemen for a combined assault. This battle organization proved sufficiently successful that eventually whole artillery and tank armies were formed to be shifted from front to front as the need arose. Lacking the ability to direct accurate artillery fire the Russians replaced it with saturation bombardments of the target area, similar to the Allies' carpet bombing of Germany after realizing that they were unable to hit pinpointed objectives.

As part of their efforts to use any and every available means of fighting the enemy, an elaborate partisan network was set up behind the German lines. At first these consisted of small groups of cut-off soldiers who on their own initiative kept their weapons and tried to survive in inaccessible stretches of forest and swamp. Soon Moscow stepped in to organize them in more formal fashion. Their expansion came from both the enlistment of civilians in the occupied areas and from reinforcements sent across the front in the form of instructors, officers, and radio experts. This liaison was mostly via small aircraft, which trudged their way night after night, bringing the partisans supplies and evacuating the wounded. These were extremely hazardous flights. The pilots lacked modern equipment, navigated by terrain features and had no parachutes either for themselves or the supplies to be dropped They not only delivered supplies without parachutes, but in winter, also men. The planes had a plywood tube installed on their belly inside which the man to be dropped would lie stretched out. Over the target area the plane would fly low and slow and jettison the man onto a deep snow bank (Myles, 77). It was only later when the partisans controlled large areas that the planes could land in designated clearings.

In 1941 a man's chance of surviving the fighting was slim; in case of capture it was nil. Before the end came the Russian soldier endured the fiercest assaults by artillery, tanks and those terrifying Stukas, which hovered over the battlefield day after day. In the end the Russians were saying that they had won the war with their wounded. From medical records it emerged that 75 percent of the wounded and 90 percent of those who fell sick were returned to the fighting units; many of these men had been wounded several times (Axell 2001, 235). All around him the Russian soldier saw his native villages and cities go up in flames. Many of them farmers, they had to watch the spectacle of endless fields of rye and wheat scorched by fire or left unharvested. For millions of soldiers their homes ended up under German rule, leaving them in continuous anxiety about their fate. Everywhere they encountered wandering children whose parents had been killed or otherwise lost and they started picking them up and keeping these kids in their units throughout the war. The Russian soldier received no mail; he was granted no home leave; was never relieved from combat duty; and when he died he knew that along with the masses of other killed men he would be buried in a mass grave without any sign of his resting place. He was alone in a storm of death and fire with little hope of emerging from it and seeing his family again. On their march routes and in their nightly bivouacs they would in the Russian manner pour out their melancholy in songs sung in chorus to the wail of an accordion — and they were searing songs. Two of these became the epitome of the Russian soldier's sense of doom. One, "Tyomnaya Notch"— "Dark Night"— was a lament of death and longing; the other, more resigned but more poignant was "Zhdyj Menya"—"Wait for Me"— addressed to one's wife or girl, a few lines of which read:

> Wait for me and I will return!
> Wait when from far-off places letters do not come
> Wait when everyone else has grown tired of waiting.
> They will not understand how amid the fires
> You saved me with your waiting.*

The gloom the Russian soldier felt seeing the country go up in flames was intensified by his having to lend a hand to it. In withdrawing, the army had orders to lay waste to anything that could serve the Germans. This was nothing new as all armies destroy equipment and supplies that may be useful the enemy. But in Bolshevik Russia this was more extreme than elsewhere; it would be exceeded only by what the Germans would do two years later when they retreated. Agricultural equipment was wrecked, mounds of grain were doused with gasoline and set on fire, factories were blown up, whole city districts were mined. Probably the most painful demolition took place on August 24 when the Zaporozhe complex was blown up. This hydroelectric installation, which took decades to erect, supplied half a million kilowatts of electricity to Ukraine and was the pride of Soviet industry. After five of its giant turbo-generators were dismantled and shipped to the east, the four others were wrecked and the dam blown up over a span of 200 yards. Even after the Germans had finished rebuilding it in 1943 it produced only 5 percent of its former capacity (Neumann, 123).

Perhaps the most somber tale of the black crusade against Russia was the fate of the captured prisoners of war. This horror story is taken up in detail in Chapter 20. Here one may only note that of the 5.5 million Russian POWs taken by the Germans 3.5 million did not survive captivity. The fate of one man only will be related here because it tells so much about the nature of his war. This is the story of Stalin's son from his first marriage, Yakov. A howitzer battery commander, he was captured near Vitebsk on July 16. The Germans then scattered leaflets over the Russian lines showing Yakov talking with German officers, the accompanying text saying that he gave himself up because any further resistance to the German army was useless. In fact the conversation between Yakov Stalin and his interrogator, Maj. Walter Holters, on July 18 went as follows:

> HOLTERS: Did you surrender on your own accord?
> YAKOV: I was taken by force.
> H.: In what way?
> Y: On 12 July our unit was surrounded. I tried to reach my men but was stunned
> by a blast. I would have shot myself, had I been able to do so.
> H: Do you believe that your troops still have a chance of reversing the war?
> Y: The war is still far from ended.
> H: And what if we shortly take Moscow?

*By Konstantin Simonov, a Russian writer who spent much of the war years with the troops.

Y: You will never take Moscow.

H: When did you last speak to your father?

Y: I rang him up on June 22. Upon hearing that I was leaving for the front, he said "Go and fight" [Axell 2001, 74–5].

At some point the Red Cross contacted Moscow about exchanging Yakov for a German general in Russian hands. Stalin did not reply. Yakov, fearing that in the end the Germans might force him into some sort of anti–Soviet activity, and perhaps also knowing his father's attitude to becoming a POW, committed suicide in the prison camp by walking deliberately against the perimeter fence whereupon a sentry shot him dead.

One of the foremost achievements of the Soviet leadership was the evacuation of industrial plants to the east. This entailed not merely the stupendous task of disassembling and reassembling huge and intricate machinery but a host of associated problems. The overall evacuation plan was prepared on July 4 under the chairmanship of GOKO member Voznesensky. Almost immediately shipments started from the Donetz Basin, Moscow and Leningrad, the three major industrial centers of western Russia. The work of dismantling these plants went on 24 hours a day. The immensity of the job can be gleaned from such examples as the Zaporozhe steel plant, weighing 50,000 tons, requiring 8,000 railroad cars to ship; the 498 plants evacuated from Moscow, together with 210,000 workers, needed 71,000 railroad cars. The speed with which these tasks were accomplished was astonishing. The Dniepropetrovsk tube-rolling mill, shipped on August 7, arrived in the Urals on September 6, and was in full production by the end of the year (Werth, 214–16). Between July and November a total of 1,523 installations, 90 percent of them war plants, were transferred, half of them to the Urals, the rest to the Volga region, Siberia and Central Asia. With them went 12 million workers, half of them women (Calvocoressi, 480). An indication of their contribution to the war effort can be gleaned from the output of the relocated aircraft factories which in 1942 alone produced 25,000 airplanes (Hardesty, 31).

This was a unique feat not just on part of the organizers but perhaps even more so of the masses of ordinary citizens. They labored endless hours dismantling and loading the equipment and stayed with the machinery, riding the flatcars in heat and rain, very often assembling them en route. By the time they arrived at their destinations in the Urals or Siberia, winter was upon them. There were no prepared buildings to house either the men or the facilities. There was little food and no warm clothing. In subzero weather and driving blizzards engineers and workmen labored under the open skies to erect shops and assemble the machinery. They worked at night under strung arc lamps, hacking at the frozen soil with pickaxes and spades. Usually within two or three weeks shelters had been erected for the machines and the men and women went to work on the assembly lines. In the years to follow they labored from 12 to 15 hours a day, seven days a week. Most of them were given lodgings some distance away so that in addition to the long hours they had to walk three to five miles to and from work. Large numbers of them died on the job from overexertion.

The amazing performance of these industrial workers was but one facet of the dedication and sacrifice exhibited by the entire population. With the men at the front nearly all the agricultural work was performed by women and mostly by manual labor as all tractors and most horses had been requisitioned by the army. The young women, too, were gone, 2 million of them serving in the army including in combat units. It was a literal fulfillment of Stalin's July 3 dictum that in order to win this war it would have to be a fight not just by the Red Army but by the entire population. And the nation heeded it.

But the price was immense. Since most villages and towns were ashes and rubble large numbers of people lived in holes and ruins, with only a stovepipe sticking out of the ground to indicate the presence of humans. Food rations were allotted according to a person's usefulness to the war effort so the old and the very young starved. This starvation raged not only near the front but across the continent because not only was there a shortage of food but a lack of transportation to distribute the little that was available. The most elementary commodities were unavailable throughout the war. When the US Embassy in Moscow lost its windowpanes during an air raid, no replacement glass could be found and the windows had to be boarded up (Harriman, 84). Thus all across the Soviet Union, from Byelorussia to the Far East a starved, rag-clad populace died en masse from malnutrition, epidemics, overwork and cold.

All this was in striking contrast to the effort put out by Germany. German industry was not on a war footing, there was no allocation of labor and except for a system of rationing and the disappearance of such import items as coffee or cigars the German people led a more or less normal life without undue hardship. Despite the war in Russia the output of consumer goods in 1941 was higher than the year before (Cecil, 142). Germany's powerful industrial capacity had simply not been utilized to provide the machines and updated weapons the Wehrmacht needed. The best indication of this lassitude is that when eventually an effort was made to boost production the output of planes and tanks in 1944 was seven times that of 1941 and this despite devastating bombing raids which forced many industries to disperse and go underground.

At a strategy conference in Orsha on November 13, 1941, the führer stated that it looked like the enemy would not be defeated that year because it had "inexhaustible supplies of manpower." This is a hackneyed, false phrase in the description of the Russo-German war used repetitively by sundry commentators and historians. In the summer of 1941 the opposite was true. Germany had twice the manpower of the USSR. When the invasion began Germany had at its disposal nearly all of Europe — a total of 290 million people — whereas Russia had at the beginning something like 195 million. Within a month Russia lost 40 million to the invader; by November 1942 she had lost 80 million inhabitants (Ziemke and Bauer, 440). In 1941 this gave Germany a manpower pool of 330 million people compared to Russia's 155 million. Moreover Germany's human pool consisted of industrious, skilled people inhabiting a compact area with excellent communication and transportation facilities whereas in all these respects Russia lagged far behind.

The reasons for Germany's mishandling of its human resources fits in with the overall nature of Hitler's war. Hitler remembered World War I when the German population endured severe shortages, including widespread hunger, which contributed to the collapse of Imperial Germany. Hitler did not want to lose popularity with the masses; he wanted to keep their loyalty and keeping their stomachs full was the most direct way to assure that. That by doing so he at the same time was digging their grave was something that the Germans, he was certain, would not see, and didn't. Even after Stalingrad and later on when Goebbels pushed for "total war" Hitler kept putting him off and, of course, he had his way. Actually Hitler underestimated the Germans' loyalty to him. Given that in the last two years of war under a hail of bombs with defeat following defeat on all fronts the Germans steadfastly went on loving and obeying him, he certainly had no reason to worry that by tightening their belt he would shake the Germans' fealty to their führer.

But the bigger reason for the negligence to harness the nation's capacity for fighting the war was ideological. Whereas Stalin, as the war went on, kept discarding more and more pages from the Bolshevik Manifesto, Hitler kept insisting more and more on following the Nazi creed to a point that in the last stages of the war the accepted combat tools were not guns, tanks and airplanes, but faith, willpower and fanaticism. It was Nazi doctrine that a woman's place was with the three K's—*Küche, Kirche, Kinder*—and so in 1941 few women were employed in factories, forcing the military to give men deferment to run the machinery. While Stalin began to empty his gulags, sending many prisoners to the front and rehabilitating arrested generals, Hitler as the war expanded littered his empire with extermination, concentration and slave labor camps, which tied up large numbers of trains, building materials and SS troops to run the installations and do the killings. Tied to this ideological angle was the sheer contempt for the Russian adversary in that Hitler would not stoop to the proposition that the total strength of his Aryan race was needed to overcome a bunch of Mujiks led by hook-nosed commissars. In that, as in everything else, he was adamant and consistent to the end.

• CHAPTER 17 •

Death of Barbarossa

The Germans had won great battles and inflicted grave damage on the Red Army. However, Barbarossa's objective of staging a victorious superblitzkrieg had not been achieved. The Russians fought on, more stubbornly than ever. It was time to try again.

The period of vacillation described in Chapter 15 ended in the last week of August. This was triggered by the audacious OKH memo that the next move should be an operation against Moscow. Instead, on August 21 Hitler issued an order for launching offensives on both wings, in the north to seize Leningrad and join up with the Finns, and in the south to seize Ukraine. Only then would Moscow be tackled, an echo of the führer's original super-plan. Before long the northern attack was scrapped. Directive No. 35 of September 6 laid down what was to be the second phase of Barbarossa, aimed at annihilating the enemy before winter. It was to be implemented in two stages. First by combining the right wing of AGC with the left wing of AGS Ukraine was to be seized by a deep flanking movement east of the Dniepr arc. With this operation completed, the detached AGC forces would be returned to von Bock so that by the end of September he could launch an all-out assault on the central front.

After Hitler had rebuffed the OKH on the Moscow plan and had issued his order about an offensive in the south, Halder had so informed Guderian since his PzG 2 would be the force to attack in Ukraine. Guderian immediately set about implementing the projected switch from an attack east to a southern direction. In terms of distances, combat area and number of troops involved the Ukraine scheme was to be the greatest single battle in history. It was also very simple. As sketched in Fig. 17.1 the southern front at the end of August ran from Starodub near the Desna to Gomel from whence it followed the Dniepr along its southeastern course. This formed a huge semicircular salient thrusting westward into German territory. On the northern periphery of this semicircle was Guderian's PzG 2. To the south was Kleist with PzG 1, freshly arrived after his victory at Uman. The plan was for Guderian to head south and for Kleist to head north along the base diameter of this semicircular area in order to encircle the enemy manning the Dniepr bend. The Russian forces there were huge; at least 1 million men in the Dniepr arc plus Budyenny's armies on the outside of the contemplated cauldron. Both Guderian and Kleist would have to conduct their vertical thrusts exposed all the while to enemy attacks right and left of their march route.

For the job Guderian used two of his Panzer corps reinforced by von Weichs' 2nd Army. The Panzer divisions stayed on the left facing the Russian troops to the east while Weichs's infantry marched on the right. They took off from the Starodub-Gomel line on August 24. Two days later the 750-yard bridge over the Desna near Novogrod-Seversky was

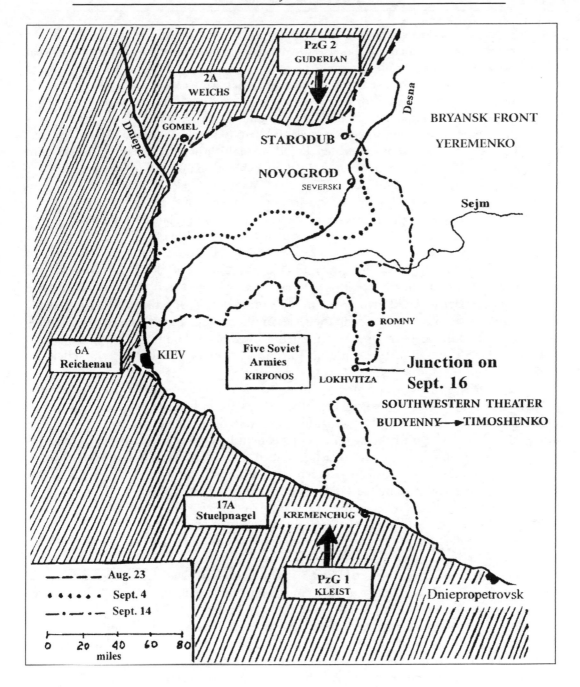

17.1. The Kiev encirclement, September '41

taken by a *coup-de-main* and the Panzers were in the open heading south across the Ukrainian plain. In order not to reveal the plan Kleist was held back for the time being so that initially only a simple south-directed thrust was apparent to Stavka. The maneuver seemed to work, for Stalin's view at that point was that the Germans were executing a wide loop to envelop Moscow from the south.

But this didn't last long. Seeing Guderian cross the Desna and then the Seym the Russians caught on to what was afoot. Yeremenko of the Bryansk front was ordered to attack the Germans' left flank. He did but failed to make a dent. Budyenny, too, realized what was happening but he was not the man to tackle a Guderian or a Kleist. He was the kind of commander who, when asked by a subordinate what to do, replied, "Do what you want. My specialty is to saber them down" (Seaton 1975, 80). So all he could recommend was that the 1 million troops in the Dniepr arc be pulled out. He was seconded by Kirponos, commanding the troops directly involved. In reply, Shaposhnikov, no doubt at Stalin's order, told him to stay put. Budyenny appealed directly to Stalin, whereupon Stalin dismissed him and appointed Timoshenko in his place. By then, evidently on Budyenny's order, Kirponos had already begun preparations for a withdrawal. When Timoshenko arrived in Poltava on September 13 he stopped it and ordered Kirponos to fight it out.

In view of what happened subsequently it is easy to view Stalin's stay-put order as a colossal blunder. But Stalin's initial considerations were not without validity. Stalin argued that whereas now the troops at the Dniepr were facing the enemy north and south, should they start withdrawing the Germans would cross the Dniepr and the Russians would face them also in the west. Next, he said, the Russians are better at static defense than mobile warfare and a retreat would involve them in a running battle with the two Panzer groups. Finally, given that in the Dniepr bend they had 1 million troops and to the east under Timoshenko were additional armies — he felt such a huge force should be able to defend its positions. He proposed instead simultaneous attacks from left and right on Guderian's wedge.

On September 12 Kleist opened his attack to the north from the Kremenchug bridgehead. It is worth noting that since September 3 a period of heavy downpours set in converting roads and tracks into their usual mud and waterholes. It stopped neither Guderian nor Kleist. This has some bearing on the subsequent battles near Moscow when the German generals claimed it was mud that had stalled their offensive; it did not stop them at Kiev. On September 17 Stalin finally agreed to a withdrawal but it was too late. A day earlier the two Panzer wedges met at Lokhvitsa closing the Dniepr cauldron 140 miles east of Kiev, trapping in it four Soviet armies, for a total of 43 divisions. When they met on September 16 the combined length of the German armored canal was 130 miles, its width a mere 15 to 25 miles. The generated cauldron formed an isosceles triangle each side 330 miles long encompassing an area of 55,000 square miles. The German incision was thrust into a combined Russian strength of at least 1.5 million troops arranged on either side of the Panzer stream. It was the height of Russian incompetence that they were unable to sever that narrow band or cause any crisis to the German armor.

Nor was there much resistance after the Panzers had done their job and the infantry, the 2nd and 6th Armies, arrived to liquidate the gigantic cauldron. They did this in a bare 10 days so that by September 26 it was all over. In terms of losses inflicted, territory occupied, resources and industries captured it was the greatest German victory in this or any other war. Six hundred sixty-five thousand prisoners were taken and at least another 300,000 were killed or wounded. The commander of the southwestern front, Kirponos, and his chief of staff, after declining to be flown out, committed suicide — though officially the Soviets claimed they fell in battle. Vast quantities of arms littered the battlefield, thousands of tractors and vehicles were burning, rifles 30–40 feet high were stacked across the plain, and a sea of defeated Russian soldiery flooded the fields and ravines.

The launching of the Kiev battle in September rather than attacking Moscow is a standard item of criticism in histories of Barbarossa. All the generals, including Guderian, were against it and most strategists consider it to have been a grave mistake. The arguments, as is so often the case with debates, center on a secondary issue rather than on the core of it. The critics claim that had Hitler attacked Moscow rather than Ukraine he would have taken it. That is quite likely. But the relevant question is not whether he would have taken Moscow but whether this would have ended the war. What took place in October — the evacuation of industries, the transplant of government offices and the diplomatic corps to Kuibyshev and many of the other steps taken — indicates that it did not even occur to Stalin that losing Moscow meant the end of the fight. Perhaps the following would give some indication of its truth. In July, fearing a possible loss of Moscow, Voznesensky was moved to Kuibishev to set up a war-production industry based on the Urals-Volga-Siberia regions (Overy 1996, 184). Also in October, when reserves were moved from the Far East and elsewhere for the defense of the capital, a substantial number of troops were held back to build fortifications along the Sura and Volga rivers in case Moscow fell (Reinhardt, 94). Thus efforts to continue the war in Soviet Asia were taken before, during and past the threat to Moscow. The only pertinent comparison is whether the Germans would have gained more by capturing Moscow than by taking Ukraine. Here the answer is straightforward. They could not have inflicted larger manpower losses on the Russians than they did at the Dniepr — 1 million casualties. The agricultural produce of Ukraine overshadows Moscow's by an order of magnitude. The industrial and natural riches of the Donetz Basin were the largest in European Russia. The argument that taking Moscow, a hub of the Russian railroad system, would have wreaked havoc with their transportation is only partly true since the Russians had a lateral loop of railroad lines to the east which would have replaced the centrality of Moscow.

* * *

The battle of Kiev was still on when preparations began for the offensive in the center, code named Typhoon. In mid–September PzG 3, which had been sent north to assist von Leeb, was recalled. Hoepner's PzG 4 was detached from AGN and sent to von Bock. Guderian was turned around in last week of September and given 100 replacement tanks. Rundstedt in the south was deprived of nine divisions, two of them Panzer and two motorized, and added to the central front. Von Bock now had a concentration of 14 Panzer divisions, 82 percent of all available armor, and 50 percent of the Ostheer's infantry and motorized divisions—close to 2 million men deployed along 20 percent of the eastern front (Reinhardt, 57; Boog, 671). Originally the OKH had 24 reserve divisions. By the end of August most of them had been fed into the line because of a shortage of replacements, eight to AGC. At the start of Typhoon the last three reserve divisions were moved to the front, so that during the upcoming battle no reserves were available.

The struggle that followed is referred to usually as the Battle of Moscow but this is a misnomer. It was not strategically, or even tactically, a battle for the Russian capital. This would have been alien to the single-mindedness and obstinacy of the führer. It was an attempt, late in the game if not too late, to reach the A-A Line, the original objective of Barbarossa. Hitler's generals understood his military intentions no better than they did his politics and labored under the illusion that they were about to do battle for Moscow. True, they were puzzled by the tactical objectives but failed to glimpse what lay behind them. When the order was given Hoepner's chief of staff, General Rötinger, recalled after the war, "The intermediate command could not completely understand the reason for such a far reaching operation which would divert the direction of the attack from the immediate area of Moscow" (Newton, 48). The operational plan, vague as usual, was based on Hitler's directive of September 6. This, as shown on Fig. 17.2, visualized a parallel assault of all three Panzer groups in a northeasterly direction headed not at Moscow itself but flanking it from all sides. Guderian was to head for Tula, 100 miles south of Moscow while Hoth was to move on Kalinin 100 miles north of the city. In the center Hoepner's PzG 4 and 4th Army were to split into two prongs, bypass Moscow from north and south to enclose it from the rear. By the führer's wish the capital was not to be occupied but obliterated; should it try to capitulate it was not to be accepted. Moscow was to be besieged, gutted, and its 4 million inhabitants starved, a second Leningrad. At a later point the führer visualized that the city area would be flooded and converted into a lake.

The operation was scheduled to start on October 2. Since Guderian was still far to the south, 300 miles from his Tula objective, he requested that his attack be advanced and was assigned a starting date of September 30. Guderian gave his troops three days rest and on the assigned date struck out from his assembly area near Glukhov (see Fig. 17.2). On October 2 Hoth and Hoepner, deploying from north and south of Smolensk, joined in the assault. For zero hour Hitler had issued an order of the day to the troops proclaiming that the concluding phase of the war had arrived; that in the last few months the Wehrmacht had created the conditions to destroy the enemy with a last mighty blow before winter; and that along with the Soviet Union this would also bring about the destruction of England, the instigator of the whole war" (Boog, 672).

A most unusual thing now happened. The troops had barely left their jump-off positions and before any of the future successes or failures became apparent, Hitler out of the blue announced victory in the war with Russia. On October 3, delivering the traditional *Winterhilfswerke* speech in Berlin, Hitler proclaimed that only now was he "permitted to tell the German people that the foe was already broken and would never rise again" (Seaton 1971, 86). A day later Hitler dispatched his press chief to Berlin where in a press conference amid great pomp and a huge map of Russia he proclaimed, "For all military purposes Soviet Russia is done with" (Bullock 1992, 734). And, as shown in Fig. 17.3, on October 10 Goebbels had his *Völkischer Beobachter* print the giant headline DER FELDZUG IM OSTEN ENTSCHIEDEN — the Campaign in the East Decided.

What prompted this wild assertion remains a puzzle. It could only have surfaced from those murky depths of the führer's psyche that had spawned his other heinous or ludicrous visions. Since he had said he would knock Russia out in four months perhaps he felt he must claim that he in fact had done so. He knew that a mere lie would not be held against him by his compatriots; they never did. Perhaps he felt that by announcing victory he would compel his Junkers to fulfill what their führer claimed had already happened. These are speculations. The fact remains that Hitler had announced to have won the war against Russia and that everyone outside and inside the Third Reich had heard it.

Hitler's speech about having won the eastern campaign had an important effect on the Soviet Command. Stavka had not expected the October offensive on Moscow. This was partly because the Kiev battle was still on and also because they knew the Rasputitsa was about to break loose upon Mother Russia. They were also sidetracked by Guderian's drive on Tula. It was Hitler's boast that awoke them to what was happening astride Moscow. At that point the Russians had in front of the capital fewer than a million men, and only a third of their armor, an inferiority of 1:2.

Typhoon started in brilliant fall weather. The forces on the northern and central axes

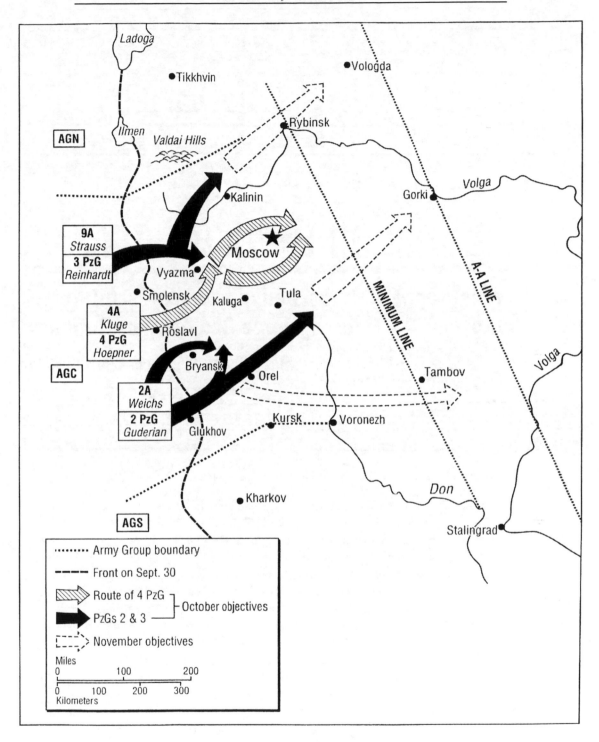

17.2. Objectives of Operation Typhoon, October–November 1941

17.3. Press announcement of German victory over the Soviet Union, October 10, 1941

jumped off at 5:30 A.M. on October 2, when PzG 2 had already been on the march for three days. Taking advantage of the initial surprise Guderian roared ahead 150 miles in five days, taking Orel on October 3. Two things then happened. On October 6 the weather turned. Wet snow fell that night turning next day into slush; then steady rain; then a deluge which went on for weeks. As he advanced on Mtsensk, northeast of Orel, he was attacked by large formations of T-34s. It was a major encounter with these tanks and Guderian was impressed both by the superiority of the Russian vehicles and the improved skill of their crews. The Panzers lost the battle suffering "grievous casualties" (Guderian, 179). When Guderian visited the battlefield he found more German tanks knocked out then Russian ones. Also for the first time Russian planes appeared in force. The advance on Tula stalled.

On October 10 Guderian was ordered not only to resume his attack but to accomplish an additional task; turn left to encircle the troops of the Bryansk front, a move of a 100 miles to his rear. With the help of the 4th Army Guderian succeeded in trapping three armies of Yeremenko's Bryansk Front. An even bigger cauldron was formed on October 7 by Reinhardt's and Hoepner's Panzers (Reinhardt had replaced Hoth on October 5) near Vyazma, which contained six armies of Konev's west front. When by the third week in October the two cauldrons were cleared the Germans bagged 673,000 prisoners, 1,200 tanks and 4,000 guns. Hoepner in the center then breached the Mozhaisk defense line and came within 50 miles of Moscow. Reinhardt captured Kalinin on October 14 and established a bridgehead across the Volga. After taking Kalinin PzG 3 was ordered to continue north-east to prevent the escape of the "remaining" Russians from around Moscow. Likewise in the south the 2nd Army was detached from the main thrust and diverted southeast to capture Kursk and Woronezh, the latter actually a part of the AGS front. In the middle PzG 2 was ordered to circle around Moscow and lay siege to it from the east.

Yet with all these victories the Germans were in trouble. The OKH was bewildered by the persistence of Russian resistance after their latest debacles. Since the middle of September alone, the Russians had lost in prisoners and other casualties at least 2 million men. Being worn out by their victories the Germans could not fathom the appearance of new Soviet armies, better equipped and fighting more stubbornly than ever. Moreover, from now on the Germans faced not one but two adversaries— the Russians and the Rasputitsa. They had met the latter before but not in the dimensions it emerged now. Rain and mud they experienced during the summer but these were short bursts lasting hours or at most days when all they had to do was wait, the sun would be out and the roads dry. Not so the autumn Rasputitsa. The skies were a permanent dirty gray; the rain poured incessantly; fog and snow showers drove through the murk; and the floods and mud deepened with no hope of letup. Great expanses of water a foot deep filled the landscape as far as the eye could see. In some places the slime was knee or waist deep without any way of sidestepping it. Roads and tracks became canals and most local bridges were swept away. The mudholes were so treacherous that soldiers roped themselves together so that if someone fell in he could be saved from drowning (Degrelle, 19). The very nature of the war underwent a metamorphosis. It affected not only the fighting but every detail of the soldier's existence; his tools, clothing, health, food, not to speak of his mental state.

In an ironic twist it was now the Panzers that could not keep up with the foot slug-gers, unlike the summer days when the infantry lagged 100 or 200 miles behind. With tracks too narrow for the swampy terrain, slithering and sinking, the tanks were incapable of making much headway in the autumn slush. They also suffered from lack of fuel. Guderian on his march to Orel had to have 100,000 drums of fuel flown in by air. Other provisions, too, such as calks for the tracks were lacking. Guderian had to have bundles of rope dropped to him by aircraft because they were short of chains and couplings to drag the tanks out. Logistical difficulties led to a shutdown of most repair shops. Lacking spares and tools they could not repair damaged tanks even when the problems were minor. At first great attempts were made by all hands to keep the Panzer divisions moving; corduroy log roads were laid for miles and men and horses were shanghaied to pull them out of the mire. But the weather won out. Toward the end of October the Panzers were being left behind, unfit for warfare. The order went out that the crews were to abandon the immobilized armored vehicles and fight as infantry. Combat units were assigned to railroad construction and maintenance as the problem of logistics soon emerged as the most critical aspect of the eastern campaign.

The letdown by the tanks was accompanied by a breakdown of the regular motor traffic. The trucks and trailers of the supply columns sank into the morass and were out-paced by the infantry. At one stretch between Gzhatsk and Mozhaisk, a distance of 40 miles, 2,000 to 3,000 vehicles stood immobilized for weeks unable to move either forward or back. The German army had large numbers of motorcycles with sidecars and those sank to their handlebars; the drivers, unable to extricate them, wept with rage. As the ruts and water-holes deepened eventually the horse-drawn convoys, too, stalled. The horses sank to their bellies and the carts tipped and broke beyond repair, often wasting the supplies. A dozen or more horses were needed to pull one artillery gun and its limber. Eventually the artillery, too, was lost to the mud. Thousands of men were employed for traffic control to keep moving whatever still moved. Eventually most of the supply trains came to a halt.

So the infantry — the sole fighting force capable of movement — was ordered forward without the necessary ammunition, rations, and all the other daily paraphernalia. They were not only to do the fighting but provide for themselves as best they could. When attacked they were to expend a minimum of ammunition and were to live off nearby villages. They stayed wet for days on end without a chance of drying out or getting warm. Their clothing disintegrated into rags. They lacked razor blades and soap, even needles and thread to mend their torn uniforms. They fell ruthlessly upon the local population, stripping them of their few miserable possessions, their last boots, jackets and hats. They became lice-ridden and, unable to steam bathe or boil the garments, they stayed that way. The shortages were such that when PzG 4 was offered an additional two infantry divisions, Hoepner declined saying he couldn't feed them. The troops formed foraging commandos venturing deep into the hinterland, risking death from partisans and snipers. The already-despoiled countryside had little to offer and the soldiers often devoured rotten and frozen potatoes, bringing on stomach ailments. Diphtheria, dysentery, and a kind of local malaria were common and because of lice the most-feared illness, typhus, soon spread among the troops.

When on October 22 Guderian resumed his attack on Mtzensk he was again repulsed with heavy losses. It wasn't till he gathered enough reinforcements from his wings for a concentrated push that he took the place two days later. He then advanced on Tula both frontally and from the west. The Orel-Tula highway had disintegrated and log roads had to be laid along his march route so it wasn't until a week later that he reached the vicinity of the city. But despite repeated attacks Guderian never captured Tula, which proved to be a dagger in his foot preventing him from attempting any larger operation south of Moscow. Things were not any better along the two other axes of advance. The central drive got within 50 miles of Moscow but no farther. Reinhardt's initial success in taking Kalinin was also his last. On October 28 he received an order to move on to Yaroslavl and Rybinsk — 160 miles north of Moscow — but he was barely capable of holding on to Kalinin and never even attempted to execute it. At the end of October none of the assigned objectives had been reached and Bock ordered a stop to any further advances. The entire central front came to a halt.

In a curious way Typhoon now began to mimic Barbarossa as a whole for despite the stupendous initial successes at Bryansk and Vyazma the strategic goals eluded the Germans. When autumn weather set in Guderian was only halfway to his initial objective, Tula; Hoepner in the center hadn't even started to envelop Moscow; and Reinhardt, who had gotten the farthest, had yet to cross the Volga and take Rybinsk. Aside from the strategic factors behind this failure, of which later, there were several fiascos in the conduct of operations. The biggest was the breakdown of supplies, partly due to the weather, but mainly because of the recklessness or negligence of the high command. By November only 75,000 serviceable motor vehicles remained of more than the half a million the Ostheer had started the campaign with (Overy 1996, 216). Aggravating the situation was the fact that these consisted of a bewildering variety of models, pirated from all over Europe by past victories. It was impossible to assure spare parts for all of them. Nor was the situation better with the horse-drawn supplies. Unused to the climate and requiring decent fodder the large German horses died from lack of feed and exertion whereas the Russian ponies could survive on very little. Even their wagons were inadequate because, being low slung, they sank in the mud.

The discrepancy between the generals' understanding that they were involved in capturing Moscow and Hitler's obsessive lunge toward the A-A line was bemoaned by Bock, "As at Smolensk ... here too, my Army Group will scatter to all winds" and, looking further ahead, despaired "What will become of us in the winter?" (Bock, 331–2). But there was here an additional crisis of understanding, in fact a deception. Already at the end of August, the OKW had concluded that the campaign would have to be continued into 1942. An OKW memorandum of August 27 reads, *inter alia,* "If it proves impossible to realize the objective ... during 1941, the continuation of the eastern campaign has top priority for 1942" (Kershaw 2000, 417). This was, presumably, accepted by Hitler also in a discussion with Halder and Brauchitsch (Boog, 684n). In October the OKH took various steps to prepare for this contingency. Regroupings were initiated to gain good starting lines for next summer's campaign and some preparations made for fixing winter quarters. Hitler ignored all this and drove the troops relentlessly beyond Moscow in a frantic attempt to live up his original conception of Barbarossa, the A-A line and his October boast that he had already won the war against Russia.

* * *

With the start of Typhoon the Russian leadership began making preparations both for a defense of Moscow and for its possible evacuation. On October 6, the 24th anniversary of the Bolshevik Revolution, Stalin reviewed the troops from atop Lenin's mausoleum and delivered a speech. After what the Russians had suffered in the past three months Stalin no longer spoke, as he did at the start of the war, of distinctions between Hitler and the German people. His words were direct and brutal. "The German invader wants a war of extermination.... Very well then.... Our task will now be to destroy every German to the very last man who had come to destroy our country" (Werth, 242). Work began on building three defensive rings around Moscow, with barricades and tank traps erected in the city itself. Half a million Muscovites, most of them women, went out to build fortifications. They dug 60 miles of antitank ditches; 200 miles of barbed wire fences; and 500 miles of trenches. All bridges leading to the city were mined. Eventually several defense rings 65 miles deep were formed in front of the capital. One hundred thousand men were trained after working hours, forming 12 civil guard divisions of which three were immediately sent to the front. The Russians for the first time departed from mass attacks and formed assault units to tackle the Germans. Likewise they started employing tanks in concentrated formations often assisted by the reborn Red air force. Zhukov was recalled from Leningrad to take over the defenses west of Moscow. Konev was shifted north to lead a newly named Kalinin front while Yeremenko, just flown out from the Bryansk encirclement, was to flank Zhukov to the south at the head of a reconstituted Bryansk front. All three fronts numbered perhaps 750,000 men, half of what the Germans flung at them.

As the Germans came ever closer to the city a decision was taken on October 12 to start evacuating it. Some of the ministries and the diplomatic corps were moved to Kuibyshev on the Volga, 500 miles to the east. On October 17 Stalin convened a meeting and ordered the evacuation of all important state and party figures with the government going to Kuibishev and part of the General Staff to Arzamas (Volkogonov, 434). All major scientific and cultural institutions including the Academy of Science and the university were relocated to the interior. The gold deposits had been moved already on October 11. The documents of the Foreign Ministry were packed and buried in the Ural Mountains. Major industrial plants were disassembled and shipped out. With the previous evacuation of children Moscow shrank from its original 4 million to 3 million people. Lenin's embalmed corpse was removed though the guard in front of the mausoleum remained in place so as not to reveal it to the public. Stalin's library and papers were likewise shipped out. Planes stood by to fly out the top leadership though for the time being members of GOKO, Stavka and Stalin himself remained in Moscow.

When the Mozhaisk defense line was breached on October 13 and Kalinin fell the next day the Muscovites for the first time woke up to the danger facing the city. This was given a fillip by an official communiqué of October 16 which said, "During the night of Oct 14-15 the position of the West Front became worse.... The German fascist forces ... in one sector broke through our defences" (Werth, 233). Something resembling panic broke out. Residents began swarming out of the capital, joined by families of government officials. Sporadic looting occurred and enemy agents plastered the walls with anti–Soviet slogans. It did not last long. Martial law was declared on October 20. Looters were shot on the spot and squads of NKVD troops were posted at the city gates to intercept deserters and stragglers. Under the high-sounding motto of "No retreat — only forward" it was announced that Moscow would be defended. The city quieted down and soon returned to the task of building fortifications.

By the end of the month it became clear to Stavka that the German offensive was losing momentum. It then felt sufficiently confident to start pulling out troops from the front for reequipping. This confidence stemmed not from the fact that the Germans were stuck in the mud; the Russians knew that they were only waiting for the ground to freeze to renew their attacks. The confidence came from the well-kept secret of Russian reserves. The Germans in starting Typhoon had a clear appreciation of the strength of Russian armies facing them but no notion of their existing or potential reserves. This was true of the entire campaign. Hitler was negligent about this as he was about most aspects of his eastern campaign. And his generals went along assuming that since they, as victors, fought their battles without reserves— Bock for Typhoon had a reserve of only two divisions and the OKH none — the loser, they reckoned, certainly could not afford to hoard any. The story of Russian reserves is, in fact, one of the more dramatic features of the way Stalin directed his war. It was one of his principles, old-fashioned perhaps, not to fight a major battle without substantial reserves. A body of troops was kept in the hinterland of Moscow throughout the October fighting. What is amazing is that while the fate of Moscow hung by a thread and the front-line troops held their positions by their fingernails, Stalin, with nerves of iron, kept his reserves back, only now and then releasing a small number of troops to prevent a collapse. As a forerunner of a later practice Stavka now formed special artillery divisions to be used at vital points of battle. This was done that October by depriving fighting formations of their support guns even though these troops were barely able to hold their positions. This hoarding of reserves, a basic feature of Russian war-making, was first demonstrated at Moscow, and repeated in striking fashion at Stalingrad and in most later battles.

In addition to the local reserves there were the troops from the Far East. This is a familiar story. Sorge, the top Soviet agent in Tokyo, had been feeding his superiors information that the Japanese intended to wage war on the Western powers rather than on Russia as pressed on them at this stage by the Germans. Based on this and other intelligence

Stalin thought it sufficiently safe to transfer some of the Far East forces to the west. These amounted to 29 infantry divisions and nine armored brigades, all splendidly equipped for winter warfare; on the battlefield the Germans referred to them as Siberians. They began to move west at the beginning of November. Giving drivers and locomotives no respite the trains ran uninterruptedly, covering 500 to 600 miles at a stretch and at night only. All other rail movement, including supplies to the troops, was suspended. Cadres were siphoned off to form new divisions from local manpower. Together with the new classes called to arms Stalin raised during October–November nine new armies. This boosted the strength of the strategic reserves to 800,000 men (Bullock 1992, 734). Of these fresh forces only 100,000 men were released for the defense of Moscow. The bulk was kept for later strategic tasks. Even so, by the time the Germans renewed their offensive Zhukov, who had absorbed the Bryansk front, had doubled his forces in front of Moscow. Also, in anticipation of winter fighting, Khrulev, the Red Army quartermaster, raised 76 sled battalions, a total of 20,000 teams, to handle transport over the snow-decked country.

* * *

Immobilized on both wings and in front of Moscow, the German generals at the beginning of November were at a loss how to proceed. But one thing they knew — the troops were at the end of their tether and incapable of further offensives. Hoepner even advocated a withdrawal of some 150 miles to better lines (Seaton 1980, 136). What resting the troops and a partial withdrawal would have accomplished in the overall context of the war the Junkers dared not think or say. But there was no doubt what the führer thought. He had stated in his Barbarossa Directive that this would be a blitzkrieg and he had declared on October 3 that the blitzkrieg had already been accomplished. Therefore there could be no withdrawal. Mud it was that had stopped the Ostheer but the mud was about to end. As soon as the ground froze, Barbarossa would be resumed. Accordingly, this second phase of Typhoon was referred to by the eastern troops as *Flucht nach Vorn* — an Escape Forward.

When the October battles ended the strength of German motor vehicles and tanks was down to 30 percent. The evaluation of the General Staff was that the combat effectiveness of the infantry was 65 percent and that of the armor 50 percent; the Ostheer's total of 136 divisions was equivalent to 83. The army had zero reserves (Reinhardt, 115). At the same time General Thomas of the OKW submitted a report on USSR's war potential. The invasion, it said, had not substantially affected its war economy; should all the territory west of the Volga be occupied its industry would not collapse; a breakdown would occur only if all the territory west of and including the Urals was seized (US Army, #20-261a, 78–84). The military paid no heed to this prognosis.

After long peregrinations at the OKW and OKH Halder journeyed to Orsha on November 13 for an all-day conference with the commanders and chiefs of staff of the three army groups. Halder informed them of the next operational plans which had been dictated by the führer. With the onset of cold weather the offensive would be resumed. The Ostheer was to advance to a line Maikop-Stalingrad-Gorki-Vologda, essentially the A-A Line. At the minimum the line Lower Don-Tambov-Rybinsk was to be reached (see Fig. 17.4). There could be no talk of withdrawal; the führer had ordered that no rear defensive positions be prepared (Seaton 1980, 136–40). These operations, ran the rationale, would eliminate the "remaining" industrial and armament centers of Russia. The enemy forces, it said, were at their last breath and large stretches of his front were devoid of troops. Reinhardt in the north was to start on November 15 and aim for Vologda, 150 miles to the northeast; Guderian was to start on November 17 and aim for Gorki, 300 miles away; and Hoepner with the 4th Army would move straight ahead to encircle Moscow.

The winters in Russia are overpowering at any time but the one in 1941-42 was particularly onerous throughout Eastern Europe. It did relieve the Ostheer of the mud but heaped upon them miseries of which they had no inkling. If the German Command failed to provide for the Rasputitsa it prepared its troops even less for the Russian winter. When earlier in the campaign Paulus mentioned the possible difficulties of transportation in winter Hitler flew into a rage: "I won't listen to any more of this nonsense ... there isn't going to be a winter campaign. That you confidently leave to my skill as a diplomat.... I herewith formally and emphatically forbid anyone to mention the phrase winter campaign" (Goerlitz 1963, 35). It is worth noting that the OKW did place orders for winter clothing but only for about a third of the Ostheer, the 50 divisions Hitler had assigned for occupation duties after victory in the east. Even these provisions were still in German depots and were not to arrive at the front till spring. The full effects of this negligence would not be felt until later in the season but already in November they were grim enough.

The problems started with attempts to extricate the sunken tanks and vehicles after the ground froze. This was no solidification known in Europe due to a few or dozen degrees below freezing. In the long arctic nights the density of the soil induced by -10 to -40 F made the soil hard as concrete. In efforts to pry loose the stuck vehicles tracks and axles were broken, shafts bent and parts left in the frozen ruts. The tanks had the usual cold weather problems: engines wouldn't start, batteries went dead, radiator coolants froze. There were no stocks of antifreeze fluids or low-viscosity oils and such crude methods as lighting fires under the vehicles or using acetylene torches were employed to thaw out the gelled fluids and greases. Many drivers resorted to starting the engines at frequent intervals to keep them warm which wasted precious fuel. Inside the tanks the crews' breath condensed and formed ice on the walls. In combat the tanks encountered unfamiliar problems of falling into snowdrifts, sliding down icy slopes and of gun sights obscured by mists and blizzards. To cross frozen rivers the vehicles had to be lowered on ropes and hoisted up the opposite shore, the banks usually being too steep to negotiate on their tanks' traction. Nor would the weapons function properly at these temperatures, if at all. The slides on machine guns jammed and there was no graphite to restore them to order. In the artillery pieces the hydraulic fluid in the recoil mechanism froze, leaving only the mortars as effective weapons. Those howitzers and guns that did function had their range and accuracy affected by the dense winter air and the contraction of the barrels so that their salvos often fell short, wasting ammunition and, worse, hitting their own troops.

One of the greatest crises arose with respect to the supply of fuel. By the end of October the oil needs were supplied from current production, which was insufficient to satisfy the needs of both the Wehrmacht and industry. With winter the situation worsened. What was usually enough fuel for a 100-kilometer stretch now covered only 35–40 kilometers. The other bottleneck was the railroads. Due to Stalin's scorched earth policy the Germans had to import from home 2,500 locomotives and 200,000 railroad cars. But these locomotives were unsuitable for Russia's winter condition. The water pipes on the German locomotives were installed externally, whereas in Russian locomotives these ran through the boilers' hot water system. Consequently by the beginning of December 70 percent of the German locomotives had broken down.

But the most excruciating impact was on the fighting troops. The soldiers wore nothing more than their standard gear. This had worn threadbare by the long campaigning, particularly during the mud period when the men were soaked to their underwear for weeks on end. The Germans' hobnailed boots were particularly inadequate because the nails conducted the cold; so were the steel helmets, which the Germans religiously wore during battle. Without proper gloves the skin of their hands came off when they touched the metal of their weapons. When Guderian mentioned the difficulties of stopping the T-34s Hitler asked why he didn't use the 88 mm guns to which Guderian replied that he needed them to blast shelters in the ground for the infantrymen to sleep in, otherwise they would freeze to death. The soldiers rarely had a hot meal and the frozen rations had to be hacked open with a bayonet or a saw. They stripped the living and the dead of the lice-ridden rags the Russians wore and robbed them of the last morsels of food, even of such primitive items as straw and paper which they stuffed into their boots and helmets to ease the cold. Draped in this local garb they ceased to look like soldiers and when replacements arrived they often burst out laughing at these apparitions until their own ears and noses turned blue in the frost. The men suffered by the thousands from dysentery, scarlet fever and typhus. Soon the number of frostbite victims exceeded the casualties suffered in combat. There was little chance to thaw out and firefights erupted for a village or a few hovels in order to secure shelter from the howling blizzards. For the wounded death came swiftly and even if retrieved they were hauled long distances on horse carts or in unheated railway wagons and usually died on the way. For lack of transport some were placed on saucer-shaped boards and dragged on the snow behind available vehicles. The dead were left unburied since the only way to dig graves was to dynamite the soil and there was a shortage of explosives; they were kept in stacks waiting for spring when the earth would be willing to oblige them. When the winter ended the High Command awarded all men that had been at the front special awards, which the Germans with their sordid humor nicknamed *Gefrierfleisch* Order — Frozen Meat medals.

These were the conditions under which the second phase of Typhoon got underway in mid–November. Guderian's PzG 2 had the most difficult task. He was to take Tula, then head for Kolomna, partway to his objective, Gorki — 300 miles from his starting line. Weichs' 2nd Army, which had been part of Guderain's striking force, was to cross over from left to right and head for Kursk and Voronezh, effectively taking it out of the fight around Moscow. Even before Typhoon started Guderian had grave doubts about its outcome and it did not improve after the October fighting. On November 6 he wrote home, "How things will turn out, God alone knows. We can only go on hoping and keep our courage up, but this is a hard time we are passing through" (Guderian, 188). Earlier he had asked that OKH change the assignment for his Panzergruppe as he felt it could not be carried out. He was told to abide by orders.

One day late, on November 18, Guderian started his drive. He made little progress. He bemoaned having had an average of 500 frostbite cases per regiment. Next was the appearance of the Siberians on his sector. In white smocks, with white-painted submachine guns, many of them on skis, they slipped into his lines with ease and as easily eluded the Germans. His 112th Infantry Division broke and panic spread to a depth of 20–30 miles to the rear. In a letter of the 21st he wrote, "The icy cold, the lack of shelter, the shortage of clothing, the heavy losses of men and equipment, the wretched state of our fuel supplies, all this makes the duties of a Commander a misery and the longer it goes on the more I am crushed by the enormous responsibility" (Guderian, 190,192). In this mood he flew off two days later to AGC HQ to tell Bock that the orders he had been given could not be carried out. After contacting OKH the objective was changed to reaching the line Michailov-Zaraisk with the stipulation that a raid be staged on Kolomna in order to destroy its important rail junction. Except for taking Michailov on November 27, a bulge of some 50 miles, Guderian could not implement even this restricted task. He was then told to just take Tula. Employing all his strength, on December 2 he reached the Tula-Moscow highway north of the city so that he now had it surrounded from three sides. But his troops could do no more. They were cold, exhausted, their spirit gone. On December 4 the temperature in his sector dropped to -31 degrees F and his troops froze in their positions. Next day at nightfall Guderian made a decision to break off all attacks and withdraw to the upper Don and the river Upa. He took this decision all on his own. On December 8 Guderian informed Bock that a crisis existed with the top leadership and Bock replied, "Either one held out or let himself be killed" (Bock, 385). Following this exchange Guderian started his retreat. Like Hoepner earlier he actually thought the retreat should be to the Oka near Orel, 100–150 miles back, but for the moment he merely retreated to south of Tula, his starting line of two weeks ago. By then he no longer thought in terms of local conditions for in a long letter of December 8 he said, "I am not thinking about myself but rather about Germany, and that is why I am frightened" (Guderian, 201).

As with Guderian the objectives for the two other Panzer groups, too, had to be altered in view of the paralyzing cold and enemy resistance. Instead of Rybinsk and Vologda, Reinhardt was told to head for the Volga-Moscow Canal. This complex waterway containing dikes and locks was part of the innermost Moscow defense line. From the starting date of November 15 it took Reinhardt the rest of the month to reach the canal where he formed a narrow bridgehead south of Dimitrov. From there he ordered his troops to head into the hinterland north and east of Moscow. But his troops were at the end of their strength and they faltered. OKH then ordered him to give up the bridgehead and turn toward Moscow along the western bank of the canal. He was counterattacked from both east and north and the closer he got to Moscow the fiercer was the resistance. On December 5 Reinhardt informed Bock that "a fight for large objectives is no longer possible. It is necessary to reach a decision about choosing a line which could be held during the winter." He then ordered a stop to all attacks; by coincidence this happened on the same day Guderian had issued his halt order. And, like Guderian, he too made plans for a withdrawal without approval from above.

Hoepner started his drive on the 18th and made even less progress than the two other Panzer groups. This was partly due to an OKH decision to keep 4th Army from participating in the offensive. The aim was to tie down Russian forces in front of Moscow while a breakthrough was secured on the wings. Since the Panzer groups, both north and south, failed in their mission the result was that 4th Army remained idle throughout the desperate November battles. Hoepner reached the Klin-Moscow highway on the 23rd and Istra on the 26th ending up eventually at Swenigorod, 20 miles northeast of Moscow; this was the closest the Germans came to the Russian capital. By then Hoepner had already warned OKH that his troops were nearing exhaustion. He supplemented this warning with the following report on December 3: "Physical and spiritual overexertion no longer endurable. In the view of the commanding generals troops no longer have any fighting capacity. The High Command is to decide about a withdrawal." Without waiting for a reply Hoepner ordered a three-day rest for his divisions.

At the very time that the three Panzer commanders were sending in their reports that the troops were incapable of further operations, Bock on his own sent a report to the OKH saying the offensive could not be continued because the troops were "ausgebrannt"—burnt out. To his request for fresh troops Halder replied that "the Army has no voice in this matter" (Bock, 385).

While the October–November battles raged in the central front, the two other Army Groups, too, had been given objectives to be reached before the onset of winter. On November 21 Hitler ordered AGS to push beyond Rostov and, starting from the Crimea, "take" the Caucasus, particularly Maikop where the oil was. In addition, the 17th Army was to take Stalingrad—a rehearsal for the 1942 campaign. In his grand strategy this scheme was also intended to sever the link with Persia and stop the flow of Lend-Lease materiel. Through mud, rain, ice and snow Kleist badgered his way into Rostov. The bridges on the Don were blown, resistance grew hourly and his hold on the city soon became untenable. On November 30 the Germans were forced to abandon Rostov and give up hope of reaching the Caucasus. Under continuous pressure Army Group South fell back to the river Mius, a retreat of some 40–50 miles. Similarly in the north after von Leeb had captured Tikhvin in an attempt to link up with the Finns the troops there broke. In December the salient around Tikhvin was abandoned.

With the armies faltering all along the front and commanders initiating withdrawals without approval from above, Hitler on December 8 issued his momentous Directive No. 39. It said: "The severe winter weather which has come surprisingly early in the East and the consequent difficulties in bringing up supplies compel us to abandon immediately all major offensive operations and to go over to the defensive" (Trevor-Roper 1964, 107).

* * *

The führer's decree of December 8 put the official stamp on the failure of Barbarossa. It had been launched as a blitzkrieg to destroy Russia within two to four summer months but ended with an exhausted German army immobilized in the face of the oncoming winter and a Red Army relatively stronger than at the start of the campaign. Unlike its namesake, Barbarossa drowned not in a clear river but in mud and snow.

It is typical the way Hitler phrased his order to halt operations. One reason he gave was that winter came "surprisingly early." There was, of course, nothing surprising about it and it was not early; mid–November was when winters started for millions of years. The other reason given was failure of supplies. Therefore, all this had nothing to do with him. The guilt for Barbarossa's demise lay with God and the quartermaster general.

Aside from failure of the campaign as a whole there was something perverse about its specifics. Having driven some 800 miles into Russia the German army came within sight of all its major objectives yet failed to take any of them. From north to south these were Murmansk and its railway which would go on functioning throughout the war, bringing massive Allied aid to Russia; Leningrad, which tied down large German forces and prevented a junction with the Finnish army; Moscow with its rail hub, industrial and armament works and importance as the country's capital; and Rostov, the gateway to the Caucasus with its oil fields. The only worthwhile objective the Germans did take was the Donetz Basin. Except for Rostov, held for a few months in 1942, the Germans would fail to conquer any of these objectives throughout the war.

The causes for the failure can be easily stated. One was that the Germans had insufficient forces for the task and particularly a deficient logistic organization. This comprises two components. One was that the Ostheer was not large enough and its mobility

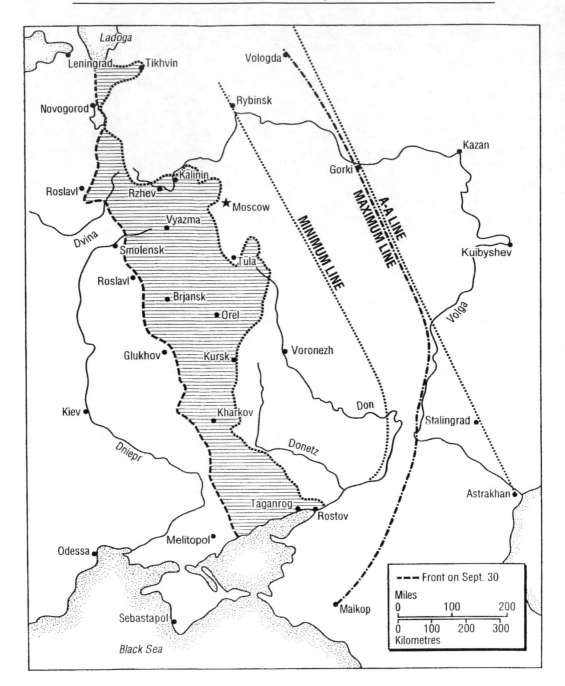

17.3. Maximum German advance during Operation Typhoon vis-à-vis stated objectives

inadequate for tackling a 1,000-mile front from the White to the Black Sea, far from their home bases. Second, was their underestimation of Soviet resources not with regard to the much-touted "inexhaustible" manpower (which was not true) but in armament production. After the occupation of western Russia most of the arms came from the Urals and Asia, which the Germans severely misjudged. In the fall of 1941 a stream of new modern weapons—T-34 tanks, Katyushas, ground-attack Shturmoviks and PPsh submachine guns—began streaming in profusion to the front and the Germans soon felt their effect. The other reason was the climate, likewise ignored by the planners. This, too, had two sets of consequences. One was the breakdown of the supply system involving not only amenities, but also spare parts, fuel and ammunition. The other consequence of the weather was the wretched state of the troops who were permanently wet during the Rasputitsa and froze during the winter. Bock in his wartime diaries gave the reasons for the failure of Barbarossa as the breakdown of the supply system but more cogently as due to the "underestimation of the enemy strength" (Bock, 383). In the Russian campaign these shortcomings combined to produce a strategic fault in the functioning of the German army. After successfully trapping large numbers of the enemy, the Panzer divisions could only throw a thin ring around them but were not equipped to liquidate the cauldrons they had created. In effect the encircled enemy immobilized the victors, for unlike the Western armies the Russians continued to fight within the encirclements, attempting and often succeeding in breaking through the porous tank pickets. The Panzers had to sit idle and wait for the infantry divisions. These, trudging on foot, accompanied by their horse-drawn artillery, were usually hundreds of miles behind. For weeks the armored divisions were unemployed while the enemy was given pause to reorganize and prepare new defense lines—cardinal impediments in the dictates of blitzkrieg. Moreover, and this was the crucial flaw, time was lost. When upon arrival of the infantry the Panzers resumed their advance the process repeated itself—each time, due to the increasing distances and wear and tear of machines and troops, in more unfavorable conditions. Thus instead of a continuous campaign the German army progressed in fits and starts, each pause resulting in an enforced immobility of the armor and a loss of precious time. By the time the Germans approached their major objectives such as Rostov, Moscow, or Leningrad—not to speak of the A-A Line—the campaigning season in Russia was over and Barbarossa was off his horse.

These are all analytical reasons. The reality was that there was but a single reason behind all of them. It is unfair to blame the führer for not having prepared the troops to fight in conditions of mud and ice, for he harbored no such intentions. He had not planned to fight in Russia during the fall and winter. He had stated in his Directive No. 21 that this was to be a "lightning campaign" to be won in two to four months maximum. So it all reduces itself to saying that the cause of failure was the proposition that the Soviet Union could and would be defeated in a blitzkrieg. And the basis for this assumption was the usual one—the führer's private will. Hitler had lived his life for the idea of destroying Russia. Ergo she would be destroyed. And it would have been sacrilege to suggest that the Russian *Untermensch* could possibly thwart the German army.

When Barbarossa ended and the German troops hunkered down in their igloos, one-quarter of their 3.2 million soldiers had fallen out of the ranks. On December 10 there were 775,000 battle casualties of whom 195,000 were dead or missing. And if those alive had hoped to be left alone to lick their wounds in half-decent shelters during the coming winter they again deluded themselves as to the kind of war they had unleashed. For simultaneously with the führer's gracious decision to go over to the defensive, the Russians released their reserves and launched their winter offensive which would inflict new unknown terrors on the Ostheer.

CHAPTER 18

December 1941

December 1941 was the month when Hitler irrevocably lost the war. The events that month were swift and decisive. On the 8th Hitler was forced to cancel Barbarossa. Simultaneously and unexpectedly, the Russians launched a counteroffensive driving the Germans back from their snowbound holes in front of Moscow. On December 7 came Pearl Harbor and hard on the heels of the Japanese attack Hitler found himself at war with the USA.

There had been two other occasions when it became clear that Hitler was bound to lose the conflict he had unleashed with the invasion of Poland. One was September 3 when against Hitler's expectations and wishes England and France declared war, converting the brief campaign he had envisioned into a European war of unforeseen duration. Yet there had been hope. Perhaps the Allies were merely playacting and would settle for a compromise peace. If not, Hitler had a great project up his sleeve. He would, as he was certain he could, defeat France after which a helpless Britain would have no choice but to quit. In June 1940 France was duly knocked out of the war but England, left alone to face Germany, Italy and possibly Japan, too, yet said no to Hitler's peace offer. Still all was not lost. Already Hitler was preparing to invade the Soviet Union which would create an entirely new political constellation. With the Russian continent in his grip an unbeatable super–Germany of immense economic and strategic power would arise. There was also a chance of the West acquiescing in his crusade to extinguish Communism, that archpoison of Western civilization. Thus though on both of these occasions— September 3, 1939, and June 1940 — Hitler's pending downfall was writ large there had yet been illusions for a change in Germany's fortunes. There were none whatsoever after December 1941.

Of the above events the most telling long-range impact was bound to be America's entry into the conflict. That Hitler was the one to declare war on the USA was another instance of the führer's private furies overriding all else. For neither by the terms of the Tripartite Pact nor by Germany's self-interest did he need to have done that. Article III of the Tripartite Pact obligated the signatories to join in war if one of the partners was "attacked." Japan, fearful of getting entangled in a war against its wishes, had insisted on an amendment that whether a signatory had been attacked was to be decided by agreement of all three parties. Letters to that effect had been exchanged between Berlin and Tokyo. In mid–November, when Japan had already decided on its Pearl Harbor venture, General Okamoto asked Ambassador Ott what Germany would do if Japan went to war with America. Ott sent the inquiry to Berlin. At that time Hitler knew nothing of the Japanese plans but a query of that sort was clear enough. Back came the answer that yes, Germany would join in.

After Congress, in response to the Pearl Harbor attack, declared war on Japan, Roosevelt refrained from asking for similar action against Germany and Thomsen of the German Embassy notified Berlin. Roosevelt, evidently, preferred it came from Berlin. Hitler obliged. The act was consummated with full premeditation. First a military alliance supplementing the Tripartite Pact between Germany, Japan and Italy was hastily prepared. Signed by Ribbentrop, Oshima and Alfieri the alliance committed the partners not to conclude a separate peace with the Anglo-Saxon enemy. Leaving behind a frozen Barbarossa the führer hastened from the Wolfschanze to Berlin. There, on December 11, he delivered to the Reichstag an oration saying that Roosevelt was bent on "world domination and" of all things "dictatorship." Whereupon he declared war on the USA. The declaration of war was handed to the American Embassy in Berlin shortly after 2 P.M. The same day at 3:05 Washington time the Congress passed a joint resolution that "the state of war between the US and the Government of Germany which has been forced upon the USA is hereby formally declared."

When the USA finally came into the war Churchill's dogged, far-reaching vision came to pass after 19 lonely months of facing Hitler. That night, Churchill wrote, he went to bed "satiated with emotion and sensation and slept the sleep of the saved and thankful."

* * *

One of the reasons Hitler gave for declaring war was that the US has been involved in warlike acts against Germany for some time. This, as we shall see, was true as far as it goes. But we shall also see what a cardinal difference there was between America helping Hitler's enemies and her being formally at war. For this purpose the preceding events have to be divided into two phases: pre–June 1940, and June 1940 to Pearl Harbor. They highlight the ironic fact that the more victories Hitler had won the closer he came to war with the United States and his ultimate downfall.

During the '30s Roosevelt's attitude to the rising tide of Fascism and belligerence paralleled that of the statesmen in Europe, more nearly that of England; whatever the threats uttered, or aggressions committed, by Germany, Italy or Japan as long as they did not directly affect me it was easier and seemingly safer to be aloof. That eventually the price the nation was to pay for this would be incomparably higher than action taken at an early stage — that would have been poor politics and a sin against "public opinion." Just as England looked upon its continental neighbors as a bunch of martinets unwilling to follow London's wise statesmanship, so did America see Europe, England included, as an outmoded continent that failed to emulate and learn from the American experience. Moreover, quite frequently the conflicts in Europe provided opportunities to a peaceful, industrious America — much in the spirit of a Founding Father's motto of letting the New World thrive on the follies of the Old. This political line was known in America as isolationism.

This isolationism, and it, too, to a large degree had its origins in World War I, was adhered to throughout the various crises that plagued Europe and Asia throughout the '30s. It coincided with Roosevelt's presidency since both he and Hitler came to power within a month of each other (they also died the same month). When the first overt aggression occurred — Italy's 1935 attack on Ethiopia — Congress enacted the Neutrality Act which forbade both Italy and Ethiopia from buying arms in America. Law knows no favorites so that both rich and poor are forbidden to beg. Roosevelt concurred in the enactment of the various provisions of the Neutrality Act except those that were likely to encroach on his executive powers. The president would not subscribe to the League of Nations' attempt to impose sanctions on Italy. The main aim of the USA, he announced, was to "avoid being drawn into a war"— not to prevent war but to have no part of it. The primary role for America was to provide an example to mankind of the virtues of peace and democracy. When Franco, with the help of Italy and Germany, started the civil war in Spain, America extended the Neutrality Act to cover civil strife thus preventing Spain's legitimate government from obtaining arms. When Japan attacked China in 1937 the Neutrality Act, which had been a temporary measure, was made permanent. Since neither China nor Japan declared war on each other, the Neutrality Act was not invoked but when Japan imposed a blockade on China's coastline Roosevelt forbade American ships from sailing there, which amounted to an embargo of trade with China. When the major powers convened a conference in Brussels to deal with Japanese aggression the American delegate was instructed by the president not to endorse the use of force or sanctions against Japan. Predictably, the conference ended in failure, actually condoning the Japanese in their Chinese adventure.

Inaction prevailed in Washington throughout Hitler's progressive violations of the Versailles Treaty. No protests were delivered when the Germans reoccupied the Rhineland and annexed Austria. During the Sudeten crisis Roosevelt did intervene. He implored all parties to negotiate and, proposing to Hitler a conference for a peaceful solution, he emphasized that the USA would not attend it and "will assume no obligations in the conduct of negotiations." Moreover, there was a touch of callousness in the president's view of the crisis. In a letter of September 15, 1938 to Walter Phillips, US ambassador in Italy, the president wrote, "Perhaps when it [war] comes the US will be in a position to pick up the pieces of European civilization and help thus to save what remains of the wreck" (Divine, 23). And when England and France declared war Roosevelt announced on September 5 that "this nation will remain a neutral nation" though he allowed that in their hearts they need not be so.

Throughout the Phony War, from September 1939 till June 1940, there was one departure from US neutrality. On November 4 the arms embargo was repealed, that is the Allies could now place orders and buy ordinance from America. But the cash-and-carry provision of the Neutrality Act remained in force. The Allies would have to pay cash for everything they bought and American ships were forbidden to ferry the purchased goods. Otherwise there was precious little America contributed to the face-off between Hitler and the democracies. Whatever the president did was not aimed at strengthening the Allies in fighting their war but toward peace — a throwback to Chamberlain's Munich delusions. America felt safe relying on the Europeans to handle Hitler and forestall any potential discomfort or threat to US interests. The last episode in America's role of impartial observer occurred during the death throes of the French Republic. Reynaud's appeal in mid–June for some American gesture — a massive supply of arms, a promise to join the war, a warning to Hitler — was rejected outright by Roosevelt. Not that it would have prevented the German occupation but it may have kept France and its empire in the war. This rebuff terminated one phase of America's role in the history of World War II.

Then came June 1940 and the collapse of France. Stunned by an unimagined new reality across the Atlantic "public opinion" and its elected representatives suddenly realized two things. One was on the purely visceral level. Though isolationist there were few Americans who did not sympathize with the Allied cause. Suddenly they awoke to the realization that it was not just a matter of cant and sympathy. The prospect of having to deal with a Europe under the sway of Nazi slogans and practices, that from now on this would be a radically different Old World with which their diplomats, businessmen, students and millions of tourists would have to fraternize, struck the American people as distasteful. With this would come great damage to America's business and trade relations with the rest of the world. They bristled at such a prospect. The more important factor, however, was national security. As the situation looked in June 1940 it may not have been too clear that there was any threat to the US, but one had only to go one step further and visualize what the situation would be like should England, too, collapse — and the US military had indeed concluded that, left alone, England could not win. Should England fall, Spain, Portugal and the entire African continent would become Axis property and with it all the outlying Atlantic islands — the Azores, the Canaries and Cape Verde. The Europe Hitler would rule had 350 million inhabitants as compared to 125 million in the USA. America's enemies would dispose of the naval fleets of five maritime powers: Japan, Germany, England, France and Italy. From Dakar in Africa there was only a moderate distance to Brazil. It was South America that worried the Americans most. All its countries were dictatorships, many of them with large German communities of great influence on the ruling military and business oligarchies; in World War I Germany had indeed attempted to enroll Mexico to its side. A German foothold there by internal aggression was a possibility. This could occur at the same time Japan embarked on her Greater East Asian Co-Prosperity drive for hegemony in the Pacific, with America left alone to defend herself against an onslaught from both East and West.

Hitler did, indeed, among his other fantasies, spin a weave of eventually defeating America. For, unlike the English whom he accepted as Aryan cousins, Americans were to him their very antithesis. America was a mongrel nation run by hooknosed plutocrats just as the Russians were a subhuman race led by hooknosed politruks. When on July 7, 1940, Raeder talked to Hitler about expanding the navy the grossadmiral was told that this would have to wait for the post-peace period when Germany and England would together defeat the US. He reiterated this prophecy in his Table Talk of September 8–9, 1941, when he said, "I will not live to see it but one day the German people will see how a united England and Germany will move against the USA" (Hillgruber 1965, 147).

Faced with a new situation Roosevelt took a leaf from the Spanish Civil War when Germany and Italy had won the battle for Franco without going to war. He decided to do all he could for England, short of war. For Roosevelt this turned into a struggle not to overstep the bounds of limited belligerency, not to jolt his isolationist opposition, and, most of all, not to jeopardize his 1940 reelection to which, as noted previously, he was committed with a compulsive hunger. There was one additional hesitation. The US that June had less than a million men under arms and needed all its armaments for equipping new divisions. The dilemma was whether to equip its own forces or ship the arms to England where the war was. The risk was that should England fall the arms would be lost; by not shipping them England might be lost. The US military, naturally, preferred to keep the new production at home. But after some hesitation Roosevelt overruled them. Thus began a steady and rising flow of military aid to England and the Middle East. Eventually the US participated with its own forces in securing and keeping open the sea lanes for these shipments.

It began with a delivery of the most rudimentary items. Between June and October Britain was shipped 1 million rifles, 87,000 machine guns and even 200,000 revolvers. Then came the first substantial boost to Britain's defense — the destroyer deal. Up to June Britain had lost 32 out of its 100 fleet destroyers and Churchill asked for 50 old World War I American destroyers, the basic weapon against U-boats. To give away such a fleet congressional approval was needed so the deal was arranged in the form of a barter. The US would receive bases on British possessions in the Western Hemisphere plus a commitment that in case of defeat Great Britain would transfer its fleet to the New World. Churchill accepted it and on September 3 the deal was made public.

In January 1941 British Ambassador Lothian died and was replaced by Halifax. With him came representatives of the British Chiefs of Staff, disguised in mufti, for talks with their American counterparts. They had been invited by the president in December to discuss common strategy in the event the US entered the war. The discussions lasted till the end of March, producing what is known as the ABC-1 and ABC-2 protocols. It was agreed that Germany would be Enemy No. 1 with the war in the Pacific relegated to the defense, and that protection of the sea lanes in the Atlantic were a strategic priority. As part of this emphasis the president ordered on March 25 the seizure of 30 Axis and Danish ships blocked in American ports (Friedlander, 205).

When Halifax arrived he brought with him the sad news that England's coffers were nearly depleted so that she would shortly be unable to pay for the orders placed in the USA. This gave rise to Lend-Lease, the most sweeping American initiative in aiding Britain. It took more than two months to enact the bill but when it was signed on March 11 it authorized the president to "sell, transfer title to, exchange, lease, lend or otherwise dispose" of armaments and other defense materiel to any government if he considered it "vital to the defense of the US" (Dawson, 9). The president was now free if he so chose to give away to any country at no cost any quantity of weapons and defense aid. This essentially eliminated the "cash" provision of the Neutrality Act.

Nineteen forty-one was a grim year in the antisubmarine war so that in May the rate of sinkings was triple the shipping England could replace. Therefore the next assault the president opened was on the "carry" provisions of the Neutrality Act. Such help involved not only supplying new ships but securing bases, providing escorts and instituting patrols against the prowling enemy. In agreement with the Danish minister in Washington, Greenland was taken over by the US Navy on April 10. On the same day the Red Sea was declared a noncombat zone so that US ships could deliver war materiel directly to the Middle East. By May, 40 cargo vessels and 50 tankers were en route to Egypt, taking over from Britain the burden of supplying the forces fighting in Libya. Also in April, America began building bases in Scotland and Northern Ireland using equipment and workers shipped directly from home (Reynolds, 198). Following the German invasion of Denmark, British troops had been occupying Iceland, a crucial station on the cross–Atlantic route, and to relieve both the troops and the British naval units there the US on July 8 landed 4,000 Marines and undertook to supply them.

Utilizing the incident of a German U-boat firing on the US destroyer *Greer*, Roosevelt delivered on September 11 a speech to the nation saying, "From now on if German or Italian vessels of war enter waters the protection of which is necessary for American defense, they do so at their own peril." Orders went out to protect US as well as Allied ships all the way to Iceland. Together with the previously extended Western neutral zone up to 26 degrees West this entailed US convoys over nearly three-fourths of the Atlantic Ocean where the navy was under orders to shoot on sight at any Axis ships present in these waters. To end the tedious escalation, Roosevelt in December prevailed upon Congress to repeal the most restrictive clauses of the Neutrality Act. Henceforth US merchant ships were armed and free to carry goods all the way to British ports.

One year after Roosevelt had decided to aid England the question arose of helping Russia. Here one element instrumental in giving help to England —communality of language and political institutions— was absent. The opposite was true — the Communist state was a vile, alien world to which the public's attitude in both England and America ranged from excommunication to indifference. But there was here a more telling factor — self-interest — and it prevailed. Unlike Stalin, who until and beyond the fatal hour hoped to be spared the Nazi onslaught, Churchill, thanks to Enigma, anticipated it and was ready for it. A week before the invasion he told Roosevelt that when the attack came England would give "all encouragement and any help we can spare to the Russians following the principle that Hitler is the foe we have to beat." On Saturday, June 21, Roosevelt replied that he would support publicly "any announcement the Prime Minister might make welcoming Russia as an ally." With this backing Churchill, in the evening of June 22, delivered a talk to the nation in which he announced, "We shall give whatever help we can to Russia and the Russian people.... If Hitler imagines that his attack on Soviet Russia will cause the slightest divergence of aim or slackening of effort in the great democracies who are resolved upon his doom he is woefully mistaken.... The Russian danger is, therefore, our danger and the danger of the US just as the cause of any Russian fighting for his hearth and home is the cause of free men and free peoples in every quarter of the globe" (Churchill Vol. 3, 369–73). That night Churchill must have been smiling in his sleep throughout the night; in June 1940 Hitler had squashed England's continental ally that provided the land armies to fight her war. Now, in June 1941, Hitler handed England a new continental ally whose armies would prove to be the stuff of legend.

In a succession of statements during the first week of the invasion Washington announced that Hitler remained the main enemy, that the USA would provide aid to Russia and that the Neutrality Act would not be invoked in the conflict. At the end of July the president sent his closest advisor, Harry Hopkins, to Moscow; he spent July 29–30 in conferences with Stalin. Like most visitors Hopkins was impressed with Stalin's grasp of the situation, his cool manner, his cordiality. He was also struck that in the midst of unmitigated disasters Stalin remained confident the Red Army would prevail, contrary to all the experts in the West who gave Russia one to three months to live (the same experts who judged the French army the strongest in the world). When at their first meeting Hopkins asked Stalin what the West could do to help, Stalin answered that yes, the thing to do was to join the fight by invading the continent. He had said the same thing to a British delegation 10 days earlier when he recommended two invasions, one in France and one in northern Norway (McNeil, 53). Like the British, Hopkins sidetracked that remark and turned to the subject of material aid.

Hopkins' initial contact was followed on September 9 by an official US–British mission led by Averell Harriman and Lord Beaverbrook. The talks resulted in a protocol to provide aid to Russia over the next nine months worth a billion dollars. This included an initial monthly shipment of 500 planes and 500 tanks. A Russian purchasing commission came to Washington to administer it. But the question of payments impeded the efficient implementation of the program. Consequently on November 7 Russia was made eligible for Lend-Lease on the basis of an interest-free loan to be repaid after the war (Divine, 84). Thus both England and the USA had in the most expeditious way made a commitment to provide aid to Soviet Russia in its struggle with the German army.

The alacrity with which the Western powers rushed to the aid of the Soviet Union; Stalin's talk, as early as July, of the need for an invasion of the continent; and the West's willingness to forget Soviet misdeeds in the Baltics and Poland — these were the initial rumbles of a long history that would dominate East-West relations for the rest of the war. All the basic parameters of wartime cooperation, or lack of it, were already present in these initial exchanges. When the news reached Washington about the outbreak of the Russo-German war, US Secretary of War Stimson sent Roosevelt a memo saying that this is "like a providential occurrence." Indeed, the West could not have received a more divine gift. It fell into England's wartime strategy like a Samson telling a groggy David to go home and rest; he would take care of Goliath. As Averell Harriman put it, "It was self-interest to keep Russia in the war. If Russia would stand up to the Germans this might well make it possible for us to limit our participation to Naval and air power" (Harriman, 74). Even when initially they were not sure Russia would endure Americans considered it a godsend providing the USA the time needed to manufacture armaments and train troops. Later the Russian war became not just a respite, but rather the primary sledgehammer used to demolish the German army. The greatest concern of the West was that under the crushing blows and bloodletting Russia might make a separate peace. This worry appeared as early as September 5 when, after a talk with Maiski, Churchill confided to Roosevelt that he had heard overtones that Russia might be compelled to make peace. This conversation occurred at a time when Stalin had again suggested the British make a landing, if not in France, at least in the Balkans and Churchill rebuffed it. Instead Churchill made an offer reminiscent of the worst features of Chamberlain's 1939 negotiations with the Soviets—that he send two British generals for discussion! Stalin declined the offer (McNeill, 54–5). It was Churchill's conversation with Maiski that prompted the post-haste dispatch of the Harriman-Beaverbrook mission to Moscow and the agreement for a billion-dollar aid package to Russia.

The strategy of leaving Russia to deal with the German army was of such cardinal importance to England and America that they were willing to take on Japan as long as this helped keep Russia in the war. This policy, formulated as early as June 23 by the Far Eastern desk of the State Department, ran as follows. In the short run it would be advantageous to induce Japan toward attacking Russia rather than the Dutch and British possessions to the south. However this most likely would mean the end of Russian resistance after which the West would be left to deal with the Wehrmacht — a much more formidable client than the Imperial Japanese Army. It was thus in America's long-range interest to bait and deflect Japan to attack the Western powers rather than Russia (Dawson, 123). A parallel view was expressed by Churchill when on his way to Washington after Pearl Harbor he cabled Eden, "Russia's declaration of war on Japan would be greatly to our advantage provided, but only provided, that the Russians are confident that it would not impair their western front either now or next spring" (Miner, 182). The buttressing of Russian war-making capacity became and remained a top priority in the West's World War II strategy. It promised a quicker end to the war and, most important, at a minimal cost in British and American lives. All this would become ever clearer in the years to come.

Thus at the time that Hitler found himself at war with America his hopes of June 1940 had come to nought. His certainty of being able to conquer Russia was ground into mud and snow; rather there was doubt whether the Ostheer would survive the winter. The hope that England and America might acquiesce in his crusade to save Western civilization had turned into the exact opposite; vast quantities of weaponry and munitions were being readied for shipment to the Red Army. A formal alliance between England and Russia undertook to stay in the fight until Nazism was eradicated, the two parties pledging never to make a separate peace with him. After 28 months of spectacular victories in all four directions of the compass—Hitler ended up in December 1941 at war with America, Russia and the British Empire, the world's three most powerful states.

Nor did his contention that he declared war because America had already been a belligerent for some time have any validity. Whereas in 1940 the US armed forces were less than a million strong, after she entered the war they grew to 12 million. In December, Roosevelt invited Churchill to Washington for discussions, known as the Arcadia Conference. After the two leaders, now cobelligerents, reaffirmed the strategy of Germany being Enemy Number One, appropriate joint staffs sat down to formulate production goals for arms and munitions to be manufactured in the USA. The figures for the next two years that Roosevelt announced were so overwhelming that his own countrymen accused him of a "numbers racket." These quotas are listed in Table 18-1. While US production was already hefty in 1941 Germany's entry into the war doubled the quotas for the next year and quadrupled them for 1943. Not only were these goals met but some were exceeded. From now on there would be an ever-denser forest of smoke rising from German and American industrial plants; those in Germany would come from the ever-growing devastation caused by Allied bombing; those in the USA from producing a veritable flood of trucks, guns, tanks, airplanes and ships culminating in the development of an atomic bomb. All of this—and much besides—could not have happened on the scale it did, were not America officially at war with Germany.

Table 18-1
USA Arms Production Goals for 1941-43

	1941	1942	1943
Aircraft	28,600	45,000	100,000
Tanks	20,400	45,000	75,000
A-A Guns	6,300	20,000	35,000
Shipping (in millions of tons)	6	8	10
Antitank Guns	7,000	15,000	—
MGs	168,000	500,000	—
Bombs (in tons)	84,000	720,000	—

Source: Harriman: 113

* * *

While the Germans assaulted Moscow and the Russians just managed to hang on to their positions, the Stavka had been accumulating reserves just to the east of the capital. The Germans were unaware of it and whatever information filtered through Hitler furiously dismissed as fantasy; instead he hectored his commanders that the Russians were on the verge of collapse. There are no reliable figures what these reserves amounted to; the best estimate is of some 700,000 troops hidden in the forests and marshes around Moscow, including whole divisions of artillery and parks of airplanes. These were now released in stages, in step with the escalation of Stalin's ambitions for the winter offensive.

The battle opened on a minor key. Zhukov, who was given three new armies, intended a frontal attack on the enemy directly facing Moscow. Before he started, however, the Stavka made some changes in his plans. Noting that the Kalinin front ran for almost 120 miles east to west, Zhukov was told to link his attack to both Konev's Kalinin front and Timoshenko's southwest front. This extended the battle line to almost 700 miles.

The offensive on the northern sector started on December 5 and a day later on the southern end. From the beginning the Russians noted that there was no continuous front and that the Germans clung primarily to settlements and roads, leaving huge gaps in between. Bypassing the strong points they advanced steadily across open country and by mid–December had gained some 30 miles in the north and 50 miles in the south. On the southern wing they had eliminated the bulge around Tula, all that Guderian had won in bitter fighting in November. Thus after one week the Russians had pushed back the Germans from the immediate vicinity of Moscow. Provided he got additional reinforcements, Zhukov planned to continue his attack and hopefully recover all the territory the Russians had lost during Operation Typhoon.

Instead, impressed by the initial successes, the Stavka upped its objectives. They now aimed at nothing less than the destruction of the entire AGC. This was to be achieved by launching two powerful prongs, one in the north by Konev, and another from the south. To coordinate the planned encirclement, a Bryansk front was reestablished to assist the left prong in its pincer movement. The two thrusts were to head in the direction of Vyazma, some 150 miles behind German lines. In accordance with this new plan the bulk of Stavka reserves went to the Kalinin and Bryansk fronts; in the center Zhukov's mission was to pin down the enemy in front of him. This new plan formed the second phase of the Russian winter offensive.

The Bryansk front failed to capture either Orel or Mtsensk, its immediate objectives. Instead it was Zhukov's left wing which produced the deepest penetration in the German lines heading for Sukkenichi — a major German supply depot — and for Yukhnov on the direct approaches to Vyazma. As a result of this more northerly breakthrough Guderian's 2nd PzA was pushed southeast, out of the intended encirclement, and a huge gap of some 50 miles appeared between Guderian's tanks and 4th Army. In the north, the advance was slow but relentless, with Reinhardt's 3rd PzG and 9th Army being pushed back toward Rzhev. What was in the making was a giant semiellipse, subsequently referred to as the Horseshoe, with the easternmost German troops at the apex leaning on the Ruza River and both their flanks bent westward for some 50 miles. The Russians aimed to close off its mouth by driving from north and south on Vyazma. The city, located on the Moscow-Smolensk highway with a rail network running in all directions, was a key supply and communication center for all AGC armies.

A deep crisis soon developed in von Bock's Army Group. The Germans had gotten a taste of winter warfare during last November's fighting, but now it was late December and whatever was bad then only got worse. The daytime temperatures hovered around -4 F; at night they dropped to near -40 F. In addition to the breakdown of road transport, the railway system came to a complete standstill. The troops lacked winter clothing and were freezing. Men were forced to wrap their hands in rags with pieces of wood stuck into them to pull the triggers. When urinating the penis was wrapped in a rag and the urine passed over the men's cold fingers to keep them from freezing. Unable to position their heavy weapons in the frozen ground they placed them inside dwellings (Fritz, 117; Seaton 1980, 212). This was not the best tactical position; it did not offer a good field of fire and was an obvious target for the enemy. In deep snow any artillery shell below 155 mm was useless for the snow absorbed the shrapnel. Hitler had ordered that upon leaving, all dwellings be burned but this was a clear signal to the Russians who fell upon the Germans in the midst of their retreat. With the ground frozen to a depth of five to eight feet no dugouts could be built and the only defensive positions possible were above-ground parapets of snow and ice, occasionally reinforced with timber. A particular affliction was the powdered snow which made men and weapons sink into it as in quicksand; the same snow driven by the prevailing evening winds covered within minutes the tracks and roads that had taken days to clear. As a consequence the Germans in their retreat were losing their heavy weapons. Some they managed to destroy but much equipment was abandoned in the snowdrifts, along with the dead and often the wounded, too. In winter the Russians did not use paved roads because shoveling away the snow exposed the surface to cracking. They built separate winter roads parallel to the old ones or cross-country. They also resorted to attacking the Germans in deep snow by tunneling channels in the snow at right angles to the enemy positions and unexpectedly appearing over their heads (Höhn, C-034). After one week's retreat Hoepner lost half his artillery. By the end of December, out of Guderian's original 970 tanks only 70 were still operational. In the first two weeks of December the Ostheer lost 1,000 tanks (Hitler 1953, 275–6; Ziemke 1988, 91). Facing them were troops relatively well clad, using an abundance of skis and motor-sleds. Their T-34 tanks had compressed-air starters that could ignite the engines in the coldest weather and whose wide tracks carried them over most of the wintry terrain. Ironically, it was now the Germans— kings of Panzer warfare — that developed a phobia of Russian tanks. For the first time in the history of the German army there were occasions of troops throwing away their weapons, of entire units gripped by panic and of commanders unable to carry on and asking to be relieved.

The failings in the ranks were soon overshadowed by a profound crisis in leadership, culminating in Hitler's dismissal of the entire top command of the Ostheer. It started in November when Rostov was abandoned—the first of the winter retreats. After taking the city Kleist found himself wedged into a narrow corridor at the tip of the Azov Sea, threatened to the north by furious Russian counterattacks. On November 28 his 1st PzA was on the point of being encircled. To forestall it Rundstedt approved a retreat of 35 miles to the river Mius. When Hitler heard of it he countermanded it and ordered Kleist to stay put. Rundstedt then faced Hitler with a demand that either the retreat be approved or he be relieved. On December 1 Hitler dismissed Rundstedt and replaced him with Reichenau, the most Nazi of generals. Reichenau proved no superman and to save the 1st PzA had to agree with his predecessor.

Having dismissed the AGS commander, the next in line was the commander of AGC. It was von Bock's view that the AGC should be withdrawn, preferably east of Smolensk or at least to the Winter Line. This line, formally the Königsberg Line, ran from Lake Seliger past Rzhev, Gzhatsk and along the Oka to Orel. In his view, as well as in the views of nearly all other top commanders, this would preserve the troops, straighten out the front, and release divisions for a mobile reserve. Hitler opposed it but von Bock kept pressing it onto Brauchitsch. The latter was too timid to broach it to the führer. Exasperated, Bock told Brauchitsch during a visit on December 13, "I have no more suggestions to make. I made them earlier. The question that has to be decided now goes beyond the military" (Bock, 391). These views became known to Hitler. On December 16, just as the second phase of the Russian winter offensive was getting underway, Hitler dismissed von Bock. He was replaced by von Kluge, whose 4th Army was taken over by Kübler. Not only was von Bock dismissed but so, too, were nearly all his top officers. Then came the dismissals of Weichs of the 2nd Army and of Stülpnagel of the 17th Army. The process was the same in all cases. Under the onslaught of winter and enemy attacks the troops gave ground. When Hitler heard of it he fired admonitions to immediately stop the retreats. This proved impossible and the result was the cashiering of their commanders. On December 8 Hoepner was fired for "insubordination and cowardice" (Warlimont, 233) and replaced by General Ruoff. On the 12th Strauss of the 9th Army was replaced by Model — another Nazified admirer of the führer. On the 21st the just-appointed Kübler was thrown out and replaced by General Heinrici, a fellow Austrian. Along with them 35 other corps and divisional generals were dismissed.

Then came Guderian's turn. When the familiar cycle of führer injunctions and defeats at the front inundated his headquarters, Guderian decided to have it out with the führer. On December 20 he flew to the Wolfschanze and talked with him for five hours. Halder was not invited to the conversation; instead Keitel and Schmundt attended. It is worth quoting a small portion of the exchange because, as described in Chapter 1, it illustrates the technique of argumentation practiced by Hitler even with his top professionals, not to speak of when dealing with lesser souls. After describing the condition of the troops and the situation at the front, Guderian requested permission to withdraw to the Oka-Susha line. When Hitler heard the word "withdrawal" he exploded, "No, I forbid that." Guderian related that the retreat forced on the troops could not be halted. "Then they must dig into the ground where they are," was the answer. Guderian explained that the ground was frozen to a depth of five feet. Hitler persisted, "Then they must blast craters with heavy howitzers. We had to do that in World War I in Flanders." Guderian said that the soil in Russia in winter is not like that in Flanders; a howitzer shell will make a hole the size of a washtub, no bigger. Besides, such fighting would lead to a war of attrition.

"Do you think" — Hitler's voice rose — "Frederick the Great's grenadiers were anxious to die? … I believe that I, too, am entitled to ask any German soldier to lay down his life" (Guderian, 204–5).

On December 25 Guderian was dismissed. By Hitler's instructions he was forbidden to issue any farewell order to his men with whom he had fought since September 1, 1939 (Ziemke 1986, 100). The command of 2nd PzA was taken over by Gen. Rudolf Schmidt.

On January 12,1942, the last Army Group commander, von Leeb of AGN, was cashiered. His end came when he tried to pull back his troops from the Demyansk salient. Feldmarschall von Leeb left and Demyansk was encircled to the untold misery of the 100,000 men trapped there. He, too, was replaced by a Nazi sympathizer, Georg von Küchler, commander of the 18th Army, a rare specimen who had supported Hitler during the Blomberg-Fritsch affair.

The culmination of these purges occurred on December 19 with the dismissal of the commander in chief of the German army, Feldmarschall Walter von Brauchitsch, sent away without ceremony and without a handshake. As soon as he left Hitler appointed himself *Oberbefehlshaber des Heeres.* In 1938 he had made himself minister of war and commander in chief of the armed forces; he now also became commander in chief of the army. On the day of his self-appointment he fired the OKW chief of personnel, the brother of Wilhelm Keitel, and had his adjutant, Schmundt, take over the administration of this office under his supervision. From now on all nominations, not just confirmations, and all appointments in the armed forces would come directly from Hitler.

When Halder was told who his new boss was Hitler expostulated to the chief of staff, "Anyone can do this little job of directing operations in war. The task of Commander-in-Chief is to educate the Army to the National-Socialist idea and I do not know any Army general who can do this as I want it done. I have therefore decided to take over command of the Army myself" (Görlitz 1954, 406). On the day of his self-appointment Hitler issued a proclamation to the troops: "Our struggle for national liberation is approaching its climax! Decisions of world importance are about to be made…. I have therefore as of this day myself taken command of the Army" (Ziemke, *Moscow*, 83). One of the motivations for the purge was to shift the blame for the failed campaign and lack of winter equipment onto his military chiefs. In this Hitler was, as usual, most successful. The news of his taking command brought elation and a surge of confidence among all ranks. The soldiers felt that now there would be no more mishaps and failings. The troops would be cared for and the enemy beaten, for at last the führer took things into his own hand (Seaton 1980, 217). Halder, hailed after the war as one of the more independent spirits, joined the general chorus. On December 25, in addressing senior commanders of the Ostheer he said, "We can and should be proud that the Führer himself is now at the head of the Army," and on a subsequent occasion, added, "We shall master (the situation) ... if a single will, the will of the Führer prevails from the highest levels down to the soldier at the front" (Boog, 718, 724).

Hitler now issued his famous stand-fast ukase forbidding any further withdrawals. An order of December 18 from the OKH said that "The Führer had ordered: Large-scale retrograde movements must not be conducted.... The troops are to be forced to resist fanatically in their positions, paying no attention to the enemy breakthroughs at the flanks or in the rear" (Piekalkiewicz, 240). From now on the troops, isolated or not, about to perish or not, whether their stand did or did not benefit the tactical situation on other sectors, were to hold their ground to the last. To reinforce this new dictum, instructions went out that commanders were personally responsible for staging any withdrawal. What that meant was the following: Hitler forbade withdrawing; this was to be passed on by army to corps and from there to the divisional commanders. With this the duties of Hitler, army and corps commanders were fulfilled. Should the troops knuckle under and retreat, the low-ranking commanders would pay for it. The troops received a Manual for Winter Warfare in which they were informed that in winter fighting the German soldier is superior to the Russian and the question of snow and cold is only a matter of "attitude." These crisis control steps were crowned with a spiritual appeal by the German clergy which preached to the troops that, compared to Abraham willing to sacrifice his son when God asked him to do so, a German soldier's death for the Fatherland is small coin (Kluge, 39, 51). Then Hitler ordered Colonel Martin, OKW liaison to the Propaganda Ministry, to compile a list of all OKW and OKH officers who "are fostering defeatism" so they can be dealt with. In no time at all, Martin delivered such a list to Goebbels for submission to the führer (Goebbels 1948, 37).

While these events were unraveling the high command and the traditions of the German army, the Russian offensive rumbled on. By the time Hitler had fired his last army group feldmarschall, the outlines of the intended AGC encirclement became apparent. In the south Zhukov's armies reached the Kirov-Yukhnov line, some 50 miles south of their objective, Vyazma. In the north Konev's 39th Army was approaching Sychevka, likewise some 50 miles from Vyazma, separating thereby 3rd PzA from the 9th Army. In mid–January all four major formations of AGC were struggling each on its own to hold their positions while the Russians were about to close the 100-mile mouth of the Horseshoe.

Just then Stalin decided on nothing less than an overall offensive from Lake Ladoga to the Black Sea. In the north Leningrad was to be liberated by the northwest and Volkhov fronts. In the center the penetration was to be extended beyond Smolensk to a battlefield depth of some 200 miles; except for the Kiev cauldron, not even the Germans ever attempted such a vast envelopment. In the south Timoshenko was given two objectives. His northern wing was to invest and take Kharkov. His southern prong was to aim for the Dniepr where it would swing south and take Melitopol on the Azov Sea. This would cut off the

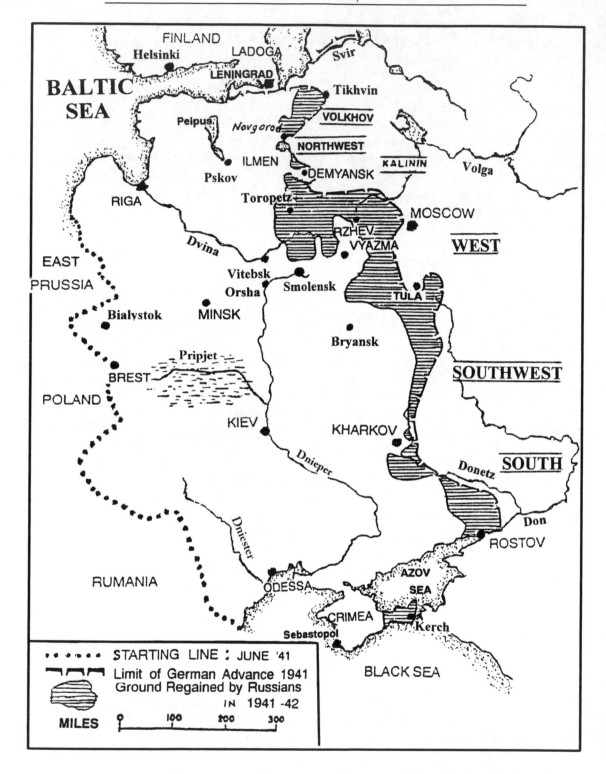

18.1. Ground gained in Russian 1941/42 winter offensive

entire AGS, liberate the Donetz Basin and isolate the Crimea, which was already being assaulted across the Kerch Straits (see Fig. 18.1). On the eve of this all-out offensive Stavka instructed its field commanders "to adopt the practice of concentrating in a single direction" (Ziemke 1986, 142). What it advised its troops Stavka failed to heed itself; instead of concentrating all its efforts at Vyazma where things were going well, it now dissipated its forces along a 1,500-mile front. Aside from not achieving its inflated objectives this grand design doomed the pending encirclement of AGC.

For the general offensive Kurochkin in the north had received much of the available reserves. The attack was to form a thrust parallel to the north Vyazma prong, aiming as far west as Vitebsk. Unlike the Vyazma operation this parallel drive had no second prong to meet it. Kurochkin opened his offensive on January 9 from south of Lake Seliger slicing his way along the boundary between AGC and AGN. His gains were rapid and carried great operational promise, for by the end of January he was near Velikye Luki, having covered 170 miles in that period. His push also produced great gains for Konev. Two thrusts adjoining Kurochkin brought Konev deep into the German rear. One element, Belov's 1st Cavalry Corps, started operating behind the German lines and joining up with large partisan formations concentrated between Vyazma and Smolensk. Compressed within an ever-narrowing salient south of Rzhev were Model's 9th Army and the 4th PzA. At the mouth of the Horseshoe, the 4th Army was being attacked by Zhukov's forces including Efremov's 33rd Army, which soon penetrated close to Vyazma. To complete the encirclement the Russians began landing on January 18 an airborne brigade along a 40-mile front at the mouth of the Horseshoe. These forces were to combine with the partisans, Belov's cavalry and Efremov's troops and close the trap.

At this stage Russian and German formations were so intertwined that no continuous front existed. The various Russian penetrations formed behind the Germans a convoluted serpentine making it unclear who was enveloping whom. An answer to this, however, was already in the making as two things made themselves felt. One was that the Russians were becoming exhausted. It was difficult and costly to attack across deep snowdrifts whereas snow helped the defender. And the further the Russians advanced the more cumbersome became the supply problem. Then, too, the AGC was getting reinforcements — 70,000 men in February alone. On January 30 Model, whose 9th Army was hemmed in south of Rzhev, attacked to the west, linked up with PzA 3 and cut off Konev's 29th and 39th armies. Konev eventually extricated one of them but the 29th Army was trapped in a pocket south of Rzhev. A few days later PzA 4 from the north and the 4th Army from the south attacked across the base of Efremov's 33rd Army which had gotten within a few miles of Vyazma and severed it from Zhukov's main forces. Then the 2nd PzA far to the south joined in the fray by attacking from the Orel-Bryansk line and drove the Russians back some 40 miles to the north. Stalin ordered that Zhukov rescue Efremov's 33rd Army and Konev do the same for his 29th Army — but neither succeeded. The resistance of these encircled armies, as well as of the dropped airborne troops, was to last into midsummer, but they were eventually destroyed.

On April 30, with the Rasputitsa in full bloom, the AGC went over to the defensive along the jagged lines the winter fighting had created. The Russians, bloodied in the encirclements north and south of Vyazma — where they themselves not long ago were only 10–20 miles from closing the gap round the AGC — halted all further attacks.

As in the center Stalin's general offensives in the northern and southern sectors also ended in defeat. In the attempt to head for Leningrad the Volkhov front started its attack on January 7 and managed to advance some 20–30 miles. Then the Germans counterattacked and surrounded two Soviet armies in the very bulge they had won. Vlasov, the general who would later become the head of a Russian Liberation Army serving the Germans, was sent in to lead the troops out of the pocket but was himself trapped with the remnants of the two armies ending up in German captivity. South of Lake Ilmen the Russians surrounded more than 100,000 Germans in the Demyansk pocket but failed to destroy them. Eventually a narrow corridor was sprung by a German rescue force under the command of General Seydlitz and the Demyansk salient remained part of the German lines.

In the south Timoshenko opened his offensive on either side of Izyum, with one thrust aiming at Kharkov and the other heading for the Dniepr. Just as the offensive got underway von Reichenau, commander of AGS, died of a combination heart attack and plane crash. On January 17 Hitler asked von Bock to take over Army Group South. One motivation for recalling him was that there were widespread mutterings about Hitler's cashiering of his top commanders; even Sepp Dietrich, his devoted stormtrupper-general, as well as Josef Goebbels complained about it. So Hitler relented. On January 18 von Bock reached Poltava, headquarters of AGS, and went to work; the results were not long in coming. Timoshenko had gotten to within 15–20 miles of Kharkov but failed to take the city. In the south, too, he came close to the Dniepr, covering a distance of more than 70 miles. But in mid–May the Germans launched a major operation and within 10 days Timoshenko's armies were shattered. As in his heyday von Bock even managed to create a cauldron in which he took close to a quarter million prisoners. At the end of May here, too, the fighting came to a standstill.

* * *

Despite the blows the Red Army had suffered in the last phase of the winter fighting the counteroffensive can be considered as having changed the situation at the front in favor of the Russians. On the AGC sector the front line was shifted by some 130 miles to the southwest, relieving Moscow of any danger of being assaulted, not to speak of being taken; on December 15 the Russians had felt sufficiently confident to bring back to the capital the evacuated Central Committee and the government ministries. Aside from relieving Moscow and Tula such major cities as Kalinin and Kaluga were retaken and the jagged front left by the fighting put a severe strain on German resources. The salients of Rzhev, Belyy and Demyansk required large forces to sustain them. The character of the Germans' tactics and new command practices are reflected by the story of Demyansk. The area had been encircled on February 8, trapping six divisions of the 18th Army, a total of 103,000 men, 30 miles behind the front. After a month of desperate slugging through snow and furious resistance, Seydlitz managed on April 21 to open a narrow corridor to the pocket. Everyone expected that the purpose of this rescue operation was to evacuate the trapped men. But no—the order from above was to leave the troops in place even though they continued to suffer supply interruptions and severe losses in men. Early in May, Küchler and Seydlitz flew to the Wolfschanze to prevail upon Hitler to evacuate; it would shorten the front by 120 miles and free large forces. Halder agreed with this and so did Jodl. When pressed for a decision the führer said no, he needed the outpost for staging a new offensive. When Seydlitz started to say that the marshy terrain was unsuitable for tanks and so on, the führer snapped, "These are my orders." The pocket was kept alive mostly by air supplies. Over 30,000 replacements were fed into it and 35,000 wounded flown out. In the course of this air shuttle 262 Ju-52s were lost which, on top of the losses in Crete, effectively crippled the Air Transport Branch of the Luftwaffe. The troops stayed there for nine months but in the end had to be withdrawn.

In addition to loss of territory the Ostheer suffered a manpower attrition it could not replace. Battle casualties in the four months from the end of November to the end of March were 376,000, of which 108,000 were dead or missing. The losses to frostbite requiring hospitalization were 228,000; those due to exhaustion and epidemics close to a quarter million. The latter losses totaling 478,000 men exceeded battle casualties by 25 percent. Altogether the losses in manpower at the end of winter was approaching a million, producing a shortfall of 625,000 men (Seaton 1980, 291). The losses in tanks and self-propelled guns amounted to 4,240 machines so that by the end of winter the army was left with 140 operational tanks. The Ostheer survived but it was a damaged instrument. The AGC, in fact, was never again capable of offensive operations. It remained in place unemployed and eviscerated for more than two years until it was destroyed in 1944 by a Russian onslaught of tidal proportions.

Territory and manpower weren't the only casualties. When the winter ended the Ostheer was a different army; its very nature had changed. It had lost much of its heavy weaponry and, not having planned for a long war and not having harnessed industry for mass production, no adequate replacements were in the pipeline. An ominous factor was the silencing and crippling of the officer corps. One of the great strengths of the German army had been that every officer was a feldmarschall in his own right. When the situation demanded he had the talent and initiative to conduct battles without compulsion or guidance. With the new stand-fast order and personal responsibility for any retreat the German officer was robbed of his greatest asset. Contrary to this Stalin was giving his generals more and more freedom of action. Russian plants were beginning to pour out a flood of new tanks and airplanes. Ironically, November 1941, just when the Germans exhausted themselves in front of Moscow, was the nadir of Soviet industrial production; whereas in 1940 there were 31.2 million industrial workers, in November 1941 this had dropped to 19.8 (Seaton 1971, 228). By spring this was being reversed.

Like the arguments about Moscow versus Kiev in the late summer of 1941, Hitler's stand-fast order versus his generals' preference for a withdrawal is a favorite topic of discussion in historical writings. A convincing case can be made for either side, but this again would be arguing a secondary issue. That standing fast according to Hitler's ukase did not help him win the war in Russia is a fact. But what would a major withdrawal have achieved? What would that have done as far as beating the Red Army? Neither Hitler's nor the generals' choice could have had a telling effect on the ultimate outcome. The conflict between Hitler's stand-fast order and his generals' desire for tactical retreat centers on a different issue altogether. Hitler's spastic decisions to hang on to any captured position were subsequently repeated throughout the war to the ongoing puzzlement of his commanders. But it was the generals who in this confrontation seemed ridiculous because, as on most previous occasions, they did not fathom their warlord nor did they understand the war they were fighting for him. The German generals, being professional men, thought and operated in terms of their trade. They considered what was reasonable or likely and were concerned with cost, risk and trade-offs. In terms of soldiering, if retreat would yield fewer casualties, better tactical deployment for present or future battles—well, that was the thing to do. Even at the high levels of strategy and war aims rational factors held sway. Thus if, as it seemed, it was impossible to "conquer" Russia then perhaps by withdrawing and erecting a German Maginot Line they could retain Ukraine and the Baltics and that should be good enough. If the situation turned grim then, for the sake of national interest, one could retreat to the old borders or ask for an armistice — as Germany had done in 1918 and France did in 1940. Perhaps a separate peace? War and statesmanship contain a gamut of escapes and arrangements practiced ever since war was invented. Therefore one's moves and operations are tailored in conformity with one's prospects, as Bismarck had done when victorious and Hindenburg when a loser.

But, of course, here is where they were blind as blindness can be. These were not the norms Hitler operated by. His life had always been, in his own words, *"Entweder Oder"* an either-or proposition. He would not consider a partial occupation or partition of Russia any more then he would ask for an armistice. Hitler would never make peace with Russia and the West would never make peace with Hitler. Either Hitler was going to achieve his aims — not just conquer but extirpate Russia's "life force" — or there would be armageddon for all, including Germany. He had said so countless times. They were involved in a war which their warlord was either going to win as he defined it — or there would be nothing. When Hitler insisted on his stand-fast order or refused to withdraw the Rzhev and Demyansk salients it was because from these springboards he was going to resume his march on Moscow, the Caucasus and the A-A Line. What was the point of withdrawing when this flew in the face of the core of the enterprise? The same reasoning applied throughout the rest of the war when he would not abandon Stalingrad, or the Kuban, or the Crimea and would let the entire AGN be trapped in Kurland rather than use it in the defense of the reich. These scattered anchors, large and small, were to be platforms for a Barbarossa Redux.

Faced now with three powerful enemies, all alive and growing in strength, then *Quo Vadis Gröfaz?* What were Hitler's thoughts at that juncture, what measures did he envisage to deal with a hopeless situation? Why did he go on? This subject is taken up in some detail in Chapter 31, when following the fateful events of *Annus Irae* 1943 the impending doom emerged in full force. At this stage, the end of 1941, Hitler offered no reasons why he went on with the war for another three and a half years. What prevailed at this stage was a fanatic adherence to his immutable *Weltanschauung*, a steadfast repetition of his past convictions and prophecies immune to the history that had intervened between Munich 1938 and December 1941. Thus the reason propounded for the failure of Barbarossa was the refusal of his blockhead generals to follow his strategic blueprint. On November 25 he confided to Engel, his army adjutant, his concern about the eastern campaign, saying, "We started a month too late. The ideal solution would have been the fall of Leningrad, capture of the southern area, and then, in that event, a pincer attack on Moscow.... Then there would be the prospect of an eastern wall with military bases" (Kershaw 2000, 438). A few months later (March 20) this was repeated during an intimate meeting with Goebbels: "The Führer described how close we were during the past months to a Napoleonic winter. Had he weakened for but one moment, the front would have caved in and a catastrophe ensued.... Brauchitsch bears a great deal of responsibility for this ... a vain cowardly wretch.... The Führer had no intention whatever of going to Moscow, he wanted to cut off the Caucasus. But Brauchitsch and his general staff knew better ... a coward and a nincompoop.... The Führer again has a perfectly clear plan for the coming spring and summer. He does not want to overextend the war. His aims are the Caucasus, Leningrad and Moscow.... He intends possibly to construct a gigantic line of defense and to let the eastern campaign rest there.... Possibly this may mean a hundred years' war in the East, but that need not worry us" (Goebbels 1948, 135–6). Those who attribute to the führer a touch of insanity the above argumentation could serve them better than any psychiatric test.

Another Hitlerian vision that surfaces during these dismal winter discourses is the lifelong obsession with England. After the rebuff suffered with his peace offensive in the summer of 1940, after the lost air battles in the subsequent fall, after America's relentless march toward belligerency alongside the British, after the formal and factual commitment by the Anglo-Saxon powers to aiding Russia, nothing had changed in Hitler's strategic dreamland. We are back to *Mein Kampf*. One month after launching Barbarossa, Hitler informed his dinner guests on July 22, "I believe that the end of this war will mark the beginning of a durable friendship with England," and on August 8, "I rejoice on behalf of the German people at the idea that one day we will see England and Germany marching together against America" (Hitler 1953, 11, 22). This was at the peak of his victories in Russia when he expected a quick end to the campaign after which, as he said, England would eventually line up with Germany. When the situation at the front turned more precarious the plans he had had for England shifted to the present. On October 26 he talked into space as if the British were eavesdropping: "If the English are clever they will seize the psychological moment to make an about turn — and they will march on our side" (Hitler 1953, 76). In January when the situation turned catastrophic the alliance with Britain received a quantum leap in time — now it was likely to happen any day. Twice during that bitter month he mentions it; on the 7th he prophesizes, "In my view it is not impossible that England may quit the war.... and it will be a German-British army that will chase the Americans from Iceland," and on January 15 he repeats, "It's not impossible that a miracle may take place and England may withdraw from the war" (Hitler 1953, 154–5, 170). Consistent with keeping his distance from the realities of Germany's situation he didn't say a word about his rush to Berlin to declare war on the USA. After his return on December 13 to the Wolfschanze in his first Table Talk he expostulated on Negro taboos, the Eucharist, paradise, St. Paul and Christianity. There was no need to talk about the new war with the USA because, as he informed his audience on January 7, "I don't see a real future for the Americans. In my view it's a decayed country."

Like his *Weltanschauung* so his personal traits stayed ironclad; they were only reinforced, driven to the brink. He had always disliked snow — now, after his experience in Russia it grew into a phobia. On March 20 Goebbels went to see his mentor at the Wolfschanze and his diaries record the impact of the visit. The landscape, the discussions, the recollections were all about snow, as if that winter's snow had been a new ecological phenomenon, like the biblical flood. Goebbels found the führer turning gray, lonely and, in a most appropriate phrase, living like "in a concentration camp." Talking about the last few months, Goebbels said, "His aversion for the winter has received cruel and terrible vindication. He certainly never imagined that a time would come when winter would so unrelentingly take advantage of his instinctive antipathy and inflict such suffering upon German troops." The führer's only consolation was "a little dog that was presented to him [which] now plays about his room. His whole heart belongs to that dog. The canine may do anything it wants in his bunker" (Goebbels 1948, 131–8).

On April 26 Hitler went to Berlin to deliver a speech. Goebbels, who saw him, wrote that "the dominant thought with the Führer is his joy at the majestic coming of spring.... During the coming years he doesn't want to see any snow at all; snow has become physically repulsive to him." The speech, delivered the next day at 3 P.M., was a sort of state of the union message about what had happened on the eastern front. He spoke of the generals who had botched their jobs, of officers who at critical moments had lost their nerve, of the fact that he had to employ drastic measures. Perhaps to show that one reason for these failures was that he, Hitler, had not wielded enough authority, he requested that the Reichstag grant him plenary powers to directly dismiss or punish any functionary — whether he be a general, bureaucrat or judge — when Hitler considered this necessary. In essence he requested that he be made what one German historian termed *Oberste Gerichtsheer* — supreme judge. Amid thunderous applause the Reichstag granted him that power.

The führer now needed a rest and he left for the Berghof. Within a day snow began to fall on the Obersalzberg. The führer packed up and departed. As Goebbels recorded, "It was impossible for him physically to look at snow.... It was," says Goebbels with his customary sarcasm, "so to speak a flight from the snow."

CHAPTER 19

The Subhuman East

The looming invasion of the Soviet Union had fueled feverish expectations among the nations incorporated into the Communist empire. These were located mainly along the western rim of the USSR — the three Baltic states, the Ukrainians, the Byelorussians, and even the Poles who lost their eastern territories as a result of the Nazi-Soviet Pact. The other populations that were stirred by the prospect of a German victory were the Turkic tribes at the southern rim of Russia — the Crimea, the Caucasus, and beyond. It was by all reckoning a plausible vista and the degree to which they have misunderstood the nature and intentions of their potential friends will be seen in the case of two of these ethnic groups, the Lithuanians and the Ukrainians. It should give a very first indication of what lay ahead for the "liberated" territories.

On June 16 the president of Lithuania, Smetana, crossed over illegally into Germany expecting to be greeted as a friend and ally. Subsequently, the former Lithuanian envoy to Berlin, Colonel Skirpa, residing in Germany since Lithuania became a Soviet republic, informed Ribbentrop of the formation of a clandestine Lithuanian government to rule over an expected free Lithuania. Along with this, Skirpa informed the German military that an insurrection had broken out in his home country with guerilla formations ready to assist the Wehrmacht in the liberation of Lithuania. The German reaction was swift. Skirpa, who was intending to return to his country, was on June 22 ordered to remain in Berlin and to register every day at police headquarters (Kaslas, 344). On instructions from home the OKW issued on June 26 a directive to the troops not to recognize any Lithuanian authorities and Lithuanians must take orders only from the German military. All independent organizations that had been formed were disbanded on July 28 and a newly appointed generalkomissar, von Renteln, was installed to rule the country. On the same day, Weizsäcker requested of the Vatican — which had continued to recognize the Baltic states — not to have any dealings with representatives of these countries. Lithuania's future, as well as that of Latvia and Estonia, was to be a part of a much more grandiose scheme, as envisaged by Adolf Hitler.

More weighty than the dismissal of the Baltic states' pretensions was the treatment meted out to the Ukrainians with their large population, fertile soil, and vast mineral resources, compulsively in love with Germany. The 1920 resurrected Poland had contained a sizeable portion of western Ukraine and its largest city Lwow (now Lviv) had been a hotbed of Ukrainian irredentist agitation and violence. Ukrainian nationalists had, therefore, looked to Germany, particularly Nazi Germany, to liberate them from both Polish and Soviet domination. Its largest clandestine organization was the OUN with a radical faction led by Stepan Bandera. In April 1941 the OUN submitted a petition to Governor Frank calling for the establishment in the GG of a Ukrainian enclave after expelling from its territory the Poles and the Jews. This had been refused but now with German troops in occupation of eastern Poland, including Lwow, the OUN proclaimed an independent Ukrainian state. Within days the newly formed Ukrainian government and Bandera himself were arrested. In order to splinter what had now become a territorially contiguous Ukraine, Hitler in mid–July ordered that the erstwhile Polish Ukraine, with its cherished city of Lwow (or Lviv), be made part of the GG. Moreover, a chunk of Belorussian territory was attached to East Prussia, ominously making the reich a neighbor of Ukraine. Later on Hitler induced Antonescu to take over Transnistria, part of Soviet Ukraine, performing thereby a trisection of Ukrainian territory. Bandera, first carted off to a Gestapo prison in Berlin, was subsequently shipped to Sachsenhausen; two of his brothers, shipped to Auschwitz, died there. Two other Ukrainian leaders, Habrusevich and Kardyba, were taken to Sachsenhausen and executed there.

When in the latter half of 1942 German troops reached the Caucasus Ribbentrop, yielding to the entreaties of neutral Turkey, convened at the hotel Adlon a number of representatives from the Turkic regions. During the conference the chieftains urged the German government to proclaim independence for their communities. Ribbentrop, supported by the erstwhile ambassador to Moscow, von Schulenburg, an Ostpolitik advocate, duly consulted the führer and returned with the message that "it is all nonsense.... In wartime nothing can be achieved with sentimental scruples. The Führer has made a definite decision" (Dallin 1957, 135). A number of émigré Russian groups, expecting the liberation of their homeland, had formed a Council of Russia and a General Biskupski had begun to recruit cadres for future governance of the freed Russian territories. They were prevented from moving to Russian territory and anyone attempting to do so was arrested. Biskupski, a pro–German, even pro–Nazi individual, concluded that "the war is not being conducted against Bolshevism but against the Russian people."

The treatment accorded the sympathizers and potential allies of Nazi Germany was, of course, not accidental. It was a direct result of the plans Hitler harbored for the continent he was about to conquer. The major outlines of this program had been postulated back in *Mein Kampf*. As early as spring 1934 he had told Rauschning "We are obliged to depopulate, as part of preserving the German population. We shall have to develop a technique of depopulation, I mean the removal of entire racial units. And that is what I intend to carry out" (Rauschning, 140). In planning Barbarossa, Himmler projected the exact scale of depopulation when, on January 1941, he told a gathering of SS men that a prerequisite for German settlement in the East was the destruction of 30 million Slavs (Koehl, 146)—a prescient arithmetic, as this was about the death toll of Russian civilians in the war. The formal edict for the colonization in the East came from führer headquarters on July 17. Some of is provisions read:

- The Russians have started a partisan war which is actually to our advantage as this gives us the opportunity to exterminate anything that is in our way.
- We shall never allow any alien armed formations west of the Urals, not even Ukrainians or Kozakhs.
- The entire Baltikum is to be part of the Reich. Crimea must be totally cleared and settled by Germans. It would be allotted a sizeable rear area, likewise to be part of the Reich. So will Galicia. In addition, the Volga region and Baku will be annexed.

- The area of Leningrad will be given to Finland after the city itself is completely leveled.
- A wall will be built some 300 miles east of the Urals beyond which will be dumped some of the surviving Russians while to the west of the Teutonic wall all of Russia will be ruled by Germany [Holldack, 486–91].

Even the name Russia was to disappear for after apportioning vast tracts of Russian territory to Ostland and Ukraine the remainder was to be renamed Reichkommissariat Muscovy. Germany, in fact, declared itself the legal successor to the Soviet Union, including the three Baltic states (Calvocoressi, 275).

Hitler did not even contemplate an end to the conflict in Russia since a continuing state of war would enable the Germans to perpetuate the expulsions and the colonization of the eastern landmass, a project expected to take 20 or 30 years. In case there would be a shortage of Germans, Hitler intended to settle there Danes, Norwegians, Dutch people and Englishmen! He indulged in some high-level psychohistory. Ending the war, he argued, would again expose the Germans to the soft European civilization. Instead he intended to breed a generation of soldier-peasants, a new species of land Vikings, who would settle and hold the East in perpetuity. On October 19 in the presence of Todt and Sauckel Hitler elaborated, "We shan't settle in the Russian towns, and we'll let them go to pieces without intervening…. To struggle amongst the hovels, chase away the fleas, provide German teachers, bring out newspapers—very little of that for us…. For them the word 'liberty' means the right to wash on feast days…. There is only one duty: to Germanize this country by immigration and to look upon the natives as Redskins." Ten days later he added, "Nobody will ever snatch the East from us…. To exploit the Ukraine properly—that new Indian Empire—we'll need only peace in the West" (Bullock 1992, 724). Echoing the führer, Göring added, "The best thing would be to kill all men in the Ukraine over 15 years of age and then send in the SS stallions" and in November 1941 he told Ciano, "This year between 20 and 30 million persons will die in Russia of hunger," a recapitulation of Himmler's higher mathematics (Dallin 1957, 123).

Though Hitler had been talking a lot about a New Europe the fact remained that, except for some minor annexations, the boundaries of Western Europe remained remarkably in place. Not so in the east where a new geopolitical and demographic chart was being drawn by master cartographers—Hitler, Himmler, Göring, Rosenberg, Koch, Lohse and a herd of minor draughtsmen. According to these plans the continent of what was once Russia would look like the map in Fig. 19.1. Parallel to what was now called das Grossdeutsches Reich the new imperium would be renamed *Das Grossgermanische Reich*. Everything was clearly labeled except when the chief cartographer crossed the Urals his magic marker faltered; he had run out of captions. Recovering, he opined that if there was any trouble there the Germans would continue their march eastward, into Siberia (which they eventually did).

By the fall of 1941 occupied German territory roughly extended to the line Leningrad-Vyazma-Kharkov-Rostov and this, as shown in Fig. 19.2 was parceled out into two major enclaves, Reichskommisariat Ostland which included the Baltic states, and Reichskommissariat Ukraine—the first to be administered by the Schleswig-Holstein gauleiter Hinrich Lohse residing in Riga, and the second by East Prussia's gauleiter Erik Koch in Rovno, not in Kiev, the capital of Ukraine, which was to be eradicated. When in 1942 the Germans penetrated the Caucasus a Reichskommissariat Kaukasus was created under Arno Schikendanz, editor of the *Völkischer Beobachter*. The envisioned Reichskommissariat Muscovy was

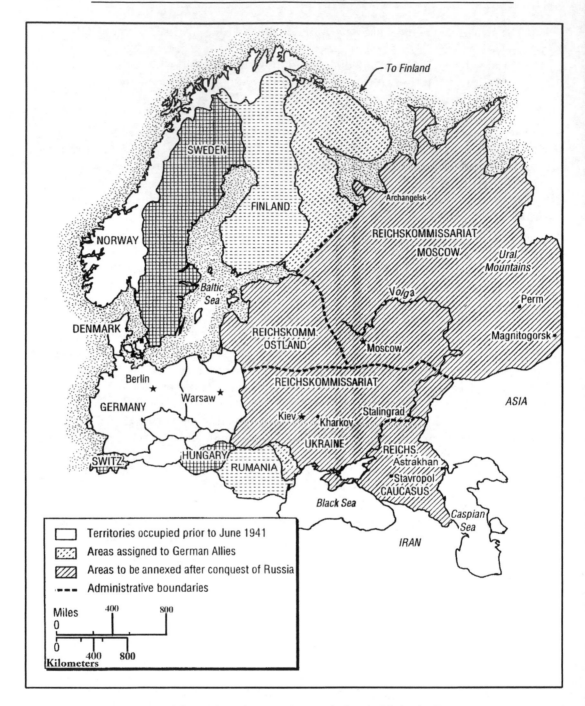

19.1. The projected Gross-Germanisches Reich in the East

also assigned a ruler, Siegfried Kasche, although by fault of the German army he never set foot there. All the occupied territory was subordinated to Alfred Rosenberg's Ostministerium in Berlin. In addition to this administrative construct Hitler lopped off a wide north-south corridor, designated Rear Army Area, which remained under army control. Beside the Ostministerium and the army at least three other state organs exercised authority in

19.2. Administration of conquered territories

the East — Himmler's SS and SD; Göring's Four Year Plan, in charge of exploiting the Russian economy; and Sauckel for the procurement of slave labor. Let loose, these multiple agencies and their subagencies were in perpetual fight with one another over jurisdiction, turf, loot, and much else.

* * *

The agricultural riches of the area occupied by the Germans were enormous. Its 100,000 collective farms represented 40 percent of all cultivated land and the livestock 45 percent of Russia's total. The residents of these kolkhozes and sovkhozes were another potential source if not of collaboration at least of sympathy with the invader for they resented, if not hated, the Soviet system of collective farming. But as ordered from above the kolkhozes were kept intact and for two reasons: because it was easier to enforce the collection of produce, and their land was not meant for Russians to own anyway; Minister for Agriculture Backe, in fact, stated that had there been no collective farms the Germans would have had to invent them. For propaganda purposes the Germans changed the name of the collective farms to Gemeinwirtschaften, which meant the same as the Russian acronym; from time to time, too, they announced plans for privatization which inevitably fizzled out. It was only in the last few years that in some local regions privatization was introduced but by then it was too late to affect the attitude of the peasants, or boost agricultural production. Moreover, by that time the dragooning of Russians for forced labor in Germany robbed the farms of the manpower to work the land. Rounded up without regard to health or age, these laborers, were housed in isolated barracks and forced to wear the label OST. Any intimacy with a German woman was punished by hanging. By the end of 1943 there were 2.1 million Ostarbeiter in Germany, half of them women.

In their advance into Russia the Germans had already found a land denuded of much of its possessions and work force. When retreating the Russians had taken with them everything they could and the young men and women had been conscripted either into the army or for work in evacuated armament plants. By order of the OKH the occupied land had now to feed 3 million German soldiers, plus another 2 million German administrators and executioners while some produce was also shipped to Germany. Not only did the Russian peasant have to provide the official quotas but individual soldiers singly and in groups continually raided and robbed private homes of whatever food they found there. There was both method and malice to the German policy of starving the Russians. Ukraine, rich in surplus food, usually fed the other parts of the country but now the Germans issued the following directive: "Efforts to save the population from starving to death by bringing in surplus food from the black soil region to the northern areas (Byelorussia) ... undermines Germany's ability to hold out in the war. From this there follows forcibly the extinction of industry as well as of a large percentage of human beings in the hitherto deficit areas of Russia" (Dallin 1957, 311). The induced starvation was so extreme that animal cadavers were being exhumed as food; in Leningrad meals were made of carpenter's glue, and cannibalism was frequent (Boog, 1171). The previously cited directive attests also to the intent of the Germans not to revive or promote Russian industry. And indeed, except for mining and oil, the policy was to suppress all Russian industrial activity. The exploitation of the natural resources, on the other hand, was pursued with extreme ruthlessness. There had been no abundance of consumer goods under the Soviets but with the extermination of Jewish artisans and the closure of factories and civilian workshops, the supply of the most

The ruined Russian city of Murmansk in 1942. (From *The Russian War 1941–1945* by Daniela Mrazkova and Vladimir Remes copyright ©1975 by Daniela Mrazkova and Vladimir Remes. Used by permission of Dutton, a division of Penguin Group [USA] Inc.)

primitive needs— shoes, cloth, needles, paper —fell to nil. As a result of its policy to devastate the country, Germany during its occupation got out of Russia less than she received in the trade agreement prior to the invasion.

When after years the Red Army began regaining the lost territories, the Germans instituted the most sadistic implementation of scorched earth tactics. On September 3, 1943, Himmler ordered that "Not one person, no cattle, no quintal of grain, no railway track must remain behind…. The enemy must find a country totally burned and destroyed." Four days later Göring supplemented this with one of his own orders which stated that "all agricultural products, means of production and machines serving the food industry are to be removed…. The population engaged in agriculture … is to be transported westwards." As a result, during the retreat 15,000 freight cars loaded with agricultural machinery including 7,000 tractors, 20,000 generators, a quarter million ploughs and 3 million scythe blades had been shipped to Germany (Dallin 1957, 364–6).

Along with economic prostration, the other basic policy was to depopulate the country and make it ripe for German colonization. The primary instrument for this was induced starvation which along with mass executions was the main cause of the enormous loss of life under German rule. Given the Russian distances and lack of adequate rail and motor transport in the German army the order to live off the land certainly alleviated the Ostheer's provisioning problems. But as in all other domains this was not simply a pragmatic choice but was meant to serve the overall objective of extirpating the "life force" of the Russian people. That this was deliberate is indicated by a number of ordinances like the one cited previously of forbidding the transfer of food from Ukraine to Byelorussia. In the May 2, 1941, instructions attending the formation of Göring's *Wirtschaftsstab Ost*, the rules laid down were that "The war can be pursued only if ... the entire German Armed Forces can be fed at the expense of Russia and thereby tens of millions of men will undoubtedly starve to death if we take away all we need from the country" (Dallin 1957, 39). And again as in all other German depredations in the East the behavior of individual soldiers aggravated the plight of the Russian populace. For the troops collectively and singly robbed the civilians of any crumbs and leftovers still in their possession. The OKW order that no German soldier be prosecuted for crimes committed against civilians launched the process; and the individual soldier improved on it without a second thought or a shred of pity.

While the civilian population — particularly in the larger cities— was dying by the tens of thousands from hunger, dystrophy and attendant epidemics, an even graver loss of life resulted from the simple butchery perpetrated on the population by the SD, police units and army troops alike. Ten days after Göring's "starvation" decree had been promulgated came one from führer headquarters. Issued on May 13 it contained inter alia the order that, "all irregulars" are ... to be executed" and that "collective measures are to be taken against localities from which attacks occur" (Schulte, 321–3). The above guidelines were applied usually under the guise of antipartisan warfare. Russian partisans were made up of two major groupings. One, dating back to the first summer of the war, consisted of Red Army soldiers cut off from their units by the rapid advance of the German troops or caught in the kesselschlachten. In small groups or singly they took to the woods and the remote countryside trying to avoid capture. The others, organized either locally or directed from Moscow, consisted of bona fide guerrillas engaged in sabotage and intelligence who did not come into their own until 1942. All these men either lived off the land or frequented the isolated villages to solicit or steal food after which they would retreat to their haunts. These partisan groups sprouted mostly in the forests and marshes of Byelorussia. Some of them permanently occupied large tracts of the remote countryside. In an attempt to eradicate the partisans, army troops together with SD and police units from the rear banded together to sweep the areas suspected of harboring them. As is the case with guerrillas most of the time they eluded their pursuers, leaving behind only traces of their existence and of course the villages and hamlets they once roamed. Unable to pin down these bands the Germans wreaked their vengeance on the inhabitants left behind. It thus became an established routine that across the entire area the partisans had evacuated dozens of villages were burned to the ground and the peasants— often enough the women and children included — were massacred. The only profit of this collective killing was that upon return to base the troops claimed the civilians as partisans killed in battle. In reports compiled after such sweeps one reads German-partisan kill ratios of the order of 100 or 1,000 to one, an extraordinary achievement in combating guerrillas. Thus the 207th Infantry Division in Byelorussia in one month shot 10,431 "partisans" for the loss of two of their soldiers; and when the sleds of the 12 ID struck mines all the male inhabitants of the nearest village were shot and the village burned down (Overy 1997, 181; Bartov, 120). Occasionally the reports were frank enough to state that so many Russians were executed in reprisal. These antipartisan operations were all under army command even when they employed SD and police units. In the cities roundups occurred daily with groups of civilians executed for spying, sabotage,

A street scene during the siege of Leningrad, 1941–43. (From *The Russian War 1941–1945* by Daniela Mrazkova and Vladimir Remes copyright ©1975 by Daniela Mrazkova and Vladimir Remes. Used by permission of Dutton, a division of Penguin Group [USA] Inc.)

shirking work, trying to escape, or as one order specified for a "cross look" at a German soldier. The largest killings in this category occurred under the hostage system. The orders from the OKH were unique in their sadistic intent. "For the life of one German soldier," the orders read, "a death sentence of from 50 to 100 'communists' must be generally deemed commensurate. The means of execution must increase the deterrent effect." The firing squads were instructed "to aim below the waist of the executed hostages ... and as when children are present such persons may escape death ... [they] should then be dispatched by hand by the officer in charge" (Clark, 153).

Another cause of widespread civilian loss of life was deprivation of the most rudimentary means of survival in the fierce climate and brutal conditions of wartime Russia. The most cruel instances of this treatment occurred in winter, in particular during the extraordinarily cold winter of 1941-42. Without the slightest hesitation Germans threw occupants out of their homes letting whole families roam the frozen wastes to slowly freeze to death. When retreating, or for other convenient reasons, they set peasant huts on fire, dooming the people to a slow death. Being short of proper clothing that first winter the soldiers stripped the peasants of their boots and clothing, no longer fussing about lice and infections. They would dismantle houses to build themselves shelters and dugouts and sometimes just for fuel. These acts did not constitute pilferage but death sentences.

As it fought the Red Army the Ostheer did not forget the caveat that this was a war of extermination. Consequently a disproportionate number of casualties during combat consisted of civilians. Of course, the Luftwaffe was an old hand at it, a practice going back to Warsaw, Rotterdam, Belgrade and numerous other cities. But there was much more to it in the East. Given that the Luftwaffe's days of glory had dimmed, here the role of butchers was taken over by the army. All extermination techniques employed throughout Russia — induced starvation, exposure to the elements, and mass killings— were applied to the Russian cities caught in the fighting. The only distinction one can make is that in place of execution battalions the tools used were artillery and air bombardments employed for no particular military profit. The most notorious case, as is well known, was that of Leningrad (St. Petersburg). A city of over 3 million inhabitants was by Hitler's order deliberately besieged rather than taken and then methodically destroyed. During the long siege, 1,000 days by one reckoning, shorter or longer by others, the city was starved, frozen out, shelled by artillery and raided from the air. During the siege agents from Einsatzgruppe A were sent across the lines to examine the destruction which prompted Heydrich to write to Himmler on October 20, 1944, that what was needed was a more "massive use of incendiary and blast explosives" (Müller, 161). As one writer describes it "Leningrad resembled some prehistoric mastadon, frozen in its tracks, in darkness, stillness, and falling snow ... with thousands of corpses lying in the streets, on the embankments, and in the houses" (Goure, 219). In one month, April 1942, over 100,000 corpses were buried in mass graves. For nearly three years Leningrad starved and froze while from the German lines fire and steel rained down on the dying city. The result was 1.5 million dead. Some grim statistics noted that for infants less than one year old the death rate was 75 percent. The same fate had been scheduled for Moscow in 1941. When in March 1943 the Russians temporarily retook Kharkov they found an empty city; a quarter million people had perished during the 15 months of German occupation, 80,000 of them due to starvation (Overy 1997, 168), with the rest either scattered or carted off to Germany. Minsk upon liberation in 1944 looked like Hiroshima, as did dozens of other cities.

In dealing with the German practices in the East, particularly when it comes to outright killings of the civilians and "hostages," it should be clear that the bulk of these acts had never been documented or even reported to the perpetrators' superiors. Much of the evidence that did exist had been either deliberately or otherwise lost. What really transpired lies buried in the forests and ravines of the Russian hinterland where the killings took place and they are silent; they are also buried in the memories of the German soldiers and administrators that had trampled across Russia — their numbers when including rotations and replacements being 6, 7, 8 million?— and they too remained silent. But the extent of their heinous activities is attested well enough by the toll it took on the Russian people. The Soviets had talked of 20 million; during Gorbachev's perestroika this had risen to 27 million. With the release of wartime archives following the demise of the Soviet Union, the number of Russian dead has now grown to 50 million, more than one-quarter of the total population (*New York Times*, 2/21/04). This includes the millions of lives lost on the Russian side due to starvation and exhaustion caused by the ongoing war. In the grim task of "rounding off" these statistics it seems that after subtracting the 12–15 million fallen Russian soldiers, the civilian death toll due to the German invasion was close to 35 million people.

• CHAPTER 20 •

The Russian POWs

The next chapter relates the Germans' deed of murdering all the Jews of Europe under their domination which in scale and thoroughness constitutes the greatest mass slaughter in human history. The killing of the Russian POWs is next in scale to that perpetrated on the Jews.

In the first six months of the war the Germans captured 3.35 million Russian soldiers; the AGM alone took 1.4 million, the AGS close to a million and the AGN the least, 84,000 (Streit, 83). By the end of 1942 the total number had risen to 5 million, and by the time the war ended it stood at 5.73 million. The treatment of these masses of soldiery was, of course, a function of Hitler's scheme of making the Russian continent part of a gargantuan reich, after the partial extermination and enslavement of its 190 million inhabitants. But there was an extra dose of attention given to the captured soldiers as they were young men, the source of the country's "life force." So in addition to the general guidelines about the treatment of the natives there flowed both an overt and covert stream of directives about how to treat the millions of conscripts and the result, as stated, was, excepting the Jews, a crime exceeding all other German abominations perpetrated during World War II.

One can start with the commissar order in which the Ostheer was ordered to kill upon capture all Politruks and Communist functionaries. The commissar order, dated June 6, had been promulgated by the OKH and reads, in part, "In the struggle against Bolshevism we must not assume that the enemy's conduct will be based on principles of humanity or of international law…. To show consideration to these elements … or to act in accordance with international rules of war is wrong. As a matter of principle they will be shot at once whether captured during battle or otherwise" (Kershaw 2000, 357–8). If this were all — as the German generals kept claiming — their record of criminality would have been trivial, and the losses among the prisoners would have been in the thousands instead of millions. But the Ostheer's intent and practices had little in common with this one category of captured men. It aimed, instead, at the entire population of Russian POWs, a mass of humanity close to 6 million. A few months before Barbarossa started, on March 30, 1941, in a talk to the Ostheer's commanders and chiefs of staff, Hitler told them, "We must forget the notion of soldierly camaraderie. The Communist is never before a Kamerad nor is he after [capture] a Kamerad. We are here dealing with an extermination struggle [Vernichtungs-kampf]." On October 13, with winter at the doorstep, he made sure that the exterminations continued by saying, "We used to say 'let's take prisoners' but now we think, 'What are we to do with all these prisoners?'" adding on January 23 that "I see no other solution but extermination," and he added, "Why should we look at a Jew other than if he were a Russian POW?" (Hitler 1953, 45, 193).

The administration of prisoner affairs and of the POW camps lay in the hands of the army. The army's quartermaster general, Eduard Wagner, was responsible for provisioning the Ostheer as well as the prisoner camps. The man running the whole POW camp system was Gen. Hermann Reinecke, who was part of the OKW. The split of jurisdiction was arranged so that in the theater of operation and in the rear areas the OKH was in charge; in the interior zones the OKW ruled. Thus in the early stages of captivity, at the front, in the collection centers, in the rear and during the long marches to permanent camps in the interior army group commanders and their subordinate officers were in charge of the prisoners. The camp commandants, appointed by Wagner, were reserve officers who had served under the kaiser. They were mostly middle-aged or elderly men; a 1941 survey showed an average age of 56 (Schulte, 310–11). In the interior zones—the reichskommissariats, the GG, and in reich territory—*Wehrmachtbefehlhabers* were in charge of the camps. They had precedence over the civilian authorities (under Lohse, Koch, etc.) in matters relating to military affairs but had to cooperate on all "political" issues.

The torment of a Russian prisoner of war began the moment he was apprehended and continued over a track of thousands of miles until for most of them death terminated it all. Immediately at the front thousands of them were shot out of hand by the German soldiers right after capture and their numbers never even turned up in the POW statistics. The bulk of prisoners came from the mass surrenders and the vast encirclements that characterized the first summer of the war. When officers eager to gain intelligence from the prisoners asked that the shootings be stopped the soldiers ignored them and went on with the sport. Even deserters weren't spared. In the rear areas no provisions had been made for housing or feeding them so that starvation, thirst and exposure set in at the very beginning. Even if there was water in the neighborhood the men were not permitted to fetch it. Kept in the open they were exposed to the fierce summer heat or freezing temperatures in the winter. The wounded could be treated only by Russian doctors who, if available at all, had neither instruments, bandages, nor medicines; no German doctor was allowed near them. At these collection centers behind the front Einsatzkommandos would arrive to launch their "selections" after which thousands of commissars, "Communists" and Jews would be separated out and executed outside the compounds. The next chapter of a POW's nightmare were the marches to the rear. Mountains of prisoners, hidden in a wall of moving dust, hundreds of thousands of them, were driven for weeks under the scorching heat of the 1941 summer, deprived of rest, food, and water. When the local population offered bread they were driven off at gunpoint. The attempts to deliver food to the marching prisoners were made mostly by women and youngsters. When threats were not effective enough, guards fired into the crowd, killing and maiming. When the peasant women took to tossing parcels from a distance, the soldiers stomped on and destroyed the food. The guards, army soldiers, shot anyone who fell out of the ranks, anyone who stumbled, anyone who impeded the march, anyone "suspicious looking," anyone "ready" to escape, or just for practice shooting. Thus on a march from Smolensk to the rear 5,000 men were gunned down before they reached camp (Fugate, 281).The empty freight trains or trucks going to the rear were forbidden to transport Russian prisoners, the official reason being that they would be infected with lice or disease, or simply Russian filth. After week-long marches the survivors were brought into camps. These were vast open spaces surrounded by strands of barbed wire where tens if not hundreds of thousands of men were dumped on the ground and left to linger for months with perhaps a watery turnip soup a day for nutrition. The grounds onto which the prisoners were dumped were soon bare of all grass, needles, weeds,

A minor German atrocity on the Kerch Peninsula in the Crimea. (From *The Russian War 1941–1945* by Daniela Mrazkova and Vladimir Remes copyright ©1975 by Daniela Mrazkova and Vladimir Remes. Used by permission of Dutton, a division of Penguin Group [USA] Inc.)

all trees denuded of bark. Mass starvation would set in and assisted by sickness, epidemics and executions by the guards and the visiting SD, it soon produced a harvest of thousands of dead each day. When winter came the frost killed off those still alive, now huddling in dugouts or coops made of tarpaper, until by the dawn of the new year the camps would usually be empty.

An official army report about one camp containing 11,000 prisoners stated that "The prisoners receive nothing to drink. When the water carrier brings the water for the kitchen a ferocious brawl always breaks out which can often only be ended by shooting … hunger revolts with incessant shooting are also the order of the day…. Lacking latrines the prisoners are compelled to relieve themselves on the spot." The report noted that this was in an area which afforded accommodation, cooking implements and running water, deliberately left unexploited (Bartov, 195). In a camp near Rzhev up to November the daily death rate was 2 percent; in mid–December this rose tenfold to 20 percent (Schulte, 200). In Stalag 307 near Deblin there were at the end of 1941 100,000 prisoners. In a short period 80,000 of them died. In Stalag 344 near Opole where 200,000 prisoners lived in dugouts, with 700 people in each pit, 40,000 died in the camp and 60,000 were worked to death. In the GG of the 360,000 prisoners brought there over the summer 293,000 died by the end of winter (Streit, 134). The sight of what was transpiring in the camps was such that the guards had to be given special allotments of alcohol to be able to carry on with their tasks.

The dying was on such a scale that it prompted Rosenberg of the Ostministerium, who contrary to the führer was interested primarily in exploitation of the East, to write on February 28, 1942, to Keitel, "The fate of the Soviet prisoners of war is a tragedy of the greatest size. Of the 3.6 million prisoners only several hundred thousand are today fit to work. A considerable proportion has died of hunger or due to bad weather.... In the Soviet territories the local population was willing to deliver food for the benefit of the POWs.... In most cases they were prohibited the delivery of food.... Statements could be heard 'The more prisoners will die the better for us'" (Datmer, 218–19).

The Soviet prisoners were also subjected to ingenious sadistic practices. At intervals the men were branded. Some Germans invented a special Russenbrot to feed them, the contents of which can only be imagined. When it was decided to use some prisoners for work it was often mooted to increase their rations by shooting or poisoning the rest. As with the civilian populations, the Germans stripped the prisoners of their jackets, boots and hats leaving them to freeze. They were used for clearing minefields by making them walk across them. Before Auschwitz went into operation the poison gas Zyklon B was successfully tested on a sample of 900 Russian prisoners (Streit, 25).

These practices frequently rebounded to the detriment of the Germans themselves as when the front shootings deprived the staffs of intelligence and dissuaded desertion from the Soviet side. The induced epidemics among the prisoners often spread to the army and the civilians around the camps. None of this altered the by now routine treatment of the Russians. On the contrary, it was from time to time reinforced. In an open letter to the *Soldaten der Ostfront*—before Operation Typhoon — Hitler reminded them that the enemy was not composed of soldiers but animals (Schulte, 191). Jodl on September 26 added that from now on any Russian soldier cut off in the rear after combat be treated as a partisan and shot. And Heydrich extended the commissar order to include state officials, leading personalities of industry and, generally, "the intelligentsia" (Streit, 91). Accordingly the number of "commissars" eventually became so huge that in May 1944 a tally of executions performed by the SD Einsatzkommados yielded 490,000 men selected from the OKH and 540,000 from OKW areas—a total of 1 million executed prisoners (Streit, 105).

In the spring of 1942 a shortage of manpower in Germany prompted several economic agencies to start utilizing Russian prisoners for work. This meant lifting the ban on bringing the Russians into the reich, originally forbidden by the führer. This coincided with the utilization by the Ostheer of some of the prisoners as coolies, called hiwis. By 1943 large numbers of them found themselves on German soil. There they were kept separated from the POWs of the Western countries, while a number of them were shipped outright to concentration camps. The condition of the men arriving from the East is described by one French POW: "The Russians arrived in rows five-by-five holding each other by the arms as none of them could walk by themselves.... The color of their faces wasn't gray, it was green. Almost all squinted as they lacked the strength to focus their sight. They fell by rows, five men at a time ... of the 10,000 who arrived in November by February only 2,500 were alive" (Datmer, 236). Following the July 20 attentat the administration of the POW system was transferred to Himmler, a fit finale to that gruesome tale. Toward the end of the war most of the POWs in the concentration camps of Auschwitz, Bergen-Belsen, Lublin, and other such places were gassed to prevent them from falling into the hands of the Red Army (Streit, 221).

Most writers on the subject cite a number of 3.5 million dead out of 5.7 million Russians captured during the war. Of the 3.5 million, 600,000 were executed by army troops during their common "cleansing" of the assembly areas behind the front (Schulte, 181). In

Table 20-1
Death Rate of Russian Prisoners of War in German Captivity

Period	Total No. Captured	Increment	Alive in POW Camps	Died in Captivity
		In Millions		
End '41 from June 22	3.35 (in 6 months)	3.35 (in 6 months)	1.16 (after 6 months)	2.19 (after 6 months)
End '42	5.00	1.65	1.50	3.50 (after 18 months)
End '43	5.60	0.60	0.82	3.50 to 4†
End '44	5.73	0.13	0.086 (+0.650)*	As above

*Number of POWs employed in Germany as slave laborers
†Includes estimated number of Russian soldiers killed upon capture
Based on Streit: 245

May 1944 the OKW provided the following tabulation: Of the 5.2 million POWs 2 million died of "wastage"; 1 million were shot either by the troops or the SD; and 0.3 million disappeared (Fugate, 281). For the entire war the numbers cited are: 2 million died in the military camps; 1 million died in the rear areas; a quarter million in transit; and a half million while in the GG or in Germany (Calvocarossi, 278). Of the 77 Red Army generals taken by the Germans 26 died in captivity (Maslov, 222). Table 20-1 provides a summary where the cited 4 million figure includes an estimated number of prisoners killed immediately upon capture, never accounted for in the POW tallies. Thus the loss of life of Russian soldiers in captivity is of the order of 60 percent. Compared with this, the mortality rate for all Western prisoners was 3.5 percent; for the French, 1.58 percent; the British, 1.15 percent; and the Americans, 0.3 percent. As a side note, the toll among the Russian war prisoners under the kaiser, also in the millions, was 5.4 percent — under Hitler 10 times as high.

• CHAPTER 21 •

The Final Solution

There is an enormous literature on the history of the eradication of Europe's Jewry by the Germans. It contains, in addition to the facts, a plethora of spiritual, mythological, sociopsychic and other such elaborations. All these commentaries have little to do with the history of the event. What happened is of such an extent and totality that it constitutes history's greatest mass killing committed on the most defenseless and innocent of people. It has been impossible to name it so that it has been called variously Tremendum, Immanitas, War, Shoah, Holocaust, and others. A neologism was coined for the occasion — genocide. But no sooner had this gained currency when it was immediately corrupted by calling the Russian war in Chechnya or what the Serbs did in Bosnia genocide. So there is nothing left but to call it what the Germans did — the Final Solution.

Given the profusion of works on the subject what will be offered here is the bare outlines of the deed. To give an idea of what transpired one would have to go and stand alongside the tens of thousands of ordinary human beings lined up along the execution ditches, watch a battalion of helmeted Germans fire their guns and witness the gore and screams and convulsions as they were being mowed down into the pits; or to peer through peepholes the Germans had installed in the gas chambers and watch masses of humanity writhing and choking in the process of being asphyxiated and later follow the bulldozers as they plowed a mountain of corpses into the crematoria. But this would amount to imitating the German soldiers in the East taking photographs of the executions because it was all *sehenswürdig* — worth seeing. All this will be left out of the accounting here. What will be done is look at the Final Solution not from the Jewish or human angle but from the German viewpoint — that is to say, what the Germans decided to do with the Jews of Europe, how they went about implementing it, and the extraordinary results they had achieved, unique in recorded history. One has to stress an additional point. The mass slaughter was done not in the heat of combat, not out of passion, not even out of hatred; and not for any material gain. The opposite was true; it was done against their self-interest and with great harm to their war effort. One of the more straightforward books on these events is that by Goldhagen. Its main thesis is that what made it possible for the Germans to perpetrate this deed was their unique kind of anti–Semitism which he called "eliminational." But it is quite clear that the anti–Semitism of the Poles, Ukrainians, Rumanians, Croats and others superseded by far that of the Germans. There had not been a pogrom in Germany for centuries and the one on Kristallnacht was staged, not by the populace, but by the government. But all the critics who pounced on Goldhagen's book did the Germans no favor and the German critics would have been kinder to their kin had they let the thesis stand. For this raises the specter that even not hating the Jews the Germans were capable of murdering them simply because they were told to do so, then had they been told to murder all Albanians or Belgians they would have done so. In other words, all they needed was an order and the job would have been done — as they had nearly done so to the Russians. There is, though, one qualification to this dismal conclusion. What helped them in murdering specifically Jews was their Christianity. For in the Christian catechism the Jews had been branded as deicides and condemned for the rest of history.

* * *

Hitler had started World War II partly in order to be able to achieve one of his life's basic goals, the biological eradication of the Jewish people. Whenever he said, as he often did, that he must rush for no one else would be capable of performing what he intended to do "for the German people" what he had foremost in mind was his Final Solution. Thus one cost to Germany of its leader's kink was the premature start of the war. He knew that without a war it would be impossible to carry it out. Yet it would be misleading to link the killing of the Jews with the ongoing war. The war was a necessary screen for its implementation but the deed itself was above and beyond it. It was an autochtonous project that could be carried on best under the umbrella of a Europe occupied by Germany. And its origins go back to days preceding even *Mein Kampf.*

There has been sufficient mention of Hitler's obsession with Jews. In a number of speeches he announced his intention to exterminate — *ausrotten* — all the Jews in case they provoked another world war. This he had done in his January 30 speeches over three consecutive years, 1939, 1941 and 1942; in his new year speech of 1943 and again in February that year; and in numerous pronouncements during his table talks. But in view of what will be told in this chapter it needs to be stressed that this compulsion goes back not only to the murk of his mind but to the very murk of his growing up; and that as extreme as his *Ausrottung* speeches sound they pale in comparison with his inner hallucination on the subject. In 1922 the journalist Josef Hell asked Hitler what he would do with the Jews once he succeeded in taking power. In a state of extreme agitation Hitler answered as follows: "My first and foremost task would be the annihilation of the Jews. As soon as I have the power to do so I will have gallows built in rows ... as many as traffic allows. Then the Jews will be hanged indiscriminately, and they will remain hanging until they stink; they will hang there as long as the principles of hygiene permit. As soon as they have been untied, the next batch will be strung up, and so on down the line, until the last Jew in Munich has been exterminated. Other cities will follow suit, precisely in this fashion, until all Germany has been completely cleansed of Jews" (Fleming, 17). Here we have a perfect cameo of Hitler in his facet number three.

Aside from the diplomatic and political fallout of his racial policies the killings had a direct impact on the military operations on the eastern front. On November 12, 1941, in the midst of the most severe transportation crisis during the battle of Moscow Feldmarschall Bock noted in his diary, "At the same time I received a report that several trains carrying Jews from Germany are being sent to the AG's rear areas" (Bock, 356). At the beginning of December AOK 11 supplied trucks, drivers and fuel to Ohlendorf's EG D to enable him to execute the Jews of Simferopol. This author, at work on the railroad near the Bug, watched in puzzlement as German troops and equipment were stranded along the tracks for lack of rolling stock during the height of the summer offensive in July 1942 while several trains carrying deported Austrian Jews passed the station on their way east (Pinkus,

71). When Lohse of the Ostland objected that the EG was taking outskilled laborers from his camps for extermination, which would jeopardize the economy behind the front, he was told by the Ostministerium that "in principle economic consideration must be overlooked in the solution of the problem." Likewise when Kube in Minsk objected that the killing of artisans would strike a blow at the well-being of the troops he, too, was told to cease his objections. Both he and Lohse were informed that this is "the Führer's wish" (Dallin, 206).

Hitler's intent and determination to eradicate all ethnic Jews did not seem obvious in the early period of the war. For one thing Hitler's plan embraced the totality of Europe's Jews, by his experts' count some 11 million. During the 1939–40 period all he had in his hands, including Czech and German Jews, was some 3 million souls. He had to await future acquisitions. After the conquest of Russia, when the Baltics, Rumania and Hungary are included, he would have in his hands some 80 percent of the continent's Jews (see Table 21-1). This would not be realized till the midsummer of 1941. Still, already in 1939 preparations for the eventual deed were set in motion. We have seen the order that Heydrich issued on September 21 (Chapter 6) that in preparation for "the final goal the Jews in Poland should be concentrated in localities close to major railroad lines." There seems in the history of the Final Solution a train of thought on Hitler's part similar to his surreptitious way of achieving his geopolitical goals. The territory he was bent on usurping and which he later in fact invaded — Poland, Russia, Rumania, Hungary — were also countries that contained the bulk of Jews, 80 percent of the total. So while waiting to implement his scheme he let float a bit of *Dichtung* to deflect attention from the preparations for the real thing. The most known of these deceptions was the Madagascar scheme. On May 25, 1940 Himmler said, "I hope that the concept of Jews will be completely extinguished by the possibility of large scale emigration of all Jews to Africa or some other colony." Ostensibly the Germans were serious on resettling the Jews to some tropical haven. Particularly eager to float that idea was the crowd around Ribbentrop. This reached its peak with the French collapse when on July 3, 1940, the Foreign Ministry proposed to include the Madagascar plan in the peace treaty with France. Frank in a July 12 speech announced that upon his request not to have more Jews dumped into the GG the führer informed him that Madagascar was being considered as a solution (Docs.,Yad Vashem, 198, 216–8). Later on when Franco took a beneficial interest in Sephardic Jews, there was talk about settling them in Morocco.

Hitler let all these speculations hover about — like his presumed intention of invading England, Malta, Gibraltar, etc. — while he himself kept silent, only from time to time reminding the world that if they wouldn't let him win, all Jews would be dead. But while on the surface not much seemed to be happening in the first two years of the war, this was a delusion. While Heydrich's ukase to concentrate all Jews near railroad lines could be interpreted as a preparation for a trip to Madagascar it should have raised some geographical questions for if indeed Madagascar, wouldn't ports instead of railroads be a more practical place for the Jews? No one asked such questions, then or later. But the implementation of Heydrich's order started as soon as it was promulgated. The first ghetto was established on October 28, 1939 in the town of Piotrkow, 40 miles south of Lodz. Lodz itself was cramped into a ghetto on May 1, 1940; the order for it had actually been issued as early as December. On the 15th of November the biggest of ghettos was set up in Warsaw. A wall was erected around its periphery into which were also driven all neighboring small settlements as well as deportees from the western annexed territories, a population close to

Table 21-1
The Death Toll of European Jewry in the Final Solution*

Country	Jewish Population in '39	Deaths	%
Poland	3,350,000	up to 3,000,000	90
USSR	3,020,000	over 700,000	23
Romania	800,000	270,000	34
Czechoslovakia	315,000	260,000	83
Hungary	400,000	over 180,000	45
Lithuania	145,000	up to 130,000	90
Germany	240,000	over 120,000	50
Netherlands	140,000	over 100,000	71
France	270,000	75,000	28
Latvia	95,000	70,000	74
Yugoslavia	75,000	60,000	80
Greece	74,000	60,000	80
Austria	60,000	over 50,000	83
Belgium	90,000	24,000	27
Italy†	50,000	9,000	18
Estonia	4,500	2,000	44
Norway	2,000	1,000	50
Luxemburg	3,000	1,000	33
Total	9,190,000	5,100,000	

Note: Borders refer to 1937. Converts to Christianity are included, and refugees are counted with the countries from which they were deported.

*The statistics for 1939 refer to prewar borders, and postwar frontiers have been used for 1945. The figure of 80,000 for Germany includes 60,000 displaced persons.

†Includes Rhodes.

From Hilberg, R. *The Destruction of Europe's Jews*, 1985 edition. By permission of Yale University Press.

300,000. Anyone found outside the ghetto there and throughout the GG was shot. The establishment of the ghettos had a purpose beyond the need to enclose and concentrate the Jews for future deportation. It was already meant to serve as part of the Final Solution. With the jamming of hundreds of thousands of people into deliberately confined areas and depriving them of all contact with the rest of the country, leaving them without food, fuel or medicines, what had been set in motion here was a process of decimation to ease the future task of physical killing. The induced starvation, epidemics and death from freezing paralleled the methods the Germans used to decimate the Russian civilian population. Over the next year or so, particularly over the very harsh winter of 1941-42, anywhere from 10 percent to 15 percent of the ghetto populations throughout the country died of hunger, cold and disease — an induced death of some half a million people. In addition Jews were taken by the hundreds of thousands to forced labor camps where they slaved on dredging rivers, paving roads and all kinds of needed and unneeded projects, where they were over-worked, flogged, starved and beaten to death as a daily routine. Throughout the occupied territories gendarmes, policemen, Arbeitsamt personnel, clerks, soldiers and visiting Volks— and Reichsdeutsche — indulged in an orgy of sadistic antics that required effort and inventiveness for the variety of torture and killings committed.

The establishment of the ghettos dovetailed with regulations forbidding Jews from emigrating from anywhere under German rule to anywhere outside of it. From the ostensible hatred of Jews and the resulting eagerness to get rid of them, all at once this transformed itself into a convulsive need to hold onto them whatever the cost. The first ordinance to that effect, dated June 24, 1941, came from Heydrich to Ribbentrop in which he said that the "entire problem of the approximately 3.5 million Jews in the territories under German domination can no longer be solved by emigration. A territorial final solution (*Endlösung*) therefore becomes necessary." This decision must have been taken early in the year because there is a State Department document dated March 28 which takes note of the fact that Jews in the GG were no longer permitted to emigrate (Garland, 64). When on February 2, 1941, the Madagascar Plan was mentioned to Hitler, his interlocutor recalled him saying that, "He has now other ideas, not very kind ones, to be sure" (Lukacs, 131). This was applied not only to the general Jewish population under German jurisdiction but also all of Europe's neutral and Allied countries. Thus on October 24, 1942, the Italians offered to take in Jews from occupied Croat territory but the Croatian government had to inform the Italians that "it [Croatia] was bound by an agreement with the German Reich not to meet such requests." Moreover Mackensen was told that in the future he was to reject any similar demands by the Italian authorities. When on December 12 Antonescu had agreed for payment to let 80,000 Jews emigrate to Palestine Killinger told the Rumanians that Berlin wouldn't permit it. Luther from RSHA cabled the embassy in Bucharest that such a refusal was mandatory as it "represents an intolerable PARTIAL solution of the Jewish Question" (Garland, Docs. NG-2366 & NG-2200). Likewise Franco's scheme of bringing some of the Sephardic Jews to Morocco was rejected.

* * *

June 1941 was an apocalyptic month for two national communities in Europe, the Russians and the Jews. It was the month when the long-conspired onslaught on Russia was launched that would bring with it the deaths of some 50 million or more of the eastern peoples; and it was the month that launched the Final Solution that would result in the killing of 6 million Jews; and perhaps also for the Yugoslavs who, with the start of Tito's rebellion in that period, would suffer the loss of 1.5 million people. Thus though it was France and England that had declared war on Hitler the resulting cataclysm would be inflicted on the East.

In the spring of 1941 Hitler had set the date for the start of Barbarossa for May 15; due to the Balkan campaign this had to be shifted to June 22, a Sunday, as usual with Hitler a weekend. The Final Solution was to begin sometime early in the year — the exact date is unknown but by circumstantial evidence in March, with some giving the date as March 21, the start of *Frühling* (springtime). Several facts point to this as accurate, among them that on March 26 Frank told his subordinates that in a recent talk with the führer he was promised that the GG would be made *judenrein* in the near future (Gross, 73). Another is that it was in March 1941 that Adolf Eichmann was appointed head of office IV-B-4a, the section dealing with Jewish affairs. Sometime that March Hitler had called in Himmler and said that he wanted him to start the implementation of the Final Solution. This was an oral order and he wanted no written piece of paper spelling this order out, neither now nor ever. It was to start with the opening of the invasion of Russia and it was to start with the killing of all the Jews on the territory of the Soviet Union. Including the Baltic states, eastern Poland and Bessarabia-Bucovina, all now part of the USSR, this amounted to an order to execute 5 million people, complete, without exceptions. At a somewhat later date, but still during that spring of 1941, Hitler gave the order to extend the executions to the remainder of Europe — north, west and south — likewise without any exceptions, a total of 9 million people. The modalities of the executions he left to his underlings.

Himmler passed on Hitler's order about the Russian Jews to Heydrich and he, in parallel to the army's General Staff, set up execution troops to kill an estimated 5 million people to be found on Soviet territory (including the annexed areas). The name give to these outfits was *Einsatzgruppen* (EG) which means task forces. Four such groups were formed. In parallel with the three Army Groups (AG) these were named A for the North, B for the Center, C for the South. The fourth group, D, was assigned to extreme south Ukraine and the Crimea and when in 1942 the Germans occupied the Caucasus they were in charge of that region, too. The four groups were of battalion strength each, a total of 3,000 men and with rotations they counted 6,000. Another 38 police battalions participated in the killings raising the number to 19,000 men. Three SS brigades in Russia also took part, boosting over the years 1941–43 the total to an army of 25,000 men. Prominently the *Ordnungspolizei* — traffic cops — were busy on the program. They were made up of Germans unfit for army service with no ideological training or SS background; from 131,000 in 1939 they grew by 1943, due to work in the East, to 310,000 strong (Goldhagen, 182). In the operational area the EGs also employed local constabularies made up of Latvian, Lithuanian and Ukrainian nationals. They were also assisted now and then by army personnel. The EGs were subdivided into Kommandos and *Sonder-* or *Teil-kommandos*. Their leaders were bureaucrats who had officiated over the various departments of the RSHA. Three of the four early top leaders of the EGs were a Dr. Franz Stahlecker, a Dr. Otto Rasch and a Dr. Otto Ohlendorf, the latter a doctor of law. The middle ranking commanders also had an educated background. Highly qualified academics, civil servants, lawyers, a Protestant pastor, and even an opera singer were among them (Kershaw 2000, 382). The EGs started training at a special school at Prezsch, northeast of Leipzig, where Heydrich schooled them from time to time about what the führer expected of them.

There was one incident when a subordinate commander of the EG, a Dr. Bradfish, inquired of Himmler in April 1941 who had given the order to kill all Jews. According to Bradfish, "Himmler answered in a sharp tone that these orders had come from Hitler, the supreme Führer of the German government and that they had the force of law" (Fleming, 51). Not only that but the führer took a direct interest in the workings of the EGs. On August 1, 1941, Gestapo Chief Müller sent the following order to the heads of the EGs: "The Führer is to be kept informed continually from here about the work of the EGs in the east." Later on Himmler frequently met with the führer to provide both details and a summary the Final Solution.

The logistics of the EGs — ammunition, food, supplies, amenities — were attended to by the Army's QG. On occasion Army troops either demanded or actively assisted in the executions. This cooperation ranged from the very top of the military hierarchy to the ordinary soldier. On June 14 the QM informed the Ostheer that behind each Army Group there would be two EG Kommandos and behind each army one Sonderkommando. Some of the execution squads moved together with the forward units, often at the request of the army commanders. So the killing of the populations followed immediately upon the capture of a hamlet or town. Thus Sonderkommando 1a followed the forward units of AOK 18 which took Libau on June 27 and already in the next days it indulged in a mass killing at Scoudas east of Libau (Streit, 110) In Zhitomir the first panzers that entered town were followed by thee vehicles of EG. Cooperation was particularly good with Hoepner, the man who, like Nebe, who commanded one of the EGs, was scheduled to be a leader of the New Germany had the putsch against Hitler succeeded. Strongest of all was the intimacy at the southern front where the bulk of Jews lived. On October 10 Reichenau issued a poisonous order to the soldiers against the barbarous East in which he said, "the soldiers must understand the need for hard, though just treatment meted out to the Jewish subhumans." This followed an earlier proclamation by Manstein who on September 17 announced to the troops that, "Jewry constitutes the middleman between our enemy in the rear and the still fighting remnants of the Red Army…. The Jewish-Bolshevist system must once and for all be exterminated (*ausgerotted*)." Generals Hoth, Stülpnagel, Wohler and others followed suit with lesser and stronger incitement against the true enemy of Germany (Streit, 110–15).

The spasm to eradicate any Jew anywhere was implemented by the execution squads with a zeal equal to Hitler's own derangement. During the offensive against Moscow when amid rain, snow and fierce Russian resistance the Germans took Kalinin on October 21 (though it would soon be lost) right on Reinhardt's heels came an EG *Sonderkommando* who, lacking the time to organize a proper execution, led the local Jews to a high cliff to dump them to their death into a ravine (Bross, 146). It was only when one of the victims grabbed two SS men and pulled them with him to their death that they requested gas vans from the rear to finish the job. *Sonderkommando* 4a in the south persisted in following the army all the way to Stalingrad in search of the few Jews there. The planning was meticulous, so that the killings were conducted from east to west lest the Russians recapture some territory.

The job the EGs performed was of a uniquely horrendous nature in both scale and form; it was unique in human history. Miles-long ditches were dug, the populations of whole towns from old men to infants lined up naked along the edges or piled sardine-like into the ditches while still alive, and killed at close range. The slaughter lasted for hours and days on end. After one town was emptied of people the Germans went to the next and the next. In between they ate three meals a day, wrote letters home to their parents and wives while outside their barrack windows the earth heaved with the blood and gases of a slaughtered nation.

As in training for any profession their leaders— the three doctors included — saw to it that men of the EGs slid into their routine without undue difficulty. At the beginning during June and early July they took out only young men. This was partly to give the impression that they were being taken to work but more importantly to "accommodate" themselves to the grisly task of later killing women and children, too. In eastern Poland and the western parts of the USSR they thus initially took from each hamlet or town anywhere from 1,000 to 5,000 men and executed them in the neighboring ravines and forests. But within a month or so they were ready to kill without regard to age or sex. Among the many colossal slaughters the most notorious is the one at Babi Yar where in the two days of September 29–30 the Germans executed 33,000 Kiev Jews. In a ravine called Drobitski Yar the EGs executed 22,000 Kharkov Jews (Temkin, 72). In October after Odessa fell to the Rumanian-German troops they killed a total of 36,000 people. In a place called Ponary they murdered 100,000 from Wilno and its environs. And so on and so on. In the first six months of their activity the EGs killed by shooting half a million Jews; in the two years of their operation in Russia they killed a million (Crankshaw, 164).

* * *

Soon after Hitler had ordered Himmler to launch the killing of Russian Jews, he ordered the extension of the Final Solution to all Jews within the reach of Germany's power, influence and coercion. This, too, was an oral directive but here there are written documents attesting to the initiation of the European program. The relevant document passed on from Göring to Heydrich — the chief implementer of the program for both east and west — is dated July 31, 1941 — and its key paragraph reads:

"As supplement to the task which was entrusted to you in the decree dated 24 January, 1941, namely to solve the Jewish Question by emigration and evacuation in a way which is the most favorable in connection with the conditions prevailing at the present, I herewith commission you to carry out all preparations with regard to organization, the material side and financial viewpoints for the final solution of the Jewish Question in those territories in Europe which are under German influence" (Garland, 19).

This order is preceded by an exchange indicating that the original Hitler directive came much earlier and may have been issued simultaneously with the start of EG operations in Russia. Already in June Heydrich had told Ribbentrop that "the Jewish problem cannot be settled anymore through immigration but must be a territorial solution." The reason that this went to Ribbentrop is, of course, that were emigration on the books, whether to Madagascar, Morocco or Devils Island, Ribbentrop as foreign minister would have been the chief negotiator for implementing it. Ribbentrop is thus relived of this burden, though a new one would soon be imposed on him — that of coercing Germany's allies into participation in the program. At the same time the future chief of Auschwitz, Rudolf Höss, was, according to his testimony in Nuremberg, called in to Himmler's office who, dismissing his adjutant, had said to him, "The Führer has ordered that the Jewish Question be solved once and for all and that we, the SS, are to implement the order…. I have earmarked Auschwitz for this purpose…. I have decided to entrust this task to you…. You will learn further details from Sturmbahnführer Eichmann…. After your talk with Eichmann you will immediately forward to me the plans for the projected installations…. Every Jew that we can lay our hands on is to be destroyed now during the war without exception" (Docs., Yad Vashem, 351).

The most known official preparation — and one unusual for the whole history of the Final Solution since otherwise everything was kept supremely secret — was the convening of the Wannsee Conference. This is often misread as the start of the extermination program; instead, as we have seen, it took place when the process had been in operation for over half a year with a million Jews already dead, half by direct execution and half from starvation and epidemics in the locked-up ghettos. What the conference amounted to was a mobilization of the entire state apparatus in Germany — the bureaucracy, transportation, diplomacy, etc. — toward the implementation of a program that had been in the works since September 1939 and in full execution since June 1941. The conference was convened on January 20, 1942, at the lakeside Wannsee on the western edge of Berlin. The participants included assistant secretaries of various ministries, the Nazi judge Freisler, representatives of the Four Year Plan, experts from the GG and others. Present also were Gestapo Chief Müller and Adolf Eichmann, now named special assistant for the final solution of the Jewish question, who took notes, later issued as the Wannsee Protocol. Presiding over this assembly was Reinhard Heydrich. The protocol issued on January 26 with a covering letter from Heydrich bears the title *Endlösung der Judenfrage* and contains the following points:

- Prohibition of further emigration for Jews.
- There are 11 million Jews in Europe to be handled.
- Jews will be displaced to the East where in one way or another they will disappear.
- Europe will be cleared of Jews from west to east.

Thirty copies of the document were distributed to the relevant agencies so that they could fulfill their part under the overall program.

In addition to this statewide alert Heydrich proceeded to develop the necessary tools for the essential part of the Final Solution — that is the physical method of killing, by his estimate, of 11 million people. This task he assigned to two men. One was Odilo Globocnik, a former gauleiter of Vienna and presently chief of police in Lublin. The other was Dieter Wisliceny, Eichmann's RSHA representative in Bratislava where since April 1940 he served as advisor on Jewish affairs to the Slovak government. The project of coming up with a system of extinguishing at one go 11 million lives was named Aktion Rheinhard.

As a preparation for 1942, the year scheduled for the elimination of Europe's Jews, the Germans extended the establishment of ghettos throughout the east. Overall the Germans created 400 ghettos in Poland alone; this in addition to over 1,000 forced labor camps and a network of 50 concentration camps with numerous satellites— all complementary institutions to the eradication of Europe's Jewry. By 1942 the bulk of the Jewish population in the East had been locked in ghettos and various other enclosures, the overstepping of which brought instant execution.

While still relying on the EGs to complete the annihilation of Russia's Jews the immensity of the task was such that the Germans had to look for more efficient ways of mass killing. One of the schemes they came up with was the gas vans. These were closed trucks or vans with the engine exhaust pumped into the interior packed with the condemned people. This proved unsatisfactory as in the throes of dying the victims soiled the interior of the vehicles. So while mobile gas vans were used in the first killing centers established by Aktion Reinhard the organizers— which included architects, landscape artists, chemists, physicians, scientists and other learned specialists— were looking for something that would measure up to the stupendous task ahead. What was decided upon was large permanent facilities with Zyklon B to be used as the killing gas.

Five such extermination factories were erected on the erstwhile territory of Poland. Two of these had existed as labor camps and they were transformed to serve the new function. These were Chelmno, in existence since the fall of 1941, which went into operation in December 1941. The other was Auschwitz, in existence since 1939 as a labor camp. It was now vastly expanded into nearby Birkenau to serve to the very end as the largest of the slaughterhouses; it was here in September 1941 that the 900 Russian prisoners were gassed as a test of its proper functioning. There were three newly established facilities. One was at Belzec, 20 miles northwest of Lwow finished by Christmas of 1941. The Jewish laborers that worked on it were the first to be killed there, and the first mass gassing of an arrived transport took place in March 1942. The second new facility was at Sobibor, 40 miles northeast of Lublin abutting the river Bug. The third facility was that of Treblinka, also on the Bug, 40 miles northeast of Warsaw. These locations were chosen for their proximity to large ghettos. There had been all along one other major facility, that of Majdanek, where executions had been taking place even prior to the official institution of the Final Solution. Next to Majdanek was the camp Trawniki where the operators of the gas chambers and the camp guards were trained for proper execution of their jobs. When fully operational these death factories were capable of the following daily killing rates: Chelmno—1,000; Treblinka — 6,000; Auschwitz —12,000 (Calvocarossi, 250–1).

Nineteen forty-two was the year when the bulk of Europe's Jews was murdered in the above five facilities. From all over the continent trains rushed to these centers into which as into a cosmic black hole an entire nation disappeared without a trace. The frenzy with which the EGs pursued the Jews in Russia extracting them from the smallest hamlet and from localities still under enemy fire was matched by the relentlessness with which the Eichmann establishment searched out Jews in the remotest corners of Europe. From remote little islands in the Aegean little packets of Jews were shipped out; from Norway two boats took away 900 Jews; from the Channel islands occupied by the Germans 20 Jews were deported — all of them to disappear in the maelstrom of

The empty town of Losice on August 22, 1942, after the Jews have been taken out for extermination.

destruction. The trains carrying the Jews to their deaths were classified as military transports and given the highest priority, often, as was related earlier, in preference to military needs. And the compulsiveness of getting at the surviving Budapest Jews as late as 1945 will be related later when with the enemy East and West already on German soil, Hitler shipped his best Panzer divisions to the Hungarian puszta to get at these survivors.

Throughout all of this Hitler, at his specific instructions, was kept updated on the rate and total count of the ongoing exterminations. This was in conformity with Müller's instructions of August 1, 1941, reported earlier. In December 1942, just at the tail end of the EGs' work in the East, Report No. 51 for the period of August 1 through November 1942 informed him that 362,311 Jews were executed. When in the summer of 1942 Hitler moved to Vinnitza to keep a hand on the Caucasus-Stalingrad offensive he had Himmler settle down in nearby Zhitomir and had a special 50 miles of road paved between the two headquarters so he could be kept informed on the progress of the war — against the Jews.

When the end of the Third Reich approached the orders were to march all inmates still alive to the rear so they wouldn't fall into Russian hands. Of the nearly 700,000 prisoners, most of them Jews, that were marched out of the dozen concentration and slave labor camps in the eastern parts of Europe at the beginning of 1945 a third perished on the roads or in the freezing cattle cars that winter (Gelately, 252). Those that could not be moved were to be killed in the camps and the facilities destroyed.

The toll of the Final Solution is given in Table 21-1. There is zero one can add to the scream of these numbers. But one side comment will be made here because in the vast literature on the subject this has not been alluded to. And it is this. The Jews in Nazi propaganda were portrayed as being plutocrats or Bolsheviks, often both wrapped in one. As it turned out Hitler got none of the Jewish plutocrats and few Bolsheviks. Most Jews of the Soviet Union were beyond Hitler's reach. While three-quarter of a million Jews in the prewar Soviet Union were killed by the Einsatzgruppen and another quarter million died in the general Russian catastrophe, some 2 million survived. As to Jewish plutocrats, they could be found only in the USA, Great Britain and perhaps in some South American countries and Hitler didn't quite get there. As for the German Jews, 65 percent of them managed to get away and they, of course, were the wealthiest and most influential of that community. In France, too, the native French Jews who were the most active in commerce and the intellectual life of the country survived under Vichy while the ones shipped to extermination camps were immigrants from Eastern Europe, a solid part of the French proletariat. The 6 million the Germans murdered were the Jews of Poland, the Baltic countries and the Russian pale — the huddled masses of tailors, shoemakers, shopkeepers, fiddlers, laborers and beggars — exterminated in toto. They had been the core of the Jewish people, a colorful community with their own speech, music, traditions, cuisine, wit and moral standards. With the obliteration of European Jewry a unique people and culture were wiped out — never to return.

• CHAPTER 22 •

Stalingrad

General Blumrentritt, since June 1942 deputy chief of army General Staff, later recalled that following the failure of the Moscow offensive there was discussion at the OKH as to the best course to follow in 1942. In the preceding two months AGC and AGS had been forced back an average of 150 miles over a frontage of 650 miles and German manpower stood at a little over 3 million whereas the Soviets had 5.5 million men at the front with 1.5 million in the reserves. Most of the participants, including Halder, felt that the Ostheer did not have the strength for another all-out assault on Russia and the best it could do was to hold its present lines. Of the three AG commanders von Rundstedt and von Leeb even thought they should withdraw to their departure lines and set up a defense belt on a much-shortened front. This was what they said to one another but not what they would dare tell the führer. Besides, within a short time both Rundstedt and von Leeb had been dismissed and their replacements, flattered by the promotion and driven by ambition, were even less likely to broach anything of the sort to Gröfaz.

Hitler had his own clear-cut plans for the coming year. It was simple; what hadn't been achieved in 1941 would be done in 1942. To convince his generals all he had to do was to change the argument. Barbarossa had been predicated on the total destruction of the Red Army in the western borderlands, following which, the Soviet state would collapse. This did not happen. The Soviet state was now to be shattered by a different stratagem. It was only necessary to rob it of its industrial base and victory would follow. The pillar of any industrial complex is oil; oil was in the Caucasus and that is where the German army would strike. The generals, not good even at waging war, were, as he had often told them, complete ignoramuses when it came to economics and would be likely to challenge this logic even less than the prospects of victory in one fell swoop.

In preliminary discussions before the plans for 1942 gelled, Hitler outlined for some of his staff at the OKW, but not to the army, his basic plan. A thrust would be launched on the southern front toward Stalingrad. Once the Volga was reached a left swing would be made toward Kazan (500 miles east of Moscow) and further north; there would also be a swing south along the Caspian Sea to capture Baku (see Fig. 22.1). From these new lines "patrols" would be sent to the Urals to finish the job (Clark, 190). Examining the direction of these thrusts, one quickly realizes that Hitler was again after the A-A Line. The scheme predated Barbarossa, when he had proposed to conquer Russia by a final giant pincer closing some 500 miles east of Moscow, 1,500 miles from his starting line. As with his love for England and his determination to eradicate Slavdom, Hitler was not one to change a concept merely because of new realities that emerged in the course of pursuing it. He was back to December 1940 when he first decided on ways and means of destroying Russia.

All this was completely unknown to the OKH — nor, by Hitler's dictum, should it have known. It was therefore a very confusing directive that spelled out the objective and operational plans for the summer campaign. The preamble to Directive No. 41, issued on April 5, said that it would be "our aim to wipe out the entire defense potential remaining to the Soviets." For this purpose "all available forces will be concentrated on the main operation in the southern sector with the aim of destroying the enemy before the Don in order to secure the Caucasian oil fields." But in the conduct of operations the Caucusus was ignored. Instead it went on at great length to discuss the attack to the Volga. All three projected thrusts—from near Orel, Kharkov and the Sea of Azov — were to head straight east and converge on Stalingrad. It already had the usual Hitlerian flavor when it said that "every effort must be made to reach Stalingrad itself, or at least to bring the city under fire from heavy artillery so that it may no longer be of any use as an industrial or communications center." The only mention of the Caucasus is in a vague aside at the end of the operational plans which says, "Swift progress of movements across the Don to the south in order to attain the operational objective, is essential in consideration of the season" (Trevor-Roper 1964, 116). What this sentence meant was anyone's guess.

For the generals to whom Directive No. 41 was a command of how to lead hundreds of thousands of men in battle this was a maddening document. In the preamble it stated that the Caucasus was the objective but the operational plan ignored it and in paragraph after paragraph went on detailing how to reach the Volga at Stalingrad. Thus while the objective lay in the south the campaign ordered was to the east. The allocation of forces, too, was in keeping with this contradiction. As will be seen, while the bulk of forces was allotted to the eastern thrust, a much smaller force was given the task of taking the Caucasus. The main question that immediately arises is this: If oil was the objective why not employ the entire force of the Army Group for this purpose, keeping only a screen to the northeast to secure its flank? The Caucasus is an extensive mountainous area and to seize and hold it required all the Germans could spare and here the main forces were directed away from the presumed objective. Furthermore, why Stalingrad at all? Presumably it was meant to sever transportation upriver from the oil wells in Grozny and Baku. But if these were captured there would be no oil to ship in the first place. Directive No. 41 thus makes sense only if it is seen against Hitler's original intent. With the main forces heading for the Volga he could subsequently turn north to seize his coveted A-A Line from where only "patrols" to the Urals would be needed to finish off the Soviet colossus. So determined was Hitler for this to be the scenario that before the campaign started the Germans, using the Danube, had transferred 430 vessels to the Black Sea, many of them originally designed for the invasion of England; and an admiral had been appointed to command the naval forces in the Caspian Sea, with Makhach-kala chosen as the main naval base (Boyd, 217).

On his part Stalin was convinced that the German offensive would be at Moscow via a thrust from the south. This was not what the Germans planned or did but in a lopsided way Stalin wasn't far off Hitler's innermost intentions. Stalin was so convinced of it that not even a fortuitous incident which handed him a copy of the German plans succeeded in swaying him. On June 19 a Major Reichel flew to the front carrying with him a copy of the initial operational plans of AGS. The pilot lost his way, the plane was shot down over the Russian lines, and both Reichel and the pilot were killed. The plans were soon on Stalin's desk. The ease with which the plans had been obtained only made Stalin more suspicious and he labeled them a plant. Accordingly, Russia's two main tank armies were positioned near Orel and Moscow, ready to pounce on the German lunge for the capital.

More than getting ready, Stalin decided on a preemptive strike. In May he ordered Timoshenko to launch a spoiling attack on the German assembly areas at Kharkov to upset their preparations and timetable for the coming offensive. The attack started on May 9 from the Issium bridgehead across the Donetz which projected 40 miles into enemy territory. From here the southwest front comander attempted to punch a deep penetration into the German concentrations. The Germans let them plunge ahead and then counterattacked from north and south the base of the salient. In 10 days of fighting several Russian armies were encircled, the AGS taking in the process a quarter million POWs. This followed the loss of 200,000 prisoners in the Crimea where with the coming of spring Manstein had taken Sevastopol and cleared the Kerch peninsula of Russian troops that had landed during the winter. It was an inauspicious beginning for the Russian Command.

In January 1942 two new appointments had been made in the AGS. On the 5th Paulus took command of the 6th Army and on the 20th, following the death of Reichenau, von Bock was recalled to lead the Army Group, only a month or so after he had been cashiered. For the coming offensive one of the most formidable armored formations, Hoth's 4th Panzer Army, was transferred from the center to the southern front. To increase mobility AGS was allotted all the motor vehicles of the other two army groups, giving the AGS 85 percent of its former motor fleet. Additional formations were brought over from the West. By June there were in the AGS 65 German divisions, 11 of them armored, as well as four allied armies—an armada of 90 divisions. They counted more than a million German and three-quarter million satellite troops. This force outnumbered the Russians in men, armor and in the strength of its air forces. But already then there were ominous indications about the grave state of the Ostheer's transportation and supply systems. Two divisions that were unloaded in Grodno could find no transportation and had to march 500–600 miles to the front.

The code name for the offensive was another color, Blau, tiered into three stages, Blau I, II and III. This was dictated by the staggered timetable for the troops joining the attack. The first to march was the northern force, Hoth's 4th Panzer Army, abutting the upper Don near Kursk. They were to head southeast keeping the Don River on their left as a buffer. In the center aiming straight for Stalingrad was the 6th Army under Paulus which, as Blau II, was to open the attack three days after Hoth. The last to join in were the forces assembled at the extreme south, along the Azov Sea. Bock naturally assumed that all the 90 divisions of AGS were under his command to dispose of as he saw fit. He had a surprise coming. Unbeknownst to him a new Army Group headquarters had been organized in Germany which arrived at the end of May to set up quarters in Stalino. At first Bock was not much concerned about it, particularly when Blau envisioned all three groupings to be attacking in unison eastwards, as Directive No. 41 demanded. Bock therefore assigned to this southern grouping the role of right prong to Hoth's main forces coming from the upper Don.

On June 1 Hitler flew down to Bock's headquarters at Poltawa for a discussion of the impending operation. Hitler listened to Bock's presentation and agreed with his plans. He then launched into a typical peroration: "If we don't get Maikop and Grozny, I shall have to pack up (*liquidieren*) the war." This was a perennial refrain of his prior to any major offensive. Combining imprecation with a threat he would stress that this or that particular venture was a life-or-death issue and failing to achieve it meant the end of it all. More often than not the venture would fail to come off and Hitler neither quit nor ended the war and no one subsequently ever heard of it. Soon another event would surface as the fateful key to the entire war, only to be forgotten in its turn.

The offensive opened on June 28 with a powerful thrust by Hoth's Panzers down the right bank of the Don and three days later Paulus' 6th Army lunged eastward over the open steppe. Both armies made good progress. As the southernmost grouping was about to go into action Bock received a jolt. On July 9 the Stalino headquarters was designated as a new Army Group A under the command of Feldmarschall List, brought over from occupation duties in the Balkans. The other forces Bock had were designated AGB under General Weichs. With his Army Group split in two Bock moaned he was uncertain whether he commanded both of them, only one, or none. This frustration was soon compounded by an operational disagreement with Hitler. As the northern prong headed southeast its left flank stretched and overran ever greater distance and Bock became apprehensive over a Russian flank attack across the Don. Consequently he kept much of Hoth's armor along the Don; moreover he crossed the river and took Voronezh on the left bank to forestall a Russian attempt to attack him. Hitler became furious. He wanted the Panzers to race on, pin down and destroy the Russian armies in the Don bend and here Bock was worrying about his flank. On July 13 Hitler again sacked von Bock, appointing Weichs in his place.

There were perhaps deeper reasons for firing von Bock. One had to do with commanding the now double-headed AGS. With Bock eliminated each of the two southern Army Groups was now directly subordinated to Hitler as army commander in chief and he could order them around without Bock's interference. A still more fundamental cause was that already then the campaign was not going as planned. One of the stipulations of Directive No. 41 was to trap and destroy the Russian armies west of the Don. This was not happening and for several reasons. As stated, Stalin was expecting an attack on Moscow and kept his main forces opposite AGC; there were thus no great Russian concentrations facing von Bock in the first place. Also the railroad from Moscow south was cut at the very beginning of the offensive and Russian reinforcements had to travel first east before being routed south and thus avoided encirclement. Finally, learning from the past, Stalin had ordered a strategic retreat. The Russians moved fast and on time and their ability to elude the Germans was aided, as in the past, by Hitler's ignorance and disregard for Russian spaces and Russian weather. True, there was no snow and only occasionally mud. But the German supply system failed in the summer heat as it did in the winter snows. Every few days Hoth's Panzers came to a dead halt, empty of fuel. There was only one railway bridge across the Dniepr, the distances were enormous and, as all along, the Germans had insufficient motor transport to keep up with the troops; in the Caucasus the distances were such that the trucks hauling fuel consumed it nearly all themselves during the trip. Thus what few Russians they did see the dried-out Panzers could only sit and watch disappear over the horizon. Unlike the summer of 1941 no cauldrons materialized. The Don country was open steppe, roadless, swirling with dust, seemingly endless. The weather was described as hotter than Africa. The Russians polluted what few wells there were and water had to be brought from the rear like fuel. At night Russian planes dropped phosphorous bombs, setting the steppe vegetation on fire. The soldiers described the landscape as an "ocean of sorrow." Forced to lap up whatever water they found the soldiers incurred dysentery and many had to keep marching while soiling their pants.

Stalin's retreat order, issued on July 6, specified that the Germans be allowed to advance into the void of the Don steppe but that the hinges of the offensive at Voronezh and Rostov be held. When a copy of this order fell into German hands Hitler convinced himself that the Russian armies that had eluded him at the Don were concentrated near Rostov and he ordered that every effort be made to trap and destroy them before they retreated into the Caucasus. With Bock gone Hitler decided to take a more direct hand in the operations. Together with the entire OKW and OKH he moved from the Wolfschanze to Ukraine. He arrived on July 16 and installed himself in a hut in the village of Skrishevka, some 10 miles from Vinnitza where because of the heat and the mosquitoes his temper had reached the choleric. Before moving he had ordered Hoth to proceed posthaste toward the presumed Russian concentrations at Rostov and for this purpose he temporarily transferred AGB's 4th Panzer Army to AGA. This was the operational area of Kleist's 1st Panzer Army and so it happened that by the third week of July some 25 divisions, including all German armor on the southern front, were milling around in a 40-mile arena in search of an enemy who wasn't there. When the two Panzer armies joined hands on July 20 they discovered that the ring they had formed was empty.

On July 23 Hitler issued new orders, Directive No. 45, which seemed to bring some order to the armies scattered from Voronezh to the Kalmyk steppe. Like all his utterances it was a stunner. The directive opened with the statement that in "little more than three weeks the broad objectives ... have been largely achieved. Only weak enemy forces from Timoshenko's Army Group have succeeded in avoiding encirclement." As for the coming operations the "most important task of AGA ... will be to occupy the entire eastern coast-line of the Black Sea thereby eliminating the Black Sea ports and the enemy Black Sea Fleet." The directive then went on to say that part of AGA, namely its fast formations, would head inland to occupy Maikop and Grozny following which a drive along the Caspian Sea would capture Baku. AGB would follow the previous plan of investing Stalingrad and blocking the Volga, to which was now added a rider that after taking the city, a drive south along the Volga would capture Astrakhan, the southern anchor of the A-A Line (Trevor-Roper 1964, 129). Thus, according to Hitler, after three weeks the objectives of the summer offensive had been fulfilled and only weak enemy formations escaped encirclement. This fabrication was fed not to a gullible public in Germany but to his top commanders in the field. Already earlier he had told Halder, "The Russian is finished" to which Halder responded, "I must admit it looks like it." (Clark, 209).

According to the new directive the two army groups were now to march away from each other at a 90 degree angle, AGA to the south and AGB east. AGA itself was split in two. While its main task was the capture of the Black Sea coast to the west, another force was to head for the oil fields near the Caspian Sea in the east — a 180 degree divergence. The oil fields were dispersed in three localities. A very small amount was produced in Maikop, 180 miles away; another small output came from Grozny, 400 miles away; but 80 percent of all the oil in the Caucasus was at Baku, 700 miles from Rostov (Seaton, 1971, 266–7). Moreover, Baku was across the Caucasian mountain range, its highest peak, Mount Elbrus, reaching 18,500 feet.

At least it was now clear who was going where. By the end of July AGA began to wheel south to enter the Caucasus while 4th Panzer was returned to AGB for its drive on Stalingrad. The two army groups now had the following establishment: List's AGA had two armies, the 17th under Ruoff and Kleist's 1st Panzer Army, while Weichs' AGB had three German armies and four satellite armies, two Rumanian and one each from Italy and Hungary.

As seen, the Stalingrad expedition was three to four times as strong as the one allocated to the Caucasus. However, it contained four satellite armies which could not be compared to the Germans; on the other hand 6th Army was twice the normal establishment comprising five corps totaling 20 divisions, six of them Panzer or motorized, 270,000 men in all (Toepke, 421). While originally AGA was promised the 11th Army under Manstein,

which was to cross over from Kerch as soon as AGA reached the Taman peninsula opposite it, in the end most of 11th Army's divisions were moved north for an assault on Leningrad which never came.

By splitting the southern front into two army groups two distinct campaigns were now
fought in southern Russia with no coordination and no mutual support between the two.
As shown in Fig. 22.1, there was in fact a yawning gap between AGA and AGB in the Kalmyk
steppe nearly 200 miles in extent, manned by a single German division at Elista, which bore
the character of a foreign legion outpost in the desolation of the Sahara. Despite Hitler's
assertion of the primacy of the Caucasian oil fields, AGA turned into a subordinate operation and its eventual fate depended less on its own fortunes than on the success or failure
of the main drive to the Volga.

* * *

Even though AGB met little opposition on its march eastward it took, largely because
of supply difficulties, a full month to reach and seize the arc of the Don. When the projected encirclement near Rostov came to nothing, 4th Panzer Army was on July 31 returned
to AGB and ordered to swing toward Stalingrad. After taking the city it was to be withdrawn into reserve for further tasks.

In the first week of August the Germans crossed the Don and entered the Don-Volga
land bridge. Both 4th Panzer from the southwest and 6th Army from the west now converged on Stalingrad. Here resistance stiffened. While up to now the Russian retreat had
been deliberate and Stalin felt he could afford it — now that vital areas were being approached
he issued on July 28 a "stop order" phrased in the most brutal terms, "We have lost more
than 70 million of the population, more than 12 million tons of grain and ten million tons
of metal a year…. To retreat farther would mean to destroy ourselves and with us the Motherland…. Not one more step backwards … the retreat mentality must be decisively eliminated" (Volkogonov, 460). Over the past six weeks as the German push toward the Volga
made it clear that this was the main offensive, Russian armies had been shifting in a steady
stream from the north to the Stalingrad front. Though they were fed into the lines spar-
ingly — Stalin had bigger plans for them — it was enough to keep the Germans busy. Against
rising opposition and with rising casualties, the Germans gnawed their way ever closer to
the city. Why this compulsion for Stalingrad remained, as did many other features of this
war, unclear; if traffic on the river was to be interrupted it could have been achieved more
easily by reaching the Volga north or south of the city. But in a spiraling fury the place was
turning into a magnet to Hitler and he shoved all available forces toward the city that bore
the name of his nemesis. According to one report Hitler's orders were that all women and
children were to be expelled and the male population exterminated. When the troops
reached the outskirts Hitler, as he did with Warsaw and Belgrade, ordered a massive air
attack on it. On the night of August 21 a stupendous bombardment was launched using
every available bomber and fighter, including planes from as far away as Kerch and Orel;
at a distance of 40 miles German troops could see the flames of the burning city. Unlike in
other places no statistics of civilian dead were ever compiled by the Russians but whole sections of the city collapsed into ruin. The German soldiers were soon to regret these piles
of rubble that Hitler heaped in their way.

The city of Stalingrad stretched along the west bank of the Volga for some 20 miles,
its width no more than a couple of miles. With their back against the water which, includ-

ing the midstream islands, was here about two miles wide, the Russian defenders were essentially separated from the hinterland. Given its ribbon-like geography and isolation, it should not have been too difficult to penetrate it, but the air attacks and heavy artillery fire that Hitler had ordered turned the city into a moonscape of concrete and twisted iron. And it was in this 20-mile stretch of wreckage that the Russians decided to make their stand — to some extent perhaps for the same reasons that Hitler was determined to take it. The defense of the city was in the hands of Chuikov's 62nd Army consisting of eight depleted divisions. Chuikov's tactics were to "hug" the Germans so they would not be able to unleash concentrated air and artillery bombardments on his troops. Eventually his army was hemmed into four separate bridgeheads, the front lines no more than 600 feet from the water's edge.

Hoth's Panzer Army reached the Volga at the northern tip of Stalingrad on August 23 and as soon as the remainder of 6th Army came up Hitler ordered it to storm and take the city. While Stalin and Stavka were making plans for the winter, the orders to Chuikov were not to launch any attacks but to keep the 6th Army pinned down in relentless defensive combat. Chuikov decided to depart from the customary Russian mass battle tactics. He broke up his troops into small units, often no more than platoons or squads training them to fight a close combat war for each street, house, and often a single floor of individual buildings. In addition, Chuikov instituted a routine of night fighting, a practice the Germans usually shunned. Thus began a three-month Battle of the Rubble fought at close quarters with submachine guns, explosives, hand grenades and knives — a war in which the Russian soldier was more than a match for the Germans. The house-to-house fighting was termed by the Germans *Rattenkrieg*. Much of it was psychological, such as the Russian tactic of firing flares every night to feint impending attacks and keep the Germans from sleeping. With it went extreme cruelty to friend and foe alike. The western bank of the Volga was littered with thousands of Russian wounded as the ferries were allotted to more important tasks before the wounded would be attended to, if at all. The boats bringing fresh troops were under continuous German shelling and should a Soviet solder panic and jump overboard the orders were to fire at him to keep others from doing the same. In the city itself the cannonade was so intense that dogs unable to bear it jumped into the Volga where they drowned. Such memorable spots as Mamayev Hill, the Tractor Factory or the Red October Steelworks, for which men fought for weeks on end, reflect the gang-like killing to which the Germans' erstwhile blitzkrieg had degenerated on the eastern front.

Just as the war in general was Hitler's own affair, so Stalingrad became his private vendetta and he relentlessly goaded the troops to take the city. To make sure that they would not fail Hitler, as with his victory claim before Moscow, announced in a speech to the German people that yes, Stalin may rest assured he would take Stalingrad. Consequently, the entire 6th Army, a quarter million men, was shoved into the maelstrom of smoke, soot and cordite and step by step, ruin by ruin, infantry and sapper battalions clawed their way through the craters. The first major assault was a murderous air attack on August 23, conducted by the hero of Guernica, von Richthofen. In continuous waves his air armada dropped 1,000 tons of bombs on the city, killing in one week an estimated 40,000 civilians (Beevor 1998, 106). The follow-up ground attack was sufficiently successful that one morning Eremenko, getting out of his bunker, found Russian troops gone and had to transfer his HQ east of the river. As artillery fire and Stukas rained death and destruction on the shrinking perimeter held by Chuikov's men, Stalin, in spoonfuls and driblets, fed replacements from across the river to make sure the tiger was held by its tail. On October 14 the last major assault was launched on the parts of the city still held by the Russians. Further gains were made and the Germans came within 300 yards of Chuikov's command post near the brickworks; using the river he transferred to the chemical plant, one of the wider pockets still held by the Russians. The Germans crept deeper and deeper into the skeleton of Stalingrad until come November they had bottled up the defenders into three small bridge-heads clinging to the west bank of the river. By now 90 percent of the city was in German hands; still Hitler could not claim that Stalingrad had fallen.

Nothing as dramatic as the Stalingrad meatgrinder developed on Army Group A front. After taking Rostov on July 23, it, too, initially encountered little resistance as it drove into the south's maize and sunflower fields, befriending on the way the smiling natives— Kalmyks, Tatars, Chechens and assorted Mussulmans. But List was achieving neither of the two assigned objectives. Though plunging deep into the heart of the Caucasus he seized neither the Black Sea coast nor the Caspian shore with its oil fields. If one looks at Fig. 22.1 one can partly see why. Whereas the northern ground between the two seas is accessible, the Black Sea coast and Baku are blocked by the Caucasian mountain range — steep, road-less, with violent rainbursts, and early snow. In these mountains the Russians made their stand and it was here that by mid–August the 17th Army and Kleist's Panzers came to a halt. List's front, anchored at Novorossisk at the extreme northwest could neither drive south along the constricted seacoast nor get to it from the east across the Caucasian range. Instead Hitler kept raising his demands, insisting that he reach Batum, on the Turkish border. To accomplish it List was given three mountain divisions and Alpini units were brought over from Italy to tackle the Caucasus. With mules and climbing gear these troops reached a few places Kleist's Panzers could not; on August 28 they even succeeded in scaling Mount Elbrus and planted the swastika there. But it was no more than a mountain-climbing feat and such it remains in the history of the war.

At this point it must have become clear to Hitler that the 1942 offensive had miscar-ried. It failed not only in terms of his grand design, but even in the limited sense he had phrased his directives. Fig. 22.1 shows the maximum German advance reached in the 1942 campaign. There had been no great encirclements of Russian forces; Stalingrad had not fallen; the Black Sea coast had not been reached; and the oil fields at Grozny and Baku remained in Russian hands. It was time to launch his usual two-pronged post-mortem; to claim, as he had done in Directive No. 45, that success had in fact been achieved; and to find culprits for the failure to realize those grand schemes he, Hitler, had so clearly shown how to go about achieving.

It had all started with von Bock and his insistence on securing his left flank while Hitler wanted his Panzers to repeat what they had done in France and Byelorussia — push on and on; as will be seen, the catastrophe that was to strike the 6th Army in the coming months was due precisely to neglecting its left flank. Hitler now decided to get rid of List, soon to be followed by a wider purge reminiscent of the one following the failure before Moscow in 1941. On August 26 List sent an appreciation to the OKH that should his right and left wings not achieve their objectives soon, his Army Group would have to halt offensive operations and take up winter quarters. This decision, said List, should not be put off beyond September 15; there was already snow in the mountains (Ziemke 1986, 375–7). Hitler, already unhappy with him, jumped at the occasion. On September 7 Jodl was sent down to List's headquarters to find out what lay behind his lack of success; for sure he had not been following orders. Jodl conferred with List and his staff and reported back to the führer that from what he had seen and heard, List had scrupulously followed directives.

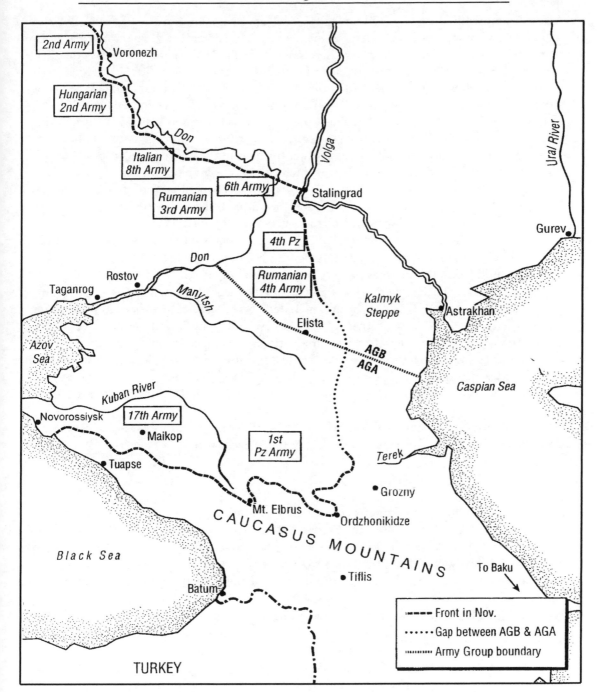

22.1. Furthest German advance during the 1942 Summer Offensive

Screaming, "that's a lie" (Beevor 1998, 123) a hurricane ignited in the führer's psyche: the cause of failure was being attributed not to the generals' incompetence, cowardice, and treason but directly to him. The first counterstroke was the dismissal of List on September 9, with Hitler himself taking command of Army Group A. To punish Jodl for his blasphemy the führer banned him from the meals they usually shared and refused to shake his hand.

A similar punishment was meted out to Hitler's very own man, Keitel. Next came the turn of Halder, army chief of staff throughout the war. On September 27, he was replaced by General Zeitzler, a man with neither talent nor personality. Instead of Jodl it was now Zeitzler who presented the situation report on the eastern front. Next, Hitler ordered stenographers to be flown from Berlin to transcribe verbatim every utterance he made at the situation conferences so that history would know the truth. He then locked himself in his hut, ate alone, and demanded that the situation reports be held at his place instead at the usual conference room. It is revealing to note Jodl's reaction to this confrontation. In a conversation with Warlimont Jodl confessed that his behavior was wrong because a dictator's strength comes from his self-confidence which should never be questioned (Jukes, 74). In his diary entry of May 10, 1943, Goebbels noted Hitler's overall view of his commanders: "All generals lie; all generals are disloyal" and the reason he had stopped having meals with them was that he "just can't bear the sight of generals anymore."

Following the purges came the official pronouncement of the successes that had been achieved. This was more or less a restatement of the claims made in Directive No. 45 but with the implication that no more was to be expected in 1942. Order No. 1 issued on October 14 by Chief of Staff Zeitzler but actually dictated by the führer stated, "This year's summer and fall campaigns ... have been concluded." It ordered the Ostheer to prepare for winter quarters "in the present lines ... to be held without withdrawals or maneuvers, even if ... outflanked, cut off, encircled, overrun by tanks, enveloped in smoke or gassed." With this announcement the fighting was declared over until next spring and the Ostheer was hereby ordered to repeat last winter's miracle and remain in their positions regardless of any actions the enemy might undertake even when "outflanked, overrun or gassed" (Ziemke 1986, 450).

Transferring command of AGA to von Kleist Hitler now left the Ukrainian headquarters and on October 13 returned to his lair at the Wolfschanze.

* * *

As in Stalingrad the Germans continued to capture yards of rubble and their mountain troops scaled the 18,500 Mount Elbrus, Stavka was busy finalizing its plans for a winter offensive. There were discussions as to its scope ranging from a simple frontal attack to push the 6th Army away from the Volga to visions of a southwesterly sweep to cut off both German Army Groups in the south. What emerged was something in between, executed in three phases with varying degrees of success.

The first Russian dictum was to accumulate the necessary reserves. As mentioned, some of them came from the central front once it had become clear there would be no attack on Moscow. But fresh armies were drawn from the hinterland, the Urals and the Far East. The arriving troops were assembled mostly north of the Don and east of Stalingrad. All this traffic moved exclusively at night and mostly by rail. To transport the hundreds of thousands of men and mountains of supplies six branch lines of a total length of 700 miles were laid from the north to the middle Don; the other main railroad trunks were the southeastern and Ryazan-Ural branches. As the time for the offensive approached trains were run in continuous echelons disregarding the usual control system by employing men carrying lanterns and spacing the trains at 12-minute intervals. In the last stages the rail stock after being unloaded was simply thrown off the tracks to enable only one-way traffic to the west. From the railheads 27,000 trucks and horse-drawn wagons lugged the materiel to the

Top: A Russian counterattack; the soldier at left carries an anti-tank rifle. (From *The Russian War 1941–1945* by Daniela Mrazkova and Vladimir Remes copyright ©1975 by Daniela Mrazkova and Vladimir Remes. Used by permission of Dutton, a division of Penguin Group [USA] Inc.) *Bottom:* Russian infantry during an attack. The soldier in the foreground carries the popular Pepeshka submachine gun. (Courtesy the United States Army.)

assembly areas while the men marched 200–250 miles to the front (Ziemke, 464). One of the problems was to get the forces across the Volga. The buildup was taking place in muddy terrain with both the Volga and Don in flood so that to ferry across the Volga took four hours instead of the normal half hour. Seventeen false bridges were constructed over the Don to deflect the Luftwaffe from those actually used to assemble the troops. When day dawned the flatlands east of the Volga and the steppe north of the Don looked empty of man and beast.

Including the troops at the front the Russians had accumulated around the Don bend a force of 1 million men with 13,500 guns and mortars, half of it concentrated over a single 40-mile stretch of front. There are conflicting reports about how much the Germans knew. One is that they were completely in the dark. Another is that they had strong suspicions that something was brewing on their northern flank but did not react because there was little they could do. Whatever the reason, they did nothing.

Vasilevski, at the time Red Army chief of staff, prepared what was to become stage one of the offensive, code named Uranus. This was approved by Stalin on September 13 and Vasilevski was charged with coordinating the three fronts involved. These were the southwest front under Vatutin; the Don front under Rokossovski; and the Stalingrad front under Yeremenko. Orders were given that only a few people were to know about the plan and it was forbidden to put anything connected with it in writing. Not even Chuikov was informed about it. On September 28 Rokossovski and Yeremenko traveled south and took over their respective commands.

Stage one, planned as a pincer movement to trap 6th Army in its Stalingrad lair, opened on November 19. It was a foggy morning and at 8:30 out of that fog came lumbering shadows of T-34s followed by specter-like lines of infantry. This was Rokossovski's 5th Tank Army coming out of the Serafimovich bridgehead on the Don, 110 miles north of Stalingrad. They turned southeast hitting the Rumanian 3rd Army arranged on Paulus's left wing. Within hours the Rumanians panicked and fled. One day later another phalanx of tanks and infantry belonging to Yeremenko's front emerged from the fog south of Stalingrad. Headed northwest they hit the Rumanian 4th Army guarding Paulus's right flank. Here too the Rumanians fled at the first sight of Russian tanks. Three days later the two prongs met at a place called Sovetskyi, 40 miles west of Stalingrad encircling in it the entire 6th Army plus parts of the 4th Panzers and two Rumanian divisions. Pushing the remaining 4th Panzers away from the Don the Russians turned and clamped a vise on the 6th Army. By November 28, 94 Russian divisions held a solid ring around the Stalingrad pocket which at this stage was 50 miles long and 20–25 miles wide, containing in it a quarter million men.

Evidently believing his own assertion that for now the fighting was over, Hitler on November 7 left the Wolfschanze for a prolonged stay at the Berghof. From there, on November 17, two days before the start of the Russian offensive he had sent a message to Paulus that he expected him "getting through to the Volga and the gun factory and the metallurgical plant and taking these sections of the city." Accordingly, Paulus kept chipping away and, on the very day the Russian offensive started, took several more blocks of houses. When Hitler was informed of the double-pronged Russian attack, a flood of orders spewed forth from the Berghof. On the 20th Manstein, who was kept in Vitebsk waiting for a special assignment, to rush south and form a new Army Group Don. When Hitler heard there was talk about extricating the 6th Army from the threatened encirclement, Hitler sent orders on November 22 that, yes, the 6th Army could withdraw, but not west, only eastward, where it was to form a defensive hedgehog until contact was reestablished (Jukes,

96) and he ordered Paulus to move his headquarters into Stalingrad. At that time Paulus was at Nizhni-Chirskaya where the 6th Army's winter quarters were being prepared. When he got Hitler's order Paulus flew into the about-to-be closed cauldron, setting up his command post at Gumrak, four to five miles from the city. Hitler then returned to the Wolf-schanze after a 16-day absence. There he received a message from Manstein who was forming his new Army Group Don that, in his view, there was no need yet for the 6th Army to withdraw; if worst came to worst a relief operation could be organized at a later date (Ziemke 1986, 474).

The story of Stalingrad is, among other things, a lesson in parallels—as if history was an exercise in geometry. The model was the Demyansk pocket of the previous winter. There 100,000 Germans had been surrounded in frost and snow but on Hitler's orders had stayed put. Supplies delivered by air had kept the besieged troops alive through the winter and a relief launched in the spring opened a corridor to Demyansk. Although the losses both in the pocket and in the battles to keep the corridor open were out of proportion to the tactical value of Demyansk, and although in the end it had to be evacuated, the official view was that it had been a German success. All this was now to be duplicated in Stalingrad even though the number of besieged men and the supplies needed were three times those of Demyansk; the distance to the pocket was not 10 but 80 miles; and neither the German nor the Russian army of 1942 was the same as of a year ago. Ironically, General Seydlitz, who led the relief operation to Demyansk, was now himself in the bag.

In taking over AGB, now renamed Army Group Don, Manstein wasn't given much to work with. The 6th Army was surrounded, the two Rumanian armies had disintegrated, and the 4th Panzer had lost much of its strength. His task was no less than to "bring the enemy attack to a standstill and recapture the positions previously occupied by us" (Clark, 251). This was partly made easier for him by the Russians concentrating their main forces around the pocket to make sure no one escaped. Manstein's mission to reestablish contact with Paulus was designated Winter Storm. Undermining this effort was the usual dichotomy between Hitler's and his generals' understanding of what was being attempted. Manstein outside and Paulus inside the pocket understood Winter Storm as an attempt to make contact with the 6th Army and provide it with enough fuel and supplies to break out. Hitler's expectations were entirely different. Yes, a road was to be opened and the 6th Army supplied but only in order that it would remain in place as a nucleus for a third round.

During the crucial military conference at the Wolfschanze on December 12 about possibly evacuating the Stalingrad pocket Hitler rambled on as follows: "To think that it would be possible to do it a second time [capture Stalingrad] ... is ridiculous. They [the troops] cannot take everything with them. The horses are tired, and they don't have any more strength to pull. I can't feed one horse with another. If they were Russians I'd say one Russian eats up the other one. But I can't let one horse eat up the other horse.... We won't come back here, so we can't leave" (Heiber 1963, 28).

Winter Storm commenced on December 12. The plan was worked out in strict cooperation with führer Headquarters. A corridor was to be breached and the 6th Army supplied and reinforced so that it formed a "cornerstone ... with regard to operations in 1943" (Beevor 1998, 296). The attack, led by Hoth's Panzers, started from near Kotelnikovo toward the pocket's southern edge, 75 miles away. Initially Manstein preferred that 6th Army stay put and tie down the Russian forces there; when close enough he intended for it to break out and link up with Hoth's Panzers. But by November 30 the Russians felt that the pocket was sufficiently secure and began to shift forces to the main front. When they realized that a relief operation was underway they withdrew 150,000 troops from the ring, pulled in a fresh Guards Army and sent them against Hoth. By December 19 Hoth was halfway to his target and needed another 35 miles to reach it. At the southern perimeter of the pocket 100 tanks were waiting to break out. There was optimism among the surrounded troops that they would be relieved; donations were collected — several hundred thousand Reichsmark — as a Christmas gift for Manstein when he appeared in the pocket (Kluge, 142). Paulus's tanks in the pocket had fuel for about 20 miles so they had to wait for Hoth to advance another 15 miles. Besides, they needed the führer's permission to break out. Neither happened and under Russian pressure Winter Storm dissolved into the first winter blizzards.

Parallel to failure of the relief operation was the failure of the airlift to supply the pocket. Göring, whose star had dimmed because of the Luftwaffe's poor performance in the Battle of Britain and more so because of his inability to stop the bombing of German cities, sensed here a chance to redeem himself and accomplish what the army could not — another echo of Demyansk. Nearly 1,000 Ju-52s and bombers were assembled to fly in supplies to the beleaguered army. In a patriotic gesture six luxurious private planes belonging to Göring, Ribbentrop and Company were hitched to serve the airlift. The requirements of 6th Army were 500–700 tons per day. At no time was the delivery higher than 300 tons and over time the daily average was only 100 tons (Jukes, 108).

In the end the 6th Army was abandoned to die a prolonged death. This took 10 weeks. On January 1, 1943, Paulus received a message from the führer: "Every man of the 6th Army can start the New Year with the absolute conviction that the Führer will not leave his heroic soldiers on the Volga in the lurch and that Germany can and will find the means to relieve it." This grandstand performance was preceded by a Hitler pronouncement similar to that he had made to Bock about the live-or-die importance of the Caucasian oilfields. On December 12 he told Zeitzler, "If we give up there [Stalingrad] we give up on the whole sense of this campaign" (DDR, XVIII, 78). Zeitzler had nothing to say, nor did Paulus comment on the führer's new year's message. The 52-year-old Friedrich Wilhelm Ernst Paulus was a 6-foot 4-inch tall, thin-lipped, ramrod-stiff German general not given to banter with either superiors or underlings, alone with his thoughts, if there were any. He never did, nor would he now, stand up for his views, the interests of his soldiers, or those of Germany. When the Wolfschanze asked that General Hube, commander of 6th Army's V Panzer Corps, be sent out to review the situation, Paulus instructed him to give a true picture of the pocket — the lack of food, ammunition, shelter, clothing and the sinking morale of the troops. Hube was a one-armed experienced warhorse but after a talk with the führer Hube returned to the pocket on January 8 telling Paulus that what was being ordered by Hitler was right and Stalingrad would soon turn into a German victory (Goerlitz 1963, 260).

Through December the Russians did not attempt to liquidate the pocket, waiting instead for starvation and epidemics to do a large part of the job. Several times they sent parliamentarians proposing full or partial surrender. They were rebuffed. On January 10 the Russians for the last time sent an officer asking for an end to the fighting. The offer was rejected. The Russians then opened an assault on the reduced perimeter. Under a blitz of Katyushas and Sturmoviks the pocket was split in two. The larger southern part remained under Paulus, whereas the northern enclave was commanded by the XI th Corps' General Strecker. When Gumrak was about to be overrun Paulus, on January 20, moved his command post to Univermag, Stalingrad's department store, where he installed himself in a cellar partitioned off from his staff by a curtain behind which he sat chain-smoking and brooding. When the last airstrip at Gumrak fell to the Russians the wounded could no longer be evacuated and they crawled around on all fours in the snow and mud. The caul-dron became a phantasmagoric scene of hell. All horses, dogs and cats had been eaten. Bearded, ragged men without weapons lounged in the cellars and crevices not talking to each other. Forty-thousand wounded and frostbitten soldiers roamed the ruins looking for shelter while rats nibbled on those who found some. The dead lay unburied in piles as the living had no strength to dig graves in the half-frozen earth. The pocket's perimeter along the river was not manned by the Russians and groups of men attempted to escape east-ward, but the ice on the Volga was mined and they all perished; others committed suicide. Three hundred sixty-four court-martial executions were carried out for refusal to obey orders. From January 29 on no more rations were issued to the wounded, saving whatever there was for the few fighting men; those that still received food were given soups made of motor oil and sawdust. To further depress the Germans the Russians staged a fly-past on January 30, the 10th anniversary of Hitler's chancellorship. Some 100 planes flew low just out of rifle range, in parade formation over the German positions, dropping no bombs and doing no strafing, conveying the message that they were no longer worth expending ammu-nition on (Kluge, 73). There was still one significant incident, typical of this war, before the end came. There were 3,500 Russian POWs in the pocket. When the food ran out Paulus instructed that they be handed over to the Russians. That was not how the German soldier felt about it. When the pocket surrendered no live prisoners could be found (Kluge, 197)

On January 30 Hitler sent another message of praise for the heroic defenders of Stal-ingrad and promoted Paulus to the rank of feldmarschall. Paulus thanked the führer and assured him that the German soldier would do his duty to the end. The end came the next day, January 31, when Russian infantry appeared before the Univermag. A 21-year-old lieu-tenant asked for the surrender of the cellar. Out came General Shmidt, the chief of staff, telling the Russian that he would "negotiate" on behalf of the feldmarschall. Eventually Paulus himself stepped out. He was brought before Rokossovski, who had taken Stalingrad and Voronov, the Stavka representative. When Voronov addressed him as generaloberst, Paulus corrected him that he was now a feldmarschall; the uniform happened not to have arrived yet (Beevor 1998, 389). The Russians offered him a cigarette, tea — he would take neither. They asked that he order his troops to stop fighting but he would issue no such order. They asked if he needed anything but aside from giving his name and age he refused to talk and was led away. The northern pocket near the Tractor Works under General Strecker resisted for another two days. On February 2, a blistering windy day, the Stalin-grad battlefield fell silent.

The number of men lost at Stalingrad has not been precisely determined. Figures range from 220,000 to more than 300,000 but 280,000 should be close. This includes 14,000 Rumanians and 20,000 hiwis. Thirty-four thousand German wounded had been flown out in the transport planes that had brought supplies. When the fighting ended the Russians took 90,000 prisoners, which leaves 157,000 German soldiers dead during the two-month siege. Of the prisoners taken 5,000–6,000 survived captivity so the toll of the Stalingrad pocket was close to a quarter million dead. The Russian losses were higher. Of each Rus-sian division fed into the Stalingrad inferno only a few hundred survived. Total casualties are estimated at 1.1 million with close to half a million dead (Beevor 1998, 394). From the Stalingrad ruins 10,000 civilians crawled out, among them 1,000 children, all orphans.

Among the German prisoners were 27 generals, including the recently named feld-marschall and his five corps commanders. There had been in the pocket some 1,800 guns and 10,800 motor vehicles but these had mostly been destroyed or spiked. In addition 500 transport Junkers were lost during the airlift. There had been 8,000 horses in the pocket but they were all eaten. When Hitler heard of the end of Stalingrad his reaction was a vitriolic outburst against Paulus. By making him a feldmarschall he was sending the message that since no German feldmarschall had ever fallen into enemy hands he, Paulus, should not break this sacrosanct tradition. "It takes only a few minutes to die" lamented the führer when he heard that Paulus was a prisoner. No, he would never make anyone feldmarschall again, a vow he kept no more than any other (Seaton 1971, 335). Paulus was not the only one to incur Hitler's wrath. An order went out that none of the Stalingrad wounded be brought home, that they should get no farther than the Dniepr (Kluge, 153). After the war, promised Hitler, all officers from the Stalingrad pocket would be court-martialed. Sometime later Paulus's wife was arrested — she was a foreigner anyway, Rumanian. While only a handful of German soldiers and officers survived the Stalingrad debacle, most generals did. They managed it by the simple stratagem of becoming lackeys to Stalin, as they had been to Hitler.

* * *

While the battle of Stalingrad still raged the Russians launched the second stage of their offensive, Little Saturn, a reduction from full Saturn. The start of this second phase had the additional benefit of finally scotching Winter Storm when on top of its lack of success in the field forces had to be diverted to meet the new threat posed by Little Saturn.

While the aim of the first stage of the offensive can be said to have been military — encirclement and destruction of the German troops on the Volga — the 2nd stage had both military and strategic objectives. This was to make a lunge to Rostov and cut off AGA in the Caucasus. In addition to a possible destruction of an entire Army Group, this would liberate the Caucasus and eliminate any threat to the oil fields and the rail line to Persia from where Allied aid was arriving in increasing quantities. The proper thing would have been to aim the thrust west of Rostov but Stavka did not feel confident enough to manage such a wide-ranging penetration, when in the past, most recently at Kharkov last May, such deep sweeps usually ended in defeat. Little Saturn, approved by Stavka on December 2, thus visualized a more restricted campaign. The offensive still aimed at Rostov but it was to consist of two prongs, which were to strike at AG-Don north and northeast of Rostov. The main attack was to be carried southward from the upper Don against the Italian 8th Army; the southern prong was to start from Kotelnikovo and head for Rostov (see Fig. 22.2). To accomplish their strategic objective of isolating AGA in the Caucasus both prongs had some 200 miles to cover.

The fact that after the collapse of the two Rumanian armies in November the Germans still relied on the Italian and Hungarian troops to shield their flank on the upper Don seems to settle the previously raised questions whether the OKH knew but could do little about the impending battles. Keeping the allied armies in such vulnerable positions after what had happened at Stalingrad shows that it was shortage of troops and Hitler's refusal to make any strategic decisions on the eastern front that paralyzed the Ostheer into passively accepting what was to come and merely reacting in an ad-hoc manner to each developing crisis.

As happened with the Rumanians the Italians broke under the attack. The Don was frozen and the Russians made good progress, covering 100 miles in the first four days. Manstein had overwhelming tasks, one to keep Rostov open as an escape route for the AGA

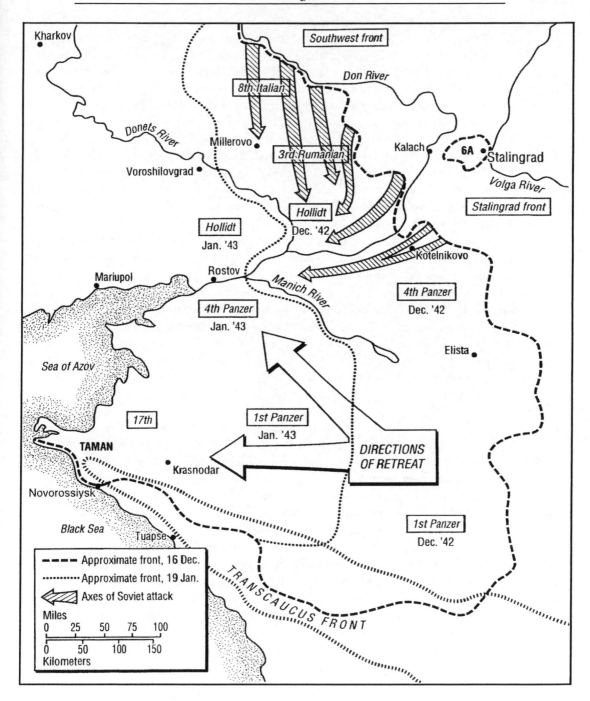

22.2. Second stage of Russian Winter Offensive, January 1943

and a second to keep his lines of communication to the rear intact. At this stage Hitler would not hear of withdrawing the AGA; even if the Russians took Rostov he would keep AGA in the Caucasus, he said. By mid–January the Russians were on the Donetz, their forward troops 20 miles from the sea. However, 4th Panzer in retreating from south of Stalingrad was now merging with the main forces of AG Don, which from a force of one corps had grown to 30 divisions, 12 of them Panzer or motorized. Fourteen of these divisions had been rushed from France. With these forces the Russians were stopped at the Donetz.

With Rostov threatened, Hitler at the end of the year finally gave permission for AGA to pull back. In doing so it was ordered to take along the civilian population of the Caucasus (Jukes, 130). The withdrawal proceeded along two routes. Kleist's Panzer Army retreated via Rostov, strengthening thereby the forces guarding it; 17th Army moved toward the Taman peninsula from where it could pass over to Kerch in the Crimea. With the start of withdrawal AGA was transferred from Kleist to Manstein. The troops of the Russian Transcaucasian front were under General Tyulenev, facing 24 divisions of AGA. Stalin kept pressing Tyulenev to prevent the Germans from withdrawing, at least to capture the Taman peninsula. But his forces were too weak and Tyulenev could do no more than trail the retreating Germans. Kleist completed his pullback in the middle of January. With this accomplished Hoth's 4th Panzers, which had been screening Kleist's movements, could now be moved west. But Hitler did not completely give up on his determination to hold on to the Caucasus. An order went out for 17th Army not to cross into Kerch but to keep its forces on the Taman. Thus several hundred thousand German troops were isolated on the peninsula, held there for a reconquest of the Caucasus.

Rostov fell to the Russians on February 14, ending stage 2 of the offensive. It achieved the strategic objective of clearing the enemy from the Caucasus and the Russians regained most of the ground they had lost in 1942. But the military success they had hoped for eluded them. The entire AGA succeeded in withdrawing, the Russians able neither to trap them nor even to seriously impede their retreat.

The third and last stage of the winter offensive started a month after the second and was conducted by the Voronezh and Southwest fronts. In general it seems to have been an attempt to capitalize on the prevailing disarray in the German ranks and regain as much of Ukraine as possible; seemingly, it also tried to achieve what the previous fighting had failed to do—cut off the German southern front. If so, the Russians were now attempting something they had been careful to avoid, as to reach the coast from the Voronezh front they had to go even farther and deeper than from the Don.

The offensive started on January 13 with an attack on the Hungarian 2nd Army arranged south of Voronezh—the last of the satellite troops still at the front. They too broke within days. Here, as well as in the south against German troops, the Russians achieved notable successes. After one week they had punched a 150-mile-wide gap between AG Don and AGB. In the north they had taken Kursk and in the south crowned their successes with the capture of Kharkov on February 15. The giving up of Kharkov was part of Manstein's plan to draw the Russians as far from their bases as possible and it was done against Hitler's explicit orders; this decision was taken by Hauser, commander of the II SS Panzer Corps. He, like another SS commander, Sepp Dietrich, found the temerity to disobey Hitler more often than did the traditional Junkers. After the capture of Kharkov the Russians were nearing the Dniepr, 100 or more miles in the rear of the German armies strung out along the Sea of Azov.

Manstein had by now accumulated in his area a substantial force. He had the 1st and 4th Panzer Armies, the II SS Panzer Corps, a number of special Combat Groups—Kempf, Hollidt, Fretter Pico—and fresh divisions brought over from France. In the north he could also count on Weich's AGB. Originally these large forces had been allotted by Hitler to relieve Stalingrad but by February this was no longer an option. Manstein had been planning a counterpunch since mid–January and on February 9 had discussed it with Hitler.

At that meeting Manstein added that it would help if Hitler appointed a single chief of staff for the entire Wehrmacht. Hitler retorted he could never appoint anyone to be above Göring (Sadaradanda, 98). When the Russians neared Dniepropetrovsk, Hitler flew down in a panic to Manstein's headquarters at Zaporozhe. After meetings lasting two days he approved Manstein's plan for the counterattack.

The operation was an unqualified success. Manstein struck on February 19 using from the south the 1st and 4th Panzers and from the northwest the II SS Panzer Corps with the attached Combat Groups. The Russians had for days been at the end of their tether, short of fuel and hemmed in on all sides by German armor. While in the north they managed to retain most of the gains, including the Kursk salient, in the south they not only gave up the territory they had won but suffered an all-too-familiar grievous defeat. Several of their armies were encircled, yielding the Germans another quarter million Russian prisoners. Kharkov was retaken by the Germans on March 14 and by the end of the month the fighting died down.

The Stalingrad-Caucasus battles of 1942–43 bear a strange resemblance to the struggles of 1941— only that each phase of it was fought at an intensified pitch and with a more devastating outcome for the German army. The city of Stalingrad Hitler fought for was as symbolic in name and as strategic a location as Moscow or Leningrad had been. As in the case of those two other cities, in Stalingrad the Germans had come close to their objective, penetrating not just to its suburbs but to its eastern limits— yet in the end unable to take it. In the Caucasus, Hitler came close to the oil fields of Grozny and Baku as well as to the rail line feeding Lend-Lease supplies but could take neither; not even the secondary objective of grounding the Russian fleet by capturing the Black Sea coast was achieved. And, as at Moscow, new and undetected Russian reserves swooped down on the Germans to hurl them back, ending the campaign in a military and strategic defeat for the Ostheer. Moreover, with all their past victories, the Ostheer in the spring of 1943 disposed of only 2.73 million men and a bare 1,330 tanks; the Red Army, after all its debacles, had 5.8 million under arms and 6,000 tanks (Glantz 1995, 151).

Part Three

THE SMART WAR

CHAPTER 23

The Reluctant Allies

Aside from a dozen or so governments in exile that had a negligible effect on the course of the war, Russia had three wartime allies—England, the USA and Poland. The inclusion of the latter may seem odd but Poland exerted a disproportionate impact on Stalin's diplomatic and military moves. More important than their mutual interaction was the effect the Polish question had on relations between the three major cobelligerents. This problem preceded the outbreak of the war and endured into the postwar period.

The official stance of the West to Hitler's attack on Russia was described in Chapter 18. The Western powers, letting out a sigh of relief, made it their task to provide Russia with material aid to enable her to withstand the German onslaught and remain a viable fighting force. This was to be of the highest priority to the point of the USA preferring Japan to attack her rather than Russia because in the latter case Russia might collapse. With Russia fighting, time would be given to mobilize America's prodigious resources while the German army continued to be ground down in the East. Ultimately the war would be won with minimal casualties to the Anglo-American armies. This approach, too, had a precedent in World War I. In the wake of the 1917 revolution the Allies tried everything to keep Russia in the war. It provided loans to the Russian government; it sent "goodwill" missions to determine Russia's needs intimating that "no fighting—no loans"; it provided railway experts to keep the trains running, especially the Vladivostok-Moscow line. And finally the US ambassador recommended sending in two to three US divisions (Churchill's two divisions). While Kerensky may have been pliable to these inducements, the Bolsheviks went their own way and ceased fighting.

There was a second unspoken element in the attitude of the West to the struggle being waged in the East. That this element was present throughout the war will become clear from the events during the next three years when Russia was left to fight alone the bulk of the German army. But hints of it surfaced soon after the invasion. On the night of June 21, a weekend, Eden was at Chequers spending time with Churchill. At 7:30 the next morning Eden was awakened by a servant who handed him a big cigar on a silver tray, saying, "The Prime Minister's compliments. The Germans have invaded Russia" (Eden 1960, 312). Thus along with relief there was glee. This inner satisfaction was soon heard on both sides of the Atlantic. In England the minister for air production said in July that he hoped the German and Russian armies would destroy each other (McNeill, 51). In the US Congress Sen. Harry Truman advised the administration, "If we see that Germany is winning we ought to help Russia and if Russia is winning we ought to help Germany and that way let them kill as many as possible, although I don't want to see Hitler victorious under any circumstances" (Dawson, 108). Except for the phrase of helping Germany if the Russians were winning, what Truman had said represented an unspoken current running through the emotions and thoughts of the Anglo-American powers. Thus the US military attaché in Moscow said, "aid to the USSR should be carefully gauged, so carefully that both Germany and the Soviet Union will find themselves completely exhausted and neither can be a dominant factor after the war." This view grew as the Russians were beginning to have the upper hand. On April 8, 1943, Hull received a memo from W.H. Gardiner, former president of the Navy League, endorsed by Sumner Welles asking the secretary of state to convince Roosevelt to change to a policy of defeating Japan first in order to stop the Russians from winning. Similar views were held by Leahy, Bullitt, Assistant Secretary of State Dunn, with Hull himself close to the above sentiments (Bennett, 42, 77). The Soviets were fully cognizant of these undercurrents as articulated by Litvinov in a January 2, 1943, report: "There is no doubt that the military plans of both countries [USA and Britain] are based on the goal of maximum exhaustion of the Soviet Union in order to diminish its role in the solution of postwar problems" (Perelmuter, 233).

The problem the Western Allies faced was how to implement their intrinsic strategy of letting Russia do all the fighting without jeopardizing the objective of sustaining her as the bludgeon to kill Hitler. This dichotomy was articulated by Roosevelt who, while setting in motion the aid shipments to Russia, told his entourage that he intended "to make haste slowly" (Mc Neill, 22). This dilemma would in the coming years produce great somersaults of deception, prevarication, outright lies, broken agreements and mutual acrimony — practiced by England and America individually and conjointly. It was sufficiently contorted to involve deception not only vis-à-vis Stalin but between England and America themselves. All this, of course did not escape the Russians' comprehension. Already on August 27, in a discussion with Eden, Maiski conveyed Stalin's view that the British were mere "spectators" in the war. When later Maiski reported the conversation, Stalin mused, "What do they [the British] want? They want, it seems to me, our weakening."

For Poland, the third ally, there was no ambiguity whatsoever; her interests and her prayers were that both Germany and the Soviet Union would collapse, as it happened in World War I, bringing with it a large independent Poland. The Poles had little reason to wish Russia well; she had been instrumental in the 1939 partition of Poland, subsequently deporting 1.5 million people from the annexed territories. And, unlike the Anglo-Americans, the Poles would not inherit the burden of winning the war should Russia collapse. In instructions to its underground in Poland the government in exile advised not to expend its forces fighting the Germans but to conserve them for such a time when both the Germans and Russians would be sufficiently weakened to offer an opportunity for a successful national revolt (Calvocoressi, 305). So beneath the diplomatic and propaganda niceties that accompanied the wartime reconciliation there lurked the conviction that for Poland the best thing would be a war in which Germany and Russia destroyed one another.

* * *

The September Protocol on aid to Russia for the period of October 1 to June 30, 1942, provided that supplies be made available but said nothing about delivery. Russia's merchant fleet was small and whatever she had was bottled up in the Baltic. The Black Sea was equally useless as the Bosphorus was closed to Allied shipping in conformity with Turkish neutrality. Eventually the Allies undertook to deliver the goods in their own vessels. Three different routes were available for reaching Russia, each with its own problems. One was from America's West Coast across the Pacific to Vladivostok. This route was completely safe as far as enemy action was concerned. Initially, American ships carried the cargos. After Pearl Harbor ships were transferred to the Soviet Union which, thanks to its neutrality pact, carried them safely across Japanese-dominated waters. This was a slow haul involving a sea voyage of some 5,000 miles. Consequently the turn-around time for the ships was long. Even after the goods reached Vladivostok they had to be transported overland for another 5,000 miles before they reached the front. In addition the Trans-Siberian Railroad was taken up much of the time with Russia's need to ferry men and supplies to the front.

The other available route was around Africa into the Persian Gulf. This was a sea voyage of 14,000 miles and the capacity of the Iranian rail link was minimal. Partly to improve this situation and partly to safeguard the Persian and Iraqi oil fields in case of a German breakthrough into the Caucasus, England and Russia jointly occupied Iran in August 1941. With the help of American engineering troops the capacity of the Iranian railroad was doubled. The Africa-Iran stretch was still relatively safe, though not as safe as the Vladivostok run because German U-boats prowled the Cape and Indian Ocean. Given the mountainous terrain, even with improvements the capacity of the Iran railroad remained low.

The third possibility was the northern ports of European Russia. In the summer that meant both Murmansk and Archangelisk; in the winter when the waters off Archangelisk froze, only Murmansk. From Iceland this sea route was only 1,500–2,000 miles long and when unloaded the supplies were close to where they were needed. From the standpoint of expeditious aid to Russia this was the best route. Here, aside from the foul weather, the big problem was the route's proximity to Norway's northern waters studded with German surface ships, U-boats and air fleets. Murmansk itself was only 20 miles from the German front lines. Because of this German threat only one-quarter of Allied assistance was transported along this seaway, a fifth of it being lost on the way (Heiber 1963, 816). As will be seen below all this had some painful consequences on the level of help Russia received and its relations with the Western Allies.

The first aid package from the West arrived in August. Following their practice at Malta, the British aircraft carrier *Argus* sailed from Iceland on August 21, launching 24 Hurricanes which landed at Vaenga airfield near Murmansk. Fifteen more crated Hurricanes along with a cargo of rubber and tin was shipped on six vessels which reached Archangelisk early in September. The first of the regular eastbound PQ convoys consisting of 10 merchantmen left Iceland on September 28 and docked at Murmansk on October 11. Churchill had promised to dispatch a convoy every 10 days but this proved beyond the Allies' shipping capacity and the subsequent convoys sailed at roughly two-week intervals. Till the end of 1941 53 ships reached Russia, supplying her with 800 fighter planes, 750 tanks and 1,400 motor vehicles (Schoefield, 31–40). These were mostly British shipments. The US deliveries were in arrears well into 1942 so that by June 1942 when the first protocol was about to expire only half of the US–promised aid had been delivered (Matloff, 205).

In 1942 the rate of Lend-Lease shipments picked up considerably as can be seen from the following tabulation (McNeill, 232).

Table 23-1
Lend-Lease Aid to Britain and Russia

	1941		1942	
	$ millions	%	$ millions	%
To British areas	1,747	Base	7,148	Base
To Russia	20	1.2	1,376	19.0

The weaponry delivered by the end of 1942 amounted to 7,652 planes, 9,848 tanks and 111,301 motor vehicles (Schofield, 224). Thus of the total arms delivered during the period of 1941–42 the proportions during each of the two calendar years amounted to the following:

Table 23-2
Levels of Aid Given Russia in 1941 and 1942

	% of (1941–42) Total	
	1941	1942
Planes	10.0	90.0
Tanks	7.6	92.4
Motor Vehicles	1.2	98.8

Thus Lend-Lease aid shipped to Russia in 1941 was, as shown in Table 23-1, only 1.5 percent that of 1942.

We have seen in Chapter 18 that the fate of Barbarossa was decided during the October to November 1941 battles. Subsequently the Russian war no longer posed a question of outcome but of the progress and cost of the Russian victory. Thus Western aid has to be viewed from two angles; one, did it have an impact on the Russians' ability to stop the Germans in 1941 and turn the struggle into a war of attrition which the Germans were bound to lose; and two, what effect did the West's material aid have on Russia's subsequent ability to gain victories at the rate they did and end up on the steps of the Reichstag on the date they did? While the latter point will be taken up when the total amounts of aid given Russia in planes, tanks, locomotives, tin, rubber, aluminum and even food and Army boots is catalogued — there can be no doubt that the trickle of weapons that reached the Red Army by the end of November — a tiny proportion of the arsenal the Red Army wielded against the Germans — had a negligible effect on the outcome of Barbarossa. There were also deliveries of industrial raw materials in that period but these could have had no effect until later in the war. It can, therefore, be asserted that Lend-Lease had no effect on the outcome of Barbarossa and that the Russians had won the 1941 campaign entirely on their own, albeit at a frightful cost.

The shipping of material aid to Russia was a Western initiative readily and gratefully accepted by Stalin. But from the very first, already at his July meeting with Hopkins, Stalin said that the only effective help in stemming the German avalanche was to siphon off 30–40 German divisions from the eastern front. This would have represented 15–20 percent of the German armada facing the Russians. And the only way to accomplish this was by a landing in France and possibly also in Norway. This was at a time when there was not a single Allied soldier on the Continent and the only land fighting that the British did in Libya was against the Italians and Rommel's three German divisions. Any thought of a cross–Channel landing in 1941 Churchill dismissed out of hand, citing the lack of shipping and the peril of launching a seaborne invasion against German troops. Stalin repeated his request on September 3 to which Churchill replied that he would sacrifice 50,000 British lives if it would draw off 20 divisions but it would not succeed, adding the disingenuous parallel that for the British to land in France was as impossible as for the Germans to land in England! (Miner, 158).

In the first week of September a bitter exchange erupted between Stalin and Churchill on the issue of sharing the war burdens. It started with a letter from Cripps bemoaning the fact that the British "consider the war here [in Russia] as a war which we desire to assist … without unduly endangering our own position" and he asked that Britain "make a super-human effort" not to lose the Russian front. To this Churchill gave a sarcastic reply: "When you speak of 'superhuman effort' you mean, I presume, an effort rising superior to space, time and geography. Unfortunately these attributes are denied us." On September 4, soon after Cripps' letter, came a communication from Stalin who, referring to an assessment by Churchill that the German onslaught on Russia had passed its peak, wrote, "The stabiliza-tion achieved on the front has now broken down due to the transfer last week of 33 fresh German divisions…. Germans consider the danger in the West a bluff." This prompted the war cabinet to note in its minutes that it was likely that the USSR was considering a sep-arate peace unless military action in the West was forthcoming. But when the CGS were consulted their view was that England could not undertake a cross–Channel attack because in France the Germans had 20–30 divisions and 800 aircraft. Churchill then answered Stalin's letter that there was no possibility of British action. He added what could only be salt on Russian wounds: "We are raising our Army in the Middle East to ¾ million men at the end of this year and to one million by the summer of 1942. Once we clear up Libya we will attack in the southern flank." Being an old warhorse Churchill knew that when under attack the best riposte is a counterattack and so he wrote to Cripps with the intention of it being passed on to Stalin that, "No one wants to recriminate but it is not our fault that Hitler was enabled to destroy Poland before turning his forces against France, or to destroy France before turning them against Russia" (Churchill Vol. 3, 1160–72). It was a shabby rejoinder unbecoming a man of Churchill's caliber. Churchill knew perfectly well that by the logic of his argument the Western powers were far more delinquent by remaining inac-tive during the occupation of the Rhineland, Austria, the Sudetenland and Czechoslova-kia; by resorting to a "phony war" while Poland was being overrun; by their frivolous maneuvers during the German takeover of Norway; and, *horribile dictu*, by their avoiding, at the very time of the Churchill-Stalin exchange, of any military action by Britain (and the USA) to help Russia fighting for its life.

If not an invasion, Stalin proposed that British troops join the fight on the eastern front and on September 15 asked that England send 30 divisions either via Archangelisk or through Iran. In response Eden on October 16 offered to send one brigade to the Caucasus (Eden 1960, 321–2). Puzzled, the Russians said that the fighting was near Rostov, not in the Caucasus, which the British took to be a rejection of their offer. Churchill also proposed to Stalin on October 12 that England take over the occupation of all of Persia thus freeing Soviet divisions for the front. After delivering this message to Molotov, Cripps reported to London, "I do not think he liked the suggestion about Persia very much" (Miner, 165). Next, the British proposed to send to Moscow Wavell and Paget for military discussions but Stalin said that he would not want "to intrude upon the generals." In December, fearing a Finnish offensive against Murmansk, the Red Army proposed a joint Russian-British landing at Petsamo, which would in addition cut off the nickel supply to Germany (Nissen, 170–3). This, too, was dismissed but something else was suggested. On December 5 Churchill promised to send 10 squadrons of RAF aircraft for the southern front, if Auchinleck was successful with his planned attack in Libya. Before Auchinleck could show success came Pearl Harbor and a rapid succession of British defeats in Malaya and Burma, whereupon, five days after having made the offer, Churchill cancelled it. This effectively ended all talk about British participation in fighting on the Russian front. That the vacuity of these British offers was transparent to the Russians surfaced in the following episode. In October 1941 a Russian mission arrived in Baghdad and the British, concerned about a possible German penetration of the Caucasus in the direction of the Persian oil fields, asked the Russians for information about their southern front so that they would be ready to defend the oil fields. To this the Russians replied, "If by chance such an event did take place and the Red Army could not stop the Germans, how in the name of heavens could you?" De Guignand, who was present at this exchange, was shaken by the Russian remark (Guignand, 102).

Next arose the question of Polish troops fighting on the eastern front. The background to this was the Sikorski-Maiski agreement of July 30,1941, restoring relations between the Poles and the USSR, severed since the Soviet occupation of eastern Poland. The pact provided for the release of all deported Polish citizens and for a Polish army to fight under Russian command. General Anders, a 1939 POW, would be its commander in chief. The physical condition of the Poles released from the various dungeons, gulags and places of exile after nearly two years of maltreatment was not good. In addition, Russia in 1941 was a country bare of the most primitive necessities, be it food, clothing or implements. The released Poles, therefore, were not fed and equipped as they should have been. Even worse was their mental outlook. After having lost their country, their freedom and often their families at the hands of the Soviets, they looked with a jaundiced eye at the prospect of fighting alongside them. A grim, hostile mood prevailed among the newly formed Polish units on Russian territory. Thus was born the idea that the best thing would be if these men were evacuated to Allied territory where they could be rehabilitated and equipped by the British. Churchill supported it, seeing in the Poles fresh troops for his plans in the Mediterranean.

Yet from a political standpoint it was in the Polish interest to have Anders' army stay in Russia. Already then it was clear that in the event of a German defeat it would be the Russian army that would enter Poland and it would be of paramount importance for Polish troops to be on Polish territory when it was liberated. Sikorski understood that. Anders, however, a typical specimen of Poland's prewar officer clique, was against it. So were nearly all the released Poles who harbored nothing but hate and contempt for their Russian hosts. Many of the men stated outright that they would rebel rather than fight alongside the Russians. With the concurrence of the Polish government, Harriman then proposed to Stalin on November 12 that Anders' army be evacuated to Persia where it could be properly equipped and trained; Harriman added that it would then return to fight on the eastern front.

A month later Sikorski arrived in Moscow for talks and on December 3 had his first meeting with Stalin. He, too, raised the question of sending out Anders's troops to be refurbished and armed after which they would return to Russia. The following exchange then took place:

STALIN: "I am an old, experienced man. I know that when you go to Persia you will not return."

SIKORSKI: "They will..."

STALIN: "If the Poles don't want to fight, let them go."

SIKORSKI: "You have annoyed me Mr. President by saying our soldiers don't want to fight..."

STALIN: "I am "prosty" (Unpolished but straight).... (But) as you wish" [Kot, 140–9].

The irony of this exchange is that Stalin, in fact, wanted these Poles to leave because already then he had plans for a different postwar Poland in which men of Anders's ilk could only become internal enemies. Already then six Polish officers had been taken from the Lubianka prison and interviewed by Beria and his cohorts to whom it was proposed they organize a pro–Soviet Polish army in the USSR. The officers agreed and one of them, Zygmunt Berling, no higher than a colonel, led the first Polish division in fighting the Germans under Soviet tutelage. The Anders troops, many accompanied by their families, started leaving Russia the following spring. By the fall of 1942 135,000 Poles, including 70,000 soldiers, had left the USSR. As soon as they were gone, Stalin formed of those remaining in USSR an alternate, Communist-led Polish army under Berling, overnight promoted to general.

Though there were altercations and reproaches about aid, the Polish question and other issues, the most wrenching and persistent contention between the West and Stalin concerned the formation of a second front. There was in it so much guile and circumvention — particularly on the part of Churchill and Brooke — that it is unprofitable to go into it. However, some of it has to be told because it reflects much of the physiognomy of this war. What stands out most is the sheer doggedness, the unsparing, relentless combat of the PM to hark to the strategy of avoiding the German army but stick to his pretense of winning the war by air bombardment, dispersal tactics and the fantasy of freedom fighters setting "Europe ablaze."

When the news broke of the Japanese attack on Pearl Harbor, Churchill immediately traveled to Washington to talk to Roosevelt. Now that the USA and Britain were, in Roosevelt's phrase, "in the same boat," Churchill brought with him a strategic plan for dealing with Germany. The document presented to Roosevelt on December 23, had three parts which read:

a. With regard to the German-Russian war the Western Allies have no other role to play but send supplies to Russia.

b. A combined bomber offensive is to be launched on Germany.

c. The North-African coast is to be cleaned up by May 1942.

This scenario Churchill named "Closing the Ring." With the ring closed he then advanced his favorite overall strategy — hit-and-run attacks on Norway, Denmark, Holland, Belgium, France, Italy and the Balkans (Beitzell, 15–6).

Roosevelt passed on these proposals to Marshall and to Eisenhower, who at that time headed the Army War Plans Division. Neither of them cared much for "Closing the Ring" or its follow-up. Being military men and American, they wanted to tackle the problem head-on and by the maximum concentration of forces. By March they had their own plan of dealing with Germany, which, as already decided on, was to be the main enemy, ahead of Japan. Named *Sledgehammer* this consisted of a limited landing by five British divisions

on the coast of France in September 1942, to be undertaken, even if it meant failure, in
order to draw German forces from Russia; this was to be followed by *Roundup*, a massive
invasion in early 1943 of the French coast between Le Havre and Boulogne by some 48 divisions, 30 of them American, and 5,000 aircraft.

Hopkins and Marshall traveled to London and presented their plan on April 8. After
perusing this document, in every fiber a departure from his plan, Churchill nevertheless
cabled Roosevelt, "Our two nations are resolved to march forward into Europe together
in a noble brotherhood of arms as a great crusade for the liberation of the tormented peoples." The American scheme with regard to both Sledgehammer and Roundup was approved
by the British Chiefs of Staff and, with Hopkins and Marshall in attendance was also
approved "in principle" by the British War Cabinet Defense Committee (Beitzell, 35–6).

A subtle redressing of Sledgehammer soon took place. While ostensibly the Americans and the British agreed to a 1942 landing, both sides seemed to have come to the following understanding. Sledgehammer would be launched in either of two contingencies:
when it looked that the Russians were about to collapse, in which case launching Sledgehammer would siphon off a number of German divisions and restore the eastern front; or
when the Germans were on the verge of collapse, making the invasion a walkover. These
stipulations were nowhere articulated in writing but such an understanding clearly existed
within the Anglo-American community (McNeill, 173). The intent and informality of this
understanding fits in with the Western Allies' unspoken policy vis-à-vis the Russian-German war. It dictated that should Russia falter an invasion in the West would be launched
to put her back in shape; but should no such exhaustion occur in either belligerent, no invasion would take place in 1942.

Armed with the ostensible British agreement to the American plan for invading Europe
and ignoring the tacit understanding not to implement what had been formally agreed to,
Roosevelt on April 10 send Stalin the good news, "I have in mind very important military
proposals ... to relieve your critical western front" (McNeill, 178). In May when Molotov
journeyed to London to sign an Anglo-Soviet Treaty, he was invited to Washington. On
May 30 he conferred with Roosevelt in the presence of Marshall and King. This was one of
the crucial exchanges that considerably colored the subsequent state of trust between Stalin
and the West. Since to the Russians a second front was of the highest priority the subject
soon took center stage. Pressed by Molotov, Roosevelt turned to Marshall, inquiring whether
"developments were clear enough so that we could say to Mr. Stalin that we were preparing a Second Front?" To this Marshall replied, "Yes." Roosevelt then authorized Molotov
to tell Stalin that "we expect the formation of a Second Front this year." When it came to
drafting an official communiqué, Roosevelt let Molotov compose the crucial phrase which
read, "In the course of the consultations full understanding was reached with regard to the
urgent tasks of creating a second front in Europe in 1942." After obtaining British concurrence this statement was released on July 11. After Molotov left, Roosevelt went to Hyde
Park where Harriman joined him. In his memoirs Harriman wrote that while listening to
the president he became convinced that Roosevelt deliberately misled Molotov in order to
keep the Russians in the fight (Abramson, 328).

No sooner had Molotov left than Churchill came to Washington to scotch any plans
for a landing in 1942. He arrived on June 18, a month before the official commitment to a
second front in Europe in 1942 was released to the public (July 11). Instead of Sledgehammer, Churchill applied all his eloquence and zest to preach an invasion of the North African
coast, part of his coveted "Closing the Ring." He even had an additional reason for shying

away from a landing in France—the vengeful Germans might vent their fury on French civilians (Abramson, 329). Listening to the prime minister, Roosevelt confessed to a great liking for a landing in Africa. Within the last month Roosevelt had, in fact, turned a sympathetic ear to all his interlocutors—Molotov, to whom he pledged a 1942 invasion; Churchill, whose enthusiasm for Torch he readily shared; and to Marshall, staunchly opposed to any diversion of American troops to secondary battlefields such as Africa. No sooner had Churchill left when Roosevelt sent his chief strategists to London to reconvert the British to American strategy. At the end of June, Hopkins, Marshall and King alighted in London, their mission being to resurrect Sledgehammer. Buttressed by Roosevelt's newborn enthusiasm for Torch, the British put up a stone wall against any idea of a cross–Channel attack. Faced with a complete reversal of decisions commonly taken only a few months ago and in violation of what had been promised the Russians only last month, Marshall in desperation cabled Roosevelt for instructions. To his utter bafflement he was told to yield and agree to a 1942 landing in North Africa instead (Abramson, 331). Soon thereafter, on July 24, the Combined Chiefs of Staff formally annulled Sledgehammer and replaced it with a 1942 landing in North Africa. Moreover, in phrasing this decision sand was thrown into the planned invasion in 1943. The draft of the new decision stated that "a commitment to [Torch] renders Roundup in all probability impractical of execution in 1943" (Beitzell, 51).

Along with the cancellation of a 1942 second front, the British suspended the Murmansk convoys. With the long daylight hours in the Arctic, German ships and planes were taking a heavy toll on the merchantmen ferrying supplies to Russia. At the Admiralty's insistence Churchill agreed to stop the convoys and on July 18 so informed Stalin. He sweetened the bad news with a solemn promise to stage an invasion of France by a million Allied troops—in 1943. This was the first Stalin heard about the cancellation of a second front in 1942. Back came a harsh rebuke telling Churchill that "the Soviet Government cannot tolerate a Second Front in Europe being postponed till 1943" (Beitzell, 51). Roosevelt played shy, insisting that Churchill be the one to reply. Churchill felt the situation to be sufficiently grave to go and see Stalin in person.

Churchill arrived in Moscow on August 12 and at 7 that evening met with Stalin. Accompanying him in addition to Ambassador Kerr was Averell Harriman as special representative of President Roosevelt. Molotov and Voroshilov also attended. Churchill started expostulating on the obstacles to launching an invasion against German troops when a glowering Stalin interrupted, "A man who was not prepared to take some risks could not win a war." Churchill kept his temper and in offering Torch as a substitute for the second front he drew a crocodile explaining that France represented its snout whereas the Mediterranean was the soft underbelly. Stalin again interjected that what he wanted and what had been agreed to was a landing in Europe perhaps of no more than six to eight divisions, say at Cherbourg, a promontory easy to hold. He then went on to accuse the British of cowardice and Churchill of duplicity. This was a painful note for Churchill's ears because it came close to what he himself felt. In February, after a series of defeats on the Malayan peninsula, General Percifal surrendered 100,000 British troops in Singapore—not to the Germans but to the Japanese; the fortress fell a month ahead of Japanese expectations. And only a few months ago while in Washington killing off Sledgehammer, he received the news of 33,000 British troops surrendering at Tobruk to a German force half their number, making Churchill blurt out "Defeat is one thing but disgrace is another." He had himself come to feel that not only were his generals incompetent but that the customary valor of the British soldier has become a thing of the past. He was now being told all this by a leader of armies whose tenacity and bravery exceeded all the predictions of military experts. It cut so deeply that Churchill crashed his fist on the table, and left the meeting.

Next day, to avoid a repetition of the previous day's acrimony, Churchill presented an aide-memoire which pointed out that with regard to a second front in 1942 Molotov had been told in London that "we can ... give no promise,"—which was only literally correct. But what was truly astounding was that in the written memorandum that Harriman likewise gave Stalin it stated that on the American side, too, "no promise has been broken regarding a Second Front" (Beitzell, 58)!

In his memoirs Churchill goes on at great length to relate that when he presented Torch—an invasion of French North Africa—Stalin turned enthusiastic, grasping immediately the astuteness and import of the scheme. To glean the intentions of Torch required the talents of a kindergarten strategist and the reason, certainly, Churchill praised Stalin so extravagantly for embracing Torch was to imbue it with a significance it did not have. The reason Stalin concurred with Torch was that he was powerless to alter a thing in his Allies' decisions. Not only this but on January 13, 1943, Roosevelt and Churchill met in Casablanca where the decision was taken that after North Africa was cleared of Axis troops, the next step would be an invasion of Sicily. To make sure that the Casablanca decisions stood, in May Churchill traveled to Washington to get the president's word that Sicily and not France would be invaded in 1943.

Stalin was not informed about the Casablanca decisions. He thereupon inquired what about Roundup? For a second time Roosevelt left to Churchill the task of breaking the bad news. Stalin was told that, yes, there will be a cross–Channel attack in 1943, but "the timing ... must be dependent upon the conditions of German defensive capabilities." This should have made sense to any military expert but evidently not to Stalin. In reply he demanded an invasion "in spring or early summer of 1943, as Churchill had promised in Moscow." This message Stalin sent to both London and Washington. Churchill's answer of March 11 again temporized, saying, yes, there would be such an attack but only in August. To end this tormented exchange Roosevelt on June 4 finally informed Stalin that there would be no invasion of France in 1943 (Beitzell, 99). Churchill followed it up on July 19 with an "I am sorry" note to which Stalin replied, "You say you quite understand my disappointment.... It is a question of saving millions of lives and of reducing the enormous sacrifices of the Soviet armies compared to which the sacrifices of the Anglo-American armies are insignificant" (Harriman, 213).

One of the pretexts why there was no cross–Channel invasion in 1943 was a presumed shortage of shipping, particularly of LCs, the poorest excuse the Allies could have floated. When it was decided that instead of Roundup Sicily would be next, the armada that sailed in July for the invasion of that island was larger than the one employed on D-Day in 1944. In fact, when Sicily was decided on, the US top priority for manufacturing LCs was downgraded to 12th place. Of the enormous number of 31,000 LC's produced by May 1944, only 2,500 were used on D-Day, the rest having gone to the Pacific despite the proclaimed Europe First strategy (Grigg, 212). The lack of LCs had become an incantation the Anglo-Americans flaunted not only in front of their critics but to each other, too, as if eager to convince themselves that the scotching of the invasion of France in 1942 and 1943 was due to *force majeure*.

Two charades were being played out with regard to the second front. One was practiced on Stalin, the other between the Western Allies. The one played on Stalin was straightforward but the one between the British and the Americans was tortured. Churchill had to

Top: The sub–Alliance: Roosevelt and Churchill having a confidential chat at Yalta. (Courtesy the Franklin D. Roosevelt Presidential Library.) *Bottom:* The full Alliance: Churchill, Roosevelt and Stalin at Yalta, February 1945. (Courtesy the National Archives.)

tread gingerly lest his opposition to an invasion of the Continent lead the Americans to reverse the Europe First strategy and concentrate on Japan. A second motive was to encourage the buildup of American forces in England in preparation for an invasion, which in fact aimed partly at assuring its defense in case of a Russian collapse, followed by a German attempt to invade the island. The result was that large US forces were kept in England for the purpose of doing nothing. This game required the British to indulge in double talk — hence the repetitive endorsement of a cross–Channel attack followed by subsequent cancellations.

Roosevelt's role was, as usual, Machiavellian. Formally he was bound to respect the views of his cabinet and his military chiefs who advocated an invasion of the Continent. There was, too, the American suspicion that "Closing the Ring" was geared to safeguarding the British Empire — Egypt, Palestine, Iraq and the road to India. Furthermore, with the Americans doing the fighting in the Pacific, Roosevelt had hoped to get Stalin to join in and was therefore more inclined than Churchill to accommodate him. Aware of Wilson's disappointment after World War I, Roosevelt was determined to set up a universal organization, more effective than the League of Nations had been, and for this, too, he needed a cooperative Soviet Union. Finally, there was Roosevelt's vanity. At the beginning of the war, particularly in 1940, Churchill had been the world-renowned warrior and statesman and it was flattering to be his intimate. But after Russia's string of victories Churchill became a secondary figure and Stalin the star, Britain a junior partner and Russia the power deciding matters of war and peace. Roosevelt soon transferred his interest and camaraderie to the Russian leader to a point of avoiding meeting Churchill — a pettiness that clouded his political judgment and deeply hurt Churchill. All this made Roosevelt behave as if he were fully for launching a second front but eventually he would side with Churchill's Mediterranean schemes. It can only be surmised that it was the covert motive of letting the two dictatorial adversaries in the East fight it out that in the end decided the common Western policy of not staging a second front in Europe either in 1942 or 1943.

* * *

By 1943 a serious crisis had developed between the Anglo-American powers and the Soviet Union. It ranged over the entire gamut of strategy, material aid, and political and diplomatic issues.

After the start of Barbarossa in June 1941 Russia was left to fight the German army alone for three agonizing years. Table 23-3 shows the number of German divisions engaged in combat by their eastern and western enemies. For one and a half years after the start of Barbarossa the British fought three German divisions in Libya while 150 to 200 divisions were arraigned on the eastern front. Thus only 2 percent of the German Army was engaged in the West. Now, the British also fought the Italians but in the east, in addition to Germans, were Finnish, Hungarian, Rumanian and Italian armies— well over a million men. For the year and a half between Torch and D-Day in June 1944 there were 14 German divisions fighting in the Mediterranean, which still left 93 percent of the German army to be dealt with by the Russians. The German occupation troops throughout Europe cannot be simply included in this arithmetic because, due to heavy losses, the German combat divisions in Russia needed 100 percent or more replacements so that in terms of manpower these divisions over the years represented double their number. This holds even more so for the turnover of weaponry, tanks, guns, and other equipment used by combat troops.

Table 23-3
Number of German Divisions Involved
in Combat and Occupation Duties*

| YEAR | MONTH | Engaged in Combat in | | Africa | Italy | France | Total in the West | |
| | | Russia | | | | | | |
		No.	%				No.	%
1941	June	151	98.5	2	—	—	2	1.5
	Dec.	166	98	3	—	—	3	2
1942	June	192	98.5	3	—	—	3	1.5
	Dec.	188	97	6	—	—	6	3
1943	June	200	100	—	—	—	0	0
	Dec.	198	93	—	14	—	14	7
1944	June	178	70	—	22	56	78	30
	Dec.	162	64	—	22	71	93	36
1945	March	166	67	—	19	63	82	33

Thus the often-cited point that over the years the Allies pinned down x German occupation divisions in the West as against the 200 fighting in the East is a feeble argument.

Of course, the Western Allies also fought in the air and here their input was substantial — but still not as overwhelming as their wide-ranging activities over the Mediterranean, France and in the bombing of Germany would lead one to expect. The available data for some of the periods show that in the second half of 1942 the Germans lost 5,000 planes, half of them in Russia. In 1943 the Germans lost a total of 12,000 planes of which a third was in Russia, a third in fighting the West, and a third in the defense of the reich (Murray, 114,148). The bitter struggle against the U-boat menace was a Western affair which had no direct impact on the war in Russia.

The second cancellation of a cross–Channel attack was followed by a second suspension of the Murmansk convoys. This came with the onset of long daylight hours in the Arctic. Consequently by September 1943 the amount of aid delivered via the Arctic route was a third of what had been shipped in 1942 (Beitzell, 373). For the entire year the number of ships dispatched to Murmansk was less than half of 1942 — 112 in 1943 versus 256 the previous year. Even though when the Pacific and Iran routes are included the total aid in 1943 exceeded that of 1942 ($2.44 billion vs. $1.38 billion) yet the stoppage of the Murmansk convoys was to Stalin another indication of the Allies' ill will. The Allies justified the suspension by the high convoy losses. Yet even in 1942, the worst year for the Russian convoys, the losses in merchant shipping amounted to only 12 percent (McNeill, 238–9). This includes the July disaster of PQ 17 when two-thirds of the convoy was sunk. This catastrophic event resulted from the Admiralty's policy that when a choice had to be made between losing naval ships or merchantmen the latter should be sacrificed. Thus when information was received that the German surface fleet was about to sortie out against PQ 17, the warships were ordered home leaving the merchantmen to make their way to Murmansk as best they could. As a result 23 out of 37 cargo ships (including two rescue vessels) were sunk, not by German surface ships — which did not, as it turned out, sortie out — but by U-boats and aircraft. Stalin may have taken a jaundiced view of the decision to sacrifice his precious cargos in order to avoid battle with the German warships (Admiral King, too, was infuriated by the decision). And Stalin may also have viewed a 12-percent loss in shipping as not too exorbitant, given that in any major land battle, even a victorious one, the Red Army's losses verged on 50 percent, or more.

Churchill and Roosevelt were planning a get-together in Quebec, known as *Quadrant*. After Churchill told Stalin that Roundup, too, had been cancelled he had, on June 19, invited Stalin to the meeting, perhaps to mollify him. Stalin said he was too busy fighting the war and declined to attend. Instead, with regard to the cancellation of Roundup, he wrote to Roosevelt that "the alliance is being subjected to severe strain." The two Western leaders went ahead with Quadrant, which took place during August 14–24. The main impetus for the meeting was how to respond to the looming surrender of Italy as a result of Mussolini's dethronement the previous month. Also, plans were being made how to proceed after the fall of Sicily. The Americans, as usual, wanted an invasion of France; Churchill stuck to his soft underbelly campaigns. Churchill said he would agree to invade France provided the following conditions prevailed:

- There must be a substantial reduction of German fighter aircraft there.
- There should be no more than 12 German divisions facing the Allies.
- The Germans should be capable of boosting this initial force to no more than 15 divisions.
- A technology must be developed for the construction of at least two artificial harbors.

Familiar with past British maneuverings the Americans insisted on drawing up a "contract" specifying that after Sicily an invasion of Italy would take place if it was accompanied by a commitment for the invasion of France in 1944.

Concurrently, serious political differences arose between East and West. On the one hand this was due to the divergence of national interests but it was certainly exacerbated by the avoidance of military action by the West. In 1940 England, alone and desperate for allies, dispatched Cripps, a left-wing maverick and admirer of the Soviet Union, as ambassador to Moscow in the hope of luring Stalin away from his German partner. As part of this campaign, on October 15, 1940, Churchill offered to recognize de-facto the USSR's annexation of the Baltic states and eastern Poland in return for no more than that "the USSR apply to Great Britain a neutrality as benevolent as that applied to Germany" (Beitzell, 8–9). When in December 1941 Eden went to Moscow to negotiate an Anglo-Soviet treaty, Stalin asked that Churchill's 1940 concessions be included. When Eden consulted Churchill and the latter, in Washington at the time, discussed it with Roosevelt the answer was to reject it; there was no need for such compromises now that, willy-nilly, the Soviet Union was in the Allied camp. When Molotov came to London in June 1942 the political questions were raised again, Stalin's argument being that certainly after winning the war Russia should not end up with less than before. At that time, when faced with a choice between a promise for a second front or insistence on the border issue, Stalin chose the first. However in 1943, with no second front in either 1942 or 1943 the problem of recognizing Russia's 1941 borders became a top priority pressed by Stalin with growing determination. The Western powers would not recognize the incorporation of the Baltic states and even though they were more flexible on Poland's eastern borders— their own Curzon Line — they would not accede to that either.

The question of the eastern territories also led to a crisis with the London-based Polish government. Before the Sikorski-Maiski agreement was signed in July 1941 the Poles had insisted that Stalin agree to a restoration of Poland's prewar boundaries. This he would not do— the best he offered was a repudiation of the Nazi-Soviet Pact of 1939 leaving the question of the eastern territories open. The Poles continued to insist on the inviolability of their old borders. They would not listen to British advice that they gain Russia's postwar cooperation by some compromise on the subject, some members of the Polish government being against the pact altogether. It is against this background that the Katyn story erupted. When in the summer of 1941 the Poles were organizing their army in Russia they noticed that few former officers showed up among the released POWs. When on his visit to Moscow Sikorski inquired about their whereabouts, Stalin said that perhaps they had escaped. "But where could they flee to?" asked Sikorski. "Well, to Manchuria, for instance," was Stalin's reply (Kot, 140). In April 1943 the Germans announced that in the Katyn forest near Smolensk they found a mass grave of some 6,000 executed Polish officers, a deed they attributed to the Soviets. The Poles, deeply disturbed by the news, tried to find out the truth of the German allegation. Long after the war it was revealed that on an order from Beria issued on March 5, 1940, nearly all Polish officers as well as high functionaries of the Polish police and government in Russian hands had been murdered during April–May 1940 and the number was not 6,000 but closer to 20,000, among them 12 generals and 250 colonels (Sudoplatov, 477). But in 1943 all this could as well have been a German provocation. Churchill counseled Sikorski to be prudent, saying, "If they are dead nothing will bring them back to life" (Churchill, IV, 759). It is questionable whether Churchill — a man not lacking in empathy — would have said this had it involved 20,000 murdered British officers. The Poles ignored his advice and endorsed a Red Cross investigation of the affair. Whereupon Stalin, accusing the Poles of abetting German propaganda, on April 25 broke relations with the Polish government.

The next political fallout related to the surrender of Italy in September 1943. Negotiations between Italian envoys and the Western Allies had been going on since July, following Mussolini's overthrow. The terms of surrender had been agreed on by Churchill and Roosevelt at their August 14–17 Quebec meeting. When Stalin was eventually informed about the impending surrender, he wrote back on August 22, "To date it has been like this. The USA and Britain reach agreement between the two partners, a third party looking passively on. I must say that this situation cannot be tolerated any longer" (Beitzell, 159). Roosevelt refused to answer this communication. Subsequently Stalin demanded that Russia be given a share of the Italian fleet transferred to the Allies as part of the surrender agreement. The loot had been considerable. Beside the naval fleet (listed in Chapter 32) this included a large commercial tonnage. In addition to the 1 million GRT of Italian shipping there were 150 ships of 650,000 GRT of French shipping which fell into Axis hands during the occupation of Vichy France in 1942. Roosevelt answered Stalin that the ships would be used wherever it suited the Allies best.

The consequences of all this were not long in coming. Early in the year Roosevelt started laying plans for a private meeting with Stalin. On March 18 he wrote to Churchill, "I tell you that I think I can personally handle Stalin better than either your Foreign Office or my State Department. Stalin hates the guts of all of your top people. He thinks he likes me better and I hope he will continue to do so." In June Harriman informed the prime minister that Roosevelt intended to meet alone with Stalin prior to a possible Big Three conference, the objective being to "take Mr. Stalin out of his shell, so to speak, away from his aloofness, secretiveness and suspiciousness" (Harriman, 134, 216). Stalin kept saying he would like very much to meet the president. When in June Roosevelt wrote that there would be no second front in 1943, Stalin cancelled all plans for a meeting.

Next Maiski was recalled from London and on July 28 it was announced that he would not be returning to his post. On August 16, Litivinov, too, was withdrawn from Washington. Both of these ambassadors were known to be pro–Western diplomats. In Moscow two significant initiatives were launched at about the same time. Two months after severing ties with the London-based Polish government, the Congress of the Union of Polish Patriots was organized which in due course would spawn a Communist government for postwar Poland. On July 12 and 13 a Free German Committee was set up in Krasnogarsk with the participation of the prewar Communist functionaries Ulbricht and Pieck, which would likewise yield a Communist government for East Germany. This Free Committee was later joined by a number of German officers, including Feldmarschall Paulus.

The biggest fallout of the East-West tensions was a surge of reports about a possible separate peace between the Soviet Union and Germany. These peace feelers remain a murky affair for obvious reasons. The contacts were clandestine and no records were either written or preserved. While some of the low-level meetings were observed or deliberately leaked, meetings of prominent personalities—if they indeed took place—were kept secret. Not only are the mechanics of the contacts obscure but their motives, too, cannot be ascertained with any assurance. Absent also are any clues what were the offers or conditions for a cessation of fighting. For all these reasons one could have been excused for consigning these events to the realm of planted rumors except that such contacts did take place, sanctioned evidently by the highest authorities on both sides.

This whirlwind of activities orbited primarily in neutral Sweden, its center the Soviet Embassy in Stockholm run by Ambassador Alexandra Kollontay. Of the Soviet contacts the main figures were A.M. Alexandrov, chief of the Central European desk at the Foreign Ministry, and two Soviet embassy officials, Semionov and Nitutin, counsellor and trade representative respectively. On the German side two were agents of Ribbentrop, still fond of his 1939 pact and his Moscow "comrades." One was Peter Kleist, an erstwhile member of the Ribbentrop Büro and a participant in the 1939 pact with the Soviets; the other was Paul Schmidt, chief of press and information at the German Foreign Ministry. The main figure, however, was one Edgar Klaus, employed in the film department of the Abwehr station in Stockholm and thus a Canaris man. He was of Jewish origin though officially listed as the son of a German general under the Tsar. Aside from his claim of having connections with officials in the Soviet Embassy what influenced his choice may have been that in Soviet eyes his being a Jew lent credence to his sincerity in pushing for an end to the war; to the Germans, "Jewish traitor" would be a handy label should the affair become public.

The peak of activity occurred in mid–1943. In June Kleist came to Stockholm; Alexandrov, too, was there at that time. Also in June Schmidt met with Nitutin at the Swedish spa Saltsjobaden and again in August. Their first meeting was reported in the Swedish newspaper *Allehand,* which prompted an official denial by Ambassador Kollontay. The denial was repeated on June 18 by Tass, adding that the rumors aimed "at spreading misunderstanding between the allies." Another meeting between Alexandrov and Kleist was arranged for the first week of September but miscarried apparently due to faulty timing. When after waiting for nine days Alexandrov left Stockholm he told Klaus that the Russians would be watching for some "gesture" from the Germans (Fleischauer, 158, 191). Aside from being the middleman, numerous other contacts were independently run by Edgar Klaus with various members of the Soviet Embassy. Some of these meetings were monitored by Swedish agents and recorded in the police files. In addition there were purportedly contacts via the Rosenberg ministry; von Papen in Turkey; and the former ambassador to Moscow, von Schulenburg.

It is also of some relevance to note that it was at this period that Maiski and Litvinov were recalled from the western capitals. Both diplomats were Jews and it served as a wink to the Germans. In the case of Litivinov it duplicated his dismissal as foreign minister just before the Nazi-Soviet pact was consummated.

Aside from these surreptitious or inveigling acts some of the others were quite direct and official. Three of them came in quick succession from the Russians. On September 16 Gromyko handed Hull a communication from Molotov that on September 13 the Japanese Government proposed to mediate a separate peace between the USSR and Germany and that the offer was rejected. Ten days later in a talk with the first secretary of the Soviet Embassy, K.W. Winogradow, the US ambassador in Sweden, H. Johnson, inquired about the ostensible peace feelers to which Winogradow replied that in fact "some persons" had tried to act for Germany but that there had been no direct approach from official circles. The most revealing statement, however, was made on November 12 by Molotov himself when he handed Harriman a memorandum stating that in mid–October 1943 Ambassador Kollontay received an anonymous letter about a possible end to the war. Molotov confirmed that Soviet Embassy officials met with the sender who turned out to be Edgar Klaus. The latter conveyed the following message: "A group in Germany in close contact with Ribbentrop ... [are] for a separate peace with the Soviet Union.... They will agree to all Soviet demands and are ready to restore the boundaries of 1941." Klaus wanted to hear whether there was "a possibility for this group to meet with Soviet representatives and whether a Soviet representative would be ready to meet with Ribbentrop." Molotov said that the instructions to Stockholm were to discontinue the contacts (Fleischhauer, 199–20).

While it is quite common for individuals and organs of nations at war to make soundings about a possible end to the fighting — using the familiar sequence of secret governmental endorsement and public denial — there seemed to have been more to the goings-on in Stockholm. Given the timing of these events and the tenor of the official Soviet denials — a typical Soviet practice of floating a story by denying it — the most likely motive for all this must have been to frighten the West over a possible separate peace and cajole them to launch the promised invasion of France. Molotov's note alluding to the German willingness to recognize the Soviet 1941 borders was also directed at the West's reluctance to do the same. Judging by their responses the Western Allies seemed not to have been overly concerned, apparently recognizing these maneuvers for what they were.

· CHAPTER 24 ·

British Strategy

By the summer of 1943 Great Britain had been at war with Germany for nearly four years — the total duration of World War I. Throughout these years there had been no British victories over the Germans on the European continent nor did a front exist where British and German armies were in combat. This was as the British wished it. The reason for this mode of waging war lies, as discussed earlier, in the trauma of World War I. The British were determined not to repeat that experience. Tied to this, and partly as a result of it, hovered their leaders' awareness of the abject performance of the British army in whatever combat they engaged with the Germans. Worse than the performance of the troops was the caliber of British generalship. They were obsolete men devoid of the competence and imagination required in modern warfare. Some of the failures had the marks of burlesque. A decision was taken on February 1941 to occupy the tiny island of Castelorizzo, midway between Cyprus and Rhodes. A Commando of 200 men landed while the main force lounged offshore. A counterattack by the Italian garrison scared the Commandos whereupon the entire expedition returned home. Churchill was sufficiently unsettled to order that no communiqué about the adventure be issued. A similar conquest of the even smaller island of Pantelleria was planned for December 1941. But in the estimation of the High Command this was considered not feasible because the British did not have "adequate forces" and moreover it was discovered that the island had lately installed artillery guns. The army's ineffectiveness showed not only in combat but also in its organization, planning and discipline, not to speak of "lack of imagination and daring on part of the High Command" (Churchill Papers Vol. 3, 804 et al.). Even the British navy did not escape the onus of lack of vigor in World War II. During the *Bismarck* affair the Admiralty was naturally shocked by the quick demise of the *Hood* and Churchill fumed why the *Prince of Wales* had broken off contact because she had been hit by a few shells. And it was only an Enigma decrypt that helped locate the *Bismarck* after she had eluded the British fleets. The *Bismarck* had notified the Naval Command that she was heading for St. Nazaire but the British did not read the naval Enigma at the time. However Jeschonnek, who had a son serving on the *Bismarck*, inquired about her fate. The answer delivered in Luftwaffe code was that she was due at St. Nazaire. It was this Luftwaffe Enigma which the British read that sealed the *Bismarck*'s doom (Bercuson, 243)

The disappointment with the British army and its generals was often enough lamented by the British leaders themselves. On May 24, 1940, Churchill wrote to General Ismay with regard to the fighting in France: "Apparently the Germans can go anywhere and their tanks can act in twos or threes all over our rear.... Our tanks recoil before their field guns but our field guns do not like to take on their tanks.... Of course if one side fights and the other

326

does not, the war is apt to become somewhat unequal" (Churchill Papers Vol. 2, 138). And again in writing to his wife from Egypt two years later he says, "This splendid Army, about double as strong as the enemy, is baffled and bewildered by its defeats ... a kind of apathy and exhaustion of the mind rather than body has stolen over our troops" (Winston and Clementine, 466). When after invading North Africa Eisenhower proposed taking Sfax to prevent the junction of the Libyan and Tunisian German troops, Brooks stopped him as being "too risky" (Grigg, 75). On September 16, 700 reinforcements for the British 10th Corps disembarked at Salerno, but refused to join their units, saying that they were supposed to rejoin the 8th Army or be shipped to England—the only case of open mutiny. After listening to General McCrery, 500 soldiers obeyed but 192 did not, and were shipped out for court martial. Three ringleaders were sentenced to death, but were pardoned (Graham and Bidwell, 93). In Malaysia 60,000 Japanese, facing twice that number of British troops, landed 700 miles from Singapore and—crossing jungles and mountains on foot and bicycles—took Britain's greatest fortress on February 15, 1942, capturing in Singapore 100,000 prisoners and enormous booty at the cost of 3,500 dead. What happened in Malaysia was repeated in Burma, which was swiftly conquered by the Japanese against a much larger force. General Wavell, commander in chief in India, was compelled to inform the War Office that, "Until we have again soldiers capable of marching twenty or thirty miles a day ... and his idea [is] to come to grips with enemy ... whatever the difficulties and odds, we shall not recover our morale and reputation" (Bierman, 244). Moaned Cadogan, "Our Army is the mockery of the world."

It did not help when in trying to mask their mediocrity and stodginess British generals resorted to the stiff upper lip, dismissing their American colleagues as crude greenhorns. This had been the pattern before America's entry into the war and it persisted thereafter. With the exception of Churchill this superciliousness extended from the very top to the lowliest officer. When Churchill decided to send Halifax as ambassador to Washington, he confessed in a letter to Baldwin that he was loath to take the appointment because "I don't think it is particularly my kind of country and I have never liked Americans.... In the mass I have always thought them dreadful!" (Churchill Papers Vol. 2, 1268). In Alexander's view "the American soldiers are mentally and physically soft and very green.... They simply do not know their job as soldiers and this is the case from the highest to the lowest; the result is that their men don't really fight" (Hastings 1984, 25; Whiting, 47). After having breakfasted with Eisenhower on March 6, 1944, Brooke opined, "there is no doubt that he is a most attractive personality and at the same time [has] a very limited brain from a strategic point of view" (Beevor, 2002 139). This view of Eisenhower was shared by Montgomery who on the other hand considered Brooke "a genius." Also in commenting about Stilwell Brooke said that he had "little military knowledge and no strategic ability of any kind ... he did a vast amount of harm" (Allen, 387).

In addition the British generals resorted to bombast. Thus at the end of the Sicilian campaign Alexander cabled Churchill, "Island taken in 38 days. Sicily has a coastline 600 miles and area 10,000 square miles. Island is heavily fortified with concrete pillboxes and wire. Axis garrison: Italian 9 divisions, German 4.... Total forces 405,000 soldiers.... On August 17 the last German soldier fled Sicily" (Agarossi, 40). This report reduced to the reality that prevailed on Sicily would read as follows: Discounting grounded Luftwaffe formations there were not four but two German divisions and they had not fled but left the island in good order, taking all their equipment with them; and as for the Italian nine divisions, they chose not to fight. In his January 24, 1940, radio address aimed at America in which he tried to reassure it that it need not actually go to war Churchill enunciated the ringing pledge, "Give us the tools, and we will finish the job." In view of the performance of British arms whenever they met the Germans it seemed more correct to recall Bismarck's remark that "should the British Army land on the continent he would send the Berlin police force to arrest them."

Still, a war waged with the intention of winning must be prosecuted by some means or other. When Churchill met Roosevelt in Newfoundland for the Argentia conference he brought with him a blueprint of how to win it. The major points were as follows:

- Defeat of the U-boats.
- Bombing of Germany, and
- "If necessary land in 1943 armored spearheads in several occupied countries to link up with the local resistance groups."

As Churchill summarized it a month later, "We shall undermine them by propaganda; depress them with the blockade; and above all bomb their homeland ceaselessly, ruthlessly, and with ever increasing weight of bombs" (Churchill Papers Vol. 3, 1254).

In general, thus, the British plan for achieving victory can be subsumed in three domains, discussed below in the order of its authors' presumed strategic weight. (Defeat of the U-boats was a strategy not to lose the war, as opposed to winning). By far the most important British weapon was to be the bombing offensive. There is in conventional historiography a semantic laxity when dealing with Britain's policy of bombing Germany. Generally, one can distinguish three forms of aerial combat. One is tactical, in which airplanes are used as flying artillery to support the fighting troops; not being engaged in land combat such usage of the RAF in the European theater did not arise. The next form is strategic bombing, which is a directed effort aimed at destroying a specific industry, economic sector or a particular infrastructure of the enemy's war-making capacity. Finally there is the third mode, when bombing is done against the enemy's cities and civilians. It is in confusing the last two that a misnomer arises for it is quite clear that the British bomber offensive in the years 1940–44 — commonly referred to as strategic bombing — was in fact of the third kind, here to be innocuously called air war. For sure there would be strategic bombing but not until 1944 when the invasion of France was set in motion. What had occurred till then was the use of bombers for the leveling of German cities and the shattering of the morale of its inhabitants. It was this form of air war that the British relied on to bring Germany to its knees.

Churchill's second weapon for crushing Germany was a mass uprising of the oppressed peoples of Europe. Except for a few isolated corners, Sweden, Switzerland or the Iberian peninsula, Germany had by 1943 subjugated nearly all of Europe counting about a dozen nations. It was their wrath and thirst for "freedom" that in Churchill's vision were to erupt into an angry flame to devour the locust that had settled on the Continent. Here too it is necessary to be clear about what Churchill meant by resistance in the occupied countries. He did not have in mind partisans operating behind the front lines to assist a fighting army. He was referring to rebellions inside the subjugated countries which would rise to such a pitch as to make it impossible for the Germans to keep Europe under their boot. These revolts springing up from the Pyrenees to the forests of Poland would be supplied with agents, weapons and sabotage experts by the recently formed SOE branch of British intelligence.

Complementing these resistance movements would be a British campaign of raids on the European continent. After dinner with his military chiefs Churchill informed them, "We shall plan large scale 'butcher and bolt' raids on the continent and Hitler will find himself hard put to it to hold 2,000 miles of coast line" (Churchill Papers Vol. 2, 511). After France collapsed the British started forming commando or combined operations units, trained in special combat and sabotage techniques. Their activities would consist of raiding the occupied coast of Europe from the Spanish border to the North Pole and inflicting grievous damage on the German troops and their arsenals. These commandos together with the resistance fighters would, in Churchill's phrase, "set Europe ablaze." Churchill appointed Mountbatten to lead these commandos and to stress their importance his position was put on par with the other chiefs of staff.

The third strategic weapon, which in World War I had indeed been a potent factor in the collapse of Imperial Germany, was economic blockade. This weapon, however, foundered early in the game. Much of its effectiveness was diluted even before the war started by the Nazi-Soviet pact of '39 when Russia undertook to ship Germany enormous quantities of foodstuffs and raw materials. A year later the blockade was further undermined by the occupation of Western Europe. Given the eventual German occupation of the entire Balkans, their stranglehold on Swedish steel and, after June 1941, their possession of vast stretches of Russia, the weapon of economic blockade was retained by the British even when it was clear it could have no noticeable effect on the war.

While the above war-making methods were touted quite openly one other strategy stayed unacknowledged and would have been vehemently denied had anyone alluded to it. This policy consisted in provoking the Germans to disperse their strength over the widest possible area. In retrospect it seems clear that all British initiatives prior to D-Day were aimed at having the Germans thrust themselves into as many countries as possible so as to tie them down in occupation and pacification duties. It explains much of the piecemeal engagements and rapid flights staged repeatedly by British expeditionary forces which, it turns out, were not due to incompetence alone. They were rather planned stage-sets. The botched occupation of Norway was the first in the series of dispersion tactics and was so perceived by Sweden, which had rebuked Britain for trying to embroil it, too, in the conflict. A bare six months after the French armistice, in December 1940, Churchill contacted Pétain and Weygand trying to induce Vichy to resume the war from its colonies, promising to help out with as many as six divisions (Churchill Papers Vol. 2, 1373). When the Vichyites declined the offer Churchill growled, "No scrap of nobility or courage has been shown by these people so far." While it failed with Sweden and Vichy it succeeded well enough with Yugoslavia and Greece. As we have seen, Britain intended to withdraw from Greece before it even landed. Great efforts were expanded on trying to draw in Turkey. As early as January 1941 Churchill wrote to Inönu that in view of the impending German move into Bulgaria he was prepared to send Turkey several squadrons of British planes and 100 AA guns. Moreover, it was added that such a move would prevent Russia from joining Germany in the dismemberment of Turkey. In fact one of the main arguments for helping Greece later on was to embroil Turkey in the Balkan war. Stark light on the whole affair is thrown by a letter from Churchill to Air Marshal Portal, of May 5, 1941: "Personally I never expected the Greek venture to succeed, unless Turkey and Yugoslavia came in." Britain attempted the same with Spain and Portugal without success. This intent probably also lay behind failing to occupy Tunisia during Torch so as to lure German troops there and siphon them off from the European continent. And, as will be seen subsequently, as late as fall 1943 during Italy's surrender Eden insisted that the Allies refrain from landing but rather let the

Germans disperse their troops over the Italian mainland, the Balkans and the Dodecanese islands. This was in conformity with a British war cabinet memorandum approved as early as November 1942 (Agarossi, 17). To a large extent this was what subsequently happened, for except for the southern tip of Italy the Allies left all the other vast territories occupied by the Italians to fall into German hands. And some of it indeed paid off. When D-Day came there were 300,000 German troops holed up in Norway and another quarter million in the Balkans and the adjacent islands never used against the Allies. This policy was kept under wraps for good reasons. One was, as Sweden complained, it was at the cost of invasion and suffering of a number of small countries. It is also likely that behind the wish to see the extinction of as many European states as possible lay a calculation that this would make America more prone to intervene. Soon after the Greek fiasco much of this was acknowledged by Churchill at a cabinet meeting where it was recorded that Churchill "felt no regret over the decision to send troops to Greece. Had we not done so, Yugoslavia would not now have been an open enemy of Germany. Further the Greek war had caused a marked change in the attitude of the United States." These remarks were not recorded in the cabinet minutes but in a confidential annex (Churchill Papers 3, 563).

When the USA came into the war the British were soon faced with the specter of being forced into combat with the German army on the Continent. According to the American military this was the proper course to take. To deal with this threat Churchill came up with the soft underbelly theory. This he had first articulated to Stalin when he fobbed him off with Torch in place of a second front in Europe. In Churchill's crocodile simile Occupied France represented a pair of iron jaws rigged with double or triple rows of razor-sharp teeth whereas its underside, Europe's Mediterranean coastline, was mush, vulnerable to the slightest pinprick. Henceforth, whenever the notion of taking on the German army was broached the place to do it, according to the British, was along the underbelly of the Nazi crocodile — Pantelleria, the Ballearics, Sicily, Sardinia, Italy, Greece, Rhodes, Turkey, even the Black Sea. As will be discussed later, this soft belly of Europe was anything but that — far from the vital centers of Germany and blocked by a convoluted geography and multiple mountain ranges and rivers. Instead of being the vulnerable spot into which to thrust a dagger to reach the heart of the beast, it was for any attacking army a *cul-de-sac* leading to stalemate.

There were several reasons for generating this crocodile simile. One was the often-mentioned British dread of getting involved with the German army. Then, too, Churchill knew well enough that the British military was incapable of conducting a mobile war involving large tank and motorized formations. By contrast, any attack along Europe's Mediterranean coast was bound to bog down in the rugged terrain. And, regardless whether it entailed victory or defeat, attacking any of the Mediterranean islands would be no more than a local engagement. None of the above campaigns could lead to massive battles such as were likely in northern France. Finally, whatever local gains were to be achieved would serve the interests of the British Empire, of which Churchill was an impassioned advocate.

• CHAPTER 25 •

The Bombing of Germany

We are concerned here with the attempts of the British to bring about a decision in the war by a bombing offensive against the German heartland. This covers the period between the fall of France in June 1940 and early 1944 when preparations were begun for the invasion of France. The first few months of the war saw some attempts at bombing of military targets. In three of these, conducted against warships near Wilhelmshaven, a total of 63 aircraft reached their target of which 25 were lost — 40 percent. The clinching disappointment occurred on December 18 during a raid on Helgoland when out of 22 attacking aircraft only 10 returned home. No damage was done to any of the sites. These were the first and last attempts by the RAF to attack Germany in daytime.

With the start of the Western campaign in May 1940, when a German raid on Rotterdam killed 980 civilians, the British started bombing German cities. Soon after France collapsed Churchill, in a letter to Beaverbrook of July 8, stated explicitly the course England was to take in her war with Germany: "When I look around to see how we can win the war I see that there is only one such path. We have no Continental army…. The blockade is broken … [but] there is one thing that will bring him down, and that is an absolutely devastating, exterminating attack by heavy bombers from this country upon the Nazi homeland" (Churchill Vol. 2, 567). The centrality of this policy was emphasized in a poignant note sent to Halifax on October 13 in which, referring to a Swiss proposal to adjudicate alleged violations of the rules of aerial warfare, Churchill wrote, "Even if Germany offered to stop bombing now we should not consent to it." Likewise he opined, "It may well be that the application of superior air power to the German homeland and the rising anger of the German and other Nazi-gripped populations, will bring the agony of civilization to a merciful and glorious end." The matter was formally considered at a war cabinet meeting on December 12, 1940, and the decision taken was to start a "crash concentration" of bombing which would

- "rely largely on fires … [in] closely built-up towns where bomb craters in the streets would impede the fire fighters"
- "since we aimed at affecting the enemy's morale we should attempt to destroy the greater part of a particular city."

The cabinet's approval contained the proviso that "preference should be given to a town which would be recognized as having a predominantly industrial character" (Churchill Vol. 2, 940, 1191, 1217). The wording is interesting in that "enemy morale" appears here two years before it was officially targeted at the summit meeting in Casablanca.

Of the British hierarchy that saw bombing as a decisive instrument of the war two men besides Churchill stand out in particular. One was the prime minister's scientific gray eminence, Professor Lindemann. Unmarried, a teetotaler, a vegetarian, a lover of pets and lifelong bigot, he fed Churchill technical and statistical data on the British war effort. Postulating that humans are more distraught at losing their homes than having a relative or a friend killed, he argued that since 22 million Germans live in 58 large cities, destroying most of them would leave a third of the German populace homeless. The other zealot was the commander in chief of Bomber Command, nicknamed Bomber Harris. A stubborn, blinkered automaton he was immune to any evidence and to all other needs that might encroach on his professional turf. Of the countless memoranda that flowed from his desk a few may be cited. In June 1942 he wrote to Churchill, "We are free ... to employ our rapidly expanding air strength ... in such a manner as would avail to knock Germany out of the war in a matter of months"; on August 29 he wrote to the chief of air staff, Portal, "Bomber Command provides the only means of physically weakening and nervously exhausting Germany ... the only force which can, in fact ... secure our victory" and on November 3, 1943, he minuted Churchill, "We can wreck Berlin.... It will cost between 400–500 aircraft. It will cost Germany the war" (Saward, 160, 164; Hastings, Bo, 295). These views were in November 1942 presented to the war cabinet by Portal in a paper entitled "Estimate of the Effects of an Anglo-American Bomber Offensive Against Germany." It stated that after building up a combined Anglo-American force of 4,000 to 6,000 bombers the following would be achieved in the next two years:

- The destruction of 6 million dwellings leaving 25 million Germans homeless.
- 900,000 Germans would be killed and 1 million seriously injured.
- One-third of Germany's industry would be destroyed and to provide a minimum subsistence to the civilian population, its entire war industry would have to come to a stop.

The superciliousness of Britain's army generals echoed also in the ranks of the RAF when — and this after Stalingrad and Kursk — Air Vice Marshal Inglis, intelligence head of the air staff, said on November 5, 1943, "We are convinced that Bomber Command's attacks are doing more toward shortening the war than any other offensive including the Russians." In keeping with this diagnosis a plan, code named Rankin, was readied which visualized the rapid occupation of the European continent when the bombing offensive caused an incipient collapse of the Third Reich (Hastings, 296, 314).

* * *

In pursuing their air offensive the British did try to locate and damage industrial centers of the enemy. This would have been a more efficient utilization of their air power and more in keeping with the British stance of upright war making. But it soon transpired that this was an impossible task. So it reduced itself to carpet bombing of densely inhabited city centers. Following the cabinet approval of this policy the first city thus attacked was Mannheim, which was struck by 200 bombers on the night of December 16, 1940, causing the death of 34 civilians. Seven planes were either shot down or crashed, a 4 percent-loss rate which, peculiarly, was to be maintained throughout the bombing campaign. Depending on the availability of planes and the weather, bombers were subsequently sent into Germany in smaller or larger groups. It was soon realized that even the crude form of area bombing presented difficulties. The bombing was done at night, the weather most of the time was foul both in England and *en route*, and keeping formation was both a challenge and a hazard. Finding the designated objective in a blacked-out Germany was not always possible. Once reached, the target itself was usually under cloud cover and AA fire distracted the crews. A pattern soon developed called "creep back" a result of the eagerness of the crews to get rid of the bombs as soon as possible so that they started bombing up-target, with each successive wave dropping the bombs even earlier than the previous one. This not only missed ground zero but caused a scattering of the bomb load nullifying the intended effects of a concentrated mass eruption of explosions and fires.

While Bomber Command repeatedly claimed success, reconnaissance flights provided disturbing evidence that all was not well. An investigation committee set up in 1941 that interrogated crews and examined the reconnaissance photos discovered the following. On moonlit nights a third of the crews did not even claim to have bombed the target, whereas another third did no better than bomb within five miles of it; in the Ruhr, where the AA defenses were strongest, only one in 10 claimed to have bombed within a five-mile radius. On dark nights the number of aircraft that bombed within a five-mile radius was 7 percent, one in 15.

Various techniques were developed to improve navigation and to assure concentration of bombs on the targets. These relied mostly on sophisticated radio and radar devices, often utilizing the enemy's own electronic beams. One of the simpler tactics to ensure good aiming was the institution of pathfinder units. These were experienced crews equipped with special devices for locating the targets and marking them with parachuted flares which hung over the target long enough to lead the bombers to it. These efforts were, of course, counteracted by the enemy's deception measures, by the rising concentration of AA guns and the appearance of night fighters. Still, night remained a formidable protector of the British raiders and the bombing of Germany grew in intensity and spread to ever wider areas of the *Vaterland*.

Although the choice of targets remained arbitrary, Harris liked to assign tactical names to the various stages of his air war. One such stage was the 1,000 bomber raids. These in his view were bound to subdue deficiencies and have a decisive effect on the Germans. To dispatch such a force was at the limit of his resources and he had to empty repair shops and hangars to assemble it—but he did it. The first such raid was staged on the night of May 30, 1942, on Cologne. For 90 minutes 900 bombers rained down 1,500 tons of explosives on the city. Not much was achieved; fewer than 500 people were killed and 50,000 were made homeless. The attackers lost 40 bombers, the reliable 4 percent. Two nights later Harris sent 956 aircraft against Essen with even poorer results. The weather was bad and the bombing was aborted or scattered resulting in a loss of 31 planes. Then on June 25 he sent 909 bombers against Bremen, causing very little damage and losing 44 planes. The mobilization of practically all available aircraft for these attacks wreaked havoc with the training of new crews and other essential operations. Harris was soon forced to scrap his 1,000-bomber missions.

The next labeled campaign was Battle of the Ruhr, to be followed by the Battle of Berlin. From the spring of 1942 to mid–1943, some 60 major raids were concentrated on the small enclave around Essen, the Ruhrgebiet; 14,000 bombers took part in the attacks dumping 36,000 tons of explosives and 7,000 incendiaries. The idea was to have the explosives first blow off the roofs of buildings into which rained the incendiaries to start fires and set in motion a self-sustaining process of destruction. The ultimate aim was to generate what was called a firestorm. Its mechanism is essentially the same as that of a chimney over a fire grate where the column of heated flue gases sets up a draft, sucking air into the burner. Only that here the chimney was miles high, temperatures reached thousands of degrees, with the sucked-in air reaching hurricane force. In the areas surrounding the cauldron of flames winds racing toward the center of the firestorm uprooted trees, tore down buildings and flung people into the flaming inferno. This continued until there was nothing left for miles to feed the flames.

The generation of a firestorm depended not only on the concentration of the explosive-incendiary bomb load but also on climatic and urban conditions and the British succeeded in producing such a firestorm only on a few occasions. The most notorious was that of Hamburg. Even this was made possible only by the use of a deception called *Window*. This consisted of strips of metal dumped by the incoming bombers which on the Germans' radar screens looked no different from oncoming aircraft. The British had had this device for some time but delayed using it lest the Germans themselves employ it in raiding England. But in the spring of 1943, after Stalingrad and Tunisia, they were confident enough to go ahead with it. The German AA and fighter defenses were completely swamped and the bombers had a free run of the city. A total of 2,149 bombers attacked in close succession on the three nights of July 24, 27 and 29. During the day USAAF planes kept the fires going. A never-to-be-duplicated catastrophe overwhelmed the port city. The firestorm that erupted destroyed half its buildings, killed between 30,000 to 50,000 people, and forced a million residents to flee the city. While on October 22, 1943, there was a second "minor" firestorm in Kassel in which 9,200 people perished it was not until 1945 in Dresden that the bombers produced another catastrophe similar to that of Hamburg.

* * *

During the Casablanca Conference held in January 1943 the British policy of area bombing was confirmed by the following directive to the Anglo-American strategic air forces: "Your primary object will be the progressive destruction and dislocation of the German military, industrial and economic system and the undermining of the morale of the German people to a point where their capacity for armed resistance is fatally weakened."

This directive coincided with the first American attempts to join in the bombing of Germany. The US Air Force general Ira Eaker had arrived in London in January 1942, just when Harris was appointed to his post; after setting up the necessary infrastructure, Eaker took command of the 8th US Strategic Air Force in England. The Americans' approach was different from their ally's; they were going to do precision bombing and do so in daylight. Their confidence rested on the characteristics of their B-17 and B-24 bombers. Unlike the British Wellingtons and Lancasters, which had a ceiling of about 20,000 feet, theirs was well over 30,000 feet, so much safer from antiaircraft fire. For a defense against fighters, each B-17, named Flying Fortress, mounted 13 0.505 Browning machine guns arranged for all-around defense with a range larger than the German fighters' cannon. When a squadron of seven B-17s flew in a staggered tight formation an attacking fighter faced 91 heavy machine guns and the Americans felt the formation would give a good account of itself. To ensure precision bombing the visual advantage provided by daylight was enhanced by a new aiming device, the recently developed Norden bombsight, superior to anything available heretofore. With hundreds of bombers flying tight boxes and bristling with 1,000 or more machine guns, the US air strategists were confident of being able to bomb Germany with acceptable losses even in daylight.

The first year or so the Americans practiced short sorties, accompanied by fighters, over occupied France. Starting in 1943 they began to nibble at Germany, mostly port cities of the North Sea. This way they avoided flak and fighters at least while en route to the target. For the first four months of 1943 the loss rate was 4 percent; after six months, which included an attack by 252 bombers on Wilhelmshaven on June 11, the loss rate climbed to 6.6 percent, with a third of the attacking planes damaged. Already then Eaker was beginning to worry about the presumed ability of the B-17s to fend off the German fighters. The American bomber formations were routinely accompanied by a fighter escort, but the available P-38 had a limited range and had to leave the bombers just when the going turned onerous. But Eaker persevered. In July he launched six missions of about 300 planes each in quick succession, still on coastal cities except for one on Kassel. The casualties were severe and the results meager. One hundred bombers with 1,000 airmen were lost; many of the crews experienced frostbite or anoxia since the B-17s were neither heated nor pressurized; and a number of men suffered emotional breakdowns (Coffey, 218).

The real test was yet to come. When it was time to tackle the interior of Germany the Americans relied on the British Ministry of Economic Warfare to provide suitable targets. These, in order of priority, were given as submarines, aircraft and ball bearing factories, oil, synthetic rubber production, and military vehicles. The target chosen for the first major daylight precision attack were the ball bearing factories in Schweinfurt, east of Frankfurt. These supplied two-thirds of Germany's total production of these bearings—a vital component in aircraft, vehicles, guns, and a host of other military paraphernalia.

The operational plan was elaborate. The formation was divided into two groups. One hundred forty-six bombers were to act as a decoy by attacking the Messerschmidt plant in Regensburg, 150 miles southeast of the main target; after the attack they were to fly on and land in North Africa. The main group of 230 B-17s was to attack Schweinfurt and return to England. It was hoped thereby to confound the defenses as to the real target and scatter the fighters over a large area.

The attack took place on August 17 in good weather accompanied part of the way by friendly escorts. Despite the fierce opposition by flak and fighters both targets were struck and damaged. Both groups, the one headed for Africa and the other back to England, were pounced by fighters over the entire route. The cost of the raid was prohibitive. Of the Schweinfurt group 63 planes were either shot down or had to be written off, nearly a quarter of the force; of the Regensburg group only 60 eventually returned from Africa to England—a loss of 60 percent. For both groups the total loss amounted to 147 machines (39 percent) and 550 personnel.

The post mortem of the raid included an examination of what had been accomplished. No independent assessment of the Regensburg raid is available, but as for Schweinfurt, Speer's immediate estimate was that after the destruction of the two main plants total production was down by a third. What is, however, symptomatic is that reconnaissance flights soon brought evidence that the factories were being reconstituted at an astonishing pace and postwar evidence confirms that within two months they were almost back to original production—a typical aspect of the bombing offensive of that period. When this became known to the American planners a second attack was staged on Schweinfurt. On October 14, 227 bombers attacked and this time the mauling of the bombers was even more severe; 60 planes were shot down (28 percent) and 142 came back damaged.

Between the first and second Schweinfurt raids a number of other attacks had been launched on the interior of Germany by the 8th AAF. The loss rate continued to climb.

Whereas in the first six months of the year this amounted to 6.6 percent, in the second half, when the Americans ventured deep into Germany, the loss ratio reached a forbidding average of 17 percent.

Following these events the 8th AAF concluded that on their own B-17s and B-24s were unable to withstand the fighters in daylight attacks. Major operations were suspended until long-range fighter planes became available to accompany the bombers to and from the target. This materialized with the appearance of the P-51 Mustang fighter, which began arriving in early 1944. The Mustang had a range of 950 miles and could accompany the bombers to Berlin and back. This, however, coincided with the launching of a truly strategic offensive accompanying the invasion of France. Bomber Command, however, even in 1944 and 1945 continued to indulge in area bombing. By then millions of Allied soldiers were engaged in a land war and the much touted Victory-by-Air-Alone was a discarded pipe dream.

* * *

Considering that by the end of 1943 the British had 1 million personnel in their air forces whose major function was the bombing of Germany and for which their industry had labored to produce 40,000 aircraft (the Americans had 2.4 million men in their air forces and produced 75,000 planes)—what were the results of these efforts? These can be examined in four areas—industrial damage, civilian casualties, morale, and the German resources tied down by the air attacks.

The bombing offensive had as one of its goal the disruption of Germany's economy. The estimates are that damage to industrial output in 1942 was anywhere from 0.7 to 2.5 percent, whereas Britain's commitment to the bombing consumed 33 percent of its war economy. Throughout the war only 12 percent of the bombs fell on industrial targets and even in carpet bombing only 24 percent fell on housing in major cities (Mitcham 1988, 202; Magenheimer, 225). Overall, German industrial losses throughout the war ranged from a few percent to a maximum of 30 percent. If instead of persisting with the air war merely to avoid an invasion of Europe the British had been serious about the bombing they would perhaps have realized two salient features of the German economy. One was that there was a widespread slack in its wartime capacity. This was due to several factors. Hitler did not want to subject his people to undue hardships as had happened in World War I, so he left much of the private sector alone. Then, too, he had started the war earlier than planned so that a number of plants scheduled for a war in 1942 were only now coming into being. The Germans could thus activate the dormant potential of these industries and more than make up for damages caused by bombing. The other major feature of the economy was its adherence to the familiar German thoroughness and craftsmanship in manufacturing goods. The American way of automated mass production was inimical to the Nazis as coming from a mongrel civilization. When in February 1942 Speer took over the Ministry of Armaments this is exactly what he resorted to—rationalization and standardization of production methods and exploitation of heretofore unexploited German industrial capacity.

The result was a veritable leap in the output of armaments and industrial goods. In the period under discussion (1941–1944) everything increased by 200 to 300 percent. The

Opposite, top: Formations of American B-17 bombers heading for Germany. *Bottom:* The bombed-out city of Cologne, on the Rhine. (Both photographs courtesy the United States Army.)

effects of bomb damage were completely overshadowed by the utilization of Germany's latent economic potential of which the British planners were either genuinely or deliberately oblivious as they peddled their war-winning strategy of aerial bombing. It wasn't until a specifically directed strategic assault was launched on such essentials as oil and transportation combined with the march of invading armies that deprived Germany of vital territories with their plants and sources of raw materials that its economy started to crumble. This did not commence until late 1944 when the enemy was already entering German soil from both east and west.

Table 25-1 shows a listing of German fatalities for a number of individual air raids. In 19 air raids on Berlin, which involved 10,000 bombers dropping 33,000 tons of explosives and incendiaries, 9,650 civilians lost their lives (Middlebrook, 321). It took a heavy bomber dropping 10,000 pounds of explosives to kill one civilian. In London during the Blitz 2,000 pounds of explosives was enough to kill a civilian (Ch.Pprs 2, 912). This startlingly low civilian casualty rate bespeaks of the superb network of shelters and civil defense measures organized in wartime Germany. When one recalls the thousands of dead inflicted in Warsaw, Rotterdam, Belgrade and Leningrad by a few scores of German Heinkels, German casualty figures reflect an astonishing feat. These numbers stand out against the nearly total destruction of most major German cities, which at the end of the war had become nothing but heaps of rubble. The total figure of German bombing victims after four years of assault eventually stood at about 600,000 dead, of which 100,000 were due to the two firestorms in Hamburg and Dresden. While the low casualty figures are a monument to civil defense measures, more impressive was the extraordinary hardiness and discipline of the German populace — and here we touch on the subject of morale. First the morale of the führer himself. And it

Table 25-1
Civilians Killed in Germany in Allied Bombing

City	Date	No. of Planes	Dead
1940			
Berlin	8/30	140	10
Hamburg	11/5	97	7
Mannheim	12/16	200	35
1942			
Luebeck	3/29	234	320
Cologne	5/30	1,047	474
Essen	6/1	956	
Bremen	6/25	909	
Cologne	6/28	540	3,460
1943			
Berlin	2/15	891	320
Berlin	3/2		700
Dortmund	5/23		600
Düsseldorf	11/6	1,542	1,200
(2 raids)	11/11		
Mühlheim	6/22	557	500
Cologne	6/28	540	3,460
Schweinfurt	8/17	230	200
Peenemunde	8/17–18	595	120*
Frankfurt	11/26	300	79
1944			
Frankfurt	2/11	2,050	798
Berlin	2/15	891	320
Rüsselheim	7/20	100	157
Augsburg	2/25–6	584	1,500
Wolfsangel	8/26	116	21†
Braunschweig	10/14	233	561

*and 500 foreign workers
†and 177 foreign laborers

comes as no surprise that it was not affected in the least. One way of dealing with the sight of destroyed cities was not to see it; the führer rarely traveled through them and when it was unavoidable he ordered the curtains to be drawn over the windows of his special train (Rumpf, 123). Moreover, in his view "the devastation actually works in our favor because it is creating a body of people with nothing to lose — people who will therefore fight on with utter fanaticism" (Overy 1997, 332). The logic that when one achieves a lot it is a good idea to lose it, because then one fights ever more willingly to repossess it, may seem puzzling but Hitler knew his people well. The Germans endured the raids with an equanimity that baffled the officials in charge of the bombing victims. In ruined cities Germans stood in lines at makeshift offices to pay their taxes. After the heaviest raids employees never failed to show up at their workplaces; even after the Hamburg firestorm, when a million inhabitants fled the city, the workers soon returned to the still-hot ruins and resumed work with undiminished vigor. Following the Lübeck raid in March 1942 the chief of police reported the "behavior of population extraordinarily stoic and calm, as well as of the wounded" (DDR, XIX, 67). Bombed-out people immediately started fixing whatever could still be fixed while others settled down in cellars and cement holes without complaint or protest. They identified the dead, put up notices for the missing and walked off stolidly to their routines. Speer wrote, "Neither the bombing and the hardships that resulted from them weakened the morale of the populace. On the contrary.... [Losses] were amply balanced by increased effort" (Hastings 1979, 265). This comportment endured to the end of the war when nearly all German cities had become wastelands and the death toll rose to over half a million with 1 million injured. There was no outcry, no spasm of protest or pain. In April 1945 after Göring had blown up his Karinhall Palace and was leaving Berlin for the hospitality of the Western enemy, he had to take refuge from a bombing raid in a public air raid shelter. The people huddling there treated him with exuberant affability, exchanging jokes and clapping the Fat One on the back. When neighboring shelters heard of Göring's presence he was invited to visit them. They had no complaints against their Luftwaffe chief, or the regime, or their recent history.

In reading about the reactions of the Germans to the ruin of their lovely medieval cities and the killing and maiming of family and friends what emerges is that this was not an act of holding back pain and regret, not a defiance of the enemy but the strange spectacle of an absence of any emotion; a spectacle of stony hearts and brains which needed no effort to subdue grief either in the name of patriotism, personal dignity, or any other such restraint. There was instead callous equanimity and indifference as if their mental and emotional responses had gelled into a catalepsy that no horror would shake. It makes it easier to comprehend how the same people managed to indulge in industrial mass murder without so much as the quiver of an eyebrow.

There were, of course, consequences of area bombing on the arithmetic of the war but it was neither in such strategic returns as crippling Germany's arms industry, or the cracking of its citizens' morale. The benefits came in tying down resources which the Germans could have used elsewhere. By the end of 1943 nearly 1 million Germans were busy with the Allied bombing; in 1944 the number was closer to 2 million, though a large proportion of them were women and teenagers. The 12,000 AA guns deployed on the home front needed the services of 440,000 people, this at a time when the vaunted 88 mm Flak guns were being employed at the front with great effect against tanks and strongholds. Thus, of the 20,000 88 mm guns produced during 1942–44 only 3,170 went to the army (Saward, 309). And it required 16,000 rounds by an 88 mm Flak 36 to shoot down one bomber.

Nearly 1,000 fighters had to be kept operational and continuously replaced to fend off the bombers by day and night. The diversion of guns, planes and personnel did siphon off considerable resources from the Wehrmacht. Still, when tallied up against the enormous turnover of men and weapons on the fighting fronts— this drain on Germany's economy was a small percentage of its total war effort.

• CHAPTER 26 •

Ultra-Secret

Wars are accompanied by prodigious efforts to learn the enemy's plans and resources from agents, defectors and military intelligence. In World War II, instead of infiltration and spying, the main effort lay in deciphering the enemy's communication traffic. The greatest scoop in this cryptographic war was obtained from the German cipher system Enigma. It is no exaggeration to say that access to its codes was equivalent to having British leaders and strategists sit in at the table at which Hitler and the High Command of the Wehrmacht made their fateful decisions. Enigma's role was so crucial and unique that the British had to invent a classification for it, *Ultra-Secret*. At the end of the war Churchill, with some hyperbole, told the king "It was thanks to *Ultra* that the war was won" (Brown, 671).

Oddly enough it was the Poles who took the first steps to decode Enigma, contributing to the Allied victory more than many an army. Another strange aspect of it was that the cipher machine started as a commercial product in Holland as early as 1919. The German army adopted it in the '30s after modifying it to suit their purposes. A Polish agent working in the plant where Enigma was being produced shipped parts of it to the Polish Secret Service which reassembled them and with the help of Polish mathematicians decoded and read the ciphers for a number of years. As war approached the Germans made Enigma more and more complex and the Poles gave the machine to the Deuxième Bureau. In turn the French, with help from a spy in the German cipher office, made further progress on reading the device. Eventually Enigma had 200 different keys which the Germans changed every 24 hours—enormously increasing the number of permutations. The encoding was done via three rotating drums, carrying on each face 26 electrical contact points that constituted the secret alphabet. The permutations on the 3-rotor model amounted to 17,576 possible readings. The rotor positions could be rearranged in six different modes yielding 105,456 permutations. The encoded message was radioed to the receiver who decoded it automatically on a similar machine. With additional manipulations the number of permutations could be in the trillions. To make it still more difficult to decipher, the three services in Germany used different codes and models: the Kriegsmarine, for example, used an 8-rotor setup.

After the collapse of France the work on Enigma was taken over by the British. In mid–April they had captured an Enigma machine complete with operational codes from a German plane downed off Norway. Thus the first code the British broke was that of the Luftwaffe. And, as was noted, it was the Luftwaffe Enigma, not the naval one which had not yet been broken, that enabled the British to track and sink the *Bismarck*. Enigma was used not only by the three services but also by Hitler's headquarters, the OKW, the Abwehr, the SS and even the Foreign Ministry. In fact some of the raids on the coast of Norway were staged not to liberate Europe but to secure the naval Enigma codes. In the Lofoten raid the demolition of the oil factories was a cover for the actual objective. On May 1941 the British navy captured a U-boat complete with its Enigma and operating chart which opened the German navy code to British cryptographers.

The employment of Enigma throughout the war by the British is given by the following timetable:

Luftwaffe: May 1940–End of war
Navy: May 1941–February 1942 and December 1942–End of war
Army: Early 1940–End of war

The decoding, itself, was not the only part that made Enigma such a powerful tool. The decoded messages by themselves often seemed minor. The British attached intelligence staffs to the cryptographers who collated the bits of data into important strategic and tactical information.

The information gleaned from Enigma was of the highest order. In the summer of 1940 the British learned the date of Adlertag, the number of Luftwaffe formations scheduled to attack and their targets; and they eventually intercepted Hitler's order to postpone the invasion of Britain. After breaking the naval code every convoy across the Mediterranean was known as to its complement and route with disastrous consequences to Axis shipping and Rommel in Africa. When the army's code was broken the impending attacks on Greece and Crete were learned to the smallest detail, as were the preparations for the invasion of Russia. Further crucial information obtained via Enigma were Rommel's plans for an attack on the Quattara Depression preceding the El Alamein offensive; the Germans' appreciation that the allies' mid–1943 landing in would *not* be in Sicily; a May 1944 report that 50 V-1s were ready for launching, which prompted Churchill to press for a June landing; the decision to keep four reserve Panzer divisions away from Normandy on D-Day; Hitler's order to attack Avranches which resulted in the Falaise disaster. Even the weather report over the Continent was read which helped Bomber Command plan its operations. At the end of 1942 the U-boat code was also broken; the British then listened in on both Dönitz's orders to his submarines as well the U-boats' operational reports to him. In large measure this led to the defeat of this greatest menace to Allied war making.

Enigma's headquarters was at Bletchley Park, 50 miles from London, where the British Secret Service moved at the outbreak of war. The main administrators of the complex, Denniston and Travis, were subordinate to Maj. Gen. S.G. Menzies, known as "C." The amount of work performed was prodigious. In the summer of 1942 Bletchely decrypted 39,000 signals a month; in 1943, 84,000. While at the start it employed 1,800 people by the war's end there were 9,000 (Brown, 402). Relevant information was received by those in need within minutes, often before the Germans did. A sensitive issue was who should know about this fountain of truth and who should be given its intelligence, if not the source. Churchill received all important signals in a locked box to which only he had the key. The commands which received it had a special unit attached to them, called SLU, to handle Enigma material according to a strict security routine; after being perused the messages were retrieved and destroyed. The pervasiveness of the penetration into the German war machine was such that some British generals felt guilty for reading "other people's mail."

The heaviest burden on those handling Enigma was preventing the Germans from discovering its usage by the enemy. The urge to exploit it to the full entailed the peril that the more used the more likely was its give-away. A variety of measures were employed, including some painful ones. No one likely to be taken prisoner had access to it. Commanders were not to act immediately on the information received. Before attacking convoys, reconnaissance planes were dispatched over the target to give the impression they had discovered the convoy. Some of the steps taken to protect Enigma posed moral dilemmas. When the British learned in 1940 that Coventry was about to suffer one of the heaviest raids Churchill faced a bitter choice — to evacuate the town and risk compromising Enigma, or subject the populace to death and injury. The city was not warned but much was done to mitigate the blow such as concentrating in the vicinity firefighting equipment, ambulances and rescue teams. Another case occurred when in order to mask the cause of the Mediterranean sinkings the British sent a decipherable message to its "agent" — an Italian admiral — thanking him for the information and raising his pay. As a consequence the admiral was nearly shot and eventually dismissed. It was one of the Germans' major failures that for four years they never caught on to the leak. The negligence is the more striking when one recalls the episode with the U-boats. At the turn of 1942–43 the British navy passed to its ships and aircraft orders based on what could only be data received from Enigma. The Germans at that time read the British naval code but never stopped to investigate how the British obtained information that could have come only from Enigma sources.

The Soviets, too, were aware of Enigma and tried to break its code, but never succeeded. On the other hand the British, via Enigma, learned which Soviet codes the Germans had deciphered and warned the Russians accordingly. A final episode, which has not been confirmed but also never disproved, can be explained only by a link to Enigma. This is the Swiss spy case, Lucy. A bespectacled, inconspicuous man who ran an antiquarian shop in Basel was a Soviet agent code named Lucy. Throughout, he supplied Moscow with first-rate intelligence on Germany's plans and doings regarding the war in the East. The quality of the information was so high that the Soviets distrusted it and inquired of Lucy from whom he was getting it. His answer was that it came from an agent within the German High Command. The Soviets wanted to know who the man was. Lucy's reply was he had given his word not to reveal it and should he do so the flow of information would cease. The Soviets remained suspicious but the data supplied was so important and accurate that the Soviets put up with Lucy's answers. Even after Germany's defeat and the death of Lucy no hint and no trace was found of the mysterious German agent. The most likely scenario is that, eager to prevent the collapse of Russia, Lucy was receiving Enigma information from London which had either committed him to secrecy or had generated a bogus German superspy for him. The Russians, naturally, were never told of Enigma, though Churchill did share the secret with Roosevelt and the Americans used it as extensively as the British.

Enigma was not the only super-secret German code the Allies succeeded in reading. There was a German army code used primarily by the Army Groups on the eastern front called Vulture, which Menzies ("C") passed on to the Russians prior to major German offensives (Churchill Papers Vol. 3, 1293). Another code system, second in importance only to Ultra, was Purple or Magic, employed by Oshima in transmitting to Japan information from Germany, including records of his frequent talks with Hitler. Thus already in April Göring had told Oshima about Barbarossa, which served as one of the warnings transmitted to Stalin. Oshima was also informed by his government on July 22, 1942, that there would definitely be no Japanese attack against Russia.

CHAPTER 27

African Laurels

Having decided not to invade the continent in 1942 the Western Allies felt that they ought to do "something" to ease the struggle of the Red Army against the German minions who at the time were at their deepest penetration into Russia. If one scrutinized the map of Hitler's empire stretching from the North Pole to the Sahara and from the Atlantic to the Volga and was asked where would be the easiest and safest spot to take a nibble at Hitler's dominion, the obvious answer would have been the campaign the Allies chose — a landing in French North Africa. Aside from it being a preliminary to Churchill's soft-belly strategy, the main reason was that there were no Germans in the French colonies. Second, it would be an overseas battlefield, isolated from the Axis' homeland by two powerful navies. Whatever the Germans might do in the wake of an Allied landing, they would be hostage to shipments of supplies from across the sea — a perilous and tenuous link. With the African hinterland and the sea lanes under Allied control the Germans, if they chose to fight, would be waging war on an island. By the same token the Allies would never get mired in a protracted campaign because the end in Africa also meant the end of the undertaking; it would be up to them to either venture into new incursion or be satisfied with what they had achieved. They would have cleared the Mediterranean for Allied shipping, possibly reengaged the French in the war against Hitler and would menace the Germans with potential landings from the Dodecanese Islands to Spain — a 2,000- to 3,000-mile stretch of coast to be guarded and defended. It would be the culmination of the strategic principle of dispersion.

There remained one minor point to be attended to. While there were no Germans or Italians in French North Africa there were Vichy troops there and it was uncertain how they would greet the invaders. Little as they worried about French military capabilities the Allies wanted to forestall any potential hostilities. Keeping in mind Mers-el-Kebir and Dakar where the British had shed French blood, it was decided to portray Torch as primarily an American affair. The Americans chose to disarm the French even before they stepped ashore. Secret negotiations were conducted with the French in Algeria on several levels. This started back in midsummer when the Allies orchestrated General Giraud's escape from German captivity to have him lead the French army in Africa into the Allied camp. Then Robert Murphy traveled to Algeria to work on the diplomatic front. On October 22, General Clark, Eisenhower's deputy for the African invasion, landed from a submarine on an Algerian beach and negotiated with French General Masti, a corps commander in Algiers. The Vichyites were cajoled, bribed, or convinced of the need for cooperation with what was after all their own redemption.

There were, as said, no Axis troops in French North Africa but there were four German divisions in Egypt, 2,000 miles from where the Allies were to land. To keep them pinned down a British offensive was planned to start shortly before Torch. By normal reckoning these four divisions, with whatever Italian troops hung to their coattails, would be crushed between two plunging pistons, the British 8th Army from the east and the Anglo-American troops from the west. Given the overwhelming air, naval and land superiority over a Rommel cut off from his supplies, the whole affair should take no more than a few weeks.

The 8th Army offensive at El Alamein was scheduled for October 23, some two weeks ahead of Torch. Led by General Montgomery, the fourth commander in chief on the scene, this would also be the fourth British attempt to oust the Axis from Africa. But this time it was bound to be different, for two reasons. One was the great advantage in arms and men the British possessed, including an uninterrupted supply of fuel, vehicles and ammunition, whereas Rommel would be starved of all this. The second and more important operational element was Rommel's no-win situation, because no matter what he accomplished against Montgomery there were Allied armies to his rear which were bound sooner or later to stab him in the back. Symbolically, on sick leave in Germany, Rommel was not on the scene when the battle opened.

The forces at the disposal of Montgomery were 200,000 men, over 1,000 tanks, 2,300 guns and 530 serviceable aircraft. The Germans had 50,000 men, 211 tanks, 644 guns and 150 planes with the Italians disposing of about an equal complement of men and weapons. Thus the ratio of British to German forces was 4:1. The Germans had two Panzer and two motorized divisions and at the start of battle enough fuel for 11 and ammunition for nine fighting days (Gelb, 157). While some supplies did get through, all tankers on the way to Libya were sunk. Furthermore, of the fuel available in the rear much if not most was consumed in delivery to the front, the distance from Benghazi being 800 miles. To compensate for all these weaknesses Rommel had laid a five-mile-wide minefield from the sea to the Quattara Depression, a 40-mile-long belt containing half a million mines.

At El Alamein Montgomery fought a battle in his fashion. In Field Marshal Alexander's words, "It was a battle of grueling attrition like World War I lasting 11 days." The overall concept was an attack at the northern end, near the coast, the idea being to take the whole "door off its hinges." After a heavy artillery bombardment the infantry was to make a frontal attack to, in Montgomery's phrase, "crumble the enemy front." A partial function of the artillery barrage was to explode as much of the minefield as possible. Two corridors would be opened through the minefield. Armored divisions would get through and cut Rommel off from the sea so that the door would fly off its hinges. From Enigma Montgomery knew every detail of the enemy's dispositions and plans.

At nightfall of October 23, in the glare of a full moon, 900 artillery pieces opened fire on the Axis lines, first on the enemy batteries in the rear then on the forward positions, each gun firing that night for a total of five and a half hours. The Germans' artillery response was sporadic for they had orders to save ammunition. Rommel, suffering from liver and stomach ailments as well as bouts of depression, was away in Germany. His replacement was General Stumme. On the first day of battle Stumme had gone to the front, suffered a heart attack, fell off the command car and died in the desert. So, for a day or two, the Axis army was leaderless. On October 25 Rommel was back at his command post and immediately staged a counterattack. It failed in the face of the formidable British defenses, which included 1,500 anti-tank guns. The other reason was that by the end of the counterattack Rommel had fuel for only three more days of fighting. Montgomery's crumbling job went on for eight days without achieving its objective; no corridors were open for the armor. By now Rommel, realizing where the main effort lay, moved the 21st Panzer Division from the south to join his 15th Panzer Division in the north. Thus the hinge at the coast, which was supposed to have been broken to leave Rommel dangling in the desert, was now in the hands of the concentrated Afrika Korps.

Montgomery then changed his plans—which went against his grain—and staged a second crumbling assault to the south aimed at the junction of the German and Italian armies. This lasted through the first two days of November. By then the losses in tanks and guns were heavy on both sides. However, while Montgomery could afford them Rommel was running out of strength. Consequently, after 11 days of battle the British broke through the Axis lines. A single corridor five miles south from the coast had been opened and the armored divisions of the British 10 Corps went through. An attempt was made to pin Rommel's forces against the coast but they withdrew in time. On November 4 Rommel ordered a general retreat.

Rommel reached the Libyan frontier on November 8, the day the Allies landed in North Africa. Any thought now of a German counterattack, even if it were to succeed, was out of the question. Axis troops had shrunk to half their October numbers suffering a total of 20,000 casualties, 30,000 POWs and losing practically all their tanks and guns (Strawson 1969, 170). The distance they had to travel from El Alamein to Tunisia was 1,785 miles on a single road, with little motor transport and even less fuel. What now transpired is one of the more curious spectacles in the history of war. Rommel moved on the coastal road while slightly to the south and parallel to him traveled the 8th Army. After reaching Tobruk some generals suggested the British make a dash to Benghazi—to cut Rommel off the way O'Connor had done to the Italians in 1940—but Montgomery was afraid lest he even now suffer defeat at the hands of the Germans. Thus, as the wounded tiger shuffled along the coast licking its wounds, packs of hounds followed him at a safe distance. Not only did Montgomery's land army not attempt to cut him off or maul him, but neither the navy nor the RAF did much to interfere. The navy, of course, could have landed troops on Rommel's long trek to the west but no such attempt was ever made. The RAF had a magnificent target—columns stretched for miles in the open desert with no place to hide—something the Germans would have destroyed in a day—but the RAF accomplished precious little. They did appear from time to time, but only to drop bombs, a mighty ineffective way of dealing with troops. The British pilots never strafed the enemy forces, claiming that they were not trained for it; besides, they argued, low-level attacks were dangerous. Rommel reached Benghazi on November 19, crossed into Tripolitania and continued west. Following him the British entered undefended Tripoli at the end of January 1943, three months after the start of their offensive. By mid–February Rommel was on the Mareth line in southern Tunisia boosting the German forces that had landed there in response to Torch.

In September Rommel had been given his feldmarschall baton at the Wolfschanze to the overwhelming praise of the führer and his entourage. That was after he had reached the gates of Suez. When the fighting in Egypt started to go badly for the Germans, Hitler sent Rommel an order on November 2 that "there could be no other course but that of holding out to the last man and that for the German troops there was only one choice, victory or death" (Winterbotham, 116). When eventually forced to retreat, Rommel suggested to the German-Italian Command that his army be evacuated before it was destroyed. Mussolini refused. On November 27 Rommel decided to see the führer, arriving in Rastenburg the next day. In a preliminary talk with the chiefs of the OKW they seemed to agree with his stand. In the evening Hitler received him in the presence of Göring.

"How are things in Africa?" asked the führer, as if he didn't know.

ROMMEL: "They have better material, more powerful artillery, more tanks and supremacy in the air.... We had no fuel"

Appropriately instructed by the führer, Göring took over: "But your trucks fled in their hundreds.... There was fuel enough for that."

ROMMEL: "We also had no ammunition."

GÖRING: "Nevertheless you left 10,000 artillery shells behind..."

ROMMEL: "We also had not enough weapons"

GÖRING: "The weapons were thrown away on your flight."

HITLER, rejoining the fray: "But anyone who throws away his weapons deserves to rot."

Red in the face, Rommel jumped from his seat crying "Mein Führer."

Hitler banged on the table and repeated, "Anyone who throws his weapons away and has no gun left to defend himself with must be left to rot."

Rommel pressed on to have his army saved by evacuation, but Hitler shouted, "Never."

ROMMEL: "Let me withdraw the Panzer Army to Italy so that it can defend the Continent against Eisenhower's anticipated invasion."

"I no longer want to hear such rubbish from your lips.... North Africa will be defended, as Stalingrad will.... That is an order, Herr Feldmarschall" [Carell 1980, 305–7].

In Britain, starved for years of any success, the eviction of the four German divisions from Libya was hailed as the victory of the century. Church bells tolled throughout the British Isles. A solemn Mass was held in Canterbury Cathedral in the presence of the country's leaders. Field Marshall Alexander, chief of the Middle East Theater, sent a telegram to the prime minister, pronouncing, "The orders you gave me on August 10, 1942, have been fulfilled. His Majesty's enemies together with their impedimenta, have been completely eliminated from Egypt, Cyrenaica, Libya and Tripolitania," for the British untypically heavy verbiage, not to speak of the geographical eye-raiser as if Libya were something different from Cyrenaica and Tripolitania. Montgomery was hailed as the modern Wellington, promoted to full general, later on to field marshal bearing the epithet Montgomery of Alamein. In Montgomery's view, this was the least he deserved because, said he, the battle of El Alamein was "one of the decisive battles in history" (Jacobsen, 204).

* * *

Torch had been on the planning boards since June when Roosevelt, against Marshall's objections, approved the scheme. The expedition, part coming from the USA and part from Britain, sailed on the very day the battle of El Alamein opened. The Western Task Force from the USA was to land on three locations of the Atlantic coast, Safi, Casablanca and Fort Lyautey; the Central and Eastern Task Forces from England were headed for Oran and Algiers in the Mediterranean. Originally the British wanted to land also in Tunisia but the Americans demurred; they were concerned lest the Germans occupy Spain and sever sea communications with the disembarked troops; hence the landings on the Atlantic coast. Once landed the troops from Algiers would make an overland dash for Tunisia and bottle up Rommel in his retreat across Libya.

The Anglo-American armada consisted of 111 transports accompanied by 216 warships including battleships and aircraft carriers. They arrived at their destinations without interference either from the air or by U-boats. They carried 110,000 troops. Though the majority of them were British the key role was assigned to the Americans, who were to be present at all locations, from Safi to Algiers. To play their role they came with US flags and military bands. From Casablanca to Tunis, a stretch of 1,300 miles, the French fielded 135,000 men, mostly native contingents without heavy weapons, carrying World War I rifles (Blumenson, 24). To enhance the spirit of fraternization Roosevelt, at midnight of November 7 and 8, broadcast an appeal to the French asking for no-resistance, ending his proclamation with "Vive la France eternelle." De Gaulle had not been let in on the plans for Torch, partly for security reasons and partly due to the Allies having picked Giraud as their man in North Africa.

The commander of French land forces in North Africa, General Juin, was in on the secret; consequently there was little ground fighting and whatever small arms fire erupted was because not everyone was aware of the deal. But the French navy was under the command of Darlan, a notorious Anglophobe and his warships opened fire on the Allied flotillas at Casablanca and Oran. This turned out to be less of a problem than the mechanics of disembarkation. The landings were in disarray due to crew inexperience and inadequate equipment. The coxswains of the landing crafts had difficulties with the rough surf, mishandled their jobs and caused many boats to be swamped; men overloaded with 60 pounds of equipment were disembarked in deep waters and many drowned. In the end losses from landing mishaps and drownings were higher than from French resistance. Still they were low. The Americans forecast 18,000 casualties; the actual toll was one-tenth of that with some 500 men dead. The fatalities for the entire Allied force were 1,000 men. On land local cease-fires were fairly soon arranged. Eventually the Allies were in luck with the French Fleet, too. Darlan, who normally officiated in Vichy, happened to be in Algiers at the time of the landings attending to his son stricken with poliomyelitis. Eisenhower, mixing threats with promises, persuaded Darlan to come over to the Allied side who ordered a general cease fire to take effect at midday November 10. Three days later Darlan set up a provisional government in North Africa and the USA recognized it. Giraud was appointed commander in chief of the French armed forces. On November 20 an official agreement was signed bringing colonial France into the Western Alliance.

* * *

On November 7 Hitler was traveling from the Wolfschanze to Munich to address his *Altkämpfer*, a traditional panegyric to past triumphs. At dawn of November 8 reports reached the führer's train about the Allied landings. Earlier, when informed of the massive convoys passing Gibraltar, the führer's intuition was that they were headed either for Malta or a landing on the European coast. When the facts became clear Hitler issued the following orders:

- Kesselring was to establish a bridgehead in Tunisia.
- From Tunisia Kesselring was to drive west, taking port after port and chasing the Allies back onto the ships.
- Rommel was to get ample supplies from Sicily and Tunisia and halt the 8th Army as far east as possible.
- Vichy France was to be occupied and the fleet in Toulon seized.

Interestingly enough Mussolini urged the occupation of Spain to close off the Mediterranean and take the Allies in the rear but the führer rejected it (Jacobsen, 212–3).

Anticipating such orders, Kesselring had started dispatching planes to Bizerte and Tunis already on November 9. By 3 P.M. he had over 100 aircraft there. The Germans met no French resistance. Admiral Esteva, commander in chief of the fleet at Bizerte, declared neutrality. The army commander withdrew from Tunisia westward, eventually joining the Allies. German and Italian reinforcements poured in by air and by sea so that by the end of the month there were 17,000 German and 11,000 Italian troops in Tunisia. Eventually a total of four German and two Italian divisions were ferried across (Gelb, 181) to form the 5th Panzer Army. Simultaneously 10 German and six Italian divisions marched into unoccupied France and some troops landed on Corsica. The French Armistice Army was disbanded. Even though Darlan had ordered the French fleet to sail for African ports, when the Germans approached Toulon the fleet scuttled itself.

The Allies attempted to follow up on their plan of capturing Tunisia. From Algiers the British 1st Army, consisting of two divisions supported by some US troops, set out for their objective, 500 miles away. They had at their disposal two roads and a railway and they used them to transport the troops, the tanks lashed to flatcars. Some airborne units had been dropped near Bone and Tebessa as early as mid–November. The weather was bad with much rain and waterlogged terrain. In one place the Allies got as far as Djedeia, 15 miles west of Tunis— see Fig. 27.1.

On December 3 there was another conference at the Wolfschanze regarding Africa. For this meeting the commander of the 39th Panzer Corps fighting near Rzhev, von Arnim, was called in. A dour, limping Prussian the general was promoted to generaloberst and designated commander in chief in Tunisia. The orders given to von Arnim were a repetition of the old ones: capture first Bone and Philipville harbors, advance along the Algerian coast and drive the Allies onto their ships. In addition, the German Command was to stage an Arab revolt against the Allies— the führer had a high regard for Islam's martial spirit in fighting infidels (Carell, 324). With von Arnim's appearance in Tunisia neither shortage of supplies, nor bad terrain nor lack of roads damped the Germans' usual speed and initiative. In a series of counterattacks they retook most of what the Allies had gained in Tunisia. All through December heavy local battles were fought, particularly at Longstop Hill, where the Allies suffered serious casualties and lost much of their equipment. Von Arnim did not drive the Allies back onto their ships but he stopped them from taking Tunis and Bizerte and bottling up Rommel. By Christmas Eisenhower had to concede that the Germans had won the race to Tunisia and suspended all major operations till the end of the rainy season. That meant waiting for the spring of 1943.

By January the front had stabilized some 20–50 miles inside Tunisia with a large bulge to the east in the center anchored on the mountains of the Eastern Dorsal. At the southern borderlands near the old French defenses against Libya, the Mareth Line, there was a gap in the front line which the Allies left unoccupied. It was toward that fortified line that Rommel was retreating, fearing that the Allies would forestall him and reach the coast in his rear. They did not. On February 12 Rommel, completing a trek of 2,000 miles, reached the Mareth Line bringing with him 70,000 mostly German troops. Rommel now had the option of either continuing north to join von Arnim near Tunis or stay at the southern perimeter and have a chance of driving northwest into the rear of the Allied armies. Typically, he chose the latter. The German bridgehead was now more or less a continuous 400-mile periphery manned by what would soon be a quarter million Axis troops. At Mareth Rommel resumed his nominal command of what was now AG Africa, von Arnim commanding the 5th Panzer Army in the north and General Messe in charge of the newly named German-Italian Panzer

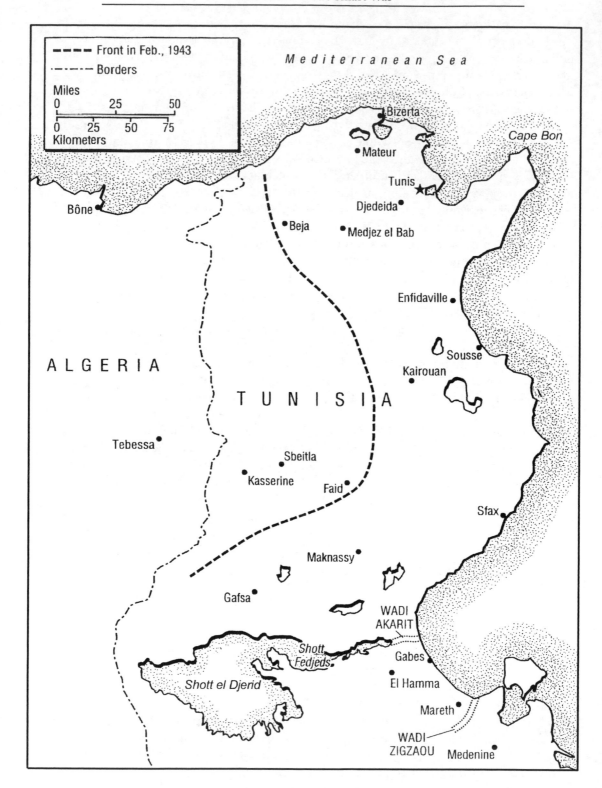

27.1. The Tunisian Bridgehead

Army in central and south Tunisia. In effect, Arnim ran the show in the north and Rommel in the central and southern sectors. The Allies, too, had reshuffled commands, Field Marshal Alexander as of February 15 in charge of both the British 1st and 8th Armies.

It was in the central bulge near the Faid Pass that the Allies were concentrating strong forces threatening to separate Rommel from von Arnim's army. Von Arnim decided to eliminate the threat, and more. After attacking the Faid Pass he planned to roll northward, force a retreat on the Allies and bring about a major change on his sector of the front. Rommel, free of Montgomery who was still plodding through the Libyan sands, decided to join in the battle but his idea was more ambitious. From his southern position he proposed to attack deep into the Americans' flank, take Tebessa in Algeria and head for the sea to cut off and destroy the Allied armies in Tunisia — an African *Sichelschnitt*. Von Arnim's was thus the minor vis-à-vis Rommel's major plan.

The northern army opened its Faid Pass attack on February 14 using the 10th and 21st Panzer divisions, the latter taken over from Rommel. The green American troops broke under the onslaught of the two Panzer divisions. Large numbers were encircled near Sidi Bou Zid and their armor destroyed; others retreated from the battlefield in semipanic, abandoning most of their equipment. A day later Rommel joined in by swinging northwest, taking Gafsa on the 15th and Feriana a day later. By taking Feriana and the nearby Thelepte airfield Rommel found himself on the flank of the US II Corps fighting von Arnim's troops. Impressed by Rommel's success the führer, after initial hesitation, gave Rommel the green light for his dash to Tebessa and thence to the Mediterranean.

To get to Tebessa, his pivot point for the drive north, Rommel had to get through the Kasserine Pass in the Western Dorsal. The enfilade is topped on either side by 4,000-foot crests and at its narrowest point is less than a kilometer wide. The weather was bad, the ravine full of rocks and mud, taxing terrain even for tracked vehicles. On the 20th, with the armor of three divisions massed on a seven-mile front and skipping the customary artillery barrage, Rommel charged across the pass causing supreme havoc among the US troops. No one expected him in that place and no defenses had been prepared; 3,000 POWs were taken and 250 tanks and armored vehicles destroyed or captured. Many of the attacked troops simply melted away. Leaving enough men to deal with the trapped Americans, Rommel headed for Tebessa. Half of the "major" plan seemed to have been accomplished.

But the remaining half if not 90 percent of the undertaking never came to pass; this was 1943 not 1940. From all over, the Allies pulled in reinforcements and reserves. Those Americans who had panicked returned to their posts. Most tellingly the Allied air forces rushed to the scene and launched a massive assault on any German infantryman and vehicle they could spot. And finally, two weeks after Rommel's arrival at the Mareth Line, the 8th Army made its appearance from Tripolitania, impinging on the rear of Rommel's army fighting 150 miles away on the Algerian frontier and posing the danger of its being overrun from the south. In a conference with Kesselring, commander in chief south, who had flown in from Italy, it was decided to call off the offensive. On February 22 Rommel disappeared through the Kasserine Pass as swiftly as he had arrived.

This was the end not only of the African *Sichelschnitt*, it was also the end of Rommel. Worried about the prospects of the war in Africa, Rommel once again requested a meeting with his leader. It was granted with unusual dispatch. On March 9 Rommel left Africa. The details of his visit are not known but the outcome is; told that he was a defeatist, Rommel was ordered to "take a cure." He never returned to Africa. His place as commander of AG Africa was taken over by von Arnim — and not for long.

When Montgomery reached the Tunisian border, aside from the enemy a further advance was blocked by the Schott Jerid-Fedjeds, a 120-mile-long marshy lake stretching from the Algerian border almost to the coast. To hook up with the Allies Monty had to overcome two obstacles: the Mareth Line and Wadi Akarit, the narrow 18-mile-wide land bridge between the lake and sea. On the Mareth Line Montgomery met the Afrika Korps again, alive and kicking. Following a tremendous artillery barrage the 8th Army launched its attack on the night of March 16. The main thrust was to be along the coast with two supporting moves, a northwest attack to its left and Patton's troops heading toward Gafsa. The main attack ran into trouble from the start and Montgomery shifted his attack to the auxiliary northwest prong. Patton took Gafsa and headed toward Maknassy, threatening to come into the rear of the Mareth Line, whereupon the Germans abandoned it on March 28. Following them Montgomery took Gabes and came astride Wadi Akarit, the cork that blocked entry into Tunisia. Starting on the night of April 4 a two-day duplicate of El Alamein was fought with tremendous expenditures of ammunition, hand-to-hand fighting and crumbling attacks that eventually made the enemy give up. Crossing Wadi Akarit, the 8th Army linked up two days later with Patton's troops coming from the west. A continuous Allied front was now formed, manned by 160,000 British, 90,000 American and 50,000 French troops. A general assault against the Tunisian bridgehead was not long in coming.

For the impending spring offensive several reorganizations took place. Up till now on the main front the British held the northern and the US II Corps the southern end with the French in between. Now the II Corps was moved to the extreme north, Bradley replacing Patton on April 15. The central portion of the front line was assigned to British V Corps with the French placed at the junction of the 1st and 8th Armies. The 8th Army, which after overcoming Wadi Akarit was advancing north was, to Montgomery's ire, assigned a holding position along the southern perimeter. The US II and the British V Corps were given the main task of taking, respectively, Bizerte and Tunis.

The offensive was launched on April 22 by 300,000 men supported by 3,200 aircraft and 1,400 tanks. Compacted into a tight pocket the Germans held their positions so that after three days the assault ground to a halt. It was decided to pull out a whole corps of the 8th Army and position it south of the British V Corps. While this shift was going on the Americans in the north broke through the German lines and took Mateur on May 3; from there Bizerte was only 15 and Tunis 25 miles away. The new British assault was launched on May 6 accompanied by the most intense aerial bombardment the war had seen thus far, as well as a ceaseless artillery barrage as the infantry moved to the attack. By now the Axis bridgehead had shrunk to 25 square miles which received ever more withering fire by land, sea and air. It soon broke into two, one around Bizerte and another around Tunis. As the Germans were beginning to destroy their dumps and equipment an order arrived from the Wolfschanze: "The German people expect you to fight to the last bullet." But the Germans were already packing for a comfortable life in Allied POW camps.

After the last pocket of resistance on Cape Bon collapsed, von Arnim capitulated at noon May 12. The last communiqué of May 13 from General Cramer commanding the Afrika Korps ended with the words "The German Afrika Korps must rise again." At the same time Alexander was signaling Churchill, "Sir, it is my duty to report that the Tunisian campaign is over. All enemy resistance has ceased. We are masters of North African shores"—compared to El Alamein a more sober message for an incomparably greater victory.

The number of enemy POWs taken in Tunisia falls into two sets. Most sources cite 250,000 to 300,000, half of them Germans. But two more reliable numbers are 150,000 POWs cited by Alexander in his message to Churchill, and 170,000–180,000 given as the ration strength in a report from AG Afrika to Rome headquarters. Among the prisoners were nine generals taken in the Bizerte pocket alone, among them von Arnim. Only 600 or so Germans got away. It is instructive to note the casualties suffered by the Allies in their African campaigns. By the end of 1943 the British had been fighting in Africa for three years, incurring in that period 35,500 dead. The Americans suffered in half a year 16,500 fatalities (Carell 1980, 354). Thus a British-USA 6:1 span of warfare resulted in ratio of 2:1 fatalities. This would indicate that on the average the fighting waged by the US forces in Africa was three times as intense as that of the British.

The events in North Africa mirror much of the nature of the war between the Western Allies and Germany. In military terms the Germans managed everywhere to come out on top. At El Alamein a German force only a quarter as strong with a weak air force and disastrous logistics managed to elude Montgomery's juggernaut, for four months keeping a whole imperial army at bay. The German command faced the *fait accompli* of a North African invasion supported by a vast armada of ships and aircraft and, lacking transport and a navy to speak of, managed to rapidly set up a bridgehead in Tunisia which vitiated the main Allies' objectives; it prevented them from attacking Rommel in the back; and by occupying Tunisia it for a time completely prevented Allied ships from passing the Straits of Sicily. These were clearly tactical victories in the familiar mold of the 1939–41 German military prowess.

But in the end these tactical successes brought with them strategic defeat. In Libya the Germans had perhaps 50,000 men who, had Hitler not been hell-bent on putting good money into bad, would perhaps have been lost. By succeeding in his Tunisian venture he had lost — even taking the lower POW estimate and adding to it the casualties — at least 150,000 men. To maintain the Tunisian bridgehead 107 ships with a total of 400,000 tons were lost just during the January-February period alone, a loss the Axis could ill afford. All the weaponry of a quarter-million men, including at least four Panzer divisions, had gone to ground if not to the enemy. With Tunisia lost, at one fell swoop the Mediterranean was clear sailing for the Allied armadas. Thus all the local victories eventually added up to a crucial defeat, which was to have repercussions in the immediate future.

Aside from the military victory in Tunisia the Allies gained much in their surreptitious conduct of the war in general. It is unlikely that the neglect to seize Tunisia was not premeditated; that being remiss in destroying Rommel on his retreat was not deliberate; that the stretching out of the Tunisian campaign over six months did not serve a purpose. It rather fits in comfortably with general Allied strategy, a perfect case of Roosevelt's dictum of "making haste slowly." While the war in Africa lasted there were no pressures on the Allies to open a second front. There was no need for Roosevelt to take sides in the dispute between Marshall and Churchill as to the proper direction of the war. American industry was given time to set new records in production. Most of all, the Russians were given another half year to bleed and maul the Germans so that, if meet them the Allies must, they would be so much weaker, they and the Russians, too. It was an overt and covert gain for the Western powers with which they could be very well content.

Part Four

ANNUS IRAE 1943

• Chapter 28 •

From Kursk to Kiev

In 1943 the implications of December 1941, when Hitler's doom had irrevocably etched itself on the course of the war, materialized in a series of swift, crushing debacles. Whereas at the end of 1941 these could only be surmised, they now took place all around *Festung Europa*—on land, sea and in the air.

When the second attempt to subdue Russia the previous fall ended with the Stalingrad-Caucasus fiasco, Hitler for a change had no new schemes up his sleeve. He had no "unalterable" plan to impose on his underlings, nor did he, as in the past, foist on them ersatz projects meant to hide his real intentions. In meetings with his commanders he thought out aloud, mumbled, shuffled possibilities, even listened to suggestions and remained noncommittal. Of course, it never came down to fundamental issues or a radical change in the conduct of the war. These were outside the permissible framework because his generals, the führer had stated often enough, understood nothing of geopolitics, economics, the destiny of nations or the place of genius in history. The only permitted question was: What should the Ostheer do next in the positions and the condition it was in now?

A number of proposals were tabled by the OKW, OKH, and the field commanders. Zeitzler proposed to build an east wall along shortened lines so that reserves could be built up; that was also Mussolini's advice. This Hitler declined. Manstein offered two plans, both inspired by previous successes. One, labeled the "backhand stroke," was to await the expected Russian offensive in Ukraine, give ground and then counterattack, a duplicate of his Kharkov success in the spring. Otherwise Manstein proposed to attack the Kursk salient and wheel south to encircle the bulk of the Russian armies in Ukraine — a repetition of the 1941 Kiev holocaust which he called the "forehand stroke." The backhand stroke was dismissed by Hitler because it entailed surrender of territory. The second planted in Hitler's head the word Kursk, which would resurface later. Then there was Hans Guderian, whom Hitler had dismissed in December 1941 for failing to storm Moscow. But in 1943 there was a crisis in the German armored divisions. Most of the old tanks lay rusting in the mud and snows of Russia and those that still ran — in January 1943 the Ostheer had only 500 of them left (Cross 49) — were no match for Russia's T-34s. In February Hitler had appointed Guderian inspector general of armored troops, charged with equipping Germany's Panzer arm with new and better tanks. Guderian was to report directly to the führer, bypassing both the OKW and OKH, thus setting up another chain of command responsible to no one but Hitler. Guderian now proposed that the Ostheer take a breather for all of 1943 while the Panzer arm was being rebuilt to its former glory. In the spring of 1944 the Ostheer would then launch a new Barbarossa.

On March 23 Hitler retired to the Berghof to mull over the situation. On May 3 he summoned his generals to Munich for a conference to announce his decision. It was to be Kursk, code named *Zitadelle* to indicate that the Wehrmacht now operated from an unassailable fortress. On Kursk both Model and Manstein, the two commanders scheduled to conduct the operation, were hesitant. Subsequently, when alone with Hitler, Guderian asked why Kursk — and the führer admitted that, yes, "it makes his stomach turn" when he thinks of it but he must do something "for political reasons" (Clark, 325). In 1941 the Germans had been strong enough to attack along the entire Russian front; in 1942 they were capable of attack only in the south; in 1943 they were no longer capable even of that for Kursk was a local engagement which, even if successful, would amount to no more than the elimination of a Russian salient. Next arose the question whether to launch it soon before the Russians had time to fortify their positions there or wait for the arrival of Guderian's new tanks, which were still in the workshops. Despite his having made a "decision" Hitler was still wavering because deep inside such a minor venture was repugnant to the core of his being.

The Kursk operation had been mooted in early March but Hitler's Order No. 6 for Zitadelle did not materialize till April 15. It set as its objectives the encirclement of the enemy forces in the Kursk salient and the straightening of the front line. The deployment was to be timed so that as of April 28 the offensive could be launched within six days. When it came to phrasing his directive Hitler could not restrain himself from indulging in his standard bluster of imbuing each operation with transcendental import. Said he in the Kursk order, "I have decided to launch the *Zitadelle* offensive.... The offensive is of decisive significance.... The victory at Kursk must have the effect of a beacon seen around the world."

The distaste for the Kursk venture made the führer procrastinate for two months. A few days after issuing Order No. 6, Hitler, on Manstein's urging, called in Zeitzler proposing a frontal instead of a pincer attack on Kursk, arguing that the latter was too obvious a battle plan; Zeitzler said it was too late to redeploy the troops. On June 10 the backhand stroke was resuscitated, then abandoned. A week later the OKW recommended a new strategy altogether: pull from the front a number of armies, concentrate them into strong reserves along the major communication lines to await the Russians' summer offensive. Buffeted by all these proposals Hitler on June 20 finally ordered the attack on Kursk to be launched on July 3, later postponed to July 5.

When he finally got himself to issue the order to attack, Hitler seemed to have been reinvigorated somewhat by the scent of impending bloodshed. A few days before the offensive, Hitler told Zeitzler that he now felt that all previous failures had been caused by the Italians, Magyars and Rumanians and that from now on there would be no more retreats. "Where we are, we stay," announced the führer. And in his proclamation to the troops going into battle, he rose to his tried rhetorical heights by telling them, "This day you are to take part in an offensive of such importance that the whole future of the war may depend on its outcome" (Clark, 329).

The Russian salient at Kursk, a leftover from the messy Russian winter offensive of 1941-42, projected like a balcony, into the German lines abutting it on three sides. Its frontage had been static for more than a year, as it was along the rest of the central and northern fronts. The salient projected to a depth of some 80 miles while north to south it was 120 miles long. Its north and west sides faced Kluge's AGC; the southern periphery faced AGS under Manstein. The German plan visualized assaults into the two inner corners of the salient. The northeast corner was to be tackled by Model's 9th Army disposing of 15 divisions, six of them armored. The southeast corner was assigned to Hoth's 4th Panzer Army fielding 18 divisions, 11 of them Panzer or Panzer-Grenadiers. Model was to breach the Russian lines with infantry, pioneers and massive artillery following which the armor would form the northern prong of the pincer attack. Hoth's 15 full or semiarmored divisions contained the best units of the Ostheer, the most formidable Panzer force ever concentrated on only 28 miles of frontage. Hoth planned to accomplish his penetration by standard blitzkrieg methods. The two prongs were to meet east of Kursk.

By the time the battle opened the Germans had received 200 of the new 45-ton Panzers equipped with 75 mm guns and 90 of the 60-ton Tigers mounting the formidable 88 mm gun. In gunnery and armor these tanks were superior to the Russian T-34s. However, they were slower and, by some peculiar reasoning, the Tigers had no MGs, making them vulnerable to infantry attacks. More seriously, they had been rushed to the front without eliminating the teething problems inherent in new designs and were prone to mechanical breakdowns.

Given the constricted geography and the delays in the German deployment, the Russians were fully aware of what was brewing. Moreover they had received the most detailed intelligence of the German plans, mainly from Lucy's network in Switzerland. Already on April 20 they were sent the gist of Hitler's Order No. 6. Following a last battle conference at the Wolfschanze on July 1, Lucy the next day alerted Moscow that the attack would open sometime during July 3–6 (Cross 1993, 154).

In the three months the Russians had to get ready they converted the Kursk salient into a steel and fire-spitting concrete hedgehog never equaled before or after. Using 300,000 civilians they dug five concentric belts of trenches, three around Kursk and two in the hinterland so that the defenses extended 100 miles deep. Streams were dammed up so that floodwaters could be released to trap the advancing tanks. One hundred and fifty airfields were erected as well as 50 dummy ones. They laid 400,000 mines. Disposing as they did of 6,000 anti-tank guns they converted each hillock and ravine into a tank trap. Of their 3,500 armored vehicles 2,000 were positioned in the salient and 1,500 in the rear. A complete front faced each of the two endangered corners with two powerful reserves stationed in the rear, one directly to the east and another at the southeast corner where Hoth's assault was expected. Including the reserves the Russians assembled 1.3 million men, and three-quarters of their armored strength (Overy, 1997, 244). They were commanded by the most experienced generals of the Red Army, Rokossovsky, Konev and Vatutin. The several fronts were overseen by Zhukov and Vasilevsky, sent down by Stalin to coordinate their moves and serve as a link with Stavka. The Russian buildup was so formidable that come July Manstein recommended Zitadelle be abandoned. But it was too late.

Before they got wind of Kursk the Russians had planned an offensive of their own but then decided to wait. There were also suggestions for a preemptive strike against the German assembly areas at Kursk; this, too, was abandoned. The decision was to let the Germans attack and exhaust themselves before a counterattack was launched.

Along the southern periphery the Russians had a topographical advantage in that the German lines ran behind a ridge that obstructed their view of the battlefield. Thus Manstein opened a preliminary attack a day earlier to capture the high ground. On the following morning, the day of the general assault, there also occurred an unplanned clash of large air forces when both sides were on their way to a preemptive strike against the other's troop concentrations. Thus when the Russian armada of 450 planes approached the German lines, instead of the surprise they had hoped for, they found the Luftwaffe up in the air. As usual in such encounters, the Russians suffered a stinging defeat. Although their bombers were accompanied by 285 fighters the Russians lost 120 planes against a loss of 20 for the Germans, without inflicting any damage on the troops below.

The attack in the south opened at 3:30 on the morning of July 5. The Germans had been fed Peruitin (Benzedrine) for some time and so, too, at Kursk. The attack was preceded by a massive artillery barrage during which the Germans, in one hour, expended more shells than during the entire Polish and French campaigns (Cross 1993, 170–71)—an indication of the kind of combat to come. Hoth planned to advance straight north which would bring him just east of Kursk, the junction point with Model. But several factors interfered with this plan. One was the weather. On the very first day torrential rains, sometimes turning into cloudbursts, converted roads into mud streams and the rivers into swollen rapids requiring bridging equipment to ford them. The other problem was Hoth's gnawing fear of the Russian reserves loitering to the southeast of his advance—thus the tendency for his troops to veer eastward. It also did not help when Abteilung Kemp, meant to shield his right flank, failed to make a dent in the Russian lines as Hoth pushed his way into the salient.

In the north the attack opened along a 50-mile front. Here, too, one of Model's problems was to safeguard his left flank from the menacing steppe front. He made strenuous efforts to capture Maloarchangelsk at the hinge of his advance, but failed. In pouring rain Model advanced five miles during the first day and it is a measure of the ever-stiffening Russian resistance and the heavy losses of his troops that during the remainder of the offensive he gained only another seven miles before he was brought to a complete stop. Here, as in the south, the fighting resembled the worst of World War I—an expenditure of mass and firepower in place of mobility and leadership. The German fighting machine proceeded at the pace of a gigantic rotary drain cleaner, gouging out chunks of terrain without achieving a breakthrough.

Given its preponderance of armor, Hoth's 4th Panzer Army was having somewhat better luck than Model as it pushed its way along the narrow corridor between the Donetz and Psel rivers. After heavy and costly fighting Hoth eventually gained a bridgehead across the Psel where he hoped to block the Russian reserves while proceeding across open country to Kursk. After a week of bitter and costly fighting he advanced for a distance of 37 miles but this was as far as he would go.

On the third day of battle Russia's elite armor, Rotmistrov's 5th Tank Army, started moving up to the southeastern corner of the salient. He had 200 miles to cover and by July 11 reached the front at a place called Prokhorovka, Hoth's farthest advance. The clash that occurred next day between the 4th Panzer Army and Rotmistrov's tanks was the culmination of the battle of Kursk and remains the greatest tank battle in the history of warfare. What was pathetic was that here the flower of Germany's Panzer arm, celebrated for its skill in maneuvering and fielding tanks and superior in armor and gunnery, became locked in a battle with Russian tanks that can be best described as hand-to-hand fighting. It was a head-on collision in which individual tanks fought at the closest range, a gigantic melée of dueling ironclads. A total of 1,300 tanks, 850 of them Russian, fought each other in a narrow strip of land between a railroad embankment and the Psel river with no room for maneuvering, envelopment, or escape. The new Panzers and Tigers lost the advantage of thicker armor, longer range guns and the superior skills of their crews and commanders.

In stifling heat, amid raging fires, smoke, and cordite fumes the battle went on all day long by the end of which Hoth's offensive was blunted. Of the 916 tanks the 4th Panzer Army went into battle with, 450 had been lost in the week-long struggle. Rotmistrov himself lost half of his strength. Overall the Russians lost 1,500 armored vehicles but remained master of the battlefield and their repair shops were better than the Germans' so that by August they were back to a strength of 2,750 tanks (Cross, 1993 230).

The day following the Prokhorovka battle Kluge and Manstein were summoned to the Wolfschanze where Hitler ordered them to call off the offensive. Clearly the battle was lost but this usually would not have led to the cancellation of an undertaking sanctioned by the führer—it would have been fought to the cruel end until the defeat was worse still. Hitler gave his generals two pieces of bad news—one, that on July 10 the Allies had landed in Sicily and he needed to transfer troops there, and two, that the Russians had just started an offensive at Orel which not only threatened the German front there but also menaced the rear of Model's 9th Army. These were surely sufficient reasons to call off the doomed offensive but the deeper motivation was probably that Hitler had no stomach—or a turned stomach—for the whole business. The battle of Kursk would turn out to be the last offensive the Germans managed to launch on the Russian front.

* * *

In considering a summer offensive Zhukov tried to persuade Stalin to avoid the mistakes of the first winter and employ encirclement tactics instead. Stalin felt the Red Army was not ready for it. They agreed on a battle plan employing a series of hammer blows at diverse sectors of the front and exploit success to primarily liberate territory. This, in fact, became the basic Soviet operational doctrine; a series of multiple piston-like strikes along a wide front to keep the Germans guessing where the main effort would be until at some point a breach was achieved whereupon reserves were rushed there for a deep drive behind enemy lines. The main objective in the summer of 1943 was to regain the Donetz basin with its mineral resources and fertile soil. Its symbol was Kharkov.

Stavka opened its attack at Orel on the day of the Prokhorovka battle. Three fronts, including the one blocking Model, launched the assault. In view of the faltering Kursk offensive the German field commanders suggested withdrawing to the base of the Orel salient, the Hagen Line, so as to shorten the front, but Hitler rejected it. Orel fell on August 5 and to celebrate it Moscow for the first time was treated to a display of gun salutes and fireworks, soon to become a standard celebration whenever a major city was liberated—a string of salutes that was to last to the end of the war.

The main weight of the Russian summer offensive was to be not at Orel but near Belogrod aimed at Kharkov to the southwest. In order to siphon off forces from Hoth's powerful Panzer formations lurking to the north of Belogrod, the Russians as early as July 5 attacked along the river Mius as if intending a major drive along the Black Sea. Fearing a collapse there Manstein rushed two Panzer corps to the south; it was what the Russians had hoped for. On August 3 a powerful thrust from the Belogrod area achieved a breakthrough almost at once and the Germans had no forces to stem it. Within days a huge gap opened up between the southern and central Army Groups, into which the Russians charged with an avalanche of tanks, covering 70 miles in five days headed straight for Kharkov. Hitler ordered the city be held at all costs using the familiar political whip that its loss "would have an unfavorable effect on the attitude of Turkey and Bulgaria" as if this mattered one way or another. On August 22 Rotmistrov's tanks reached the outskirts of the city and the next day Kharkov was in Russian hands—this time for good.

Kharkov had been one of Hitler's obsessions. When, following the Stalingrad-Caucasus debacle, he had reorganized the AGS he had allotted half of the dissolved AGB, including three Panzer divisions, to form Detachment Lanz for the specific purpose of defending Kharkov. But its attempt to repeat Manstein's feat of the previous March failed and Kharkov was lost. Alarmed, Hitler on August 27 flew down to AGS headquarters in Vinnitza. There Manstein, far from making excuses for Kharkov, told him that they should withdraw from the Donetz basin altogether as the Russians, in addition to their attacks against the Central Front, had renewed their drive along the Mius. Hitler ordered that the Donetz basin be defended and flew back to his lair.

By the end of August the events of the last two months and the grim prognosis for the future produced some soul searching in Manstein and Kluge. On September 3 they journeyed to the Wolfschanze with an astounding proposal. Given the fractured leadership structure and the conflicting demands of the various war theaters, why not establish a supreme command under a single chief of staff, in essence a merger of the OKW and OKH under a professional military man. Without even bothering to reject it Hitler told the two feldmarschalls they didn't understand the situation and sent them back to a continuation of piecemeal retreats laced with rages of the führer for having done so. Sometime earlier the same two men had put forth a plan to build an east wall from the Black Sea to the Gulf of Finland, which properly fortified would perhaps stem the onrush of the Red Army. It was to utilize natural topographical features and run from Melitopol along the Dniepr, from north of Kiev along the Desna to Czernigov, east of Gomel and Vitebsk to Lake Pskov, and from there to Narva on the Gulf of Finland. Hitler had declined the project lest the line become a license to retreat. But by mid–August the situation looked sufficiently critical for Hitler to authorize the erection of the East Wall, also known as the Panther Line. By then it was too late. In September the Russians had reached and crossed the line in several places. As by now it was clear that there would be no invasion in the west the only thing left to do was to rush reinforcements from France. Of the 36 divisions stationed there 27 were that summer transferred to Russia and replaced by burned-out units.

On September 8 Hitler was again at AGS headquarters, this time at Zaporozhe. The urgent request of his commanders to allow a retreat behind the Dniepr was dismissed. Instead of attending to current woes Hitler had past and future problems on his mind. He finally authorized the evacuation of the Taman peninsula where for more than eight months 400,000 troops had been kept bottled up for the sake of a fantasy, while at the front commanders were begging for single regiments. On this visit Hitler in particular stressed the scorched-earth policy he had recently ordered. Upon withdrawal from Russian soil it was of the highest priority to leave behind no able worker, not a building, not a live animal, no useful implement, not a well, not a yard of rail or highway—Russia must be turned into an uninhabitable wasteland.

While Hitler was at the stage of mulling over defunct projects—building of an east wall, evacuation of the Taman peninsula, laying waste to a wasted land—the Red Army, after taking Orel and Kharkov, was racing over the entire extent of the central and southern fronts for the Dniepr. The order to the Red Army was to reach and cross it on the run. In their fashion they did just that. In order not to give the Germans time to establish themselves on the high western bank, the forward echelons did not pause to wait for sappers to build even improvised bridges but resorted to any and all means to get across. Timber, gasoline drums, ripped-off doors, discarded tires, and straw bundles wrapped in ponchos were used to ferry men and weapons across the Dniepr; many simply swam across, dragging guns and horses behind. In this manner the Russians erected 40 small bridgeheads which typically in dribs and drabs they kept reinforcing until they were securely anchored on the west bank of the formidable river. The largest of these was on Rokossovski's central front, a 15-mile enclave straddling the Pripet delta from where, come winter, he would be the first to cross the old Soviet border.

Barely ahead, and often lagging the Russians, the AGS retreated along a 450-mile front dragging with it 200,000 wounded, hundreds of thousands civilian evacuees and livestock and attending with the utmost zeal to Hitler's scorched-earth order. In the center AGC lost Smolensk after which it too fell back on a non-existing wall. In the extreme south in mid–October the fourth Ukrainian front attacked Melitopol, the Black Sea anchor of the east wall, and by the end of the month the Russians had advanced across the open triangle between the lower Dniepr and the Black Sea. The Ostheer, having just extricated its men from the Taman peninsula to Kertsch, had to watch the repetition of another quarter million men bottled up in the Crimea — which Hitler again insisted on keeping there — this time for the sake of Rumania. To account for the defeats Hitler on October 27 dismissed Kluge, replacing him with Busch. On November 6 the Russians captured Kiev — the last symbol of Hitler's Ukrainian condominium.

* * *

On December 27 Hitler held his usual military conference with Zeitzler at the Wolf-schanze. With the events of 1943 in the background — Stalingrad, Kursk, the surrender of Italy, and other symptoms of the approaching end — it is instructive to listen to the concerns and guidance dispensed by the führer during this critical review of the situation in the east. Zeitzler tries to retrieve troops from lost positions, most urgently from the Crimea about to be cut off. Hitler then comes forth with his familiar views.

> H: To give up this thing [Crimea] — Zeitzler, we can talk big now and say that it is lost anyway.... Herr Manstein wouldn't bear any responsibility. We will bear it.... A major crisis will appear with the consequences that this will immediately extend over to Turkey ... they want to blackmail Turkey into joining them. The results are catastrophic. They will be catastrophic in Rumania.
>
> Z : Yes, sir. But if we can't do anything and allow it to continue the same thing will result.
>
> H: Be careful because we have already experienced cases like this where it was said it couldn't be repaired. Then afterward it suddenly turned out that it had all stopped for good.
>
> Z: It's just that it's a very deadly place for us.
>
> H: He has to run out of steam at some point. In my view the critical thing is that these troops really don't have good morale any more. If someone tells me that's impossible to have influence on the morale of the infantry — Zeitzler, I will tell you something. I am someone who has personally built up and led what is perhaps the biggest organization in the world and who still leads it today.... We must not forget, either, that last winter we were in a tragic situation, nevertheless we advanced so far by May that we almost believed that we could attack ourselves, and in July we finally did attack [Kursk].
>
> Z: It's just that the tension in the line is so very high.
>
> H: We just have to take the commanders from the dreadful divisions. If a com-

mander says that any influence on the people is useless I can only say: your influence is useless. I know that, too. During the four-year war (World War I) I got to know regimental commanders who—in the worst situations—got things in order again in the shortest time and stabilized the troops. It depends on the man [Heiber 2003, 338–40].

At the next day's military conference much of Hitler's concern was with his erstwhile headquarters in Vinnitza about to be evacuated. Hitler insisted with great vehemence, "There must be a unit in Vinnitza that burns the whole thing down and blows it up"; and, evidently instructed by the führer, Schmundt adds, "No furniture must be left in there — otherwise it will be sent to Moscow and exhibited."

One cannot read and comprehend the above high-level military discussion unless one approaches it from the completely different universe of the führer's psyche — a subject taken up in Chapter 31.

CHAPTER 29

The Fall of Italy

The successful Allied landing in French North Africa and Rommel's retreat from Libya augured the end of the Axis presence in Africa. Though the inexperienced American troops may have here and there faltered in their first engagements with the German army and though Montgomery may have continued to procrastinate to the full extent of his ability — it was certain that the Tunisian bridgehead would crumble and the Allied troops would be unemployed. The question would then arise what to do next. It was largely to thrash out this issue that Roosevelt and Churchill met in Casablanca during the third week of January 1943.

Torch had been launched on November 29 and as soon as it got underway Churchill, in a memo to his chiefs of staff, instructed them to study expeditions to Sicily, Sardinia, Italy, Greece, Turkey and the Balkans so as to "march overland to meet the Russians." Roosevelt seems to have gotten wind of this strategic master plan for even ahead of Torch he anticipated Churchill by writing to him on November 12 in pure Churchillian prose, "It is hoped [for] a forward movement directed against Sardinia, Sicily, Italy, Greece and other Balkan areas and including the possibility of obtaining Turkish support for an attack through the Black Sea against Germany's flank" (Feis, 96). All this despite the fact that ahead of his visit to Moscow as well as in his talks with Stalin Churchill had solemnly stated that a million-man invasion of France would take place early in 1943. Ahead of his coming to Casablanca Churchill had prepared a scenario which would consist of a further buildup of American forces in England while the actual fighting would take place in the Mediterranean. To substantiate the merits of this strategy, the British Chiefs of Staff brought with them a freighter loaded with statistics and study papers and on the way Churchill advised his military shadow Brooke to apply to the Americans, who were opposed to a further embroilment in the Mediterranean, a spot of Chinese torture, the "dripping of water on a stone" (Beitzell, 80–1).

Prior to the arrival of the two leaders there was a conference of the Combined Chiefs of Staff at Anfa, outside Casablanca. It met in 15 sessions and lasted 10 days, the Americans struggling manfully against the avalanche of paperwork the freighter had brought from England. The documents contained such irrefutable facts as British military experience, diplomatic acumen, and historical wisdom, all stacked against American naiveté. And it was at the very opening of these debates, on January 14, that Eden came forth with his astounding policy statement, which he sent on to Roosevelt and the State Department. This has been alluded to in a previous chapter, but it gives such insight into British intentions and overall wartime plans that it should be quoted more fully. "Our aim" the document read, "must be to knock Italy out of the war as quickly as possible and this could be achieved with almost equal effort whether Italy made a separate peace or whether dissatisfaction and disorder within the country attained such serious proportions that the Germans were forced to establish a full scale occupation. In the latter event it is to be expected that the Germans would not only have to provide troops for the occupation of Italy, but also be forced to replace the Italian troops on the Russian front, in France and in the Balkans.... It may well be in our interest that Italy should, as a member of the Axis, develop into a German commitment and become as such an increasing drain on German strength.... The view of His Majesty's Government is ... that we should not count on the possibility of a separate peace but should aim at provoking such disorder in Italy as would necessitate a German occupation. We suggest that the best means of achieving this aim is to intensify all forms of military operations against Italy, particularly bombardment, and to support the military operations by a firm line on our propaganda" (Higgins, 1968 40–1). Ensconced safely in Africa without an enemy to fight the Allies were thus to revert to the established strategy of avoiding the German army but aim at its dispersion, bombing of the cities, and internal subversion.

When the Casablanca conference convened on January 23 in the presence of Churchill and Roosevelt, Brooke presented a post–*Torch* strategic plan of "threatening attacks on the Dodecanese, Greece, Crete, Sardinia and Sicily." The original rationale for *Torch* had been that were the Allies not to open a second front in 1942 there was a need to do "something" to help Russia, hence North Africa. With this venture near completion, the vision of Torch as a temporary palliative seemed to have been shelved and converted instead into a completed major venture, per se. As to a second front, it was now decided that a cross–Channel attack would be undertaken only if either Russia or Germany were about to collapse. Still the British were not about to go back on their word; as with the 1942 promise they were going to be literally correct. Not to have lied about their commitment to a cross–Channel attack in 1943 they proposed that the Allies invade Guernsey and Jersey, two microscopic, German-held British isles in the Channel, pop. 2,000 (Beitzell, 95). Marshall, having gone to Casablanca to work out plans for an invasion of France, returned to Washington with an Allied decision to continue the war in the Mediterranean.

Although Eden's scenario was not followed verbatim, in essence it was adhered to throughout the Italian imbroglio. This manifested itself first in the planning of military operations, which will be termed here the *Ladder*, but more glaringly in the wake of Italy's capitulation. The British acted as they did because it was in line with their wishes that there be no serious fighting with the Germans even along Churchill's much-touted soft underbelly. The motivation of the Americans in having followed the Ladder tactics and in acting as they did during the Italian surrender is less clear. Their stated reason for not getting involved in the Mediterranean was because of the impending cross–Channel invasion. But they had agreed that the invasion of France was not to occur for another year. On the other hand, the rewards for exploiting a possible downfall of Italy were so tempting that it became embarrassing to just sit in Africa and do nothing. Hence the Ladder.

The Allies' acts of commission and omission during the Italian surrender will emerge later on — here the nature of the Ladder will be briefly encapsuled. The image of a ladder arises because one climbs it a step at a time, each next step predictable from the previous one. It is a blinkered journey in that the climber can venture neither to the left nor right, and it is enough to crack one or two rungs to bring the climber to a halt. To take a less metaphorical view, Italy had the worst geography and terrain for an invasion. In a report submitted to Il Duce in May 1943 Ambrosio wrote, "I do not believe in an invasion of the mainland because it would be a long affair and would not decide the final result of the war," (Mussolini, 28). The geography of the Apennines covering Italy from toe to the Po valley is rugged, its countless rivers run east-west, the weather in these mountains is vile — mud, rain, and sleet most of the year — and it had poor roads and bridges impassable to motor vehicles. It turned out to be the Allies' only battlefield where the fighting resembled trench warfare of World War I. Even had the Allies been more successful in crawling up the boot of Italy in the end they would have faced a dead end, the Alps. And just as a historical note, Rome had never been conquered from the south. All this was contrary to the elementary dictates of warfare so that it cannot be ascribed to the proverbial incompetence of the British generals. Even on the operational level it was conducted contrary to the Allies' crushing superiority in naval and air power. As it was to happen Berlin had fallen, Hitler was dead, the Americans and Russians had met at the Elbe and in Italy the Allies were still climbing mountains, in the foothills of the Alps.

With the Casablanca decision to knock Italy out of the war came the implementation of Ladder (see Fig. 29.1). Just off the Tunisian coast is a tiny island called Pantelleria, 8x4 miles in size, the first rung. On May 14 the Allies instituted a blockade of the island, followed by heavy air and naval bombardments. This lasted four weeks in the course of which 6,200 tons of explosives were dumped on the island. On June 11 the British 1st Division landed on Pantelleria, encountering no resistance. Immediately a bombardment was begun on the adjacent isle of Lampedusa, smaller than Pantelleria. After 24 hours its garrison surrendered. The next rung on the ladder was Sicily.

During the Tunisian campaign a German combat group of 15,000 troops was stationed in Sicily, the 15th Panzer Grenadier Division. In addition there were some 30,000 grounded Luftwaffe personnel. With the end in Tunisia the Hermann Göring Division started arriving. While some Luftwaffe personnel left, others took their place so that between the beginning of the Sicilian campaign and the peak of fighting there were between 30,000 and 60,000 Germans there. The 6th Italian Army in Sicily under General Guzzoni numbered 200,000 men. Though Guzzoni was the nominal commander, the Germans, led by General Hube, took their orders from von Senger and Etterlein, Kesselring's liaison to Guzzoni.

The low number of Germans on the island was a reflection of Hitler's treatment of the war in the South. A few days after the invasion of Sicily, Alfieri, Italian ambassador in Berlin, sent his government the following appreciation of Germany's attitude: "Germany is fully committed in her engagement with Soviet Russia, against whom she has offensive plans of a grand style…. Germany cannot commit herself fully in Italy against the Anglo-Americans because she must reserve her main effort against Russia…. The impression is forming that the Germans by leaving us unaided to fight in desperate conditions, are pursuing a plan aimed at provoking a collapse in Italy in order to install a new government completely subservient to them" (Deakin, 373). Fed up with the king–Duce duality and the un–Fascist performance of the Italian army, Hitler hoped that a crisis provoked by an Italian defeat would serve his cause. Paradoxically he and Eden seemed to have shared a common goal.

Facing the approximately two regular German divisions (plus Luftwaffe personnel) were 1 million Allied troops lined up on the shores of Africa; the Italians didn't count because they were not expected to fight, and didn't. Clearly the Germans, too, had large bodies of troops behind them, but they could not be shifted without jeopardizing Hitler's other conquests. Except for some skeleton crews to attend logistics, the Allies were free to move the African contingents anywhere, anytime. For the Sicilian landing the theater's commander in chief, Alexander, picked Patton's 7th Army, actually only a corps of three divisions with 66,000 troops, and the British 8th Army under Montgomery comprising 115,000 men. To conform to past and future struttings, Monty on May 2, signaled Alexander, "Consider proper answer would be to put US Corps under me," a request Alexander ignored. Before battle Monty also opined, "8th Army must get ashore; this is really the difficult thing ... the other points [the land battle] are easy" (Strawson 1988, 109). The reality of Monty's Sicilian war making would be just the opposite.

On the night of July 9 and 10 an armada of 2,500 ships, including eight battleships and two aircraft carriers, headed from west and south for the island. Overhead 134 gliders and other airborne troops—a total of 8,400 men — were on the way to seize strategic points. The landing sector assigned to Patton's three divisions was the 40-mile coast astride Gela; to his right Monty's six to seven divisions were assigned 70 miles of beach south of Syracuse (see Fig. 29.1). Monty's troops landed without opposition. The Americans encountered some resistance because the Hermann Göring Division happened to be encamped opposite Gela but they, too, got ashore in good order. In the first few days 160,000 troops had disembarked; another 350,000 soon followed so that the Allies had half a million men on the island. Throughout, there was no opposition from the Italian fleet. At the naval base at Augusta, north of Syracuse, the Italian admiral destroyed the coastal batteries and surrendered. In addition to Augusta the Allies soon had in their possession the ports of Licata and Syracuse, as well as the airfields near Gela. Italian army troops surrendered en masse.

Sicily has the shape of an oblong triangle, its apex pointing northeast where it is two to three miles from the mainland. Had the Germans been charged with taking Sicily, that is where they would have landed, so that not a single enemy soldier could escape, but not so the Allies. They were all lodged in the southeastern corner and had to cross the entire island to reach Messina. Along its base Sicily is relatively flat but it rises steeply toward the apex where Mount Etna reaches a height of 10,600 feet. The battle plan was for Montgomery to advance along the east coast with Messina as the objective; Patton on his left was to protect his flank. On July 13, in the wake of the Allied landings Hitler had sent in reinforcements which established themselves astride Mount Etna waiting for Montgomery's push. The British failed in breaking through the German defenses south of Catania, a third of the way to Messina. Cunningham, the theater's naval commander offered Montgomery ships to land in the rear of the enemy but Monty declined. Faced with a stalled campaign Patton flew to Alexander's HQ asking that he go over to the offensive. Reluctantly Alexander agreed. Patton then launched a two-pronged drive, northwest and north. Soon enough the first prong reached the west end of Sicily, taking its capital, Palermo. After cutting across the hump of the island the northward thrust reached the coast and turned sharply for Messina. On August 8 Hitler ordered the evacuation of the island. There followed the spectacular withdrawal of all German units toward Messina and across the narrow straits to the mainland; 40,000 Germans were ferried across along with 70,000 willing and unwilling Italians whom the Germans subsequently disarmed. In addition 10,000 vehicles and 19,000 tons of supplies were evacuated. There was no interference with this week-long evacuation from either Allied ships or planes. On August 16 Patton's troops entered Messina. The same day Alexander cabled Churchill, "By 10 A.M. this morning the last German soldier was flung out of Sicily."

The Sicilian campaign lasted 38 days, pitting a 10 to one Allied army against the Germans without managing to trap them. Montgomery's chief of staff, General de Guignand, wrote in his memoirs that there were three reasons for Montgomery's failure. One was the

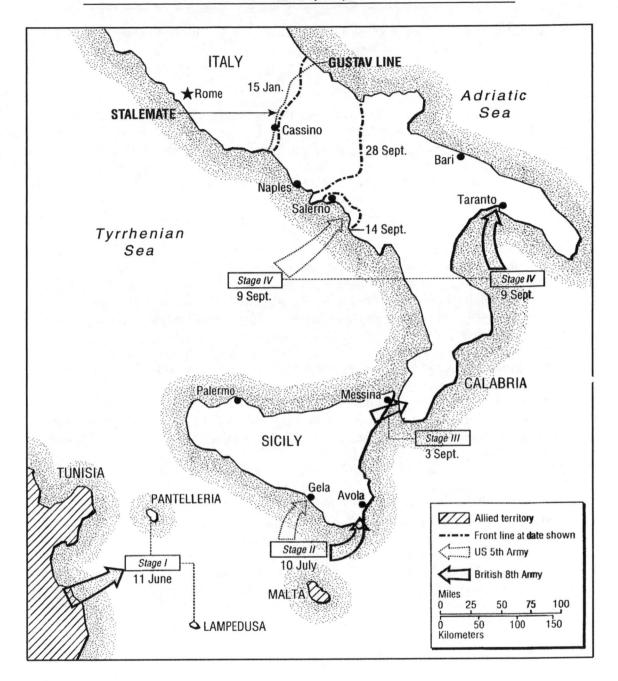

29.1. Allied moves against Italy in late 1943

strong enemy defenses; another, difficult country; and finally that the British troops were
"tired" (Guignand, 307). Still he had to add that the British military leaders were upset by
Monty's performance. As Alfieri had indicated Hitler most likely did not intend to hold
Sicily and his outright order to evacuate attests to it since he rarely issued such orders. The
fighting in Sicily was not heavy. On both sides the losses due to sickness, particularly
malaria, were higher than the battle casualties (d'Este, 607). Contrary to the Germans'

treatment of their ally, of the 137,000 Italian POWs in Allied hands 34,000 soldiers native to Sicily were released to their homes.

* * *

By mid–1943 Benito Mussolini was not the figure he had been. Never really the callous dictator he tried to dissemble he had now lost even the trappings of it. He was suffering from adhesions in the duodenum and was restricted to a diet of rice and milk. He was also in the doldrums of a mental depression. With cavernous cheeks, a scrawny neck and sunken eyes he now needed glasses to read, which he tried to hide. Consequently he rarely appeared in public. But unlike his Teutonic partner, who also needed glasses to read and tried to hide it, Il Duce made no pretense that the war he had joined was being won, nor did he spout deceptions and fairy tales of how it would yet be won. He was, in fact, in one respect more realistic than most of his realists. When they pressed and argued for an end to the war his answer was quite to the point. Because he knew Hitler better than they, which perhaps accounted for his silences whenever he met him, he told his generals and ministers that they deceived themselves if they thought Hitler would let them quit. He predicted that any such move would produce an immediate occupation of Italy by the Germans—which, in fact, happened.

Reduced to the role of a disciple at the feet of the prophet whenever he met Hitler, Il Duce was now to undergo once more and for the last time the humiliation of being summoned to a "conference" with the führer. Feeling as he did after the loss of Tunisia and the landing in Sicily, Il Duce would have jumped on the railbed rather than enter the führer's special train. But that was where he had been summoned to be on July 19. The meeting at Feltre on the Italian-German border was scheduled to last three days. As it happened it lasted only three hours.

When in February 1943 Cavallero was replaced by the new chief of the Comando Supremo, Ambrosio, he tabled a package of recommendations to Il Duce in anticipation of the events to come. These included the withdrawal of the Italian army from the Russian front, return of the troops fighting the Yugoslav partisans as that struggle was "futile" and a concentration of all resources for the defense of the homeland. Before he left for Feltre Il Duce's advisors entreated him to make clear to the führer that without ending the war in Russia and channeling large air and land forces to the Mediterranean, the situation would soon become untenable. He was urged to tell his partner that without some radical change Italy itself would become a battleground and that the Italian people were not strong enough to endure this burden. Promising to do just that, though knowing better, Il Duce departed for Feltre.

The conference ran its predictable course. At the plenary meeting Hitler launched into a two-hour monologue. He first addressed the issue of "iron, coal, molybdenum, nickel and chromium." All this was in the Donetz basin and without the Donetz basin all war production would grind to a halt, hence no peace with Russia. On the other hand, given that Germany controlled the continent from Norway to the Balkans and from Ukraine to the Spanish border, the war could be continued, he said, "indefinitely." All that is required is "willpower." He himself was "sacrificing the whole of his time and personal comfort to the task of bringing about a settlement in his own lifetime" because if not he it would never be done by the "future generations." As characterized in Chapter 1 this was a typical case of an officer who had come to discuss a military crisis receiving instead a transcendental dissertation on destiny, psychology and so on. The Germans, according to the führer, were about to inundate the battlefields with the unexpected—an avalanche of new U-boats, super-airplanes and revolutionary weapons which the führer "preferred not to enlarge upon." Just as a hint he told the Italians that come next month a tremendous new air fleet would raze London to the ground. If the Italians had any complaints it was their own fault because "every [Italian] soldier and every officer who deserted an Army or a naval battery … must be shot" (Deakin, 402–5).

The Italian delegation, swamped and silent, waited for Il Duce to speak up. But, as usual, he had been struck dumb. With the monologue over, Hitler invited Il Duce to a private lunch from which all others were excluded. During this tête-à-tête the Italians and Germans milling around the dining car overheard Hitler bang his fist on the table, rant and scream. When Mussolini stumbled out of the Pullman he was trembling. He refused to talk to anyone and headed straight for his train, which immediately left for home.

On the way Mussolini received another blow. As the Feltre conference was running its course, 500 USAAF bombers raided Rome. The city's marshalling yards, central station and Ciampino airfield were leveled, as were large sections of workers' quarters. It was a hint that were things to go on as before. Italy's precious cities would be spared no more than Germany's. Unknowingly, the raid was also a reply to Hitler's boast that next month London would be razed to its foundations. But Il Duce was not to suffer much longer. His inner if unstated wish to be done with it all was about to be fulfilled.

A few days after his return from Feltre, Il Duce was visited by Dino Grandi. President of the Fascist Council of Federations and Corporations, past ambassador to Great Britain and cabinet minister, Grandi was the great hierarch of the Fascist elite. He came to tell Il Duce that he intended to convoke the Grand Council, formally the governing body of the Fascist movement, and that at the meeting he would table a motion to have all statutory powers returned to the king. In simpler words he would ask that Il Duce be stripped of all state powers (Davis, 16). At the time Mussolini held the portfolios of prime minister, minister of air and navy, interior minister and, after the dismissal of Ciano, also minister of foreign affairs; in addition he was supreme commander of the armed forces as well as president of the Grand Council Grandi proposed to convene. During the exchange Mussolini made no objections, which could have meant one of two things; either that he did not mind or that, following this conversation, the life of Dino Grandi and perhaps of the entire Grand Council wasn't worth a shilling. As events were to show, given Il Duce's physical and mental state, he no longer cared.

At 5 P.M. on Saturday, July 24, the Grand Council convened in the Parrot Room of Palazzo Venezia next to Mussolini's office. Its 29 members sat at a trapezoidal table with Il Duce at the head. Mussolini spoke for two hours, saying that he actually never sought all the powers he had accumulated but they had been imposed on him. When Grandi spoke, telling the council that in the present conditions it was mandatory to hand back to the king the authority Mussolini had wielded for 21 years, Bufforini, a staunch Fascist, tried to stop him—whereupon Mussolini cut him off with a "Keep quiet." Near midnight a break was taken during which those who supported the motion were asked to place their signatures on a text Grandi had left on the table. The key clause in the document read, "having reviewed the domestic and international situations and the political and military conduct of the war … [the council] declares that to this end it is necessary to review forthwith all the offices of State and to assign to the Crown, the Grand Council, the Government, Parliament and the Corporations the duties and responsibilities prescribed by our national and constitutional laws; invites the Head of the Government to entreat his Majesty the King ... to assume ... not only the effective command of the Armed Forces, on land, sea and in the air, in accordance with Article 5 of the Statute of the Realm, but also that Supreme power of decision which our laws ascribe to him" (Alfieri, 303).

During that midnight break 20 members put their signatures on the motion. When the council reconvened at 2:30 A.M. Mussolini called for an open vote on the resolution. With one participant changing his mind to an abstention 19 men voted for and nine against the resolution. Mussolini, himself, then announced "Grandi's motion approved." When Il Duce stood up to leave and party secretary Scorza raised his arm to give the Fascist salute, Il Duce checked him saying, "No, let it go." He then left the room for his office (Davis, 114–24).

Not only did Il Duce acquiesce in his own overthrow, but he seemed to speed it up. By convention he saw the king every Monday but now he insisted on an appointment that very day, Sunday the 25th. The king of, course, was the main instrument behind the day's events and was prepared for the meeting. Earlier he had informed Marshal Badoglio to be ready to become the new prime minister and to be on call. After lunch the king called in General Puntoni, his military aide, and ordered that following the interview Il Duce be arrested. Mussolini arrived at the Villa Savoia, the king's summer residence, in his Alfa Romeo at 5 P.M. He was received immediately. No one was present at his meeting with the king and no record of the conversation exists. It lasted 20 minutes. When Mussolini emerged from the villa his Alfa Romeo was not at the foot of the steps where he had left it but some distance away. When he started walking toward it, a captain backed by 50 carabinieri, approached him and said, "Duce I have been ordered by the King to protect your person, please follow me."

"There is no need," replied Il Duce and tried to get into his car.

"No, not that one.... Over there," said the captain.

An ambulance backed up, its rear doors open. As Mussolini hesitated the captain took him by the elbow and helped him in. Surrounded by three plainclothes men and three carabinieri with automatic weapons he was driven away.

That same day Badoglio was called in to the king and given the task of forming a government of non–Fascists and technocrats. Badoglio then drove off in Il Duce's Alfa Romeo. That Sunday the king announced the fall of Mussolini and his takeover of the supreme command of the armed forces. Not a shot had been fired in toppling the 21-year-old Fascist regime.

The overthrow of Mussolini was part of the larger scheme of pulling Italy out of its alliance with Hitler's Germany. Attempts to get out of the war preceded by many months the events of July 25. As early as December 1942 there were peace contacts in Geneva instigated by the Royal Court. Contacts had previously been made with the Hungarians and Rumanians about forming a common bloc in approaching the Allies. Done in the shadow of Nazi terror these attempts led nowhere. But now, having taken the daring step of toppling the Fascist regime, a frightful precedent for their German partner, the Italians launched a serious effort to terminate the war.

On August 12 Ambrosio, Italy's chief of staff, instructed General Giuseppe Castellano to contact the Allies about an armistice. Castellano traveled to see Britain's ambassadors first in Madrid then in Lisbon. At that time Churchill was in Quebec attending a conference with Roosevelt. Though not publicized, one of the items on the Quebec agenda was how to respond to Italy's willingness to quit because, as early as February, the Allies had known about the impending coup in Italy (Beitzell, 118). Informed of the Castellano contact, Eden flew to Quebec bringing with him the good news. On August 18 Eisenhower was instructed to send a two-man team to Lisbon to talk to Castellano. The men chosen were Bedell Smith, Ike's chief of staff, and Kenneth Strong, head of AFHQ Intelligence section. They arrived the next day and presented Castellano with a set of 12 demands. Immediately there was a muddle. Castellano had understood his mission simply to offer a switch from the German to the Allied side — without reference to armistice, surrender, or anything else. The meeting lasted nine hours and produced no understanding.

To complicate things further a second envoy, Zanussi, was dispatched from Italy soon after Castellano left. He, too, was presented with a set of demands by the Allies, which was later to be known as the Long Term document. This was on August 27, the same day an empty-handed Castellano returned to Rome. On August 29–30 meetings took place in the presence of the king, Badoglio, Ambrosio and others at which the Italians put forth conditions of their own. One of these was not to announce the surrender until 15 Allied divisions had landed in Italy, including Rome. The core of the disarray was that formally the Allies were bound by their unconditional surrender formula though they did not intend to apply it to Italy but did not know how to wriggle out of it, particularly when Stalin was altogether suspicious of these negotiations. On the other hand, though the Italians talked of switching sides, what they really strove for was for the Allies to rescue them from the impending Teutonic fury. As will be seen later, the Allies themselves were not too eager to meet this fury head-on.

On August 30 Castellano arrived in Cassibile, Sicily, where he met the Allied negotiators plus Zanussi, of whose "long terms" Castellano had no knowledge. Badoglio's conditions were rejected and an ultimatum given that by midnight of September 1, the Italians must answer yes or no. The reason for this one-day ultimatum was that the Allies were to invade Italy within days, which of course, the Allies would not reveal. The Allied conditions for accepting Italy's surrender were that no resistance be offered to an Allied invasion and that six hours before the landing both sides announce the surrender. These were the so-called "short terms." Castellano flew back to Rome, where, after further meetings with Badoglio and the king, approval was given to the "short terms." This decision was then radioed to the Allies.

The armistice was signed at 5:15 P.M. on September 3, by Smith and Castellano in the presence of Eisenhower. Following a common dinner Smith handed the Italian general the "long terms" including a formal statement of Italy's unconditional surrender. Taken aback Castellano protested. Smith answered that Zanussi had had these terms all along and Rome must have known about them. But, as mentioned, the unconditional surrender formula was aimed at Hitler's Germany and so Smith penned an addendum to the "long terms" document which said, "The additional clauses have only a relative value insofar as Italy collaborates in the war against the Germans" (Davis, 319). For the time being things seemed to have been settled.

* * *

For the planned invasion of mainland Italy Monty was assigned the toe and heel while the Americans the southwestern side of the Italian boot. For his task Monty had his old 8th Army astride the Messina straits. Across from him, in all of Calabria, there were no German troops. Yet the British sat idle for two weeks and despite urgings from all sides wouldn't cross the two-mile straits. It wasn't until September 3, after having lined up 600 guns that dumped 400 tons of explosives on the unmanned opposite shore that they crossed onto the toe of Italy (Gelb, 243). This operation is marked on Fig. 29.1 as Stage II. Stage III, which followed a week later, the landing at Salerno, constituted the major operation of the Italian campaign.

Originally there had been a scheduled operation aimed at capturing Rome. This went back to the original Italian request that the Allies capture Rome as part of the armistice agreement. Though the Allies at the time would not commit themselves, it remained in the Italians' minds. This was only natural as all the civil, political and military organs of the state were in the city, not to speak of its million inhabitants. Following the signing of the armistice Castellano remained at Allied HQ to help plan the Rome expedition. This produced a 32-page plan to "secure the city of Rome and adjoining airfields in cooperation with Italian forces." To accomplish it the Allies had requested that the Italians secure three airfields for an airborne landing; that they neutralize both banks of the Tiber river; and, in addition to trucks and fuel, they provide a host of supplies, specifically 23,000 food rations, 5,000 wire pickets, 150 miles of barbed wire, shovels, pickaxes and others. In discussing the plan the Allies still did not reveal the date of the invasion. Remarked Italy's chief of staff, General Roatta, "If we could do all that we wouldn't have needed the Allies" (Davis, 322–34).

In preparation for the landing General Taylor of the 82nd Airborne and Colonel Gardiner from Troop Carrier Command left clandestinely for Rome on September 7. There the Italians were told that the invasion was two days away. They were dumbfounded. Somehow their information was that it would not take place until the 12th and they told the Americans their demands could not be met in such a short time. More importantly, in talking to Badoglio Taylor realized that the Italians saw the Rome operation not as a combined effort, but exclusively as an Allied shield against the Germans. With this in the background the issue of announcing the armistice flared up anew in a most critical fashion.

Badoglio now told Taylor that given the influx of German forces around Rome, Italy would like to have the armistice announcement, scheduled for the next day, postponed and asked Taylor to so inform Eisenhower. Taylor refused. Badoglio then drafted a message to Castellano to be handed to Eisenhower, that due to "the disposition and strength of the German forces in the Rome area it is no longer possible to accept an immediate armistice as this would provoke the occupation of the capital and the violent assumption of the Government by the Germans. Operation Giant II (Rome) is no longer possible because of lack of forces to guarantee the airfields." Taylor, in his own message, told Allied HQ of the Italians' inability to make the required preparations and that the planned seizure of Rome was impossible. He was awaiting instructions.

Carrying Badoglio's message, Castellano flew to Bizerte. After cooling his heels for half an hour he was ushered into a large room filled with high brass, Eisenhower himself flanked by Alexander and Cunningham. Castellano's salute was not returned. When ordered to sit down Castellano handed over Badoglio's message. Upon reading it Eisenhower said he could not accept it and brushed aside Castellano's pleas to wait and find out what lay behind his government's change of heart. Instead Ike read out to him the text of a telegram he was transmitting to Rome. Its first paragraph stated, "I intend to broadcast the existence of the armistice at the hour originally planned. If you or any part of your armed forces fail to cooperate as previously agreed I will publish to the world the full record of this affair. Today is X day and I expect you to do your part." The last paragraph warned the Italians, "Any failure now on your part to carry out the full obligations to the signed agreement will have the most serious consequences for your country. No future action of yours could then restore any confidence whatsoever in your good faith and consequently the dissolution of your government and nation would ensue." The telegram also stated that in view of the prevailing situation the Rome operation was cancelled.

That same afternoon of September 8 Badoglio, Ambrosio and several others were locked in a conference with the king over what to do next. In view of the Allies' firmness Badoglio stated that they had two choices: disavow the armistice with Badoglio resigning as if all this happened without the king's knowledge, or accept the armistice and take the consequences. At 6:30 P.M., while still deliberating, the news was brought in that the armistice was being made public. Over the Algiers radio they heard Eisenhower's voice: "The Italian Government has surrendered its armed forces unconditionally. I have granted a military armistice, the terms of which have been approved by the Governments of the U.K., the USA and USSR. The Italian Government has bound itself by these terms without reservations.... All Italians who now act to help eject the German aggressor from Italian soil will have the assistance and support of the United Nations."

With these words hanging in the air the decision taken was to go ahead with the armistice. At 7:45 P.M. Italians heard Badoglio announce over Rome radio, "The Italian Government has requested an armistice.... Beginning today, 8 September 19:45 hours, every act of hostility on our part should cease toward the Anglo-American forces. The Italian Armed Forces should, however, react with maximum decision to offensives which come from any other quarter whatsoever" (Davis, 365–80).

With the armistice wrangle settled, the Allies proceeded with the Salerno landing. This consisted of two elements. General Clark's 5th US Army encompassing 170,000 men, 20,000 vehicles, 600 tanks and 800 guns was the main force headed for the Bay of Salerno. Including US Rangers and British Commandos the first wave was made up of some five to six divisions. Montgomery, commanding the British 8th Army had been in Calabria since September 3; now, the British 1st Airborne plus additional formations were to land at Taranto, on Italy's heel. Since there were no German troops there the role of Monty's two armies on the heel and toe was to pose a threat and, if necessary, to attack the Germans attempting to throw off the Salerno beachhead. The objective of the entire operation was Naples, 30 miles to the north.

The German OB Süd, Kesselring, foresaw the Bay of Salerno as the landing place. In south and central Italy he had Vietinghoff's 10th Army, some six to seven divisions. He worked out his battle plan beforehand. North of Naples he built a string of redoubts, the Gustav Line, running from the Garigliano delta on the Tyrrhenian Sea via Cassino and along the river to the Adriatic. He withdrew his troops from Calabria and Apulia (toe and heel) and disposed them along the west coast, ready for a landing anywhere but so that they could all pounce on Salerno with the intention of driving the invaders into the sea. If this proved impossible, he intended to pivot on his right flank and take back the front to the Gustav Line. There he would bring the Allied march in Italy to a stop. This scenario he carried out to the dot.

The Bay of Salerno has a level beach surrounded by summits reaching 3,500 feet. At 3:30 A.M. on September 9 Clark's troops landed on time and in the right places to scant opposition. In the following days troops and supplies kept pouring ashore though the perimeter was not as wide as had been planned and there was a gap between the two corps, an American to the south and a British one to the north. The Germans, on their part, waited for their scattered divisions to reach the battlefield. A messenger then arrived from the führer ordering Vietinghoff not to wait; success was needed immediately "for political reasons" (Graham, 80). The plan was to attack astride the river Sele, reach the coast, then turn north and south and liquidate the beachhead.

Although due to the führer's intervention the counterattack was launched prematurely it went in with the customary German fury, led by the formidable 15th Panzer. The main blow struck the US 6th Corps in the south, which soon found itself in serious trouble. The enemy was advancing and the Americans suffered high casualties. By dark on September 13 the 5th Army saw itself in a crisis. It was grave enough for Clark to prepare his headquarters for moving out on 10 minutes' notice and he alerted a naval craft to be ready to transfer his staff to the 10th Corps sector. He also ordered the transports lumbering offshore to make preparations for reembarkation of 6th Corps troops.

Facing this crisis Alexander's command turned to Monty's 8th Army, put ashore precisely for such a contingency. But no rescue came from that quarter. On September 11, when the German attack started, the British on the eastern shore had just taken Brindisi across from Taranto and on September 13–14 when the danger of losing Salerno was at its peak they were just approaching Bari. On the toe the British were 70 miles from the southern edge of the beachhead. Despite persistent urgings from Alexander, Montgomery wouldn't rush. In fact, he actually halted his troops, arguing that he had to wait for supplies. Eventually it was the massive firepower of artillery and naval guns that saved the beachhead. The Germans had come within seven miles of the coast but the incessant bombardments from land and sea decimated their Panzers and logistics. Shattered by the high losses the Germans halted their attack on the 14th, intending to resume it two days later. They never did. On the 17th the order came down from Kesselring to begin the slated withdrawal to the Gustav Line.

The spectacle of Monty's slow crawl to Salerno was highlighted by a pathetic episode. Two journalists took off from 8th Army lines and traveled by jeep across southern Italy, reaching Clark's HQ on September 15. They had seen no Germans and no one stopped them on the way. Monty reached Salerno on September 19, four days after the journalists did when the Germans were in full retreat to the Gustav Line. When it was all over Monty recorded in his diary on September 20, "The original idea was that my Army was not to operate beyond the Cantanazaro neck. But in actual fact I had to operate some 200 miles beyond that neck, and go very quickly, too, and if I had failed to do so the whole of 5th American Army would have been pushed into the sea. As it turned out I arrived just in time to relieve the pressure, and make the Germans pull out" (Strawson 1988, 132).

Concerned about Monty's performance in Sicily and on the Italian mainland Alexander instructed the press to play down the battle at Salerno but instead praise the achievement of the British 8th Army (Graham, 97).

* * *

The events surrounding the fall of Italy constitute one of the most bizarre and revealing episodes of World War II. The Italian-held areas along the Mediterranean were the soft underbelly incarnate extolled by the British as the ideal place for defeating Germany. But when the opportunity arose to do just that the Allies walked away from it. While formally the Italians — their armed forces, arsenals, and the land they controlled — were supposed to be handed over to the Allies, the outcome was that they surrendered it all to the Germans.

Vast areas were held by Italian troops on the eve of the armistice. In France they reached to the Rhone valley and included the naval bastion of Toulon. In the Balkans they embraced the entire Dalmatian coast, Albania and, except for Thrace, all of Greece. All the islands in the Aegean were under Italian control and on Crete they occupied the eastern part of it. The Italians also had a powerful fleet with nearly a dozen capital ships. The US and British navies completely dominated the surrounding seas. The air was ruled by bomber fleets sailing from England, Africa and Sicily itself. The Mediterranean coasts Germany had to protect stretched over 10,000 miles. This was the gigantic hollow that was open to the combined Italian–Anglo-American armies and flotillas when the armistice was announced at a place and time of their choosing.

Hitler started preparing for a possible defection by his ally soon after the fall of Tunis. On May 22 the OKW laid out plans for the seizure of northern Italy under the code name *Alarich*— the Visigoth king who in 410 had sacked Rome. Another plan, code named *Konstantin*, was for the seizure of Italian areas in the Balkans. Hitler's mind, however, was not just on the military steps to be taken but just as much on blood and terror. His overall summary of the situation at the May 20 military conference regarding Italy was that "So far every difficult situation has eventually resulted in an improvement for us." Then, at the follow-up planning sessions on May 27, his mind was less on the consequences than on the "criminals" of this betrayal. A string of instructions followed, "Jodl, draw the order — without talking to anyone — to enter Rome with assault guns ... and to arrest the government, the king and the whole group.... We have to draw up a list at once. It will, of course include Ciano and Badoglio, and many others. First of all, the whole rabble — and Badoglio of course, dead or alive" (Heiber 2003, 140, 205–7). On July 1 Rommel was called to the Wolfschanze and given the job of executing Alarich. Rommel established himself at Lago Garda, commanding a special headquarters AGC while Kesselring, subordinated to Rommel, commanded the fighting troops in the south. In case of Italy's surrender Kesselring was to withdraw his forces and join up with Rommel south of the line Bologna-Firenze for the defense of the Po valley. Kesselring objected to the plan, arguing that the Allies would be too timid to land that far north and decided to stay in the south (Winterbotham, 162–4).

Definite news about Italian negotiations with the Allies was handed to Hitler when he returned on July 19 from the Feltre meeting and on July 29 intelligence intercepted a conversation between Churchill and Roosevelt about the pending armistice (Hubatsch, 54). German troops kept slithering into Italy, occupying the mountain passes in the Alps and key road junctions. During August the OKW dispatched five infantry and two Panzer divisions to northern Italy. In several instances the Italians threatened opposition but when the Germans persisted they yielded. By September there were 18–20 German divisions deployed in Italy.

Hitler had been at Zaporozhe dealing with the crisis of another Russian breakthrough and had just returned to his Wolfschanze when the news broke about the armistice. A telegram from Badoglio pleading that Italy was at the end of its tether and unable to continue the war reached the führer a few minutes after midnight of September 8; Hitler ignored it. Already four hours earlier, Jodl had issued the code word for implementing *Achse*, substituted for Alarich and Konstantin, to all three respective theaters, France, Italy and the Balkans.

In September 1943 the Italian army amounted to 83 divisions, 1.5 million men. They were distributed in roughly equal numbers between north Italy and France, central and south Italy, and the Balkans with its surrounding islands. They could count on the support of Tito's 150,000 partisans and 50,000 Greek guerrillas abutting the areas occupied by Italian troops. Behind them an Allied army 1 million strong was positioned along the African coast and Sicily, making for a 3 million man land force. And, as was noted earlier, they had complete mastery of the seas and skies in and about the contested area. There were here wider implications than the military picture. For over six months Rumania and Hungary had been looking for ways to escape Hitler's clutches. If there was hesitation on their part it was the fear that upon surrender they would be occupied by Russians rather than the West. Were the Allied armies to appear on Balkan territory they would head-over-heels have jumped into the Allied camp. Turkey, too, may have joined the Allies because her aloofness was dictated by the German presence on her border. These were the vast strategic-political vistas open to the Allies following Italy's surrender.

The first fiasco, still ahead of armistice day, occurred at Rome where, as was seen, both sides shied away from a possible fight with the enemy. In the immediate vicinity of Rome the Italians had two armored, two motorized and three to five infantry divisions. They were positioned in two concentric defense rings around the capital, outnumbering the Germans 2:1. But when it became clear that the Americans were not going through with the airborne landing, panic struck the entire top apparatus of government. The king had for some time been sending some of his possessions to Switzerland. Forty sealed railroad cars packed with objets d'art, silverware and linens crossed the Simplon Pass before the armistice date and at the beginning of September both the king and Badoglio sent their families abroad (Davis, 343–4). At 5 A.M. the day following the armistice the king and queen; Crown Prince Umberto, who was commander in chief AG South; Prime Minister Badoglio; head of Comando Supremo, Ambrosio; and the chiefs of the army, air force and navy abandoned Rome in a cavalcade of cars (Schröder, 291). Along the escape route the king's entourage stopped at Crechino Palace to have lunch, then proceeded to Ortino, a fishing community where they boarded a ship for Brindisi, already in Allied hands. As the king left Ortino some 200 generals milled about looking for a similar escape. Subsequently when the Germans arrived they wrecked the Crechino estate and shipped the duke and his wife to a KZ; Ortona was gutted to the ground and all the fishing boats — the population's livelihood — destroyed.

Following the announcement of the armistice, Badoglio had issued a Memoria 44 in which he instructed the chiefs of the armed forces to offer resistance "to any attacks from any source" without mentioning the Germans by name. This the Italian high brass ignored. Nor were they encouraged to resist by what was radioed to them by Wilson, the Allies' commander in chief Middle East. Thus for the Italian troops in the Aegean word was sent that they should head for the nearest ports — the implication being that they would be rescued by the navy, a British specialty. The result was that the general officers simply tried to save their skins by reaching, as did the king and his entourage, Allied territory. Roatta, army chief of staff, gave orders to the five divisions near Rome to assemble near Tivoli so as "not to expose the city and its people to serious and useless loss"; those divisions that were being rushed to the defense of Rome were ordered to change their route. The troops were placed in barracks where they were scooped up by Kesselring's men. The 7th Italian Army, which operated in Campania, Calabria and Apulia found itself between the Germans to the north and the oncoming Allied troops in the south. They were commanded by General Arisio with HQ in Potenza. He did not bother to instruct his men to reach the Allies but together with his chief of staff, General Pelligra, escaped to Allied territory. The objective of the Salerno landing was Naples and there the Italian XIX Corps under General

Pentimalli was supposed to hold it against the enemy, but he did no such thing. Together with the other officers he put on civilian clothes and disappeared. The abandoned troops discarded their weapons and deserted but not before they, together with the city's civilians, looted army property. In Sardinia the garrison was under the command of General Basso, who requested permission to allow the Germans to depart peacefully. The request was rejected but he complied with the German request anyway. The Germans then broke their word and seized the island which they later left only upon the OKW decision to evacuate it (Agarossi, 96–107). In all of these instances the Germans acted with their customary zeal. On the 9th of September there had been a bombing raid on Kesselring's headquarters at Frascati which leveled the complex, wrecked its communications and killed some 800 of its personnel. Yet at 9 P.M. the same day Kesselring emerged from his bunker, ordering the occupation of Rome. The escaped army chief of staff, Roatta, had left behind a General Carboni to take care of the situation. Together with General Calvi di Bergolo, the king's son-in-law, the two negotiated with Kesselring and at 3:30 P.M. on September 10 agreed to hand over the city. Posters appeared on the walls ordering the population to maintain "order, calm and obedience to the dispositions of the military authorities" (Davis, 458). There followed the spectacle of Italian divisions marching out of the city to be disarmed passing German troops marching in.

When the armistice was signed there were 24 divisions on the Italian mainland and 35 in the Balkans and the Aegean islands. In mainland Greece the 13 divisions encompassing 70,000 men were opposed by six German divisions. Athens alone contained 35,000 Italian troops facing 7,000 Germans. As soon as the Italians heard of the surrender they sold their weapons and ammunition to the resistance, and all army materiel and equipment to the locals; Athens, that morning, was described as "an endless market festival" (Mazower, 148). On Rhodes 7,000 Germans subdued 40,000 Italian after a brief engagement; Corfu fell on September 26; Crete surrendered without a fight.

In Italy and southeastern France all the Italian troops—over 50 divisions, close to a million men—were disarmed without any opposition or fighting. The only variation was that while Kesselring sent the disarmed soldiers home, Rommel had them all imprisoned, most of them to end up as slave labor in Germany. In the Balkans two separate commands were set up to deal with the situation, an AGF in Belgrade under Weichs, with AGE under Löhr responsible for Greece. There were two Italian armies in the Balkans, the 2nd in Yugoslavia and the 11th in Greece. But already on September 12 OB Südost could report that the Italians had been dealt with, including those on Rhodes and Crete. Where the Germans did have competition was from Tito's partisans who disarmed several Italian divisions and occupied a good part of their territory. Soon the Germans counterattacked and took back all the territory the guerrillas had won and much of the heavy weapons and stores Tito's men had been unable to take with them.

Greece seemed to the Germans the most problematic arena. Given the distance from the Fatherland, the presence of guerrillas and the Allies' easy access to its shores, Weichs, Dönitz and the OKW all recommended evacuating the country. But Hitler refused. The Italians there as well as on the Dodecanese islands were all taken over by small contingents of Germans. In only one instance did it come to serious fighting, and that was on the island of Celaphalonia. An attack from the air and sea by the 1st German mountain divisions was resisted for two days. When it was over, on orders from the Wolfschanze, the divisional commander, General Gandin, his deputy, 155 officers and some 4,750 soldiers were executed by the Germans. Their bodies were burned and left burning for several days as a "lesson" (Herzstein, 94; Davis, 465). There was also some opposition in Dubrovnik where General Amico and his staff were shot, as well as in Split where three generals and other officers were executed. With this the 1.5 million strong Italian army ceased to exist.

Even when it came to an episodic event it followed the general pattern of surrender. When Hitler charged Skorzeny with the rescue of Il Duce the scarfaced commando chief had no notion where Il Duce was being held or the circumstances of his detention. But no matter. Employing guile and torture he soon knew that Il Duce was being held on the 6,000 feet Gran Sasso in the Abruzzi. As described earlier Il Duce had had his day. When arrested he had asked to be taken home, promising to present no problem. From the Gran Sasso he wrote to Badoglio offering even to cooperate with the new regime. But Hitler knew better what was good for his "friend." The rescue took place a few days after the armistice, on September 12, when 108 Germans in 12 gliders descended on the rock-strewn outcroppings of the mountain. Skorzeny brought with him the Italian general Ferdinando Soleti to make sure of the guards' cooperation. These were the carabinieri, Italy's top paramilitary police units. But the general was not needed. There was no resistance from the Italians and not a shot was fired as Skorzny barged into the mountaintop hotel and fished Il Duce from his room. He then wedged him between his knees in a Fieseler Storch for the ride to freedom. There was no runway for a take-off so the plane was plunged from mountaintop into the valley leveling off just above the treetops. Haggard, sunken-eyed, unshaven, Il Duce begged to be taken home but, no, he was flown to meet his friend in the Wolfschanze. When brought before the führer, Il Duce said, "I have come for my instructions" (Davis, 474).

Although the pusillanimity of the Italian army was a result of its own proclivities, this conformed to the Allies' intentions. Had the Italians fought anywhere in France, Italy or the Balkans and called for support, the Allies would only have been embarrassed, for they had no intention of getting involved. In several instances they hinted as much to the Italians. Rome had been one case in point. In a message beamed into Yugoslavia, the British instructed the Italian troops to depart for home by land and sea; Tito's men were not to molest or to interfere with their departure; arms were to be taken from the Italians but without the use of force (Tomasevich, 360). On their own the British tried to get possession of some of the islands to bolster their traditional sea power. In Rhodes they joined a sizeable Italian garrison to keep the Germans out, but failed. They did land on three other islands in the Aegean, Kos, Leros and Samos. Since the Germans were busy elsewhere the British managed to stay there for over a month. But in November the Germans retook them with ease. The last to fall on November 16 was Leros, the Germans taking 5,000 British and an equal number of Italians prisoner (Higgins, 129).

One thing the British did not fail to attend to was to get the Italian fleet. This was an atavistic legacy of their imperial days, for by then they no longer had a naval opponent; all German capital ships had been either sunk, damaged, or immobilized. As insisted upon in the armistice terms, the Italian fleet left La Spezia on September 9. Three battleships, six cruisers and 10 destroyers headed for Malta; from Taranto more ships sailed for British anchorage. While one battleship, the *Roma*, was sunk by German bombers firing rockets, all others arrived safely, swelling an already overpowering Allied armada littering the Mediterranean waters.

While the Germans retained and even fought for the islands in the Aegean and Ionian seas they, for some reason, gave up two of the largest — Sardinia and Corsica. Sardinia's 15,000 Germans left soon after the armistice, without interference from Italian troops 10 times their size. On Corsica the Germans were attacked by partisans which eventually

Table 29-1
Dissolution of Italy's Armies in September 1943
(OKW Tagesbuch, Dec. 10 1943   DDR Vol. XX 347-8)

Area	Divs	Men	Disarmed by Germans	Comments	Disposition	Men	%
N. Italy & France	20	480,000	300,000	23,000 to Switzerland	Joined the Germans	42,000	2.8
Central & S. Italy	23	400,000	300,000	100,000 under Allies	Under the Allies	240,000	15.8
					Joined the Partisans	20,000	1.3
Rome Area	(10)		(All)	13,000 joined the Germans	To Neutral Countries	42,000	2.8
Sardinia & Corsica	9	140,000	None	Under Allies	Went Home	469,000	30.8
Balkans & Islands	31	500,000	380,000	29,000 to Partisans			
				29,000 joined the Germans	Interned by Germans	707,000	46.5
TOTAL	83	1,520,000	705,000	— —	— —	1,520,000	100

involved the Allies, the Communists, de Gaulle and his challenger, Giraud. The Germans fought them off for a while. but then decided to withdraw and were gone by October 3. The reasons for this remain obscure when one considers that the island, wedged in between Italy and France, presented potential staging areas for an invasion of either of the two countries.

The tally of the Italian army's collapse was collated by an OKW entry of December 10 and is given in Table 29-1. Some figures may be doubtful — such as the number that joined the partisans quoted by some as 50,000 or even 150,000 — but in general, as customary for the OKW, the tally seems correct. Thus about half the troops ended up in German stockades while a third dispersed for home. Eventually 430,000 Italian soldiers found themselves in German labor camps (Herztein, 104). The Germans also took over 44,000 Allied prisoners held by the Italians. The booty taken by Germans was substantial and included the following:

two battleships	1,250,000 million rifles
six cruisers	33,000 machine guns
11 destroyers	10,000 artillery pieces
60 E- and torpedo boats	920 tanks
11 U-boats	4,500 planes
61 merchantmen	15,500 motor vehicles
32 million gallons of fuel	uniforms for 1.5 million men

(Schröder, 309). Said Jodl only half facetiously, "militarily it was the greatest service that Italy rendered its ally" (Davis, 467).

* * *

A peculiar aspect of the events accompanying the fall of Italy was that when it was all over little seemed to have changed in the overall physiognomy of the war. There had been an earthquake, but when it subsided everything had settled back into place. It had the character of a recoil after which the jolted components return to their previous positions, the firing itself a dud. This was true for the Allies. Not so for the Axis powers and of the two it was Italy that suffered the most grievous consequences.

Even before the surrender Il Duce and his generals had been mere pawns shuffled about by the Germans. Now Italy became another occupied country, treated with an extra dose of contempt. Mussolini was installed as leader of a Republican regime in Salo on Lago Garda to preside over a government of German lackeys. He was a virtual prisoner sliding more deeply into depression. Humiliation was heaped on Italy from both the Germans and the Allies. On both sides Italian armed units were formed to fight "the enemy." While Il Duce continued to be at war with the Allies, Badoglio was forced to declare war on Germany on October 13. Trieste and South Tirol were annexed to the reich. Albania was given independence to become the latest German ally. Il Duce had to convene a tribunal to try his erstwhile Fascist cohorts, including his son-in-law Ciano, as traitors for their votes on Grandi's motion, Grandi himself having absconded to Portugal. Five of the participants in the Grand Council, including Ciano and the 80-year-old de Bono, were sentenced to death and executed. Still, the greatest victim was the country itself, subject now to the familiar Nazi terror, hostage-taking and executions on top of being leveled by air and artillery bombardments accompanying the Allies' climb up the ladder which turned each village and town into a battlefield.

The Allies took the Italian campaign in their stride; given the topography and their strategic blueprint it could not have been otherwise. Ike and Montgomery left for England and Alexander took command of an army made up of Americans, Britons, Canadians, New Zealanders, Poles, Frenchmen and black colonial troops—a total of 17 divisions. Naples fell on October 1. From there the Allies trudged on north and in three months covered 30 miles. By the new year they reached the Gustav Line and there the campaign stalled. They were to stay there all winter and spring fighting skirmishes tabled as the battles of Cassino. In mud and snow, with mules for transport, they fought for yards of rock and the banks of swollen rivers, up desolate mountains that became ever steeper. For the Allied strategy this was an ideal battlefield. The width of Italy was less than 100 miles with no chance that the Germans would outflank them or stage one of their fanatic Panzer drives to form cauldrons or provoke major battles. The international hodgepodge of troops involved no more than a couple of divisions from each of the Anglo-Saxon powers. Stalemated at the Gustav Line, the Allies reverted to their previous year's hectic preparations for a war yet to come.

The actions and inactions of the Allies corresponded closely to what was going on in the minds of its leaders. Although not much of this was articulated, enough seeped out to tie in with the ongoing events. Days after Mussolini's fall Churchill announced in the House of Commons that the best thing would be to let the Italians "stew in their own juice" (Davis, 227). In his usual fashion of ostensibly disagreeing with the prime minister, Roosevelt on July 26 cabled Churchill that all of Italy and the Italian-occupied Balkans should be taken over. In response Churchill, without throwing out the president's grand strategy, cabled back that why, yes, what should be aimed at is to occupy the Aegean islands, take possession of the Italian fleet and secure the release of the 74,000 British POWs in Italian hands

(Higgins, 94). On the morning of the Salerno landing Churchill had told Roosevelt that instead of pushing for the Po valley it would be best to dig in the Apennines so as to free troops for a landing in the Balkans or ... France. This, Churchill argued, would have a good effect on Rumania and Hungary. The last act in the duet between the two leaders occurred when on August 10 Roosevelt agreed he did not really wish to go beyond Rome (Davis, 262).

Astride two fronts—the never-implemented second front in France and the ongoing second front in Italy—Churchill cabled Eden who was in Moscow on October 20 to inquire of Stalin whether he would approve of the following Allied plan: enter the Balkans, seize the Bosphorus (echoes of Gallipoli) and link up with the Russian armies along the Danube, all in place of an invasion in France. As a bonus Churchill proposed to bring Turkey into the war and ... Sweden. Before showing this to Stalin, Eden approached Cordell Hull, who had accompanied him to Moscow, and asked for his support; Hull would have nothing to do with it (Beitzel, 190). The above was no fly-by-night scheme for, on November 22, at the meeting in Cairo with the president, Churchill proposed to seize Rome by January and stop; turn either left to grab southern France or right into Yugoslavia; then in February take Rhodes and open the Dardanelles (Higgins, 142). This was reminiscent of 1940 when the great Franco-English alliance bandied similar decoys hoping thereby to keep the Germans away from French soil.

For the Germans the situation soon reverted to routine. With operation Achse completed AGB was disbanded and Rommel transferred to France to bolster the Atlantic Wall. Kesselring, now OB Southwest, took command of all forces in Italy consisting of two armies, the 10th under Vietinghoff and the 14th under von Mackensen, 22–25 divisions in all. When the Allies landed in southern Italy Hitler opined, "No more invasions for them. They are much too cowardly for that. They only managed the one at Salerno because the Italians gave their blessing" (Strawson 1988, 134) The propaganda line was peddled that the fall of Italy was a blessing in disguise. Goebbels, however, felt that the Germans needed to hear the führer's voice, which had worked magic on them for over a decade now. Hitler had been shy about speaking to his Volk as he had nothing good to tell them. In the end Goebbels persuaded him and he delivered a radio talk on September 10. It was a fairly vapid speech explaining to the Germans that it wasn't Italy's military weakness nor lack of German support that led to the collapse but that it was the work of cowards and traitors. But he didn't fail to use the occasion to utter a warning against drawing parallels to his own position, saying, "The attempt of the international Plutocrat conspiracy to undermine German resistance similar to that of Italy's is childish. The hope to find in it traitors as in Italy is based on a complete ignorance of the nature of the Nazi State. Their belief to produce in Germany a 25th of July rests on the basic misconception they hold about my own personal attitude, as well as of my political fighters, my Feldmarschalls, Admirals and generals." Despite the subsequent events of July 20, it was quite a correct estimate of his people.

* * *

Like Italy other Axis satellites, too, attempted to disengage from Germany's lost cause. Most active was what had seemed all along the staunchest of the partners, Rumania. On January 10 Antonescu came for a two-day visit to the Wolfschanze for what was already a Stalingrad post mortem. He reminded the führer that last fall he had warned about the precariousness of the bulge on the Volga, to which Hitler replied that it was all the fault of the Rumanians and Italians who ran from the enemy. Unfazed Antonescu stuck to his view that the whole summer campaign was misconceived and urged the führer to make peace with the West — the most galling suggestion one could have made to him. Stepping out of the führer's HQ Antonescu confided to his entourage, "Germany has lost the wider war" (Axworthy, 119).

After this visit Mihai Antonescu contacted Mussolini and proposed that Germany's allies as a bloc approach and offer peace to the West to forestall the bolshevization of Europe. When Hitler learned about it he on April 12 summoned Antonescu to Schloss Klessheim, where he demanded Antonescu fire his foreign minister as well as his ambassadors in Spain, Portugal and Switzerland, as they were all involved in treason. Instead of showing remorse Antonescu demanded the Axis make peace with the West and once again remonstrated with the führer that the entire strategy on the eastern front had been mistaken. He knew what he was talking about. A quarter of a million Rumanian soldiers had been killed in the east. Six of his remaining eight divisions were bottled up in the Kuban bridgehead, 800 miles from home; when extricated, they were next bottled up on the Crimea. Soon, he said, Rumania would be left without an army to face its real enemy — the Hungarians.

When he returned home Antonescu openly encouraged his foreign minister to continue his search for peace. This proceeded mainly through British embassies in several neutral countries. The Allies told the Rumanians they must simultaneously offer peace to the Soviet Union. It was a bitter pill to swallow but the Rumanians were desperate enough to acquiesce. The first contacts took place in Stockholm and although they produced no immediate results they led in the fall of 1944 to Rumania's capitulation to the advancing Red Army.

A similar course was followed by Hungary, though Horthy did not have Antonescu's courage to face up to Hitler. The Hungarian prime minister, Kallay, met on April 13 with Mussolini urging common steps to withdraw from the war. Independently Kallay dispatched envoys abroad, primarily via Istanbul, to directly contact the West (Horthy, 256). On April 16, in the footsteps of Antonescu, Hitler summoned Horthy to Schloss Klessheim, raging at him for his approaches to the West, for lack of fighting spirit in his army, and for not having yet extirpated his Jews. Horthy prevaricated. In a letter to the führer of May 7 he denied the peace feelers and claimed to be Europe's foremost anti–Semite. As for lack of fighting spirit, he reminded the führer that out of the 200,000 Hungarian troops on the Don, 143,000 became casualties, 80,000 of them dead. As with Rumania it would take another year before Horthy gathered the audacity to offer surrender to the Allies.

In the fall of 1943 Finland, too, took the first steps to end the war. They approached Mme. Kollontay, the USSR's ambassador in Stockholm, offering to cease fighting if they could have back the 1939 frontiers. This the Russians rejected. The talks were broken off but resumed again culminating in a cease-fire in the fall of 1944.

The willingness of Italy, Hungary and Rumania to cease fighting all about the same time threatened to open a fatal hole in Festung Europa. Combined with a rapid switch of Allied forces it could conceivably have cracked the entire German front and brought about the junction of Allied and Russian armies across the entire extent of the Balkan peninsula and taken the war to the doorstep of Austria. This is what was alluded to previously when it was asserted that an extraordinary strategic opportunity during Italy's surrender had been squandered, in part willfully, by the Allies.

CHAPTER 30

Defeat of the U-boats

Along with Stalingrad, loss of Ukraine and Italy's defection, 1943 saw the demise of the U-boats, the most viable threat to the Allies' lifelines. Three major causes led to this collapse, two inherent to Hitler's overall conception of the war — the third due to the Allies' superior technology, including a dose of good luck.

The first fault in the whole U-boat edifice harks back to the beginning of the conflict when, as was seen, Hitler had no intention of fighting the British. Consequently, along with scrapping the Z-plan for the construction of a mighty surface fleet, he felt no need to build submarines. It was only natural that Raeder and Dönitz should have ceaselessly argued for the construction of a large U-boat fleet. Theirs was not the pleading of turf-conscious bureaucrats—it was indeed Germany's most promising weapon against England. Employed massively from the start it could conceivably have brought England to its knees. At Nüremberg Dönitz testified that Germany could realistically have had 1,000 submarines in 1939 (Miller, 24). Instead it had entered the war with a bare 57 U-boats, 39 of them operational. After the fall of France Raeder on several occasions pleaded with Hitler to forget an invasion but embark instead on a rush program of U-boat construction. Such a program was launched neither before nor after the outbreak of war. Since of the total number of available boats most were either headed for or returning from operations while others were undergoing repairs or were being used for training, the outcome was that throughout 1939 and 1940 there were only 10 U-boats engaged against the enemy.

In Dönitz's estimate he needed at least 300 operational U-boats to subdue England. In a conference with the führer on August 26, 1942, Dönitz reported that of the 304 boats built 105 were lost, leaving a total of 200 boats. Given that by that time Hitler, along with his armies, had scattered his U-boats over half a dozen combat zones— the Baltic, the Murmansk run, the Atlantic, the Mediterranean, the coasts of North America and South Africa — mighty few ships were left to fight specifically England. The above tally was at the heyday of Germany's U-boat campaign, known as the "happy times" and it was not to last. As Fig. 30.1 shows soon the losses would amount to 70 to 80 percent of construction, bringing not an end to England's lifelines but to the U-boat campaign itself.

Along with the shortage of numbers there were other weaknesses. The two main types of U-boat used were of 750 tons possessing the following characteristics:

Type of Boat	Surface/Submerged Speed (knots)	No. of Torpedoes	Range (miles)	Number Built
VII C	17/7.6	14	6,500	660
IX C	18.2/7.3	22	11,000	146

These two models made up 80 percent of the 1,053 boats built during the war. The bulk of them, Type VII C, was not particularly suited for oceangoing missions. They were slow in maneuvering around convoys and it remains a fact that of the millions of Allied soldiers transported between America, England and Africa not a single troopship was ever sunk by the U-boats. It was not until 1944 when the fight was nearly over that the Germans came up with an advanced submarine — typical of their belated introduction of other innovations such as jet aircraft or rocketry. The new 1,200-ton type XXI boats were equipped with Schnorkels and had an ideal hydrodynamic configuration so that they actually cruised two knots faster under water, 17.5 knots, than on the surface. The Germans built 120 of these but only three ever departed on operations. By the war's end they gave up building ocean-going U-boats altogether and switched to midget submarines carrying two torpedoes. The 63 that were built became a minor nuisance along the British coast during the last few months of the war.

Lack of a sizeable fleet was the main but not the only problem with the U-boat campaign. Germany had no naval air arm, similar to Britain's Coastal Command. The U-boats needed eyes to spot and trail the convoys plying the waters around England, Africa, the Murmansk lanes and the Northern Approaches. Long-range reconnaissance planes would have been of immense assistance to the near-blind boats in locating and pursuing their quarries. When later aircraft became the main U-boat killers, a fleet of long-range planes could have alerted and in extremis defended the nearly helpless boats. By 1943–44 when the decisive Atlantic battle was fought half of all U-boat sinkings were due to aircraft. Here, too, not intending to fight the West, Hitler saw no need to invest in a naval air arm. Tactical airplanes, Stukas, Heinkels, Messerschmidts, yes; to conquer Russia there was no need for a naval or strategic air force. Repeatedly Dönitz and Raeder pleaded to have Göring build or divert planes for service with the Navy and Hitler would nod his head in agreement. At the naval conference on May 13, 1942, it was recorded "the Führer recognizes the fact that the submarine war will in the end decide the outcome of the war." But it was only a left-over tune from the *Dichtung und Wahrheit* play he had enacted after the fall of France. For at the same conference one day later he told Dönitz "it was impossible to build a naval Air Force during this war." And none was built or attempted.

But typically the Germans did well for a while with whatever they had. The first successes came in the latter part of 1940 when the U-boats sank 298 ships of 1.6 million ton (MT), mainly on the approaches to England. This period the Germans knew as the "happy times." There were a number of reasons for this. Thus far the Germans had been using track-less electric torpedoes which tended to run either too deep or off-course, missing their targets. They soon reverted to contact detonators. Then after the fall of France, Dönitz moved the U-boat bases from Wilhelmshaven to the Atlantic coast. This brought them 500 miles closer to the operational sea lanes. All this happened while England kept many of her destroyers and other ships in home waters for fear of an invasion. Finally it was at that time that the Germans broke the British naval code which they went on reading till 1943 when the Allies caught on to it.

The year 1942 brought spectacular results. In the first six months of the year the U-boats sank 826 ships of 4.2 MT; for all of 1942 the Allies lost 1,664 ships of 7.8 MT, 80 percent inflicted by the U-boats (Wilt, 209). The averages for the year approached a monthly sinking rate of 0.7 MT, projected by Dönitz as required for winning the submarine war against England. And indeed by 1942 imports had fallen to one-third of prewar levels leaving England with only a two-month supply of oil.

While achieving tactical victories, just as typically there was something fundamentally wrong with the U-boat strategy, a flaw that ultimately could only bring failure. Britain had started out the war with 3,000 oceangoing vessels, a merchant fleet of 18 MT. With the fall of Norway, Denmark and Holland and the confiscation of Axis and neutral ships Great Britain acquired an additional 600 ships of 4 MT. To this must be added the ongoing ship construction throughout the British Empire and in the USA, which in 1941 amounted to 2 MT and by 1943 reached the astounding level of 14 MT per year. Thus the strategic imperative was not merely to sink ships wherever found but to sever the lifeline to England — an island that depended on most of its food and all of its oil and raw materials from overseas, not to speak of the ongoing buildup of huge armies for the invasion of the continent. Were the Germans able to cut the flow of goods (and troops) to the British Isles it wouldn't have mattered much how many other ships the Allies had sailing worldwide. Instead, the Germans resorted to what will be here called chessboard tactics. Whenever operations in one sector grew too hazardous they moved to a different square of the chessboard where success was more promising. True, were the Germans to have persisted in attacking primarily the Western and Northern Approaches to England the defenses there would have risen accordingly. But the point is that success elsewhere could not bring victory; the only place where victory was at all conceivable lay on the sea lanes to England. But like the penchant for flinging his armies in all possible directions here, too, Hitler scattered his meager U-boat force across all the seas and oceans, drunk on the tonnage game.

The first diversion was Norway. During April 1940 no fewer than 42 boats were directed to Norwegian waters, sinking a pitiful eight ships for a total of 0.03MT, losing four boats in the process. Nor did the end of the Norwegian campaign bring an end to this drain. Hitler was obsessed with a possible invasion there — perhaps because of Swedish iron ore, or because he feared a northern link-up between the Allies and the Russians. In typical fashion he told Dönitz on December 1941 that such an event would be "decisive for the war" and on February 15 insisted that 20 U-boats be dispatched there (Blair 1996, 157, 443). This was to persist to the end of the war when, ironically, with the bases in France lost and those in Germany under a hail of bombs, all U-boats were moved to Norwegian ports.

In midsummer of 1941 the Germans had 25 boats in the North Atlantic — a maximum to date — when the war with Russia was launched. Hitler then ordered a breakup of this force, sending 10 of them into the Baltic and another six off Murmansk against a Russian navy which was no more a match for the Germans than was their air force (Miller, 184). Simultaneously he began to draw off forces to the Mediterranean to rescue Mussolini. By the end of the year nearly all VII C boats — the bulk of the fleet — were committed to assisting Rommel. Of the 37 boats dispatched in December 1941, three were sunk in attempting to get past Gibraltar, six were damaged, but the rest did get through. Their attacks were mostly on warships, a strategic mistake of both place and target. Of the 22 that did get into the Mediterranean 13 were lost within the first six weeks. Since the remaining XII C boats were all sent to American waters there was a total absence of U-boats in the North Atlantic during 1941–42 (Blair 1996, 403). What emerges from all this is that Hitler hitched his U-boats to the land campaigns in Russia and North Africa to the despair of both Raeder and Dönitz who, like the army generals, never mustered the courage to stand their ground. Thus instead of using the U-boats as the strategic arm they were meant to be, Hitler, in parallel with his air force, converted then to a tactical weapon to support his land battles. All this got worse with time. The minutes of the naval conference of November 21, 1942, recorded the following decisions: "The number of submarines in the Arctic Ocean is not to be permitted to fall below 23.... The number [in the Mediterranean] is to be brought up to 24 again.... [The führer] desires that measures be taken against enemy shipping to Egypt and the Middle East, via South Africa.... Furthermore it must be possible to reinforce the submarines in Norway immediately in case of an invasion there.... The führer also wants to build transport submarines. The reason he gives is that since the Americans took over Iceland, he has again taken up the idea of a sudden invasion and establishment of an air base there" (FNC, 300–1).

The biggest diversion was launched, almost with relish, after war was declared on the USA. With all restraints dropped, nearly all available U-boats were rushed to the Western Hemisphere. There they inflicted considerable damage. Their favored pickings were tankers hauling oil from the south to North American ports. In the first half of 1942, 143 tankers were sunk (Blair 1996, 696). The USA had no convoy system, the view being that convoys merely offered a concentration of victims. Confident of their geographical sanctuary they did not bother about blackouts and the U-boats had a great time picking out ships silhouetted against the lights of coastal cities. Thus the great successes of 1942 were in a way deceptive, for they were due mostly to the rampage in the peaceful waters of the American coast. Of the 4.2 MT sunk in the first six months of 1942, 75 percent, were off America; for all of 1942 when 8.2 MT were lost, 5.3 MT or 67 percent occurred there.

Once goaded, the Americans produced a massive response. By July 1942 escorts were established all along the coastline. Typical was the response to the tanker problem. Rail traffic and barges took over much of oil haulage; in addition a huge pipeline, two feet in diameter, 1,380 miles long, was built from Louisiana to the northern ports which by midyear carried 160,000 barrels of oil a day. While in January 1942, 85 percent of all oil was transported by ship, by the end of the year only 10 percent was by tankers and 90 percent overland (Blair 1996, 696). By that time the Americans even had enough tankers to afford handing over 124 of them to the English. In the latter part of the year the U-boats found it unrewarding to operate off the US coast. They shifted, first to the New Indies, and from there to the Gulf of Mexico. Eventually these waters, too, became perilous and the U-boats swung back north to the Greenland Gap. This was a 600-mile-wide area in the North Atlantic beyond the reach of Allied aircraft. As will be seen later, that hole was soon plugged. By then the U-boats had floundered all over the oceanic chessboard and Dönitz was at his wits' end.

While the shortage of boats and the flawed chessboard strategy were of the Germans' own doing, the third factor in their defeat was due to the Allies' cryptological and engineering achievements. The two aspects of defeating what FDR called the "snakes of the ocean," were detection then destruction, two tasks almost independent of each other. Given the vastness of the Atlantic, the tiny size of the attackers and their capacity for three-dimensional maneuver, detection was a most difficult task. But it was here that the Allies excelled. The greatest scoop was, of course, Ultra. The German naval Enigma was more complex than that of the other services. But the British also gave it more attention. Naval intelligence was located in the Admiralty next to the U-boat Tracking Room, which helped to coordinate the two activities. The first inroad made into the German naval code was in February 1940 when parts of the three-rotor Enigma were taken from U-boat 33. The more important haul, however, occurred on May 9, 1941 when Kapitan Lemp, commanding the *U-110* abandoned his damaged boat without having it properly scuttled. An Enigma machine together with its code books was retrieved from the boat and a disinformation campaign launched via the U-boat's prisoners that the boat sank before it was boarded (Blair 1996,

281). To safeguard their success the British for a while refrained from attacking the U-boats themselves, whose location they now knew, but simply rerouted the convoys. This lasted until January 1942, when the Germans added another rotor to their encoding machine increasing the number of permutations enormously. Throughout the remainder of the year Bletchley could not read the new ciphers and this was indeed the year of the Germans' greatest successes. The new Enigma code was eventually broken in December 1942. Bletchley now read the German naval ciphers to the end of the war.

A number of electronic devices assisted the Allies in tracking the enemy's boats. One was radar. The Germans had it too, but they were behind the Allies in its technology and application. Already in 1941 radar sets were installed on the masts of ships which could detect a surfaced boat. This ended the U-boats' immunity during night attacks. Another, more effective means, were the HF/DF sets. These homed in on the boats' radio signals as they communicated with each other or with shore headquarters. A destroyer equipped with an HF/DF set could by triangulation home in on the jabbering boats, which they did a lot. The combination of Enigma and the new homing devices was so effective that in a report on June 5, 1943 (FNC, 334), Dönitz told the führer that 65 percent of boats sunk were lost not during an attack but while still en route or lying in wait, be it good weather or foul. He suspected that it was due either to a new radar or treason. It never occurred to him that his ciphers were being read.

When it came to actually destroying the spotted enemy, it was primarily aircraft that did it, though there were some advances in the tactics and weaponry of surface ships. Whereas originally convoying extended only partway into the Atlantic, by June 1941 in a cooperative effort with the Canadians these were extended all across the ocean. When the USA came into the war, the Atlantic was subdivided, north of 40 degree latitude under British-Canadian guard which embraced all east-west convoys; while south of 40 degree, the routes to the Mediterranean and Africa, were under US surveillance. By then the convoys were accompanied by strong escorts of destroyers, trawlers and other craft. They were equipped with new hedgehog mortars which could fire a number of charges from a distance, whereas the conventional depth charges required the attacker to be on top of the U-boat. The Americans also instituted hunter-killer groups whose mission was not to wait for an attack but to range over the open seas in search of the "snakes." Their only restriction was not to venture so far as to be unable to rejoin the convoy in case of an attack by the wolf packs.

In the early days the British resorted to almost desperate means to deal with the German spotter planes trailing the convoys. They installed catapults with a single Hurricane on deck which after being launched on its mission could come back only by ditching, the plane lost and the pilot fished out of the water. In September the British started using merchant ships able to carry six planes. But it wasn't really until early 1943 that specially built escort carriers each with 20 planes aboard began accompanying the convoys. They operated in two groups, one close to the cargo ships, the other ranging out in search of U-boats before they reached attack positions. When eventually an air base was established on Newfoundland the entire Atlantic from Greenland to the Azores was under an Allied air umbrella.

But the main new weapons were the long-range reconnaissance and bomber aircraft. The U-boats now found themselves in a perilous situation. With the help of radar and HF/DF the planes detected their quarry long before the boats had any inkling they had been spotted. By the time they heard or saw an attacking aircraft it was too late to escape the bombs and gunfire. The U-boats set up lookouts on the deck; they armed themselves with 20 mm AA guns; they floated buoys and balloons to act as Window; by night they ran on a single diesel to at least hear the oncoming plane but they were all poor palliatives and the planes continued to take a heavy toll on Dönitz's fleet. Even if not sunk the mere presence of an airplane overhead made the U-boat ineffective by forcing it to dive.

By the spring of 1943 all of the above elements converged and weighed in on the U-boats. Failures and blows mounted with each passing month. The defeats began in April when in sinking 0.33 MT of shipping Dönitz lost 15 boats. At the same time the US hunter-killer groups destroyed all the milch-cows in the Atlantic that were resupplying the boats with fuel and torpedoes so they could remain longer at sea. The exchange rate worsened in May, when for 0.27 MT sunk the Germans lost a staggering 40 boats. Among these was the *U-954* with Dönitz's son aboard (May 14); when informed, Dönitz showed no emotion, nor was he to show any when next year he lost his second son. On May 26 Dönitz suspended "temporarily" all operations in the North Atlantic (Syrett, 146). In order to disguise this from the Allies Dönitz directed 13 VIIs to remain at sea to broadcast dummy radio messages simulating ongoing operations. The Allies learned of it from Enigma and sank three of the decoy boats. The mood in the U-boat bases darkened, morale sank. This soon showed in a sharp decline in the crews' combat aggressiveness.

Dönitz then directed his boats off Gibraltar to intercept the convoys between the Mediterranean and England. But this too proved hazardous. The area was heavily patrolled by Allied aircraft so that it took a boat 10 days merely to cross the Bay of Biscay, if it crossed at all. Desperate, Dönitz pleaded with the führer at his June 5 conference to occupy Gibraltar; but the führer dismissed it (NFC, 335). Dönitz then disbanded the wolf packs and scattered his boats to West Africa, Brazil and the Indian Ocean. Throughout the three-month period of June–August, 1943 the boats sank only one ship for a loss of 15 of their own. At the naval conference of July 8 Dönitz told the führer, "We are at present facing the greatest crisis in submarine warfare since the enemy, by means of new location devices, for the first time makes fighting impossible." Yes, the führer commented, "something must be done about it" (FNC, 329).

In September the U-boat arm was given two advanced weapons, acoustic torpedoes as well as better AA guns and were returned to the North Atlantic. Not only did they not achieve any successes but were unable even to get close to the convoys. They were then shifted back to the north-south run. There they came upon a convoy of 60 ships with 10 escorts headed from Capetown to England. When no results came in, Dönitz sent out on October 31 a desperate plea: "Something must be sunk out of the convoy tonight." The cry produced the sinking of one ship for the loss of two boats (Syrett, 230–3). In mid–November a second convoy, escorted by 20 warships, passed these waters and although there were now 35 U-boats on station not one ship was sunk. From mid–November 1943 one can consider the U-boat war as having been lost. Whatever the U-boats still undertook was in the nature of a harassing or guerrilla activity. As was the case with the other branches of the Wehrmacht — better tanks, automatic infantry weapons, jet aircraft, the V's— toward the end of the war better submarines, running on hydrogen peroxide and using snorkels, made their appearance but by then it was too late for them to make an impact on the course of submarine warfare.

The overall history of the U-boat campaign can be gleaned from Fig. 30.1. In 1943 for each Allied ship sunk three new ones appeared on the sea lanes while sinkings of U-boats reached 90 percent of construction. They were driven from the North Atlantic and remained

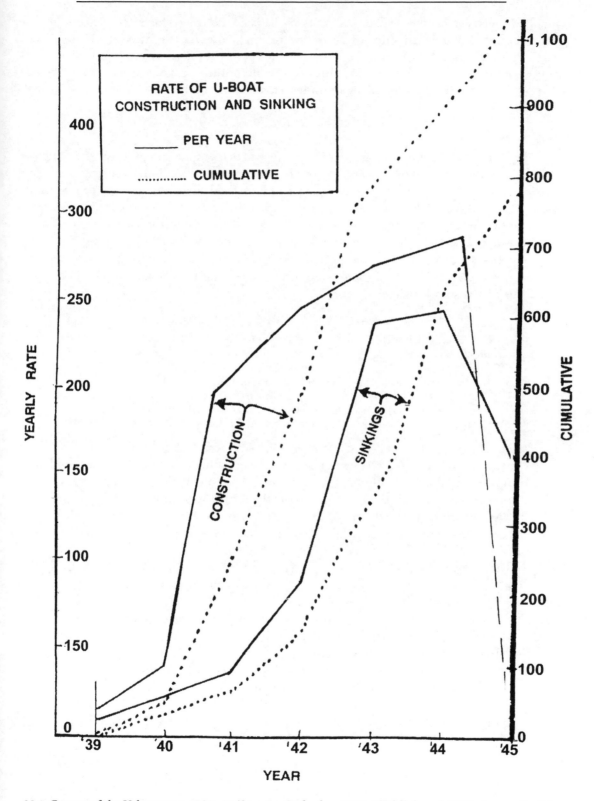

30.1. Course of the U-boat war, 1939–45 (Source: *Oxford*, p. 1060; Middlebrook 1976, Appendix 6.)

ineffective elsewhere. By war's end 782 U-boats had been destroyed for a loss of 30,000 crew. Even though 5,300 Allied ships of 23 MT were sunk, 70 percent of it by the U-boats, at war's end the Allies' net gain was 20 MT. This fares poorly vis-à-vis World War I when only 200 U- boats were lost causing the Allies at the end of the war a net deficit of 6.4 MT of shipping. So much for Hitler's vow to do better than the kaiser.

* * *

The end of the U-boats as an effective naval arm marked the end of the German high-seas fleet as a whole. When the war started Germany had, or was about to complete, seven battleships and heavy cruisers. The Z-plan had visualized the tripling of the fleet within the next five–10 years. This had been scrapped when Hitler prematurely started the war in 1939. So the German navy went to war with England with whatever it had. By the time the U-boats met their doom the rest of the German fleet, too, had given up its ghost.

The first to go were the destroyers, of which Germany had 22. During the Norwegian campaign in April 1940 half of them were sunk just off Narvik. The fate the German capital ships met is shown below:

The Loss of German Capital Ships

1. *Graf Spee* (battleship)	sunk at Montevideo	December 17, 1939
2. *Blücher* (cruiser)	sunk at Oslofjord	April 8, 1940
3. *Karlsruhe* (cruiser)	sunk at Kristiansund	April 9, 1940
4. *Bismarck* (battleship)	sunk in the Atlantic	May 26, 1941
5. *Gneisenau* (battleship)	crippled at Kiel	February 26, 1942
6. *Tirpitz* (battleship)	crippled in Norway	September 1943
7. *Scharnhorst* (battleship)	sunk in the Arctic Sea	December 26, 1943

Thus all of the original capital ships were eliminated by the end of 1943.

On the last day of 1942 a German task force consisting of two capital ships and six destroyers ventured out to intercept a Murmansk-bound convoy. Far from sinking any ships, in its encounter with the convoy's escort the *Hipper* was damaged. In a rage, Hitler told Raeder on January 6 that unlike the army, which was continuously in combat, the German high fleet shrank from battle. The führer said that he was "strongly opposed to any further engagements of the surface ships since, beginning with the *Graf Spee*, one defeat followed another. Large ships are a thing of the past." He then issued an order that the capital ships be scrapped, their heavy guns converted to coastal batteries and the released manpower and materials utilized elsewhere.

On January 15 Raeder met the führer to present a memorandum on how to decommission the large ships and dispose of their naval and AA guns. At the same time he voiced his view that a grave error was being committed. In response, Hitler dismissed Raeder as commander in chief of the German navy and appointed Dönitz in his place.

While Dönitz later managed to mollify the führer's ukase somewhat, essentially the big ships went into mothballs. Thus in 1943 Hitler himself eliminated the German navy from playing any further role in the war.

• Chapter 31 •

Satan as Prophet

Seriously warped for some time, in 1943 Nazi Germany had begun to tilt toward its inevitable crash. It was the year when all previous forecasts had become flesh providing friend and foe with the spectacle of its approaching collapse.

As mentioned previously, there had been stages when the ultimate defeat should have become discernible to the Germans and their führer. The fact that in 1939 the war could not be confined to Poland and resulted in the intervention of the Western Allies should have been enough to call off the venture. But then there was Hitler's certainty that he would defeat the French armies and by depriving England of its continental vassals compel it to quit the war. When the collapse of France did not lead to peace there remained the führer's central design of demolishing the Soviet Union with the two-pronged hope of England acquiescing in the elimination of Bolshevism and of yielding Germany massive economic and geopolitical clout to outlast the British. But the Soviet Union was not defeated and England chose not to acquiesce in its destruction if the winner was to be Hitler. These events were followed by the most dreaded fact of the USA entering the conflict. Hence the assertion made in Chapter 18 that in December 1941 Hitler had irrevocably lost the war.

All the implications of that conclusion materialized in Annus Irae 1943 — on land, in the air, and the seas. In January came Stalingrad; in May the collapse of the Axis in North Africa; the debacle at Kursk in July; the capitulation of Italy in September; the collapse of the U-boat campaign by the end of 1943; and all through the year the massive destruction of German cities by British and American air armadas — pillars of fire illuminating Hitler's edifice toppling.

By September 1943 the war had been going on for four years. Germany was to prosecute it for roughly another two years at a cost in lives and devastation exceeding what it had suffered to date (see below). And the question arises: What was it that made Hitler carry on the doomed adventure? He was not the kind of leader to let history carry him passively along; he was not one to count on rescue by others, or the intervention of God. At all stages in his life he had clung to a plan. Never disclosing them to either friend or foe he always worked to fixed, single-minded schemes — and large ones at that. What was on the führer's mind when faced with Germany's situation in the fall of 1943? What stratagems, hopes, illusions or delusions did he harbor while assaulted by massive armies in the east, west and south, the roof of Fortress Europe blown off by fleets of bombers, and his allies committing treason? What did the führer think and plan regarding a war already lost but unwilling to end it because on September 1, 1939, he, the Austrian from Brunau, had said he would never capitulate?

Two scenarios can be construed from the little that is available on the führer's state of mind — and his state of mind was all that had mattered in the past and all that mattered now. Such an insight would clearly have to take note of whatever the führer and his cohorts let drop on the subject. However, given his iron determination never to reveal his true intentions, one must rely even more on his known proclivities and goals, as well as on the events that followed 1943. Given, as has been repeatedly shown, that throughout his career and the war he had unswervingly pursued his once-and-for-all chosen path, his subsequent acts should reveal his 1943 intentions better than official statements issued at the time for propaganda and deception purposes.

One scenario is that of clinging to some semirational prospects, illusory as they might seem to a detached observer. These hopes consisted of several unrelated possibilities, each promising to bring about a radical change in the political and military situation. One was miracle weapons. Ignorant of the atomic bomb being readied in America, what the Germans were developing seemed to them revolutionary. One was rocketry, the subsonic V1, followed by the supersonic V2. The first could somehow be countered with conventional means but against the second there was no defense. While not a military weapon in the sense that these unguided missiles could not be aimed at a specific target — an airfield or industrial facility — they were potent terror bombs threatening urban sprawls like London or Antwerp. The other new weapon was jet aircraft. Its operational novelty was high speed, nearly twice that of existing fighter planes and could have given the Luftwaffe a considerable edge over the Allied air forces. In the press and official addresses the miracle weapons were given great emphasis with a palpable effect on the morale of the country. Intelligence reports by the SD confirmed that in the last two years of the war the expectation of miracle weapons was the ordinary German's main hope for reversing the course of events.

Hitler also placed great emphasis on a possible rift between East and West, even anticipating the Western Allies joining Germany in destroying Bolshevism. As usual Hitler picked some incident from history to validate his forecast. The example was the Seven Years War when Frederick the Great, facing a coalition of nearly all European powers, was about to be overwhelmed. In 1762 the Tsarina died and Russia pulled out of the coalition, saving Prussia from defeat. Said the führer, "World history shows that coalitions eventually collapse. One has only to await the proper moment, no matter how difficult the situation.... Under all circumstances we will continue this struggle until — as Frederick the Great said — one of our accursed enemies grows weary of fighting on" (Schramm 1971, 169–70). Accordingly, wherever he moved the führer had a portrait of the Prussian king staring down at him. This vision of a breakup of the East-West alliance was carried beyond the war's end when, after approving the establishment of the Werewolf in an Alpine redoubt, Hitler predicted that the moment Werewolf partisans attacked the Soviet troops, the West would join Germany in the fight against the Russians (Cookridge, 96).

From these delusions there was only a short step into mysticism with Hitler resorting to astrology and horoscopes to extract from the stars promises of victory he could no longer extract from his generals. This stargazing should not strike one as strange for a leader who all along believed that Will and Geist will conquer all. Another leap and Hitler seemed to embrace religion. In most proclamations and addresses the führer now invoked Providence. As with the wonder weapons the turn to Providence found a ready response in the nation. In the utterances of ordinary Germans, in sermons from the pulpits and the exhortations of Nazi officials there nestled a faith, a conviction, that somehow a mighty Christian nation like Germany could not possibly fall prey to the godless hordes from the East. All this constitutes a fairly conventional fallback on illusions, a familiar response of terminally ill or doomed individuals clutching at visions of some wonder medicine, at inflamed religious faith, or some other superrational force that would remedy what reality cannot. In relying on the above visions for ultimate salvation Hitler would have been in tune with ordinary Germans.

All of the above may have been the things that he peddled to his people but was this what Hitler himself knew and believed in the privacy of his skull? Was his decision to continue the war really driven by a belief in a turnabout to be effected by the V's, astrology or religion? It is quite noteworthy that many histories of World War II end either with the German stalemate at Moscow in December 1941 or with the Stalingrad fiasco a year later. To this day one stumbles when trying to go beyond these two terminal events which cover only 40 percent and 60 percent of the duration of the war. And understandably so. It is of the greatest difficulty to continue in any coherent or plausible way with the events that followed these two critical periods. There has to be some other illogical logic to the history of Germany's counsels, battles and convulsions that seethed for the last half or two-thirds of the war. As all along we must here, too, turn to the individual who had been the centerpiece of German history for the past 10 years to unearth the motivations and spasms that dictated the course of the latter half of World War II.

As in the summer of 1940, we are here again in the realm of *Dichtung und Wahrheit* where the scenario of new weapons, historical precedence and divine intervention represent the façade whereas the reality was something else entirely. This reality had two aspects. One, was it accepted by Hitler that the war was lost? And if so, what motivated him to continue it for another three years? By all accounts December 1941 seems to have been the watershed in Hitler's prognosis for the outcome of the conflict. This emerges from his own utterances; from the testimony of his underlings; and very tellingly from the führer's moods, comportment and physical health. Following his failure to defeat the Soviet Union the atmosphere was so bleak that the führer even claimed to have lost the war before it had started. In notes dictated to Borman in February 1945 he said that 1939 was too late to have started the war. "We should have gone to war in 1938. That was our last chance to keep it localized. But they [Chamberlain, et al.] gave in everywhere. Like cowards they yielded to all our demands. So it was difficult [in '38] to initiate hostilities" (Fest 1977, 97).

Most written and oral evidence of Hitler having despaired of victory harks back to the winter of 1941-42 when his failure before Moscow, followed by a Soviet counteroffensive, had triggered a deep crisis in the Ostheer. Hitler's conclusions from the failure of Barbarossa were that the defeat of Russia was no longer possible. This he enunciated in a talk with, of all people, two foreign ministers— Scavenius, of Denmark and Lorkovic of Croatia — as early as November 27. It was on this occasion that he uttered the fateful words, "When the German people is no longer sufficiently strong and ready for sacrifices as to give its blood for its existence, then let it disappear and be destroyed [*vernichtet*] by another stronger power. It then no longer deserves the place it has acquired for itself" (Haffner, 120; Reinhardt, 180; Hillgruber 1967, 22). This was buttressed by a statement to Oshima the following January that "How one is to defeat the USA he does not yet know." These three interlocutors were foreigners. To Halder, however, as part of his deception, he said that it may come to peace negotiations. In peddling his *Dichtung* he even resorted to transparent nonsense, as on November 8 in a speech to his Altkämpfer in Munich, he said that the reason the war was taking so long was that, because of Russia's size, it was taking the foot soldier a long time to cross it!

The most authoritative report that Hitler knew he had lost the war as early as December 1941, and certainly in 1943, comes from his closest military advisor who stood by him to the last and even remained loyal beyond his master's death. This is Alfred Jodl, chief of staff of the OKW throughout the war. There are three statements, two referring to the winter of 1941-42; and another for the period of 1942–43. The OKW diary contains the following note: "In particular, once the catastrophe of winter 1941/1942 intervened it was clear to the Führer and Colonel General Jodl that from this climax at the New Year 1942 on, victory was no longer to be had" (OKW, 1503). During a May 15, 1945, situation conference of the Dönitz government Jodl reported "that it was clear to Hitler and himself ... when the catastrophe of the winter of 1941/1942 occurred that after that point of culmination at the beginning of the year 1942, victory could no longer be achieved." As a prisoner in Nuremberg, Jodl wrote in a deposition that "earlier than anyone in the world Hitler realized and knew the war was lost" and that after Stalingrad "when toward the end of 1942 Rommel, defeated before the gates of Egypt, fell back on Tripoli as the Allies landed in North Africa, it was clear not only to the responsible soldiers but to Hitler himself that the god of war had now turned from Germany and gone over to the other camp" (Schramm 1971, 161).

Sometime in 1943 Hitler abandoned the reichs chancellor part in his signature, retaining only the title of führer (Steinert, 187). He also turned away from addressing directly his Volk and no amount of persuasion from his acolytes made him change his mind. His agenda no longer needed the enthusiasm of his people — all he now needed was time to implement the last act of his 12-year-long rule. His decrees were now accompanied by threats. On November 27, 1943, he issued a proclamation: "The struggle for the existence of the German people and for the future of Europe is nearing its climax," and promised to restore the fighting strength of the army "with the most ruthless methods and ... draconian penalties." After the decrees to "strengthen the front" were issued — such as the transfer of 1 million heretofore deferred men to the army, engagement of female labor and others — Hitler issued the following admonition: "If after January 1944 I am informed of cases where for reasons of indifference, egotism, and disobedience, orders are not executed I will treat the responsible superior as a war criminal" (Steinert, 228).

A profound change in the führer's stance and mood took place during the winter of 1941-42. He was not seen or heard from, confining himself to a crab-like existence at Rastenburg. The denial of reality was almost symbolized by his keeping the window curtains permanently drawn, even on sunny days. On a visit in March 1942 Goebbels recorded that "the whole atmosphere at GHQ is truly depressing.... The Führer this time truly worries me. I have never seen him so serious and grave as today. Will this winter never end?.... [He] has gone through exceedingly difficult days, and his whole bearing shows it." A year later, in March 1943, the story continues: "The Führer has become such a recluse.... He does not relax. He sits in his bunker fusses and broods.... One can understand his present mood of sometimes being fed up with life and occasionally even saying that death holds no terrors for him.... A little dog that was presented to him now plays about his room. His whole heart belongs to that dog" (Goebbels, 1948, 137–8, 266). During the following year Goebbels paid several more visits to Rastenburg at which the führer unburdened himself of his worries as to the outcome of the war. One of the visits took place when the Tunisian bridgehead was about to fall and the führer explained that it is all "a matter of movement. We lost Stalingrad because of the impossibility of mastering this problem of movement. We are now passing through a serious military crisis in North Africa because of mastering this problem of movement. Whoever has the organizational power to solve the problem of movement will be victor" (Goebbels, 1948, 359). Clearly, there was no doubt in the mind of either of the two who indeed had the greater means and freedom of "movement." Talking to Goebbels after the Kursk fiasco Hitler confessed that Zitadelle had been a minor thing. The real grand design in Russia had been the original 1941 plan; this was now a lost dream (Cross 1993, 143).

Absorbing these laments Goebbels attempted to help by hinting that perhaps the time had come to make some radical move. "No matter what the situation may be now," said Goebbels, "we have to come to terms with one side or the other. Never has the Reich won a two-front war." Employing a bit of *Dichtung* the führer said that there was no hope of approaching Churchill or Roosevelt because they are "consumed with hatred; he may, however, be willing to negotiate with Stalin." Goebbels then prepared a 40-page memorandum for peace negotiations with Russia, which the führer dismissed by saying that Stalin would never cede his, Hitler's, demands in the East (Goebbels 1948, 477). Hitler also confided his loss of faith to two foreigners he considered closest to him. To Antonescu he said on April 22, 1943, "as far as the outcome of the war.... either we win or there will be total extermination" (Hubatsch, 12n); and in a conversation with Oshima in mid–July 1943 Hitler told the Japanese ambassador that "the Soviets cannot be militarily exhausted this year" (Fleischhauer, 215). On July 25, 1944, he specifically told Feldmarschall Kluge that he was no longer a master of his own decisions— no longer could he dictate the course of events (Cross 1993, 241).

After Stalingrad Hitler withdrew into complete solitude and for several months ate alone with his Alsatian dog. When this became wearying he resumed eating in company but not with his military entourage. The company consisted of his female secretaries, his adjutant, Dr. Morell and, after 1944, his cook. One of the secretaries related that after Stalingrad "Hitler could no longer bear listening to music and every evening we had to listen to his monologues which were always the same — Vienna, the *Kampfzeit,* cosmic philosophy; war and politics were forbidden subjects" (Hitler 1953, XIII). There came a point in late September 1944 when he simply refused to get up. His adjutant reported to the staff that "The Führer is completely apathetic about events around him. He is not even interested in the eastern front although we have a real crisis on our hands" (Morell, 88).

As a result of the stress and depression that engulfed him his health and physique deteriorated. Most of this information comes from a diary his personal physician, Dr. Morell, kept during the war. In January 1940 a medical examination and appropriate tests showed little out of the normal. According to Dr. Hesselbach, one of Hitler's physicians, prior to 1940 Hitler appeared to be younger than he actually was; from 1940 to 1943 he looked his age; after that he gave the appearance of having grown old. In December 1941, Morell recorded a medical episode during which Hitler's systolic blood pressure shot up to 200 mm (versus 120 mm normal). When Goebbels saw him at that time he noticed that Hitler's hair had turned gray. In August 1941 in response to complaints about dizzy spells Morell called in a cardiologist who, after tests, diagnosed Hitler as suffering from coronary sclerosis, akin to, but less serious than, meningitis. When Hitler moved to Vinnitza in the summer of 1942 to oversee the Caucasus offensive he suffered what Morrell termed "brain fever" which people at headquarters called "Russian headache." It was early in 1943 — the period coinciding with Stalingrad and North Africa — that Morell first noticed a tremor in Hitler's left arm and leg which got progressively worse and eventually assumed extreme forms. When in 1945 Hitler gave Speer a signed photograph as a birthday present he apologized, "Lately it has been hard for me to write even a few words in my own hand. You know how it shakes. Often I can hardly complete my signature. What I have written for you came out almost illegible" (Speer, 439). The only way he could read documents was through a magnifying glass or when it was prepared in enlarged lettering, the special "Führer script." He also took to walking with a cane. Among the hysterical afflictions Hitler suffered from were insomnia, headaches, spastic constipation, arterio-spasms, impairment of vision, swelling of joints, and flatulence. Morell plied him with an array of pills—Hitler consumed every day at least half a dozen drugs and daily injections as well as frequent enemas and bloodletting by leeches. Characteristically, Hitler himself often specified what medicines or treatment to administer. Morell later confessed that he gave the führer "what he wanted."

By the end of 1944 his condition was such that postwar medical opinion tends to diagnose Hitler as having had Parkinson's disease. Here is a witness' description of him on April 23, 1945: "A physical wreck who could barely walk, doing so with a stooped back and a shuffling gait, his right leg dragging, his head shaking, and his left hand violently trembling on the limply dangling arm. His handshake was soft and flabby, his gestures those of an old, old man — only the eyes still had their old flickering gleam and penetrating power" (Morell, 272). The last detail will be expanded upon later.

It is worth supplementing the above with a look of what his allies and Nazi chieftains felt and said about the war. Among the first to have foreseen the collapse of the Axis enterprise was Mussolini who, in one of his frequent switches from buffoonery to reason, forecast the end as early as mid–1941. His wife related that when on the night of June 21-22 she had awakened her husband with the news of Hitler's attack on Russia, Il Duce exclaimed, "My dear Rachele that means the war was lost" (Schramm 1971, 162n). Following the Stalingrad debacle Hitler wrote on February 16 a long, mournful letter to Mussolini plying him with the usual turgid prose, excerpts of which read, "You can hardly imagine how much I want to spend a couple of days personally with you…. For what I am to Germany, Duce, you are to Italy; and what we both are to Europe, posterity alone can judge…. No episode on any front can be considered and examined in isolation, since they are part of a vast chain of events which will ultimately be decisive for the destiny of the whole of Europe, decisive in the sense of those great historical upheavals like the Persian and Punic wars, the invasions of the Huns, the expansion of Islam and the Mongol raids. But I can assure you that I am happy to be alive at such a time and be able to fight in the defence of those immortal values which have taken shape on our continent" (Deakin, 184). To Mussolini's Italian mind, however, what came through was that Hitler considered the war lost and that despite it Hitler would go on fulfilling his own private mission.

Hitler's second ally, Antonescu, came to similar conclusions. After visiting führer HQ in May 1943 he concluded that "militarily the war could no longer be won…. This is the last hour for returning to the political method." He also told the führer that if the Western Allies refused to deal with him then he should be concerned more "with writing the history of his people, not his own biography." That phrase Antonescu took from Hitler's own rhetoric — a shining example of the führer's use of *Dichtung* when suppressing his true intentions (Deakin, 310). Come October even Franco requested the return of the Blue division from the eastern front, promptly executed within 10 days of the request.

Goebbels seemed to have lost faith in victory at the same time the führer did. On the day Hitler explained to his Nazi stalwarts the problem of Russia's size and the slow pace of the German infantry Goebbels wrote in *Reich* magazine, "there is for none of us any longer a way out…. More important than the question when this war will end is the question how it will end…. If we win we win all … should we lose it then everything is lost … the discomforts that the war imposed on us pale in the face of the inferno which awaits us if we lose" (Reinhardt, 134). In a Sportspalast speech on January 30, 1943, he prophesied, "in this war there will be neither victors nor vanquished, but only survivors and annihilated" (Overy 1996, 306). Talking to his adjutant in 1943 Goebbels said "If all our exertions, our work, our struggles are to prove futile, then [echoing the führer] death would come to me as a release" (Schramm 1971, 162). It was this personal conviction that led him to repeated attempts to persuade Hitler to make peace with one side or the other. A no-less-loyal comrade, Martin Borman, likewise worried aloud that "it is so difficult to extract decisions from the Führer and yet with high morale alone one cannot win wars" (Hubatsch, 20). Ribbentrop, too, torn by premonitions repeatedly urged Hitler to approach Stalin. In rebuffing him Hitler came out with one of the most lucid statements about himself and the war Germany was waging. Said Hitler to his foreign minister, "You know, Ribbentrop, were I today to make an accommodation with Russia, I would to-morrow attack it again — I could behave no different" (Fest 1963, 89). Were Germany ever to erect a monument to the Second World War it fought that statement, cast in blood and iron, could well serve as its motto.

Visiting the Wolfschanze at the end of 1942 Göring told Speer, "We will be lucky if Germany retains the borders of 1933 after this war" (Paul, 230). Himmler was at that time aware of the anti–Hitler scheme but already toyed with the idea of letting the plot go through to subsequently join the West as he eventually did via Sweden and Switzerland. The following June, on a visit to Hitler, Baldur von Schirach said that he considered the war lost, to which Hitler replied that he knew this very well but "what am I to do except blow my head off" (Below, 326). Thus at that stage not only did Hitler expect defeat but had already decided what to do with himself when the end came; the theme of his own death reappeared frequently in those days in his table talks and in his conversations with Dr. Morell. With the onset of winter and failure of Barbarossa, Todt concluded that there was no longer any hope and he pressed his views on the führer. He did this in a most emphatic way on November 29, 1941, at the Reich Chancellery in the presence of Brauchitsch. Hitler responded that he saw "hardly any way of reaching a political conclusion" and pressing his *Dichtung* added that victory was a matter not just of armaments but of will. Even Keitel, the most submissive of lackeys, had begun to have doubts about victory, most likely just parroting his boss. In June 1945 he told his interrogators that he came to his conclusions around 1943 and as for the führer's views he said, "The Führer always kept to himself. I believe, however, that already in the winter of 1941/42 the Führer was well aware that this war could not be brought to a rapid conclusion" (Overy, 2001, 344).

Another key man in the war, the army's intelligence chief, Reinhard Gehlen, party to everything that was known about the Red Army, concluded by the end of 1943 that the war could no longer be won (Cookridge, 67). And in the fall of 1943 Sepp Dietrich, head of the *Leibstandarte* and a darling of the führer, announced that in view of the sheer numerical superiority in men and materiel the Soviets enjoyed, decisive victory over them was no longer possible (Messenger, 118). These sacrilegious words were picked up by Rosenberg and Himmler and passed on to the führer but quite unlike him he chose to ignore them. Another military hero whom Hitler much admired, Luftwaffe Feldmarschall von Richtoffen, appeared one day at headquarters and in the presence of Adjutant Below asked Hitler to put an end to the war. Richtoffen was not shot; Hitler merely commented that he saw no chance of obtaining a "tolerable" peace from his enemies (Below, 370). Two more feldmarschalls faced Hitler with a demand to stop the bloodshed. On July 17, 1944, Rommel as commander of AGB wrote that in about two to three weeks he expected the Allied armies to break out of the Normandy beachhead, adding, "I must ask you to draw the consequences from this situation without delay." Hitler told him to mind his own business. A month later, on August 18, OB West Kluge likewise wrote to the führer, imploring him "to take the decision on ending the war. The German people endured such unspeakable sufferings that it is time to end this horror." Hitler was spared having to give an answer because after sending this letter Kluge killed himself.

* * *

In the previous pages Hitler's realization that the war was lost was paired with a serious deterioration in his health and physical condition. A specific detail had been alluded to, namely that while physiologically a wreck, the gleam and fury in his eyes remained undiminished. This was cited advisedly because in the face of all these cataclysmic events, Hitler's murderous instincts not only did not abate but reached a terminal form. In the very first chapter Hitler was characterized as embodying three personalities: the Austrian *petit-bourgeois*, the quasi–Bismarck, and the third persona — a ghoul devoured by a craving for ruins and corpses. By 1943 only the last facet remained. It is here that we must look for the motivations and aims that made Hitler prolong the war to the last possible moment.

Hitler's stance throughout his career was always, in his singular phrase, "*so oder so*" (either this way or that way). When one reads his speeches and harangues one discovers that he rarely said that the Germans would win. He spoke much about the German soldier's virtues, about willpower and *Geist*, crowning it with a solemn promise that, unlike in the Great War, he would never capitulate. Thus the first "*so*" meant that blessed with Nazi ideology and his infallible leadership, Germany ought to win the war. The other "*so*," however, meant that should victory be denied him he would take the "world" with him into apocalypse. This intent he put on par with his will to win the war.

This he started flaunting as soon as he became chancellor, which is not surprising given that his taking power meant war. He spelled it out early in 1934 in a conversation with Rauschning. When in response to Hitler's warlike plans Rauschning asked what would happen if the European powers resisted, he answered, "That would be the end. Even if we could not conquer then we should drag half of the world into destruction with us and leave no one to triumph over Germany," and again, to his generals "even if we won't conquer, then we should drag half the world into destruction with us, and have no one to triumph over Germany" (Rauschning, 125–8). He had said a similar thing to Sumner Welles when the latter came on his peace mission in 1940. Hitler talked little about peace terms but told the American envoy that Germany was going to fight, win or lose, but if she lost she would drag everyone with her. They had better let him have his way because the world would be worse off if Germany lost.

One is accustomed to hearing Hitler ramble on about the Jews being parasites, the Slavs nitwits, the Americans mongrels, and so on. But those that heard him out shortly before the Third Reich collapsed were aghast by the latest verdict Hitler pronounced on — of all people — the Germans themselves. The Germans were cowards and laggards; Germany should be destroyed because it proved to be weaker than the "eastern" peoples and he accordingly issued orders to scorch and destroy the country's. As with everything else this was nothing new for the führer. He had been heading in that direction for some time. To his generals he said, "If the war were not won, that would mean that Germany had not stood the test of strength; in that case she would deserve to be, and would be, doomed." He was even more specific during that fateful winter of 1941. As quoted earlier, on November 27 he said to the Danish foreign minister, Scavenius, and the Croatian foreign minister, Lorkovic, that the Germans deserved extermination and that he would shed no tears for them when they perished (Haffner, 120). A most interesting twist in that theme were his instructions to Goebbels regarding the tone the press should adopt in connection with the Yalta Conference in December 1944: "those warmongers in Yalta must be so denounced, so insulted and attacked that they will have no chance to make an offer to the German people. Under no circumstances must there be an offer.... Surrender is absolutely out of the question" (Speer, 426).

The Jews had been condemned to death in *Mein Kampf*. One of the reasons Hitler had started the war before Germany was ready — which was to be 1942 — was to be able to eradicate the Jewish population of Europe, 11 million by Nazi count, fearing that he might die or be assassinated before accomplishing it. Goebbels quotes a number of instances where Hitler gloats at the opportunity provided by the ongoing war. "Fortunately — he says — a whole series of possibilities presents itself for us in wartime that would be denied in peacetime. We shall have to profit by this" or, "He is right in saying that war has made possible for us the solution of a whole series of problems that could never have been solved in normal times. The Jews will certainly be the losers in this war" (Goebbels, 1948, 148, 314). The death-cum-slavery sentence on the Russians had also been hatched as early as Mei*n Kampf* and its implementation had been going on since June 1941. Now, with the Germans having shown themselves to be weaklings and traitors to their own cause, the führer pronounced a death sentence on them, too, to be carried out by the Germans themselves in cooperation with the enemy.

With such a wide agenda on his hands the führer needed time. Hence the war had to continue for as long as possible. The first task was to finish off any Jews still to be found on the Continent. Although the program for the biological extermination of European Jewry was a unique and separate abyss in his psyche and, although employing it as a threat was as monstrous as it was pathetic, yet he used it to warn the "world" against going to war against him. The first time he openly declared his intention of killing all the Jews of Europe was in a Reichstag speech on January 30, 1939: "I want today once again to make a prophecy: In case the international Jewish financiers within and outside Europe succeed once more in hurling the peoples into a world war, the result will be not the Bolshevization of the world and with it a victory of Jewry, but the annihilation of the Jewish race in Europe." January 1939 seemed an odd occasion to have come out with it — Munich had given him what he had demanded and peace seemed assured — but in retrospect it becomes clear why. Infuriated by having had his demands met, he was just getting ready to do what he had planned in the first place — occupy all of Czechoslovakia. He rightly feared what the West's reaction might be to this aggression after he had signed the Munich agreement. Therefore the lunacy of his threat.

When by the end of 1941 the debacle in Russia had become apparent, similar prophecies about murdering Europe's Jews followed, on the 1st and 30th of January, on February 24, on September 30 and on the 8th of November. These statements were now accompanied by glee, typical of which was that proclaimed on November 8, 1942: "You may still remember the meeting at the Reichstag when I declared ... that the outcome will be the extermination of Jewry in Europe. I have always been laughed at as a prophet. Of those who then laughed a countless number are no longer laughing today, and those who are still laughing will no longer be doing so in a little while" (Haffner, 138). The Germans, therefore, must continue fighting because some Jews were still "laughing."

Indeed, in 1942 the Nazi program of total extermination—begun in Russia in July 1941—grew rapidly in extent and intensity. While half a million Jews had been murdered in Russia by mass shootings, special extermination facilities had now begun to spring up: Chelmno, north of Lodz, in December; Belzec and Sobibor near Lublin in the spring of 1942; Treblinka on the Bug in July; Auschwitz-Birkenau in the fall. On January 20, 1942, the Wannsee Conference was convened to coordinate the extrication and transportation of the Jewish communities from south, central and western Europe, requiring the cooperation of all bureaucratic and military authorities of the reich. The plan embraced every conceivable nook and cranny where Jews lived, including those not yet in German hands but which the German soldier was to conquer to make the führer's words come true. In his talk with the mufti of Jerusalem on November 28, 1941, Hitler said that "Palestine Jewry is just another center of Jewish destructiveness. Germany is determined step by step to demand from each European nation a solution to the Jewish problem, and at an appropriate time address a similar appeal to the nations outside Europe.... From Russia he would reach the exit from the Caucasus. The German aim would be the destruction of Jewry living in Araby" (DDR, XVIII, 138). And in his Table Talk on the evening of January 27, 1942, he announced that "they [the Jews] will also have to clear out of Switzerland and Sweden."

By 1943 some 4 million out of the 6 million Jews the Germans were eventually to kill were already dead. The bulk of those living, some 760,000, were under Hungarian jurisdiction. A great diplomatic and military offensive now began in order to lay hands on this one remaining community thus far unscathed. On April 16, 1943, Regent Horthy came to Schloss Klessheim at the urging of the führer. Great issues were at stake. Stalingrad had just played itself out; a 200,000 strong Hungarian army had been lost at the Don; North Africa was about to fall; there were Hungarian feelers to the West about quitting the war. Horthy expected to discuss all this—instead he received a standard führer monologue. When Horthy attempted to broach some of the urgent issues Hitler lashed out at him for harboring a mass of Jews at home and asking what the regent intended to do with that plague. When Horthy argued, that "he had done everything that could be done against the Jews but one couldn't murder them or let them die after all" the führer screamed, "the Jews had to be handled like tubercular bacilli ... beasts who want to bring us 'Bolshevismus' should not be spared." The Jews were brought up again on the second day of the conference, April 17, with Horthy repeating that after all "he cannot kill them." Chiming in for the führer, Ribbentrop told Horthy that the Jews "had to be either destroyed or brought into concentration camps. There was no other alternative" (Fenyo, 128–9).

The diplomatic offensive to have Hungary deliver its Jews for extermination continued unabated throughout 1943 and 1944. In his talk with Prime Minister Sztojay on June 4 Hitler went back to the Jews, telling him that the Hungarians must listen to him because "should the Jews win 30 million Germans would be exterminated and many more millions starved" (DDR, XXII, 113). As diplomatic talk did not seem to help, on March 19, 1944, Horthy was summoned again to Berlin and given a treatment similar to Schuschnigg and Hacha — that is, kept in Berlin while German troops and Nazi contingents occupied Hungary. And in May the first freight trains packed with Hungarian Jews started rolling for Auschwitz.

Back in Budapest Horthy, who had been assured that the occupation would be temporary, wrote to the führer saying that the quarter million German troops kept in Hungary would be more useful at the front and asked they be withdrawn. On June 7 Hitler summoned Sztojay and told him outright that the occupation would last "until the Jewish problem would be solved" (Horthy :306). Pressed by the USA and the Vatican, Horthy then ordered a stop to the deportations.

On August 23 Rumania signed an armistice with the Soviet Union and Russian armies surged into Rumania and approached Hungary. On October 15 Horthy likewise announced an armistice with the Russians. But the Germans were faster. Under the threat of murdering his only son (one had been killed on the Russian front) whom the Germans had kidnapped, Horthy was forced to resign and a Fascist leader by the name of Szalasi took over as prime minister. Effectively the Germans now ruled the country. While this was taking place the Russian armies approached Budapest and by December 15 had the city under siege. Whatever Jews were still left in the country were now shipped en masse to their death but nearly a quarter million remained in the besieged capital. Hitler's dedication to the slaughter of Jews is nowhere more prominent than in the story of Budapest. More on this will be told later in connection with the military operations. What is pertinent here is that at a time when the Russians were already on German soil, Hitler dispatched his elite SS Panzer divisions to retake Budapest. When at the situation conference on January 23 the staff protested against the Budapest gamble, Hitler retorted, "On top, is the Hungarian oil" (Schramm, 78). To Szalasi Hitler said, "Budapest is important because it is a main railway center." Alternately, "he needed it for prestige reasons" (DDR, XXII, 182). With Berlin about to fall and the Ruhr surrounded the best German troops were kept battling in the puszta to retrieve a quarter million Jews so they could be gassed.

The next part of the "world" meant to go down the abyss was Russia. As the 1941 winter approached Hitler renewed his previous admonitions about not conquering but erasing the major Russian cities. On October 7 instructions went out to the AGN that "the Führer has again decided that a capitulation of Leningrad and later Moscow, must not be accepted even if offered by the enemy.... No German soldier must therefore enter these cities. Anybody attempting to leave the city in the direction of our lines is to be repulsed by force.... The same applies to all other cities; before capture they are to be worn out by artillery bombardment and aerial attacks" (Carell 1966, 207). He repeated this at his Table Talks on August 6, 1942: "St. Petersburg must therefore disappear utterly from the earth's surface. Moscow too. Then the Russians will retire to Siberia."

One of the ingredients of the apocalypse was the Germans' scorched-earth policy in Russia initiated in 1943. Stalin, too, had during retreats practiced something akin to scorched-earth tactics. But this was an integral part of warfare meant to delay the enemy and give Russia time to gather strength to repel the invasion. What Hitler meant by scorched earth had no strategic or tactical aim. It did not delay and would have meant little even if it had delayed the Soviet armies— the outcome of the war was set regardless of how slow or fast the Russians moved. There was no prospect of a German comeback or Russian collapse. It was slaughter and destruction for its own sake. If anything, it laid the ground for retribution by Russian troops once they stepped onto German soil, but this was, in fact, what Hitler wished for his Vaterland.

The Scorched Earth order issued on September 7, 1943, reads inter alia:

- All agricultural produce, facilities, and machinery will be evacuated.
- The production base of agriculture, in particular basic facilities and installations (stores, etc.) of food supply and collecting organizations are to be destroyed.
- The population employed in agriculture and the food industry is to be taken ... west (Carell, 524).

The order signed by Göring was supplemented by one issued on the same date by Himmler. This empowered a certain General Stapf with overseeing the following: "In the evacuation of the Ukraine it must be seen to that no human being, no head of cattle, no grain depot is left behind; that no stretch of rail track is left intact; that no house remains standing; that all mines are destroyed for years to come; that no well is left that has not been poisoned. The enemy is to find a completely scorched and destroyed countryside" (DDR, XVII, 611).

Accordingly, as the Germans retreated every house, barn, wagon, well, bridge, tree, stretch of road or railway was methodically destroyed. A special device called *Schienenwolf*, a massive steel plow towed by a locomotive, was used to tear up the rail lines. Men, women, cattle, horses and pigs were driven to the west. When retreating from just the Donetz the Germans dragged with them 200,000 head of cattle, 153,000 horses, 270,000 sheep followed by 40,000 peasant carts (Temkin, 144). What live inventory could not be taken was slaughtered. Thus in May 1944 when the Germans evacuated the Crimea they had on their hands 50,000 horses. They proceeded to shoot them and when this proved too cumbersome they drove the mass of horses to the edge of a precipice and opened machine gun fire with most of the horses stampeding and toppling over the ledge to crash to their death in the incoming tide (Carell 1966, 469).

Whatever the material losses the cost to Russia in human lives was even more appalling. By 1943 Hitler had exterminated over 3 million Russian POWs. He still had about 2 million more. Some of them served as Hiwis, coolies to the Ostheer, while others were being worked to death in slave labor camps. Twenty million civilians had already perished as a result of the German invasion. In the following two years of Hitler's apocalypse, 10, and by some accounts, 20 million more would lose their lives.

* * *

If, as it is asserted here, Hitler's actions after December 1941 were guided primarily by a wish to see the realization of his apocalypse then the implementation of it started in that very month. The most drastic act in this program was declaring war on the USA. As has been pointed out, there was no such clause in the Tripartite Pact; whatever there was, Germany's joining was predicated on Japan being a victim of aggression. Not even Japan saw Pearl Harbor as an aggression by America. In August 1941 Churchill had to confess to the combined chiefs of staff that in the privacy of his talks with Roosevelt, the president had frankly told him that "he would wage war but not declare it" (Divine, 214). Thus, while the USA had been in an "undeclared war" with Germany since mid–1940 this pales with an America officially at war. To announce his war on the USA Hitler had arrived in Berlin at 11 A.M. on December 9. There he found a message from Thomsen, his charge d'affaires in Washington, confirming that Roosevelt, despite Pearl Harbor, had no plans of declaring war on Germany (Weintraub, 646). That this was so was evident during the Argentia Conference in August. Moreover, Churchill revealed something more definite that could have come to him only during a tête-à-tête with FDR. When Smuts urged him to appeal directly to Roosevelt about declaring war, Churchill informed him on November 9 that when he had mentioned the subject to FDR his answer was, "I shall never declare war, I shall make war" (Churchill Papers Vol. 3, 1423). Still Hitler declared his war. As one historian views it, "A speedy declaration of war on Japan (by Britain after Pearl Harbor) ensured that the English-speaking peoples had one common enemy, but for a few days (November 7–11) the horrific prospect opened up of the new Allies waging a common war in the Far East but not in Europe…. Such was the outrage in America about the nature of the Japanese attack that the pressure to ignore Germany and pursue an all-out war in the Pacific might well have been irresistible … [and] the British and Soviets would have found some of their supplies drying up" (Charmley, 44). The only explanation reason can provide for Hitler's declaring war on America is that it was an act of spite and revenge aimed at his own people. With America as an opponent the cost of waging war in the West was now bound to exceed anything the British could ever have inflicted on Germany.

Along with the declaration of war on America, Hitler's simultaneous second act of revenge was his order in December 1941 for the Ostheer to remain where it stood in face of the oncoming winter and the Red Army's offensive. It remains moot whether the order not to give an inch had saved the Ostheer from a Napoleonic retreat. But there is little doubt that had Hitler pulled back his troops to prepared positions in time, as soon as his October offensive had stalled, that the debilitating losses due to combat, frostbite, sickness and exhaustion, as well as the collapse of morale never to be regained, could have been avoided. The Ostheer, having failed to subdue Russia, was now to be destroyed in attrition-like fighting without winter clothing or shelter, without an adequate supply system, the piecemeal withdrawals through blizzards and a pursuing enemy marked by panic and loss of the heavy equipment. It was the first deliberate punishment of the army, to be followed later by the sacrifice of a quarter million men in Stalingrad, and the willful abandonment of entire armies in the Kuban, Crimea, Kurland, East Prussia and other doomed outposts of the crumbling eastern front.

A clear indication of Hitler's willful handling of the ongoing war from 1943 onward emanates from both the substance and tenor of his daily military conferences. After Stalingrad the deliberations had become finicky marathons thrashing out logistical and numerical minutiae and leaving the impression that they were deliberately so conducted as to avoid all strategic or operational discussion about the war. All measures were merely ad-hoc reactions to events imposed by the enemy with no general review of what to expect or what was to be done. Whenever his arguments fell flat Hitler ended the discussion with a standard, "There is no doubt about it at all." Following is a typical excerpt taken from the July 25, 1943, conference, a time when the overriding concerns should have been the fiasco at Kursk, the Russian offensives at Orel and in Ukraine and the pending Italian defection. Instead, what we have is the following:

> ZEITZLER (Z): The following total losses … have been reported.
> HITLER (H): Fifteen tanks, six Panzer IIIs, long, seven Panzer IVs, 13 Panzer VIs. Those are the total losses.
> BÜHLE (B) (OKH liaison to the OKW): That's absolutely correct.
> H: Hermann Göring seven Panzer IVs — also long — and 13 Panzer VIs.
> B: In this matter it's absolutely correct.
> H: There it's totally correct: Hermann Göring seven tanks.
> JODL (J): Not the 15 Grenadier Panzer Division.
> H: Seven Panzer IIIs, long, and 12 Panzer IIIs short.
> B: That's 19.
> H: That's seven Panzer III short. There are 42 in total here. These 16 — these are the long ones?
> B: Those are command vehicles.
> Z: Those could only be self-propelled anti-tank guns.
> H: Yes, self-propelled anti-tank guns. Then 12 Panzer IVs, long,15 self-propelled mounts with 7.5 guns on the Panzer IIs, 14 assault guns (Heiber 2003, 173).

And so on...

Late July 1944 was probably the period of greatest military crisis for the Third Reich. The Russian summer offensive resulted in the total destruction of the central front and the encirclement of AGN; while in the west the Americans broke out of Normandy (Cobra) inundating France and heading for the German border. At the July 31 Conference Hitler, in the presence of Jodl, Warlimont and five others, delivered a colloquy on the political and military situation which elliptically veered into getting the generals to participate in his apocalypse. To set the tone he starts off by saying that is it not good that the front has now shrunk from Russia to Poland with the communications lines so much shorter, making it now possible to defend the Reich and win the war. This astonishing argument he peddles not as propaganda but to men intimately familiar with what has actually transpired. Instead of having followed his generals' repeated pleas to preserve the available forces by retiring to short, prepared positions he finds it possible to say to them that it was better to be forced back and lose on the way half of the Ostheer, all because retreat is against Grofaz's principles. But if indeed there has been failure and defeat, he tells his listeners, obviously this was due to treason, because the General Staff has "poisoned" the military with treachery. This too is an amazing flip-flop. Hitler prided himself as being the head of a Reich led on the führer-prinzip meting out instant perdition to anyone opposed to the Nazi regime. Now to blame lost campaigns on a bunch of shabby spies and traitors is a supreme act of mental daring. Being a leader of such proven insight and vaunted instincts capable of shattering internal and external enemies in the blink of an eyelid, how did he let the Third Reich be outwitted by another "stab in the back"—something he promised his Germans that, whatever else, this would never, never happen again.

If one reads the transcripts of Hitler's sessions with his top commanders* one gets the impression that his monologues were designed to test his listeners' mental and even physical endurance. The seminars contain usually two features, both in the nature of Chinese torture. One consists of a string of non-sequiturs. The other element in the führer's dissertations is the elevated metaphysics of the topics he flung at his listeners—transcendental and peripheral—sidetracking the issues of the hour and irrelevant to either the present or the future. These lectures were not only high-falutin but also predictable—World War II sliding into his own experiences in World War I; the next Soviet offensive presented as Jewish conspiracy; the shortage of fighter aircraft to be remedied by the exertion of willpower and Geist.

These performances were, of course, willful acts aimed at avoiding all discussion and any references to the ongoing war, a dyke against any attempt of his interlocutors to bring up issues relevant to the fighting going on in Russia, Italy, France, and the skies over Germany. Hitler had to accomplish his stagecraft not only vis-à-vis his listeners but he needed supreme self-control lest that amidst the flood of verbiage he himself not blunder into subjects he was bent on avoiding. It was an exhibition of Dichtung of the highest order sailing through it with aplomb either by virtue of the intellectual and moral caliber of his cohorts or, in extremis, by the use of abusive language and bursts of rage. There was even an element of mockery—in fact of revenge—revenge not only on the Jews, the Russians, the Yugoslavs, the leftists, the aristocrats, but now even on his own entourage for they—

These verbatim transcripts are stored at the Institute of Contemporary History in Munich under the title of Hitler's Lagebesprechungen; Die Protocolfragmente Seiner Militarischen Konferenzen, 1942–1945. *An English translation can be found in Heiber and Glantz 2003.*

he would say — didn't follow his strategic Superplan. And after all he had done for them — glory, medals, baronial estates — they went ahead and lost the war.

Parallel to the deliberate military wastage there was the price Hitler exacted from his Germans by his treatment of "strategic" bombing. The year 1943 saw the bombing at its most intense, coming as it did just when the US and British air fleets had come into full power in numbers and tactics — and before 1944 when the air forces were diverted for the invasion of France. Round-the-clock raids turned city after city into rubble and ashes. When at the end of 1944 the Allies returned to bombing Germany they had difficulty finding targets as its cities had become a wasteland. To the civilians' ordeal was added that of the front-line soldiers to whom the fate of their homes and families became an added preoccupation. While a formidable array of anti-aircraft artillery was defending the cities, this was by far insufficient to stem the air armadas which came first from the north (England), then the south (Italy) and soon also from the west (France). What Germany needed was, on the one hand, a far larger fighter arm, and on the other hand, anti-aircraft missiles capable of homing in on their targets from both the ground and the air. The increase in fighter strength was implemented much too late when the cities had already been leveled and Germany was out of fuel and trained pilots. Vast resources went into producing V-1s and V-2s, the V standing for *Vergeltung* (Revenge), a weapon of no relevance to either air defense or anything else. The technology that went into producing V rockets was applicable to anti-aircraft missiles and could have been channeled into advanced anti-aircraft weaponry. Another diversion of effort from effective war-making was the story of the Walter submarines. This was a very advanced boat propelled by hydrogen peroxide which gave it an underwater speed of 15 knots — compared to two to three knots of the old types. One of the reasons for neglecting the project was a shortage of hydrogen peroxide, the very fuel used in the V-2s. By Hitler's order rockets heading blindly toward the English coast and fantastic 200-meter-long artillery barrels capable of firing a few shells at London were attended to with zeal while cities burned and millions of homeless people wandered the landscape in search of shelter. When traveling through this growing desolation the führer ignored the appeals of his gauleiters to stop and visit the stricken cities; when his *Sonderzug* passed the bombed-out area he ordered the curtains drawn and forbade any discussion of what could be seen outside his Pullman windows.

Hitler put his own cohorts and hanger-ons on notice that there was no way for them to abandon the doomed ship because the bridges to desertion had all been burned. On October 6, 1943, a distinguished gathering of gauleiters, generals, ministers, and state and party officials had been assembled, no doubt on Hitler's orders, to hear Heinrich Himmler convey to them an important piece of information. In Posen, on the afternoon of that October 6, Himmler informed the audience that just in the past two years the Germans had murdered in toto, infants and grandmothers included, all the European Jews in German hands. Said Himmler, "The simple sentence 'the Jews must be exterminated' is easily spoken, *meine Herren*.... For he who has to implement its demands it is the hardest and most difficult task there is.... The question that arose for us: What about women and children? I have decided to find an entirely clear solution here too. The fact is, I did not feel entitled to exterminate the men ... and to allow the avengers in the shape of their children to grow up.... The difficult decision had to be taken to make this people vanish from the face of the earth.... It was carried out without ... our men and our leaders suffering injury to spirit and soul.... You now know the facts.... I believe it is better that we — ALL OF US — have borne this for our nation, we have taken the responsibility on ourselves." Following the speech the audience was invited to a festive meal to which the participants ambulated, according to a witness, "in stony silence" (Fest 1999, 184–5).

In the previously quoted February 1943 letter to Mussolini the führer had told Il Duce, "The National Socialist Party will mobilize everyone, down to the last man and the last woman, in its inexorable resolve not to capitulate to our enemies in any circumstances whatsoever" and this was what he proceeded to do. The two means of extracting the last available cannon fodder were his *Volkssturm* and *Werewolf* schemes. Having always admired Stalin's methods of ruling his empire he now also aped his tactics. One such instance was the introduction, after the assassination attempt of July 20, of Nazi commissars into the army along with a mandatory Nazi salute. The Volkssturm was an imitation of the city militias Stalin had thrown at the enemy in the opening phases of the war. By a decree of September 25, 1944, all males between 16 and 60 were to be mobilized into the army. Since most men in the intermediate age brackets had long been conscripted, this Volkssturm consisted of boys 16 to 17; old men over 55; recuperating soldiers; and semicripples invalided out of the Wehrmacht because of hearing, gastric, and other health problems whom the soldiers dubbed the Ear and Stomach Battalions. These millions of teenage, old and sick men were given no proper training, no heavy weapons and frequently no uniforms. They were armed with Panzerfäuste, deadly for tanks and its users alike. And to make sure that they would fight and die an order went out on March 5, 1945, that "anyone who falls into captivity without being wounded or without proving that he fought to the end would have his family pay for it" (DDR, XXIII, 25). How they would fare facing the by-now mechanized, experienced Red Army glutted with tanks and planes, was a foregone conclusion.

The other machinery for self-destruction was the Werewolf, an imitation of Stalin's partisans. The name comes from German folklore wherein men are capable of reincarnating themselves into ravenous wolves; a ballad by that name was often recited at Nazi Youth rallies. The approval for activating the Werewolf was given by Hitler on February 27, 1945, but a school for guerrilla fighters under Col. Paul Krüger had existed since 1943. On April 1, the Werewolf numbering some 350 men, was ordered into action with instructions, "To stay behind, evade capture and then harass and destroy supplies of US troops in the rear." The men as well as Colonel Krüger wore mostly civilian clothes, each member carrying a Lilliput pistol firing eight rounds (Melchior, 150–3). By wearing civilian clothes they, of course, forfeited their lives, once captured.

Probably the heaviest blow Hitler inflicted on his beloved *Volk* in the context of his apocalypse was the eastern refugees. As the Russian armies entered East Prussia in the fall of 1944 and the German mainland the following January, the authorities in the east pleaded for an early evacuation of the local populace who to a soul dreaded falling into Russian hands. Although in postwar debates the Germans posed as having known nothing of what they had perpetrated in the East, the panic that gripped these otherwise staunch and callous people can only be explained by their knowing only too well and feeling they had very good reasons to flee. But orders from above forbade any such evacuations. This was contrary to the orders in the West where the civilians, glad to fall into Allied hands, were to be forcibly evacuated to the east.

Thus the German inhabitants of East and West Prussia, Brandenburg, Upper Silesia, and Saxony the Sudetenland took to their heels anyway, using horse-drawn wagons, hand sleds and baby carriages during the particularly severe winter of 1944-45. Strafed from the skies, mauled by convoys of tanks and trucks, felled by frost and exhaustion they died by the hundreds of thousands along the snow-covered treks and forests. A veritable *Völker-*

wanderung resulted when some 10 million Germans took off in an attempt to escape to the West in the course of which 1.4 million Germans died from the effects of winter, exposure and at the hands of vengeful Russian troops (DDR, XXIV, 471).

The above was only the preliminary scenario of what Hitler planned for all of Germany. The first instructions for a scorched-earth policy in Germany were prepared in September 1944. The führer laid down the following: "No German was to inhabit territory occupied by the enemy. Those wretches who did remain would find themselves in a desert.... Not only the industrial plants, and not only the gas, water, electric works and telephone exchanges were to be completely smashed ... food supplies were to be destroyed, farms burned down, cattle killed" (Speer, 403). Before leaving, the cities must be set afire. Any house that showed a white flag, all men in it were to be shot on the spot. In brief, a Russian Germany!

The order to go ahead with its implementation, often referred to as the Nero Order, was released on March 18, 1945. On the same day Hitler delivered himself of the following to Speer: "When a war is lost so, too, is the nation. This fate is unavoidable. It is not necessary to provide for a primitive existence for the nation. On the contrary, it is better that we destroy everything. The nation had proved itself to be the weaker and the future belongs exclusively to the stronger eastern peoples. Those left after this struggle will be the inferior ones, for the good ones will have fallen" (Schramm 1965, 79). The instructions given to the gauleiters contained essentially the items in Speer's description above. On March 19, Bormann issued a supplementary führer ukase that "in case transportation is not available, evacuation should be undertaken in horse- or ox-drawn wagons. If necessary the male part of the population should proceed on foot" (Speer 439–40).

It was estimated previously that the prolongation of the war by Hitler's desire to drag the "world" into the abyss with him had cost the lives of an additional 2 million Jews and 10 to 20 million Russians. German fatalities accruing after the failed attentat of July 20 are according to one estimate (Fest 1977, 3–4) as follows:

Duration of War	German Dead
September 1939 — August 1944: (60 months)	2.8 million
August 1944 — May 1945: (10 months)	4.8 million

Our framework extends from Italy's capitulation in September 1943 to the end of the war in May 1945, a total of 20 months. If one takes from above the average losses for the period of September 1939 to July 1944 (0.046 million per month) then up to Italy's capitulation the Germans lost 2.3 million people. The extra duration of the war from Italy's capitulation to the war's end in May 1945 brought death to an additional 5.3 million Germans. Given that the average German losses during 1939–1943 were much lower than those obtained from the 1939–1944 period, the above 5.3 million calculation represents a low estimate. Thus as part of the fulfillment of Hitler's apocalypse the last year and a half of the war caused about two and a half times as many dead Germans as the first four years of the war, or a sevenfold rate increase in fatalities.

Part Five

EXTINCTION

• CHAPTER 32 •

Barbarossa in Reverse

Three years to the day after the Germans launched Barbarossa the Russians staged a Barbarossa of their own. Although in historical and moral terms it had nothing in common with Hitler's onslaught, it bore such an uncanny resemblance that one may attribute this campaign to some deity in charge of setting things right. In terms of bloodshed it could never match the Germans—Barbarossa cost the Russians first hundreds of thousands, then millions of lives—but in military and strategic terms it outdid the Germans. And unlike the German campaign this armageddon was never to be repaired or repaid.

All through 1942 and 1943, very little had happened on the central front, the one tasked with tearing apart the Soviet Union. Except for Kursk, all major battles and Russian advances took place in the south. As a result, by the spring of 1944 the eastern front was split in two. Its northern and central sectors were deep in Russia. In the southern half, however, from the Pripet marshes to the Black Sea, the Germans, as shown in Fig. 32.1, had been pushed back beyond the prewar Polish and Rumanian borders. The two halves were telescoped along a 200 mile east-west axis, the Pripet marshes fulfilling again their historical role of splitting the front. Despite this each German half clung to where it stood with no attempt made to connect or straighten out the line. This was as the führer wished it.

Sharp local fighting had been going on in the northwest corner of the protruding ledge throughout the winter and early spring. In accordance with the principle of yielding nothing and losing much, the Germans parried each Soviet push with counterattacks and a stubborn defense of local fortresses. Fortress Kovel in the AGC's area of operation had been encircled by the Russians; after costly efforts it was relieved on March 25. It was a complete backwater, an area without roads, or major railway, infested with swamps and partisans where the lodged German divisions could at most achieve local successes.

Looking at the map there seems little doubt from where the next Soviet thrust would come. Below the Pripet marshes the Russians stood astride the Kowel-Mozyr line, their front facing north. From the knee of this ledge there were only 200 miles to East Prussia; another 80 miles and there was the Baltic Sea. In fact the Russians would have stepped right onto what Stalin called "the beast's lair"—Hitler's Wolfschanze at Rastenburg. The intervening Polish plain was ideal for mobile warfare, its rivers parallel to a northern thrust to the sea. Once there, not only would Russian soldiers be on German soil but both Army Groups, AGC and AGN, would be cut off with incalculable consequences to the course of the war. This was clear to any amateur. And this, Hitler insisted, was where the Soviet summer offensive would strike.

Not only amateurs and Hitler thought that the Russians would strike from the Kovel ledge, so did the entire German military establishment. Evidently by then Hitler and his

413

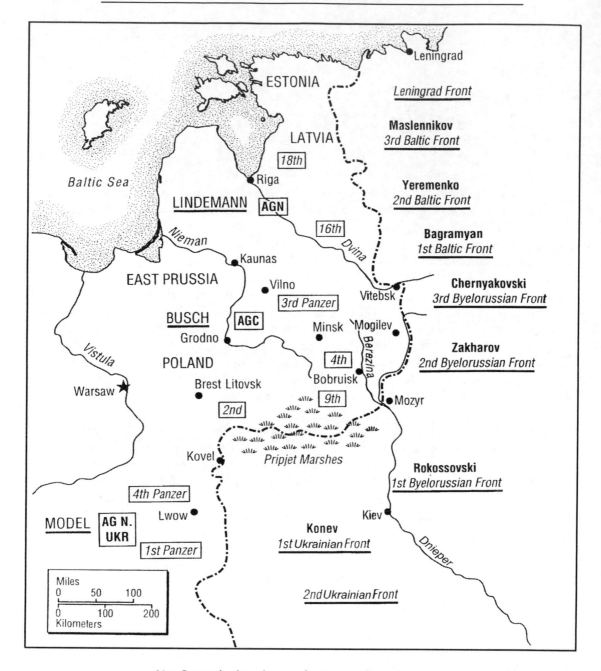

32.1. Strategic situation on the Eastern Front in June 1944

toadying generals had forgotten their own maxim of never attacking where the enemy expects it. They also forgot their contempt for Russian generalship which could never match the German genius of executing a flanking movement over an immense distance such as a thrust from Kovel to the Baltic sea. Ever since November and into the spring of 1944, army intelligence under Gehlen argued that the main Russian effort would be directed against Army Group North Ukraine where the bulk of enemy forces was concentrated. Their only uncertainty was whether the attack would be directed southward into the Balkans or toward the Baltic. This was also the view of the OKH as well as of the commanders and staffs of individual Army Groups. Even when Russian preparations pointed more and more often to the central front Gehlen's FHO dismissed these as a deception. The Germans' certainty that nothing would happen there was such that even after the offensive opened, they doubted that it was the real thing, which reminds one of Stalin's disbelief in a German attack three years earlier.

That this misjudgment was not an unavoidable by-product of the imponderables of war, but due in large part to the submission of the top ranks to Hitler's ideas is attested to in the diaries of Gen. Hans Jordan of AGC's 9th Army. On the eve of the Russian attack he wrote, "One thing is certain: In the last few weeks the enemy has completed an assembly on the very greatest scale opposite the Army and the Army is convinced that that assembly overshadows the concentrations of forces off the north flank of Army Group North Ukraine.... The Army has felt bound to point out repeatedly [that] ... this year's main Soviet offensive ... [is] aimed at the reconquest of Byelorussia.... The Army looks to the coming battle with bitterness knowing that it is bound by orders to tactical measures which it cannot in good conscience accept as correct.... The Commanding general and Chief of Staff presented these thoughts to the Army Group in numerous conferences but there, apparently, the courage was lacking to carry them higher up" (Ziemke 1971, 316).

The disposition of German forces and whatever reserves the OKH had corresponded, naturally, to its preconceptions. Since FHO had predicted that the central front would stay quiet, which matched the General Staff's views, Zeitzler proposed taking units from both the Central and North Ukraine Army Groups to form a reserve ready to meet an attack from the ledge either toward Rumania or toward the Lvov-Lublin area. The reserve created was the LVI Panzer Corps. While Zeitzler meant to use it as a defense against the expected offensive Model, who headed the North Ukraine Army Group, proposed on May 15 to use it instead in a preemptive attack against the ledge. Always eager for staging attacks, Hitler concurred and transferred the LVI Panzer Corps on May 20 to Model. In this way AGC lost 15 percent of its divisions, 88 percent of its tanks and 50 percent of its tank destroyers virtually denuding AGC of armored strength (Ziemke 1971, 314).

The complacency about the situation at AGC had much to do with both the state of the troops in that sector and the personality of its commander in chief, Feldmarschall Ernst Busch. He was a Nazi and a zealous conformist. More than the other yes-men in Hitler's entourage, he had no views of his own and no willpower to express them even if he had any. He accepted Hitler's pronouncements about the offensive occurring at the ledge without demur. When his troops were withdrawn to form the LVI Corps reserve he collaborated in the transfer. When at a conference on May 20 at the Wolfschanze he did bring up the weakness of the AGC, Hitler mocked and derided him; Busch registered no reaction. Another element contributing to the subsequent collapse was the lassitude of the troops. As the central front had been relatively quiet the troops there lived in comfortable shelters, had adequate provisions, swam in the rivers and enjoyed home leave. It was the usual malaise of a fighting force that did little fighting commanded by a brain that did little thinking, both troops and feldmarschall confident the führer knew what he was doing.

As signs multiplied that something big was brewing in front of AGC, Model's planned preemptive strike was cancelled. However, the troops of the LVI Corps were not returned to Busch's command but stayed with Model. An order came down to designate Vitebsk, Orsha, Mogilev and Bobruisk "fortresses"—defense islands that would break the flood, should it occur there. By June 10 reconnaissance patrols had discovered the presence of Rotmistrov's 5th Guard Tank Army and an avalanche of new divisions in front of AGC—but neither Hitler nor the OKH were deflected from their assessment that the strike would come in Model's sector.

On the eve of battle AGC disposed of 38 divisions manning a front of nearly 1,000 kilometers—about 600 miles. In the last week before the storm broke it was assigned three armored divisions which were still en route when the fighting broke out. As reserves Busch had two divisions. AGC's order of battle consisted of four armies: the 3rd Panzer (without Panzer divisions), the 4th, 9th and 2nd armies, the latter tied down along the northern rim of the Pripet marshes. Excluding the 2nd Army the front-line strength of the AGC was some 400,000 men plus another 400,000 in rear services and security.

As the Germans had surmised Stavka did consider the ledge as a possible platform for the summer offensive. But they knew that the Germans expected it there and felt that slicing their way to the Baltic risked a major defeat. The other options were a drive into Rumania or into the Baltic states. The first would have disrupted Germany's primary oil supply, the second could conceivably have cut off the AGN. What probably nudged Stavka in the direction of the central front—besides the weakness of the AGC and the element of surprise, was the urge to liberate the last portion of Russian soil still occupied by the invader. It was not an easy choice for several reasons. The Central Front had been the scene of repeated Soviet failures ever since the 1941-42 winter offensive. Nor was the terrain suitable for the kind of major drive envisioned by Stavka. The southern sector abutted the Pripet marshes, impassable even for tracked vehicles. The ground up to Minsk was wooded, swampy and only in patches suitable for tanks. The Dniepr, Drut, Berezina, Svisloch and Ptich rivers all formed potential obstacles to a rapid advance. Because of the difficult terrain the Russians created new formations consisting of a mix of cavalry and mechanized units capable of operating in terrain unsuitable for tanks. For the attack two main axes and one reserve axis were laid out. The tactics for breakthrough were the ones worked out in the past as best suited to Russian troops. This consisted of concentrating troops at narrow segments but at disparate locations of the front. Infantry supported by heavy weapons were first to make a breach in the enemy lines following which the armor would be inserted for long-range envelopment. The night before the attack four assault walkways were laid in front of each leading regiment. At river crossings six-ton ferries were set up and shallow bridges prepared. The piers for the bridges were laid early and the decking brought up during the artillery preparation. Whichever location proved more profitable the reserves would be brought in for operational deployment. To facilitate the campaign two major feints were planned. One was to maintain the threat to AG North Ukraine. The other was an offensive against the Finns in Karelia, expecting the Germans to rush reinforcements there to forestall a collapse of their northern partner.

The offensive was to be sprung over a stretch of 300 miles set to the following schedule. First the "fortresses" which constituted strong points and communication hubs would be reduced by heavy artillery and air bombardments. Two prongs, from north and south, would envelop Minsk and the 4th Army defending it. Simultaneously strong columns would head for Molodechno and Baranovici to block the Germans' escape route. The last phase aimed at reaching East Prussia and the Baltic Sea. For this the Russians organized four fronts as shown in Fig. 32.1. Vasilevsky was assigned by Stavka to oversee operations of the two northern fronts while Zhukov was to do so for the two southern fronts. The role of the 1st Baltic Front was to block any German interference from the north while that of the 2nd Byelorussian Front was to mop up stragglers and pockets left behind the main sweep.

The two southern fronts, the 3rd and 1st Byelorussian fronts, commanded respectively by Zakharov and Rokossovsky, were given the main task of the offensive. The number of front-line troops was 1.2 million men; with the available reserves the number was 2.5 million. They disposed of 4,000 tanks, 25,000 guns and mortars and 5,300 aircraft (Ziemke 1971, 315).

A prodigious effort was undertaken at *maskirovka*, the Russian term for camouflage and deception. This involved the following steps:

- All troop concentrations were hidden from both friend and foe.
- Officers and tank crews were ordered to wear ordinary soldiers' uniforms.
- Except for special cases all reconnaissance was suspended.
- Absolute radio silence was imposed.
- No artillery registration and no air attacks on the enemy were undertaken.
- Elaborate earthworks were erected at the front to simulate a defensive posture.
- Train drivers were not told of their destination and only small groups of soldiers were let out during stopovers.

The opposite of all the above was instituted at the front facing AG North Ukraine.

While Russian partisans had been active practically from the start of the war, it was only during the 1944 summer offensive that they made a notable contribution to the operational success of the Red Army. Because of the nature of the terrain the area behind the AGC had the highest concentration of partisan detachments, by some count as high as 400,000 men (Adair, 76). During the spring and early summer AGC staged several large operations to eradicate these concentrations, the last conducted just prior to the start of the Russian offensive. As is the case with antiguerrilla warfare, the successes achieved by the German troops were soon followed by the reappearance of the partisans in the same and other locations. The main task assigned by the Red Army to the partisans, aside from general harassment, was interference with German supply and communication lines, particularly the railways.

The decision to proceed with the central front offensive was taken at a meeting with Stalin on April 12. Zhukov at that time had commanded the 1st Ukrainian Front after its commander, Vatutin, was assassinated by Ukrainian nationalists. He was recalled to Moscow and along with Antonov of the Stavka charged by Stalin with preparing a plan for the offensive. On May 20 the plan was subjected to a final review and approved, whereupon Stalin was asked for a code name for the operation. He picked *Bagration*, a Georgian general killed at Borodino in the 1812 war against Napoleon. Signed by Antonov, the order for the offensive went out to the individual fronts on the last day of May. The timetable for the main and auxiliary attacks was staggered; against the Finns around June 10; Bagration to start on June 19 and against AG North Ukraine four weeks later. As it developed, due to the congestion on the roads and railways, Bagration was shifted to June 22 — the third anniversary of Barbarossa.

* * *

It is not possible to portray the course of the Bagration offensive either chronologically, operationally or in any other coherent sequence. The reason for that is that unlike most campaigns which consist of either a frontal displacement, or of prongs cutting through the opposing army to be eventually encircled and destroyed — Bagration resulted in a unique

German collapse. It can best be compared to a plate of glass shattered under a sudden impact. The shards and splinters of the AGC were then swallowed up by capture, annihilation or dissolution in the forests and swamps of Byelorussia. This course of events was due both to the tactics of the Red Army and the by-now almost routine submission of the German military to Hitler's dictates. To this one may add the supposition that at this stage of the war (see Chapter 31), Hitler's refusal to forestall the fate of the Central and Northern Army Groups was a deliberate act of demolition for the army's failure to win the war in the East.

Most accounts of the fighting deal with the activities of particular corps, divisions or regiments. From our standpoint such a scrutiny is of little interest. The operational and political consequences will be discussed, but the course of the battle itself will be given a bird's-eye view only. It will endeavor to take in the progress of the Soviet army as it swallowed territory, along with hordes of German troops, from its jump-off positions till it reached the Baltic Sea and central Poland.

While the opening of Bagration had to be delayed to June 22, problems in communication tied the partisan groups to the original order to start operations on June 19. Since the Germans had intercepted the Soviet instructions to the partisans, instead of the planned 40,000 explosive charges the partisans managed to place only a third of that number of which the Germans defused 3,500. Still the disruption was considerable; 10,500 sections of track were blown, stopping traffic completely for one day and interfering with German communication and transport for the duration of Bagration.

On June 22 the First Baltic and 3rd Byelorussian fronts began their attacks astride Vitebsk with company- and battalion-size strength to locate weak spots in the German defenses. This was preceded by air attacks on every major locality behind the front. The attack came to the Germans as a complete surprise so that already on that day the Russians punched a hole seven kilometers deep by 12 kilometers long (four miles by 7.5 miles) on the left wing of 3rd Panzer Army. The full-scale offensive started the following day at 5:00 A.M. preceded by a one-hour artillery bombardment and massive air attacks. It began in the north and rolled southward until it engulfed the entire front. The first wave consisted of plow tanks to clear the minefields. They were followed by infantry accompanied by sappers and supported by self-propelled artillery and tanks. The German defenses crumbled fairly swiftly whereupon mechanized divisions rolled through the breaches. The Soviet commanders had orders to bypass pockets of resistance and roll forward to prevent the formation of new defense lines. The main breakthrough occurred on the Polotsk-Vitebsk stretch and led to the encirclement of Vitebsk. When on the same day the main forces, the 2nd and 1st Byelorussian fronts, went into action they shattered the 9th Army in front of them and headed for Minsk, the offensive's initial objective.

When the offensive opened on June 22, the supreme commander of the German army, Adolf Hitler; the chief of the army General Staff, Kurt Zeitzler; and the commander in chief of Army Group Center, Ernst Busch, were all away from their posts getting ready for another conference. Busch immediately, and Zeitzler a day later, rushed back to Minsk. The main fighting at this juncture was against the 3rd Panzer Army near Vitebsk and the goings-on there are a mirror of the loss of direction attending the German handling of the offensive. The sequence of events on this front was as follows (Buchner, 151–3).

- June 23. 3rd Panzer Army being enveloped on both wings orders withdrawal of the three divisions of LIII Corps from the Vitebsk salient. When Busch gets wind of it he countermands it.

• June 24. Busch asks Zeitzler to authorize withdrawal. Citing a führer order, Zeitzler refuses. By now Vitebsk is partially encircled and General Gollwitzer, commanding LIII Corps, asks permission to pull out. A call from the Berghof orders that the three divisions are to allow themselves to be encircled. By evening the roads to the west are severed, isolating the Germans in the city. At nightfall a new directive arrives from the Berghof. Two divisions are given permission to break out. One division under General Hitter is to stay in the city and fight to the last man.

• June 26–27. Two divisions of the LIII Corps break out of the city. They are caught by Russian troops that have overtaken Vitebsk and are captured or destroyed with General Gollwitzer himself a prisoner. General Hitter of the fortress division tries to break out, too, but fails. His troops are destroyed.

• June 29. In the one week following the start of the offensive 3rd Panzer Army loses two of its three corps, opening up a critical gap between AGC and AGN.

Abutting the 3rd Panzer Army to the southeast was the German 4th Army. Unlike the rest of the AGC it was still holding on to territory east of the Dniepr including the cities of Orsha and Mogilev. When the offensive started the army requested permission to withdraw from east of the river. Hitler refused. When the Russians broke through the right wing of the army, severing its contact with the 9th Army to the southwest, 4th Army troops began to withdraw against orders. It was not until June 26 that Hitler approved the withdrawal, provided Orsha and Mogilev were held as fortresses. This authorization came too late, for the next day the two cities were invested by the Russians whose spearheads were already at Borisov, 200 kilometers (125 miles) behind the 4th Army. The taking of Borisov left the 4th Army with a single road to Minsk and a single bridge over the Berezina. In scenes reminiscent of 1812 a nightmarish panorama enacted itself at the Berezina crossing as troops, stragglers, supply columns, vehicles, guns, civilians, horses and cattle tried to get across the bridge at Berezino. A 30-foot span of the bridge was knocked out by the Red Air Force and when the Germans repaired it the next air attack knocked out a 45-foot span. There was no intervention from the German 6th Air Fleet as it had only 40 fighters left while all flak batteries were tied up in the ongoing land battles. Most of the divisions did get to the western side but by then the two Byelorussian fronts were already converging on Minsk behind their back.

On the 29th Hitler sacked Busch and replaced him with Model. One of the first things Model did was to scrounge up some 13 divisions from various war theaters as a relief for the central front. At that time the 4th Army was still lumbering between the Berezina and the river Svisloch. Minsk was a nodal road and rail hub and had been the headquarters of Army Group Center. Thousands of wounded from the recent fighting were kept in its many hospitals. Unable to cope, the 4th Army handed over Minsk to the 9th Army, a proverbial switch of musical chairs. After a brief fight with the surrounded garrison Minsk was taken by the Russians on July 3. To the east of it troops of the 4th Army still trudged on hoping to reach their own lines. But the German front line was already out of Byelorussia leaving the 4th Army at the mercies of the Red Army.

The upper rim of the Pripet marshes angles in a northerly direction and this channeled the progress of Rokossovsky's 1st Byelorussian Army. His opponent was the 9th Army centered on the city of Bobruisk. There the attack opened on June 24 when both northern neighbors of the 9th Army were already in great turmoil. In the course of the first five days its XXXV Corps in the north was half destroyed and half surrounded while the XXXXI Corps in the center was being slowly squeezed into a pocket near Bobruisk. On the 26th Busch, in the company of General Jordan, commander of the 9th Army, had flown to the Berghof to plead for a withdrawal of the army. Instead, Hitler relieved General Jordan on the spot and Busch three days later. This was followed by an order to make Bobruisk a fortress manned by one division. At this stage both Bobruisk and the divisions outside it had been cut off by Rokossovsky's prongs which were already far beyond the Berezina. The entire XXXXI Corps was trapped, either inside or outside the city, a total of 70,000 men. On the 28 Hitler ordered a break out to the north along the Berezina river. With nightfall coherent and incoherent masses of German soldiery attempted to get out of the burning city, leaving behind 3,500 wounded. Some units were gunned down at the periphery of the cauldron; those that broke through ran into advancing tank divisions further to the west and were annihilated. Of 70,000 men originally in the Bobruisk pocket some 15,000 survived.

The capture of Minsk can be considered the end of a major phase of Operation Bagration. For one thing, it marked the end of German occupation of Russian soil. It also seems that Stavka had no plans for the continuation of the offensive because it exceeded their expectations. But the disorganization of the German front and the plight of the AGC armies were so severe that it propelled the Soviet Command to exploit a rare turn of events in the war. There were three possible headings— all of major import. One was into the plains of Poland, another a drive into East Prussia, and the third a thrust to the Baltic. It is not clear what motivated Stalin to choose the first and third options. It is puzzling because the urge to wreak a little havoc in East Prussia must have been overwhelming. Stalin may have felt that East Prussia would fall into his lap without a murmur from anyone. But a takeover of eastern Poland and the Baltic countries— Stalin's 1939 gains by the grace of Hitler — the Western Allies had never recognized. These were territories Stalin may have wanted to absorb while the Allies were still busy fighting the Germans. And a drive to the Baltic, if successful, promised to cut off Army Group North with grave consequences to the German position in the east. And so he did; the southern fronts headed for eastern Poland while the fronts in the north lunged for Lithuania.

Stavka assigned the 1st Baltic and the 3rd Byelorussian fronts, to head for Dvinsk, Vilniuis and the general direction of the Niemen. The operations of these two fronts are an integral part of the fate of the German Army Group North and will be discussed later; here we shall concern ourselves with the Russian offensive into Poland. This was the task of the 1st Byelorusssian Front under Rokossovsky, who was to head for Baranovici and Brest, screened on the right by the 2nd Byelorussian Front. On July 8 Rokossovsky captured Baranovici, a key railroad hub, the Pripet marshes still channeling him into a northwesterly direction so that he debouched into central Poland from the northeast. In mid–July his armies opened a wide gap between Bialystok and Brest on the Bug. The Bug is the second largest river in Poland and there Model had hoped to stop the Russians. It was a plausible hope as the river presented a considerable tactical barrier and the Russians had by now been uninterruptedly on the attack for five weeks and were bound to have outstripped their supplies. But the Soviet armies came to the river not from the east but from the direction of Bialystok. On July 26th 2nd Army declared it could not hold Brest. Hitler, as customary, delayed and when at midnight he gave his approval for a withdrawal an entire corps had been surrounded in and around the fortress. The Germans threw everything they had, including several Panzer divisions, in the area of Siedlce to keep a route open for the troops in the Brest encirclement. The effort was wasted because a few days earlier the Russians had opened an attack from the ledge cutting into the rear of the German forces fighting between the Bug and Vistula rivers.

Though several Panzer divisions had been drained off it to stem the flood at the center, AG North Ukraine still represented a formidable force. Facing the sub–Pripet balcony were two Panzer armies, the 4th opposite Kovel and the 1st south of Lvov with the 1st Hungarian Army manning the foothills of the Carpathian Mountains. Together they counted 900,000 men, 900 tanks and self-propelled artillery as well as 6,000 guns and 700 aircraft. Facing it was primarily the 1st Ukrainian Front under Konev with over a million men and about twice the number of heavy weapons (Zaloga, 73–4), not a very conspicuous Russian superiority. The offensive against AG North Ukraine opened on July 13, aimed at the seam of the two Panzer armies, the main objective being Lvov. Due to the time the Germans had had to prepare themselves as well as the very heavy rains, the assault was not successful. As was now their practice the Russians on July 18 shifted the main effort against the 4th Panzer Army aiming at the hinterland of AGC struggling to contain Rokossovski's troops at the Bug. Within days a major breakthrough was achieved to the northwest with Konev's troops heading for the Warsaw-Brest highway. From the July 22 breakthrough at Chelm the Russians covered the 40 miles to Lublin within a day and Stalin immediately installed there what he later named a provisional Polish government to the complete exclusion of the London Poles. At the same time the attack toward Lvov was resumed, this time trapping three divisions near Brody. Of the 30,000 men encircled there 5,000 to 10,000 managed to break out while the rest were either killed or captured. With the elimination of the Brody pocket the road to Lvov was open and the city was taken on July 27, three years after it had fallen to the Germans. Konev's troops were now split into two prongs, one headed for Stanislawow to the south and the other toward a junction with Rokossovsky's men coming in from the northeast (see Fig. 32.2). The troops of the 1st Byelorussian Front reached the Vistula at Deblin, south of Warsaw, while Konev's troops cut the Warsaw-Brest highway east of Biala Podlaska. The Germans were now forced to stage a precipitous retreat to the west bank of the Vistula. The Brest fortress was struck from the south on July 27 and, unlike the saga of June 1941, the last pockets of resistance surrendered within a day. Before the fighting died out the Russians managed to establish three major bridgeheads west of the river, one at Magnuszew about 50 kilometers (30 miles) south of Warsaw; one 60 kilometers (37 miles) upstream near Sandomierz at the easternmost bend of the Vistula; and another at Baranov, near the San inlet — important platforms for future operations. With this the summer offensive against the Army Group Center came to an end. There still remains the story of Army Group North.

While the disintegration of AGC represents the largest loss in men, weapons and territory that the German army suffered, strategically the consequences for Army Group North of the Russian offensive were the more portentous. The AGN had only two armies, the 18th and 16th. Due to a previous Russian attack during which the 18th Army suffered heavy losses and the Russians liberated the Oranienbaum pocket, von Küchler, commander in chief of AGN, flew to the Wolfschanze on January 22nd to propose a withdrawal to Luga. As was by then standard von Küchler was relieved of command, the AGN being taken over first by Model and then by Lindemann. Bagration had started with an attack on the extreme left of AGC so that already on the first day contact with AGN was broken. By June 24 the left flank of the AGC collapsed, leaving a 90-kilometer (56-mile) gap between the two army groups forcing 16th Army to withdraw behind the Dvina. OKH, however, ordered the army to reestablish contact with AGC. Both Lindemann and Model at the AGC, judged the order

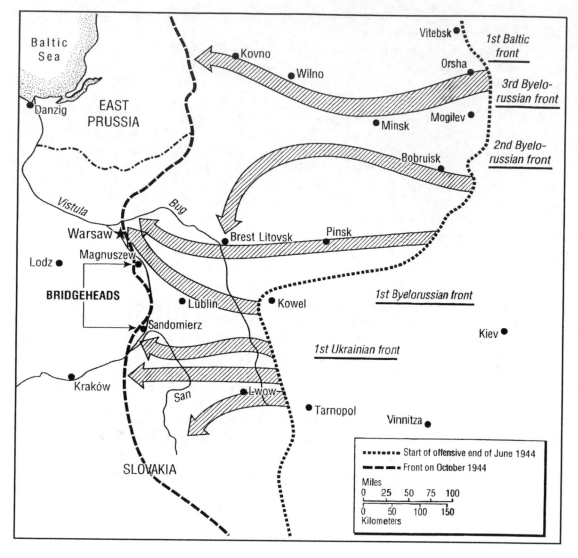

32.2. Results of the 1944 Russian summer offensive

impossible to execute and so informed OKH. Hitler's response was to attack in order "to cut off the lead elements" of the enemy. On July 1 Lindemann talked to Hitler for an hour but was again told to attack south, toward Polotsk. Hours later Lindemann called the Wolf-schanze again saying that "I don't believe we can execute the ordered attack" to which the führer replied, "The attack is to be executed with all means and with utmost energy" (Haupt, 228). The next day Polotsk fell to the Russians and the subject of the attack lapsed. Hitler's predictable follow-up came on the stroke of midnight on July 4th when Lindemann was sacked and replaced by Friessner. A week later Friessner informed the führer that it was impossible to reestablish contact with AGC. When Model proposed the solution of pulling back AGN to the Riga-Dvinsk line Hitler used Dönitz as a prop saying that such a move would be ruinous to the navy's position in the Baltic. Then there were also the crucial issues of Latvian oil, Swedish ore, Finnish nickel — things which he had said often enough his generals did not understand at all.

On July 14 Hitler summoned Model and Friessner to a conference at the Wolfschanze during which the latter was told that the Baltic countries must be held at all cost. This took place while the gap between the AGN and the AGC had grown to 120 kilometers (75 miles) and Maslennikov at the extreme north had gone over to the attack aimed at splitting the two AGN armies. In his request to withdraw AGN to the line Riga-Kaunas, Friessner pleaded in a letter to the führer, "I cannot reconcile with my conscience not having made every effort in this fateful hour to spare these loyal troops the worst that could befall them and not having found for them an employment that would make it possible to hold the enemy away from the eastern borders of our Homeland." Otherwise, Friessner asked to be relieved of his command. In the wake of this missive which Hitler termed a *Drohbrief* (a threatening letter), Friessner was fired and replaced by Schörner (Friessner, 20–21). What Model was to achieve at the AGC in place of Busch, Schörner, another furious Nazi general, was to do for the AGN in place of Friessner. When Schörner arrived AGN had a strength of about 700,000 men including two SS Latvian divisions; between him and the AGC's 3rd Panzer Army was a gap of more than 30 miles. Before he had time to lower himself into Friessner's saddle, Tuckum, on the Baltic, just west of Riga, was taken by the Russians on July 29, cutting off AGN from the rest of the eastern front. It did not faze the führer a bit who now switched from AGN reestablishing contact with AGC to a vehement demand that the AGC rush north for the deliverance of AGN.

The rest can be briefly told. Commanders were again switched, Model went to the West and Reinhardt took over AGC. The army chief of staff, Zeitzler, was sacked and forbidden to wear his uniform, clear proof as to who was responsible for the collapse of two army groups. The attack to relieve AGN went in on August 16 just as Czerniakovsky's troops reached the borders of East Prussia, stepping for the first time onto German soil. On August 20, 3rd Panzer Army recaptured Tukums, opening a narrow escape corridor for the encircled northern divisions. While at the OKH the leaders were euphoric, Reinhardt informed them that it would be difficult to hold the opening and urged that AGN be speedily evacuated. This Hitler ignored. When Schörner took over the AGN had been reduced to 570,000 men (Mitcham 2001, 130, 142). After a brief pause the Russians renewed their attack further south and on October 10 reached the Baltic at Polangen north of Memel in Lithuania, this time isolating the AGN for good. Thus, as shown on Fig. 32.3, an army of close to half a million men was bottled up in a triangular area, 40 kilometers (25 miles) wide at its base and 80 kilometers (31 miles) in height, and stayed there unemployed for the duration of the war.

* * *

Taken as a whole the defeat inflicted on the Ostheer that summer was the most telling of the Russo-German war. Army Group Center was destroyed, Army Group North was surrounded and eliminated from military operations, and the Germans were driven beyond the Soviets' 1941 frontiers. The political consequences, as will be discussed later, were to leave Hitler without any allies or satellites. In the midst of it all Hitler himself nearly lost his life.

The fate of the AGC was the most grievous. The overall course of the offensive on that sector is shown in Fig. 32.2. Seventeen divisions were totally and 50 others partly destroyed with a loss of approximately 350,000 men (Zaloga, 44). Of 4th Army's original 25 divisions 20 were lost while 3rd Panzer Army lost 10 divisions. The losses include 130,000 dead

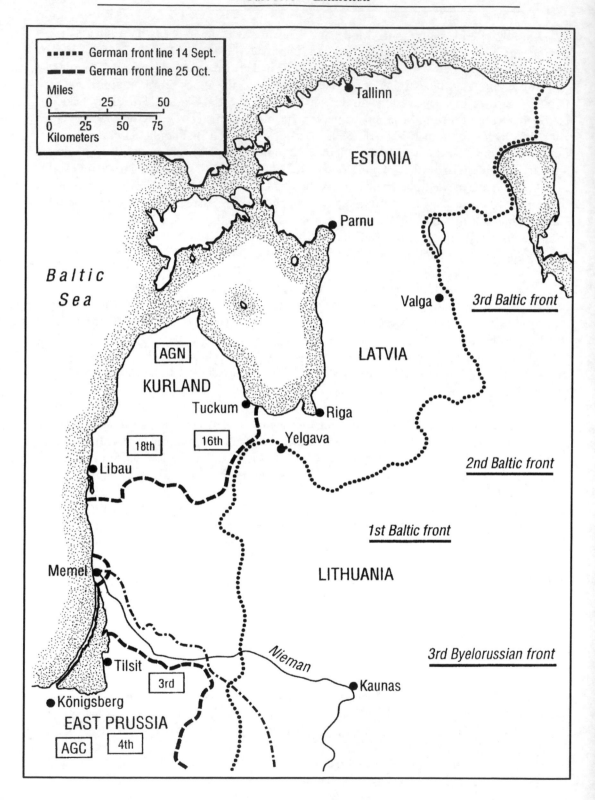

32.3 The fate of Army Group North, August 1944

(Hinze, 4), while 150,000 were captured by the Russians, half of whom did not survive captivity. Those troops that did escape were, naturally, mostly supply and rear-echelon personnel so that in essence AGC ceased to exist as a combat force. The AGC had 47 corps and divisional generals at the start of fighting; seven were killed, two committed suicide and 21 went into captivity — a loss of two-thirds of its top commanders (Carell 1966, 508–9); among those who died in captivity was the last commander in chief of the Kurland pocket, General Hilpert, promoted to generaloberst on the last day of Hitler's life. The similarity to Barbarossa is uncanny. In six weeks the Russians surged from Vitebsk to Warsaw, the same as the distance from the Bug to Smolensk the Germans had covered in the first six weeks in 1941. In its precipitous retreat the AGC lost, along with men and territory, all its heavy equipment and its logistical stores. The fate of those formations that escaped encirclement and of the small bands of men trying as stragglers to rejoin their units was a repetition of the fate of Red Army men in the scorching summer of 1941. It was in a way more desperate because while the Russians had been taken in large cauldrons the Germans ended up in countless small pockets which made the fate of the scattered troops more precarious. Those troops that set out in retreat across the flatlands of Byelorussia suffered the same despair as the Russians three years earlier — with the additional scourge of being plagued by bands of partisans. The latter set ambushes, burned bridges, felled trees and often impeded the retreat sufficiently for the Germans to fall into the hands of the pursuing Red Army. The retreating Germans were continuously strafed and harassed by hordes of Sturmoviks. They never saw a plane of their own. There was a complete breakdown in communication with neighboring units and headquarters so that even disciplined groups led by able commanders never knew whether they were heading toward their own lines or those of the enemy. The men marched on foot and the supplies were drawn by horses while the Russians, as the Germans had done three years before, rushed past them on American trucks and hordes of T-34s, overtaking them, blocking roads and river crossings. Hospitals had to be abandoned and the wounded left to their fate while the survivors, avoiding the few roads, found themselves in swamps and impenetrable forests. The heat was brutal, and the troops lacked water and food. Though in typical Russian fashion some peasants offered the stragglers a piece of bread, in most cases the Germans used violence to extract food from the emaciated inhabitants of the burned-down villages.

The pursuers did everything to impede the Germans' retreat. German-speaking Russians in uniforms taken from captured officers infiltrated the columns and led them to Soviet lines. Special detachments were formed to comb the woods and countryside for stragglers; later on, they left the Germans to their fate, certain they would not survive anyway. Those that fell into Soviet hands and survived transportation to the rear had to undergo another sort of humiliation. After vegetating for five days in the large assembly camp at Zhlobin, 57,000 of them were, on July 15, paraded through Moscow. The mass of German soldiery was led by 18 captured generals and 1,200 officers escorted by Cossacks on Tatar ponies. While the Russian crowd stared in silence, many Russian women who had lost sons and husbands wept at the sight of the defeated enemy.

In contrast to the total destruction of the central front, AGN suffered the trauma of being cut off from their comrades and homes and left to an uncertain or, rather, predictable fate. In mid–August, when there was still hope, an infantry division was actually flown into the pocket but later on the traffic was reversed. When the Germans abandoned Tallin, most of the troops were evacuated by air but 13,000 wounded were left behind. Characteristically, while the wounded were left behind 23,000 Russian POWs were taken along (this was practiced on numerous other occasions). Abandoning Riga the German divisions, as shown on Fig. 32.3, were squeezed into the Kurland corner and supplied by sea. At the beginning of 1945 the besieged AGN was blessed with the following führer announcement: "The Army Group [Fortress Kurland] stays where it is. I am expecting a change in the situation soon, then we will deal with Kurland" (Haupt, 345).

The political repercussions ranged all the way from the nearly successful assassination of Hitler to the defection of all of Germany's war partners. While these events had their origins in the past, they materialized in the wake of the collapse of the Ostheer in the summer of 1944. The most immediate was the defection of Finland. Prior to Bagration the Russians had staged an offensive in Karelia, inflicting painful losses on the exhausted Finns who, seeing the German debacle in Byelorussia, finally asked for and signed an armistice with Russia on September 4. By its terms the Finns were obligated to clear the Germans from their territory, if not peacefully then by force. The 200,000 strong German army in Finland then began a most arduous trek along the Arctic to Norway where it joined the unemployed Norwegian occupation force. In some places it did come to bloodshed. After the truce the Germans attacked the island of Hoegland but the Finns repulsed them, inflicting 400 German dead and taking over 1,000 prisoners whom they handed over to the Russians—a painful experience at the hands of their most admired ally (Haupt, 262). Preceding Finland's defection, Rumania on August 23 abandoned the Nazi camp and switched over to the side of Russia, inflicting another catastrophe on German troops stuck along the Prut between the Rumanians and Russians. On September 9 Bulgaria too went over to the Russians and Hungary was about to follow suit when Hitler preempted it . On October 15 the Germans for the second time invaded Hungary, arrested Horthy and installed a Fascist regime in Budapest.

There remains the question as to the sense of all the convolutions practiced by the führer in the course of the summer fighting; and there is no rational or half-rational explanation except through the labyrinth of Hitler's mind as portrayed in the previous chapter. With maddening predictability scene after scene repeated itself. Vitebsk, Bobruisk, Minsk, Vilniuis, Brody, Grodno, Brest and others were declared fortresses to be defended "to the last man"; orders arrived for outside formations to liberate the besieged garrisons; with the failure of each rescue attempt, orders were given for the besieged garrisons to break out for which there was no longer a chance. After Riga was taken on October 13 Schörner twice proposed an offensive to the south to join the troops defending East Prussia — already under attack by the 3rd Baltic Front — and Hitler vetoed it both times; likewise, when Guderian proposed evacuation by sea to mainland Germany, Hitler wouldn't hear of it. No plan was put forth to salvage the situation operationally or tactically by regrouping or disengaging from the enemy. Instead, there was a hysterical insistence on clinging to each swamp and hamlet — which meant only more bloodshed and ruin to his troops whether by death, capture, or plain dissolution in the eastern wilderness.

This manner of handling the German forces had started, of course, in the winter of 1941-42 when the troops had been ordered to stay put, freeze and die; and it was repeated on a strategic scale in Stalingrad the following winter. In both of these cases one can come up with führer-like justifications for the decisions. In the first case the argument went that a withdrawal would have been worse, though none of the generals agreed with that. In Stalingrad the excuse was that it made possible the Caucasus evacuation via the Rostov bottleneck. This high-strategy apologia was patently a hoax for most of the Caucasus army retreated across the Kerch straits and could have done so without sacrificing the 6th Army.

In the summer of 1944 no excuse, not even a propaganda ploy was ever offered by the führer for the willful sacrifice of Army Group North.

Hitler handled the Ostheer in the summer of 1944 in a manner consistent with his deliberate will to cudgel his army for its failure in the war against Russia. That he had lost the Russian campaign he had known since the end of 1941. He now implemented — as he had implemented his other satanic schemes — his threat that if he was not to have his way Europe and Germany itself would go down with him to perdition. He insisted on keeping the Baltic countries so as to have the nickel from Petsamo and iron from Sweden, he needed the Crimea to keep Turkey neutral, he fought for Kovel to retain the Ploesti oil — deceptions on his generals as he bamboozled his diplomats with "military" rationales. He shuffled commanders, fired orders, shifted divisions from one lost battlefield to another, acting out the role of supreme warlord, all meant to gain time and implement his determination to take the army and the Germans with him to a common doom.

· CHAPTER 33 ·

Liberation of France

The invasion of France took place three years after the German attack on Russia and two years after it had originally been promised to Stalin. There were a number of pressing reasons why the invasion was finally launched in the summer of 1944. By that date the Russians had stepped onto what had before the war been Polish and Rumanian territory and were at the doorstep of East Prussia, raising apprehensions as to what kind of regimes Stalin would install in Eastern Europe. Should they penetrate further west, similar fears arose about a possible communization of Germany as well as of France and Italy where large indigenous Communist parties dominated the resistance movements. The Western powers also harbored a suspicion that once Russian soil was liberated Stalin might stop the war or even conclude some sort of armistice, leaving the Allies to face the German army alone. One concrete element in the decision to invade was the appearance of the German V weapons. By November 1943 British intelligence discovered at least seven launching sites at Pas-de-Calais and Cherbourg ready for firing. Each of these ballistic missiles — of which the Germans were to produce an astounding 32,000 — had a range of 200–250 miles and carried a one-ton warhead. The threat of these missiles to London and southern England was one of the reasons why Churchill had finally acquiesced in an invasion of the continent.

But the determining factor in launching Overlord had to do with America's struggle against Japan. In the Far East, except for Burma, the US carried on single-handedly the war on land, sea and in the air, the fighting getting fiercer the closer the Americans got to Japan's home islands. (The conquest of Okinawa in April 1945 cost the Americans 50,000 casualties and 36 ships sunk). The prospect of having to fight the Japanese on their home territory gave the American military nightmares. And in 1944 the atomic bomb was still no more than a gamble. Roosevelt, therefore, looked to Russia for help in subduing Japan — an inverted parallel to its role in defeating the Germans. FDR had attempted something of the kind as early as June 1942. After promising Molotov to launch a second front that year, Roosevelt followed up on June 17 with a message to Stalin saying he had reliable information that Japan was about to attack the Soviet Union (Feis, 70). He then added, "We are ready in case of such an attack to assist you with our air power, providing there are available landing fields [in Russia]" and suggested that secret staff talks be started at once. It was a transparent attempt to get Russia into conflict with Japan — at a time when Roosevelt had no intention of opening a second front, with Russia facing a German summer offensive to the Volga and the Caucasus. Not only would that have imposed on Russia the perhaps unmanageable burden of fighting on two fronts, but it would also have had dire consequences on the delivery of Lend-Lease supplies. For despite all the attention lavished on the convoys to Murmansk, 50 percent of all military supplies delivered by the Allies came to Russia via the Pacific, Russian freighters having unrestricted passage through Japan-dominated waters. Had Russia gotten into a war with Japan these deliveries would have come to an immediate halt. It did not take a man of Stalin's cunning to dismiss Roosevelt's stratagem.

As the specter of invading the Japanese islands drew nearer, Roosevelt returned to the idea of inducing Stalin to join in the war in the Far East. He proceeded along two paths. With American troops and weapons now exceeding those of Britain, he was no longer hampered by British opposition to an invasion of France. And he decided to formally ask Stalin for participation in the war against Japan. Without letting Churchill know he arranged to meet Stalin. Churchill learned about the impending meeting from his ambassador in Washington and complained to the president. When it was agreed that he join the two at Teheran, Churchill frantically tried to meet the president prior to the conference. The president refused, saying, "it would be a terrible mistake if Stalin thought we have ganged up on him" (Beitzel, 264). On the way to Teheran FDR stopped off in Cairo to meet Chiang Kai-shek. There he avoided any opportunity to be alone with Churchill; and at Teheran FDR stayed at the Russian Embassy compound, presumably for security reasons, where he had a chance to talk to Stalin alone.

The Teheran Big Three meeting lasted three days, November 27–29, 1943. As an opening gambit FDR went along with Churchill when the latter once again proposed a delay in Overlord in favor of a Mediterranean operation, arguing that since Overlord could not be launched till spring, the Allied armies would remain idle for nearly six months. While he talked, Stalin stuffed his pipe with tobacco and, screwing up his small eyes, stared at his two Western allies. Roosevelt was then observed to wink at Stalin (Overy, 1997, 269). Addressing Churchill, Stalin said, "Just because the Russians are simple people it was a mistake to think they were blind and could not see what was before their eyes" (Beitzel, 330). At subsequent meetings things sorted themselves out and a mutual commitment was arrived at. Russia would join the war against Japan at an appropriate date and the Allies would go ahead with Overlord, tentatively on May 1, 1944. The Western Allies also extracted a commitment from Stalin that simultaneously with Overlord the Red Army would start a major offensive on the eastern front.

If the Americans had thought that this put to rest the British anti-invasion jitters they were disabused of it as soon as Teheran ended. The top British planner, General Kennedy, wrote soon after the conference, "Teheran has committed us ... to a course of action which, it is true to say, we should not have adopted had the conduct of war been entirely in our hands" (Wilt, 107). On January 25, 1944, Brooke, as was his wont, noted gloomily, "The possibility of Hitler gaining a victory in France cannot be excluded," adding the insight, "The hazards of battle are very great." As late as June 5, Brooke was still writing, "I am very uneasy about the whole operation ... it may well be the most ghastly disaster of the whole war" (Hastings 1984, 60).

Soon Churchill joined the fray with full vigor. Utilizing an *Ultra* message that Hitler deemed the war lost if he lost the Balkans he conceived of a fresh strategic push, no longer at the soft underbelly but what he called the Armpit or Right Hand to Russia scheme. This envisioned Allied armies landing in Istria — the Armpit — slicing through the Ljubliana Pass into the Danube plain to capture Prague and Vienna. This would not only help Russia (the Right Hand) but also forestall the occupation of Central Europe by the Red Army. Even after the invasion had started Churchill still pressed for a shift of the main effort away from

France to Armpit and so cabled FDR. The president dismissed it and on June 29 the proposal was formally rejected at a meeting of the Joint Chiefs of Staff.

Nor was Stalin convinced that the Allies would honor their word this time either. On the evening of June 5 he received a message from Churchill that the invasion would start at dawn next day. Dining with Milovan Dijlas that night Stalin remarked to his guest, "Yes there will be a landing if there is no fog. Until now there was always something that interfered. I suspect that to-morrow there will be something else. May be they will meet up with some Germans. What if they meet some Germans?" (Dijlas, 390). But America's interest was now at stake and, furthermore, FDR faced an election that fall and needed a military victory to secure a fourth term and so the invasion was going to take place after all, not on the 1st of May to be sure, but a month later.

* * *

Four years after Hitler squashed the French army the Western Allies returned to France in force. The place chosen for a landing was Normandy, halfway along the English Channel. A special staff, code named *Cossac*, had been planning the invasion since March 1943 and in December Eisenhower had been appointed supreme commander.

The campaign plans for the conquest of France visualized that after the initial lodgment the right wing of the Allied armies would head for Cherbourg, Brest and the Loire river ports, that is west and south; while the left wing would face off the German armies to the south and southeast. The first mission was assigned to American troops placed on the west end of the bridgehead, closer to the supply ships coming from the USA; while the eastern end would be manned by British and Canadian troops. No *coup-de-main* was planned against a major port, perhaps a lesson of the failed Dieppe raid. The landing was to be assisted by formidable air and naval armadas as well by paratroop, glider, and commando formations. To deceive the enemy as to the landing site a fictitious army headquarters was set up in Kent, opposite Calais. It was ostensibly the 1st American Army Group under Patton, larger than the 21st Army Group scheduled for the actual landing. Another fictitious force, the VII British Corps, was installed in Scotland to pose an invasion threat to Norway. While the latter did not deceive the Germans, the ghost army in Kent fulfilled its role, not only on D-Day, but for weeks thereafter. Since the supreme commander was an American, this was compensated by appointing Englishmen for all three subordinate commands: Montgomery on land, Ramsay at sea, and Leigh-Mallory for air. Particularly grating to the Americans was the appointment of Montgomery to command all land forces. This did last so that after the initial lodgment Bradley was given command of the American forces and Montgomery of Commonwealth troops only, both reporting to Eisenhower.

The forces assembled for the invasion were awesome. These included:

- 12,000 aircraft, 5,100 of them bombers and 5,400 fighters.
- At sea were 1,213 warships and 4,126 landing craft which together with ancillary vessels constituted a fleet of 7,000 ships, 80 percent of them British.
- The land forces were to number 2.88 million men including 45 full-strength divisions heavily armored, all motorized. By D-Day+ 90 the Americans alone were to have on land 1.2 million men.

Since initially no major port was to be invested, artificial harbors, called mulberries, were constructed. Each harbor consisted of 200 major elements weighing .75 million tons.

The parts were towed across the Channel and assembled at the landing sites, one at St. Laurent for the Americans, and one at Avranches for the British troops. An underwater pipeline was laid to pump motor fuel to the troops on land.

The preliminaries to the invasion saw the most grueling bombing of the enemy's transportation system and fuel facilities, assisted to some degree by the sabotage activities of the French underground. For this purpose Eisenhower was in April given the Allies' Strategic Air Force. Prior to the Allied bombing offensive the Germans in France ran 100 supply trains a day; by the end of May this had fallen to 20 and to less than that after D-Day (Mitcham 2001, 41).

Facing this armed might was a German army debilitated in manpower and crippled by severe shortages. When the invasion in the West became a serious threat Hitler sent in Rommel to take command of the troops facing the British Isles. While the overall commander in the West was Rundstedt, Rommel's group in northern France was designated AGB. It had two armies; the 7th, extending from the Loire estuary to eastern Normandy, and the 15th, embracing the rest of northern France and the Benelux countries. The total number of divisions in AGB was 42, including six Panzer divisions. For once the British strategy of "dispersion" paid off. Excluding Russia, the 42 divisions facing the English Channel constituted only a third of the total German strength on the continent. When the invasion came, most of the available German manpower, lodged from the Arctic Circle to the Greek islands, was not involved in combat. They were there merely as a result of Hitler's rapacious extension of rule every which way. When it was suggested to quit some of these areas and transfer the forces to France Hitler refused. In late 1943 his own OKW recommended pulling the front in Italy back to the Alps and transferring the released divisions to France (Harrison, 151–2). Rommel wanted to evacuate southern France and transfer the troops, which included three Panzer divisions, north; he also wanted to bring back the 35,000 men from the Channel Islands. Hitler brushed all these suggestions aside.

The small number of available divisions was only one of several problems facing the Germans. The second was the quality of the troops. Essentially France had become a sort of a sanitarium for soldiers after their ordeal on the eastern front, brought there to recoup and be reequipped. But as the fighting in the East intensified the army, as soon as groups of soldiers recovered, yanked them out of their units and shipped them piecemeal to the East. Consequently the divisions stationed in France were in a permanent state of disrepair. In addition the forces in the West contained what the Germans disparagingly called "ear and stomach" formations, men with ailments invalided out of the services but recalled to fill in the gaps. Some of these units the army called Whipped Cream troops because they required special diets to keep going. Then there were whole regiments made up of conscripted non–Germans not, as the phrase has it, of "doubtful" but of a very "definite" loyalty, certainly not to Germany. They were Poles from the annexed Polish territories forced to enlist; Russian POWs who enlisted to escape death by starvation; and an assortment of Uzbeks, Tatars, Chechens, Azerbijanis and Mongols whose aim in joining was to desert to the Allies. In September to October 1943, 45 battalions of these eastern troops were transferred to France, so that by May 1944 the 7th Army that faced the Normandy invasion had in its ranks 17 percent of Ostruppen (Harrison, 146). Furthermore, the few sound divisions that were in France were woefully short of motorized transport and they, as well as the Luftwaffe, suffered severe fuel shortages which affected not only operations but also their training.

The third dilemma, never resolved, was a proper strategy to meet the invasion. This had two aspects. One was to correctly anticipate where the Allies would land; the other was the proper positioning of the available forces. The two suspected locations were Normandy and Pas-de-Calais. Rommel changed his mind several times and so did some other experts. Hitler stated his views in the usual authoritative manner. On March 20, addressing his commanders, he predicted a landing in Brittany and Normandy and gave his usual admonitions about the significance of the forthcoming battle: "The enemy's entire invasion operation must not, under any circumstances, be allowed to survive longer than hours, at the most, days.... Once defeated the enemy will never again try to invade.... For one thing it will prevent Roosevelt from being re-elected.... The 45 divisions that we now hold in Europe ... are vital for the Eastern Front and we shall then transfer them to revolutionize the situation there.... So the whole outcome of the war depends on each man fighting in the west" (Mitcham 1993, 31–2). Subsequently, Hitler switched his prognosis to Calais and would stick to it even after the Normandy invasion had taken place, calling it a feint.

The other issue was how to deploy the available forces. There was no question about the so-called static divisions, troops dug in along the coast that could be used only in positional defenses. But there was a serious discrepancy of views of what to do with the motorized and Panzer divisions. Rommel was a determined advocate of stationing them in the vicinity of the landing site arguing, as did Hitler, that the invasion must be defeated at the very beginning; in addition he forecast that given the overwhelming superiority of the enemy's air forces the Germans would be unable to move troops from the interior to the coast. Others thought that given the uncertainty of the Allies' landing location it was mandatory to keep the main fighting troops back and move them once the landing took place; they also feared having the best troops exposed to naval gunfire. Guderian, the Panzer expert, wanted the armored units in the rear. Hitler's views seemed to coincide with Rommel's but stemmed from different motives. He scotched any plans that implied a possible success of the invasion — it was defeatism to even consider it. It followed therefore that success must be achieved on the very beaches where the enemy landed. Rundstedt on the other hand, considered that, given the superiority of the German mobile troops, the counterattack should take place only after the Allies had reached the environs of Paris. Thus whatever reserves were assembled, Rundstedt kept them near his headquarters, southeast of Paris. These originally comprised nine Panzer divisions, nearly all the available armor. Following Rommel's protests three of these divisions were moved to the boundary of the 7th and 15th armies so they could reach either of the two suspected locations— Normandy or Calais (see Fig. 33.1). Eventually, OB West was left with a reserve of six army and four Panzer divisions—a compromise satisfying neither of the two strategic options. These reserves were not to be moved without Hitler's permission.

In addition to their weakness on land the German forces were practically devoid of naval and air support. Neither their navy nor the Luftwaffe could interfere with the steady flow of supplies to the invaders nor with the concentration of the Allied troops for a break-out from the beachhead. They also had no planes to defend themselves against the nearly permanent umbrella of fighter-bombers over their own lines which not only prevented any major movement by rail or road but wrecked any single vehicle that ventured out during daylight. And if all this was not enough, whatever the Germans planned or did was immediately known to the Allies via *Ultra*.

* * *

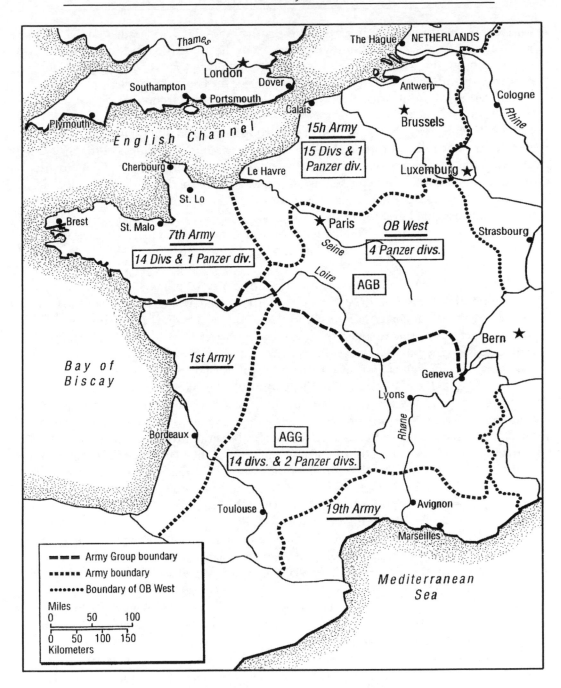

33.1. Disposition of German forces in France in June 1944

Hidden in the predawn mist of June 6 an armada of 5,000 ships was edging its way toward the coast of Normandy. Tucked in among the thousands of transports were nine battleships, 23 cruisers, 124 destroyers and 71 corvettes (Hastings 1984, 80). Abreast hundreds of minesweepers cleared the waters of the mine fields the Germans had laid almost to the middle of the English Channel. Overhead thousands of aircraft kept vigil so that not a single German plane detected the convoys. Hundreds of patrol boats scurried about to insure that no enemy vessel wandered into the path of the ships. The weather was bad, clouds covered most of the sky, a 20-knot wind blew from the west lifting five- to six-foot waves over the choppy sea — the tail end of a gale that had nearly cancelled the expedition. But they were now underway, soon to be within sight of the French coast ahead.

The sailing of the invasion fleet was preceded by airborne troops dropped at the flanks of the projected beachhead. Two American air divisions, 13,000 men strong, were flown over by 850 transports; the 5,000 British paratroopers were on 400 transports. The British troops jumped at midnight, their mission to secure the area and bridges of the river Orne in the east; the American troopers, landed an hour later, were to hold the major crossroads at the base of the Cotentin peninsula in the west. Though the British units landed on the assigned spot while the Americans were scattered as far 30 miles afield, neither of them fulfilled their assigned missions. Their unintended impact was to induce confusion and chaos in the enemy garrisons which did not know what to make of it. The Americans' main achievement was to secure the town of St. Mère Eglise which they held till the ground troops arrived.

The first wave scheduled to land in Normandy consisted of 130,000 Allied troops. The 55-mile long stretch of beach to be invested was divided into five sectors — Utah and Omaha in the west were the American sectors, and Gold, Juno and Sword were British. The landings took place at low tide to avoid the underwater obstacles erected by the Germans. One division was assigned to each sector except that Omaha was given two divisions. Covered by a barrage of naval guns and rockets the first troops landed at 6:30 A.M. There was only light resistance at all sectors, except for the landing on Omaha, which almost failed to come off. At one point Bradley was even contemplating canceling the operation. The difficulties on Omaha were due to terrain and the presence there of an undetected extra German division. The Omaha landing strip was a narrow pebbly beach abutted landward by steep bluffs, the curving strand shut off on both ends by cliffs, almost like Dieppe. At the center of the strand the distance from the water to the bluffs was 200 yards, at the corners a mere few yards. Even before they reached land and when ashore the invaders were met by withering fire from the German 352 Infantry Division which had come there for maneuvers. It took most of the day before, due to the initiative of small groups of men, the troops made their way over the bluffs to get at the enemy. While casualties on Utah among the 23,000 troops were 19, on Omaha they were over 2,000. Though isolated from each other and short of their objectives, by the end of the day all landed divisions had secured a lodgment on the Normandy coast (Hastings 1984, 88).

At the disposal of the Allies on D-Day were 5,000 bombers screened by 5,400 fighters and fighter-bombers. While they could not directly assist the fighting on the beaches because of the proximity of enemy and friendly forces, they hammered away at the rear gun positions and prevented any supplies and reinforcements from reaching the Germans. In the hinterland they destroyed highway bridges and railroad crossings leaving the defenders in Normandy isolated. Two single German fighters braved the air screen on D-Day, strafed one of the beaches, and managed to get away. All other German intruders were either shot down or turned tail.

The cost to the Allies of the first day of the invasion was 4,650 casualties among the 55,000 American troops landed as well as 1,240 among the 23,000 American airborne troops. The total casualties for the Allies were 9,500 of 150,000 men that went ashore, or a little over 6 percent. The pre-invasion estimates were that the casualties would be anywhere from 20 percent to a third of the invading force (Nofi, 127).

D-Day, June 6, 1944. American troops disembark at Normany from a coast guard landing craft. (Courtesy the National Archives.)

* * *

Due to the scattered landings of the airborne troops, the first reports of a possible invasion started coming in before the Germans spotted the Allied fleet. At 4:45 A.M. the 7th Army notified AGB headquarters that "a large-scale enemy assault" was about to take place. When the naval bombardment started both the 15th and 7th Armies informed AGB about the impending landings. At 5 A.M. Rundstedt ordered the Panzer divisions assigned to Rommel as his reserves to be ready to move up, but when he so informed OKW, it countermanded the order, afraid to authorize it without the führer's approval. And the führer was asleep with no one daring to wake him — of which more later on. The deterioration of the garrison troops in France seemed to have affected their commanders as well. At 21 Panzer the incoming British gliders were immediately spotted. Its commander, General Feuchtinger, was away — reputedly spending the night with a woman — and the staff of the division failed to move its headquarters to an operational location. The chief of staff of the entire AGB, General Speidel, at La Roche Guyon, Rommel's fancy headquarters near Paris, was exploiting Rommel's absence to invite a number of officers for dinner and drinks. After dinner Speidel received a report from 15th Army stationed near Calais of the BBC's signal to the French underground about the start of the invasion and that the army had been put on alert. When Rundstedt was asked whether the 7th Army in Normandy, too, should be alerted the answer was no. When von Salmuth, commander of the 15th Army, was told about the start of the naval bombardment he asked his staff whether they could handle the situation and when told yes he went to bed — this on the morning of D-Day. So did Speidel and the rest of the guests at La Roche Guyon. Moreover, General Dollman, commander of the 7th Army, wanting to keep his troops in good mettle, had ordered a map exercise to which he had summoned all divisional and regimental commanders. Thus only General Pemmel, chief of staff, was left with the 7th Army — just as Speidel was alone in charge of the entire AGB. Of the two 7th Army divisional commanders who were away on D-Day, von Schlieben did not reach his headquarters till noon and Falley was killed on the way by Allied paratroopers. But the most conspicuous absentee from the battlefield was Rommel. June 6 was his wife's 50th birthday and he went home to celebrate. He also intended to see the führer at the Berghof to once again plead for reinforcements. Before leaving he checked the weather report and when told a storm was expected, he left early on June 4 for home in Herrlingen.

There was complacency, if not negligence, within the German leadership as a whole. Admiral Krancke had scheduled patrols in the Channel for the night of June 5 but when reports came in of the blowing storm he cancelled them. Göring, who had been shifting fighters from the West to Germany, withdrew on the eve of the invasion a whole fighter wing from Metz where it had been within range of Normandy. When Gestapo agents who had infiltrated the French underground reported to Dönitz about the agreed-upon invasion signals from the BBC, Dönitz ignored it. The same BBC messages were intercepted by the intelligence officer of the 15th Army which he passed on to both OB West and the OKW. Gen Jodl did nothing assuming OB West would attend to it; OB West did nothing assuming AGB would handle it — all this with the invasion hours away (Mitcham 1983, 54). And it is reported that when the approach of gliders was reported, Rundstedt dismissed it saying they were probably "seagulls."

But, as always, the darkest shadow over the German response was cast by Gröfaz. As was his custom Hitler, at his Berghof hacienda, went to bed late, probably just as the invasion fleet halted off the French coast. He was there expecting the next day to meet with the Hungarian foreign minister, Sztojay. He had important business to settle with him — rumors about Hungary intending to desert his new Europe; and, more important, the problem of Hungary's 800,000 Jews, the one unscathed Jewish community still left in Europe which Hitler intended to exterminate. It wasn't till 9:30 A.M. when Eisenhower had officially broadcast the news about the invasion that Hitler's entourage at Bertchesgaden became perturbed at Hitler's long nap. Thus at 10 o'clock General Schmundt, Hitler's faithful adjutant, woke the führer. He was not particularly distressed at hearing the news and ordered the general to summon Jodl and Keitel. He then left for Klessheim Castle to meet the Hungarian minister. The OKW staff officers, maps and bulletins under their arms, trooped after him to the castle. At 2 P.M. they finally got a chance to discuss the situation. Hitler's comportment at this conference contains revealing details. According to Warlimont, who was present at the conference, Hitler "as he came up to the maps chuckled in a carefree manner and behaved as if this was the opportunity he had been awaiting to finally settle accounts with the enemy" (Warlimont, 427). He then authorized the release of the two Panzer divisions the OKW had previously vetoed. By then the weather had cleared and the Allied air force made it impossible for them to move, so that it was not until June 8 that they reached the battlefield.

Hitler's reaction to the Normandy landing and Rundstedt's own procrastinations were partly due to their belief that Normandy was a feint and the main assault yet to come would be at Calais. At 7 P.M. Jodl telephoned OB West that the Normandy landing should be "cleaned up" with what was at hand because, said Jodl, "According to the reports I have received, it [Normandy] could be a diversionary attack.... I do not think that this is the time to release the OKW reserves" (Mitcham 1983, 67). What, of course, was at stake was not just that the OKW reserves near Paris were held back but that the 15th Army, more powerful than the 7th fighting in Normandy, was kept idle waiting for a phantom force to come across Pas-de-Calais.

* * *

The tactical objectives of the wings of the invasion forces were for the Americans to capture Cherbourg and for the British to take Caen and debouch into the flat country south suitable for tanks and the building of airfields. In overall terms Bradley's troops fulfilled their mission, though not as speedily as hoped for, while the left wing, despite many attempts, failed in its mission. One of the reasons for this development was that the Germans considered the left wing — closer to Paris and Germany itself — the more critical sector and placed their main strength in that area. The British faced 14 divisions, seven of which were armored with 600 tanks; the US front faced nine divisions, two of them armored possessing 100 tanks. But there were also other reasons, which eventually led to a serious crisis between Eisenhower and Montgomery.

Two days after D-Day the Americans and the British linked up their sectors just north of Bayeoux and in another two days Omaha and Utah beaches were joined. By June 12 the various landing sectors had formed a solid beachhead 90 miles long. The Americans then launched their drive into the Cotentin peninsula. In about a week they had cut it in half isolating Cherbourg and its defenders. Holding off the Germans to the south the Americans began their drive on the port city. They made good progress over open country but the city with its fortress put up a stout resistance. Still, two weeks after launching their offensive, on June 27, Cherbourg capitulated. The success was only half a success. Immediately after the invasion the Germans began to demolish the port facilities and they did it with such thoroughness that experts considered it the greatest wrecking job in history. The basin where Atlantic liners used to dock was filled with 20,000 cubic yards of masonry for which Hitler awarded Admiral Hennecke, in charge of the operation and taken into captivity, the Knight's Cross. While some usage of the port was made within a couple of weeks it never fully served the Allies' needs. With the Cotentin peninsula in American hands the beachhead by the end of June contained a little under a million troops and 177,000 vehicles. The ratio to Rommel's forces was 3:1 with the Allies increasing their strength at a rate of two to three divisions per week.

The two Panzer divisions Hitler had sent to the beaches with the order to "clean them up" suffered a severe defeat, the 12th Panzer being nearly destroyed in the process. Rundstedt and Rommel had been pressing Hitler to review the situation and come to some appropriate decision. On June 16 Hitler summoned both feldmarschalls to Margival, a western Wolfschanze he had built himself in 1940, ostensibly to oversee the invasion of England. It took Rommel 21 hours to get from Normandy to his HQ near Paris and from there he had to endure a 140-mile ride over damaged roads to reach Margival. The next morning Hitler and Jodl arrived. Speidel, who was present at the conference, described Hitler as looking pale and ill, wearing spectacles and playing nervously with a pack of colored pencils. He sat hunched on a stool while everybody else, including the geriatric Rundstedt stood around. He denounced both his feldmarschalls, holding them responsible for the success of the invasion. As usual Rundstedt did not face up to his commander in chief and turned the presentation over to Rommel who in frankness made up for both of them. Rommel described the situation as hopeless, and predicted the course of events in France as follows: a breakthrough from the direction of Caen and Cotentin in the direction of Paris with a second operation in the direction of Avranches to cut off Brittany, the German army incapable of stopping these operations. He also stated that, contrary to the führer's belief, there would be no landing at Calais and demanded operational freedom to withdraw the armies eastward, though even for this it was perhaps too late. Except for Caen it was a pretty accurate forecast.

Hitler dismissed all he had heard and announced that "We have only to keep our heads.... Hold the enemy in the East, defeat him in the West. If we ward off the invasion Britain will sue for peace under the effect of the V weapons." The two feldmarschalls requested that the V weapons, which had started falling on London a few days earlier, be rather directed at the landing sites and at least on the embarkation ports in southern England. Hitler vetoed it saying he wanted to destroy London to make England sue for peace. Rommel then came up with the ultimate sacrilege. Turning to the political situation he said that the fronts would collapse both in the East and West unless Hitler sued for peace, whereupon a flushed Hitler retorted, "Don't you worry about the future course of the war but rather about your own invasion front." The conference lasted seven hours ending with Hitler's admonition that victory would be gained by "holding fast tenaciously to every square yard of soil" (Mitcham 1983, 101–3).

On June 29 Hitler called another conference at the Berghof. It is not clear why — perhaps because of the death of General Dollman, who had died of a heart attack just when the führer intended to shuffle commanders in the West. Keitel, Jodl, Rundstedt, Rommel, von Kluge and, ominously, Goebbels and Himmler were asked to attend. When Rundstedt arrived at the Berghof he was kept waiting six hours, making that Prussian mannequin moan that he might go down the way Dollmann did. To this fairly large audience Hitler expounded on his latest strategy for the West. It was no longer throwing the enemy into the sea, the failure of which he had warned would amount to the war being lost. Given the air superiority of the Allies, he observed, "We must not allow mobile warfare to develop.... Thus everything depends on our confining him to his bridgehead ... fighting a war of attrition ... using every method of guerrilla warfare." Confounded by this strategic lesson, Rundstedt and Rommel twice requested a private meeting. Hitler wouldn't do that, but agreed to hear them out in front of the gathered audience, hoping to avoid a confrontation similar to that of June 17. But it turned out to be even more dramatic.

When Rundstedt passed up to Rommel the honor of presenting their case, the latter began, "I am here as Commander of AGB ... [but] I should like to begin with our political situation. The entire world is arrayed against Germany ..."

"Feldmarschall," Hitler cut in, pounding his hand on the table, "please stick to the military situation."

"Mein Führer," Rommel persisted, "history demands of me that I should deal first with our overall situation."

"You will deal with your military situation and nothing else," Hitler ordered.

After hearing out the military report, Hitler reprimanded Rommel for failing to relieve

Cherbourg as he had commanded; he informed Rundstedt that the AGB would not be allowed to retreat behind the Seine; southern France would not be evacuated as OB West had recommended; and Rommel would not be given the 15th Army divisions because they would be needed when the real invasion came. Hitler then passed on to a vision of a rain of V-1s and V-2s bringing the enemy to his knees. When it was over Rommel again asked the führer point-blank how he imagined the war would be won and turned to Goebbels and Himmler, who before the conference had promised Rommel their support. But they, as well the other dignitaries, remained stone silent. Rommel turned back to Hitler. "Mein Führer, I must speak bluntly; I can't leave here without speaking on the subject of Germany."

"Feldmarschall," Hitler retorted, "be so good as to leave the room. I think it would better that way."

The consequences of this exchange came swiftly. On July 2, two days after this encounter, Rundstedt was dismissed and replaced by von Kluge. General Schweppenburg of OB West reserves was likewise dismissed. As Rommel witnessed these proceedings he was heard to say, "I will be next." But his fate was to be much more tragic (Harrison, 445–7; Mitcham 1983, 123–4).

* * *

From the Allied standpoint everything was proceeding smoothly except for Caen. Before the invasion Montgomery, musing about his assigned combat zone, spoke in his usual swaggering style. In a memorandum, a copy of which he sent to Churchill, the main emphasis, he said, would be "a rapid armored penetration after the landing" for which he stressed he was "prepared to accept any risk in order to carry out these tactics"; and he promised Bradley to reach Falaise on D-Day in order "to knock about a bit down there" (Hastings 1956, 56). The goal for his troops was a line 32 miles inland including Caen, an important road junction. Caen, only 10 miles from the coast, was not taken. According to German accounts, on D-Day the city was not defended in strength and such troops as there were escaped under the cover of darkness. Even the next day, June 7, "the city and the whole area could be taken within a few hours." Instead, the penetration of the British bridgehead on D-Day was three to six miles deep (Mitcham 1983, 72, 76).

After hunkering down Monty later launched three offensives to capture Caen. The first one was Epsom on June 25. One objective was Hill 112, a dominating position southwest of Caen, but neither Hill 112 nor the city were taken. On July 8 he launched a bigger assault, code named Charwood. For this he asked for and received the support of Bomber Command. On the night of July 7, 450 heavy bombers plastered Caen in a bombardment reminiscent of Monte Cassino. The city of Caen, heavily damaged, suffered large civilian casualties but little harm was done to the Germans. Afraid to strike their own lines the planes bombed far behind the German positions. While by July 10 a part of the city was captured, the British did not succeed in breaking into open country. The third offensive, Goodwood, launched on July 18, was a veritable bludgeon involving nearly a quarter million men. The plan was for three armored divisions to surge down a corridor blasted for them by a massed bomber stream, the objective initially being Falaise. On the morning of July 17 a two-hour air attack took place which was till then the greatest tactical bombardment in history. A thousand British and 1,500 American heavy bombers, followed by 600 medium bombers and 2,000 fighters blasted an 8,000-yard sector with 12,000 tons of bombs. Naval guns and

720 artillery pieces added their fire. In anticipation of the attack Rommel had set up five defensive lines, leaving in front the infantry but its heavy weapons and tanks in the rear. Though heavy losses were inflicted by the carpet bombing when the British Armored Corps rushed into the "corridor" they met such fanatical resistance that the offensive was halted on the first day (Mitcham 1983, 148–9). There was one notable casualty among the Germans. On the eve of battle Rommel's car was hit by one of the prowling fighters; Rommel was severely wounded in the head and face and had to be evacuated home.

It was a painful defeat for Monty. While the Canadians did take the rest of Caen, the ridges to the south remained in German hands. There was no breakout from the confines of the bridgehead into open country. In the battle the British lost 400 tanks, a third of their armored strength, in addition to 5,500 casualties. After the three offensives the tactical situation around Caen remained essentially unchanged.

Montgomery was a pedestrian general who refused battle unless he had a crushing superiority of men and munitions and who, after a breakthrough, shied away from inflicting defeat on the enemy; he preferred the role of an aging dog trailing his wounded quarry from the safest possible distance. So it was in Libya, in Sicily, in Calabria and now in Normandy. What made it worse was his bunkum talk and distortion of the facts. Had he stuck to the reality that the Germans' armored strength along his sector had prevented the British from achieving major successes it would have been understood and perhaps accepted. But no! The reason he gave for the lack of success at Caen was that his mission was to "attrite" the Germans or, alternatively, to "pin" them down so as to permit the Americans to win their battles. This being familiar Montyswagger, his reputation after Goodwood took a dive. Eisenhower fumed in private; Tedder considered Montgomery's use of strategic bombers to have been a deception; and in Brooke's words, "Churchill felt that Monty played for safety and was not prepared to take risks." Eventually Eisenhower felt compelled to meet with him in private. From the recorded remarks it seems that as another justification for failure Montgomery cited the British reluctance to incur casualties, to which Eisenhower replied that "while we have equality in size [of troops] we must go forward shoulder to shoulder with honors and sacrifices equally shared" (Hastings 1984, 240). On August 1, after the Americans had staged their breakout from the bridgehead, the command over American troops was taken from Monty and transferred to Bradley, who now commanded two armies, the 1st under Hodges and the 3rd under Patton. Monty's command was restricted to British contingents.

Since the left wing of the Allied forces was stuck at Caen it fell to the American forces to attempt a breakout for the conquest of France. The plan was for the 1st Army to attack from around St. Lo while Patton's activated 3rd Army was given a twofold mission: wheel into Brittany and seize the Atlantic ports of St. Nazaire and Nantes, and shield the 1st Army's drive in the direction of Paris. It was, of course, anticipated that Monty's 12th AG would join the Americans in the drive across northern France.

The American offensive, code named Cobra, started on July 25. It was preceded by a tactical bombardment by 1,600 Flying Fortresses primarily against the Lehr Panzer Division. When the next day von Kluge sent a messenger to its commander, Bayerlin, ordering him to stand fast, the general answered, "Out in the front every one is holding out.... My grenadiers and my engineers and my tank crews—they are all holding their ground.... They are lying in their foxholes mute and silent, for they are dead" (Mitcham 1983, 163). When reports started coming in that the German defenses were crumbling General Collins, commanding VII Corps, released his mobile divisions. Soon they were out of the bocage country that had given them so much trouble and von Kluge had to report to the führer that "Whether the enemy can still be stopped at this point is questionable." Pushing his way past the 1st Army, Patton on July 30 took Avranches, the pivot point to Brittany as well as to the southern periphery of the 1st Army's advance to the east. Here Patton staged his first major show. At Avranches there was only a narrow corridor between the sea and the Germans with a single road out of the city. Not put off, Patton pushed his entire 3rd Army through the bottleneck, managing to get two infantry and two armored divisions past it in 24 hours. He was soon in open country south of the 1st Army. Sending one corps into Brittany and the Atlantic ports, he wheeled left in the direction of the Seine and Paris, overtaking by a leap Hodges, busy fighting the German 7th Army. While on August 16 Patton took Charters and Orleans, 30–40 miles from Paris, Hodges' 1st Army was still 50 miles or more to the rear of him, see Fig. 33.2. Hodges was also meeting increasing resistance as the Germans were being squeezed between the British to the north and the Americans to the south into an oblong box which came to be known as the Falaise Pocket.

The semi-disaster that befell the Germans at Falaise was in large part due to Hitler; that it did not turn into a total disaster was due to Monty. After Patton's army broke through the Avranches gap, a tempting idea was to launch an attack from near Mortain in the direction of the sea and then not only would the 3rd Army be cut off, but the Germans would be behind the 1st Army, too—a strategic blow for all American forces. And this was what Hitler ordered, saying "We must wheel north like lightning and turn the entire enemy front from the rear." The fact that the Germans had no air force and that the three divisions assigned to the counterattack had only 145 tanks was ignored. During the evening of August 6, *Ultra* codebreakers deciphered the news about the impending attack, including the timing and disposition of forces, which was immediately passed on to Bradley. Hitler sent over General Buhle to make sure the attack was executed. After the attack was launched and its failure to advance was reported, an order from Rastenburg came for the attack to be resumed, "recklessly to the sea, regardless of risk … the greatest daring, determination and imagination must give wings to all echelons of command. Each and every man must believe in victory" (Mitcham 2000, 121). The next day the handful of German tanks were destroyed by swarms of fighter-bombers while Hodges' armored divisions struck the southern flank of the attacking Germans. It was over before it got going and the best the battered divisions could do was to join the 7th Army being squeezed into the Falaise box. Given the rapid advance of his troops, who reached Le Manson on August 8, Patton decided to give a hand to the 1st Army and instead of continuing east sent his XV Corps north toward the cauldron forming at Falaise. Patton's troops arrived at Argentan, the southeastern corner of the box, on August 13, three days before Hodges' army got there. The troops of AGB were now surrounded on three sides with a narrow escape open to the east. What was left to do was to close that door by a simultaneous attack by the British from the north and the Americans from the south.

The failure to close the Falaise cauldron harks back to Goodwood. That operation, launched on July 18, aimed at forming the northern steamroller for the pending Cobra offensive toward Paris. With the failure of Goodwood a new British offensive, Totalize, was planned specifically as the northern pincers of the Falaise Pocket. It started on August 7 just when Patton sent his troops north. After three days of fruitless fighting it was abandoned. It was then resumed on the 14th under the name Tractable just when Patton reached the outskirts of Argentan. The boundary between the two Allied armies had been set south of Argentan in the belief that by the time the Americans reached it the British would be

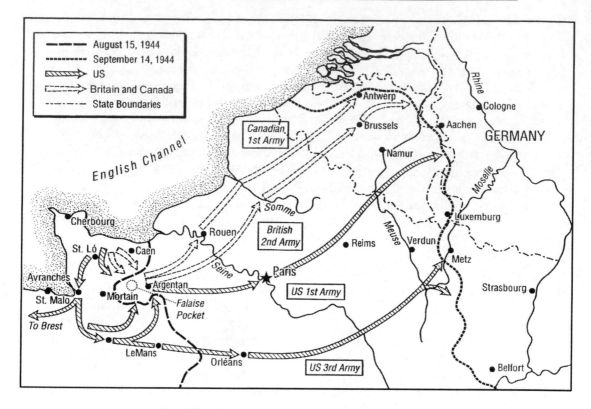

33.2 Allies' breakout into France, July–September 1944

there. But it was not to be. When the first troops of the 3rd Army reached Argentan the commanding general asked Patton's permission to continue north in order to "find" the British, whereupon Patton sent Bradley the sarcastic message, "We have elements in Argentan. Shall we continue and drive the British into the sea for another Dunkirk?" (Hastings 1984, 289). Bradley contacted Monty and suggested shifting the boundary line so that his troops could proceed north. Monty refused. Bradley then ordered Patton to halt at Argentan. By then Collins, released from dealing with the counterattack at Mortain, was heading east and the diary of the 1st Army records him as saying that he could take both Argentan and Falaise and close the pocket. He was told of Monty's refusal to adjust the boundary line and that he was not to go north of it. By then there was also a change of plans. Both Monty and Bradley now opted for a "wider" encirclement. The two Allies were now to close the pocket at Chambois, 10–15 miles east of Falaise. All this gave the Germans time to start a pell-mell escape from the encirclement. It was left to the Allied air force and the artillery north and south of the pocket to inflict grievous losses on the masses of German soldiery escaping through a hole only a few miles wide. Falaise became one the major fields of carnage and destruction inflicted on the German army. When the Americans finally took Chambois on August 20, the pocket was empty. Some 50,000 Germans were captured, 10,000 had been killed while anywhere from 20,000 to 40,000 escaped (Terraine, 662).

Far from the war in northern France were two German armies, the 1st facing the Atlantic, and the 19th guarding the Mediterranean, both under General Blaskowitz, commander in chief of AGG. As early as July Blaskowitz recommended evacuating southern

France and joining up with AGB; Soderstern, commanding the 19th Army, was of the same opinion; on August 8 both von Kluge and Speidel suggested putting AGG on the Seine-Loire line to help stem the avalanche of Allied armies heading toward Germany. Hitler rejected them all. Moreover, he ordered Blaskowitz to resist any invasion on the seashore even though his best divisions had been transferred north (Giziowski, 291–5).

On August 15 two Allied armies—the American 7th and the French 1st—landed at St. Tropez, encountering no resistance. By the end of the first day 86,000 men and 12,000 vehicles were ashore. Two days later AGG HQ received permission from OB West to withdraw north and join the retreating AGB. There was only one retreat route for the 19th Army—a narrow corridor along the banks of the Rhone River. By the end of August all German troops were in full retreat to the German border. On their heels were six Allied armies, four in the north and two coming up from the south.

As the Allies neared Paris a special command was established for the city under General Choltitz whose appointment was due to the fact that he "never questioned an order no matter how harsh it was." The general himself confessed that "since Sevastopol it has been my fate to cover the retreat of Armies and destroy the cities behind them"; this, of course was true for Russian cities but, as we shall see, it would be different for cities in the West. For the fulfillment of his assignment General Choltitz was summoned to führer Headquarters. After a long seminar about his role in the Nazi Party and past triumphs, Hitler in a semirage came to the point. "Since the 20th of July, Herr General, dozens of generals—yes dozens—have bounced at the end of a rope because they wanted to prevent me, Adolf Hitler, from continuing my work, from fulfilling my destiny of leading the German people." He then instructed Choltitz "to make Paris a frontline city ... to stamp out any civilian uprising" and ordered that Paris be made a fortress and suffer a corresponding fate. When Model informed OKW that Paris could not be held, the response that came down on August 11 was that "the Führer repeats his order to hold the defense zone in advance of the city.... The Seine bridges [more than 70] will be prepared for demolition. Paris must not fall into the hands of the enemy except as a field of ruin" (Mitcham 2000, 183–9). Choltitz, and with him the rest of the German command, ignored these orders despite Hitler's screams from far-off Rastenburg, "Is Paris burning yet?"

Paris fell on August 25 and all major French cities soon thereafter. The pursuit of the Allied armies was so swift that on September 2, Eisenhower, one day after he took over command of all ground troops, ordered a full halt because of severe shortages of fuel and supplies. Except for Alsace-Lorraine in the Rhine river bend the Allies were on the German border and on September 16 crossed it at Aachen. From the start of Cobra on July 25 the liberation of France took five to six weeks—about the same time as it took the Germans to vanquish it in 1940. Parallel to calling the Russian summer offensive a Barbarossa in reverse, one can also say that the Western Allies staged a reverse 1940 blitzkrieg.

A summation of the forces and casualties of this reverse French campaign yields the following numbers:

- Total Allied forces in France on September 16: 2.1 million men and 460,000 vehicles.
- Allied casualties: 224,000 including 40,000 dead. The ratio of US to British casualties was 3:2.
- German losses: half a million, including 80,000 dead; half of the casualties were POWs in Allied hands.

- 200,000 Germans remained bottled up in French coastal cities which Hitler had declared fortresses.
- For both fronts east and west the German losses over the three-month period July–August amounted to 1.2 million men.

CHAPTER 34

Loss of the Balkans

In the wake of the military defeats on the Russian and French fronts which brought the enemy to the eastern and western borders of Germany, the third collapse occurred in Rumania, bringing the Red Army close to the southern borders of the reich, as well. Though Rumania was properly a part of the Russian front, the repercussions of the collapse there were much wider, forcing the Germans to abandon the Balkans and bringing about the defection of the few remaining allies.

Rumania under Antonescu had been the staunchest of German partners and consequently paid the highest price. To remain Hitler's friend it had to yield up territory to Bulgaria and most of Transylvania to Hungary, the latter amounting to a national trauma. Its population of 20 millions decreased by 6.7 million, half of them ethnic Rumanians. By joining in the invasion of Russia it brought upon itself Britain's declaration of war on November 1941; and on December 12 it was forced to declare war on the USA. Its war on Russia cost the Rumanians 300,000 dead, an astounding death rate for the 20 divisions it had fielded. Of the 13 divisions employed at Stalingrad and the Don bend only a few battalions survived. The seven divisions evacuated from the Kuban bridgehead to the Crimea were cut off at the end of 1943, only part of which escaped. Much of this willingness to accommodate the Germans was due to Antonescu's feeling that the führer "liked" him. And indeed Antonescu saw Hitler more often than any other Nazi vassal. At the first meeting in November 1940 Hitler supported Antonescu's seizure of power in preference to the Nazi-like Iron Guard. In the first half of 1944 Antonescu met the führer three times. When he saw him at Klessheim on March 23, just after Hitler's first occupation of Hungary, he was told Rumania would now get back Transylvania and was promised that the Crimea would never be surrendered. The last meeting took place at the Wolfschanze on August 2–3 against the background of the July 20 attentat and the double defeats east and west. According to a witness (Gherghe, 398) Hitler met his guest with the question whether Rumania was going to stay in the war — yes or no? Though he had come determined to say no, Antonescu said yes. Shaken by his own spinelessness Antonescu suffered some sort of anxiety attack and began to gesticulate wildly, making the Germans laugh. In the evening Hitler, aware of Rumania's contacts with the enemy, would not attend dinner with his guest. As a result Antonescu, too, refused to eat and left for home.

As indicated in a previous chapter Rumania's attempts to leave the war go back to the autumn of 1942 when Foreign Minister Mihai Antonescu talked it over with the Italians. It was followed up by the dictator himself during a visit to Mussolini on July 1. The Rumanians clutched at the hope they could surrender to the Western Allies only but were told on January 16 that they must approach the Soviets. A few months later the Rumanian ambassador to Sweden broached the subject with Mme. Kollontai, Russia's envoy there. The conditions Moscow set down for an armistice were:

- Bessarabia and Bukowina to remain part of the USSR.
- Transylvania would be returned to Rumania.
- Reparations to be paid for damages caused by Rumanian troops.
- Rumania to switch sides in the war.
- Free movement for Red Army troops across Rumania for prosecuting the war.

On April 12 Rumania acceded to the terms. It then waited for an opportune moment to stage the coup (Hitchins, 496).

In midsummer 1944 the front in Rumania ran astride the Dniestr-Pruth-Sereth rivers. Army Group South Ukraine holding the front was manned in an alternate fashion by Rumanian and German troops. The commander of the front was General Friessner, dismissed, after only three weeks, from leading AGN where he had committed the cardinal sin of suggesting it be shifted for the defense of East Prussia instead of ending up surrounded in Kurland. When in July he took command of the Rumanian front Hitler assured him during a personal interview of two things: not to worry about the "political situation" as Rumania was the most steadfast of allies, and not to expect an offensive in his sector because "the Russians had expended all their strength against the AGC." Friessner commanded 47 German and Rumanian divisions with a total strength of 900,000 men, more than half Germans. After reviewing the situation Friessner wanted to withdraw the Army Group into the Carpathian ridge, which would not require large forces to defend. Months earlier Antonescu had recommended that they give up Bessarabia and withdraw into Transylvania in which he was supported by Schörner. Predictably Hitler vetoed all of this (Büchner, 244). Facing them were the 2nd and 3rd Ukrainian Fronts, under Malinovski and Tolbukhin, respectively, who together had some 930,000 men — not a great superiority in men but incomparably heavier firepower (Axell 1997, 109).

The Russian offensive opened at 6 A.M. on August 22 with a barrage of 4,000 guns. The main attack came near Jassy, where the front receded from the Pruth and ran almost in an east-westerly direction. The story of this battle is nearly a duplication of the Stalingrad fiasco, and, as will be seen, the defeat was of the same magnitude. The sectors the Russians attacked were held by Rumanian troops and these abandoned their positions as soon as the attack came. On the very first day Malinovski's troops rushed southward at an unprecedented pace. This was soon supplemented by an attack, 125 miles farther south across the Dniestr, by the 3rd Ukrainian Front, both prongs to meet behind the reconstituted German 6th Army. Eighteen German divisions were trapped and annihilated. Further west the 8th Army was likewise battered and remnants of it pushed into the Carpathians. On the 22nd Hitler gave permission for the 6th Army to be withdrawn but it was, of course, too late. On August 30 Malinovski took the Ploesti oil fields as well as Bucharest, completing the occupation of Rumania. The Russians took more than 100,000 prisoners; among the casualties were four generals killed and 18 captured (Hillgruber 1954, 352; Mitcham 2001, 200). The total German losses amounted to 270,000 men — a Stalingrad redux. In essence Army Group South Ukraine was destroyed as a fighting force.

On August 23, following the Russian breakthroughs, the young King Mihai brought in Antonescu and asked him to acquiesce in an anti–German coup. When he refused he was locked in a vault and later handed over to the Russians. A new government was installed and at 10 P.M. that day the Rumanians broadcast acceptance of the armistice terms, ordering the Rumanian army to cease operations against the Russians. When informed about the coup Hitler ordered Friessner to suppress it and arrest the king together with his "camarilla." Friessner, worried about extricating not only the fighting troops, but also the many hospitals, depots and noncombat personnel, responded that this was not possible as all Rumanian commanders were obeying the king's orders. Hitler then ordered the bombing of the royal palace and the government quarter while a contingent of 6,000 troops was to storm Bucharest and link up with its German garrison. He also ordered the engagement of the 40,000 strong paramilitary Volksdeutsche units in the country. However, unlike what happened later in Hungary, troops and civilians took to the streets, thwarted the takeover and held the city until the Russians arrived. On August 25 Rumania declared war on Germany and ordered its troops to join the Red Army. With the Russians on their heels the shattered and disoriented Germans now had to contend also with hostile Rumanians and the Carpathian Mountains blocking their retreat to the west. It was remnants of the 8th and 6th Armies that completed their arduous trek into Hungary, Croatia and on toward the Austrian border there to join the big German exodus from the Balkans.

The first collateral casualty was Bulgaria. Though Bulgaria allowed the use of its territory by the Wehrmacht and had participated in the dismemberment of Greece and Yugoslavia, it refrained, for historical and ethnic reasons, from joining the war on Russia. Nevertheless, when the Russian armies reached the southern borders of Rumania Moscow on September 5 delivered a note that, by assisting the Germans, Bulgaria had defacto been at war with the USSR and, therefore, the USSR was at war with Bulgaria and the country was swiftly occupied. Together with the occupation of Rumania this gave the Red Army a 500-mile long flank against German Army Groups F and E deployed across Greece and Yugoslavia. The thrust of the Red Army could now be directed either southward into Greece and Yugoslavia or northwest toward Hungary and Austria. There were a number of reasons why Stalin decided on the latter. By then he had a pretty clear idea what parts of Europe he would end up dominating and Greece was not one of them; in fact he was shortly to formalize it via the notorious slip of paper with Churchill which assigned Eastern Europe to Stalin and Greece to the British. As for Yugoslavia, Stalin deferred to Tito's partisans who, protected by the Red Army, could now proceed to take over the country. Aside from these political considerations Hungary was on the direct route to Vienna and the "beast's lair."

On the 2nd Ukrainian Front the Germans retreated to the Muresol River along the Carpathian chain slowing down Malinovski's troops. Stalin then transferred one army each from the 1st and 3rd Ukrainian Fronts to Malinovski with orders to shift his main effort south. This brought swift success and by the end of October Malinovski's troops were 60 miles southeast of Budapest, the Germans being forced to evacuate Transylvania. At the same time Tolbukhin, finished with Bulgaria, turned into Serbia and on October 20, together with the partisans, liberated Belgrade. He then joined Malinovski in the forthcoming battles for the capture of Budapest which, as discussed in the next chapter, offers another telling episode about Hitler's intentions in his conduct of World War II.

After Rumania's surrender and the disintegration of the German front there, Horthy dispatched a delegation to Moscow to negotiate an armistice. On October 11 both sides initialed a surrender document leaving to the Hungarians the time of its implementation. Hitler kept a close eye on these proceedings and dispatched two experts to Hungary, SS General von dem Bach Zalewski, a specialist on ethnic exterminations, and the commando wizard Colonel Skorzeny. When on the afternoon of October 15 Radio Budapest broadcast the armistice with the USSR the Germans simply took over the country. Accompanied by a small band of warriors Skorzeny rushed the royal palace and facing down a plethora of guards who did not lift a weapon or finger took Horthy prisoner. The total casualties amounted to seven men killed. Whatever he was then ordered to do, Horthy did. He appointed the Arrow Cross Party leader, Ferenc Szalasi, prime minister and he asked to be given asylum in Germany. With Horthy gone, Szalasi proclaimed himself nador, führer in Hungarian. Throughout the country, whatever army or government installation was impounded by the Germans, no resistance was offered by either the Hungarian army or police. With rare exceptions the Hungarian troops and their commanders stuck with the Germans. For the Hungarians the war was now to last to the end of the Third Reich itself, with miserable consequences for their cherished capital city, Budapest.

As early as November 1 Hitler had ordered that Budapest be defended not at, but beyond, all cost. As the Russians advanced on the city from east and south they faced a for-midable ring of semicircular defenses, anchored on the Danube River. When on November 3 the Russians broke into the ring's outer defenses, Hitler ordered that AG South Ukraine, renamed AG South (no more Ukraine), use all its forces to cut off the Russian penetration. For the next two days savage fighting raged in and around the city's perimeter coming to a stop only after the Russians ran out of ammunition (Ziemke 1968, 380). The reprieve did not last long. Shifting the main effort Tolbukhin assaulted and took Cse-pel Island, crossed the Danube and headed west on a wide loop to encircle Budapest from the rear. On November 26 he took Esztergon and linked up with Malinovski coming from the north At the time Budapest was encircled the city had 800,000 inhabitants plus 180,000 German and Hungarian troops with no provisions for food or fuel during the severe winter of 1944-45.

Friessner, of course, wanted to take all his troops across the Danube which meant abandoning the major part of the city east of the river. It was, naturally, refused, but merely to have suggested it was enough. On the night of December 22 Friessner was ordered to "immediately" hand over the Army Group to General Wöhler, commander of the 8th Army. Friessner wanted to know why and inquired of several people at the OKW for the reason. None of them knew. When Friessner insisted he wanted to hear the reasons from the führer the message he received was "*Der Führer dankt,*" whatever that meant.

* * *

Following the Italian surrender the Germans took control over the entire Balkan penin-sula with Maximilian von Weichs as commander in chief of all forces there. These con-sisted of two Army Groups: AGE under Löhr in charge of Greece and the adjacent islands, while AGF ruled the rest of the Balkans with Weichs, its commander, subordinate to him-self. Not counting the multiple Allied and collaborationist troops there were about 20 Ger-man divisions in the area. No steps were taken either by the OKW or Weichs to evacuate these troops in view of what was happening further north. When on September 2 Tolbu-khin crossed into Bulgaria and the latter declared war on Germany, the German army faced a 425-mile open eastern flank from the Aegean Sea to Hungary. In September they did start to withdraw by air and sea from the islands. This proceeded at a leisurely pace without inter-ference by the British fleet. The Allied air force was mostly busy, assisting Tito's partisans and the Soviets in their advance into Serbia. Likewise there was no interference from the Allied side when Löhr started withdrawing AGE from the Greek mainland. On the con-trary, there seemed to have been coordination in AGE's movement north and the follow-up by the British. The aim seemed to have been to forestall the takeover of the country by Communist partisans, the dominant force there, the non–Communists in Greece having long ago negotiated a truce with the enemy.

The story of this collaboration harks back to 1942. Dr. Hermann Neubacher had been Hitler's economic plenipotentiary for the Balkans and as such had extensive contacts with both German and indigenous authorities. At the end of 1942 he received a message from the Greek mayor of Athens that a high-ranking British Intelligence officer wanted to talk to the Germans. After receiving permission to do so Neubacher sent two representatives, one from the Secret Field Police and the other from the Abwehr, to meet the Allied officers at the mayor's house. The two came in uniform, a captain and a colonel, one of whom looked Greek. The gist of the British concern was that the Communist partisans in Greece were becoming too strong. One way to correct that would be to assure that the arms delivered to the partisans by British submarines ended up in non–Communist hands only. This was not official British policy, they emphasized, but that was the reason they had come. They promised to contact the Germans again but were never heard from. Further, according to Neubacher, when the Germans started evacuating Greece the British again sought to contact him, their concern being not to let the Communists take the place of the retreating German troops. Presumably British general Scobie himself was looking for Neubacher but, by then, he had left Greece (Neubacher, 203–4).

Even after the loss of Belgrade and Nis, which nearly cut the retreat route north, the AGE took its time withdrawing. Löhr, its commander, had at his disposal seven divisions on the mainland, three on the islands and six fortress brigades. He started evacuating Greece on August 23, cleared the Peloponnese in September, left Athens on October 13, and Saloniki on October 31. On November 1 he finally crossed the Greek border leaving behind on the islands 30,000 German troops who surrendered to the British. On October 10 the British started landing on the Peloponnese. The Germans moved north at the same pace it took the British to replace them, leaving no vacuum between the two armies. Nearly all of AGE reached safety in Croatia joining the AGF there. By the end of the year, barring a few pieces of foreign territory east and west, what was left of Hitler's empire in January 1945 was the German-Austrian-Czech *Lebensraum* he had had before he started the war.

Chapter 35

Raking the Ashes

As postulated in Chapter 31, from 1942–43 on Hitler continued the war, though aware that he had lost it. The summer of 1944, which brought the political and military collapses in Russia, France and the Balkans, saw Hitler busy implementing his *So oder So* (All or Nothing) agenda. Since the All had failed the job left was to attend to the Nothing. As with his presumed war-making on England in 1940 this was accompanied by dissimulation which by then could not have even fractionally succeeded had his audience been of a different intellectual and moral caliber. But these people were in 1944 the same as they had been in the past. The major part of the apocalypse — such as the extermination of Europe's Jews and a large fraction of the Russian population, including the bulk of Russian prisoners of war — had already been accomplished. He now directed the war in a way that would leave behind a maximum of slaughter and ruin on foreigners and his compatriots alike before he himself took off for Valhalla.

The most glaring evidence of his terminal handiwork was his command of the German army. On the last day of July when the AGC and AGN ceased to exist as fighting Army groups he told Jodl at the Wolfschanze, "I cannot for the moment see further than the problem of stabilizing the eastern front and I am wondering whether ... it is altogether a bad thing that we are, relatively speaking, being squeezed" (Baumbach, 146). During an inspection of new weaponry in December 1943 soldiers and officers complained that whereas the Russians were profusely equipped with submachine guns, German infantry still carried the heavy bolt-action Mauser 98 carbines from World War I. Hitler responded that he was against automatic weapons because they would diminish the troops' aggressiveness in combat (Speer, 319). It was no coincidence that under such different battle conditions as the forests of Byelorussia, the mountains of Rumania and the plains of France, the sins of omission and commission in his orders were tediously the same: no realignment or shortening of the front when facing an overwhelming superiority in men and weaponry; not a step backward during battle; orders to leave troops in "fortresses" until surrounded; staging offensives a priori doomed to failure; willful expenditure of lives, which for Hitler carried the bonus that he could fill the ranks with invalids, old men, and young boys — revving up the punishment on his people, since it was not he but they who had let him down. Consequently, whereas up to the middle of 1944 (58 months) Germany lost in the war 2.8 million dead, in the subsequent 10 months it suffered 4.8 million dead, a 10-fold increase in the death rate (Fest 1996, 3, 4).

One of his deceptions on the Germans was the promise of wonder weapons which would decide the war. Foremost was the V rocket. During the Normandy invasion Hitler was urged they be used against enemy concentrations, the ships offshore, or at least the embarkation ports in England. While there was some difficulty in doing this in that the V's would miss anything but large targets, the main reason for the refusal was, as the letter V for *Vergeltung* (Revenge) implied, that they were meant primarily to punish England. The effort that went into developing and producing these weapons was enormous; 200,000 workers were busy on the projects, ultimately producing 32,000 V-1s and 6,000 V-2s. The V-1s were unguided ballistic projectiles 25 feet long flying at 470 miles per hour carrying a one-ton warhead; 10,500 of these were fired of which over half hit England. While these were subsonic bombs which a fighter aircraft could frequently intercept, there was no defense against the V-2s. They were 50 feet long and flew above the atmosphere at a supersonic speed of 3,600 miles per hour. London was hit by 517 of these, other parts of England by 537. Together the V's destroyed 25,000 houses and damaged a quarter million. They caused over 10,000 dead and three times as many wounded. But even as a terror weapon the V's were ineffective. Even 5,000 of them, a five months' production, delivered only 3,750 tons of explosives; one large raid by Anglo-American bombers could deliver a good 8,000 tons (Calvocoressi, 558–9). Far from bringing the promised final victory this wonder weapon brought the Wehrmacht no relief whatsoever.

Another new tool was the jet aircraft Me-262. While far from being a "wonder" weapon it was a major advance on existing aircraft. It had a maximum speed of 524 miles per hour, a ceiling of near 37,000 feet, and a rate of climb of 4,000 feet per minute — performance characteristics superior to all existing Allied fighters. Produced in quantities it could have had a substantial impact on both the bombing by the Allies and over the invasion beaches. But in the midst of production Hitler suddenly ordered that the projected fighter be converted to a bomber — a catastrophic switch in terms of plane mission and production schedules. The reason for this change parallels the employment of the V rockets— terror rather than combat effectiveness— because Hitler intended to use the jet bombers to punish England. Not using the jet fighters in the defense of the cities had the additional advantage of punishing the civilians. In a talk with Hitler in the autumn of 1943 Speer reports, "Hitler was shaken less by the casualties among the populace or the bombing of residential areas than by the destruction of valuable buildings, especially theatres.... [He] seemed primarily interested in public architecture and seemed to give little thought to social distress and human misery. Consequently, he was likely to demand that burned-out theatres be rebuilt immediately" (Speer, 299).

While this destruction of the German army and German cities proceeded without letup, several extraneous events in 1944 enabled Hitler to expand on his apocalypse program. These were the July 20 attentat; the AK Uprising in Warsaw; and his moves attending the siege of Budapest.

* * *

The July 20 attentat on Hitler's life was only the last of a series of assassination attempts, none of which succeeded. This latest and most serious of the lot likewise failed to kill or even seriously hurt him. The convoluted history of the preparations, ideas, actions and nonactions taken by this group tells a tedious and fruitless tale. Since our main interest here is the handle that the putsch of July 20 gave Hitler to wreak vengeance on his compatriots, little of this history will be gone into. Still, from the overall perspective of World War II as it was waged by the German people it is worth noting the following: Unlike the proficiency, cunning and readiness to kill that characterized the Germans, whether in the army, police or as satraps in the conquered lands, the conspirators showed a remarkable talent for the opposite — inefficiency, procrastination, clumsiness and, lo and behold, moral scruples to kill — to kill a ghoul causing the death of millions. Part of the reason for this disarray was that they were not motivated by an organization with an established political platform. The more important blockage was the awesome awareness that they were acting against the emotions and beliefs of the bulk of the German people. They knew better than anybody how strongly the ordinary soldier and the man in the street admired and believed in Adolf Hitler — and that far from being heroes they would be condemned as renegades and traitors (this persisted even in the Bundesrepublik). This was a moral dilemma they never surmounted so that in the end only a severely crippled man was found willing to plant the bomb. It is thus not surprising that in a nation of some 80 million people those involved in the July 20 conspiracy counted fewer than 200 people, half of them officers.

What will be attended to here is an examination of the kind of men that made up this circle of plotters; what they envisaged after the overthrow of the Nazi regime; what were the reasons for their failure; and the revenge Hitler wreaked following the bomb plot. The circa 200 men involved did not come from any particular ideological, political or religious body. They were all individuals motivated by their own convictions. The only common denominator that can, perhaps, be attached to them is that they all came from the upper strata of German society; there was not a single bourgeois or proletarian member among them. Who were these men? What were their views on their country's recent history and the war ? What was their vision of a post–Nazi Germany? Table 35-1 lists the major figures involved in the bomb plot from which half a dozen names will be culled to illustrate the range of personalities and propensities involved.

Table 35-1
List of Major Paticipants in the July 20 Plot

Name (Age in 1944)	Position Held in 1944
Beck, Ludwig (64)	retired army chief of staff
Fromm, Friedrich (56)	head of Replacement Army
Gersdorff, Rudolph (39)	chief of staff 7th Army
Gisevius, Hans (69)	Abwehr
Gördeler, Carl (60)	retired mayor of Leipzig
Hellsdorf, Wolf (48)	Berlin chief of police
v. Moltke, Helmuth (37)	legal expert in OKW
Nebe, Arthur (50)	head of reich's Criminal Police
Oster, Hans (57)	Abwehr
Olbricht, Friedrich (56)	general in Fromm's office
v. Stauffenberg, Claus (37)	chief of staff in Fromm's office
Stülpnagel, Carl (58)	military commander in France
Tresckow, Henning (43)	chief of staff 2nd Army
v. Trott zu Stolz, Adam (35)	Foreign Ministry
Witzleben, Erwin (63)	retired feldmarschall

Gördeler, Carl: He was the outstanding civilian leader of the group, his opposition dating back to the prewar period. In 1935 he resigned his office as mayor of Leipzig in protest against the Nazis' shenanigans in the city. Had the coup succeeded he was scheduled to become chancellor. He was an outspoken opponent of the Soviet Union: when a plan was formed to send the former ambassador Schulenburg to Moscow across the front lines to deal with Stalin he vetoed it. He was also a proponent, one may say, of a *Grossdeutsche Reich*. He was against killing Hitler because the Bible says "Thou shalt not kill"; when he later heard of Stauffenberg's failure he said it was a "judgment of God." (Fest 1996, 305). Following are the demands— promulgated in January 1944 — regarding the borders the new Germany would insist on when the Hitler regime was overthrown:

1. In the East the 1914 borders were to be reestablished (the "Corridor," Warthegau, Silesia, etc.). As compensation, Poland would be told to annex Lithuania, solving its problem of access to the sea.

2. The Sudetenland and Austria to remain part of the reich.

3. South Tirol to be taken back from Italy.

4. With regard to Alsace-Lorraine two possibilities were offered: a.) Give the area independence, a second Switzerland, or b.) Partition along linguistic lines.

5. Denmark's area of Schleswig-Holstein must also be "solved" (Venohr, 264–5).

When he was interrogated after July 20 he spoke openly about the aims of the movement. Trusting that his honesty would impress the Gestapo, he implicated in the process many of his fellow plotters. Moreover, he insisted on talking to Hitler, convinced he could persuade the führer to reverse his policies. Because of his volubility he was kept alive till January 1945, months after most others had been executed.

Stauffenberg, Claus: A career officer and a practicing Catholic, Stauffenberg was the most determined activist of the group. Earlier he, as well as his two brothers, admired what the Nazis were accomplishing. He was a frequent guest at the Stefan George circle, a non–Nazi symbolist poet who advocated a life of spiritual loftiness to be found in a new reich led by exalted leaders. While a tolerant man, Stauffenberg considered that foreigners and Jews, being un–German, should be kept apart from German society. He supported Hitler's annexation of Austria and the Sudetenland and, initially, also the attack on the Soviet Union. This was consistent with his views then and later that the Russians should be fought while making peace with the Western Allies. The event that triggered his hatred of Hitler was Stalingrad when he told Feldmarschall Manstein that Stalingrad was not just a matter of a lost battle but of *Führungsystem*— a leadership problem and the war would be lost unless this leadership was changed (Venohr, 173). His personality was also affected by the wounds he received on April 17,1943, in North Africa: his right hand was mangled, the left had only three fingers left and he lost an eye over which he wore a dark patch. Fellow rebels described him as restless, moody, eager for a super act. Some of his mentality can be gleaned from the oath he drafted to be administered to the soldiers of the new Germany, which read in part, "We wish ... to make all Germans supporters of the state, guaranteeing them justice and right, but we despise the lie that all men are equal, and [we] accept the natural ranks. We wish to see a people with its roots deep in the soil of its native country.... We wish to see leaders from all classes of society, bound to the divine forces, taking the lead on the grounds of their high-mindedness, virtue, and spirit of self sacrifice" (Hoffmann, 321).

Count von Moltke, Helmuth: As the name implies Moltke came from the highest stratum of society and was a relative of the famous Moltke, the Warrior. He was a lawyer by profession and worked during the war as an expert in international law in the OKW. A very religious man he was a long-standing opponent of the Nazi regime and preached it freely. He was against the assassination attempt on both religious and ethical grounds. He was arrested even before the putsch but it was only then that the Gestapo learned of his involvement. From prison he wrote a number of letters to his wife which show that if Stauffenberg wafted somewhat of mysticism he was a mere novice compared to Moltke. Writing about his encounter with Freisler, the notorious Peoples Court judge, he said that Freisler refused to deal with facts but merely accused him of "defeatism" of which he Moltke is glad, since "this gives it a religious aspect. It gives us an inestimable advantage of being killed for something that (a) we really have done and (b) is worthwhile. All we did was think.... And it is before mere thoughts ... that National Socialism now so trembles" (Fest 1977, 315–6).

Nebe, Arthur: The Third Reich produced during World War II a record number of gruesome mass killers. But if one must single out those who can claim to have been at the head of this horde of butchers in the scale and sheer horror of the staged executions of hundreds of thousands of women, children and old men, it is surely the commanders of the four Einsatzgruppen that went into Russia with the task of executing all Jews living there. Arthur Nebe was one of them. Nebe, an SS general and head of Germany's Criminal Police, was one of the earliest members of the conspiracy circle, from 1938 on. In June 1941 he followed the German army as head of Einsatzgruppe B, that is the battalion in charge of killing the Jews behind Army Group Center. He saw no contradiction between his membership in the anti–Hitler cabal and his assignment; moreover several of the conspirators, among them Oster, a devout Catholic, urged him to take the job as this would provide good cover for his illegal activities.

Other figures loosely aware of the plot included most of the army's feldmarschalls—Rundstedt, Manstein, Kluge, Rommel, von Bock, as well as Speidel, Falkenhausen, Heusinger, Canaris, Halder and others. Like Gördeler and von Moltke, Halder said in 1948, "In the thinking of a German officer there are deep and serious qualms against the thought to shoot down an unarmed man [Hitler]" (DDR, XXI, 271). These men had another overriding "moral" scruple — violation of the oath they had taken to the führer. This weighed on them more than genocide and the destruction of Germany and none of them would commit themselves to an anti–Hitler plot, not to speak of assassinating him. Thus Manstein, "Prussian Feldmarschalls do not rebel," or von Bock, "I shall stand before the Führer and defend him against anyone who dares attack him" (Hoffmann, 271). But they all agreed that "something" had to be done to extricate Germany from the bind. Thus Beck, chief of state designate, and Gördeler submitted on April 12 via Allen Dulles in Switzerland a program for the Western Allies which specified that the opposition was prepared to negotiate with the West but under no circumstances with the Soviets. As part of the scheme the generals would assist the Anglo-Saxons in the liberation of France. A wider group involving Rundstedt, Rommel, Stülpnagel and Speidel proposed on May 24 to withdraw German troops behind the Siegfried Line, but in the East a defensive front would have to be formed from Lithuania to the Vistula and the Danube. There should, they demanded, be no dismemberment or military occupation of Germany at war's end (Hoffmann, 353). On June 16 Gördeler presented to the civilian member of the underground the following platform to be submitted to the Allies:

- immediate cessation of the bombing of Germany.
- Germany's borders in the east those of 1914.
- evacuation by the Germans of all conquered countries in the North, West and South.
- continuation of the war in the East.
- retention of a portion of the Sudetenland.
- autonomy for Alsace-Lorraine.
- no occupation of Germany (Venohr, 306).

During this meeting, Leber, the interior minister designate, objected to the retention of the Sudetenland and Alsace-Lorraine but all other participants sided with and adopted

Gördeler's proposals. Finally on July 8 — that is following the collapse of the eastern front and the Normandy invasion — a courier on behalf of the Stauffenberg group went to Switzerland with a proposal that Germany start liquidating the war in the West and withdraw all its divisions to the eastern front. There was no response from the Allies to any of the above proposals.

What is ironic about these offers is that the policies they advocated were distressingly close to the führer's own — peace with the West and war in the East against Russia. The difference was that the anti–Hitler Germans wanted to fight Russia presumably to save Germany from a Communist takeover — whereas the Hitlerian Germans wanted to "annex" Russia. Another aspect of the above peace feelers is their naiveté as to what was still open to Germany; they had no inkling how the outside world viewed Germany in 1944 and the revulsion everyone felt for their having gratuitously started another world war and for the manner in which they had waged it.

There are various indications that Himmler himself was an elusive party to the conspiracy. This evidence stems from his behavior at the time and from Himmler's known activities in the last months of the Third Reich. It is quite certain that Himmler's office was aware for some time of the conspiracy. He must have known, for example, about Gisevius' travels to Switzerland and Trott zu Stolz's to Sweden and England. The conspirators were quite careless in their dealings with each other and with men who rejected their approaches; conversations with men like Halder, Rundstedt and Canaris could not have escaped the Gestapo's notice. Thus Moltke was arrested as early as January, while Gördeler's arrest was planned long before July 20. After the putsch Himmler kept Gördeler alive for five months, one of the reasons being that Himmler had hoped to use him for negotiations with the Allies when he himself was ready for it — which happened only a few months later. Significantly, during the attentat on July 20, Himmler did not use his SS to squash the rebellion, waiting to see which side prevailed. And eventually he did contact the Allies, with Hitler disowning him and ordering his arrest.

Stauffenberg was the man who eventually performed the deed, primarily because there was no one else to do it. For this purpose he was posted on July 1 as chief of staff to the Replacement Army located at Berlin's Bendlerstrasse whose head was General Fromm, a member of the conspiracy. The posting had a two-fold purpose. One was that its representatives had to appear from time to time at the führer conferences in the Wolfschanze and Stauffenberg could be the man. The other reason was that the coup d'etat following Hitler's death was to be directed from the Bendlerstrasse in response to a presumed rebellion by the country's millions of foreign workers—code named Valküre. After a couple of cancellations the day that proved appropriate was July 20. On that day the conference was to start earlier than usual, at 12:30 P.M., due to the expected afternoon visit by Mussolini.

Stauffenberg left his office at 8 in the evening of July 19. In Dahlem he attended church for evening mass. He then met his brother with whom he spent the rest of the evening. He showed him the attaché case in which the bomb was hidden, wrapped in a clean shirt. At 6 A.M. July 20 he drove to Rangsdorf airfield, south of Berlin. A Ju-52 flew him and his adjutant, von Häften, to the Wolfschanze, landing there at 10:15 A.M. Häften carried the attaché case that contained two explosive packets. Stauffenberg went to the conference area carrying a briefcase with his documents and told Häften to join him there at noon with the attaché case containing the explosives. At noon Häften arrived. The two went to a staff officer's bedroom presumably to change into clean shirts. Stauffenberg transferred one of the bombs to his briefcase. It weighed about 1 kilogram (2.2 pounds), had no metal jacket, its potential effect due exclusively to the blast. Stauffenberg was equipped with special pliers he could operate with the three fingers of his left hand and he activated one of the bombs. A courier opened the door and announced that Stauffenberg was wanted; this stopped Stauffenberg from activating the second bomb which remained with von Häften. Two minutes late Stauffenberg arrived at the conference, held as usual in the barracks serving as a tea room. There were 25 people in the room gathered around a heavy wooden table on which maps were spread out. He tried to get next to the führer but managed only to land opposite him. He put his briefcase under the table some six feet from Hitler. An aide stumbled over it and shoved it out of the way so that it was separated from Hitler by a massive oak stanchion. Stauffenberg excused himself and left the room. Together with Häften he waited outside, observing the barrack. At 12:42 a massive explosion erupted sending up a geyser of black smoke and splintered wood. Stauffenberg and Häften immediately drove to the airport from where they flew off to Berlin. At the Wolfschanze General Fellgiebel, in charge of communication and a member of the conspiracy, telephoned the Bendlerstrasse that the attentat took place.

Hitler, who had been sitting on a stool with his elbow resting on the table, was thrown off his seat and flung against the door post. His black trousers and white underwear were in shreds. In the pandemonium the first voice heard was Keitel's shout, "Where is the führer?" As Hitler rose from the floor Keitel embraced him crying, "My führer, you are alive." Hitler's aide Schaub and valet Linge arrived and led Hitler to his nearby quarters where he sat down on a chair. He suffered a variety of injuries. There was a contusion on his left arm from the blow of the heavy table and a gash on his head which affected his inner ear; the shockwave caused his eardrums to burst and there was blood in his right ear; his eyes kept flickering and had a nystagmus to the right; a hundred oak splinters had to be removed from his legs. Strangely the explosion seemed to have eliminated a previous tremor in his left leg which now shifted to his right arm. While several others were seriously wounded so that four of those present, including Hitler's faithful Schmundt, eventually died, Hitler comfortably survived. For military men with such wide experience with explosives their expertise was poor. While in a cement bunker the bomb used would perhaps have been sufficient it was not so for a flimsy barrack which, in addition, had a hollow space beneath the floor, so that the explosion dissipated itself both outward and downward. Experts also claimed that had Stauffenberg used both bombs he had with him it would have killed everybody (Venohr, 369; Hoffmann, 404).

By all accounts Hitler was composed. According to Morell Hitler greeted him with a grin. "I am invulnerable — he shouted — I'm immortal" (Morell, 168). Referring to the shaking of his right hand he even joked that as long as his head was not shaking everything would be all right. Subsequently there was glee at what happened — though no one guessed its motivation. When he caught his breath he exclaimed, "I will smash and destroy these criminals who have presumed to stand in the way of Providence and myself!" (Mitcham 1983, 160).

He was in form to greet Mussolini that afternoon and he took him on an inspection of the demolished tea house. Later the führer, Mussolini and a number of German and Italian guests attended a tea party. After a brief period of bonhomie the führer suddenly had a fit of frenzy and, foaming at the mouth, shouted that he would take revenge on all traitors. Providence had just shown him once again that he had been chosen to make world history. He ranted about terrible punishments — all traitors would be thrown into concentration camps, none who set himself against divine Providence should be spared. He finished his outburst with the words "I'm beginning to doubt whether the German people are worthy of my great ideals" (Trevor-Roper 1947, 31–2).

The story of the scheduled coup-d'état after Bendlerstrasse was erroneously informed Hitler was dead is a sorry tale of incompetence that doomed the enterprise from the start. Neither the leaders nor the troops called upon to overthrow the regime believed in the cause and either neglected or refused to carry out their missions. And as soon as the news arrived that Hitler had survived, the conspirators turned on themselves, the condemned acting as their own executioners. The most flagrant case was that of General Fromm, the key to the events at the Bendlerstrasse. Told by Keitel that the führer was alive he ordered the execution of Stauffenberg and Häften. That very night the two were shot. He gave Beck a pistol ordering that he shoot himself and when Beck bungled the job he had a sergeant kill him. This did not save Fromm, who was shipped to a concentration camp to be killed near the end of the war shouting "Long live the führer!" as the firing squad loosed its salvo.

As a result of these events Hitler found two new allies: "Treason" to explain past misfortunes and "Providence" to guarantee future victory. This double-edged thesis was launched on the day of the bomb plot, properly enough at the bewitched hour of midnight when he addressed the German people. "If I speak to you today—he began—it is first in order that you should hear my voice ... and secondly that you should know of a crime unparalleled in German history.... I myself sustained only some very minor scratches, bruises and burns. I regard this as a confirmation of the task imposed upon me by Providence.... This time we shall get even with them in the way to which we National Socialists are accustomed" (Bullock, 744). He issued orders that "these criminals ... be expelled from the Wehrmacht and brought before a People's Court. They are not to be given a respectable bullet but will hang like common traitors" (Hoffmann, 717). The military conspirators were not to be tried by a court-martial as entitled to but by a Nazi kangaroo court. For this the soldiers had to be first expelled from the army. This task was performed by that universally respected upright soldier Feldmarschall Gert von Rundstedt, assisted by another honorable soldier, Hans Guderian. This court of honor was convened on August 4 and without any hearings or presentation of evidence it expelled 22 fellow officers from the Wehrmacht, handing them over to Ronald Freisler, an erstwhile Communist and now a fierce Nazi judge. Hitler next called in Freisler and the individual who was to perform the executions, saying, "I want them to be hanged, strung up like butchered cattle" (Fest 1996, 297). The trials began on August 7 in a large hall decked with Nazi flags with Freisler in red robes sitting under a portrait of the führer. The accused were forbidden to wear neckties and some were also deprived of their suspenders so that they had to hold up their trousers throughout the proceedings. All those tried on August 8 — some 100 men — were sentenced to hang.

Then comes the grisly story of the mode of execution. At the express wish of the führer the proceedings were recorded from the start to the last gasp of the hanged men by movie cameras and photographers. Under strong floodlights SS men followed the condemned men as they shuffled across the prison yard in their wooden clogs to the specially constructed gallows. These consisted of looped metal wires suspended from hooks attached to the roof's girders. The men were lifted up and the wire loops slung over their necks. There are two versions of the next step—one that the men were dropped and another that they were slowly lowered. In either case the usual severing of the spinal cord did not occur and the men endured prolonged agonies as the cameras were filming. To go on with the job the executioner and his assistants had to fortify themselves and for this purpose had brought a flask of brandy which they drank between hangings. That very night the films of the executions were flown out for the führer's perusal and it is said that he could never have enough of looking at them. Ten days later Speer, when in the Wolfschanze, still saw these photographs scattered on the führer's desk. An SS man explained to him that the photo he was looking at was that of the Witzleben execution and asked him if he wanted to see the others; he was also invited to attend the screening of the film of the execution that night in Hitler's private cinema and Speer had to invent a reason for absenting himself from the show. Hitler intended to show the film to the troops but his cohorts objected and the matter was dropped (Fest 1996, 303–11; Hoffmann, 719).

As in the case of the SA killings in 1935, Hitler utilized the occasion to get at people he deemed to be in his way. Thus aside from the 600 connected with the July 20 plot, 5,000 parliamentarians of the old regime were arrested. The families of various suspects saw their property confiscated and close relatives were shipped to concentration camps. Stauffenberg's wife and mother were sent to Ravensbrück and his children placed in an orphanage under changed names. The hunt after suspects continued nearly to the end of the war. In a talk with Krebs on August 31 Hitler said, "Kluge intentionally brought about the collapse in the West, otherwise it is unexplainable" (DDR, XXI, 284). Consequently, when summoned to Berlin von Kluge committed suicide to spare himself the fate of the other conspirators. On October 14 Rommel was supplied with poison and ordered to kill himself, which he did. The army as a whole was placed under the command of the OKW, Hitler's personal office. Canaris, Oster, Fromm, and others were executed at dawn of April 9, 1945. The reactions of the populace and the Army were uniformly against the attempt on the führer's life. All over the country the news of the attentat produced a reaction "of deep shock, dismay, outrage ... and immense relief at the outcome.... Women burst into tears on the streets of Berlin and Koenigsberg at the joy of the Führer's safety" (Kershaw 1987, 215). No event of the war had so deeply moved the broad masses as this murder attempt. This was also the official response of the Catholic and Protestant churches which, even after the war, continued to condemn the attempt on Hitler's life (Steinert, 268). Two minor examples reflect the general anger against the conspirators. After the failed coup Gördeler managed to stay in hiding for some time. When he went one day to visit his parents' graves he was recognized by a woman who tailed him; after he managed to elude her he was then recognized by another woman who reported him to the police. Nebe first eluded his captors by using all known police tricks— staging a suicide, dyeing his hair — but he, too was recognized by a woman and denounced. On the Russian front the troops, regardless of their opinions on the war, considered the deed a "stab in the back"— another footprint of World War I — and the soldiers made a point of letting the leadership know of their feelings (Hinze, 6). Within a very short time, Rundstedt, Manstein, and Kleist lost their jobs; Zeitzler was dismissed as chief of staff and forbidden to wear his uniform; his predecessor, Halder, was sent to a concentration camp. Still on June 26, 1944, in an unpublished speech to factory managers Hitler had said, "Another 1918 will never come as long as I live and one of my guards lives, anyone merely thinking such thoughts will be destroyed.... And because that November 9th will never come we will win this war; for Germany has never been conquered by foreign armies but always in the final analysis by Germans; but those Germans who could conquer Germany are no longer here today" (Steinert, 262).

Radical changes now entered the German army. The office of the Replacement Army was given to a new military expert, Heinrich Himmler; soon he was also given command of an Army Group. A decree creating a chief of Nazi army operations staff was issued to instill the correct political orientation in the army. From then on military saluting was to be done the Nazi way. The administration of POW camps was taken away from the army and given to Himmler. A peculiar trend made itself felt in the structure and even the tactics of the German army. This was a growing imitation of Soviet practices; Nazi commissars attached to the military staffs; "hurrah" to be shouted during an attack; use of guerrilla tactics; orders to be rigidly followed regardless of a commander's judgment; the arrest of deserters' families, and others. On Hitler's orders Guderian started preparing trench positions behind the eastern front manned by security troops whose mission was to prevent soldiers from running away or retreating during battle (Heiber 2003, 998). The reasoning presumably was: Aren't the Reds winning by these methods?

* * *

Like most resistance movements the Polish underground's *Armia Krajowa* (AK) waited until liberation was imminent to mobilize and activate its forces against the Germans. In the Polish case there was an additional consideration to staging a revolt just before the Soviets arrived. As mentioned, Stalin had broken relations with the Polish government in London leaving the AK — the major and in many areas the only partisan grouping — unrecognized by the Soviets. There was, therefore, the fear that upon liberation the much smaller, Communist-led *Armia Ludowa* would be installed as the legitimate authority. It was decided to face the Soviets with a fait accompli and have Warsaw liberated by the AK before the Soviets took it. That this fear was not unfounded became clear when, upon crossing the Bug, Stalin had on July 22 installed in Chelm, soon to be transferred to Lublin, a Communist-led Polish Committee of National Liberation charged with administering the liberated Polish territories.

On the evening of July 31 the decision was taken to start the uprising the next day at 5:00 P.M. This hour was chosen to permit the mobilization of the AK members before the nightly curfew and to facilitate their posting under the cover of rush hour. The number of available fighters was 40,000 with enough weapons for only a fraction of them. They dispersed 1,400 rifles, 120 machine guns, and one grenade per man (Korbonski, 186–7). At that time the Russians were 20 miles east of Praga, Warsaw's suburb on the eastern bank of the Vistula. Unknown to the AK command was that in the last days of July the Germans had opened a counterattack against the Red Army east of Praga.

The insurrection started on the evening of August 1 at the appointed hour, the AK managing to establish themselves in many vital parts of the city. But already then they failed to secure access to the four bridges across the river, crucial if there was to be liaison with the Russians. Together with the troops of the 9th Army around the city the Germans fielded 50,000 men, including two Panzer divisions. When he heard of the uprising Hitler appointed SS general von dem Bach-Zalewski, notorious for his antipartisan exploits in Russia, as overall commander, including army troops, in charge of subduing the rebellion. He was to report directly to Hitler.

In the first two weeks of fighting the AK suffered two crucial defeats. They were pushed away from the city's main arteries and from access to the Vistula. Of the two city centers in their hands, Srodmiescie (Midtown) and Stare Miasto (Old Town), the latter, which had been surrounded for some time, fell in mid–August. Here one of several major tragedies occurred. In order not to fall into German hands tens of thousands of fighters and civilians plunged into the city sewers to escape to Srodmiescie. The canals, dark, half-filled with liquid excrement and branching into various directions, became a nightmare for those trying to escape and many perished in the catacombs. The Germans also frequently tossed smoke bombs, grenades containing a special explosive gas called Taifun and, according to some, poison gas canisters through the manholes and shot the survivors as they emerged into daylight.

There are two panoramas in the Warsaw Uprising that followed Hitler's agenda for the apocalypse. The Germans did not try to recapture the city using the military means at their disposal; they were also in no rush. Instead they employed demolition tactics to eradicate the rebellion. For weeks on end artillery, mortars and tanks bombarded the city. This included 20 75mm guns, six of 150 mm, two howitzers of 280 mm, two of 380 mm and they even imported the monster 600 mm (25 inch) mortar used against Sevastopol, to lob explosives on the city. No less a figure than Ritter von Greim, the future chief of the Luftwaffe, was assigned as air force commander for Warsaw. Fleets of bombers, including Stukas, flew morning and evening low over the city (there was no flak) obliterating whole streets and districts by methodical bombing. When toward the end of the uprising Allied planes came to drop supplies to the insurgents they reported that not only could they not locate the drop zones but the very outlines of Warsaw had disappeared. Along with the demolitions a methodical slaughter of the civilian population went on. Starting with Wola, the western part of Warsaw, the SS and two special outfits, the Dirlewanger and Kaminski brigades, known for their proficiency in such matters, went about slaughtering the civilian population by mass executions. All this, of course, was no accident. When the uprising started Hitler personally indicated on a map the city areas he wanted destroyed and directed that mines be dropped on the ruins to assure that nothing whole remained there. When Bach-Zalewski arrived in Warsaw on August 5 to take command and saw the slaughter in Wola, he asked the commanders what was going on. He was told it was Hitler's orders (Zawodny, 56,63).

The end of the uprising came after two months of lonely and hopeless struggle. Following Bach-Zalewski's promise to treat the surviving insurgents as POWs, the AK capitulated on October 2. Hitler then ordered that the entire population be driven from the city and whatever had not yet been destroyed be thoroughly leveled. Special demolition squads (*Raumungsstab*) entered the ruins and obliterated whatever was still left. Sappers using special machinery tore everything apart, including underground electric cables which were chopped up into five-foot segments. As demolition troops moved in, 800,000 civilians were driven out leaving the city devoid of inhabitants. The cost to the AK was 17,200 dead and 5,000 gravely wounded, small compared to what had happened to the civilian population. Anywhere from 200,000 to a quarter of a million civilians were executed by the Germans in the course of retaking the city (Zawodny, 210–211). This did not occur as a result of the fighting but by deliberate extermination of whole city districts. It was one of Hitler's greatest successes on his satanic agenda. He had not succeeded with Moscow but did so with the Polish capital.

Late in 1944 the Allies were at the frontiers of Germany. In the east the Russians abutted East Prussia and had crossed the border as early as September 16. They were only 40 miles from the "beast's lair" in Rastenburg. In the west the Allies had crossed the German border near Trier at about the same time. Both the western and eastern armies had paused to catch their breath, getting ready for the last remaining task — an invasion of Germany itself. With the German military agonizing over how to stem the avalanches from nearly all directions, including the skies, and the civilian population cringing at the thought of being inundated by the eastern "hordes," Hitler suddenly plunged into a completely unexpected campaign to hold onto Budapest on the Hungarian puszta. Eventually he was to launch three offensives to relieve or recapture the Hungarian capital, which since December 26 had been under siege by Tolbukhin's 3rd Ukrainian Front. To his dumbfounded generals who produced subdued murmurs as to why there and why now he might as well have given the answer he had given them at the eve of Barbarossa: "I do not expect my generals to understand me, but I expect them to obey me." He offered various answers to his interlocutors: one was that Budapest represented a morale-booster; another was that it was the high road to Vienna; a third was that he would attack where the enemy expected it least; a fourth that losing Budapest would reduce the effect of victory in the West by 50 percent; and more. But the most frequent argument was that, with Ploesti lost, he needed the Hungarian oil fields. Still there were problems with this pretext, too. Hungary's two oil fields were located at Nagykanizsa and Komarno, the first southwest and the other northwest of Budapest — and both were behind the German lines. Budapest was irrelevant and even an impediment to their defense because it tied down German troops east of the Danube. More relevant is that they were insignificant to the German oil economy. This should be clear from the figures in Table 35-2. While both production and its share delivered to Germany rose through the war years, it amounted in 1943 to only a little over 3 percent of German production. While it is true that Germany's oil facilities had suffered from the bombing so that domestic production in 1944 fell by 30 percent from that of 1943, but so had Hungary's. The contribution of the Hungarian oil fields was so small that it was not even mentioned in German oil statistics and General Tippelskirch, unaware of the führer's motives, could only say that this area "had become an obsession" for him (Heiber 2003, 1096). When Hitler kept insisting the oil fields must be retained, the commander in chief of AGS, Wöhler, cabled back that the führer ought to look at aerial photographs of Nagykanizsa and Komarno; there are, said Wöhler, no oil fields in Nagykanizsa and Komarno, only "fields of craters."

To track down the most likely motivation for Hitler's centrifugal lunge for Budapest we must go back to early spring. It has been described in Chapters 31 and 34 how during his meetings with Horthy and his dignitaries Hitler kept reverting to the Hungarian Jews. Including Transylvania there had been 800,000 Jews in the country — in 1944 the last major Jewish population center in Europe. As Horthy did not catch on what Hitler meant by a "solution" of the Jewish problem Hitler lost patience and on March 19 invaded Hungary. As part of the agreement for letting Horthy continue as regent he consented to "the solution of the Jewish Problem" (Horthy, 289). With the arrival of the German army came the Gestapo and Eichmann. Within three months in a genocidal blitzkrieg, the Germans, with help from the Hungarians, rushed trainload after trainload of Jews to Auschwitz where they were gassed at an all-time rate. By the beginning of July most Jews in the provinces, something like half a million, had been deported and killed. By the Horthy-Hitler agreement the Germans were now to vacate the country. But this didn't happen. During Hitler's meeting with the new Hungarian PM, Sztojay, on June 6–7, 1944, Hitler, instead of attending to the Allied invasion which had just taken place, conferred at length with Sztojay telling him that there would be no withdrawal until "the Jewish problem has been settled perfectly" (Horthy, 306). The problem was the Jews of Budapest.

It is not quite clear why the previous attention had been on Hungary's provincial Jews. Some sources claim it was due to Horthy's attempt to retain the prosperous and professional Jews because of their importance to the Hungarian economy. But this is unlikely. What did happen was that in a rare incident in the history of the Holocaust there was out-

Table 35-2
Oil Produced in Germany[a] and Hungary
(In thousands of barrels per day)

Year	Germany[b]	Hungary			
		Production	Percentage of German Production	Percentage Exported to Germany	Delivery as Percentage of German Production
1940	103	5.1	5	0	0
1941	123	8.7	7	12	1.2
1942	142	13.8	10	19	1.9
1943	168	17.4	10	24	3.4
1944	120	17.2	14	?	?

[a] Includes Austria
[b] 75 percent synthetic
(Source: De Golyer and McNaughton.)

side intervention; both FDR and the Vatican had written to Horthy that postwar Hungary and, Horthy personally, would be held responsible for the ongoing genocide unless the deportation were halted. Not happy about them in the first place, and worried about the consequences, Horthy stopped the deportations. This coincided with Horthy's attempts to sign an armistice, an effort which failed. The result was a second occupation of Hungary on October 16, the expulsion of Horthy, and the complete takeover of the country by the Germans. For once Hitler was late. The October occupation took place against the turmoil engendered by the collapse in Rumania and the rapid incursion of the Red Army into Hungary. When the Russians showed up in front of Budapest its Jews were still there and when on December 26 Budapest was encircled they were effectively outside the Germans' reach. Hence Hitler's fury and spastic lunge to recapture Budapest. He had just had his 200,000 dead Poles in Warsaw; here in Budapest there were another 200,000 potential corpses to be had. And he would do the impossible to get them.

The struggle for Budapest consists of two phases. In the period December 1944 — February 1945 two major attacks were launched to break the siege of the city, followed by a grand offensive in March to "liberate" it after it fell to the Russians. Before Budapest was surrounded there was the usual altercation between the local commanders and Hitler on how to proceed. On December 18, Friessner had flown to Zossen especially to persuade Hitler to evacuate Budapest, but was told that Budapest was to be a fortress to be defended house by house. To ensure compliance tactical command over the fighting there was taken over by führer Headquarters — that is, by Guderian, the new army chief of staff, and Hitler. When on December 23 Friessner repeated that the city should be evacuated he was sacked that very night and General Wöhler ordered to take over his command. Wöhler was told by Guderian who, due to his promotion, had suddenly become Hitler's ventriloquist, that from now on the German soldier must know only one word, "Attack." He went on to echo the führer that Budapest was a matter of grand strategy; losing it would reduce the Ardennes victory [sic] by 50 percent and that the order of no withdrawal from Budapest was "irrevocable." When Wöhler, despite all this, reminded Guderian that historically Budapest had always been defended from the west, which meant withdrawing from the east bank, Hitler told Wöhler that both sides of the Danube must be held (the Jews lived mostly on the east side). Two days after this conversation the Russians encircled Budapest, coming to a stop 30 miles west of the city.

For lifting the siege of Budapest the IV SS Panzer Corps plus two other divisions were assigned to AG South. The IV SS was withdrawn from near Warsaw; the other divisions from Galicia. This was done 12 days before a Soviet offensive was expected on the Vistula which would bring the Russians onto German soil. The first offensive was launched from the northeast, on the evening of New Year's Day. This operation Hitler named the *Nordlösung*—an echo of the *Endlösung*. As the Germans moved along the left bank of the Danube, a Russian counterattack was launched parallel to the attacking Germans in the opposite direction. Ignoring it, the Germans charged ahead, coming within 20 kilometers (12.5 miles) of the city; the forward troops could already see the towers of Budapest. On January 10 Hitler decided that a *Südlösung*, an attack from the southwest, was a better idea and ordered that the offensive be halted and that IV Panzer Corps be shifted south forthwith. The reason for that was a boost in appetite; by attacking from the southwest not only could Budapest be relieved but the Russian troops in the Danube bend trapped and annihilated (see Fig. 35.1).

The *Südlösung* plan envisaged an attack from the northern tip of Lake Balatan with the troops reaching the Danube and then swinging north in the direction of Budapest. The operation was launched with considerable forces. Including the Hungarian 3rd Army and other units AGS had more than 13 divisions here, supported, rare at this stage in the war, by 135 planes of Luftflotte 4. The attack opened at 5:00 A.M. on January 18 and made such good progress that rehearsals were already being held to celebrate the liberation of Budapest. On January 20 the Germans reached the Danube at Dunapentele and were ready to turn north in the direction of the city. On January 26 the left arm of the German attack came within 15 kilometers (nine miles) of the Russian siege lines, the forward units already in radio contact with their comrades in the city.

With the liberation of Budapest in sight, the troops received a sudden order to fall back as quickly as possible. While the *Südlösung* progressed the Russians had launched an offensive on both wings of the German attack, from south of Dunapentele and across Csepel Island, just below Budapest. Both thrusts were heading straight west, threatening the Germans with an encirclement in the Danube bend, a complete reversal of roles. With German reinforcements still arriving from Italy as late as February 2, it was the end of the offensive and the Germans fell back 20–30 kilometers (12.5–18.5 miles) west of the Danube (Gosztony, 120–30).

Budapest in 1944 was a million sized metropolis, its bulk, Pest, located on the east and Buda on the west bank of the Danube. Hitler forbade withdrawal from Pest to Buda, saying that he needed the river bridges for a future offensive. Due to evacuations the population had fallen to 800,000 inhabitants. The estimated military personnel present varies but a reasonable figure is 70,000, half of them German. The commandant of the city was SS Obergruppenführer von Waldenbruch. He had been appointed because Wöhler feared there would be civilian unrest. The city had no water, electricity or fuel and suffered continuous shelling and air raids; fires could not be put out and neither the dead nor wounded were being attended to. SS and Arrow Cross bands roamed the city, pillaging and killing Jews and non–Jews alike, and dumping the corpses into the Danube. On January 6 there was already fighting in the streets and 12 days later Pest fell to the Russians. During the

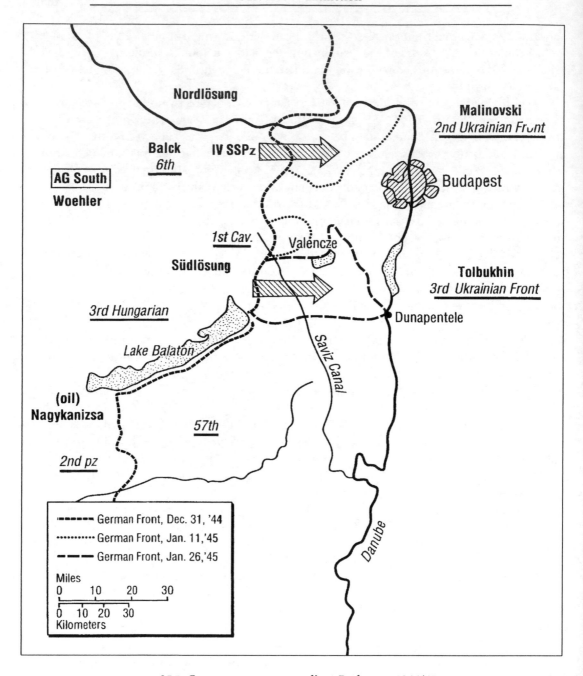

35.1. German attempts to relieve Budapest, 1944/45

withdrawal the Germans blew the Danube bridges without warning, causing many deaths. When the Russians arrived in Pest they found 120,000 Jews alive. All the shelling previously vented on Pest was now leveled on Buda. By an order of Hitler any attempt to break out of the city was to be considered desertion and punished accordingly. Von Wildenbruch decided to disobey orders and he so informed headquarters 9th Army. In order not to be countermanded the SS general ordered all radio receivers destroyed. In the evening of February 11, 24,000 Germans and 20,000 Hungarians, including 12,000 lightly wounded, assembled at the breakout point. The breakout, led by 16,000 troops, started at 8:00 P.M. leaving behind 10,000 wounded. The Russians detected the concentration and from the very beginning kept the men under heavy fire. Only 785 men reached the German lines. The siege lasted 50 days, left 20,000 civilian dead and a ruined city (Gosztony, 149–52).

It would seem that after all this the Budapest story would have been over but far from it — the greatest battle was yet to come. It was, in fact, Hitler's last grand offensive of the war. On December 16 the Ardennes offensive opened with intent to drive a wedge from Luxemburg all the way to Antwerp, another Sichelschnitt no less. The offensive was still on when on January 8 Hitler pulled out the VI SS Panzer Army containing Germany's best armored divisions from the front for refitting. On January 12 the Russians opened their winter offensive along the Vistula, broke down the German front and within days were in Germany. Guderian and the entire OKH were certain that VI Panzer would be thrown on the eastern front. But not at all. These divisions, Hitler told them, were to be shipped to Hungary. For a change all his generals, including the yes-men of the OKW, were in revolt, utterly bewildered by this decision. But it did no good. On January 31 Hitler gave his SS buddy, Sepp Dietrich, command of the VI Panzer Army and ordered them into the Puszta. Over the next 10 days 290 trains chugged across Hitler's disintegrating empire headed for a reconquest of Budapest.

When on February 25 the order reached AGS about a new grand offensive on Budapest, the Russians were already on the way to Berlin and in the west the Allies were across the Rhine. In Hungary a stupendous army, which by some accounts was larger than that facing the Western Allies, was assembled. Together with the VI Panzer and AG Balck, the five armies had a total of 30 divisions including 11 Panzer divisions. Assisting them were the Hungarian 3rd Army and German divisions from AGF, whose mission was to establish bridgeheads across the Drava. The objective was to clear the area west of the Danube and recapture Budapest. The code name for the business was *Frühlingserwache*— Spring Awakening.

Three armies including the recently arrived VI SS Panzer were arranged north of Balaton. The Second Panzer Army stayed south of the lake. The offensive opened at midnight of March 5th, the main effort located between the northern tip of Lake Balaton and Budapest opposite Tolbukhin's 3rd Ukrainian Front. Although the transfer of the VI Panzer Army was done under extreme secrecy, the Russians got wind of its arrival. After rapid consultations the decision was taken to stage a second Kursk — that is not to fight the powerful Panzer divisions in the open but to defeat them by a killing defense —fields of mines and antitank guns. After the VI Panzer achieved a breakthrough it pushed its way down the Saviz Canal toward the Danube. By mid–March they were 10–15 miles from the river along a broad front. One of the great tank battles then took place south of Velecze, involving, by some accounts, 500 German Panzers and assault guns (as at Prokhorovka). Tolbukhin found himself in great straits and did not think he could stop the Germans with the forces he had. He requested that Stavka give him the 9th Guards Army kept as a strategic reserve for the offensive on Vienna. As was his custom Stalin refused, telling Tolbukhin to hold out with whatever he had. According to Antonov the battle was one of the heaviest of the entire war and the Red Army suffered severe losses in fighting it (Brown, 656). Such was Hitler's spasm to have Budapest!

Prior to *Frühlingserwache* the Soviets had planned an offensive on Vienna for March 15, to start from Malinovski's sector. In view of what was now happening, changes had to be made. Postponed by a day the main effort was shifted further south so that it would parallel the left wing of the German attack. In this, too, it resembled the battle of Kursk when a thrust toward Orel dislodged the entire German undertaking. When the Russian Vienna offensive opened, it quickly surged westward toward the Danube and Vienna, and on the 20th a wing of the Russian attack turned south toward the northern tip of Lake Balaton. This threatened, once again, the German 6th Army with encirclement. It barely escaped via a narrow corridor between the lake and the onrushing Soviet formations. By the 25th *Frühlingserwache* was dead, with the Germans in full retreat, the Russians taking Vienna on April 4. Consistent with past practices, for failing to relieve Budapest, Wöhler was relieved of his command and replaced by Rendulic, a fellow Austrian.

* * *

From now on Hitler had no more alien people to exterminate, no plans for offensives large or small, no dignitaries of the Tiso, Pavelic or Szalasi caliber to pay him homage. He now could only go back where he had started from — his own Volk. On November 20 he abandoned the Wolfschanze. The last of his staff left on December 22 and the place, including the airfield and the railroad tracks, was blown up by Todt sappers. At about the same time Hindenburg's corpse was removed from Tannenberg and the World War I monuments to that great victory there also blown up — two German holy of holies of two world wars converted to rubble. Back in Berlin Hitler hunkered down in the subterranean bunker of the Chancellery—there to conduct his last item of business—an accounting with the Germans. He would try to destroy them for failing to win the war for him. He attached four banners to the swastika's four claws to carry along the German masses for the longest possible time during which he could wreak on them the maximum punishment. The four slogans were: He was in partnership with Providence; Wonder Weapons, of which the V's were only the tip of the iceberg; the Any-Minute-Now breach between the Allies, after which Germany, together with the West, would launch a Super-Barbarossa; and the foremost ace in the führer's hand, the Imminence of a Miracle. All these strategic concepts had been in the works for some time, but they rose to a crescendo the closer the end came; and their clarion call would survive the führer's earthly existence in his last will and testament.

The relation between the führer's will and the fate of the German nation were expressed as early as 1942. In an address to officer candidates on May 30 he explained why he was not worried about the great losses of men on the eastern front. Nazi ideology, he explained, nurtures a high birth rate which by far outstripped the death rate due to the war (Schramm 1971, 26). That this arithmetic entailed a certain moral flaw was minor; more serious was that it was untrue. There was really no point to try to eliminate him, as on July 20, he told Friessner, because "Providence has determined otherwise. I see in it once again a sign from Heaven for me to proceed with my Mission which I must carry out for the sake of the German people and the world." Hitler's closest "friends" were his valet, cook, chauffer, pilot, and female secretaries. In December 1944 Christa Schröder, a secretary, said to him, "Mein Führer, we have lost, haven't we?" Hitler denied it, for why else had Providence spared him from the July 20 bomb if not to lead the German people to final victory? In September 1944 he told his usual table companions, "My task has been — particularly since 1941— not to lose my nerve under any circumstances but whenever there is a collapse to find ways and means to repair it." As an example of such a feat he cited the destruction of AGC that year, after which he managed to restore the situation. "Without a strong will this struggle will not be won." On August 31, six weeks after the attentat, Hitler told his generals, "Since the year 1941 it has been my task not to lose my nerve, under any circumstances.... I live only for the purpose of leading this fight, because I know if there is no iron will behind it this battle cannot be won.... If necessary we will fight on the Rhine. It doesn't make any difference. Under all circumstances we will continue this battle.... I am grateful to Destiny for letting me live" (Bullock 1962, 755–6). He frankly confessed to Morell on March 6, 1945, that what upset him most, which also caused the trembling of his arm, was the blunders the generals made. In the end it turns out that he was always right (Morell, 264). In talking to cadet officers on November 20 he told them, "A nation which loses will cease to exist" and therefore this "war must end with a German victory" (Below, 340).

It became clear to the führer that the more hopeless the war the closer was the time for the fall-out between the Allies. In a speech of August 31, 1944, he assured his listeners, "The time will come when the stress between the Allies will become so great that the break will occur. All coalitions have disintegrated in history sooner or later" (Bullock 1962, 755). This held true particularly in the present situation as elucidated on December 12 in front of his military commanders, "Never before in history — said the Führer — has there been a coalition like that of our enemies consisting of ... on the one hand ultra capitalist states, on the other ultra Marxist.... This coalition is already rent by the most acute contradictions ... growing with every hour. If we can deliver a few heavy blows now, then this artificially created united front will crumble with a thunder clap at any moment" (Axell 1997, 135). When Hitler handed Friessner command of the Rumanian front he assured him that the Russians would not bother about Rumania because they were heading south toward Greece, a British domain, and this would be the beginning of the strife between east and west. He even provided a specific timetable for this to occur. In talking to Mussolini on April 22, 1944, he informed Il Duce that he, Hitler, had studied a lot of history and discovered that coalitions usually do not last more than five years (DDR, XX, 367). Friessner also quotes Hitler as saying, "The political goals of the Soviets are no longer the occupation of Germany but the Bosphorus. In two to three weeks there will be a collision there. This will bring about the decisive turn in the war to our good. Certainly England no longer wants to destroy Germany because it needs it as a buffer state." Turning to the other generals present, he continued, "You, gentlemen, must not let history judge you that in the decisive moment you have lost your nerve. I want to draw your attention to the First World War. It has been proven beyond doubt that just before the end of that war our enemies were close to a collapse. Had we kept our nerves through that crisis the German people would have been spared Versailles as well as the present war."

When these arguments were exhausted Hitler resorted to the expectation of a miracle. He cited the following historical facts: "When someone asks me how this war is to continue then my answer is that throughout history no statesman or warlord could ever answer that question. He could quote the history of the Punic Wars, the Thirty Years War and the Seven Years War as examples. In none of the above cases ... could [one] predict how the war would end and yet eventually they brought victory. In a conflict as large as the present one the main thing is to keep the goal steadily before one's eyes.... Foremost is the spiritual attitude, the fanatic determination not to capitulate under any circumstances" (Hubatsch, 18). The most frequently cited miracle was the Seven Years War waged by Frederick the Great against a coalition of European powers. He mentioned this for the first time in a letter to Mussolini on February 28, 1943, saying, "I am resolved to complete the task which Destiny has given me.... [It] is not half so harsh and fraught with peril as the fight which Frederick the Great once waged, with his 3.7 million inhabitants, against the whole of Europe.... The National Socialist Party will mobilize everyone, down to the last man and the last woman, in its inexorable resolve not to capitulate.... I shall fight until the enemy himself admits defeat." An identical faith appeared in his speech of August 31 when he told his Germans, "Under all circumstances we will continue this battle until, as Frederick the Great said, one of our damned enemies gets too tired to fight any more." In the last days of the war the above assumed the simplest possible dialectic. In speaking to General Thomale, in charge of Panzer Troops, Hitler said, "The war will not last as long again as it has lasted. That is absolutely certain. Nobody can endure it. We cannot, and the others cannot. The only question is who will endure it longer? It must be he who has everything at stake" (Schramm 1971, 171). Clausewitz would have been delighted to be able to include this maxim into his theory of warfare.

CHAPTER 36

Invasion of Germany

By late 1944 the Allies' offensive had come to a stop just short of the German border. The main reason was that supplies failed to keep up with the advance of the troops, due in part to the blockage of Channel ports by entrenched German garrisons. Antwerp fell on September 4, but the city was 50 miles inland and Montgomery failed to clear the Scheldt estuary so that Antwerp port remained blocked through the rest of the year. Other impediments to a further advance were the topographical features of the frontline. The northern area was a maze of waterways, canals, dykes, marshes and terrain liable to flooding. Below it the land was forested, hilly, cut by streams and rivers. Here as well as further south to the Swiss border was the Rhine River, a formidable barrier to infantry and mechanized troops alike. Added to this was the Siegfried Line which, though cannibalized and gone to seed, still flaunted bunkers, forts and dragon teeth easily manned again. And, most important, as a result of the Allies catching their breath the Germans were given time to reorganize and reinforce their remaining divisions. One could also expect that their morale would be boosted by fighting for their homeland, actually more a presumption than fact because the Germans were always fiercer in conquest than in defending the Vaterland. This was as true in World War I during their 1918 retreat as it would be in 1945.

By the end of the year Antwerp port was reopened, the supply system running in full gear and the invasion troops from southern France deployed along the German frontier. The Allies were now ready to start the drive into Germany proper. Yet it is difficult to detect any overall plan for this task. One reason was the infighting between Montgomery and Eisenhower, as well as between the American generals themselves. When the supplies started flowing again, Montgomery reverted to his usual swagger and demanded the lion's share, as he alone would be capable of breaking into Germany. As we shall see below, he won by dogged persistence, only to add another, the biggest, in fact, flop to his unglamorous record. The American Army commanders, too, instead of cooperating, each tried to be the first to cross the Rhine. There was also political discord about how to proceed in face of the oncoming Red Army. Despite existing agreements on zones of occupation for the major powers, Churchill and Montgomery pushed for capturing as much territory as possible, including possibly Berlin — a strategy which placed the main effort in Monty's sector. The Americans intended to abide by the agreed demarcation lines, which assigned the area around Berlin to the Soviet zone of occupation. The Americans also took more seriously the German threat of a last-ditch defense redoubt in the Bavarian Alps and intended to forestall it. This put the main effort on Bradley's 21st Army group poised for a drive into central and southern Germany. While weighing these factors, two events occurred which further dislocated Allied planning. One was an operation known as *Market-Garden*, launched by Monty; and the other, the Ardennes offensive unleashed by Hitler—both doomed operations typical of their authors.

As noted, one of the difficulties of debouching into Germany was the Rhine River stretching from the North Sea to the Swiss border. In Holland this was compounded by a maze of rivers, canals and waterways. Monty's plan was to drop airborne troops at four locations to seize and hold a chain of bridges, including those over the Rhine at Arnhem while the British 2nd Army rushed over the captured bridges to launch itself into Germany. At one stroke the Siegfried Line and Rhine barriers would be bypassed and the road to Berlin opened. The plan called for the establishment of an armored corridor 64 miles long with strong enemy forces lurking on both sides of it. While airborne troops would seize both ends of the corridor a British corps would break through the German front driving its 20,000 vehicles along a single road to join the northern end and secure the penetration. The strangest feature of this operation was that if it were to succeed it called for the utmost daring and speed—attributes that the British army and Montgomery in particular were notorious in lacking. But Ike approved it. According to the memoirs of his grandson, Ike, though convinced that it would fail, gave his O.K. in order to silence Monty in his insistence for a northern drive, sacrificing thousands of the Allies' best soldiery in the process.

The operation started on September 17 under the command of British general Browning. One American airborne division was dropped at the Wilhelmina and Wishelmsvaat canals where the Germans managed to destroy one bridge; another airborne US division landed at the Maas River where the troops captured the bridges. The two American divisions then joined hands but failed to capture the bridges further north over the Waal River. They then waited for the overland British troops. These arrived 33 hours late. On September 18 British paratroopers were dropped near Arnhem to capture the northernmost bridges over the Rhine. This they failed to do. They then waited for the British land troops to help them take the bridges. These however arrived three days behind schedule during which time the Germans destroyed most of the British paratroopers. The operation was a complete failure, the Allies suffering over 17,000 casualties and effectively destroying their only airborne army (Nofi, 176).

The other disruption in the Allied plans was the Ardennes offensive. This has been written about extensively and its only interest here is how it fits in with the führer's overall program at this stage of the war. Its psychological begetter was the glorious memories of 1940, the 1944 Ardennes offensive being an ambitious duplicate of Sichelschnitt. In practical terms, however, it was a continuation of Hitler's methodical destruction of German manpower. At the briefing for the campaign Bayerlin, commanding the Lehr Panzer Division, reported that the führer looked old and broken, reading his prepared harangue with a shaking hand. For two hours it went on with the seated generals watched over by jumpy SS men, Bayerlin afraid to reach for his handkerchief lest it be seen as another attentat. In his elucidation of the coming battle Hitler said, "If we can now deliver a few more heavy blows, then at any moment this artificially bolstered common front [of capitalists and Bolsheviks] may collapse with a mighty clap of thunder…. Wars are finally decided by one side or the other recognizing that they cannot be won. We must allow no moment to pass without showing the enemy that whatever he does, he can never reckon on a capitulation. Never! Never!" (Strawson 1971, 212–3). In keeping with his recent imitation of Soviet tactics the infantry in this campaign, shouting a mass hurrah, was to spearhead the breakthrough with the Panzers following only after the front had been breached. Hitler himself plotted the offensive down to individual units and forbade any deviations from his plans

(Lukacs, 162–8). The aim was to separate the British and American armies by driving a wedge across the Ardennes aimed at Antwerp. As Hitler told Speer he was going to force the Allies "back into the Atlantic.... That will lead to a collapse and panic among the Americans.... And there will be a huge encirclement of the entire British Army with hundreds of thousand of prisoners.... Like in Russia" (Speer, 405). For the offensive Hitler scraped together 30 divisions, close to half a million men, and nearly 1,000 aircraft. Included was Skorzeny's commandos, many of them dressed in American uniforms, to create confusion behind enemy lines. Both Rundstedt and Model, in command of the operation, opposed it, but they were ignored.

The German attack started at 5:30 A.M. on December 16, springing a complete surprise on the Allies. The main thrust was against Hodges' 1st Army, a very weakly held front. In addition the weather kept Allied air forces grounded. The Americans retreated, leaving one division surrounded at Bastogne. In the center the Germans produced a salient 60 miles deep, getting to within a few miles of the Meuse River, but the flanks of the American armies, as well as besieged Bastogne, held out enabling reinforcements to pour in from north and south. On Christmas Eve the weather cleared and 2,000 Allied planes took to the air, shattering the German supply system. In response Hitler ordered every available plane to attack the Allied airfields and as a result 300 German planes were shot down. On January 3 both Hodges in the north and Patton in the south counter-attacked the salient and though the attack, in severe cold and snow, was slow it did force the remaining German troops to retreat. The cost to the Germans was 80,000 killed and a loss of all the tanks and aircraft employed in the offensive. After the failure of the offensive Hitler's Luftwaffe adjutant, von Below, found him cowering in his bunker and fulminating against the traitors in the army, telling von Below, "I know the war is lost.... I have been betrayed.... [But] we will not capitulate. Never.... We can go down. But we will take a world with us" (Kershaw 2000, 747).

* * *

By stretching the timetable a bit one can distinguish three phases in the Allied invasion of Germany. The first consisted in clearing the approaches to the Rhine, a relatively easy task in the southern half but prolonged and costly where the Rhine ran through Germany proper. Next would come the crossing the Rhine itself. The last phase was the occupation of western Germany — a walkover, as the Germans, fearful of being overrun by the Red Army, surrendered en masse to the Anglo-Saxon invaders. At the beginning of 1945 the Allies had 73 divisions for a total strength of 3.7 million men with two new divisions arriving every month. The ratio of Allied to German strength was 10 in tanks; 3 in aircraft and 2.5 in manpower (1.5 million Germans). Of the four German Army Groups the strongest was Model's AG B, defending the Ruhr. In January Rundstedt, since September reinstated as OB West (to be dismissed again in March), proposed to shift all troops and supplies east of the Rhine to which Hitler replied that there was "no point in merely transferring the catastrophe from one point to another" (Giziowski, 383).

In a directive of January 17 Eisenhower ordered the clearing of the entire west bank of the Rhine before crossing it. He hoped thereby to be able to destroy much of the enemy before they hunkered down on the east side of the river; then concentrate large forces for crossing the Rhine by leaving only thin screens on the western bank. The largest of these initial operations was assigned to Monty's 21st AG which in addition to two British armies contained Simpson's 9th US Army. It was a double-pronged operation, the northern wing to be conducted by the British (Veritable) and the southern by Simpson's US 9th Army (Grenade). The two attacks were phased two weeks apart. Veritable began on February 8 with the objective of reaching the Rhine in 48 hours. The land was forested, marshy; the Germans, by blowing the dykes, flooded large areas in front of the attackers. The Grenade part of the attack started on February 23 with a bombardment of the German positions by 2,000 guns. Its task being to cross the Roer River and link up with the British around Duisburg. Though having started two weeks later Simpson's troops were on the Rhine on March 1 while Monty's troops were just emerging from the Reichswald. There were a number of bridges over the Rhine in the area and although Simpson's troops tried to take them on the run, the Germans blew them all. With the conclusion of this double operation by early March the Rhineland — the area between the Meuse and Rhine rivers— was cleared of the enemy, the Germans leaving behind 52,000 prisoners.

Further south were the Palatinate and Saar regions, hemmed into a triangle between the Rhine and the Moselle rivers. Here the operation, code named Undertone was conducted by Bradley's 12th AG. Timewise the campaign coincided with that of Veritable-Grenade. Most of it was conducted by Patton's 3rd Army, spurred by the feat of Hodges' 1st Army which had in the meantime secured a bridge over the Rhine at Remagen. In a rapid campaign across the Palatinate Patton came abreast the Rhine from Koblenz to Mannheim, taking in the process 87,000 prisoners. To the south Devers' 6th AG, which included de Lattre's 1st French Army, also closed in on the Rhine by eliminating the Colmar Pocket. By March 22 the Allies abutted the Rhine along the entire western bank. By fighting west of the Rhine the Germans lost a total of 300,000 men.

The task for crossing the Rhine and the resources needed were again allotted to Montgomery in the north. The reason for this was the hope of seizing the Ruhr, the industrial engine of the reich. The planning for the operation, code named Plunder, was started as early as October, the target date for crossing set for March 24. For this task Monty's accumulation of forces and equipment rivaled that of the Normandy invasion. Among the specialized troops were 37,000 British and 22,000 American engineers His three armies had 5,500 artillery pieces massed along a seven-mile river frontage. While this armada was being set up there occurred the embarrassing episode of the Ludendorff Bridge. On March 7 Hodges had reached the Rhine at Remagen where the Ludendorff Bridge spanned the river. A prisoner told the Americans that the bridge had been set for demolition at 4:00 P.M. that day. On hearing this the American troops simply rushed the bridge. The demolition charges were duly set off but, despite some damage, the bridge held whereupon the Americans cut the remaining electric wires, dumping the unexploded charges into the river. By the next day Hodges had a bridgehead of 8,000 men covered by artillery and tank fire from the west bank. The führer had, of course, ordered that no Rhine bridge was to fall into enemy hands. Those in charge of blowing the bridge who had not fallen into American captivity were all subsequently executed. An indirect casualty was Rundstedt himself, who was sacked and replaced by Kesselring.

While American troops had breached the Rhine at Remagen as well as near Mainz where another crossing was made by Patton, Plunder went ahead with its ponderous preparations for crossing the Rhine at Wesel. This was launched at 9:00 P.M. on March 23 in the presence Generals Eisenhower and Simpson. It was accompanied by a barrage of 5,000 guns and by Monty's promise that he would "crack about the plains of northern Germany chasing the enemy from pillar to post." When the troops landed on the opposite shore

U.S. 7th Army troops entering a German town. (Courtesy the United States Army.)

there was only minimal resistance. Over the erected pontoon bridges Monty's 21st AG moved into northern Germany along with the American troops debouching from the Remagen and Mainz bridgeheads. The invasion of Germany by the Western Allies was underway.

* * *

In late 1944 there were a number of similarities in the position of the Red Army facing the German homeland to that of the Western Allies. It too had come to a halt because the supplies failed to keep pace with the advancing troops. The Red Army too faced a major river, the Vistula, Poland's largest, which though not as formidable as the Rhine still presented a sizeable barrier. And like the Americans they stood just short of the German borders. There was one major difference. All the Russians had to do was wait for winter when the Vistula would freeze; also they had several substantial bridgeheads on the western bank.

Koniev opened the Russian offensive on the Vistula on January 12, followed two days later by Zhukov. The German front cracked almost instantly and the Russians swept forward over the entire length of the battle line. Warsaw, or rather its ruins, was taken on the 17th, Cracow two days later. In two weeks the German army was swept from Poland. On

German POWs led through the city of Aachen. (Courtesy the National Archives.)

the 19th Konev's troops stepped on German soil in upper Silesia and encircled Breslau. On the 29th Zhukov reached the Oder, the objective of the campaign. By the end of February the Russian armies stood along the Oder-Neisse rivers, the Küstrin fortress only 40 miles from Berlin. The offensive ignored its wings north and south, seemingly heading straight west. For a while Stalin indeed toyed with the idea of reaching Berlin but was dissuaded by his field commanders. Accordingly Stavka called a halt to the westward drive and ordered

Rokossovsky to attack into East Prussia, assisted by Zhukov who was to swing his armies north.

As can be seen on Fig. 36.1, below the Baltic the front bent sharply to the east where the Germans put up a desperate fight to keep a corridor open for the millions of soldiers

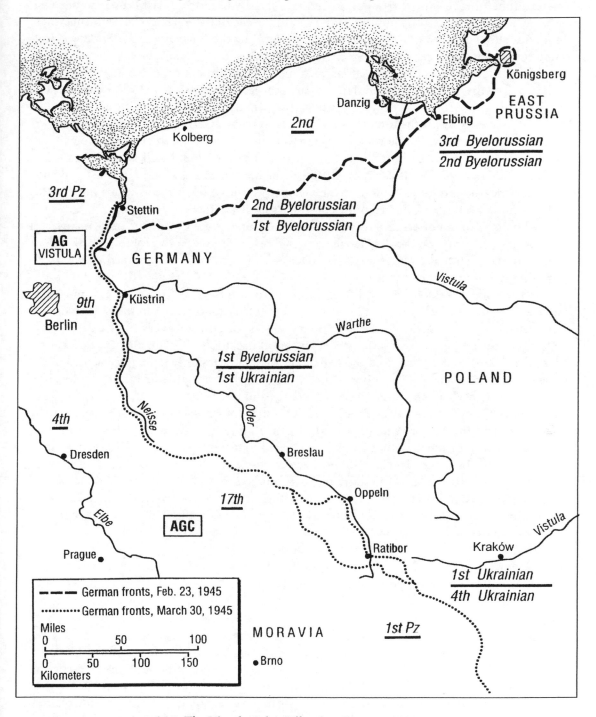

36.1. The Vistula-Oder Offensive, January 1945

and civilians trapped in East Prussia and Pomerania. Defending that stretch was AGC fielding about 600,000 men. Progress of the Russian offensive was slow and it was not till March 4 that the Russians reached the Baltic at Kolberg, cutting off all the German forces along the Baltic. Even then such places as Königsberg, Danzig and Gdynia, declared fortresses, held out helping to shuttle troops and civilians from Kurland and East Prussia to the west. Ironically one of the strong points to hold out to the end of the war was Hel peninsula where the first shots of the war were fired on September 1 by the German cruiser *Schleswig-Holstein* on a "friendly" visit to the Free City of Danzig.

Then came the last Russian offensive, aimed specifically at Berlin. On the 15th of April, a day before the offensive opened, Hitler issued the last führer directive to his eastern troops proclaiming, "For the last time our deadly enemies the Jewish Bolsheviks have launched their massive forces to the attack. Their aim is to reduce Germany to ruins and to exterminate our people.... While the old men and children will be murdered, the women and girls will be reduced to barrack-room whores. The remainder will be marched off to Siberia.... This time the Bolshevik will meet the ancient fate of Asia—he must and shall bleed to death before the capital of the German Reich. Whoever fails in his duty at this moment behaves as a traitor to our people" (Cross 1995, 214).

The task of conquering Berlin was given to Koniev's 1st Ukrainian and Zhukov's 1st Byelorussian fronts. Zhukov's offensive opened on April 16 at 5 A.M. followed by Koniev's an hour later. Zhukov's plan was to approach Berlin from the east combined with a flanking thrust from the northwest; Koniev's task was to invest the city directly from the south. Together with Rokossovsky's 2nd Byelorussian Front to the north the three groupings had a strength of 2.5 million men, 42,000 guns, 6,300 tanks and 7,500 aircraft. The morning opened with a drumfire of 22,000 artillery pieces—a gun for every 5.5 yards. By now Zhukov's profusion of weaponry was such that it backfired. Zhukov planned to push his forces forward in a night attack for which he used batteries of searchlights beamed at the terrain and the overcast. The stupendous barrage turned the battlefield into a cauldron of smoke, dust, fire and shell holes in which tanks and troops became intermingled and got stuck in chaotic traffic jams. The Seelow Heights that Zhukov had to overcome were marshy and steep and the Germans had fortified them with three parallel defense lines. It was not till the evening of April 19 that Zhukov managed to pry open the Oder line on a 44-mile frontage. This brought his troops 18 miles closer to Berlin. Koniev, too, after three days of combat, had only managed to secure bridgeheads across the Neisse River. But once across the river he was in open tank country. He swiftly moved west then wheeled northwest, surrounding in the process Busse's 9th Army. The great day for the Red Army—perhaps the greatest of the war—came on April 25 when Zhukov's and Koniev's troops linked up at Ketzin on the Havel river, closing the noose around Berlin.

While the Russians were investing Berlin the Western Allies were eliminating whatever was still left of the German army east of the Rhine. The greatest catch was in the Ruhr. While Montgomery had been dispatched to bypass Holland and occupy the Baltic coast, troops of the US 1st and 9th Armies met at Lippstadt encircling 320,000 troops of Model's AGB. The area was a wasteland after three years of sustained bombing; there was no electricity, no water and both the civilian population and the troops were short of food. On the 15th of April Model was asked to surrender but, aware of Hitler's scorched-earth and no-surrender orders, he refused. He had previously asked Kesselring for permission to withdraw from the Ruhr before the trap was sprung but, echoing Hitler, Kesselring replied, "Attack, yes; withdraw, no." Model then asked his chief of staff, "Have we done everything to justify our actions in the light of history?" and then answered his own question, "In ancient times they [commanders] took poison." He then walked off into the woods near smoldering Duisburg and shot himself. The mass of his troops had no fight left in them and the Americans collected 317,000 willing prisoners (MacDonald, 371–2).

With the end of the Ruhr Pocket on March 18 Eisenhower was ready for the final drive into Germany. For this purpose he removed the US 9th Army from Monty's command and returned it to Bradley, giving the latter the main task of overrunning central and south Germany — away from Berlin. Monty was assigned the task of covering Bradley's left wing. But he did not give up. He complained to Churchill, who appealed to Roosevelt to permit Monty to head for Berlin. The president replied that the decision should be left to Eisenhower. The 1st and 9th US armies then started a race for the Elbe to meet the Russians. This took place at Torgau, on the upper Elbe, at 3:30 P.M. on April 25 — the same day that the Russians closed the ring around Berlin. Koniev's 173rd Guard Infantry Regiment units shook hands there with patrols of the 69th Division of the 1st US Army. Thus on the same day that Berlin was surrounded the reich was sliced in two along a horizontal axis.

CHAPTER 37

Self–Immolation

As the invasion of Germany from east and west progressed toward denouement the führer was diligently at work implementing his apocalypse — this time on his own Volk. This self-immolation caught in its flames soldiers and civilians; state and civic structures; his own courtiers and henchmen; his brother-in-law and physician; his dog, his wife and finally himself. Lest this synchronized incineration be construed as accidents of war or the legends of history, it is worth hearing the utterances of the führer himself as he "prophesied" them — the term he used for his willful acts ever since he had concluded that the war was lost but would not end it.

It was shown that the realization of the war being lost came at the end of 1941. Consistently enough, the first reference to a planned auto-da-fe for Germany itself came soon thereafter. At midday of January 27, 1942, during a palaver with his companions the führer informed them: "If the German people are not prepared to give everything for the sake of their self-preservation, very well! Then let them disappear!" He followed this up on May 30 in a speech to 10,000 graduating lieutenants talking without notes, simply pouring out what was on his mind. The speech was entitled, "Was World War II Unavoidable for Germany?" and his answer was that, "based on the iron logic of nature only those who prove the fittest in the end will have earned the right to live. The principle of eternal selection," he announced, "favors the tough and superior" (Schwaab, 46). This anthropological verity he repeated on July 5, 1942, in his midnight Table Talk, saying he was "an ardent advocate of the belief that, in the struggle between peoples, those with the better average will always be the victors ... the natural order of things would be disrupted if the inferior should master the superior."

These predictions multiplied and became more focused at the approach of *Götterdämmerung*. Thus after the Normandy invasion in a talk to the Chiefs of Staff of the armies in the West he told them it was his mission to weather every crisis — unshaken by reverses — until the final moment of vindication. "My task," he boomed, "especially since 1941[!] has been never to lose my nerve under any circumstances.... If there is not a man ... who by his very nature has a will of iron, then the war cannot be won." At a gauleiter meeting in August 1944 he told his chieftains, "If the German people should be defeated in this struggle, then it would be because they were too weak to endure this test of history and were worthy only of destruction" (Heiber 2003, 1,049). On November 25, addressing the cut–off troops in Kurland, he had the following message, "The war will decide whether the German people shall continue to exist or perish.... Situations which have seemed hopeless have been redeemed by the courage of soldiers contemptuous of death" (Strawson 1971, 206). On December 12, prior to the Ardennes offensive, he told his assembled generals in one of his *weltgeschichtliche* lectures that, "It is only a question who holds out longer. The person holds out longer for whom everything is at stake.... If we were to say today we have had enough, we quit ... then Germany would cease to exist." And the only man capable of it was, as he put it, "I was convinced that in Germany in the coming ten, twenty, thirty, maybe fifty years, no man would come with more authority, more possibilities to influence the nation, and more decisiveness than myself. I also believe that after I am gone, time will prove that I assessed things correctly" (Heiber 1963, 286). With the Ardennes offensive fought and lost he, on December 28, told the generals defending Alsace that this was an ideological conflict that could end only in Germany's victory or extinction. Greeting the new year of 1945 he told the German people and the Wehrmacht in a midnight radio address, "Bringing the action into context with the overall situation we find ourselves and the problems we face and which must be solved, and which, regardless whether we solve them positively or negatively, will be solved, in the first case in our favor and in the other case to our destruction.... And I would like quickly to add, gentlemen; If I say this do not take this to mean that I am even remotely thinking of losing this war.... We are going to fight this war to the ultimate victory ... we will destroy everyone who does not share in the common struggle" (Joachimstahler, 74). And while spewing out these to frightening prognoses he provided a historical perspective for these utterances. Said Hitler on December 28, "Once upon a time my own situation was entirely different, and far worse. I say this only so that you can grasp why I pursue my goal with such fanaticism.... No matter how much I may be tormented by worries ... that would still not have the slightest effect on my decision to fight on." This decision came out with such relentlessness that two such disparate associates of his as Speer, the artist, and Himmler, the exterminator, both caught on as to what was Hitler's final goal. Testifying at Nuremberg, Speer said, "Hitler consciously wanted to annihilate the German people, and to destroy the last foundations of its existence" (Overy 2001,106). And Himmler told his doctor, Kersten, "If Germany is going to be destroyed then her enemies shall not have the satisfaction of emerging from our ruin.... They shall share in our downfall. Those are the Führer's direct orders."

While the destruction of the army had been going on since Stalingrad, the casualty rates and the number of troops that fell into Russian hands—considered a fate worse than death—took a quantum leap. The miserable state of the German armies now extended to the most primitive level. The routine tactic now was to stay in place and fight until dead, wounded or taken prisoner. If captured without having fought till wounded or to the last cartridge one was a traitor and his family was punished. Accordingly large numbers of troops found themselves surrounded or caught in "fortress" designated islands. The greatest of these was the erstwhile AGN trapped in Kurland since July 1944. Together with navy, police and Luftwaffe personnel there were, in January 1945, 400,000 men including 42 generals in the pocket. As with the Kuban bridgehead and the Crimea Hitler refused to withdraw, claiming that they represented the spearheads for a new Barbarossa. On January 29 von Vietinghoff took over the AGN and he together with the then chief of staff, Guderian, and Grossadmiral Dönitz, pleaded that the Kurland army be used for the defense of the homeland, assuring the führer they had the ships to evacuate them. Hitler's answer was, "The withdrawal of these troops is out of the question" (Haupt, 350). To give the impression that important developments were about to happen there, in March 1945 von Vietinghoff was replaced by Rendulic, who lasted only 24 hours to be replaced in turn by Hilpert. In the evacuations from Kurland on May 3 two ships, the *Cap Arcona* and the *Thieback*, were sunk by the RAF upon arrival in German ports. On board of these two ships were

6,900 concentration camp inmates who perished in the sinkings. This in the latest Hitlerian scheme had the double advantage of having the inmates snatched from possible liberation while an equivalent number of German soldiers who could have been shipped home were left to their fate (Burgdorff, 84). On May 6, 1945, the entire Kurland army went off to Siberia.

Of the so-called fortresses the largest was the capital of Silesia, Breslau. Hitler ordained that the population, the troops and the gauleiter himself stay in the city. So they did — 250,000 civilians and 55,000 soldiers (Heiber 2003, 1,102). The siege lasted 77 days, beyond the fall of Berlin. It resulted in 80 percent of the city destroyed and 40,000 civilians dead. Gauleiter Hanke, who had the mayor of the city shot for "cowardice," himself absconded by small plane. Those Breslauers that escaped the encirclement ended up mostly in Dresden where they fell victim to the February 13–14 firestorm which took the lives of anywhere from 30,000 to 130,000 people. The other great fortress was the capital of East Prussia, venerable Königsberg. The troops there were under the command of General Lasch. After prolonged fighting, with the city in ruins, Lasch capitulated on April 12. For this he was sentenced to death in absentia and his family arrested. In the last great cauldron, Berlin, when the fighting units were decimated the order came to fill them with civilians regardless how and where they were obtained.

Hitler also had his revenge on the Luftwaffe, an old scapegoat of his. Since they had failed to stop the Allied bombing he converted Luftwaffe personnel into infantry. At first 100,000 men were transferred to the army, then another 500,000, all untrained, demoralized and poorly armed, who proved useless in combat. Those who remained with the fighter wings were, metaphorically and literally, sacrificed in suicide missions. In the Budapest offensive the orders were, "No pilot is to turn back except for damage to the undercarriage; flights were to be continued even with misfiring engines; failure of auxiliary tanks were not be accepted as an excuse for turning back" (Cross 1995, 138). On April 7 Hitler ordered the German fighters to stage a mass ramming attack on the incoming American bombers. As a result 130 German planes were lost and 76 pilots killed. When on April 21 Hitler was informed that planes could no longer take off from Berlin airfields, he retorted, "We must immediately hang the entire Luftwaffe leadership" (Overy 1985, 361) — no empty threat as throughout Germany, and Berlin in particular, soldiers and civilians were being hanged from lamp and doorposts as deserters.

The most effective decimation of the civilian population resulted from the institution of the *Volksturm*. This originated with a führer decree of September 25, 1944, which called all men between the ages of 16 to 60 to the colors, a euphemism, as in most cases they lacked uniforms and were untrained for combat. Three quarters of a million men were mobilized and thrown against the Red Army. These boys and old men were equipped with Panzerfäuste and *Volkshandgranate 45* — a lump of concrete around a bit of explosive — and sent against phalanxes of T-34s where they perished before they could fire their weapons.

An adjunct to the Volksturm was the formation of Werewolves, sabotage and partisan units meant to operate behind enemy lines. The name was linked to German mysticism about the existence of man-wolves; it appeared in a novel about the Thirty Year War by one Herman Löns, killed in World War I. On September 19, 1944, Himmler assigned General Prützmann, who had studied Soviet partisan methods in Ukraine, to lead the Werewolf. An example of the Germans' desperate aping of Soviet methods at this stage of the war, was that the Werewolves were trained from translations of Soviet partisan manuals. On April 1 an appeal was made to the German people to join the Werewolf, announcing

"Every Bolshevik, every Englishman, every American on our soil must be a target. A single motto remains 'Conquer or Die.'" The slogan of the Werewolf was "Hate is our prayer and revenge our field cry." The main recruits were youngsters, many from the Hitler Jugend. Their number was close to 6,000. In addition to the use of weaponry they were also trained how to pollute wells, food or alcohol with poison; the SS had such a special school set up in 1944. In addition to operating against Allied troops the Werewolves were to deal with officials who cooperated with the occupation and civilians displaying white sheets of surrender. A number of mayors in west German cities fell victim to the Werewolves, the best-known case being that of Dr. Oppenhoff, bürgermeister of Aachen, assassinated by a 16-year-old (Biddiscombe, 12–56). Eventually the young wolves merely indulged in rampage and vigilantism, snatching passers-by as suspected deserters and either killing them or handing them over to the flying kangaroo courts.

Those civilians who were not dragged into the meat grinder of the Wehrmacht did not fare much better. Their fate under the rain of bombs had been discussed before and Hitler's approach to the problem is contained in the utterance that "the devastations actually work in our favor because it is creating a body of people with nothing to lose — people who will therefore fight with utter fanaticism (Overy 1985, 332). After the Hamburg catastrophe Göring rushed over to the führer asking that priority be given to the production of fighters over bombers. The conference ended with Göring rushing out of the room sobbing — not a frequent occurrence with the reichsmarschall. Another example of the care bestowed on the civilians during the demise of the reich was at the March performance of the Berlin Symphony Orchestra. When the audience left the dark unheated auditorium boys from the Hitler Jugend stood at the door handing out potassium cyanide capsules free of charge, courtesy of the Berlin gauleiter (Fest 1999, 261).

The largest catastrophe Hitler managed to inflict was on the civilian populations of East Prussia and eastern Germany. Evacuation of the civilians was forbidden and individuals attempting to leave had to have a special permit. The gauleiter of East Prussia, Erich Koch, was a notorious sadist and he saw to it that the order was scrupulously obeyed, though he himself escaped on an icebreaker. As the Russians headed for the Baltic coast the panicked populations took off on a precipitous flight to the west. On horse carts, sleds, baby prams and on foot millions of people, mostly women, children and the elderly, trudged over the icy roads and the frozen Baltic during one of the severest winters in Eastern Europe as Russian tanks and motorized columns sliced through the streams of refugees. Those lucky enough to get aboard evacuation boats filled to the gunwales faced prowling Russian submarines. On January 30, 1945, the evacuation ship *Gustloff* was torpedoed by a submarine with the loss of 9,000 civilians and soldiers, the greatest catastrophe in shipping history. The ship *Goya* was sunk with the loss of 7,000 passengers; two other boats were lost, with 8,250 people drowned. Of the 10 million refugees from east Germany close to 1.5 million perished on the trek, some at the hands of vengeful Russian soldiers, but mostly from hunger and exposure.

A similar fate befell the prewar and newly settled *Volksdeutsche* communities in Yugoslavia (Banat), Rumania, Hungary and the Sudetenland. They, too, were forbidden to leave and were eventually set upon by the indigenous armies which had switched sides and gone to war with Germany. The Balkans were also strewn with partisan detachments who had the most gruesome memories of what had been done to them during the occupation. In addition, these Volksdeutsche faced the wrath of the local populations. Particularly savage retribution was exacted on the Sudeten Germans—considered traitors to the country

Russian tanks roll into Germany. (From *The Russian War 1941–1945* by Daniela Mrazkova and Vladimir Remes copyright ©1975 by Daniela Mrazkova and Vladimir Remes. Used by permission of Dutton, a division of Penguin Group [USA] Inc.)

they had lived in for 20 years—who had so joyously welcomed their annexation to the Third Reich.

While attending to the demise of his own Volk Hitler also tried to get at the remnants of foreigners still in his hands. As early as September 1941 he announced, "I have ordered Himmler, in the event of some day there being reason to fear troubles back at home, to liquidate everything he finds in the concentration camps." In mid–1944 Himmler issued instructions that at the approach of the enemy, from either east or west, the camps be evacuated. If this could not be done the prisoners were to be executed, their bodies burned. Under no circumstances should KZ inmates—or Jews anywhere—fall into enemy hands. On another occasion he explained the reason for this: if Germany were to go under, its enemies should not have the chance of rejoicing over it. This started the infamous "death marches" during which the sadism of the guards and the callousness of the German population reached their peak. On January 17, 10 days before liberation, 58,000 men and women — of whom 15,000 were killed en route — were driven out of Auschwitz. From the Dora quarries 40,000 prisoners—most of them non–Jews—were shipped out and 11,000 died on the way. In East Prussia, given that the distances were large, several camps were emptied, the prisoners driven into the icy waters of the Baltic and machine-gunned (Gellately, 247). Scores of similar processions and exterminations took place all over Germany.

The cloaca of Hitler's feelings eventually burst its own dykes and spread into a miasma of hate and rampage that reached universal proportions. While the masses of German soldiery were ground into dust the greatest venom Hitler reserved was for their officers. The first recorded outbursts date back to the Moscow and Stalingrad debacles, which would not have occurred had there been no officers in the Wehrmacht. In May 1943 Goebbels recorded, "His opinion of all the generals is devastating.... He also told me why he no longer eats at the generals' mess at GHQ. He just can't bear the sight of generals any longer.... All generals lie.... All generals are faithless" (Goebbels 1948, 368). This increased after the July 1944 attentat and peaked in the last months of the war. When the head of the army operations department prematurely announced the fall of Warsaw, he and his assistant were both arrested and, when Guderian remonstrated, Hitler explained that he was not after this or any other general, but after the General Staff itself (Görlitz 1954, 487). In fact, a month later the führer abolished the entire OKH, subjecting all armed forces to the control of his OKW. On March 28, Guderian was dismissed and replaced by Krebs. On that occasion Hitler described Halder as an insufferable know-it-all, Zeitzler as lacking brains, and Guderian as a fathead. Moreover, all the defeats were due, not just to the incompetence, but to treason committed by the generals. On the night of April 20, 1945, when the news came that Germany had been split in two by the Allies meeting at the Elbe, a General Staff officer asked whether the führer really believed that the defeats were due to treason, whereupon Hitler turned to him not in anger, but with a pitying look as to how anyone could be so blind: "All the failures in the East," said Hitler, "are due to treachery." He, Hitler, regretted that he had been too lenient in these cases (Schramm 1971, 178). This fury eventually extended to the officers of his vaunted SS. During the attempt to liberate Budapest Hitler demanded that "the *Leibstandarte,* moreover the entire 6th Panzer Army be sent ... to the last man." When the SS Panzer Army, suffering severe losses, failed in its mission the führer screamed, "If we lose this war, it will be Dietrich's fault." The order sent out read, "The Führer believes that the troops have not fought as the situation demanded and orders that the SS divisions ... be stripped of their armbands." Himmler was then commissioned to fly out to Hungary to implement the punishment.

The hatred of the officer corps was extended to the country's aristocracy from whose ranks the higher military brass originated. And since many of the generals and aristocrats professed to be religious his venom extended to Christianity itself. As early as July 11, 1941, he sermonized to his pals, "The heaviest blow that ever struck humanity was the coming of Christianity. Bolshevism is Christianity's illegitimate child. Both are inventions of the Jew" (Hitler 1953, 6). On February 8, 1942, he said, "The evil that is gnawing at our vitals is our priests, of both creeds.... The time will come when I'll settle my accounts with them, and I'll go straight to the point: Our epoch will certainly see the end of the disease of Christianity" and again on June 2 he told his midnight audience, "As a sane German one is flabbergasted to think that German human beings could have let themselves be brought to such a pass by Jewish filth and priestly twaddle, that they were little different from the howling dervish of the Turks and the Negroes" and he told von Below that "We liquidated the Left in our class war, but, unfortunately, we forgot to deliver a blow to the Right. This is our great sin" (Below, 387).

Speer was present when Hitler gave orders, to be signed by Keitel, about the scorched-earth policy to be implemented on German soil by the armed forces. Hitler added that the gauleiters will receive similar instructions from Bormann for the civilian sector. When Speer was left alone with him, Hitler told him, "If the war is to be lost the nation, too, will be lost. This fate cannot be avoided. It is not necessary to worry about what the German people will need for elemental survival. On the contrary, it is best to destroy even these things. For the nation has proved to be the weaker, and the future belongs solely to the stronger eastern nation. In any case, only those who are inferior will remain after this struggle, for the good have already been killed" (Speer, 440). Similarly Hitler on April 10 told General Hilpert, who had come to plead for some resolution of the encircled Kurland army, "When one keeps in mind that Frederick the Great withstood a 12-fold superiority, one feels like a shit! This time we had the superiority. Isn't it a shame!" This was followed by the most revealing statement of Hitler's career, "When the German people loses this war it proved unworthy of me! (*hat es sich meiner als nicht würdig erwiesen*)" (Schramm 1965, 81). They let him down, not he them!

The directive issued on March 19 for the destruction of all facilities throughout Germany, often referred to as the Nero order, called for the blowing up of all military, transportation, communications and industrial installations; all food supplies, power stations, mines, waterworks, churches, castles, historical buildings, and all other valuable property, including the museum collections stored in mines and caves. Destroyed also were to be the sewage systems, telephone exchanges, the records of all municipalities, banks, and land registers. Every bridge must be wrecked and every farmstead burned. In a supplement to the order it was specified that "any concern for the civilian population can play no role." These orders had been explained to Speer as follows: "What does it matter, Speer! The enemy's advance is actually a help to us. People fight fanatically only when the war reaches their front doors.... No city will be left in enemy hands until it is a heap of ruin" (Speer, 442).

But these were not orders to exterminate Jews and Russians, so there was supreme "inefficiency" in carrying them out, nay, even disobedience! This time there were no scruples over the oath taken to the führer, no ingrained Prussian loyalty to the state. There was so little concern with these shibboleths of the German ethos that Speer had no scruples about planning to poison the führer, a personal friend no less, and would have carried it out had it not turned out that there was no need to do so. Near Essen armed miners defended the pits from destruction. Silesian workers saved the coal mines. Stöhr, the gauleiter of the Palatinate and the Saar, declared officially he would not obey the order for evacuations and destruction of property. Field commanders, including such stalwarts as Model and Guderian and the gauleiters themselves, saw to it that the Nero order was disobeyed.

In the end pure cynicism and *Schadenfreude* remained. At the 1943 gathering in Posen attended by a vast audience of gauleiters, generals and state and party luminaries when Himmler informed them in detail about the gruesome process of exterminating the millions of Jews, it was to convey the message that they had no way out but to join all the other lemmings for a collective plunge into the abyss. In one of his last situation conferences Hitler declared, "Don't fool yourselves. There is no turning back.... We have burned our bridges." And at the last meeting of the Propaganda Ministry staff on April 21, 1945, Goebbels told his co-workers, "The German people have failed. In the east they run, in the west the civilians prevent the soldiers from fighting and hang out white flags. You have earned the fate you deserve.... Why have you worked for me? Now you will have your throats cut" but as he was leaving the room Goebbels exclaimed, "when we depart the earth will shake."

· CHAPTER 38 ·

The Finale in Berlin

As the Red Army stepped onto East Prussia, Hitler left the *Wolfschanze* in Rastenburg. For three and a half years he had slouched there, bent over maps going through the contortions of defeating Russia. But it was over. Fearful of falling into Soviet hands, the führer abandoned his lair. The Wolfschanze complex covering some three square miles was dynamited and of Hitler's bunker only a pile of concrete and twisted ironwork remained. In December the führer took off for *Adlerhorst*, his western aerie, to oversee the Ardennes offensive. This, too, was now over. On January 16, he returned to Berlin. Snow was falling when the train pulled into the Grünewald station. There had been a 1,000-plane raid that morning by US bombers and a pall of smoke and brick dust hung over the city. His new Chancellery was half in ruins and he moved into the adjacent bunker. Accompanied by a valet carrying his belongings he descended into a catacomb 55 feet below ground to stay there till he killed himself.

In this cellar — removed from the living world — a pseudo–Wagnerian Walpurgisnacht was to be enacted over the next few months. The 16-foot-thick concrete roof was covered with 30 feet of soil. The walls dripped moisture, the air smelled of disinfectant and sewage. The upper level contained services. Below it were some 30-odd cubicles, three of which plus a toilet and shower were the führer's apartment. Its living room had a couch, a coffee table and three chairs. It was dominated by a portrait of Frederick the Great which Hitler always took with him to all of his 13 headquarters. Hitler's séances with the Prussian king were now so intense that when his orderly, Misch, once entered the room he found the führer gazing at the portrait in such a trance that he failed to notice his coming or leaving. A small room was reserved for Hitler's dog Blondi and her four puppies (O'Donnell, 24–5).

By all accounts Hitler was at this stage a physical wreck; an oxygen bottle had been placed in his room to help with his breathing. To all who saw him he made an unappetizing appearance. When arriving at a meeting he had to have a chair pushed under him to sit down. When he lay down his valet had to lift his legs onto the couch. He was stooped, his left side trembled and he seemed to list to one side. He often used a cane to propel himself. At meals spittle and crumbs of food clung to his chin and his jacked was blotched with food stains. His brown hair had turned white and the moustache was flecked with gray. Both hands trembled and he used his right to steady the left arm which he kept close to his body. When he held a glass or any other item the tremor of his hand was so pronounced that it produced a rattle against the tabletop which his cohorts tried to ignore.

In this catacomb Hitler continued with his usual routines. After the last military conference he indulged in a plate of sweet cakes and when darkness fell took Blondi for a walk through the garden — a duty he always performed himself. According to witnesses the dog and its puppies were the führer's only interest. He fed them himself and gave them the run of his premises. He would hold one of the puppies on his lap, ignoring his visitors. Occasionally he ventured outside to prowl the shattered Chancellery, hovering in particular at the marble table of his office now covered with dust blown in through the broken windows. In the past he had lunched there in style with 50 or so guests; he now occasionally had a snack there, alone or with his dietary cook. Most of his meals, however, were taken in the bunker and always in female company — his secretaries, his cook and, toward the end, Eva Braun. Theirs was the most congenial company for him and for good reasons. At one meeting he advised them to leave the bunker while there was still time, telling them, "Girls, the situation is hopeless." But they all pleaded to be allowed to stay, eliciting the remark, "Ah, if only my generals were as brave as my women" (O'Donnell, 115).

On a couple of occasions he performed what may have passed as a state function. The most elaborate of these was a meeting on February 24 with the country's gauleiters, two of whom were unable to appear: Hanke from besieged Breslau and Koch of East Prussia. When Hitler entered the hall his visitors were shocked to see a hunched old man. From a sitting position he spoke for an hour and a half. He reminisced about the glorious days of party triumphs and his seizing power. The year 1945, he told his men, would be decisive for the entire next century and he assured them that he knew what steps had to be taken. Then he passed on to them what was foremost on his mind. If the German people should nevertheless lose this war it would simply indicate that they did not possess the "inner value" attributed to Germans and he would have no sympathy with their demise. He used the occasion to issue a proclamation to the German people that a change in the fortunes of the war would certainly come within the next 10 months (Kershaw 2000, 780).

He also managed to deliver two other addresses. In one, on New Year's Day, he explained to the German people that the reason they had not heard from him since July 20 was because all his energies were spent on dealing with the military situation. He asked his Volk to retain their faith in God Almighty who would bring victory to those "who deserve it most…. The setbacks we have suffered are the result of a series of betrayals…. There will never be another November 9 [1918]." He threatened to annihilate anyone who attempted to weaken or undermine the resistance of the German people. (Daladier, 305–7). On January 30 this was followed by a 16-minute radio address in which he invoked the threat of the "Asian tidal wave" and called for a fight to the finish. "My life today" he informed the Germans, "is entirely determined by the duty imposed upon me — to work and fight for my people. Only He who imposed it on me can release me from it" (Sweeting, 250). It was the last time the Germans would hear his voice.

On April 15 Hitler issued his two last directives. Foreseeing the splintering of Germany into north and south regions, he assigned the north to Dönitz and the south to Kesselring in case he himself was not in one of them; but in either case he would retain "the unified control of operations by myself, personally." The second directive was to the soldiers on the eastern front, in which he admonished, "For the last time our deadly enemies — the Jewish Bolsheviks — have launched their massive forces to the attack. Their aim is to reduce Germany to ruins and to exterminate our people…. We have foreseen this thrust, and since last January have done everything to construct a strong front" and he promised them that the enemy would be defeated (Strawson 1971, 223).

On April 18 the führer had a visit form SS General Wolff who had been negotiating the surrender of German armies in Italy. He came to get an endorsement from Hitler who obliquely said to Wolff that yes, he should try to sow discord between the Allies by his uni-lateral approach to the West. But more important was, he admonished the SS chieftain, to see that the scorched-earth policy in Italy was carried out with the utmost ruthlessness. Everything standing should be destroyed, including heavy industry and all the Italian ports and with this he sent him on his way (Dulles, 177–8).

On April 25 and 27 he conducted the last two situation conferences. His verbatim pro-nouncements run as follows:

- I believe that the moment has come when the others in their self-interest will stand up against the massive Proletarian-Bolshevik Colossus. Should I falter and run … then the German Reich is lost. If I succeed in defending the capital … there is hope the Anglo-Americans would join Nazi Germany in meeting this danger. For this task I remain the only man.
- In defending the Rhineland and other places insane catastrophic blunders have been made. All the plans I had worked out miscarried because the commanders sabo-taged them.
- If there is a fallout between the Allies in San Francisco (UN Conf.)—and this *must* happen—then there will be a turnabout whereby I will deliver the Bolsheviks a blow. The others will then realize that to stop the Bolshevik Colossus—there is only I, the Party, and the German State.
- When I win the battle here it will be not for my own name, but … I will be vindi-cated. Then I will be able to deal with a number of generals including those in the SS who in critical moments failed to perform.
- I did not start the war against Russia frivolously [*leichtsinnig*].… I had information that an alliance was being hatched between England and Russia.… The question was whether one strikes first or waits until one is defeated [DDR, XXIV, 157–68].

The most interesting utterance was Hitler castigating himself. In talking to Goebbels and Mohnke at the last conference Hitler suddenly said, "It would have been better if I had waited another year or year and a half before taking power [in 1933].… There would not have been men such as Hugenburg and Schleicher [to oppose him].… Had I waited a bit longer Hindenburg would have been dead. He would have died half a year earlier because he would have been so aggravated by me being in the opposition. If anybody would have been called upon to take his place then it would have been I. I could then have acted with-out any restrictions.… As it was I had to go from one compromise to another till Hinden-burg died.… I, of course, had the intention of doing away with the entire clique [*Klüngel*]. I could have done it had I come to power by a … putsch. One regrets having been so good [*gut*]" (DDR, XXIV, 169–70). The above can be read as a retroactive diatribe against the aristocrats and generals who had, as early as 1933, sabotaged the workings of the Nazi regime. And if there was self-criticism it was that he, Hitler, had been—well—too gentle. In another monologue Hitler expressed a somewhat similar set of regrets. "The fate of this war," he said, "is that for Germany it came either too early or too late. I should have taken the initiative already in 1938.… But I couldn't help it because in Munich the French and the English met all my demands. But in terms of spiritual readiness it came much too soon. I had no time to mould the people to my politics. I needed twenty years to generate an elite which would have absorbed the Nazi ideology with their mothers' milk."

* * *

While the advance from the Oder-Neisse line was termed the Red Army's last offensive it was by no means the end of bloodletting for the Russian soldier. He still faced the battle of Berlin — and a costly battle it proved to be. Berlin's 320 square miles of territory was cut by the meandering Spree River and multiple canals and tunnels. The prewar population of 4.3 million had by 1945 fallen to less than 3 million. During February and March it had endured several 1,000-plane bombing raids, the one on February 23 leaving 22,000 dead civilians. The raid which took place on the eve of Hitler's birthday was to be the last because Russian troops were entering the outskirts of the city. Including Volksturm formations Berlin was manned by roughly 100,000 men equipped with a profusion of Panzerfäuste. In command was General Weidling, appointed directly by Hitler. They faced 2.5 million Russians, 6,250 tanks and a powerful air force (Sayer, 291). The attackers' ultimate objective was Target 106 — the Reich Chancellery. Mindful of what had happened in Stalingrad the Stavka tried to devise ways of taking Berlin without the carnage resulting from street fighting. Special assault troops drawn from experienced infantry units were to advance behind a tank and artillery curtain of fire. The central Berlin area, between the river Spree and the Landwehr Canal, designated the Citadel, encompassed the government sector including the Chancellery and its bunker. In command of the Citadel was *SS-Brigadeführer* Wilhelm Mohnke. The führer's life and death were in his hands, as he was responsible for defending the bunker and for immediately informing him when the end was near. He was also put in charge of the flying courts-martial busy executing anyone suspected of having left or not having joined his unit. On April 23 Hitler abolished the OKH and subordinated the army to the OKW. Thus in the very last days he took revenge on the detested army General Staff.

By April 20 the Red Army had reached the eastern suburbs of Berlin and shock troops began pushing their way in block by block while long-range artillery shelled the inner city. The struggle became more fierce the closer the Russians came to the city center. The inner defenses had to be broken building by building and frequently the troops had to cut passages through walls and cellars to outflank the street barricades igniting firefights in courtyards, basements and on staircases. The cellars and the U-Bahn tunnels were packed with civilians who were caught in the crossfire or were flooded by burst water pipes. By then, too, the city was without gas, electricity or food.

While the Russians battled for the city, another battle, to a large degree illusory, was being staged outside Berlin. This aimed at lifting the siege and to capture in the process its Russian conquerors. This bold strike was the brainchild of the führer himself. As shown in Fig. 38.1, there were three army groupings at some remove from Berlin. To the southwest was the 12th Army under General Wenck, presumably fighting the Americans nearing the Elbe River. To the southeast was the 9th Army under General Busse arrayed against the Red Army. Busse's army had been surrounded but Koniev, during his lunge for Berlin, ignored it. To the north was Steiner's Task Force, part of Heinrici's AG Vistula. Originally the 9th Army had been ordered to stand by until Schörner's AG Mitte came up from the southeast (fighting in Slovakia, of all places) at which time they would join the two other groupings for a triumphal march on Berlin. The führer had been warned that at any moment the 9th Army would be cut off, but he ignored it. Jodl was put in charge of the relief operation and his orders for Wenck were to turn the 12th Army around to face Koniev's left wing besieging Berlin regardless of what the Americans might do on the Elbe. Perhaps such an act, mused the führer aloud, would convince the Americans that "we intend to fight only against the Soviets" (Schramm 1965, 127). The overall plan was for the 9th and 12th

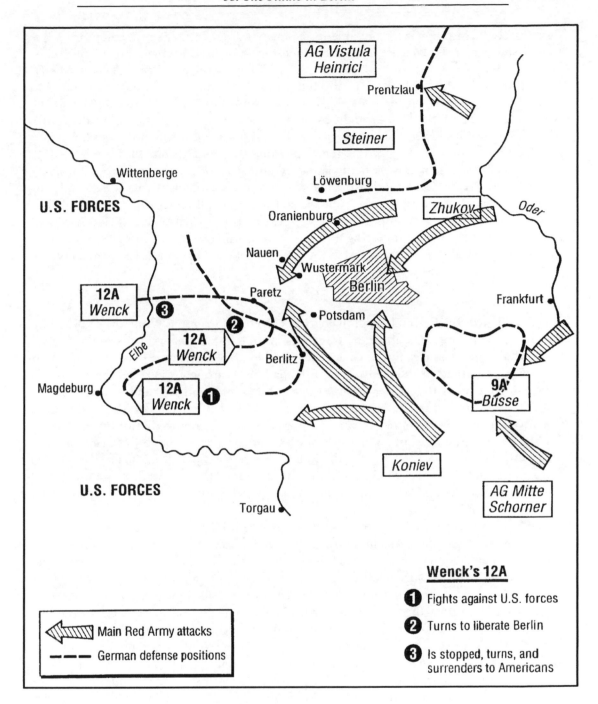

38.1. German attempts to relieve besieged Berlin

armies to join and launch an attack from the south while Steiner's task force attacked from the north. This was supplemented by an order from Hitler to completely denude the Elbe front facing the Americans and throw all troops into the battle for Berlin. Wenck, however, though ostensibly getting ready to implement the given orders was, according to his postwar testimony (Gellermann, 74), preoccupied with entirely different matters; he was desperately trying to make it possible for as many refugees and his own troops to escape to the American side. Wenck did stage an attack on April 26 and managed to establish contact with those few troops of the 12th Army that had broken out of the encirclement. Steiner, on the other hand, who had no armor and only 22,000 infantry, did not even bother to attack. By the 27th Wenck had gotten to within 20 miles of Berlin where a Russian counterattack stopped him. This brought to an end the entire scheme. Not so in the führer bunker where till the very end orders and calls and pleas and threats went out hourly for the three German armies to resume their drive on Berlin and liberate the führer.

While these attempts were being launched and abandoned, Zhukov's troops came up to the Spree River with the Reichstag just across and Koniev's men crossed the Landwehr Canal approaching the same area from the south. What still remained in German hands was a strip of real estate compressed between the east-west chausse in the Tiergarten and the Kurfürstendamm encompassing the main government quarter. By April 28 the distance to the führer bunker from the Russian lines both north and south was less than a mile.

* * *

The Third Reich, which not long ago had stretched from the White to the Black Sea and from the Atlantic Ocean to the Caucasus Mountains, had now shrunk to the dimensions of a cement bunker in the Chancellery garden. But *Gröfaz*, the Greatest Warlord of all Times, remained in all essentials what he had been throughout the dozen years of his rule. He continued to practice *Dichtung*, the system of mendacity and delusion he had resorted to from that fateful September 3, 1939, when, contrary to his wishes and predictions, Great Britain had gone to war with him. There were now only two themes to this *Dichtung*: the impending breakup of the anti–German alliance, possibly even a joint crusade with the Anglo-Saxons against the Bolsheviks; and a flip-flop in the fortunes of war brought about by a miracle deduced from horoscopes and the intervention of Providence. There had once been a third element in the deception syndrome, wonder weapons. This had now been dropped.

The imminent breakup of the coalition was gleaned from a number of events. When American and Russian troops met on April 22 at the Elbe, reports came into the bunker that there was friction among them. Hitler commented that this was "striking proof of the disagreement between our enemies.... Would not the German people and posterity brand me a criminal if I were to make peace today when there still is the possibility of our enemies falling out among themselves tomorrow? Is it not possible that any day, even any hour, war will break out between the Bolsheviks and the Anglo-Saxons over their prize, Germany?" (Boldt, 169). Moreover, he did not simply rely on this process maturing on its own but intervened to help it along. In January he gave Ribbentrop permission to offer the West peace, provided Ribbentrop alone shouldered the responsibility for it. And on March 15 Ribbentrop duly got in touch with Stockholm about peace contacts with the West. When Guderian learned about it and endorsed the move Hitler's response was that, why, this was treason. In a conversation with Speer Hitler explained the reasons for this move, so contrary to his stance throughout the war. He launched this move, explained Hitler, not really to make peace but to insert suspicion between the Western Powers and the Soviet Union about a separate peace. And as discussed earlier, the same motivation was at work when he tolerated negotiations (presumably behind his back) between SS General Wolff and Allen Dulles in Switzerland about a wholesale German surrender in Italy. The latter negotiations did, in fact, generate an acrimonious exchange between Stalin and the Western leaders.

The other strategy for a reversal in Germany's impending end was to invoke the history of Frederick the Great. In Carlyle's description of the Seven Years War between the king and the anti–Prussian coalition, the king, at the end of his tether, had set himself a deadline that if by February 15 there would be no change for the better he would take poison. Then, by the grace of good fortune — or was it the Almighty? — on February 12 Russia's tsarina died and the enemy coalition collapsed. When these passages from Carlyle's history were read to him, Hitler had tears in his eyes. And sure enough, the miracle repeated itself. On April 12 the news arrived of President Roosevelt's death. To a euphoric Hitler, Goebbels cried out, "My Führer, I congratulate you! Roosevelt is dead. It is written in the stars that the second half of April will be a turning point for us. This is Friday, April 13. It *is* the turning-point" (Bullock 1962, 781).

This faith in a turnabout was further promoted by the führer's personal demeanor. Though the Chancellery was shattered, the Berghof bombed out, and Vienna occupied, Hitler spent whole afternoons pondering the postwar aspects of Linz where after victory he was to retire and whose Nazi temples would attest for posterity the greatness of the Hitler era. The model of future Linz designed by another Hitlerian architect, Hermann Giesler, was as late as February 1945 set up in the basement of the shattered new Chancellery and the architect was continuously summoned to discuss the details of the führer's retirement. His cohorts would find Hitler slouched for hours over the Linz model lost in profound meditation about the architecture of his future, Sans-Souci.

Not only did the führer's methods keep to his past record, but his entire persona remained cast in the same concrete which had crashed onto the European scene 13 years before. In the very first chapter it was asserted that it encompassed three personalities— each hermetically sealed off from the others. Such a separation was mandatory to convincingly flaunt, in accordance with the demands of the hour, a particular facet as the Hitlerian whole. These three facets were stated to be the Viennese *petit-burgeois*, the café bohemian and gift-bearing uncle; the super–Bismarck of matchless political gifts and military genius; and the ghoul whose lust for bloodshed was so immense and immediate as to hoist him to the pinnacle of history's mass murderers. The fruits of this last facet during his rule were described in previous chapters. After losing the killing grounds of Eastern Europe, he had turned to destroying his own Volk. Locked in his bunker he now carried it to the point of trying to kill off his entourage. As the Soviets advanced to the Elbe Göring, piling his art treasures, Gobelins and cutlery on a convoy of trucks, blew up his Karinhall Palace and headed for Bertchesgaden where he had an abode next to the führer's. At some point, when pressed to start negotiations with the Allies, Hitler had sarcastically remarked that "if it comes to negotiating the Reichsmarschall can do it better than I." Göring took the remark seriously and on the evening of April 23 the bunker received the message, "My Führer: In view of your decision to remain at your post in the fortress of Berlin, do you agree that I take over, at once, the total leadership of the Reich, with full freedom of action at home and abroad.... If no reply is received by 10 o'clock tonight I shall take it for granted that you have lost your freedom of action and shall ... act for the best interests of our people and our country.... Your loyal Hermann Göring." Hitler's fury was monumental. He knew Göring was lazy and corrupt. But a traitor! He immediately ordered that Göring be stripped of all his offices, even as chief huntsman. Command of the Luftwaffe was transferred to Ritter von Greim who had come to fly the führer out of besieged Berlin. Himmler was

ordered to have the SS arrest Göring as well as Koller and Lammers. Though Göring did
not know it the commander of his SS guard had orders to execute the reichsmarschall and
all the traitors involved in the "April 23" treachery. Luckily or unluckily for Göring, this
order, too, like the destruction of Germany, was not carried out by the law-abiding Germans.

Soon came the turn of Himmler himself. Unlike Ribbentrop who acted on Hitler's
instructions, Himmler contacted Graf Bernadotte of the Swedish Red Cross on his own initiative, soon after he had been dismissed from commanding AG Vistula. Preliminary contacts took place on March 5 via Dr. Felix Kersten, Himmler's Finnish masseur. On April 23
Himmler met Bernadotte in Lübeck proposing surrender to the Western powers and asked
that the offer be passed on to Eisenhower. Bernadottte said he would do that provided the
surrender included the German occupation armies in Norway and Denmark; no mention
was made by either party of a surrender to the Russians. On the 28th Hitler was informed
that the BBC had just announced Himmler's offer of unconditional surrender. It was the
worst of all betrayals Hitler had suffered—*der treue* Heinrich, a turncoat! Since von Greim
was leaving Berlin that day he was instructed to inform Dönitz that Himmler was to be
arrested and liquidated. About the same time Hitler learned that SS Lieutenant-General
Fegelein, Himmler's liaison man at the bunker and the husband of Eva Braun's sister, had
been found carousing in Berlin dressed in civilian clothes. On Hitler's orders Fegelein was
shot just outside the bunker—even though in a day or two Hitler was to marry his sister-
in-law. Upon learning that her sister's husband had been executed, Eva Braun lamented,
"Poor Adolf, everyone has betrayed him."

The ultimate came when he was about to kill off Dr. Morell—the physician who,
according to Hitler himself, had provided him with the physical well-being and peace of
mind to carry out his gargantuan duties. In his postwar reminiscences Morell writes, "I
gave him shots of glucose. On Saturday April 21, he was very dejected.... I wanted to give
him another shot. He grabbed me and lost his temper, shouting that he knew precisely that
I was going to inject him with morphine" (Morell, 272). Suspecting that Morell wanted to
drug him so he could be handed over to the Russians he drove him from the bunker and
threatened to have him shot. The same happened to another of his physicians, Dr. Brandt,
his personal surgeon. When Hitler heard that he had moved his family to Thuringia, under
Allied occupation, he was charged with defeatism and condemned to death in absentia.

The two other facets of his persona were likewise on display during the last days in
the bunker. The Viennese uncle emerged on the führer's 56th birthday, April 20, and then
on the 29th in no less a ceremony than Herr Adolf Hitler's matrimony to Fräulein Eva
Braun. The führer's birthday was celebrated on three levels, international, national and private. The birthday broadcast by Goebbels asserted, "Today millions of people throughout
the world are looking to this man, full of hope that he may yet discover a way out of this
great evil that now plagues mankind. He will surely save all the nations, but we Germans,
in particular, owe him a great debt of gratitude." Special stamps were issued bearing his
visage and the Berliners received an extra ration of sausage and oatmeal. A telegram of congratulations was received from Il Duce to which the celebrant responded, "My thanks to
you, Duce.... Utterly unafraid of death, the German people and all those who are of like
mind will see to it that this onslaught [Bolshevism] is thwarted at whatever cost." A birthday reception was held at the Chancellery attended by Speer, Bormann, Goebbels, Göring
and Ribbentrop. The Chancellery was gutted, the floors strewn with litter, the windows
boarded up, some daylight filtering in through holes in the roof. In front stood a guard of

honor and newsreels recorded Hitler's courtiers wishing him a happy birthday. Bent and trembling, he then inspected a platoon of Hitler Youth during which the Viennese uncle did not fail to tweak the cheek of one of the youngsters. Returned to the bunker the führer officially received the congratulations from Dönitz, Keitel and Jodl. It was soon after these festivities that Göring left for Bertchesgaden to send his "traitorous" telegram and Himmler drove off to meet — of all people — a delegate of the World Jewish Congress — in the hope this would advance his "negotiations" with the West. Then followed the private part of the celebration when Hitler retired alone with Eva Braun. She emerged proudly wearing a dress of silver-blue brocade — evidently a gift from Adolf. She then invited an intimate group to the führer's apartments in the old Chancellery, still relatively undamaged. A gramophone played sentimental tunes, the guests danced and drank champagne — while explosions from the Russian guns shook the walls and made the gramophone rattle.

By the time Hitler was ready for the next Uncle Adolf act — his nuptials to Fräulein Braun — the Russians very nearly showed up at the wedding. They were by then entering the Potsdamer Platz, a few hundred yards from the bunker. Hitler's personal judgment of the military position was that "the situation in Berlin looks worse than it is." On April 21 he had ordered SS Obergruppenführer Steiner to attack from the north threatening that "Every commander withholding forces has forfeited his life within five hours.... Officers unwilling to obey were to be shot immediately," he screamed at the SS general, "even the commander's life hinged on the execution of the order" (Kershaw 2000, 802). When next day he learned that Steiner had not budged Hitler lost his self-control. After a scene of rage against the army's cowardice and treachery he suddenly calmed down and out came an astounding revelation. After six years of furious warfare, at midday of April 22, 1945 the führer and reich chancellor, Adolf Hitler, declared that Germany had lost the war. "It is all over," he sobbed. "The war is lost. I shall shoot myself" (Boldt, 146). He fetched his senior adjutant, SS Major General Schaub, who had a matching key to Hitler's safe in the study. Together they sorted out his private papers. A few were entrusted to the adjutant, but the bulk Schaub with the help of two valets lugged up the steps of the emergency exit and burned in the incinerator. When Schaub returned he found that Hitler had removed his large Walther pistol from the safe. From then on Hitler kept it on the dresser of his bedroom (O'Donnel, 114–5).

With Steiner not heard from there remained the possibility of the 12th and 9th armies joining hands to break the siege of Berlin. As noted, Wenck did turn eastward and tried to reach Berlin. He got within 20 miles from Potsdam where he was stopped. The 9th Army further east was surrounded and could not move at all. At 8 P.M. on April 29 Jodl received the famous last cry from the führer demanding he be immediately informed about the following:

- Where are Wenck's spearheads?
- When are they going to attack?
- Where is the 9th Army?
- In which direction is the 9th Army breaking through?

No answer reached the bunker either from the OKW or from the two armies. Nor was the führer ever heard from again.

And it was then that the führer got married. The ceremony took place in the bunker's conference room at midnight of April 28-29. It contained all the prescribed ingredients — witnesses, formal "I do's", a wedding feast. The registrar was an official from the Propaganda Ministry dressed in a Nazi uniform brought to the bunker in an armored car. Goebbels and Bormann were the witnesses. Following the ceremony the staff congratulated the newlyweds, followed by sandwiches, champagne and toasts for a happy future.

The previous day, April 28, Hitler had called in his youngest secretary, Junge, for a very special task. She noted that the large table usually cluttered with maps and documents was now empty. Hitler stood in front of it and dictated his last will, one private, the other political, a blueprint for posterity. In the political testament there was no mention of a lost Second World War — it was instead a beefed-up version of *Mein Kampf*. In it Hitler, in his role as a super–Bismarck, passed on admonitions to the German people and its leaders how to conduct themselves in the future. The excerpts below tell the tale:

"In the three decades [since end of World War I] I have been actuated solely by love and loyalty to my people…. Centuries will pass, but out of the ruins of our towns and monuments hatred will grow against those finally responsible for everything, International Jewry…. It is untrue that I, or anyone else in Germany, wanted the war in 1939. It was desired and instigated solely by those international statesmen who were either of Jewish descent or worked for Jewish interests…. I have, further, never wished that after the fatal First World War a second against England or against America should break out…. Above all, I charge the leaders of the nation and those under them to scrupulous observance of the laws of race and to merciless opposition to the universal poisoner of all people, international Jewry…. I also left no doubt that this time not only European children of Aryan descent will starve, not only millions of men will die and hundreds of thousands of women and children will be burned to death in bombing raids that the guilty ones, too, will pay the price, though under more humane conditions…. I beg the heads of the Army, Navy and Air Force to strengthen … the spirit of resistance of our soldiers in the Nazi sense with special reference to the fact that I … have preferred death to cowardly abdication or even capitulation…. May it become … part of the code of honor of the German officer that the surrender of a district or town should be impossible…. Göring and Himmler have conducted secret negotiations with the enemy without my knowledge … causing the nation immeasurable harm, aside from being disloyal to me and … I nominate a new Cabinet [here followed the names of 20 new ministers; with a restored presidency given to Dönitz, and Goebbels as chancellor]…. I hope that my spirit will always accompany them. May they be hard but never unjust…. may they be aware that our task remains the reconstruction of a Nazi state." In his private will Hitler left his possessions to the Nazi Party and, should it no longer exist, to the state and should the state not exist — then no instructions were necessary. "As for the paintings these I have never collected for my private needs but for the erection of a Gallery in my home city of Linz."

The testament was dated April 28, 4:00 P.M. with Goebbels, Bormann, Burgdorf and Krebs as witnesses. Three couriers rushed copies to Dönitz in northern Germany and to Feldmarschall Schörner still battling the Russians in Bohemia. In addition, von Below was entrusted with delivering a special message to Keitel, a sort of coda to the testament, which said, "The efforts and sacrifices of the German people in this war were so large that I cannot believe they were in vain. The goal for the German people remains to conquer room for itself in the East" (Lüdde-Neurath, 123–8).

As these ceremonies, conducted with the utmost solemnity, were taking their course the Russians were battling their way toward the city center. During the night of April 29 Chuikov's assault troops secured a bridge over the Landwehr Canal abutting the Tiergarten. The zoo there had been abandoned and lions and zebras roamed the neighborhood, depop-

April 30, 1945. The Soviet flag is raised atop the Reichstag on the day that Hitler committed suicide. (From *The Russian War 1941–1945* by Daniela Mrazkova and Vladimir Remes copyright
©1975 by Daniela Mrazkova and Vladimir Remes. Used by permission of Dutton, a division of
Penguin Group [USA] Inc.)

ulated but for the corpses of soldiers and civilians littering the streets. From the north the
150th Rifle Division made its way to the Reichstag, the heart of Berlin and symbol of the
German reich. Its approaches were defended by 5,000 fanatical SS and Hitler Youth troops.
Even when the first Russian soldiers burst onto the steps and through its doors, firefights
continued in the cellars, hallways and chambers of the cavernous temple. But by the end
of the day two Russian sergeants, Yegorov and Kantaryja, hoisted the Soviet flag above the
cupola of the Reichstag. It was evening of April 30.

It was also the day the German nation lost its führer. Hitler worried lest the poison he
intended to take would not work properly, so he had it tested on his beloved Blondi. At
midnight of April 29-30 Blondi was put on a toilette seat, the caretaker forced open the
dog's jaws and Professor Haase, of the medical staff using a pair of pliers crushed a prussic acid capsule inside its mouth. The dog was dead in an instant. Hitler entered the room
to inspect the result and after looking at the carcass turned and left the room. He then
started on his farewell rounds. At about 2:00 A.M. he said goodbye to his 20 or so servants
and guards. He shook hands with each of them, thanked them for their past service and
released them from their oath to him. He repeated the same with the next echelon of wor-
thies, doctors, nurses and their assistants who attended the Chancellery's emergency hos-

pital. He went to sleep not long before sunrise but was up within an hour and the attendants found him pacing restlessly back and forth without noticing or talking to anyone.

At 6:00 A.M. Mohnke was woken up and told the führer wished to see him. Instead of the study Hitler received him in his bedroom. Hitler was sitting on his bed wearing a black satin dressing gown over white pajamas and patent leather slippers. Mohnke was invited to sit on the bed while Hitler sat down on a nearby chair. Hitler asked for a situation report. He was told the Russians had occupied the Tiergarten and reached the Wilhelmstrasse, four blocks from the bunker; moreover they were in the rail tunnels under Voss Strasse facing the Chancellery. "My Führer," he said, "I cannot hold out more than one day, May 1." Hitler then confided in him a deep regret. He had hoped — said the führer — to last till May 5th, the date Napoleon died on St. Helena. "Another great career that ended in disappointment, disillusion, betrayal, despair. The fickle Europeans did not really understand him. We were *both* men born before our time. So much the worse for Europe." As Mohnke recalled it Hitler then launched into an hour-long monologue. "He reviewed his whole career, his dream of National Socialism and why and how it had failed. The German people had, in the end, proven unworthy, just not up to the supreme challenge. The war had been forced on him by the Anglo-American plutocracy, the Marxist-Bolshevik world conspiracy, Jewish international finance, the Freemasons and the Jesuits. The only reason he had attacked the Soviet Union in 1941 was because he knew the Soviet Union was about to attack Germany. He could have won, too, but for the abysmal incompetence of his General Staff, that haven of reactionary aristocrats. Even inside his own circle treason was rife. Göring, Himmler and Speer had betrayed him." As Mohnke rose to leave he complimented him on the fight of his troops; "Would that all the others have fought as tenaciously." (Sayer, 5–6; O'Donnell, 172–6). There had been no reason for this lecture except to make doubly sure that, as in his testament, future generations learned the true causes for the collapse of the Third Reich.

Hitler was breakfasting at 8:00 A.M. when he heard the artillery barrage heralding the Russian assault on the Reichstag a few blocks away. At noon he had his usual situation conference in which Weidling confirmed what Mohnke had said about the proximity of Russian troops. Even though his planned death was only a couple of hours away he ate lunch at 1:00 P.M., spaghetti and tossed salad, with his secretaries and cook; Eva was not present. At the meal he talked about the breeding of dogs, the chemistry of lipstick and such like. Dressed in his usual jacket and black trousers he appeared together with Eva to say farewell to the secretaries and the "inner" circle — the Goebbelses, Bormann, Burgdorf, Krebs, a few others. He held out his hand and uttered a few words to each one of them. He then turned toward his apartment, politely letting Eva go first. This was the last they were to see of him.

Hitler had that day again consulted Professor Haase about the most foolproof method of committing suicide and he scrupulously followed instructions to assure he would not remain alive. Hitler wore his usual uniform and a pair of black gloves. Hitler owned two pistols, the potent Walther 7.65 caliber and a smaller Walther 6.35. He also had with him two potassium cyanide vials. In the study stood a sofa and Hitler sat down at the right hand side with Eva, two feet away, on the left side, legs tucked in. He put the smaller pistol on an adjoining table in case the larger one jammed and placed a spare vial between the pistol and a vase, as a reserve. As instructed he put the barrel of the pistol perpendicular to his right temple at eyebrow level and placed the poison vial in his mouth. He pulled the trigger at the same time he bit into the poison. Eva died by using a poison vial which — by Haase's instructions — she bit into the moment she heard the pistol shot. The time was 3:30 P.M., April 30.

Hitler had left instructions to wait 10 minutes before entering the suicide room. No one heard the shot because there was a vestibule between the outside and his apartment and the doors were insulated against poison gas and smoke. His senior SS adjutant, Maj. Otto Günsche, was ordered to stand guard and prevent anyone from going inside while the self-killing was taking place. Waiting with him were Goebbels, Bormann and several others. As they waited there was complete silence except for the drone of the diesel ventilator. The group hesitated for some time to enter the room. Eventually Bormann and several others did so. It was filled with cordite smoke and a bitter almond smell typical of prussic acid. Hitler's head had drooped left and forward toward the floor with blood dripping from a hole in his right temple. His eyes were open. There was a plate-size puddle of blood on the floor. The pistol had slipped from his hand, indicating that the poison took effect before the head wound (Joachimstahler, 155).

A surgeon arrived to confirm that the two were dead. Three SS men wrapped the bodies in blankets and carried them up the bunker stairs. They placed the corpses in a shallow excavation, emptied several jerrycans of gasoline over the corpses and set them on fire. As the flames shot up the men raised their arms in a Nazi salute. Later a second incineration took place. By 8:00 P.M. the cadavers were no longer recognizable (O'Donnel, Ch. 8; Kershaw 2000, 825–7).

When the Russians arrived they found nothing but dust and wreckage. Except for the dental bridgework, which confirmed that somewhere here one Adolf Hitler had been incinerated, there was nothing left of him. Part of a skull with a bullet hole in the cranium, claimed to be Hitler's, rests in a carton box in a dilapidated Russian warehouse. The exhibit is considered to be fake — a fitting testimonial to its presumed owner.

CHAPTER 39

Unconditional Surrender

The history of World War II in Europe ends with Hitler's suicide on April 30. Since he died abandoning the state and Wehrmacht without tying up the ends of Germany's defeat it was left to his successors to implement the formalities of ending the war. But even in his death Hitler guided the hands of his successors. Though the Dönitz government lasted less than a month it indulged in all kinds of maneuvers to enable a maximum number of civilians and soldiers to reach the American and British lines. Thus even in victory the Russians ended up with the short end of the trophy. Moreover, the manner in which the Western Allies staged Germany's official capitulation contained, both legally and ethically, an offence to the Soviet Union, such that the formalities of ending the war had to be performed twice.

Dönitz, the president-designee, was in Schleswig-Holstein when, on the afternoon of May 1, he received the news of Hitler's death. At 10:30 that evening Radio Hamburg interrupted the playing of Bruckner's 7th Symphony to broadcast the news to the German people: "Führer Headquarters reports that our Führer, Adolf Hitler, having fought to the last breath for Germany against Bolshevism, has this afternoon fallen at his command post in the Reichs Chancellery." Thus mendacity was practiced even after his death, as nothing in the above announcement was true. Dönitz followed it up with a message to the German people and an order of the day to the Wehrmacht, stressing that the fight against the Russians must go on and resistance to the Western Allies would be offered only if they interfered with the fight against the Bolsheviks. This tactic and the isolation of many German armies led to numerous piecemeal and duplicitous local surrenders. The largest of these and one that had been in the works for some time was the capitulation of all German forces in Italy. This had been started by SS Obergruppenführer Karl Wolff with the connivance of the local commander in chief, Vietinghoff, as well as Kesselring and Himmler. The initial contact took place on March 8, a few days after Himmler himself had contacted Stockholm. The surrender document was signed on April 29 to take effect on May 2. A quarter million Germans laid down their weapons before any overall capitulation was even mooted, all more or less without consulting the Soviets.

About the same time came the capitulation of Berlin to the Soviet command. After Hitler's suicide, there was shock and paralysis in the bunker. Goebbels was near hysteria and Mohnke, along with a few others, was weeping. In his new role as chancellor, Goebbels convened a meeting at which it was decided to ask the Soviets for an armistice. Krebs, who knew Russian, was the spokesman. When the delegation reached Chuikov's headquarters they had to wait all night until instructions arrived from Moscow. These were plain: only full capitulation was acceptable. When it became clear in the bunker that the only outcome would be unconditional surrender, the Goebbelses decided the time had come to go the way the führer had gone. The Goebbelses had five children aged 4 to 12 and the parents decided to kill them before they themselves died. They had morphine injected into them followed by a doctor forcing prussic acid into their mouths. Imitating the führer, the Goebbelses killed themselves by swallowing poison, followed by the SS firing into their bodies. Weidling then notified Chuikov that Berlin was ready to capitulate. By midday of May 2 fighting in the city stopped. The Russians lined the streets with rows of T-34s and past them marched the surrendering German troops, including many shanghaied civilians. Russian casualties in the battle of Berlin for Rokossovsky's, Zhukov's and Koniev's three fronts amounted to 350,000, including 80,000 dead. There were 125,000 dead civilians, most certainly several times those of the German military (Beevor 2002, 424).

While the surrenders in Italy and Berlin were to opponents the German troops had been facing at the front, the next several surrenders were so manipulated as to have German divisions fighting the Soviets surrender to the Western Allies. The largest such capitulation was in northern Germany where all German troops surrendered to Montgomery. On becoming president, Dönitz handed over command of the German navy to Admiral Friedburg. On the evening of May 2 Friedburg was sent to Montgomery to propose the following: German forces in northwest Germany would surrender; AG Vistula troops (facing the Russians) would be allowed to turn around and cross the Allied lines; permit passage to the west of civilian refugees from the east as well as from the ships ferrying troops and civilians from East Prussia, Kurland, Hel, etc; and that the British provide sustenance for the civilian refugees. Friedburg and his companions reached British headquarters in the afternoon of May 3. Although Montgomery knew they were coming, upon seeing the saluting Germans he asked, "Who are these people? What do they want?" In like fashion he originally retorted that he would not permit any civilians across his lines, but soon added, "Still I am not inhuman." He demanded that all German forces in Holland and Denmark be included in the surrender; rejected the takeover of compact formations that had been fighting on the Russian front, adding, however, that individual soldiers and small units reaching his lines would not be handed over to the Russians; and he would accept refugees and sea transports coming from the east. Friedburg had no authorization to hand over the armies in Holland and Denmark so he returned to Dönitz with Monty's demands. Dönitz was satisfied with the conditions but in sending Friedburg back he had told him to accede to the demands "provided German prisoners would be honorably treated." When, back at British headquarters, Friedburg started quoting Dönitz's qualification, Monty cut him off "Is the answer yes or no?" to which Friedburg responded "Ja." The document, signed by Montgomery, was drawn up on May 4 with hostilities to cease at 8:00 A.M. on May 5 (Schwan, 85).

A more conspicuous case was the surrender of Wenck's 12th Army. As related, this army had been ordered to abandon the American front and turn eastward in order to lift the siege of Berlin. Thus during the last week or so 12th Army had been fighting the Russians. Since prior to the switch Wenck had faced Simpson's 9th US Army it was to Simpson that Wenck offered to surrender. Simpson accepted. As of May 5th Wenck's army began crossing the American lines while its rear guard continued battling the Russians. As a result of Russian protests, Simpson handed over a few of the surrendered Germans to the Red Army.

Discriminatory treatment of the Russian ally preceded these local surrenders. Since December 1944, even while the Yalta Conference was in progress, representatives of the

British Secret Service and the OSS had been negotiating with von Papen about opening the German front to the Western armies, though it is not clear to what extent the top allied leadership was party to it. In the end it proved immaterial whether an agreement was reached or not because after the Allies crossed the Rhine the Germans essentially stopped fighting in the west. According to one set of statistics, on the western front during the period of April 11– 20, 580 Germans were killed, 2,000 wounded — but the number of prisoners was over a quarter million; the corresponding numbers for the Russian front were: 7,600, 35, 000 and 26,000 POWs. The Russians, of course, were not blind to it all. On February 24, Molotov protested these goings-on and two days later cancelled his scheduled attendance at the UN Conference in San Francisco. This was followed on April 3 by a sharp letter from Stalin in which he wrote, "At the present moment the Germans on the western front have ceased the war against England and America. At the same time they continue the war against Russia, an Ally…. Such a situation can in no way serve the preservation of trust." FDR replied to Stalin that he had read his letter "with astonishment." To Churchill he confided that, with the war in Europe nearly over, they could now be "tougher" with Stalin because the considerations they had to give to Stalin in the past no longer applied (Brown, 658–9).

There was also a contretemps with the French in the way the Americans handled these surrenders. On the 5th of May the German AGG was negotiating surrender to Devers, commander of the American 6th Army Group. Devers' Army Group included the 1st French Army under de Lattre. Yet no French representative was present at the proceedings, though General Patch of Devers' 7th Army and even a U.S. corps commander attended. Sometime earlier the commander of the German 24th Army, part of AGG, had offered to surrender to the French; when he heard that AGG as a whole was surrendering to the Americans he broke contact with the French, preferring to be part of the general surrender. With this retraction, and with no French representative invited to the overall surrender, the French balked. When de Lattre was asked to put his signature to the surrender document, he refused. He demanded the German 24th Army surrender to the French. Devers ignored him, whereupon de Lattre threatened to continue the war. The French protests did them no good and the threat to continue fighting proved an empty threat — as after the AGG surrender in toto, there was no enemy to fight. What remained was another slight to the *gloire* of de Gaulle's France.

Having delayed the general capitulation as long as possible — during which millions of Germans reached the American and British lines, Eisenhower decided the time had come to officially end the war. Dönitz was told to come and sign the surrender of all German armed forces. Dönitz's headquarters were in Flensburg on the Danish border while Ike was in Reims, 85 miles northeast of Paris and it was not until late afternoon of May 5 that a German delegation arrived at Allied headquarters. Led by Friedburg it had no authority to sign, only to discuss terms, another stratagem for prolonging the interlude. He was told that Dönitz must send a plenipotentiary to sign an unconditional surrender.

At 6:00 P.M. on May 6 Generaloberst Alfred Jodl of the OKW, accompanied by his aide, Major Oxenius, arrived at Reims. With Monty's chief of staff, de Guignand at his side Jodl strode briskly into the three-story building. It then turned out that he, too, had been instructed only to "negotiate." At that time there were still a million German soldiers fighting their way to the west to escape Russian captivity: over half a million in Schörner's AG Mitte in Czechoslovakia; over 400,000 of AG South in Austria; and 180,000 of AGE in Croatia. More than that. According to Ike's chief of intelligence who was the interpreter at Reims, "Jodl told us frankly and with deep conviction that we would soon find ourselves fighting Russians and that if Germany were given time to evacuate as many troops and civilians as possible to the west there would be large resources available to help the Allies in the struggle against the Russians." Bedell Smith, Ike's chief of staff, told Jodl he must sign the document of unconditional surrender immediately and if he declined "the Allied Air Forces will resume operations. Our lines will be closed even to individual German soldiers and civilians." Jodl stood his ground and Eisenhower intervened to announce that whether he signed or not the Allied lines would be closed to all Germans within 48 hours. Jodl then cabled Dönitz, "Eisenhower insists that we sign today.... I see no alternative.... I ask you to confirm immediately by radio that I have full powers to sign capitulation." At 8:30 the next morning the reply arrived, "Admiral Dönitz authorizes signature of surrender under conditions stated — Keitel."

The official ceremony took place in Eisenhower's war room, its walls plastered with maps, charts and statistics. The representatives of the Allied powers, seated on one side of a long table, included a French general, British army, navy and air force representatives and the commander of the US Strategic Air Force. Eisenhower, who declined to meet the Germans and stayed in his office, was represented by Bedell Smith. The Soviet liaison man at SHAEF headquarters, Gen. Ivan Suslaparov, had asked Moscow for clearance to attend the signing. By the time the meeting started he had received no reply, so he decided to participate anyway. When Jodl, Friedburg and Oxenius entered the room they bowed and took seats opposite the Allied ranks. On the table were four copies of the surrender document, one for each of the four Allies. Smith asked Jodl whether he had seen the document and was prepared to sign. Jodl nodded. The main provision of the document stated that the undersigned, acting in the name of the German Oberkommando, declared here the unconditional capitulation of all land, sea and air forces to the supreme commander of the Allied Expeditionary Forces and simultaneously to the supreme command of Soviet troops. The time of the signing was 2:41 A.M., May 7, with hostilities to cease at midnight May 9-10, British time. When the signing was over Jodl stood up and spoke, "With this signature the German people and the German Armed Forces are, for better or for worse, delivered into the victor's hands. In this war, which has lasted more than five years, both have achieved and suffered more than perhaps any other people in the world. In this hour I can only express the hope that the victor will treat them with generosity." The response was complete silence. The statement, delivered in German, was not even transcribed. Jodl turned on his heels and left the room. The Germans were then taken to Eisenhower's office. They clicked heels and saluted the Allied commander. Eisenhower asked Jodl whether he understood the clauses of the surrender document. "Ja" was the answer. After a few cautionary words about adhering to its provisions Ike dismissed the Germans with a "That's all." He then sent a cable to the Combined Chiefs of Staff in Washington, "The mission of this Allied Force was fulfilled at 02:41 local time, May 7, 1945" (Botting, 87–91).

Though the piecemeal capitulations orchestrated by Dönitz and connived in by the Western commands were deliberately aimed at saving whole German armies from Soviet hands, by stretching the truth they could be fudged as tactical surrenders that occurred in the course of battle. Not so the surrender at Reims. This was a formal act of terminating the war by the unconditional surrender of all the German armed forces. By all and any precedent this had to be a solemn joint venture involving the British, Soviet, and American allies. It should have followed a prior agreement of the three combatants on procedures and held at a suitable place such Potsdam or Berlin, and attended by the war's major figures of equivalent rank and prestige. Instead the whole performance was arranged in slipshod fashion by the Americans alone. Present was an obscure Soviet general who did not rank any place in the hierarchy of Soviet military chiefs; moreover, Moscow had not given him authorization to attend. Towering over this man that signed the historic document at Reims stood Stalin as commander in chief of all the USSR's armed forces; the several chiefs of staff of Stavka, Shaposhnikov, Shtemenko, Antonov; a dozen or so Soviet fieldmarshals, topped by Zhukov, Koniev and Rokossovsky who had conquered Berlin; and other luminaries. No wonder then that no sooner was the ink dry on the Reims protocol when Moscow announced that as far as the USSR was concerned the war wasn't over.

And as it turned out there was more to it than disparagement of the main power that had brought victory over the Germans. There was also a legal violation involved for it transpired that the parties at Reims had signed the wrong document. The European Advisory Committee had earlier drafted a text to be presented to the Germans at the time of capitulation which had been agreed to by the Big Three. A copy of this official surrender document had been given to Bedell Smith. Instead, in the great rush at Reims, Smith had drafted his own version, the one Jodl had signed. This was discovered in Moscow by Antonov, and simultaneously by Robert Murphy, Ike's political advisor, who had given Smith the original version for safekeeping. According to Murphy, "I discovered that a strange document — strange to me — had been used. General Smith had gone to bed exhausted but I telephoned and asked him what had happened to the EAC-approved text. At first he could not remember, then I said, "But don't you remember that big blue folder in which I told you were the terms approved by everybody?" When they raced to headquarters and opened Smith's safe they found the blue folder. Just then a cable arrived from Washington that Moscow was furious and claiming the text of unconditional surrender was not the one agreed upon. More messages came in showing the consequences of the West's manner of handling the piecemeal and Reims surrenders. From Czechoslovakia came the news that Schörner's half a million army refused to lay down their weapons and continued to do battle. Another news item quoted the German radio broadcasting that Germany had made a separate peace with the Western Allies but not — it emphasized — with the Russians. Eisenhower was told the story of the wrong Reims document just as the American press trumpeted the end of the war (Botting, 92–3).

Early on May 7 the Soviet High Command sent a message to Eisenhower demanding that the act of Germany's surrender be held in Berlin in the presence of Zhukov as representative of the Soviet government. This message crossed one from Eisenhower informing the Russians that Germany's surrender had already taken place — the day before, in Reims. Not only to the Germans but to an incensed Stalin, too, all this sounded as if the Western powers had indeed concluded a separate peace, particularly when German troops on the eastern front continued fighting. On Stalin's orders the Reims ceremony was relegated to being merely a preliminary protocol and a "general act of surrender" was to be enacted in Berlin in the presence of Zhukov. A corresponding message was sent to Eisenhower which stated, "The surrender must be arranged as a most important historical fact, and accepted not on the territory of the conquerors but at the place where the Fascist aggression sprang from: in Berlin." Until this was complied with the war would go on. General Smith then asked his interpreter to prepare 17 Russian-language copies of the valid text of the surrender document to be taken to Berlin the next day when the German surrender was to take place in front of Zhukov. To get a Russian typewriter the translator had to drive to Paris where amid a pandemonium of officers celebrating the end of the war (for the West) the 17 Russian language copies were produced. These had to be taken back to Reims, from where the American-British delegation was to take off for the second surrender in Berlin. Eisenhower refused to attend, presumably because it would have detracted from the importance of Reims, and appointed British Air Marshall Tedder as his representative. A separate Allied plane ferried the Germans who had signed the Reims protocol, except for Jodl who was replaced by Wilhelm Keitel, still head of the OKW. General Lattre de Tassigny was the French representative, a compensation for the slight suffered at the hands of General Devers. Shipped along was the unfortunate General Suslaparov. The Russians saw to it that this would be *the* ceremony. The planes, escorted by a squadron of Russian fighters, landed at Tempelhof Airport at 11:00 A.M. on May 8 to be greeted by Zhukov's staff headed by Marshal Rokossovsky. The airport was decked out in the flags of all four Allies and the orchestra played the national anthems, including "God Save the King." General Suslaparov was whisked away by a separate welcoming party, never to be heard from again.

With Berlin in ruins Zhukov had found a two-story building in Karlhorst, an eastern suburb that had served as the canteen of a military engineering school. The furniture for the occasion was hauled in from the führer's Chancellery, including a 400-foot-long dark brown carpet from Hitler's study. Keitel's adjutant burst into tears when he saw it. At 10:30 that night the Western delegation was brought over to the large hall where the ceremony was to take place. Four tables formed a rectangle, one of them reserved for the Germans. Exactly at midnight Zhukov led all the participants into the surrender hall. Zhukov sat at the center of the top table flanked by Tedder on his right and US General Spaatz on his left. Next to Tedder sat André Vyshynski, deputy foreign minister and Stalin's political watchdog at the proceedings. Zhukov called the meeting to order and asked to bring in the German delegation. They came in through a door behind the empty table led by Keitel; with him were Admiral Friedburg, for the third time to sign a surrender, and the Luftwaffe General Strumpf. Keitel was in a blue-gray uniform hung with decorations, clutching a feldmarschall's baton. His head held high, hands swathed in gloves, a monocle in the left eye, he stepped briskly in front of the table and jerked up his baton in a curt salute. He then sat down. "Ah, the French are here, too," he was overheard to mutter. "That's all we need." Tedder rose and asked whether the Germans knew the terms of the instrument of surrender. Keitel nodded. The Germans were then asked to come forward to Zhukov's table to sign the document. Keitel pulled off a glove and signed. Zhukov and Tedder signed next. The time was half an hour before midnight of May 8. All fighting was to stop with the signing of the document (Botting, 92–99; Lüdde, 146–151).

At the time the Berlin document was signed there were still sizeable German formations in Kurland, East Prussia, Bohemia and Croatia, as well as hold-out fortresses — all on the eastern front. As late as May 5 Dönitz had sent the Kurland commander, Hilpert, a message saying that the fight against Bolshevism went on and, if necessary, his AG should convert itself into a Freikorps group — echoes of World War I — even now. Hilpert went a step further and the next day informed Dönitz that in cooperation with an SS standartenführer, named Osis, and the Latvian National Committee they were planning to set up an anti–Soviet government in Latvia. He was planning this, said Hilpert, because Frank in Czechoslovakia and Löhr in Croatia were proposing similar coups (Steinert, 262–3). However, with the signing at Reims Keitel had to inform Hilpert to forget his plans, but to negotiate with the local Soviet command. Holding out so as to enable a number of troops to board ships for Germany, the Kurland army, displaying white flags, surrendered to Marshal Godorov at 2 P.M. on May 8; 200,000 men including 13 generals went off into Russian captivity.

Next came the turn of AGE which had pulled back from the Balkans and lodged itself in Croatia. They had reasonable hopes of surrendering to the British coming up from Italy into Carinthia. But facing them east and south were not only Russians but Yugoslav partisans. Löhr gave his subordinates freedom to fight their way to the west. By then they were ringed by Tito's men who had encroached into Italian territory. Still, many succeeded in escaping but 150,000 men, including Löhr, ended up in Yugoslav or Russian prison camps.

The largest concentration was Schörner's AG Mitte, 1.2 million strong. Schörner, a rabid Nazi and ruthless commander, defied the call for surrender and continued fighting till May 11, two days after the deadline. By then Russian troops freed from other combat converged on his armies from all directions and terminated all resistance. The bulk of AG Mitte, 1 million men, fell into Russian hands, including the Nazi feldmarschall himself. Ironically, while Löhr was executed for the slaughter of civilians in the 1941 bombing of Belgrade, Schörner survived Russian captivity.

The most recalcitrant surrender occurred with Dönitz's own U-boat arm. On May 4 the Immaculate Sailor, who only occasionally machine-gunned survivors floating in the water, sent an order of the day to his men: "Six years of U-boat warfare lies behind us. You have fought like lions.... U-boat men! Undefeated and unblemished you are to lay down your arms after an unmatched heroic struggle. We recall in reverence our fallen comrades who have sealed their loyalty to Führer and Vaterland with their death. Comrades! Keep up your U-boat spirit, with which you have bravely, tenaciously and undeterred fought for long years to serve our Vaterland, also in the future. Long Live Germany" (Lüdde, 137). As stipulated in the surrender the Germans were not to destroy any of their equipment and arms. The U-boat men balked. Yes, throughout the war they had been absolutely obedient to their commander in chief, but now they ignored orders, undeterred by such an unmilitary breach of discipline and military oath. As the surrender went into effect there were 377 U-boats afloat; 151 were handed over to the Allies, while 221 or 60 percent, were scuttled or sunk by the U-boat crews (FNC, 489).

By and large Dönitz's tactics succeeded in saving many of his kinfolk from Soviet captivity. Table 39-1 lists the number of German troops that surrendered to the Western Allies in violation of the surrender terms. All the formations listed in the table had been engaged on the eastern front. More than half extricated themselves from the Russians and were allowed to cross the Allied lines in the west. Thus while throughout the war the Russians engaged 70 to 80 percent of the German army in battle, when victory came the number of prisoners taken was the reverse of the above; the Russians at the end of the war gathered some 2 million German POWs while the camps in the West teemed with nearly 8 million of them.

On the 9th of May, the first day of peace, the OKW issued its last communiqué—1,975 days after its first on September 1, 1939. Someone coming from Jupiter reading it would hardly guess that aside from German bravery and misfortune, anything else had been inflicted on Europe in the world war just concluded. The opening and closing paragraphs of the OKW *Bericht* read as follows:

"From the Headquarters of the Grossadmiral:

"In East Prussia yesterday German divisions were still defending the mouth of the river Vistula and the western sector of the Frische Nehrung. The 7th Division in particular distinguished itself. Panzer General von Saucken, the Supreme Commander, was awarded the Diamonds and Swords to the Knights Cross of the Iron Cross in recognition of the exemplary behavior of his soldiers...

Top: **The German delegation at Soviet HQ in Berlin. From the left are General Stumpf, commander-in-chief of the Luftwaffe; Feldmarschall Keitel of the Oberkommando der Luftwaffe; and Admiral Friedburg, commander-in-chief of the Kriegsmarine. (Courtesy the United States Army.)** *Bottom:* **Feldmarschall Wilhelm signs Germany's unconditional surrender on May 8, 1945. (Courtesy the National Archives.)**

"From midnight the guns have been silent on all Fronts. The Grand Admiral has ordered the armed forces to cease a struggle which was hopeless. The honorable struggle which has lasted almost six years is, therefore, at an end. It has brought us not only great victories but also heavy defeats. The German Armed Forces have been overcome, finally, by a superior force. The German soldier loyal to the oath he had sworn, has achieved imperishable things in this struggle for his people. To the end the Homeland supported him with all its strength,

Table 39-1
Extraction of German Troops from Possible Captivity in May 1945
(in thousands)

Grouping(*)	Crossed to West	Taken by Russians
East Prussia	75	150
Kurland	25	190
AG Vistula	400	—
Wenck's 12A	100	—
AG Süd	800	—
AG (E)	250	150
AG Mitte	200	1,000
TOTAL	1,850	1,490

*These were all troops fighting on the eastern front during May.
Ref. von Reimer, pp. 159–163

despite its own suffering. History will one day judge objectively this unique effort of the front and of the Homeland.... Every soldier can, therefore, lay down his weapon with pride and in this, the bitterest hour of our history, begin to work bravely and honorably for our people" (Lucas, 245).

In an ironic twist, after the surrender Japan broke relations with Germany for violating their treaty, as by the Three Power Pact none of the partners was supposed to have signed a separate peace.

On May 23 British troops arrived in Flensburg with a warrant to dissolve the Dönitz government and arrest its members. They were put on a plane and flown to what the Americans called the "Ashcan" in Luxemburg, soon to be put on trial as war criminals. On June 6 the Allies announced the formal dissolution of the Third Reich as a state. Germany was left without any indigenous governing authority, not even a collaborationist one. Partitioned between East and West, the whole country and Berlin itself was split into four zones, leaving Germany to the whim and mercy of the Soviet and Western occupying powers.

Epilogue

The present volume commenced by saying that circumstance as well as a single individual were instrumental in unleashing World War II. We can now be more explicit in specifying what were the furies that stoked the fires of the six-year war. The legacy of World War I on the Western powers was as tragic as it was for Germany. Crippled by past memories they failed to react when it would still have been possible to stop Hitler and avert the war; part of their failure consisted of not understanding who Adolf Hitler was, though he had given ample evidence of it since 1922. And when they did go to war they lacked the skills and the tools to win a modern war. As for the German malignancy that brought about the war in the first place the conclusions are in line with what was stated at the beginning of this volume, with one important amendment. And one must immediately note that the term "war" is a euphemism for what had actually transpired. For one thing the Germans had invaded 20 out of the 25 independent European states, including their own allies such as Italy and Hungary (twice). Then they did something completely unrelated to warfare, namely the assembly-line-like killing of tens of millions of war prisoners, gypsies, Jews and masses of Poles and Russians. As a consequence this "war" produced more civilian dead than combatants. In its conception and execution this apocalypse was the handiwork of Adolf Hitler. He alone wished it, he determined its course. It was not conducted for the good of a particular social class or the German people. Neither the fate of his own party, nor of the Aryan tribes of Europe, took precedence over Hitler's private obsessions. It was a war meant to satiate the kinks and hang-ups buried deep in the cloaca of the führer's psyche. As Haffner put it, it was an attempt to subordinate history to autobiography. When this private phantasmagoria proved unattainable — as Hitler realized halfway through the war — the alternative was not abdication or salvage, but the very opposite; Europe and the German people itself were to go down to extinction with him.

Thus a single individual waged this sort of war for six years. Now, it would rank with the supernatural were one man capable of such a deed. And, in fact, Adolf Hitler was not alone. While he was the one that determined the course of the six-year conflict, what made it possible was that he had a partner — the German people. A single Kapellmeister swung his baton and 80 million music lovers played the required tune, their own funeral march included. The German people implemented Hitler's programs and fought the war to the bitter end, not merely out of a sense of duty, but with love for their führer and his enterprise. The fact is often cited that in Berlin, on the day the war started, the populace seemed apathetic in contrast to the jubilation at the outbreak of World War I. If true, it is frightening to contemplate what would have happened had the Germans been enthusiastic, given that when merely apathetic they littered Europe with 60 million cadavers.

This enthusiastic commitment ranged across the entire spectrum of German society. When Nazi delegates were sent to persuade the bishops of Austria to support the Anchluss they were advised to tread gently, but there was no need for tact. When the delegates arrived the Austrian Bishops stood up and gave the Nazi salute. In Germany a few days after the outbreak of the war the bishops issued a joint pastoral letter, saying, "We encourage and admonish our Catholic soldiers, in obedience to the Führer, to do their duty." When some soldiers had qualms whether an oath to the führer was compatible with one's religious faith, the bishops stated that they could not imagine that an oath to the führer would contain anything conflicting with the word of God. When a priest, Franz Rheinish, did refuse to take the oath, the clergy would not grant him Holy Communion, saying he had violated his Christian duty (Lewy 1964, 226–41). The response of the German churches was but a reflection of the feelings of the general populace as shown in Table E-1.

Table E-1
Hitler's Rule and the Response of German Voters

Date	% of Eligible Votes Cast*	Pro-Nazi Votes, %
November 6, 1932	80.6	33.1
May 3, 1933	88.5	43.7
November 12, 1933	95.3	92.1

*Total number of eligible voters was around 45 million.

When Hitler became chancellor he got only 44 percent of the votes, but within less than a year it soared to 92 percent — this with nearly total participation of the electorate (95.3 percent). What happened then to the 56 percent of voters who had opposed the Nazis only a few months earlier? Overnight conversion of a whole people to cannibalism does not occur in nature and therefore the stampede into Nazism must have had deeper roots than a momentary madness.

What underlay this fidelity between the German people and Adolf Hitler was the German national character at this stage in history. The hysterical rallies; the screams of "*Sieg Heil*"; the nearly 100 percent support in the referenda; the loyalty to the führer exhibited by janitors, farmers, doctors, artists, academicians, aristocrats, socialists and erstwhile Communists— all this has been amply documented. Behind this collective frenzy lay the character of the ordinary German functioning above and beyond the regime's dictates. It was this that made the apocalypse of World War II possible. For alongside the state-ordered exterminations, individual Germans in the occupied territories and behind the eastern front indulged in murderous and sadistic practices entirely on their own, augmenting the official programs by their own initiatives and proclivities. A perception persists that the adulation of the führer throughout his years of triumph, defeat and impending catastrophe was the work of propaganda and image making. There was that, of course. But the apotheosis of the führer was not imposed from above but came from below, from the atavistic cravings of the general masses. As one study puts it, "The sources for his [Hitler's] popularity have to be sought in those who adored him rather than in the Leader himself. Propaganda was effective where it was building upon, not countering, existing values and mentalities ... the ready-made terrain of pre-existing beliefs, prejudices and phobias forming an important stratum of the German political culture on which the Hitler myth could easily be imprinted" (Kershaw 1987, 1–4).

The bondage to the führer and his Nazi cohorts by ordinary Germans held fast to the very end. Following the attentat of July 20 a Luftwaffe officer noted in his diary, "A wave of indignation sweeps through the German people…. The ordinary German fighting soldiers regard the unsuccessful revolt as treason of the most infamous kind." As late as February 1945 Speer, sitting unrecognized among a group of miners, listened with amazement as they voiced confidence that the führer would still remedy the situation because he understood the working class and its needs (Strawson 1971, 215). Such adulation was enjoyed also by the other Nazi bigwigs. On December 29, 1943, Goebbels inspected the heavily bombed section of Berlin near the Gartenplatz and recorded, "The men and women received me with an enthusiasm that is unbelievable…. The people wanted to carry me on their shoulders…. Women embraced me" (Goebbels 1948, 537). Göring on his way west got stuck in a flood of soldiery trying to escape the Russians. When the men recognized him they were jubilant, happy that their "Hermann" was safe and still hoping that he would bring an end to their predicament (Paul, 262).

Throughout the war the German countryside was littered with small and large concentration and slave labor camps—this in addition to the extermination camps located in the east. The inmates of these camps were frequently marched through villages and towns on their way to work or other camps and their appearance verged on death itself. As reported by nearly all erstwhile prisoners, they were never thrown a piece of bread, never detected a sign of ordinary pity on the faces of the onlookers. The German civilians looked upon these transports with hostility, often jeering and throwing stones at them (Goldhagen, 365). At best the villagers turned away, but most watched with an expression of disgust and hatred. Toward the end when the Russians were approaching there were the death marches. Of the total of 750,000 — Jews and non–Jews— 250,000 died on the road. Here there was not just the wretched appearance of the prisoners but mass killings by the escorts whenever the men or women could not keep up or collapsed from exhaustion. The response of the German civilians was the same — indifference or worse. They were callous to a point of not caring even for their own losses. As an Allied soldier related on encountering the first German civilians, "They talked about their own dead as if they were neutrals…. They seem to have lost the power of passion and sorrow. They show no sympathy for their army … or their country" (Cross 1995, 191). As a study on postwar German soldiery reported, "There was little in the way of [mental] disability pensions, nothing in the way of treatment for combat trauma," and an investigator of war guilt in Germany wrote, "I talked to approximately 80 priests, doctors, psychologists, and psychiatrists but not one of them could report a single instance of such confession." The Heidelberg psychiatrists, A. and M. Mitscherlich, likewise reported that "from the records of more than 4,000 patients it emerges that few criteria could be found for a correlation between their present day symptoms and their experiences in the Nazi era. Self-confessed Nazis virtually never appeared" (Lebert, 185–6). This compares with widespread affliction of PTSO (post–traumatic stress disorder) encountered among American veterans of the Vietnam War — a paltry affair compared to the Germans' experiences in World War II. Mitscherlich extended his findings into a more profound German characteristic — the inability to mourn — not only for strangers but for their own dead and wounded. Of course, to be able to mourn, one has to be able to feel — a response seemingly absent during the Nazi era. Readjustment to civilian life was work and more work. The same attitude prevailed to the ruins of the German cities; no regrets, no tears—just dig and dig (Shay, 59). A German observer noted, "The bombing devastation left scarcely a trace of pain behind in the collective consciousness…. There was a lack of moral sensibility bordering on inhumanity. The case histories presented by Mitschelich makes one suspect some connection between the German catastrophe ... and the regulation of intimate feelings ... the German Gleichschakltung" by which is meant that in the same breath a German family could discuss the shortage of marmalade and the just-received news that Father had fallen in Russia (Sebald, 41, 84). The Germans endured great hardships and deprivations, they had wounds and losses inflicted on them on a grand scale, but there was no introspection, no anguish — they endured, but did not suffer. Their hearts and consciences seem to have remained close to those of amoebas.

A study of the barbarization of the German army on the eastern front notes that the shooting of Russian prisoners was often done by ordinary soldiers against orders of their officers who were concerned about "discipline" in the ranks (Bartov, 114). The most gruesome of all gruesome acts were the massive executions of the Jewish populations by the Einsatzgruppen in the occupied Russian territories. The army contingents in the vicinity knew about them and whenever they witnessed them their main impulse was to take photographs of the killing of tens of thousands of men, women and children. This interest in photography eventually perturbed the higher echelons. The commanders gathered the troops and explained to them that in Russia they were in a different cosmos; whereas among Germans things were civilized and life was precious, there "in the east" life was cheap and expendable. What they are witnessing was not unusual in those parts of the world and the soldiers should not be appalled by what they were witnessing. They should, however, stop taking photographs because it might give a wrong impression back home. An ordinary infantryman (Kuby, 218–23) relates that upon returning from furloughs his fellow soldiers would tell him that they had visited the Warsaw Ghetto (half a million people dying of starvation) and told him that the place is "sehenswürdig" (worth seeing). In Russia they would frequently see batches of Jews being herded into enclosures to await execution. The soldiers knew what it all meant and coined their own term for these occasions. With typical German cynicism they called it *Schlachtfest* or *Purim*, a reference to ancient Persia where a slaughter of Jews had been planned by Haman. The congratulatory self-image expressed by the military commanders, cited above, appears even in Himmler's horrendous speech at Posen when he informed his audience about the extermination of Europe's Jews. "It is fundamentally wrong for us to try to carry our naturally innocent nature, our good nature, our idealism, to foreign peoples.... We Germans who are the only people in the world to have a decent attitude toward the animal kingdom, will hold a similar attitude to such human animals, but it's a crime against our own blood to concern ourselves with their fate or bring ideals to them" (Lebert, 43–4).

It is poignant to juxtapose the reactions of German and Italian soldiers to one particular genocidal campaign. Upon gaining a state of their own in 1941 the Croats conducted a planned extermination of Serbs in their territory. The adjoining areas were occupied by a patchwork of German and Italian troops. The Italians had or should have had a great affinity for the newly created state. Croats and Italians were both Catholic whereas the Serbs were Orthodox; an independent Croatia had for a long time been the goal of Italian policy; its führer, Ante Pavelic, had been residing in Rome for years; and the newly named king of Croatia Duke Aimone of Spoletto was Italian. For all these reasons the Italians should have been sympathetic to the Croats. Yet when groups of desperate Serbs, sometimes whole villages, in escaping the axes and bludgeons of the Croats ended up in Italian areas the Italians kept and sheltered them. When they escaped to the German occupation zones, the Germans drove them back to Croatia.

After the war the generals piled all criminal acts of the army on Hitler but this was just a synchronized whitewash. Even the military oath, which under the Weimar Republic was to the constitution, now switched to the person of Hitler, was instituted by Blomberg and Reichenau on their own initiative to read, "I swear by God this holy oath, that I will render to Adolf Hitler..."—God and Hitler side by side. In a conference with the führer on August 28, 1943, the professional soldier Jodl in discussing a retirement of the northern front, advocated "the complete destruction of Leningrad by the Air Force, and the elimination of Kronstadt, as well," outdoing the führer himself (FNC, 364). As late as April 1945, a German POW on his way to imprisonment in the USA wrote that aboard the ship the prisoners celebrated Hitler's birthday and in a speech by one of the officers it was stressed "as soldiers we have an obligation to remain true to our oath ... to trust the Führer ... and to believe in the victory of our weapons." The keeping of the faith was carried into the POW camps, where any utterance against the Nazi regime evoked not just hostility among the men, but on occasion even murder of the dissident prisoners (Hörner, 257–8).

In a compilation of letters by soldiers of the German 6th Army besieged in Stalingrad (Schneider, passim) there is very little of what one would expect of men struck by such a fate. There was no compunction, no rumination about what had transpired; why were they on the icy banks of the Volga, 2,000 miles from home; why hadn't they gone back home victorious as the führer had promised in October 1941; who was responsible for this death and misery. None of that! There were a number of common sentiments; much talk about God; a determination to live up to the heroism of their fathers in World War I; much about a sense of mission, fate, transcendental values; there is frequent mention of Goethe and Schiller; some self-pity and one man even saw Germany as the "Job of History." All along it seemed perfectly normal to the German soldier that God was on his side; any private's belt buckle had on it the motto Gott mit Uns, and between battles there were the usual Protestant and Catholic services. The text of one such prayer during the 1941–44 war in Russia read:

The German Army Prayer

Let us pray!
Your hand, oh God, rules over all empires and nations on this earth.
In Your goodness and strength bless our German nation
And infuse in our hearts love of our Fatherland.
May we be a generation of heroes,
Worthy of those who went before us.
May we protect the faith of our fathers as a holy inheritance
Bless the German Wehrmacht whose task it is
To secure peace and protect the home fires.
And give its members the strength
To make the supreme sacrifice for Führer, Volk and Fatherland.
Especially bless our Führer and Commander in Chief
In all the tasks which are laid upon him.
Let us all under his leadership
see in devotion to Volk and Fatherland a holy task,
so that through our faith, obedience and loyalty
we may find our everlasting home in Your kingdom of Your light and peace.
Amen!

[Metelmann, 206]

In a general study of the attitude of the German public to the Nazi regime and its doings the conclusions read as follows: "The regime had far more than the great majority

of the population behind it and they remained steadfast in their support up to and especially even after the coup attempt of July 1944…. Nazi propaganda was not and could not
be crudely forced on the German people. On the contrary, it was meant to appeal to them
and match up with everyday Germans' understandings…. The brutalities of the police, SS,
Wehrmacht and even the elderly members of the Volksturm seemed nearly limitless. We
cannot explain the urge to continue [the atrocities] with reference to a single motive — not
even racism — as the killers did not hesitate when the victims were German, Italian or
French" (Gellately, 257–64). Nor is it true, as one may want to assert, that under the prevailing authoritarian regime, men — be they soldiers or policemen — had to perform their
butcheries under penalty of death. The police involved in the Final Solution were not ideological warriors specifically charged with genocide but ordinary cops (Ordnungspolizei)
and they were as proficient at it as the Einsatzgruppen, and killed even when they did not
have to. For at least in eight different battalions the men were informed that they would
not be punished if they opted out, but with virtual unanimity they chose and continued
to kill. One participant, when later asked about this, gave an answer that expressed the
essence of it: "At the time we did not give it any second thoughts at all." One police unit
from Hamburg assigned to the routine shooting of Jews in the East produced a few dis-
senters. When interrogated after the war none of them expressed moral revulsion at what
they had been asked to do, but they did reveal a deep sense of shame for letting down their
fellows who had to do their work for them. Even Himmler gave his men a way out, as
testified to by the personnel chief of Einsatzgruppe C. Himmler said extermination of Jews
"could be carried out only by … the staunchest individuals…. if a man thinks he cannot
be answerable for obeying an order and you think his nerve has gone, he is weak, then you
can say: Good, retire on pension" (Goldhagen, 277–9, 578–9).

     Nor is it correct to say that the reason no protest existed in Nazi Germany was because
it would have been futile. At the end of October 1939 Hitler signed the go-ahead order for
the start of the euthanasia program in Germany. In the course of a year and a half 70,000
patients were killed. The secret soon leaked out. The reaction in the country, particularly
of the Catholic and Protestant churches was immediate. Cardinals Bertram and Faulhaber,
the bishops of Cologne, Paderrborn and Limburg, and even Nazi institutions all protested,
demanding an end to the killing. Most notable was the action of Bishop von Galen of Muen-
ster who on July 28, 1941 filed an official complaint with the public prosecutor as well as
the police chief; this he followed up on August 3 with a pastoral letter that the euthanasia
program was a violation of the fifth commandment. In response Hitler on September 3
terminated the program. None of the church dignitaries or anyone else involved in the
protest campaign was either arrested or punished in any way. Great unrest was also engendered when the Nazis tried to remove crucifixes from the schoolrooms. Similar protests
were raised when the regime tried to confiscate the large church real estate properties. The
protests were of sufficient intensity to have Hitler suspend these orders.

     One study concerned itself with the consequences for refusing to participate in geno-
cidal killings. The results of this inquiry are shown in Table E-2.

Table E-2
Consequences for Those Refusing Orders to Carry Out Executions*

Consequences	n–Number of Particular Punishments	%
No negative consequences at all	49	57.6
Sent to concentration camps	1	1.2
Sent to combat units as punishment	3	3.5
House arrest/investigations, later dropped	5	5.9
Reprimands/threats to send to front/Concentration camps	15	17.6
Units broken up after officers refused	2	2.4
Transfer to another unit or back to Germany	14	16.5
Demotion or lack of further promotion	7	8.2
Others	7	8.2

(Kitterman, 250)

*The study comprised 85 individuals. Some individuals suffered more than one form of punishment — thus n is larger than 85.

The author concludes that in his study he failed "to find one conclusively documented instance of a life-threatening situation occurring to those who refused to carry out an order to murder civilians or Russian war prisoners. In the majority of cases resulted in no serious consequences whatever" (Kitterman, 241–253) What is most telling in the above and in other such reports is that in many cases those who opted out, later on rejoined their units in their macabre job. The reason they cited was that they felt uneasy for "letting their comrades down" — a feeling stronger than massacring women and children.

In Goldhagen's chilling volume on the extermination of Europe's six million Jews, the author postulates that what had enabled the Germans to execute that deed was the prevalence in Germany of an "eliminational anti–Semitism." Clearly Poles, Rumanians, Ukrainians and others, were incomparably more anti–Semitic than the Germans. But the German critics who pounced on Goldhagen's thesis did the German people no favor; it would have been more charitable had they let the thesis stand. For if the Germans could exterminate a whole people without even hating them, then by just being given an order they could have done it to *any* nation.

The Casualties

Two nations emerged from the war crippled on a historically unprecedented scale — the Jews and the Russians. In the Jewish case the injury was beyond repair as from then on its destiny would be radically different from what it has been heretofore. The massacre produced a record in human history so that it was necessary to invent for it a new term — genocide — the total extermination of a people based on ethnic affiliation alone. The outlines of the murder of 6 million European Jews was given in Chapter 21 and the tabulation of this abyss is shown in Table 21-1. This tabulation suggests that even Hitler's military strategy was dictated to a large degree by his determination to kill every single Jew on the continent. Thus Switzerland, Sweden, Spain, Portugal, Turkey — all with minimal Jewish populations — were not touched. On the other hand, we have seen the enormous pressure on Hungary to ship its one million Jews for extermination. When it did not bear fruit Hitler twice invaded Hungary and while Germany itself was already being overrun, he had sent his best troops to "liberate" Budapest with its 200,000 Jews.

There are two sets of estimates of the Russian human losses in World War II — Soviet figures and by outsiders. The Soviet Government had conflicting interests in publicizing their wartime losses. One was to provide high or correct numbers in order to impress the world with the price it had paid for ridding Europe of Nazism and be entitled to appropriate political and economic compensation. On the other hand, these losses were so enormous as to impute to Stalin profligacy with human lives as well as incompetence in fighting the war. Following the conflict the official Soviet figure was 20 million dead. But even then outsiders estimated the losses to be closer to 30–40 million; after the fall of the Soviet Union its archives showed the number to be closer to 50 million. By most accounts the military dead amounted to some 13.5 million soldiers so that the civilian toll amounts to 35 million. The latter losses embrace not only the depredations perpetrated directly by the Germans but also the millions who died of starvation, cold, exhaustion and sickness induced by the war. Thus in Leningrad alone 1.5 million inhabitants died, 100,000 of them during the evacuations across the Ladoga ice road. Aspects of this colossal extirpation of human life — one-quarter or more of the total population — can be gleaned from the following: the war left 15 million widows; in the childbearing age there were only 31 million men to 52 million women. Added to all this Russia was left with 20 million cripples. A large part of the victorious Red Army in 1945 consisted of men who had been wounded one or more times, the Russians saying that it was the wounded who had won the war. The trauma of the Russian people showed itself even during the June 14, 1945, victory parade in Moscow when a heavy rain poured down on the parading troops. There was little celebration by the mass audience but only a hushed murmur, "Heaven is weeping for our dead."

While in the Jewish case in addition to the truncation of one-third of its biological existence there took place the eradication of an entire culture, in the Russian case the human losses were accompanied by a devastation of its civilian economy. For even though the Germans never got beyond the Volga all plants producing civilian goods all the way to Vladivostok had been converted to military usage; thousands of miles beyond the front people suffered from hunger, cold and lack of the most primitive necessities. In the occupied territories two-thirds of the national wealth was wiped out. This included:

- 50 percent of all urban living quarters destroyed.
- 75 percent of all villages burned down.
- 32,000 factories blown up.
- 100,000 collective farms laid waste.
- 90 percent of cattle slaughtered or abducted.
- 40,000 miles of railroad track ripped up (Overy 1997, 345–6).

The lack of food, shelter and clothing stayed at wartime levels for a decade after 1945. Twenty-five million people lived in caves and dugouts (Meyers, 164, 289; Salisbury, 228). The effects of this devastation persist to this day (2005).

The Yugoslav population losses are given as 1.7 million. Of these about 300,000 were due to combat, all of them Tito's partisans who at their peak counted half a million men and women; a majority of these partisans perished in the fighting. The civilian losses are close to a million and a half, a large portion of whom — estimates vary from 300,000 to half a million — were killed by the Croat Ustashes. For a total population of 15.5 million Yugoslav losses amount to 11 percent. A significant part of these losses was due to the civil war, some 40 percent of the total. Although the Germans were not the actual killers much of this civil war was fomented by them. In addition to the dead and the ruin of the country the wartime fighting left deep ethnic cleavages whose tragic consequences would emerge 50 years later.

Russia and Yugoslavia were inhabited by Slavs, after the Jews next in line on Hitler's homicidal agenda. It is therefore not surprising that the victimization agenda included the Poles. Their combat losses in both east and west amounted to perhaps 300,000 but the civilian losses were 2.5 million, a total close to 3 million people. When after the war the Poles decided to reconstruct their destroyed capital, Warsaw, it was rebuilt atop 150,000 dead buried under its ruins. A specific trauma for Poland was that the deaths were particularly high among the intelligentsia. This was due to a deliberate policy of the Germans and to some degree of the Soviets, too, such as the murder of some 20,000 officers and state functionaries in Katyn and elsewhere — the elite of the Polish nation.

The countries that emerged with the least loss of life — and by several orders of magnitude — were the Western Allies. The United Kingdom, which was in the war from beginning to end, suffered in the European theater 195,000 dead (220,000 total) plus 60,000 due to bombing. (The Commonwealth suffered another 110,000 dead.) The USA, which came into the war two years after England, lost in the fighting against Germany 174,000 men (229,000 including Japan). France, which was out of the war from July 1940 till 1943, lost 170,000 men in combat and 400,000 civilians. Italy, a sort of half-ally, suffered 120,000 combat deaths before surrendering in September 1943; afterward most of its losses were civilians, raising the total population loss to 310,000.

Placed against the total populations, the lives lost can be summarized as follows. The percentage losses by Jews and Slavs (Russians, Yugoslavs, and Poles) are of the order of two digits (35–11); those of France a single digit; those of the Anglo-Saxons a fraction of 1 percent. Including the war against Japan the cost of World War II was 60 million to 65 million lives. This compares with 9.2 million killed in World War I. But whereas in the First World War civilians made up 5 percent of the casualties in World War II the number of civilian dead exceeded the military losses.

Retribution

The price Germany paid for starting World War II and for the mass killings it committed spanned a gamut of punishments— loss of lives, loss of territory, a permanent moral opprobrium and the loss of its national persona, seemingly for good. By themselves these exactions look serious enough; seen against the injuries inflicted on the continent they will seem perfunctory. It remains a wonder that the Russians, when they overran half of Germany, did not reduce it to the void and darkness prevailing at the dawn of Genesis.

Germany's balance sheet at the end of the war adds up to the following:

- The armed forces suffered 3.5 million dead; 2.3 million German soldiers remained buried in Russia. The extent of these losses is reflected in the toll on its generalität. Of 3,363 general officers, 765, including 14 feldmarschalls, did not survive the war.
- The war left 2 million cripples.
- About 3 million civilians lost their lives. Half a million were killed in the Allied bombings. One and a half million perished fleeing the Russians, mostly from cold and hunger but also at the hands of the oncoming Russian troops. The rest perished in the various deportations from Eastern Europe and the Balkans.

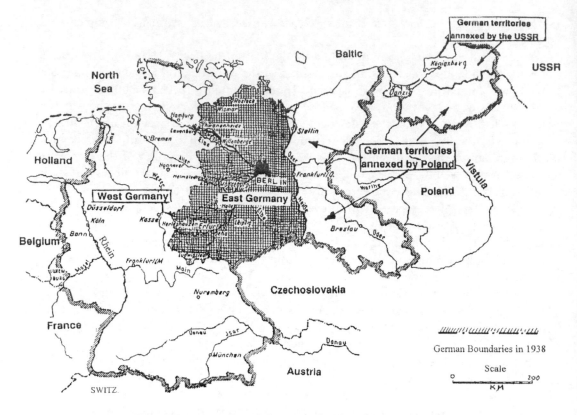

E-1. German territories lost to Poland and the Soviet Union

- Total German population losses thus amount to 6.5 million to 7 million people.
- At the end of the war 11 million German soldiers found themselves in POW camps. The Russians had 3 million prisoners of whom 1 million had been captured during the fighting and the rest as a result of the general surrender. Of the original 1 million, most died in captivity while the other 2 million were repatriated to Germany after an imprisonment of four to 10 years.
- As shown on map E-1 Germany lost a quarter of its original (1937) territory, once inhabited by 10 million people. Poland's boundary was shifted west by 150 miles while East Prussia was parceled out between Poland the USSR.
- The entire German population of the annexed territories as well as all German residents of Rumania, Hungary, Yugoslavia and the Sudetenland were expelled. Of the expellees, 9.7 million arrived in West Germany and 3.5 million settled in what was to become East Germany.
- Most German cities were fields of ruin. They contained 400 million cubic meters of wreckage. A total of 2.5 million homes were destroyed and another 2.5 million damaged. Berlin's ruins were scooped into seven giant mounds spreading the once-flat city over seven hills, like Rome. The führer's bunker was dynamited, the surface planted over with a little grove and the topography of the area so altered that both Voss and Wilhelmstrasse disappeared from the map.

While Germany's boundaries in the west stayed unchanged the territorial amputations in the east were Stalin's handiwork. On their own Stalin's demands wouldn't have achieved these results. But the Western Allies faced a dilemma. Having formally gone to war to preserve Poland's territorial integrity and having subsequently agreed to cede eastern Poland to the USSR as an inducement to keep it fighting, the solution was to compensate Poland at the expense of Germany. A quarter of German land was handed over to Poland including such ancient Germanic cities as Breslau, Stettin and Danzig while Königsberg went to the Russians. Out of the remaining three-quarters of Germany, a third was carved out by Stalin as a Communist state, its 20 million inhabitants subject to a Soviet-style polity and economy. To leave a permanent imprint, the Russians erected outside Berlin a monument to the Soviet soldiers fallen in the war against Germany of such mammoth proportions that it obscures the skies of the German capital, the tiles and marble for this complex taken from Hitler's bombed-out Chancellery. The monument straddles the graves of 13,200 Russian soldiers who fell in the battle of Berlin.

The truncation of East Prussia and the eastern provinces produced a traumatic fault in Teutonic history. Germany had been the adopted child of Prussia, a European power for centuries. With unification in 1871 the new German reich became Prussia in a larger mold, retaining the morals, manners, ambitions and pomp. The retraction of its eastern borders to the Oder-Neisse line had physically truncated both East and West Prussia, as well as Brandenburg, from the German body, depriving it of its innermost identity. Two symbolic acts accompanied the demise of the Prussian state and spirit. Hindenburg's grave was dynamited before the Germans left Tannenberg, the place of Russia's defeat in World War I; and the holy of holies of Potsdam where Bismarck had convoked the first Reichstag and where the Garrison Church contained the crypt of Frederick the Great and his father, was pulverized by an Allied bombing raid. Indeed, on February 1946 the Allies Control Council officially abolished the state of Prussia. West Germany became an imitation of the USA; East Germany a facsimile of the Soviet Union.

While the collective punishment of Germany as a state seems extensive enough, this does not apply to the individuals directly involved in the horrors of World War II. These can be divided into three groups:

1. The leaders who conceived and ordered the genocidal programs. They counted no more than one or two score of people.

2. The intermediate echelon who set up the infrastructure and supervised the implementation of the above schemes. These counted in the thousands or tens of thousands.

3. Ordinary citizens—policemen, soldiers, railwaymen, administrators, chemists, gardeners, clerks, etc.—who personally carried out the grisly tasks; the executioners of the Final Solution; the operatives of the extermination, concentration and slave camps; the guards in charge of the Russian POW camps; the troops who participated in the killing of prisoners, hostages, partisans, and entire villages in their pacification sweeps; the clerks ruling the hundreds of ghettos and the occupied territories; and so on. These categories implicated millions of Germans.

Three character traits stand out as typical in the rulers of the Third Reich. One is a stony indifference often laced with cynicism to the criminal goings-on under their very noses; this applies not only to the Nazi chieftains but to the bureaucratic and military leaders as well (Schreibtischmörderer). The other feature was that most of them were religious, often devout Christians. Lastly, one is impressed by how many of them aspired to be artistic, in particular lovers of music—indigenous, of course, to Germans in general.

The callousness and hardness of these men were applied quite ecumenically and quite often to themselves. The Germans' stubborn resistance in Holland led them to flood the lowlands, subjecting the Dutch population in the last months of the war to severe starvation. To alleviate it the Allies approached Seyss-Inquart, governor of the Netherlands, proposing to deliver food to the civilian population. A meeting was arranged between the Nazi ruler and General Bedell Smith. This took place only a week before Germany's capitulation and Smith informed the German that he ought to know that Germany lost the war. "I entirely agree," he answered. Since the German troops in Holland were surrounded General Smith proposed that Seyss-Inquart order a stop to the fighting so that the civilians can be supplied with food. Replied the German, "But what would future generations of Germans say if I complied with your suggestion — what would history say about my conduct." The American general said that if he didn't yield he would "face the wall and a firing squad." Replied Seyss-Inquart, "I am not afraid — I am a German" (Guignand, 452).

The Nazi leaders, though nihilists to the core, frequently turned to God. We have seen Hitler in the last two years frequently invoking Providence, citing his escape from the July 20 bomb as proof that God had meant it to be so. In Nüremberg Göring, in a letter to the Allies said, "Before God, my people, and my conscience I feel free from the reprehensions that my enemies put on me." On the evening of the expected executions he asked to have dinner with Captain Gerecke, the prison chaplain, so that he could receive the last consolations of the Lutheran church. The chaplain declined saying that, as attested by the trial, Göring was not a repentant sinner. In his last letter to the chaplain Göring expiates for the sin of committing suicide, "Forgive me but I had to do it this way for political reasons.... I have prayed a long time to God. Please console my wife and tell her ... she should be certain that God will take me into his grace" (Taylor, 620).

Halder, chief of staff of the Army during the horrible summer of 1941 when some 2 million Russian POWs and half a million Jews were gunned down behind his front lines had been a devout Christian before Hitler and did not stray from his Protestant faith throughout Hitler's rule and his own role in it. Neither did Feldmarschall von Leeb, commander of AGN, an even more pious man, who in addition to executions behind his lines also presided over the demise of a million civilians in Leningrad, obeying Hitler's order not to capture the city but obliterate it. Keitel of the OKW, likewise a good Christian, did not fail to admonish his wife in his last letter that in attending to their bombed out estate to resurrect the little chapel that had been there, this following the loss of three children during the war — a 30-year-old daughter during a bombing raid on Berlin and two sons in their early twenties killed on the Russian front. His wife reciprocated this callousness by instructing Keitel's Nüremberg lawyer, not to apply for clemency for her condemned husband. When Dönitz took over after Hitler's suicide he assured the German people that "after so much suffering and sacrifice God will not abandon us."

As to the artistic proclivities of the Nazis one can start with the führer whose love of paintings, architecture and the music of Wagner needs no elaboration. Next stands Albert Speer the moody architect of Nazi mastodons and Cathedrals of Light. Göring's Karinhall was overflowing with classical and medieval canvasses, Gobelins and rare furnishings. Goebbels, a Ph.D., specialized in the cinema. Heydrich, second only to Hitler in his lust for mass murder, came from a musical family and was an accomplished violinist. Ribbentrop liked to fiddle, as well as to collect art (post–Impressionist only). Other known music lovers were Seyss-Inquart and Weizsäcker. Hans Frank also spent endless time with Dr. Mühlmann, the Austrian requisitioner of Polish national treasures, not forgetting to grab much of this art loot when he fled Krakow on the approach of the Red Army; he also played the organ and the flute. Walther Funk, in charge of storing in his bank the gold teeth and eyeglasses of the murdered Jews, was a veritable one-man Philharmonic. As a child he studied harmonics; at the age of seven he could repeat entire operas, for a time he was concert pianist accompanying a famous baritone (Heinrich Schlusnus) and he was adept with both the piano and the violin. Even the morose Doenitz (who lost a brother and two sons) played the flute and staged musical soirees with Speer and his wife (Goldensohn, 16, 82).

One of the persistent excuses of the German military after the war was that as soldiers they had to obey orders while asserting that they had been opposed to Hitler's schemes. The record shows that they were as admiring of Hitler as were all other Germans. Feldmarschall Kluge, before he committed suicide in fear of Hitler's revenge for the July plot, wrote the following to him: "Mein Führer! I have always admired your greatness and your bearing in this gigantic struggle and the assertiveness of your will and Nazi ideology. You have fought a great and honorable battle. History will testify to it." This by a man who no longer had to fear or pretend; it certainly sounds as coming from the heart. The loyalty to the führer outlived the end of the war as seen in the interrogation of Brauchitsch, the first feld-marschall to be dismissed. He brushed aside questions by his interrogators by saying, "Hitler was the fate of Germany and this fate could not be stayed" (Strawson 1971, 246). In Nürem-berg, General Jodl, certainly no stooge, defended Hitler's conduct and talked of him with reverence. As to the charge of abandoning his troops by committing suicide Jodl said, "He wished to fall in battle and did so, he acted as all heroes in history did and will do.... Who-ever chooses may condemn him — but not I" (Schramm 1965, 84). Kesselring, the least Nazi of the High Command, proclaimed after the war, "Hitler was a great man — he did nothing wrong." With few exceptions this worship extended from the highest level of Ger-man officialdom to the lowest. It is almost touching to learn of the following. Hitler employed four female secretaries, all young, all single except for one Gerda Christian who divorced her husband in 1946. None of these women ever married after the war. When asked why, Gerda Christian spoke for all four of them when she replied, "How could we marry anyone after having known a man like Adolf Hitler?" (O'Donnel, 246).

Two general officers of the German army enjoyed the invariable respect of the West-ern Allies for being "upright" soldiers. One was Feldmarschall Erich von Manstein. It was inconceivable that a soldier of such immaculate ilk could have soiled his record with dis-honor, not to speak of crime. But at a time in 1941 when behind his front in the Crimea and the southern Ukraine tens of thousands of Jews and Russian POWs were being butchered, Feldmarschall von Manstein issued the following proclamation to his troops on November 20, 1941, "The Jewish Bolshevik system ... must be destroyed. The German sol-dier has the task to destroy not just the military means of this system." Despite great attempts by Allied generals including Churchill to vindicate the feldmarschall, a British court found him guilty and convicted him to 15 years in prison. The other feldmarschall for whom the west had a profound respect was Gert von Rundstedt — the 75-year-old paragon of Prussian rectitude and soldierly virtue. This was the man who together with Keitel had presided over the military court which illegally expelled the generals of the July 20 plot so that instead of a firing squad they could face the noose. There is a revealing exchange between Rundstedt and his interrogators in British captivity. Asked why he took part in the invasion of Russia when he claimed to have been against it, the answer was that he had sworn an oath as a soldier to do his duty. Asked why so, when Hitler himself had violated his oath, Rundstedt gave a nebulous answer, "The soldier is not a villain." Accept-

The Nuremberg trial of the major German war criminals. *Left to right, lower tier:* Hermann Goering, Rudolf Hess, Joachim von Ribbentrop, Field Marshal Wilhelm Keitel, Ernst Kaltenbrunner, Alfred Rosenberg, Hans Frank, Wilhelm Frick, Julius Streicher, Walther Funk, and Hjalmar Schacht. *Left to right, upper tier:* Adm. Karl Doenitz, Adm. Erich Raeder, Baldur von Schirach, Fritz Sauckel, Gen. Alfred Jodl, Franz von Papen, Arthur Seyss-Inquart, Albert Speer, Constantin von Neurath, and Hans Fritzsche. (Courtesy the National Archives.)

ing this the interrogator then asked, "But what if your superior is a villain?" Rundstedt refused to answer (Messenger, 249).

When the war ended the Allies arrested the top German leaders and gathered them in a Luxemburg enclave the GIs called the Ashcan. From there they were shipped to Nuremberg to be tried by an international tribunal. Hitler, Himmler and Heydrich, the chief trio responsible for the Final Solution, were all dead. Others involved in this enterprise, Müller of the Gestapo and Eichmann, had disappeared. According to one estimate some 60,000 war criminals had gone underground, many of them shipped to Spain, Argentina and elsewhere via the SS and Vatican-organized escape routes.

Strangely, all those responsible for creating the extermination industry — the gas chambers, crematoria, techniques of mass shooting, etc. — stayed on, evidently feeling that they had merely obeyed orders; not to speak of the rank and file who personally did the killing unaware that they had done anything out of the ordinary, whether under or over orders. Neither group feared or expected punishment. In this they had not been overly mistaken.

The top leaders of the Third Reich were tried in Nüremberg under the heading of major war criminals. Witnesses at the trial noted that whenever documentary films about the death camps were shown the accused stared impassively or turned their heads; when footage of past Nazi glory and triumphs was screened their faces glazed over with nostalgia till tears filled their eyes. Ten of this group were sentenced to death by hanging. They were executed after midnight of October 26, 1946. When facing the gallows they all resorted to the familiar clichés of God, family and Vaterland. Their last words were as follows:

- Ribbentrop, accompanied by a clergyman, pronounced: "May God protect Germany. God be merciful to my soul."
- Keitel: "I call on the Almighty to have pity on the German people.... Good luck, Deutschland!"
- Kaltenbrunner: "I served my people and the Vaterland with a warm heart.... Good luck, Deutschland!"
- Frank: "I pray to the Lord God [Herrgott], may he mercifully receive me."
- Frick: "Long live eternal Germany."
- Sauckel: "God protect Germany and make her great again.... May God protect my family."
- Jodl: "I salute you, mein Deutschland!"

Only two of the condemned offered a variation on the above theme. Alfred Rosenberg declined to say anything. Streicher, also accompanied by a clergyman, kept to the style of the Stürmer. He was brought into the execution hall shouting "Heil Hitler." Mounting the gallows he cried out "Purim Fest 1946" after which turning to the minister he said, "And now to God, Herr Pater." When the hood was placed over his head he was heard to call out, "Adele, my beloved Frau" (DDR, XXIV, 423–5).

The above individuals can be counted as belonging to group (a). A scrutiny of individuals in group (b) brought to trial indicates that most of those who were heads of the extermination camps were sentenced to death and executed. This may be due to the notoriety the camps received when they were "discovered" by the Allied armies as they entered Germany. However most of the police and SS chiefs that commanded the Einsatzgruppen or served in similar capacity had their death sentences commuted and were eventually released. However, whenever those who performed similar functions were tried in the occupied countries in the East they were without exception executed. The same story applies to the top echelon of the army commanders, not a single one of whom was sentenced to death, except Löhr executed by the Yugoslavs. Group (c) killers, the hundreds of thousands of men of the police battalions, the administrators of the occupied territories, not to speak of soldiers who committed crimes, there was no attempt to bring them to trial. Sufficient to note that, counting rotations and replacement, the Einsatzgruppen alone counted close to 6,000 men — each one of them a direct mass executioner. In the Ordnungs and Schutz Polizei performing similar duties the numbers of men involved 100,000. This also pertains to ordinary soldiers in the East who killed prisoners right upon capture, on the march routes to their assembly areas and in the POW camps. None of these men were even mentioned as possible culprits. And indeed, it would have been futile to attempt it given the numbers involved and the deliberate amnesia of both victors and losers that suited the political winds in the aftermath of the war. For all the Western occupation zones 806 Germans were sentenced to death for mass murder of whom 486 were executed.

By the late 1950s all Germans imprisoned for war crimes had been released. This was the Cold War period when the USA decided to enlist West Germany into a defensive alliance against the Soviet Union. One of the German conditions for joining was an erasure of all vestiges of World War II guilt including the release of all war criminals. The general tenor of public opinion in the Bundesrepublik was not to bring up the past. As Theodor Adorno put it, "In the house of the hangman one ought not to talk about the rope." All this did not come as a surprise to the Western Allies who themselves had been for some time scooping German officials and intelligence agents, including a number of known war criminals, and integrating them into their services for combating the Soviet Union. Thus all Germans, whether jailed for short terms or condemned for life, were released at about the same time. In response the Soviet Union, too, started to court what was then West Germany, the main trophy in the Cold War. When Adenauer buttressed this with a promise of commercial treaties and loans, the USSR started to release all German prisoners in its camps. By the end of the 1950s the process of forgetting in both East and West was complete and, except for historians plying their trade, Germany's wartime deeds were expunged from the calculus of international relations.

Appendix:
Names and Positions
of Key Personnel

Alexander, Harold: British field marshal

Alfieri, Dino: Italian ambassador to Germany

Ambrosio, Villeri: chief of Italian General Staff

Anders, Wladyslaw: Polish general

Antonescu, Ion: Rumanian head of state

Antonescu, Mihai: Rumanian foreign minister

Aris (pseud.): Greek commander of ELAS

Attolico, Bernardo: Italian ambassador to Germany

Badoglio, Pietro: Italian marshal

Bagramian, Ivan: general armii

Bandera, Stepan: Ukrainian nationalist leader

Bastianini, Giuseppe: governor of Dalmatia, successor to Ciano

Beaverbrook, Lord: British minister of production

Beck, Jozef: Polish foreign minister

Beck, Ludwig: generaloberst

Belov, P.A: general mayor

Benes, Eduard: president of Czechoslovakia

Berger, Gottlieb: SS head of POW administration

Beria, Lavrenti: head of Soviet security

Berling, Zygmunt: Polish general

Bernadotte, Folke: Swedish vice president of Red Cross

Billotte, Gaston: French general

Bismarck, Otto: counsellor at German Embassy in Rome

Blaskowitz, Johannes: generaloberst

Blomberg, Werner: generalfeldmarschall

Bonnet, Georges: French foreign minister

Bor-Komorowski, Tadeusz: commander of the AK

Bormann, Martin: Reichsleiter NSDAP

Bradley, Omar: US General

Brooke, Alan: British field marshal, chief of army General Staff

Budyennyi, Semyon: marshal Sovetskovo Soyuza

Burgdorf, Wilhelm: ADC to Hitler

Busch, Ernst: generalfeldmarschall

Cadogan, Alexander: British undersecretary of state

Canaris, Wilhelm: admiral, head of Abwehr

Cavallero, Ugo: Italian marshal, chief of staff

Chuikov, Vasili: marshal Sovetskovo Souyza

Chvalkovsky, Fratisek: Czech ambassador to Germany

Ciano, Galeazzo: Italian foreign minister

Clark, Mark: US general

Coulondre, Robert: French ambassador to Germany

Cripps, Stafford: British ambassador to the USSR

Dahlerus, Birger: Swedish businessman

Daladier, Edouard: French prime minister

Darlan, Jean Francois: French admiral

de Gaulle, Charles: leader of the Free French

Dekanozov, Vladimir: Soviet ambassador to Germany

de Valera, Eamon: prime minister of Ireland

Dietrich, Otto: reich press chief

Dietl, Eduard: generaloberst

Dietrich, Sepp: SS obergruppenführer

Dijlas, Milovan: Yugoslav partisan leader

Dill, John: British field marshal

Doenitz, Karl: grossadmiral

Eden, Anthony: British foreign minister

Efremov, Mikhail: general leytenant

Eichmann, Adolf: chief of Amt IV B of RSHA

Eicke, Theodore: SS obergruppenführer

Eisenhower, Dwight D.: US general of the army

el-Husseini, Hadji Amin: Mufti of Jerusalem

Forbes, Charles Milton: admiral, CiC of Home Fleet

Franco, Francisco: Spanish head of state

Francois-Poncet, Andre: French ambassador to Germany

Frank, Hans: governor of GG

Friessner, Johannes: German general

Fromm, Fritz: generaloberst, head of Replacement Army

Gafencu, Grigore: Rumanian foreign minister

Gamelin, Maurice Gustave: CiC of French army

Georges, Alphonse: French general

Giraud, Henri: French general

Gisevius, Hans B.: member of the Abwehr

Globocnik, Odilo: SS gruppenfuhrer

Goebbels, Josef: German propaganda minister

Gort, John S.: British field marshal

Graziani, Rudolfo: Italian marshal

Greim, Robert: Luftwaffe generalfeldmarschall

Guderian, Hans: generaloberst

Hacha, Emil: president of Czechoslovakia

Halder, Franz: generaloberst, chief of staff of OKH

Halifax, Edward Wood: British foreign minister, ambassador to USA

Harriman, Averell: US ambassador to Russia

Haushoffer, Albrecht: professor of geopolitics

Haushoffer, Karl: general (ret)

Hausser, Paul: SS obergruppenfuhrer

Heinrici, Gotthard: generaloberst

Henderson, Nevile: British ambassador to Germany

Henlein, Konrad: leader of Sudeten Germans

Hess, Rudolf: deputy to Führer

Heydrich, Reinhardt: head of RSHA

Himmler, Heinrich: reichsfuehrer SS

Hoepner, Erich: generaloberst

Hoess, Rudolf: commandant of Auschwitz

Hopkins, Harry: advisor to Roosevelt

Horthy, Miklos: admiral, regent of Hungary

Hossbach, Friedrich: general

Hoth, Hermann: generaloberst

Hull, Cordell: US secretary of state

Jeschonnek, Hans: generaloberst, Luftwaffe chief of staff

Jodl, Alfred: generaloberst, chief of staff of OKW

Kaltenbrunner, Ernst: chief of RSHA

Kasprzycki, Tadeusz: Polish minister of war

Keitel, Bodewin: general, personnel chief in OKW

Keitel, Wilhelm: generalfeldmarschall, head of OKW

Kennard, Howard: British ambassador to Poland

Kesselring, Albert: generalfeldmarschall

King, Joseph: CiC US Navy

Kirponos, Mikhail: general pulkovnik

Knox, Frank: US secretary of navy

Koch, Erich: German commissioner for Ukraine

Koestring, Ernst: German military attache in Moscow

Kollontay, Alexandra: Soviet ambassador to Sweden

Konev, Ivan: marshal Sovetskovo Soyuza

Konoe, Fumimoro: Japanese prime minister

Krebs, Hans: generaloberst

Krüger, Friedrich: SS obergruppenfuehrer

Kube, Wilhelm: German commissioner for Byelorussia

Kurochkin, Pavel A.: general armii

Kutrzeba, Tadeusz: Polish general

Kutschera, Franz: SS & police chief for Warsaw District

Kvaternik, Slavko: Croatian fieldmarshal

Lammers, Hans: chief of Chancellery

Lasch, Otto: general

Laval, Pierre: French minister

Ley, Robert: leader of German Labor Front

Lindemann, Friedrich: Churchill's scientific advisor

Lindemann, Georg: generaloberst

Lipski, Jozef: Polish ambassador to Germany

List, Wilhelm: generalfeldmarschall

Litvinov, Maxim: Soviet foreign minister, ambassador to USA

Löhr, Alexander: generaloberst

Lothian, Philip Kerr: British ambassador to the USA

Lukasiewicz, Juliusz: Polish ambassador to France

MacArthur, Douglas: US general of the army, CiC in the Far East

Maiski, Ivan: Soviet ambassador to Britain

Malinovsky, Rodion I.: general armii

Mannerheim, Carl Gustav Emil: Finnish field-marshal

Marshall, George: US general of the army, chief of staff

Matsuoka, Yosuke: Japanese foreign minister

Meissner, Otto: chief of Chancellery

Menzies, Stewart G.: head of British Intelligence

Meretskov, Kiril: general armii

Metaxas, John: Greek prime minister

Mihajlovic, Dragoliub: Yugoslav general, leader of Chetniks

Mikolajczyk, Stanislaw: Polish prime minister

Mikoyan, Anastas: Soviet trade minister

Milch, Erhard: Luftwaffe generalfeldmarschall

Model, Walter: generalfeldmarschall

Molotov, Vyacheslav: Soviet foreign minister
Montgomery, Bernard: British field marshal
Morell, Theodor: Hitler's physician
Morgenthau, Henry: US secretary of treasury
Moscicki, Ignacy: president of Poland
Moulin, Jean: De Gaulle's resistance delegate
Nedic, Milan: prime minister of Occupied Serbia
Noel, Leon: French ambassador to Poland
Ohlendorf, Otto: SS brigadenfuehrer
Oshima, Hiroshi: Japanese ambassador to Germany
Oster, Hans: generaleutnant in the Abwehr
Ott, Eugene: German ambassador to Japan
Patton, George: US general
Paulus, Friedrich: generalfeldmarschall
Pavelic, Ante: Croatian head of state
Pavlov, D.G.: general armii
Petain, Henri Philippe: marshal, Vichy head of state
Phipps, Eric: Britain's ambassador to France
Pilsudski, Jozef: marshal, CiC of Polish army
Pohl, Oswald: SS obergruppenfuhrer
Pound, Dudley: first sea lord
Quisling, Vidkun: Norwegian minister
Raeder, Erich: grossadmiral
Rashid Ali: Iraqi coup leader
Reinhardt, Georg Hans: generaloberst
Rendulic, Lothar: generaloberst
Reynaud, Paul: French prime minister
Roatta, Mario: chief of Italian General Staff
Röhm, Ernst: leader of the SA
Rokossovsky, Konstantin: marshal Sovetskovo Soyuza
Rommel, Erwin: generalfeldmarschall
Rosenberg, Alfred: minister for the Eastern Territories
Rydz-Smigly, Edward: marshal, CiC of Polish army
Salazar, Antonio: Portuguese prime minister
Sauckel, Fritz: German commissioner for labor
Schacht, Hjalmar: German finance expert
Schellenberg, Walter: SD chief of intelligence
Schmidt, Rudolf: generalmajor
Schmidt, Paul Otto Gustav: Foreign Ministry interpreter
Schmundt, Rudolf: generalmajor, Hitler's ADC
Schoerner, Ferdinand: generalfeldmarschall
Schnurre, Karl: German economics expert
Schuschnigg, Kurt: chancellor of Austria
Serrano Suner, Ramon: Spanish foreign minister
Seys-Inquart, Arthur: German governor of Holland
Shaposhnikov, Boris: marshal Sovetskovo Soyuza, chief of staff

Shtemenko, Sergei: general armii
Sikorski, Wladyslaw: general, Polish prime minister
Simon, John: British foreign secretary
Skorzeny, Otto: SS oberstandartenfuehrer
Smith, Walter Bedell: US general
Speer, Albert: German munitions minister
Sperrle, Hugo: Luftwaffe generalfeldmarschall
Stauffenberg, Claus: oberstleutnant
Steiner, Felix: gruppenführer
Stimson Henry: US secretary of war
Streicher, Julius: gauleiter, editor of *Der Stürmer*
Strauss, Adolf: generaloberst
Student, Kurt: generaloberst
Thomas, Georg: generaloberst
Timoshenko, Semyon: marshal Sovetskovo Soyuza
Tiso, Joseph: Slovakian head of state
Tito, Joseph Broz: leader of Yugoslav partisans
Tollbukhin, F.I.: general pulkovnik
Tojo, Hideki: Japanese prime minister
Tyulenev, I.V.: general armii
Udet, Ernst: Luftwaffe generaloberst
Vansittart, Robert: British undersecretary of state
Vasilevski, Alexander: marshal Sovetskovo Soyuza
Vatutin, N.F.: general leytenant
Vlasov, Andrei: general leytenant
von Arnim, Juergen: generaloberst
von Bock, Fedor: generalfeldmarschall
von Brauchitsch, Walter: generalfeldmarschall; CiC of army
von Falkenhorst, Nikolaus: generaloberst
von Fritsch, Werner: generaloberst
von Kleist, Ewald: generalfeldmarschall
von Kluge, Guenther: generalfeldmarschall
von Küchler, Georg: generalfeldmarschall
von Leeb, Wilhelm: generalfeldmarschall
von Mackensen, Hans G.: German ambassador to Italy
von Manstein, Fritz Erich: generalfeldmarschall
von Moltke, Hans Adolf: German ambassador to Poland
von Neurath, Konstantin: German foreign minister
von Papen, Franz: German ambassador to Turkey
von Reichenau, Walter: generalfeldmarschall
von Ribbentrop, Joachim: German foreign minister
von Richthofen, Wolfram: Luftwaffe generalfeldmarschall
von Rundstedt, Gerd: generalfeldmarschall

von Schulenburg, Friedrich Werner: German ambassador to USSR

von Seydlitz, Walter: general

von Stuelpnagel, Otto: generaloberst

von Thoma, Wilhelm: general

von Weichs, Maximilian: generalfeldmarschall

von Weizsacker, Ernst: German state secretary

von Witzleben, Erwin: generalfeldmarschall

Voroshilov, Kliment Y.: marshal Sovetskovo Soyuza

Wagner, Eduard: general, German army quartermaster general

Warlimont, Walter: general, deputy to Jodl

Wavell, Archibald: British field marshal

Weidling, Helmuth: German general

Welles, Sumner: US undersecretary of state

Wenck, Walter: generalleutnant

Weygand, Maxime: French general

Wilson, Horace: advisor to Chamberlain

Wolff, Karl: obergruppenführer; aide to Himmler

Yeremenko, Andrei I.: marshal Sovestkovo Soyuza

Zeitzler, Kurt: generaloberst; army chief of staff

Zhukov, Georgi K.: marshal Sovetskovo Soyuza

Zakharov, F.D.: general mayor

Bibliography

Abramson, Rudy. *Spanning the Century. The Life of W. Averell Harriman, 1891–1986*. New York: William Morrow, 1992.

Adair, Paul. *Hitler's Greatest Defeat*. London: Arms and Armour, 1994.

Adamthwaite, Anthony. *The Making of the Second World War*. London: Unwin Hyman, 1989.

Agarossi, Elena. *A Nation Collapses*. New York: Cambridge University Press, 1943.

Alfieri, Dino. *Dictators Face to Face*. New York: New York University Press, 1954.

Allen, Lois. *Burma*. New York: Ballantine Books, 1974.

Andrew, Christopher, and Vasili Mitrokhin. *The Sword and the Shield*. New York: Basic Books, 1999.

Ansel, Walter. *Hitler and the Middle East,* Durham, NC: Duke University Press, 1972.

Axell, Albert. *Stalin's War*. London: Arms and Armour, 1997.

_____. *Russia's Heroes*. New York: Carroll & Graf, 2001.

Axworthy, Mark et al. *Third Axis; Fourth Ally*. London: Arms and Armour, 1995.

Ball, Adrian. *The Last Day of the Old World*. Garden City, NY: Doubleday, 1963.

Bamm, Peter. *The Invisible Flag*. New York: Signet, 1958.

Bartov, Omer. *The Eastern Front, 1941–45*. New York: Palgrave-Macmillan, 2001.

Baumbach, Werner. *The Life and Death of the Luftwaffe*. New York: Coward-McCann, 1960.

Beaufre, André. *The Fall of France*. New York: Knopf, 1968.

Beevor, Anthony. *Stalingrad*. New York: Viking, 1998.

_____. *The Fall of Berlin*. New York: Viking, 2002.

Beitzell, Robert. *The Uneasy Alliance*. New York: Knopf, 1972.

Bennett, Edward. *F.D.R. and the Search for Victory*. Wilmington, DE: S & R Books, 1990.

Bercuson, David, and Holger Herwig. *Destruction of the Bismarck*. New York: Stoddard, 2001.

Berezhkov, Valentin. *In Dioplomatischer Mission bei Hitler in Berlin 1940–41*. Frankfurt au Main: Stimme Verlag, 1967.

_____. *At Stalin's Side*. Sergei V. Mikheyev, translator. New York: Card, 1994.

Berling, Zygmunt. *Z Lagrow do Andersa*. Warsaw: Polski Dom Wydawniczy, 1990.

Berthon, Simon. *Allies at War*. New York: Carroll & Graf, 2002.

Biddiscombe, Perry. *Werewolf*. Toronto: Toronto University Press, 1998.

Biddle, Anthony. *Poland and the Coming of the Second World War*. Athens: Ohio University Press, 1976.

Bierman, John, and Colin Smith. *Fire in the Night*. New York: Random House, 1991.

Bix, Herbert. *Hirohito and the Making of Modern Japan*. New York: HarperCollins, 2000.

Blair, Clay. *Hitler's U-Boat War: The Hunted*. New York: Random House, 1996.

_____. *Hitler's U-Boat War: The Hunters*. New York: Random House, 1998.

Bloch, Marc. *Strange Defeat*. New York: Norton, 1968.

Blumenson, Martin. *Kasserine Pass*. New York: Houghton-Mifflin, 1967.

Bock, Fedor. *The War Diary*. Atglen, PA: Schiffer, 1996.

Boldt, Gerhard. *Hitler, the Last Ten Days*. New York: Coward, McCann & Georghegan, 1973.

Boog, Horst et al. *Germany and the Second World War, Vol. IV*. Oxford: Clarendon Press, 1998.

Botting, Douglas. *From the Ruins of Reich*. New York: Crown, 1985.

Boyd, Carl. *Hitler's Japanese Confidant*. Lawrence: University of Kansas Press, 1993.

Bregman, Aleksander. *Najlepszy Sojusznik Hitlera*. London: Orbis, 1987.

Bross, Werner. *Gespräche mit Hermann Göring*. Flensburg und Hamburg: Christian Wolff, 1968.

Brown, Anthony. *"C" Menzies*. New York: Macmillan, 1987.

Brügel, Johann Wolfgang. *Stalin und Hitler. Pakt gegen Europa*. Wien: Europaverlag, 1973.

Büchner, Alex. *Ostfront, 1944*. West Chester, PA: Schiffer, 1991.

Bullitt, Orville H., ed. *For the President, Personal and Secret; Correspondence Between Franklin D. Roosevelt and William C. Bullitt*. Boston: Houghton Mifflin, 1972.

Bullock, Alan. *A Study in Tyranny*. New York: Harper & Row, 1962.

_____. *Stalin and Hitler — Parallel Lives*. New York: Knopf, 1992.

Burdick, Charles. *Germany's Military Strategy and Spain in World War II*. Syracuse, NY: Syracuse University Press, 1968.

Burgdorff, Stephan, and Christian Habbe, eds. *Als

Feuer vom Himmel Fiel. München: Spiegel, 2003.

Cadogan, Alexander. *Diaries, 1938–1945*. Edited by David Dilks. New York: Putnam, 1972.

Calvocoressi, Peter et al. *The Causes and Courses of World War II; Vol. I*. New York: Penguin, 1989.

Carell, Paul. *Hitler Moves East*. Boston: Little, Brown, 1963.

_____. *Scorched Earth*. Boston: Little, Brown, 1966.

_____. *The Foxes of the Desert*. New York: Bantam Books, 1980.

Cecil, Robert. *Hitler's Decision to Invade Russia*. New York: David McKay, 1975.

Cervi, Mario. *The Hollow Legions*. New York: Doubleday, 1971.

Chapman, Guy. *Why France Fell*. New York: Holt, Reinhart & Winston, 1968.

Charmley, John. *Churchill's Grand Alliance*. San Diego: Harcourt & Brace, 1995.

Churchill, Winston. *The Second World War*. New York: Houghton-Mifflin, 1948–60.

Churchill's War Papers, Vols. 2 and 3. Compiled by Martin Gilbert. New York: W.W. Norton, 1995 and 2000.

Ciano, Galeazzo. *War Diaries*. Garden City, NY: Doubleday, 1946.

Ciano, Edda. *My Truth*. New York: William Morrow, 1977.

Ciechanowski, Jan. *The Warsaw Rising of 1944*. New York: Cambridge University Press, 1975.

Cienciala, Anna. *Poland and the Western Powers*. London: Routledge & Kegan Paul, 1968.

Clark, Allan. *Barbarossa*. New York: William Morrow, 1965.

Coffey, Thomas. *Decision Over Schweinfurt*. New York: David McKay, 1977.

Colvin, Ian. *None So Blind*. New York: Harcourt, Brace & World, 1965.

_____. *The Chamberlain Cabinet*. New York: Taplinger, 1971.

Coogan, Tim Pat. *DeValera*. New York: Barnes & Noble, 1993.

Cookridge, Edward. *Gehlen, Spy of the Century*. New York: Random House, 1973.

Crankshaw, Edward. *Gestapo*. London: Greenhill, 1991.

Cross, Robin. *Citadel*. New York: Barnes & Noble, 1993.

_____. *Fallen Eagle*. London: Michael O'Mara Books, 1995.

Cruikshank, Charles. *The German Occupation of the Channel Islands*. New York: Oxford University Press, 1975.

Cynk, Jerzy. *History of the Polish Air Force*. Berkshire: Osprey, 1972.

Daladier, Edouard. *In Defense of France*. New York: Doubleday Doran, 1971.

Dallin, Alexander. *German Rule in Russia*. New York: Macmillan, 1957.

Dallin, David. *Soviet Russia's Foreign Policy*. New Haven, CT: Yale University Press, 1943.

Datner, Szymon. *Crimes Against POWs: Responsibility of the Wehrmacht*. Warsaw: Zachodnia Agencja Prasowa, 1964.

Davis, Melton S. *Who Defends Rome*. New York: Dial, 1972.

Dawidowicz, Lucy. *The War Against the Jews*. New York: Holt, Reinhart & Winston, 1975.

Dawson, Raymond. *The Decision to Aid Russia*. Greenwood: North Carolina Press, 1959.

Deakin, Frederick. *The Brutal Friendship*. New York: Harper & Row, 1962.

De Golyer and McNaughten World Petroleum Consulting. *20th Century Petroleum Statistics*. Washington, DC: U.S. Bureau of Mines, 1975.

Degrelle, Leon. *Campaign in Russia*. Torrance, CA: Institute for Historical Review, 1985.

de Guingand, Francis. *Operation Victory*. London: Hodder & Stoughton, 1960.

d'Este, Carlo. *Bitter Victory*. New York: HarperCollins, 1989.

Detwiler, Donald. *Hitler, Franco und Gibraltar*. Wiesbaden: Steiner Verlag, 1962.

Djilas, Milovan. *Wartime*. New York: Harcourt, Brace & Jovanovich, 1977.

Divine, Robert. *Roosevelt and World War II*. Baltimore: Johns Hopkins Press, 1969.

Documents of Belgian Foreign Ministry: 1939–40. Evans Bros., 1941.

Documents of Events Preceding Outbreak of War. New York: German Foreign Office, 1940.

Documents of German Foreign Policy, Series D. Washington, DC: Department of State, 1957.

Documents of the Polish Foreign Ministry: 1933–39. Polish White Book. London: Hutchinson, 1940.

Documents of the Outbreak of War Between Great Britain and Germany. British Blue Book. London: Her Majesty's Stationery Office, 1939.

Documents on the Holocaust. Jerusalem: Yad Vashem, 1981.

Dodd, William. *Diary 1933–38*. New York: Harcourt, Brace, 1941.

Dollinger, Hans. *The Decline of Nazi Germany and Imperial Japan*. New York: Crown, 1982.

Das Dritte Reich, Berlin: Dokumenten Verlag Herbert Wendler, n.d.

Duggan, John. *Neutral Ireland and the Third Reich*. New York: Barnes & Noble, 1985.

Dulles, Allan. *The Secret Surrender*. New York: Harper & Row, 1966.

Eden, Anthony. *The Reckoning*. Boston: Houghton-Mifflin, 1960.

Eden, John. *Brute Force*. New York: Viking, 1990.

Ellis, John. *World War Two: A Statistical Survey*. New York: Facts on File, 1995.

Enzensberger, Hans Magnus. *Europe, Europe*. New York: Pantheon, 1989.

Feis, Herbert. *Churchill, Roosevelt, Stalin*. Princeton, NJ: Princeton University Press, 1967.

Fenyo, Mario. *Hitler, Horthy and Hungary*. New Haven, CT: Yale University Press, 1972.

Fest, Joachim. *Das Gesicht des Dritten Reiches*. München: R. Piper, 1963.

_____. *Hitler*. New York: Harcourt, Brace & Jovanovich, 1974.

_____. *Plotting Hitler's Death*. New York: Henry Holt, 1996.

_____. *Speer*. New York: Harcourt, 1999.

Fleischhauer, Ingeborg. *Die Chance des Sonderfriedens*. Munich: Siedler, 1986.

Fleming, Gerald. *Hitler and the Final Solution*. Berkeley: California University Press, 1984.

Flemming, Peter. *Operation Sealion*. New York: Simon & Schuster, 1957.

Fonvieille-Alquier, F. *The French and the Phony War*. New York: Stacey, 1973.

The French Yellow Book. Published by authority of the French Government. Reynal & Hitchcock, 1940.

Friedlander, Saul. *Prelude to Downfall*. New York: Alfred Knopf, 1967.

Friessner, Johannes. *Verratene Schlachten*. Hamburg: Holstein, 1956.

Fritz, Stephen. *Frontsoldaten*. Lexington: University of Kentucky Press, 1995.

Fugate, Bryan. *Operation Barbarossa*. Novato, CA: Presidio Press, 1984.

_____, and Lev Dvoretsky. *Thunder on the Dnepr: Zhukov, Stalin and the Defeat of the Blitzkrieg*. Novato: Presidio Press, 1997.

Führer's Naval Conferences 1939–45. Annapolis, MD: Naval Institute Press, 1990.

Gafencu, Grigore. *The Last Days in Europe*. London: Frederick Muller, 1948.

Garland Series on World War II. Edited by Donald Detwiler. 24 vols. New York: Garland, 1979.

Garlinski, Jozef. *Hitler's Last Weapons*. New York: Friedman, 1979.

Gebhardt, Bruno. *Handbook der Deutschen Geschichte*. Vol. 14. Stuttgart, Union, 1963.

Gelb, Norman. *Ike & Monty*. New York: William Morrow, 1995.

Gellately, Robert. *Backing Hitler*. New York: Oxford University Press, 2001.

Gellermann, Günther. *Die Armee Wenck — Hitler's Letzte Hoffnung*. Koblenz, Bernard & Graefe, 1984.

Gellman, Irwin. *Secret Affairs — FDR, Hill and Sumner Wells*. New York: Enigma Books, 1995.

Gheorghe, Ion. *Rumäniens's Weg zum Satellitenstaat*. Heidelberg: Vowinkel & Gort, 1952.

Gilbert, Martin, and Richard Gott. *The Appeasers*. Boston: Houghton Mifflin, 1963.

Giziowski, Richard. *The Enigma of General Blaskowitz*. New York: Hippocrene Books, 1997.

Glantz, David and Jonathan House. *When Titans Clash*. Lawrence: University of Kansas Press, 1995.

Goebbels, Joseph. *The Goebbels Diaries*. Edited and translated by Louis P. Lochner. New York: Doubleday, 1948.

_____. *Final Entries 1945: The Diaries of Joseph Goebbels*. Edited, introduced and annotated by Hugh Trevor-Roper. New York: Putnam, 1978.

Goda, Norman. *Tomorrow the World*. College Station: Texas A&M University Press, 1998.

Goerlitz, Walter. *History of the German General Staff, 1657–1945*. New York: Praeger, 1954.

_____. *Paulus and Stalingrad*. New York: Citadel, 1963.

Goldhagen, Daniel. *Hitler's Willing Executioners*. New York: Knopf, 1997.

Gorodetsky, Gabriel. *Cripps' Mission to Moscow*. New York: Cambridge University Press, 1984.

_____. *Grand Delusion*. New Haven: Yale University Press, 1999.

Gosztony, Peter. *Endkampf an der Donau, 1944/5*. Vienna: Fritz Molden, 1969.

Goure, Leon. *The Siege of Leningrad*. New York: McGraw Hill, 1964.

Goutard, Adolphe. *The Battle for France*. Ives: Washburn, 1959.

Graham, Dominick, and Shelford Bidwell. *Tug of War*. New York: St. Martin's, 1968.

Greenfield, K.R. *Command Decisions*. London: Methuen, 1960.

Grigg, John. *The Victory That Never Was*. New York: Oxford Press, 1980.

Gross, Jan. *Polish Society Under German Occupation*. Princeton, NJ: Princeton University Press, 1979.

Guderian, Heinz. *Panzer Leader*. New York: Ballantine, 1967.

Haffner, Sebastian. *The Meaning of Hitler*. Cambridge, MA: Harvard University Press, 1979.

Halder, Franz. *Kriegstagebuch*. 3 vols. Stuttgart: Kohlhammer, 1962–1964.

Hardesty, Von. *Red Phoenix*. Washington, DC: Smithsonian Institution, 1982.

Harriman, Averell, and Elie Abel. *Special Envoy to Churchill and Stalin, 1941–46*. New York: Random House, 1975.

Harrison, Gordon. *Cross Channel Attack (U.S. Army)*. New York: Barnes & Noble, 1995.

Harvey, Maurice. *Scandinavian Misadventure*. Turnbridge Wells, UK: Spellmount, 1990.

Hastings, Max. *Bomber Command*. New York: Dial Press, 1982.

_____. *Overlord*. New York: Simon & Schuster, 1984.

Haupt, Werner. *Army Group North*. Atglen, Schiffer, 1997.

Hehn, Paul N. *The German Struggle Against Yugoslav Guerrillas in World War II*. Boulder: East European Quarterly, 1979.

Heiber, Helmut, ed. *Lagebesprechungen im Führer HQ, 1942–45*. München: DTV, 1963.

_____, and David Glantz, eds. *Hitler and His Generals*. New York: Enigma Books, 2003.

Henderson, Nevile. *Failure of a Mission*. New York: G.P. Putnam Sons, 1940.

Herzstein, Robert. *Waldheim, The Missing Years*. New York: Arbor House, 1988.

Higgins, Trumbull. *Winston Churchill and the Second Front*. New York: Oxford University Press, 1957.

_____. *Soft Underbelly*. New York: Macmillan, 1968.

Hilberg, Raul. *Destruction of the European Jews*. New York: Holmes & Meier, 1985.

Hilger, Gustav, and Alfred Meyer. *The Incompatible Allies*. New York: Macmillan, 1953.

Hillgruber, Andreas. *Hitler, König Carol und Marschall Antonescu*. Wiesbaden: Franz Steiner, 1954.

_____. *Hitler's Strategie*. München: Bernard & Graefe, 1965.

_____. *Staatsmänner und Diplomaten bei Hitler*. München: Bernard & Graefe, 1967.

Hinze, Rolf. *East Front Drama — 1944*. Winnipeg: J.J. Fedorowicz, 1966.

Hitchins, Keith. *Rumania 1866–1947*. New York: Oxford University Press, 1994.

Hitler, Adolf. *Mein Kampf*. Boston: Houghton Mifflin, 1943.

_____. *Hitler's Table Talk, 1941–1944*. Translated by Norman Cameron and R.H. Stevens. London: Weidenfeld & Nicholson, 1953.

_____. *Hitler's Secret Conversations, 1941–1944*. Edited by H.R. Trevor-Roper. New York: Signet, 1961.

_____. *Reden und Proklamationen 1932–45*. Würzburg: Max Damarus, 1963.

Hoettl, Wilhelm. *The Secret Front*. London: Phoenix Press, 1953.

Hoffmann, Peter. *History of German Resistance*. Cambridge, MA: MIT Press, 1977.

Holldack, Heinz. *Was Wirklich Geschah*. New York: Nymphenburger, 1949.

The Holocaust: Selected Documents. 18 vols. John Mendelsohn, editor. Donald Detwiler, advisory editor. New York: Garland, 1982.

Hörner, Helmut. A *German Odyssey*. Golden, CO: Fulcrum, 1991.

Horthy, Miklos. *The Confidential Papers of Admiral Horthy*. Budapest: Corvina Press, 1965.

Hubatsch, Walther. *Kriegswende 1943*. Darmstadt: Wehr & Wissen, 1966.

Ironside, Sir Edmund. *Time Unguarded: The Ironside Diaries, 1937–1940*. New York: David McKay, 1962.

Jacobsen, Hans Adolf, and J. Rohweher. *Decisive Battles of World War II: The German View*. New York: Putnam, 1965.

Joachimsthaler, Anton. *The Last Days of Hitler*. London: Arms & Armor, 1996.

Jukes, Geoffrey. *Hitler's Stalingrad Decisions*. Berkeley: University of California Press, 1985.

Jurga, Tadeusz. *Obrona Polski*. Warsaw: Pax, 1990.

Kaslas, Bronis. *USSR-German Aggression Against Lithuania*. New York: Robert Speller, 1973.

Kaufmann, J.E., and H.W. Kaufmann. *Hitler's Blitzkrieg Campaigns*. Conshohocken, PA: Combined Books, 1993.

Keitel, Wilhelm. *Memoirs*. New York: Cooper Square, 2000.

Kempner, Robert. *SS im Kreuzverhör*. München: Rütten & Loening, 1964.

Kennedy, Joseph. *Hostage to Fortune*. New York: Viking Press, 2001.

Kershaw, Ian. *The Hitler Myth, Image and Reality in the Third Reich*. New York: Oxford University Press, 1987.

_____. *Hitler. Nemesis*. New York: W.W. Norton, 2000.

Kershaw, Robert. *War Without Garlands: Operation Barbarossa 1941–42*. New York: De Capo, 2000.

Kiriakopoulos, G.C. *Ten Days to Destiny*. New York: Franklin Watts, 1985.

Kitterman, D.H. "Those Who Said No," *German Studies Review* (1988): 241–254.

Kluge, Alexander. *The Battle*. New York: McGraw-Hill, 1967.

Knoke, Heinz. *I Flew for the Führer*. New York: Henry Holt, 1954.

Koehl, Robert. *German Resettlement and Population Policy*. Cambridge, MA: Harvard University Press, 1957.

Korbonski, Stefan. *Polskie Panstwo Podziemne*. Paris: Instytut Literacki, 1975.

Kot, Stanislaw. *Conversations with the Kremlin*. New York: Oxford University Press, 1963.

Krosby, H.P. *Finland, Germany and the USSR*. Madison: University of Wisconsin Press, 1968.

Kuby, Erich. *Mein Krieg*. Munich: Nymphenburger, 1977.

Langer, William, and Gleason Everett. *The Undeclared War 1940–41*. New York: Harper, 1953.

Leach, Barry. *German Strategy Against Russia*. New York: Oxford University Press, 1973.

Lebert, Stephan, and Norbert Lebert. *My Father's Keeper*. Boston: Little, Brown, 2001.

Lewy, Günter. *The Catholic Church and Nazi Germany*. New York: McGraw-Hill, 1964.

_____. *The Nazi Persecution of the Gypsies*. New York: Oxford University Press, 2000.

Lipski, Jozef. *Diplomat in Berlin*. New York: Columbia University Press, 1963.

Loza, Dimitri. *Fighting for the Soviet Motherland*. Lincoln: University of Nebraska Press, 1998.

Lucas, James. *War on the Eastern Front*. New York: Bonanza Books, 1979.

_____. *Last Days of the Third Reich*. New York: William Morrow, 1986.

Lukacs, John. *The Duel*. New York: Ticknor & Fields, 1991.

_____. *Five Days in London*. New Haven, CT: Yale University Press, 2001.

Lüdde-Neurath, Walter. *Regierung Dönitz*. Göttingen: Musterschmidt, 1964.

Lukasiewcz, Juliusz. *Diplomat in Paris*. New York: Columbia University Press, 1970.

Maas, Walter. *Netherlands at War*. New York: Abelard-Schuman, 1970.

MacDonald, Charles. *The Last Offensive (United States Army in World War II)*. Washington, DC: Government Printing Office, 1973.

Magenheimer, Heinz. *Hitler's War*. London: Arms & Armour, 1998.

Manstein, Erich. *Lost Victories*. Chicago: Henry Regnery, 1958.

Martel, Gordon, ed. *Origins of World War II Reconsidered*. Boston: Allen & Unwin, 1985.

Maslov, Aleksander. *Captured Soviet Generals*. London: Frank Cass, 2001.

Matloff, Maurice, and Edwin Snell. *Strategic Planning for Coalition Warfare, 1941–1942*. Washington, DC: Government Printing Office, 1953.

Maugeri, Adam Franko. *From the Ashes of Disgrace*. New York: Reynal & Hitchcock, 1948.

Mazower, Mark. *Inside Hitler's Greece*. New Haven, CT: Yale University Press, 1995.

McNeill, William H. *America, Britain and Russia*. London: Oxford University Press, 1953.

Meacham, Jon. *Franklin and Winston*. New York: Random House, 2003.

Megargee, Geoffrey. *Inside Hitler's High Command.* Lawrence: University of Kansas Press, 2000.

Melchior, Ib. *Case by Case.* Novato, CA: Presidio Press, 1993.

Mendelssohn, Peter. *Design for Aggression.* New York: Harper, 1946.

Messenger, Charles. *Sepp Dietrich.* Washington, DC: Brassey's, 1988.

_____. *The Last Prussian.* Washington, DC: Brassey's, 1991.

Metelmann, Henry. *Through Hell for Hitler.* Havertown, PA: Casemate, 1990.

Middlebrook, Martin. *The Berlin Raids.* London: Cassel, 1988.

_____. *Convoy.* New York: Quill-Morrow, 1976.

Miner, Steven Merritt. *Between Churchill and Stalin.* Chapel Hill: North Carolina University Press, 1988.

Miller, Nathan. *War at Sea.* New York: Scribner, 1995.

Mitcham, Samuel. *Rommel's Last Battle.* New York: Stein & Day, 1983.

_____. *Eagles of the Third Reich.* Novato, CA: Presidio Press, 1988.

_____. *Retreat to the Reich.* Westport, CT: Praeger, 2000.

_____. *Crumbling Empire.* Westport, CT: Praeger, 2001.

Moczulski, Leszek. *Wojna Polska.* London: Polska Fundacja Kulturalna, 1987.

Morell, Theodor. *Secret Diaries of Hitler's Doctor.* Edited by David Irving. New York: Macmillan, 1993.

Moseley, Ray. *Mussolini's Shadow.* New Haven, CT: Yale University Press, 1999.

Mrazek, James. *The Fall of Eben Emael.* Novato, CA: Presidio Press, 1970.

Müller-Hillebrand, Burkhart. *Germany and Its Allies in World War II.* Frederick, MD: University Publications of America, 1980.

Murray, Williamson. *Strategy for Defeat, The Luftwaffe 1933–45.* Maxwell Air Force Base, AL: Air University Press, 1983.

Mussolini, Benito. *Mussolini Memoirs.* Introduction by Raymond Klibanski. New York: Sterling, 2000.

Myles, Bruce. *Night Witches.* Chicago: Academy, 1990.

Nazi-Soviet Relations 1939–41. Washington, DC: Government Printing Office, 1948.

Neillands, Robin. *The Bomber War.* New York: Overlook Press, 2001.

Neubacher, Hermann. *Sonderauftrag Südost, 1940–45.* Göttingen: Musterschmidt, 1956.

Neumann, Peter. *The Black March.* New York: Bantam Press, 1981.

Newton, Steven. *German Battle Tactics on the Russian Front.* Atglen: Schiffer, 1994.

New York Times, April 24, 1966.

New York Times, February 21, 2004.

Nicolson, Harold. *The War Years.* New York: Atheneum, 1967.

Niepold, Gerd. *Battle for White Russia.* Washington, DC: Brassey's, 1987.

Nissen, Hendrick. *Scandinavia During the Second World War.* Minnesota: Minnesota University Press, 1983.

Nofi, Albert. *The War Against Hitler.* Conshocken, PA: Combined Books, 1982.

Nüremberg Trials, Case #9. Washington, DC: National Archives and Records, 1978.

O'Donnell, James. *The Bunker.* New York: Houghton Mifflin, 1978.

OKW Kriegstagebuch 1940–45. München: Bernard & Graefe, 1965.

Olson, Lynne, and Stanley Cloud. *A Question of Honor.* New York: Knopf, 2003.

Overy, Richard. *The Air War 1939–45.* New York: Stein & Day, 1985.

_____. *Interrogations.* New York: Viking Press, 2001.

_____. *Russia's War.* New York: TV Books, 1997.

_____. *Why the Allies Won.* New York: Norton, 1996.

Oxford Companion to World War II. New York: Oxford University Press, 1968.

Paul, Wolfgang. *Hermann Göring.* London: Arms & Armor, 1998.

Peace and War — U.S. Foreign Policy 1931–42. Washington, DC: Government Printing Office, 1943.

Perlmuter, Amos. *FDR and Stalin.* Columbia: University of Missouri Press, 1993.

Perrett, Bryan. *A History of Blitzkrieg.* Briarcliff Manor, NY: Stein & Day, 1983.

Petrov, Vladimir. *June 22, 1941.* Columbia: University of South Carolina Press, 1968.

Piekalkiewicz, Janusz. *Moscow.* Novato, CA: Presidio Press, 1981.

Pinkus, Oscar. *A Choice of Masks.* Englewood Cliffs, NJ: Prentice-Hall, 1970.

_____. *The House of Ashes.* Schenectady, NY: Union College Press, 1990.

Playfair, I.S.O. *The Mediterranean and the Middle East.* 8 vols. London: Her Majesty's Stationery Office, 1954–1988.

Raeder, Erich. *My Life.* Annapolis, MD: Naval Institute Press, 1960.

Rauschning, Hermann. *Hitler Speaks.* London: Thornton Butterworth, 1939.

Read, Anthony, and David Fisher. *The Deadly Embrace.* New York: Norton, 1988.

Reck-Malleczewen, Friedrich. *Diary of a Man in Despair.* New York: Collier Books, 1970.

Reinhardt, Klaus. *Die Wende um Moskau.* Frankfurt: Deutsche Verlag Anstalt, 1972.

Relations with Germany and the USSR. Authorized by the Polish Foreign Ministry. London: Hutchinson, n.d.

Reynolds, David. *The Creation of the Anglo-American Alliance 1937–41.* Chapel Hill: University of North Carolina, 1982.

Rich, Norman. *Hitler's War Aims.* New York: Norton, 1992.

Rings, Werner. *Life with the Enemy.* Garden City, NY: Doubleday, 1982.

Rowse, Alfred. *Appeasement.* New York: Norton, 1961.

Rumpf, Hans. *The Bombing of Germany.* New York: Holt, Reinhart & Winston, 1963.

Ruge, Friedrich. *The Soviets as Naval Opponents.* Annapolis, MD: Naval Institute Press, 1979.

Sadarananda, Dana. *Beyond Stalingrad.* New York: Praeger, 1990.

Salisbury, Harrison. *The Unknown War*. Garden City, NY: Doubleday, 1978.

Saward, Dudley. *Bomber Harris*. New York: Doubleday, 1985.

Sayer, Ian, and Douglas Botting. *Hitler's Last General*. London: Bantam Press, 1989.

Schechtman, Joseph. *The Mufti and the Führer*. New York: Thomas Yoseloff, 1965.

Schmidt, Paul. *Hitler's Interpreter*. New York: Macmillan, 1951.

Schneider, Franz, and Charles Gullans, trans. *Last Letters from Stalingrad*. New York: William Morrow, 1962.

Schofield, Brian. *The Russian Convoys*. New York: Ballantine, 1979.

Schramm, Percy. *Hitler als Militärischer Führer*. Frankfurt: Atheneum Verlag, 1965.

_____. *Hitler, The Man and Military Leader*. Chicago: Quadrangle Books, 1971.

Schröder, Josef. *Italiens Kriegsaustritt 1943*. Göttingen: Musterschmidt, 2003.

Schulte, Theo J. *The German Army and Nazi Policies in Occupied Russia*. Oxford: Berg, 1989.

Schultz, Joachim. *Die Letzten 30 Tage*. Stuttgart: Steingruben, 1951. Reprint, Providence: Berg, 1982.

Schwaab, Edleff. *Hitler's Mind*. New York: Praeger, 1992.

Schwan, H., and R. Steinger. *Als der Krieg zu Ende Ging*. Ullstein Documents, 2000.

Seaton, Albert. *The Russo-German War*. New York: Praeger, 1971.

_____. *Stalin as Military Commander*. New York: Praeger, 1975.

_____. *The Battle for Moscow*. New York: Jove Books, 1980.

Sebald, W.G. *The Natural History of Destruction*. New York: Random House, 2003.

Secret History of World War II: The Ultra-Secret Wartime Letters and Cables of Roosevelt. Edited by Stewart Richardson. New York: Richardson & Stierman, 1986.

Shay, Jonathan. *Odysseus in America*. New York: Scribner, 2002.

Shirer, William. *The Rise and Fall of the Third Reich*. New York: Simon and Schuster, 1959.

_____. *The Collapse of the Third Republic*. New York: Pocket Books, 1971.

Slaughterhouse: Encyclopedia of the Eastern Front. Garden City, NY: Military Book Club, 2002.

Smith, Frederick, Earl of Birkenhead. *Halifax: The Life of Lord Halifax*. London: Hamish Hamilton, 1965.

Soames, Mary, ed. *Winston and Clementine: The Personal Letters of the Churchills*. Boston: Houghton Mifflin, 1999.

Speer, Albert. *Inside the Third Reich*. New York: Macmillan, 1970.

Stahlberg, Alexander. *Bounden Duty*. Washington, DC: Brassey's, 1990.

Steinberg, Jonathan. *All or Nothing*. London: Routledge, 1990.

Steinert, Marlis. *Twenty Three Days*. New York: Zebra Books, 1967.

_____. *Hitler's War and the Germans*. Athens: Ohio University Press, 1977.

Strauch, Rudolph. *Sir Nevile Henderson*. Bonn: Ludwig Rohrscheid, 1959.

Strawson, John. *The Battle for North Africa*. New York: Scribner, 1969.

_____. *Hitler as Military Commander*. New York: Barnes Noble, 1971.

_____. *The Italian Campaign*. New York: Carroll & Graf, 1988.

Streit, Christian. *Keine Kameraden*. Stuttgart: Deutsche Verlag Anstalt, 1980.

Sudoplatov, Pavel. *Special Tasks*. Boston: Little, Brown, 1994.

Sweeting, C.G. *Hitler's Personal Pilot*. Washington, DC: Brassey's, 2000.

Sydnor, Charles. *Soldiers of Destruction*. Princeton, NJ: Princeton University Press, 1990.

Syrett, David. *The Defeat of German U-Boats*. Columbia: University of South Carolina Press, 1994.

Taylor, Telford. *The Anatomy of the Nüremberg Trials*. Boston: Little, Brown, 1993.

Temkin, Gabriel. *My Just War*. Novato, CA: Presidio Press, 1988.

Terraine, John. *A Time for Courage*. New York: Macmillan, 1985.

Tomasevich, Jozo. *The Chetniks, War and Revolution in Yugoslavia 1941–45*. Palo Alto, CA: Stanford University Press, 1975.

Toynbee, Arnold, ed. *Hitler's Europe*. New York: Oxford University Press, 1954.

Trevor-Roper, Hugh. *The Last Days of Hitler*. New York: Macmillan, 1947.

_____. "The Blitz That Failed," *New York Times Sunday Magazine*, June 18, 1961.

_____. *Blitzkrieg to Defeat*. New York: Holt, 1964.

United States Air Force Historical Studies, The German Air Force in Russian 1941. Air Academy: Arno Press, 1960–65.

U.S. Army Pamphlet 20-230. Washington, DC: Government Printing Office, 1950.

U.S. Army Pamphlet 20-261a. Washington, DC: Government Printing Office, 1955.

U.S. Strategic Bombing Survey. Washington, DC: Government Printing Office, 1945.

Venohr, Wofgang. *Stauffenberg*. Frankfurt au Main: Ullstein Taschenbuch, 1986.

Volkogonov, Dimitri. *Stalin. Triumph & Tragedy*. Rocklin, CA: Forum, 1996.

von Below, Nicolaus. *Bylem Adjutantem Hitlera*. Warsaw: Ministerstwo Obrony Narodowej, 1990.

von Reimer, Hansen. *Das Ende des Dritten Reiches, Band 2*. Stuttgart: Ernst Klett, 1972.

Wagener, Carl. *Moskau, 1941*. Bad Nauheim: Podzan, 1965.

Warlimont, Walter. *Inside Hitler's Headquarters*. New York: Praeger, 1964.

Watt, Richard. *Bitter Glory*. New York: Simon & Schuster, 1979.

Weintraub, Stanley. *Long Day's Journey Into War*. New York: Lyons Press, 2001.

Welles, Sumner. *A Time for Decisions*. New York: Harper, 1944.

Werth, Alexander. *Russia at War*. New York: Avon Books, 1965.

Whaley, Barton. *Codeword Barbarossa*. Cambridge, MA: M.I.T. Press, 1973.

Wheatley, Ronald. *Operation Sealion*. Westport: Greenwood Press, 1978.

Wheeler-Bennett, John. *Nemesis of Power*. New York: Viking Press, 1954.

Whiting, Charles. *America's Forgotten Army*. New York: St. Martins Press, 1999.

Williams, Charles. *Adenauer*. New York: Wiley, 2000.

Williams, Wythe, and William von Narvig. *Secret Sources*. Chicago: Ziff Davis, 1943.

Wilson, Theodore. *The First Summit*. Lawrence: Kansas University Press, 1991.

Wilt, Alan. *War from the Top*. Bloomington: Indiana University Press, 1990.

Winterbotham, Frederick. *The Ultra Secret*. New York: Dell, 1975.

Zaloga, Steven. *Operation Bagration*. London: Osprey, 1996.

Zawodny, Janusz. *Nothing but Honor*. Stanford: Hoover Institution Press, 1978.

Zeszyty Historyczne, Paris: Instytut Literacki, n.d.

Ziemke, Earl. *Moscow to Stalingrad*. Washington, DC: Government Printing Office, 1986.

_____, and Magna Bauer. *Stalingrad to Berlin*. Washington, DC: Government Printing Office, 1968.

_____. *The German Northern Theater of Operations*, U.S. Army Pamphlet 20-271. Washington, DC: Government Printing Office, 1950.

Zotos, Stephanos. *Greece: The Struggle for Freedom*. New York: Crowell, 1967.

Index